INTRODUCTION TO
COMPUTERS

INTRODUCTION TO
COMPUTERS

Third Edition

GORDON B. DAVIS

Professor, Management Information Systems
University of Minnesota

INTERNATIONAL STUDENT EDITION

McGRAW-HILL KOGAKUSHA, LTD.

Tokyo Auckland Beirut Bogota Düsseldorf Johannesburg
Lisbon London Lucerne Madrid Mexico New Delhi Panama
Paris San Juan São Paulo Singapore Sydney

INTRODUCTION TO COMPUTERS

INTERNATIONAL STUDENT EDITION

This book was set in Plantin by York Graphic Services, Inc. The editors
were Peter D. Nalle, Matthew Cahill, and Annette Hall; the designer was
Joseph Gillians; the production supervisor was Joe Campanella.
New drawings were done by J & R Services, Inc.

Library of Congress Cataloging in Publication Data

Davis, Gordon Bitter.
    Introduction to computers.

    First-2d ed. (1965–71) published under title: Introduction to electronic
computers.
    Bibliography: p.
    Includes index.
    1. Electronic digital computers.   2. Electronic data processing.
3. Programming languages
(Electronic computers)   I. Title.
QA76.5.D29   1977   001.6′4   76-52465
ISBN 0-07-015825-8

KOSAIDO PRINTING CO., LTD. TOKYO JAPAN

CONTENTS

PREFACE

In 1954 an important news item was the first installation of a computer by an industrial concern in the United States. Ten years later, when the first edition of this text was written, the number of nonmilitary computers was over 13,000. By the beginning of 1977, as the third edition is being printed, every organization of any size makes use of a computer. The computer is a central force in changes occurring in many fields—production, industrial management, accounting, mathematics, and information retrieval, to name a few. It is one of the most significant technological developments of our time. As such, it is a topic of interest to everyone. For the forward-looking student, a knowledge of computers is a necessity.

The third edition represents a significant revision of the second edition. In addition to updating all chapters, the major changes are:

1 Introduction of material on the development life cycle for both data processing applications and mathematical-statistical-modeling applications (Chapter 3)
2 Greater discussion of alternative processing methodology (Chapter 3)
3 A new chapter on computer program structure and design, emphasizing programming discipline, structured design, and top-down development (Chapter 5)
4 Rearrangement of chapters to place those relating to development of computer applications and computer programs earlier in the text (Chapters 3 to 5)
5 Additional discussion of data preparation methods and alternatives for data preparation in system design (Chapter 8)
6 Addition of material on selecting application software (Chapter 12)

7 Rearrangement of all discussion of assembly language programming into a single chapter surveying the topic (Chapter 15)

8 Revision and reorientation of an introductory chapter on high-level languages to cover alternatives in language selection and the process of selecting a suitable language (Chapter 14)

9 Revision of the language chapters to reflect concepts of structured programming (Chapters 16 to 20)

10 Revision of the BASIC chapter to include both the 1977 proposed American National Standard Minimal BASIC and current developments in the use of BASIC (Chapter 16)

11 Revision of the FORTRAN chapters to present a more disciplined programming style and to include the FORTRAN changes of the proposed 1977 revision of American National Standard FORTRAN (Chapters 17 and 18)

12 Revision of the COBOL chapters to obtain a more disciplined programming style using structured programming and to reflect changes made in the newest (1974) American National Standard COBOL

Teaching a course about computers presents a recurrent problem—how much should be taught, and how much of what is taught should be tied to a single computer? A brief introduction leaves the student with little more than the impression that computers are "very, very fast." On the other hand, a course that looks only at a single computer or at a single language may give the student too narrow a view of the field.

This text arose from a course designed to avoid both the shallowness of the brief-introduction approach and the narrowness of the approach which ties the student to a single computer. The book is thus a general introduction to the concepts and basic features of computers (hardware, software, and systems). The basic elements of machine-oriented programming are explained, as are the three most popular machine-independent high-level languages (BASIC, FORTRAN, and COBOL).

Illustrations and examples in the text rely upon the equipment of many manufacturers. However, the popularity of the IBM System/370 made it appropriate to use it most frequently as the example computer. This is especially true in Chapter 15 (machine-level computer instructions), where the examples generally use the IBM Basic Assembly Language. The high-level language chapters (Chapters 16 to 20) are machine-independent, and the illustrations have been run using several different makes of computers.

A student can study the concepts and techniques related to computers without applying them to a specific computer. However, it is frequently useful to relate the general textual material to the specific computer available to the students. The text can therefore be used in two ways: (1) as a general introduction without reference to any particular computer, or (2) as a coverage of the field which is related to an actual computer through lectures or a manual. Manufacturers generally have an introductory manual for each computer system. The instructor can extract parallel reading assignments from such a manual to show how the concepts described in the textbook are implemented on the computer system used by the students.

A problem which arises frequently is the depth of study a student should have in programming and the relative emphasis on machine-oriented programming versus machine-independent high-level languages. The trend in computers is clearly toward writing most programs in high-level languages. However, a general understanding of the elements of programming at the machine-language level is useful in understanding the computer field. This suggests that one approach to the field is to have the student obtain a general understanding of the basic features of machine-level assembly language programming *and* learn one or more of the high-level languages—FORTRAN, BASIC, or COBOL, all of which are covered in the text.

Since there are many high-level languages available for programming computers, Chapter 14 describes alternatives and discusses selection criteria. In selecting one or more of the high-level languages for the student to learn, the need of the student should be considered. FORTRAN and BASIC are algebraic languages best suited for programming solutions which can be stated in terms of arithmetic processes to be performed. The algebraic languages are therefore useful to the student in research or other course work. BASIC is simpler than FORTRAN but tends to be used primarily with timesharing. COBOL is suited to data processing applications. When FORTRAN or BASIC is the only language chosen, it is advisable to also read through COBOL for familiarity with this important language. In learning a language such as FORTRAN, BASIC, or COBOL, it is very helpful for a student to code, debug, and execute programs. Almost all computers of any size have both FORTRAN and COBOL compilers. BASIC is available on all timesharing systems and many minicomputers. If both an algebraic and a data processing language are to be studied, the algebraic language should usually be studied first because it is easier to get small problems to compile and run; the problems also can be shorter with an algebraic language than with a data processing language.

The text is suitable for either a one-semester (quarter) course or a two-semester (quarter) sequence, depending on the proficiency desired and the time devoted to a specific computer and programming languages. A one-semester course can cover all topics and can include the learning of one of the three high-level languages. A two-semester (quarter) sequence can develop topics in greater depth, give a better understanding, and develop better proficiency in FORTRAN, BASIC, and COBOL.

The text is somewhat modular. For example, the chapters in Part 3, which cover computer technology, may be assigned before the chapters in Part 2, which consider development of computer applications and computer programs. An instructor may choose to skip the material on binary arithmetic in Chapter 6 and the material on internal operations in Chapter 7 if this is not appropriate for the students. Any of the language chapters (15 through 20) may be eliminated without affecting the use of the remaining chapters.

The programming assignments require sufficient elapsed time that an instructor may wish to make programming-language-chapter assignments in parallel with earlier chapters. The order of chapter use in such a case might be Chapters 1 to 3, Appendix 1, Chapters 14, 4, and 5, and then language chapter assignments alternating with Chapters 6 to 13.

The fact that the text is not tied to any particular subject area makes it suitable for students in all fields. The text is suitable for self-study. Of the 20 chapters, 8 contain self-testing quizzes either in the chapter or as part of the exercises at the end. The technique of using self-testing quizzes as an aid to the learning process is applied intensively in the BASIC, FORTRAN, and COBOL chapters.

An alternate version of this text is available for those who do not desire the six programming language chapters (Chapters 15 through 20). The alternate text, *Introduction to Computers and Information Systems,* McGraw-Hill, 1978, contains the material covered in Chapters 1 through 14 of this text plus a chapter summarizing characteristics of programming languages.

Gordon B. Davis

INTRODUCTION TO
COMPUTERS

PART

1

INTRODUCTION

The chapters in Part 1 provide an introduction to the study of computers. The first chapter gives an historical overview and surveys the equipment and other elements to be found in computer systems. Chapter 2 describes some of the uses for computers. The variety of uses provides a background for the study of computer application development, computer technology, computer operations, and programming languages.

CHAPTER

AN OVERVIEW OF COMPUTERS

The modern computer represents a fundamental advance in computation on a par with other advances such as the development of the zero or the discovery of calculus. The computer is a result of, and a major contributor to, the current technological explosion. No one can escape some contact with computers. This contact may result from such mundane computer applications as the preparation of payroll checks and department store charge account billings, or it may be from such esoteric activities as predictions of the outcome of elections or analysis of the probable authorship of ancient documents. Since the present and the future are often best understood in terms of the past, it will be valuable to an understanding of computers to briefly review their history.

Definition of a Computer

Strictly speaking, a computer is any calculating device. The name is derived from the Latin *computare,* meaning "to reckon" or "to compute," and can be applied as properly to an abacus or an adding machine as to the modern computer. However, the term "computer" has come to mean a special type of calculating device having certain definite characteristics.

There are basically two types of computers—analog and digital. *Analog computers* use electronic circuitry to represent physical processes, with changes in electric current representing the behavior of the system being studied. *Digital computers,* on the other hand, are based essentially on counting operations. A *hybrid computer* is a combination of an analog and a digital computer. Most modern computers are digital computers, and usually digital computers are meant when the word "computer" is used. For this reason, the explanations in the chapters to follow apply only to digital computers.

Several characteristics typically found in digital computers differentiate them from mechanical and electronic calculators. These features are speed, internal memory, and stored program. The speed of the electronic computer is the result of electronic circuitry. Mechanical counters are severely limited by the speed with which mechanical devices can start, move, and stop, while the speed of electronic circuitry is limited only by the speed at which electricity is transmitted (which is the speed of light). Electronic computers can hold data and instructions in an electronic representation in an internal memory unit. This feature not only adds to the speed of processing but also forms the basis for a stored program. In contrast to a mechanical or electronic calculator, which requires human direction at each step in a computational routine, the computer is automatic in the sense that the stored program will direct the performance of a long and complicated sequence of operations without operator intervention. For this reason, early writers often spoke of the automatic computer as contrasted to the existing nonautomatic calculating devices. The stored program usually includes logical tests to determine which of many possible program steps should be taken at important junctures in the program. Thus, the stored program is not just a sequence of steps to be followed in computation but typically includes all possible paths that computation might take within the scope of the problem.

Historical Events in the Development of Computers

While modern computers were not developed until the late 1940s, some important prior developments were the algebra of logic by George Boole, the punched card by Herman Hollerith, and the calculator built by George Aiken. Also important historically is Charles Babbage. His work did not directly influence the design of the first modern computer, but certain basic ideas of the stored computer program can be traced to this remarkable nineteenth-century inventor.

Babbage and the Analytic Engine

In 1812, Charles Babbage, professor of mathematics at Cambridge University, devised a machine called a "difference engine" to automatically perform simple computations needed for trigonometric and logarithmic tables. Babbage's difference engine carried out a set sequence of operations one at a time, but Babbage also conceived of an analytic engine which would execute an arbitrary sequence of operations and would have internal storage for data. Babbage's description of the analytic engine's stored program is remarkably close to the concept of the stored program of modern computers.

Boolean Algebra

The switching networks in a computer can be very complex, and the logic of a complicated program can be very difficult to analyze. Boolean algebra provides a systematic method of representation and analysis. It is named after the English mathematician George Boole, who pioneered in the field of symbolic logic. His book *The Laws of Thought,* published in 1854, represents logic in mathematical symbols and provides rules for calculating the truth or falsity of statements.

A simple illustration will show why mathematical logic is important in the design of computers. If an electronic switch is open, we shall assign the value 0, and if it is closed, we shall assign the value 1. These two states of the switch will correspond to the values of false (0) and true (1) in the symbolic logic of Boolean algebra. Two switches which operate independently such that there is current at the output line C only if both switches A and B are closed can be described by the Boolean statement A AND B (written symbolically as $A \wedge B$). A circuit in which there will be current at C if either A or B is closed is described by the Boolean statement A OR B ($A \vee B$). The results from these circuits can be described by examining all possible combinations of open and closed states for switches A and B and determining the effect on output C. The resulting tables (Table 1-1) are identical to the truth tables derived from symbolic logic. The work of Boole and others in the mathematics of symbolic logic thus provided an analytical basis for computer design.

TABLE 1-1 ANALYSIS OF SWITCHING CIRCUITS

GIVEN THESE COMBINATIONS OF SWITCH POSITIONS		AND CIRCUIT DESIGN DESCRIBED BY A ∧ B		AND CIRCUIT DESIGN DESCRIBED BY A ∨ B	
A	B	Diagram	Output at C	Diagram	Output at C
Closed	Closed		On		On
Closed	Open		Off		On
Open	Closed		Off		On
Open	Open		Off		Off

The Machine-readable Punched Card

Although not a component of the electronic computer, the punched card has become an integral part of input to data processing using electronic computers, and as such, it should be mentioned in a history of electronic computers. The use of punched cards began in 1745 when a Frenchman, Joseph M. Jacquard, designed a method for using holes in cards to control the selection of threads in weaving designs. Babbage also proposed cards with holes as input for data into the analytic engine.

The originator of the modern machine-readable punched card was Herman Hollerith. The need for mechanical tabulating equipment was seen by Hollerith while working with the 1880 United States census. During the 1880s, he developed the idea of the punched card and designed a *census machine.* The Hollerith method was chosen for tabulating the 1890 census, and the tabulation was done quickly and at a substantial savings in cost over the previous hand method. In 1896, Hollerith organized the Tabulating Machine Company to manufacture and market the machines and cards. This company merged with others to eventually become International Business Machines Corporation (IBM). James Powers, also connected with the Bureau of the Census, designed some card-processing equipment with slightly different features. This equipment was used to tabulate the 1910 census. In 1911, Powers formed the Powers Accounting Machine Company, subsequently acquired by Remington Rand (now a division of Sperry Rand Corporation). The cards designed by Hollerith used 80 columns and rectangular punches, while those designed by Powers used 90 columns and round punches. Sperry Rand has discontinued the 90-column card, and the field is dominated by the 80-column Hollerith card (Figure 1-1). A 96-column small card is used primarily in connection with the IBM System/3 computer introduced in 1969 (Figure 1-2). The small size is made possible by use of very small holes and a more compact coding scheme.

It is helpful to understand how data is encoded in punched cards. In the 80-column card there are 80 columns, and each column has 12 rows or punching positions numbered (from top to bottom) 12, 11, 0, 1, . . . , 9. A numeric digit 0 to 9 is encoded in a column by punching the corresponding row position (see Figure 1-1). An alphabetic character is encoded by a combination of a zone punch

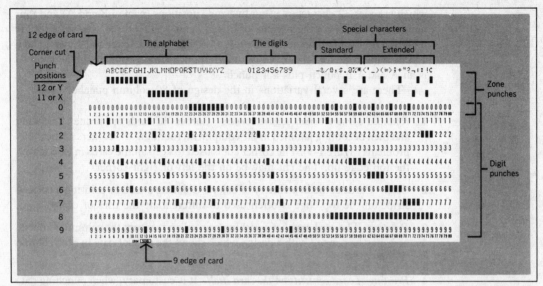

FIGURE 1-1 80-column Hollerith punched card.

in row 12, 11, or 0, and a numeric punch in rows 1 through 9. For example, the letter A is a 12 punch plus a 1 punch; the letter Z is a 0 punch plus a 9 punch. Special characters such as # and $ are encoded by a zone punch and one or more numeric punches. The 96-column card is divided into three separate areas each of

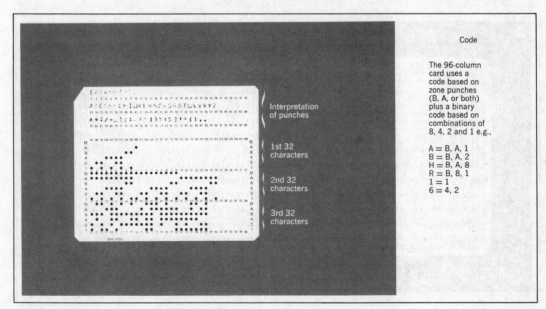

FIGURE 1-2 96-column card for IBM System/3.

which encodes 32 characters using two zone positions (named B and A) and four numeric positions having a value of 8, 4, 2, and 1. The three sets of codes are interpreted in three lines across the top. For example, the code for 3 is a 2 and a 1 punch; the code for an A is an A and a B punch and a 1 punch; the code for D is an A and a B punch plus a 4 punch.

There are several variations in the design of 80-column punched cards:

1 *Rounded corners versus square corners* Corners of cards are prone to bending and then becoming jammed in the equipment; rounding the corners reduces this problem (Figure 1-3). The corner cut is used to keep all the cards in a deck with the top edge up. The cut may be on the left or right corner.

2 *Color* Cards come in a variety of colors. Coloring a card or printing a colored stripe on the top edge is often used to differentiate the uses of cards.

3 *Printing* The card may have nothing printed on it except the column numbers, or it may be printed with a design which shows the type of data in each column (Figure 1-3).

4 *Printing of card contents on the card itself* It is customary, when punching data into cards with a keypunch, to print the contents of the card across the top, each character being printed above the punch which represents it. The contents of the card may be printed elsewhere on the card by the use of an interpreter.

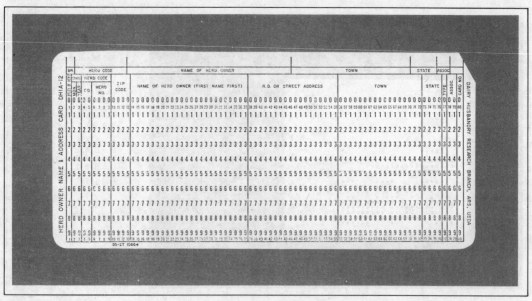

FIGURE 1-3 Punched card with rounded corners and printed format to show card column contents.

5 *Hole codes* There are two different hole codes for some of the special characters. Older style punches use one code; newer punches tend to use an expanded code. These are explained in Appendix 1.

The Automatic Sequence Controlled Calculator—Mark I

In 1937, Howard Aiken of Harvard University designed a machine that would automatically perform a sequence of arithmetic operations. Completed in 1944, the Mark I was essentially a huge mechanical calculator. It contained 72 adding accumulators and 60 sets of switches for setting constants and was instructed by means of switches, buttons, wire plugboards, and punched tape. Information was represented by patterns of open and closed mechanical relays. The Harvard Mark I was the immediate predecessor of automatic electronic computers. The ENIAC (described below), although lacking some features associated with computers, is the machine which bridges the gap between mechanical calculating machines and electronic devices.

The First Generation of Automatic Computers

ENIAC[1] (Electronic Numerical Integrator and Calculator)

The ENIAC was designed by J. Presper Eckert and John W. Mauchly of the Moore School of Engineering of the University of Pennsylvania, and was much faster than the Mark I. It did not have an internally stored memory, but was programmed instead by means of switches and plug-in connections. Completed in 1947, the ENIAC was used mainly for calculating tables. It is often identified as the first electronic computer. Eckert and Mauchly can therefore be identified as the originators of the electronic computer. As with many inventions it is difficult to identify the originator of the idea. For example, in a lawsuit relating to validity of early patents by Eckert and Mauchly, some of the key concepts for an electronic computer were traced to I. V. Atanasoff, a theoretical physicist whose ideas and computing devices were known to Eckert and Mauchly.

EDVAC, EDSAC, and IAS

During the work on the ENIAC, Eckert, Mauchly, and others working with them designed a larger machine called the EDVAC, which was different from the ENIAC in two fundamental ways. These differences were in the use of binary numbers for electronic arithmetic operations and in the internal storage of instructions written in digital form. The completion of the EDVAC was delayed until 1952, but the EDVAC design can be considered the prototype of serial computers. Another computer using internal storage, called EDSAC, which was completed in 1949 at the University of Manchester (England), is identified as the first stored program computer.

---

[1] The student of computers will find a frequent use of acronyms, i.e., words formed from the initial letter or letters of the words describing some item. Examples are ENIAC and EDVAC. The "AC" ending of names for many early computers usually stands for "automatic computer."

John von Neumann, a noted mathematician, had become acquainted with the computer work of Eckert and Mauchly during a stay at the Moore School. He became interested in the use of computers for numerical analysis and also in the design of the computer itself. The writings of von Neumann are significant because they contain a description of the computer logic being developed by Eckert and others at the Moore School. The IAS computer, which began as a joint project of Princeton's Institute for Advanced Study and the Moore School, was first described in a report prepared for the U.S. Army Ordnance Department.[1] The paper describes the features which should be incorporated into a computer. Of note is the suggestion that the proposed computer be a parallel machine rather than a serial machine. The IAS computer, not actually completed until 1952, used the binary system, a one-address command structure (explained in a later chapter), and parallel arithmetic. The EDVAC and the IAS thus introduced the basic designs for two important types of computers—serial and parallel. The differences between the two types are in the methods of moving information from one part of the machine to another and of performing addition. The parallel machine moves all the digits in a number at the same time, the serial machine moves them a digit at a time. When the parallel concept is used for addition, all corresponding pairs of digits are added simultaneously. In a serial machine, pairs of digits are added a pair at a time, in much the same fashion as in manual arithmetic.

UNIVAC (UNIVersal Automatic Computer)

The UNIVAC I is important because it was the first commercially available computer. It was built as a commercial venture by the Eckert-Mauchly Computer Company, founded in 1946 by Eckert and Mauchly and purchased in 1949 by Remington Rand (later Sperry Rand). The UNIVAC I followed the EDVAC design but used the one-address structure of the IAS.

The first UNIVAC computer went into operation at the Bureau of the Census in April 1951. The first UNIVAC installation for business use was at General Electric Appliance Park in Louisville, Kentucky, in 1954. The name UNIVAC was synonymous with "computer" for a few years until IBM, which initially showed only a limited interest in computers, changed directions and entered the computer field.

The computers discussed above are significant because they represented important new concepts in computer design. However, many other computers were developed during this period. First in operation was the ENIAC in 1947, then the EDSAC and BINAC in 1949, four separate machines in 1950, and six machines in 1951. The first year in which computers were commercially available was 1951, with two UNIVAC Is being installed.

In 1953, IBM installed its first computer, the IBM 701. Late in 1954, IBM installed the first IBM 650 computer. The IBM 650 computer was the most

---

[1] This report, entitled "Preliminary Discussion of the Logical Design of an Electronic Computing Instrument," was never issued to the public. However, it has been reprinted in two parts in *Datamation*, pp. 24–31, September 1962, and pp. 36–41, October 1962.

popular computer during the next 5 years. The computers of this period are often referred to as the "first-generation computers." They generally used vacuum tubes, were large, required much air conditioning, had little internal storage, and were relatively slow.

Computers since the First Generation

A transistor performs the same function as a vacuum tube but is smaller, less expensive, generates little heat, and requires little power. The change from tubes to transistors began with military computers in 1956 and with commercial computers in 1959 (Figure 1-4). The computers of the period 1959 to 1965 are referred to as "second-generation computers." The most widely used second-generation computers were:

Model	Size and orientation
IBM 1620	Small scientific computer
IBM 1401	Small to medium commercial computer
IBM 7094	Large scientific computer

The third generation of computers is generally dated from 1965 when IBM introduced a family of computers. The family was termed System/360 with each

FIGURE 1-4 Transistor circuit card for a computer (about 1960). (*Courtesy of UNIVAC Division of Sperry Rand Corporation.*)

size or model having a unique number. For example, System/360 model 30 was a small computer; System/360 model 65 was a fairly large computer. The System/360 continued the trend toward miniaturization. IBM chose a hybrid technique termed "solid logic technology" in which tiny chip transistors and diodes were mounted on a ceramic base (Figure 1-5). The elements were interconnected by a printed circuit. The completed module, about $\frac{1}{2}$ in. square, was enclosed in plastic. Other vendors during the period used integrated circuitry in which the entire circuit is formed from the controlled growth of a crystal structure.

The computers in the third generation from about 1965 to 1970 were characterized by hybrid or integrated circuits, by the integration of hardware with software (programming and operating aids), by an orientation to data communications, and by the handling of more than one processing program simultaneously. The third-generation idea of a compatible family of computers which allows a user to move from a smaller to a larger model without reprogramming was an important concept fully implemented by many computer vendors. The dominant third-generation computer was the IBM System/360. A small scientific computer, the IBM 1130, also received substantial use. The System/3, a family of small computers for business data processing and other uses, was introduced in 1969. It had become by 1975 the most common computer (over 30,000 in use).

The idea of computer generations having about a 5-year life can be seen from the active marketing periods for the first-, second-, and third-generation equipment just described. Although some vendors have used the term "fourth generation," there appears to be a trend away from the revolutionary changes of the three generations and a more gradual upgrading and improvement. This is illustrated by the IBM System/370 introduced in 1970. The equipment is compatible in design and concept with the predecessor IBM System/360 but uses improved, faster hardware features and more advanced storage organization and operating systems.

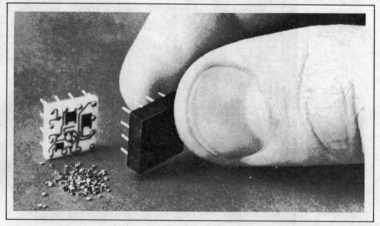

FIGURE 1-5 Chip transistor assembled onto ceramic base with printed circuit (left) and encased in plastic (right). Compare the size of this module (1965) with 1960 circuit card in Figure 1-4. (*Courtesy of International Business Machines Corporation.*)

The circuitry advances were primarily in the use of integrated circuits containing hundreds of circuits or memory elements (say, 1024 to 2048) on a single chip $\frac{1}{8}$ in. square (Figure 1-6). These circuits provide lower cost, improved speed, reduced failures, etc. Other improvements have been introduced in input and output devices and in data communications facilities.

Elements of a Computer Processing System

There are five basic elements in a system which uses a computer for processing data, performing computations, etc. These are hardware, system software, application software, procedures, and personnel. Each of these is defined in this chapter and receives further explanation in subsequent chapters.

Hardware   Hardware for computer processing involves equipment which can perform the following functions: data preparation, input to the computer, processing, secondary

FIGURE 1-6 Integrated circuit of type used with 1970s computers. (*Courtesy of Intel Corporation.*)

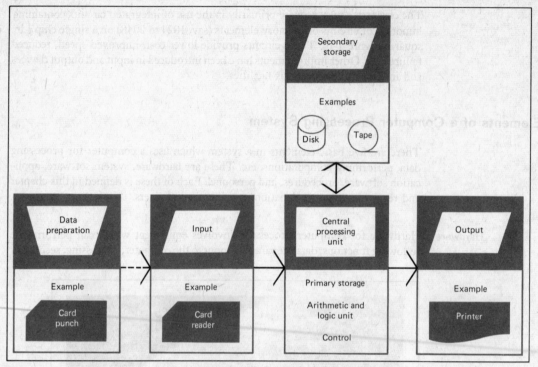

FIGURE 1-7 Equipment functions in a computer processing system.

or auxiliary storage, and output from the computer. Equipment may be online, i.e., connected directly to the computer, or offline. The relationship of the different equipment functions is shown in Figure 1-7.

System Software System software consists of nonhardware aids, namely, computer programs and computer routines which facilitate the operation of the computer by the user installation. These aids consist of computer programs for standard tasks such as sorting data records, organizing and maintaining files, translating programs written in a symbolic language into machine-language instructions, and scheduling jobs through the computer. Perhaps the most important system software is the operating system, a set of programs which directs and manages the execution of jobs by the computer. System software is as vital to effective use of a computer as the hardware.

Application Software Application software consists of programs for performing specific processing applications. A program consists of a set of instructions to the computer to perform a set of operations. Each user, whether organization or individual, normally writes some programs for unique applications; however, generalized applications programs can be purchased or leased from software organizations. The terms "routine" and "program" are somewhat synonymous. *Routine* refers to a set of instructions to perform a particular process. A *program* may consist of one or more routines—for example, an input routine, a processing routine, and an output routine. The process by which an application program is developed and placed into use may vary depending on the type of application. Figure 1-8 describes the activities to develop and use a computer program for a simple application. The cycle of activities for such development is explained in greater detail in Chapter 3.

Procedures The operation of a data processing system requires procedures for obtaining and preparing data, operating the computer, distributing output from processing, initiating new programs, etc. These procedures include control steps such as actions to be taken by users in the event they detect errors or actions by operators if the equipment malfunctions.

Personnel Computer processing requires new skills. Three major classes of positions are required in computer processing installations: systems analyst, programmer, and computer operator. Additional positions are explained in Chapter 11. Of these jobs, that of systems analyst requires the broadest background in terms of education and understanding of organizations. The position of programmer requires a skill in coding (writing computer instructions). The computer operator function involves fairly well-defined tasks which do not require high technical skill, and therefore this job requires less training than the others.

Job title	Job description
Systems analyst	Study information and processing requirements. Design the flow of operations and prepare specifications for the processing system.
Programmer	Code computer programs based on specifications prepared by the systems analyst.
Computer operator	Operate the computer.

Processing Methods

Computer processing may be performed periodically in batch mode or immediately in online mode. A computer system may be dedicated to regularly scheduled jobs, or it may be shared by many unscheduled users simultaneously. The latter is termed "time sharing."

In batch processing, data to be processed is accumulated over a period of time.

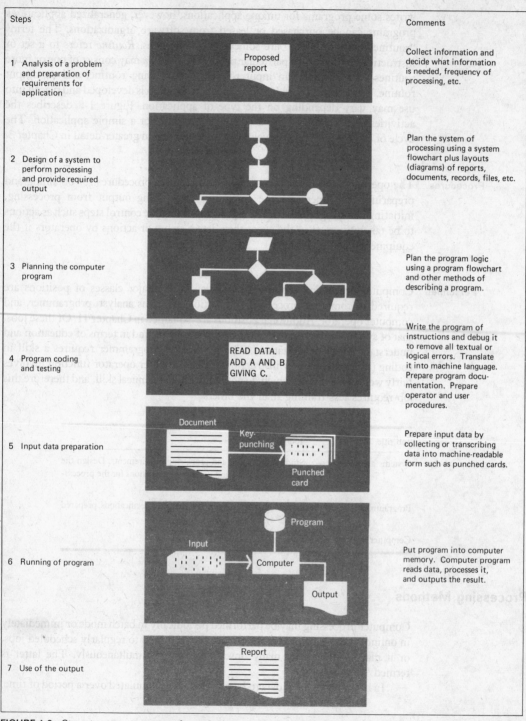

Steps		Comments
1 Analysis of a problem and preparation of requirements for application	Proposed report	Collect information and decide what information is needed, frequency of processing, etc.
2 Design of a system to perform processing and provide required output		Plan the system of processing using a system flowchart plus layouts (diagrams) of reports, documents, records, files, etc.
3 Planning the computer program		Plan the program logic using a program flowchart and other methods of describing a program.
4 Program coding and testing	READ DATA. ADD A AND B GIVING C.	Write the program of instructions and debug it to remove all textual or logical errors. Translate it into machine language. Prepare program documentation. Prepare operator and user procedures.
5 Input data preparation	Document — Keypunching → Punched card	Prepare input data by collecting or transcribing data into machine-readable form such as punched cards.
6 Running of program	Input — Program → Computer → Output	Put program into computer memory. Computer program reads data, processes it, and outputs the result.
7 Use of the output	Report	

FIGURE 1-8 Steps in using a computer for a simple application.

The accumulated batch of transactions is processed periodically. This method is very efficient, but its use means that there is always a processing delay.

In online processing (also referred to as online realtime processing), each transaction is processed as soon as it is received. There is no waiting to accumulate a batch of transactions. Online realtime processing is used especially in situations such as a computerized reservation system where an immediate response is useful.

Time sharing is the concurrent use of a single computer system by many users, each of which has an input/output device and can access the same computer at the same time. The computer gives each user a small, but frequently repeated, slice of the time, so that each user gets almost immediate response.

The Equipment in a Computer Installation

The equipment that is found in a specific computer installation will depend on the amount and type of processing being formed and on the types of equipment available for that model of computer. In general, a computer system will have a central processing unit, plus one or more units of equipment for the functions of secondary storage, data preparation, input, and output.

The Central
Processing Unit

The central processing unit (CPU) is the "computer" part of the system. It contains an arithmetic unit for computation, a control unit, and the primary storage (also called the "main" or "internal memory"). The primary storage usually contains a part of the operating system software, one or more application programs being executed, and the data required by the programs. The control unit fetches instructions from the storage, decodes them, and directs the various equipment units to perform the specified functions. The arithmetic unit performs all arithmetic, comparisons, and data manipulation. There is a control console or control panel for operator use. Figure 1-9 shows a central processor with an attached console.

FIGURE 1-9 Central processing unit with attached console (IBM System/370 model 158). Console has visual display unit with keyboard and light pen for input. (*Courtesy of International Business Machines Corporation.*)

Secondary Storage   Also called "auxiliary storage," secondary storage is supplementary to the primary storage associated with the central processing unit. It is used to hold system software and application programs not currently required in primary storage plus data files. It has large-capacity storage relative to the primary storage. When a data record or program is to be used in processing, it is copied from the secondary storage into the primary storage. After processing, the updated record is stored back in its storage position in the auxiliary storage. Punched cards can be used for secondary storage, but magnetically encoded storage media are usually more desirable. Data can be written on a magnetic surface and read as many times as necessary. The storage may be used again by writing new records in place of the old records. The concept is identical to that of a home tape recorder—once recorded, the tape may be played as often as desired, and the tape may be reused by recording on it again. The most popular magnetic storage media, magnetic tape and magnetic disk, are illustrated in Figure 1-10.

Data Preparation Equipment   Data and programs must be in a machine-readable form in order to be read into the computer for processing or for recording on secondary storage for subsequent use. The most common machine-readable input medium is the punched card. The most common device to prepare punched cards is the card punch. Data may also be keyed directly onto a magnetic disk using a keydisk system. The data on the disk is transferred to magnetic tape for input. The keydisk system has substantial use because of several operating advances over the card punch.

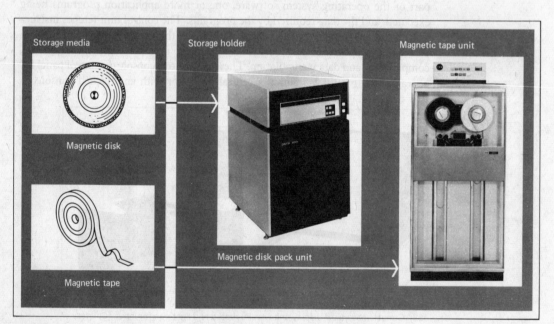

FIGURE 1-10   Examples of commonly used secondary storage devices.

Both the card punch and the keydisk systems convert data that has been captured on a document. This process is expensive, time-consuming, and error-prone. There is a trend toward eliminating manual data conversion by creating a machine-readable by-product while recording the transaction or entering data directly into the computer via a terminal device such as a typewriter or visual display unit. Some common data preparation equipment is shown in Figure 1-11; additional explanation is given in Chapter 8.

Input Devices The machine-readable input medium prepared by data preparation equipment is read by an input device (Figure 1-12) and stored in internal memory for processing, writing onto secondary storage, or output. The most commonly used input device is the punched card reader. Paper tape readers are used when input data has been placed on punched paper tape. Magnetic character readers are used mainly in banks for check processing. Optical scanners are becoming more popular. They are used for reading ticket-type data, such as gasoline charge tickets and airline tickets, and for reading typed and handwritten documents.

Output Devices Figure 1-13 illustrates output devices. The printer is the most commonly used output device. Terminals such as typewriters and visual display devices are receiving substantial use especially in systems which require persons at various locations to input data for immediate processing and then receive a fast response or to interrogate the computer files. Output may be on paper or microfilm, it may be on a display tube, it may be in the form of a graph drawn by a graph plotter, or it may be in machine-readable form, such as punched cards or punched tape.

The Computer Industry

Except for the UNIVAC computers in the early 1950s, IBM has dominated the computer industry. In the United States, IBM has furnished about 70 percent of computers (by value) to organizations other than the military. There is a vigorous non-IBM industry which has frequently been innovative in hardware and software, but it has not been able to match IBM's marketing strength or profitability. The dominance of IBM in the United States market has resulted in frequent antitrust investigations and in a major court case, begun in 1975, to decide whether IBM should be restructured to provide more balanced competition.

Other than IBM, the major computer companies based in the United States marketing a full line of computers are Honeywell, UNIVAC (division of Sperry Rand), Burroughs, NCR, and Control Data. Several large, diversified companies have dropped out of the computer business. Major examples are General Electric, RCA, Xerox, and Singer. There are a number of somewhat specialized companies. For example, Digital Equipment Company is the dominant manufacturer of small, specialized computers called "minicomputers."

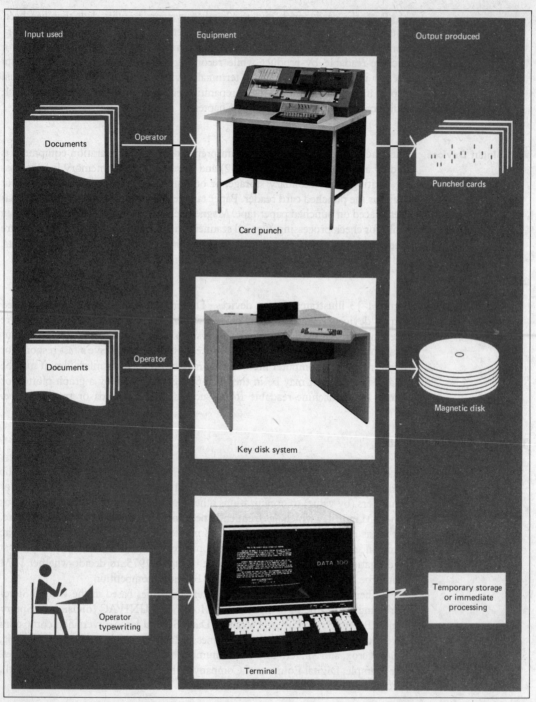

FIGURE 1-11 Examples of commonly used date preparation equipment.

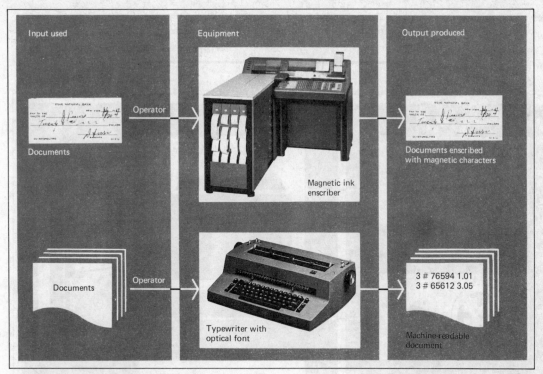

FIGURE 1-11   (*Continued*)

Although some of the earliest work in computers was performed in Europe, the United States adopted computer technology at a considerably faster rate during the 1960s. But the European growth rate in computer use exceeds the United States in the 1970s. The United States–based computer companies are active worldwide. IBM, for example, has about 50 percent of the European market. There are a number of well-established computer manufacturers in most industrialized countries. The more significant vendors are based in Europe or Japan. The U.S.S.R. has a computer industry serving primarily the Eastern European countries. Some of the major European and Japanese manufacturers providing a comprehensive line of computers are shown below.

Manufacturer	Country of origin
CII (Compagnie Internationale pour L'Informatique)—Honeywell Bull	France
Nippon Electric Co.	Japan
Hitachi	Japan

Fujitsu	Japan
ICL (International Computers Limited)	Great Britain
Siemens	Germany

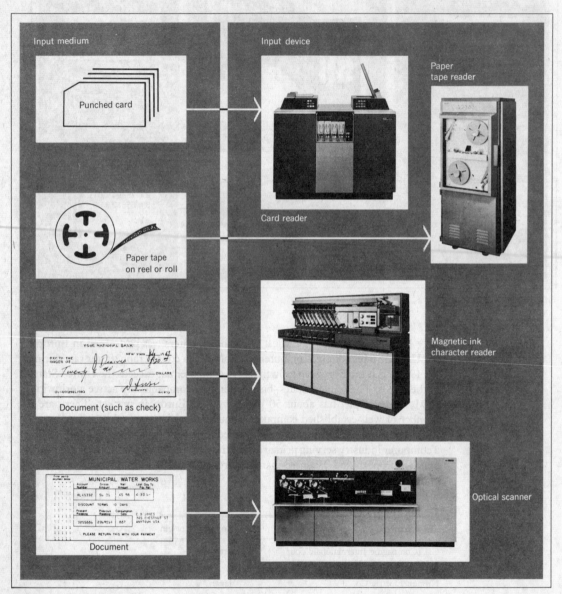

FIGURE 1-12   Examples of commonly used input devices.

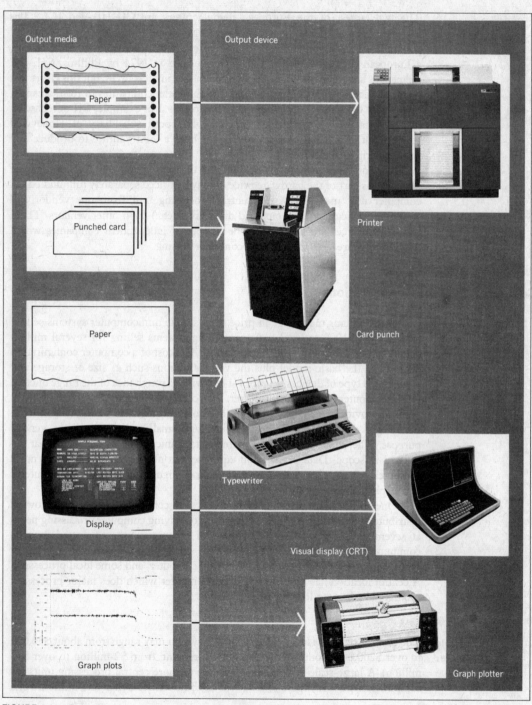

FIGURE 1-13 Examples of commonly used output devices.

The two largest of the European manufacturers are CII-HB and ICL. The European manufacturers have received considerable government subsidy and governmental direction to merge, cooperate, etc., with other vendors. For example, a European company called Unidata was formed in 1974 by Phillips, CII, and Siemens as a method of pooling design and marketing resources, but this effort was a failure. There is also some trend for the European companies to form arrangements with the United States computer companies. For example, CII purchased a majority interest in Honeywell-Bull (the European subsidiary of Honeywell computers); ICL, Control Data, and NCR have a joint venture to produce and market peripheral devices.

The computer manufacturers sell, rent, or lease equipment. Software may be furnished as part of the hardware price or may be priced separately (unbundled). A computer user may obtain the central processing unit from one vendor and peripheral devices (printer, tape and disk drives, etc.) from other vendors. These industry practices are the basis for a number of independent companies which provide software, peripherals, and computer leasing.

Computer System Configurations

Computer systems may range in price from simple minicomputer systems selling for less than $1000 to large-scale computing systems selling for several million dollars (renting for over $100,000 monthly). The cost of a computer configuration depends on the basic model plus the various options such as size of storage and number and type of devices. Figure 1-14 provides a rough idea of the range of costs for the computers of one manufacturer. Five configurations are described briefly in order to provide some idea of the type and cost of equipment a computer installation might contain. The large, medium, and small-scale systems are general purpose. The small-business computers and minicomputers are somewhat restricted in scope. Data preparation equipment is not included. Although not a computer system in the same sense as the four configurations, the microcomputer is also explained in this section.

One of the factors affecting computer system configurations is a trend toward distributed processing in which an organization having computer processing needs at several locations will use a network of computers interconnected by data communications. Each remote location has a small computer or minicomputer for input, output, communication with a central computer, and some local processing. A central location has a medium-to-large computer which does major processing tasks for the remote locations.

Large-Scale Computer   The costs of renting a large-scale computer system may range from about $50,000 to over $200,000 monthly (purchase prices ranging from $2 million to over $10 million). A large-scale system may have one or more central processing units for computation, perform operations such as an addition in less than one-millionth of a

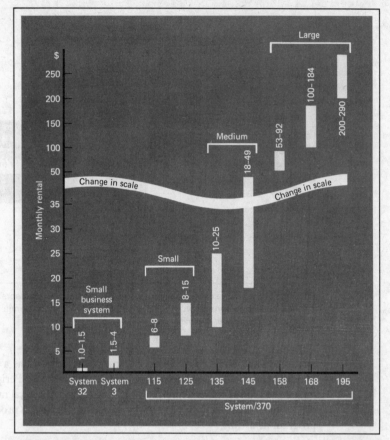

FIGURE 1-14 Monthly rental for typical configurations of IBM computers (adapted from data in DATAPRO).

second, have main storage hardware capability of storing several million characters, and include a large complement of input, output, and storage devices. Secondary storage directly accessible by the computer will range in billions of characters. The system can typically be working on a number of different programs or processing tasks at the same time, with at least some of the tasks involving input and output via data communications to remote terminals. Figure 1-15 shows the central processors in an IBM 370/168 multiprocessor system containing two processors. The input, output, and secondary storage devices are not shown.

Medium-Scale Computer A medium-scale computer system has reduced capacity and performance compared with a large-scale system. Monthly rental for typical medium-scale systems is in the range of $15,000 to $45,000. Operating speeds are perhaps one-tenth to

FIGURE 1-15 Large-scale computer system—two central processors in an IBM 370/168 multiprocessor system. The input, output, and secondary storage devices are not shown. (*Courtesy of International Business Machines Corporation.*)

one-twentieth as fast as the large system. Main storage has a capacity of several hundred thousand characters (perhaps up to 1 million). Peripheral devices will include a card reader, card punch, high-speed printer, several magnetic tape drives (say, four), and several disk drives (say, four to six). It can process more than one program at a time.

Small-Scale Computer A small-scale general-purpose configuration (relative to the large- and medium-scale systems) will have the same type of equipment but will be much slower—it may take 3 to 10 times longer to perform operations. Internal storage will be smaller—say, 65,000 up to 260,000 characters of storage capacity. There will be fewer input, output, and storage devices. Figure 1-16 shows a small-scale computer system.

Small-Business Computer A number of small computer systems have been designed for the data processing requirements of small businesses. The configurations are generally more costly than the minicomputer (although they are similar in basic capabilities), and there are more available input and output devices and more vendor support for the use of the system in data processing. The systems may also be used as part of a large-scale configuration (say, as remote devices—doing limited functions at distant sites). The most common small-business computers are the IBM System/3 (over 30,000

FIGURE 1-16 Small-scale computer system—IBM System 370/115. (*Courtesy of International Business Machines Corporation.*)

installed) and the IBM System/32, but a large number of alternatives are available. The System/3 ($1000 to $4000 monthly rental) represents a small but somewhat traditional computer configuration, whereas the System/32 (less than $1000 per month rental) has a compact integrated design that makes it suitable for an office environment. Compared with the small-scale systems, the small-business computers are about as fast but less versatile. Internal storage tends to be small—say, 16,000 to 65,000 characters, and the storage, input, and output devices tend to be slower or of lower capacity. Figure 1-17 shows two small-business computer systems.

Minicomputer Systems

A minicomputer is a small computer, but there is no clear definition of how small a computer must be to be classified as a "mini." As a rough guide, a minicomputer costs less than $50,000 and probably costs less than $20,000. Several systems at the low end of the spectrum cost less than $5000. The typical minicomputer is small in size (mounted on a rack or put on a table), weighs less than 50 pounds, and uses a standard electrical outlet. It is fast in basic operations but has a limited set of instructions. Main memory is small (say, 8000 to 32,000 characters of storage), and the number of input and output devices is very limited. The minicomputer is frequently dedicated to a specific function such as control of a manufacturing process, management of data communications, and management of access to a database. Some of the larger minicomputers provide a low-cost (but limited capability) time-sharing system. Figure 1-18 shows a typical minicomputer system. An example of how minicomputer technology may be used for limited-purpose

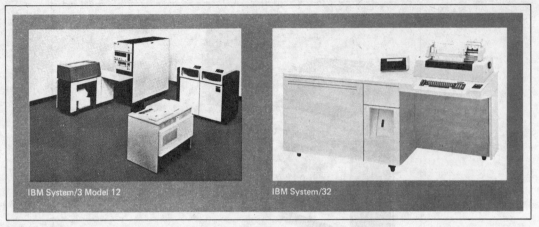

FIGURE 1-17 Two small business computers—IBM System/3 and System/32. (*Courtesy of International Business Machines Corporation.*)

computers is the IBM 5100 desk-top computer. The basic system (about $9000 for purchase) has 16,000 characters of main memory, a built-in visual display for input and output, a built-in tape cartridge for auxiliary storage, and a built-in programming language interpreter. This computer is aimed at individual users who need the capabilities of a computer for small analytical, mathematical, and statistical problems.

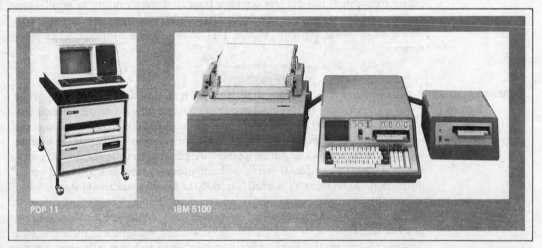

FIGURE 1-18 Two minicomputers—PDP 11 (*courtesy of Digital Equipment Corporation*) and IBM 5100 (*courtesy of International Business Machines Corporation*).

Microprocessors   A microprocessor is the "computing" part of a computer—on a chip. The microprocessor contains all the elements necessary to manipulate data. The chip is produced by etching and other processes which make and interconnect transistors, diodes, and resisters to make tiny but complete circuitry on a silicon wafer. A large number of circuits can be placed on a single chip costing less than $10 (Figure 1-19). Several chips may be combined to form a multichip processor. A power source and memory are required, as is some form of input and output to make an operational microcomputer.

The microprocessors are being used in a variety of applications. They form the computing logic for hand-held electronic calculators and desk computers. They provide a logic capability for directing the operation of machines of all types. They can add "intelligent" capabilities to data entry terminals, display devices, automobile carburetors, large household appliances, etc. For example, by using programmed logic in a microprocessor, a piece of equipment can automatically adjust itself to a variety of conditions affecting performance. Microprocessors are, therefore, likely to have a major impact on automobiles, household appliances, industrial equipment, etc.

SUMMARY   This chapter has provided an overview of the history of computers and has described the elements in a computer processing system, processing methods, the equipment found in a computer system, and typical system configurations. A computer was defined as a computational device having electronic construction, internal storage (for the program and the data being operated on), a stored program, and program modification capabilities. The history of computers starts in the 1940s with Aiken's automatic sequence controlled calculator, but the Hollerith

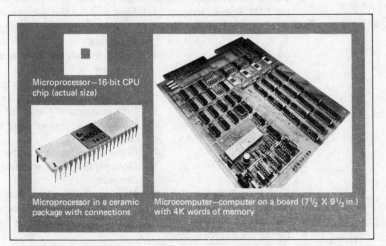

Microprocessor—16-bit CPU chip (actual size)

Microprocessor in a ceramic package with connections

Microcomputer—computer on a board (7½ X 9½ in.) with 4K words of memory

FIGURE 1-19   Microprocessor or CPU on a chip, microprocessor in a ceramic package, and microcomputer. (*Courtesy of Data General Corporation.*)

punched card was an important development preceding Aiken's machine. Babbage and Boole are also historically significant: Babbage for his idea of the computer, long before it was feasible to build one, and Boole for his mathematical logic, which is useful in designing computer circuits. In a fast-moving technological field, computer hardware is well past the first three generations—the first using vacuum tubes, the second using transistors, and the third using integrated circuits. During this period of development and change, increases in speed have been great and reductions in cost very significant.

The elements in a computer processing system were surveyed: hardware, system software, application software, procedures, and personnel. Each is explained in more detail in subsequent chapters. The hardware functions of data preparation, processing, secondary storage, input, and output were described briefly and illustrated. Methods of processing—periodic batch, online realtime, and time sharing—were defined. The computer industry in the United States and elsewhere was identified with the role of IBM noted. Computer configurations were described and illustrated.

EXERCISES

1 What was contributed to the development of computers by:
    (a) George Boole   (e) John von Neumann
    (b) Herman Hollerith   (f) J. Presper Eckert
    (c) Charles Babbage   (g) John W. Mauchly
    (d) Howard Aiken

2 What were the important features of:
    (a) ENIAC   (c) EDVAC   (e) UNIVAC I
    (b) MARK I   (d) IAS

3 Match the computer systems on the left with descriptions on the right.

(a) IBM System/360	(1) Most popular first-generation computer
(b) IBM 1401	(2) Most popular small scientific computer of second generation
(c) IBM 1620	(3) Most popular large-scale second-generation computer
(d) IBM 1130	(4) Most popular small-to-medium commercial computer of second generation
(e) IBM 7090-94	(5) First commercially available computer
(f) IBM System/3	(6) Popular small system using new-size punched cards
(g) IBM 650	(7) Compatible successor to the System/360
(h) UNIVAC I	(8) Most popular small scientific third-generation computer
(i) System/370	(9) Most popular third-generation computer family

4 What are the essential functions of the equipment in a computer center?

5 List the equipment in your computer center, classifying it by function.

6 Define the following terms:
    (a) First-generation computer   (d) Integrated circuit
    (b) Second-generation computer   (e) Transistor
    (c) Third-generation computer   (f) Analog computer

(*g*) Analytic engine   (*k*) Acronym

(*h*) Boolean algebra   (*l*) Time sharing

(*i*) Hollerith card   (*m*) Unbundled

(*j*) Batch processing   (*n*) Operating system

7   Name and define the duties of the three major classes of positions in a computer processing installation.

8   What is the difference between a minicomputer and a microprocessor?

9   Identify the major European and Japanese manufacturers and country of origin:

(*a*) ICL   (*c*) Siemens   (*e*) Hitachi

(*b*) CII-HB   (*d*) Fujitsu

10   Describe the two main shapes for punched cards and the variations in 80-column cards.

11   Explain the difference between system software and application software.

12   Prepare a short report on one of the following topics (see the selected references at the end of the text plus general business reference sources):

(*a*) The difference between IBM and UNIVAC leading to the differing market shares.

(*b*) The IBM decision for the System/360.

(*c*) The rise and fall of Unidata.

(*d*) The decision to drop out of the computer business by General Electric, RCA, Xerox, and Singer.

13   Despite the companies which have dropped out of the computer business, new companies enter. Write a short report on the Amdahl Corporation.

CHAPTER

THE USES
OF COMPUTERS

The computer is perhaps the most important technological element affecting society in the 1960s and 1970s. The computer is an important technological advance because it extends and expands human capabilities. Unaided, a human is rather puny. A person can lift perhaps 150 to 175 pounds, can move at 5 to 10 miles per hour, and can perform on the order of 10 to 15 additions of five-digit numbers per minute. Aided by equipment which extends their ability, humans may lift thousands of pounds, move themselves about at speeds of thousands of miles per hour, and perform millions of computations per minute. The computer is not only an extension of humans' ability to compute; it also expands their ability to store and retrieve data, to manipulate data, and to make decisions.

This chapter provides background for the chapters to follow by surveying the capabilities of computers and by describing a few representative ways in which computers are being used.

Capabilities of Computers

As illustrated by Table 2-1, a computer cannot perform any operation which cannot also be performed by a human, but the computer executes operations with such speed that it is in a different class. This speed also opens new approaches to problem solving and data processing. The speed of execution by computers ranges from several hundred million operations per second for a very large computer to tens of thousands of operations per second for a rather slow computer.

Although Table 2-1 indicates the ability of a human to do anything a computer

TABLE 2-1 WHAT A COMPUTER CAN DO

Operation performed by a computer	Corresponding action performed by a human
1 Hold program of instructions in internal storage.	1 Remember a set of instructions.
2 Read data in machine-readable form and store in internal memory or in secondary storage.	2 Read data in written or printed form and memorize it or file it.
3 Perform arithmetic computations.	3 Perform arithmetic computations.
4 Manipulate symbols (such as alphabetic characters or words).	4 Manipulate symbols.
5 Make comparisons.	5 Make comparisons.
6 Choose a path of instruction based on a comparison or an examination of the results to that point.	6 Make a decision as to further processing based on results to that point.
7 Retrieve any data from internal memory or secondary storage.	7 Remember data or retrieve data from a file.
8 Output the results on an output device.	8 Write or speak the results.

can do, the reverse is not true—a computer cannot do everything a human can do. Some people have characterized the computer as a very fast but somewhat moronic assistant. The computer does only what it is instructed, and these instructions must take into account every possible set of conditions relating to the action. Although a computer exceeds human capability in some activities, a human has some inherent advantages over a computer. The capabilities of computers and human clerks in performing data processing tasks are summarized in Table 2-2.

Advantages Possessed by the Computer

As seen from Table 2-2, the computer is extremely fast and almost perfect in reliability and accuracy. Once provided with a program of instructions, it will accurately retrieve information and will follow the set of directions perfectly. In substance, then, the computer is suited to any task that involves large amounts of retrieval, computation, manipulation, and comparison, so long as the procedures can be completely described in advance by a set of instructions.

Advantages Possessed by Humans

Humans are rather poor data processors. They are slow and not completely accurate. But they have two advantages—they can innovate or adapt, and they can reason heuristically. The ability to innovate and adapt means that a human's set of instructions does not have to anticipate everything that could happen because he or she can relate the new situation to old ones and make and execute a new procedure immediately.

Humans can reason heuristically. This means that they can learn by trial-and-error discovery. We do not usually reason in a simple step-by-step manner, but, in some fashion, we reach a conclusion based on trial and error, taking into account incomplete information and the effect of past experiences. A computer does not learn from past experience; a human does. Humans are aware of their environment and have their entire past experience always available; a computer has

TABLE 2-2 COMPARISON OF COMPUTERS AND CLERKS IN PERFORMING DATA PROCESSING TASKS

Basis for comparison	Clerk	Computer
Speed of execution	Relatively slow	Extremely fast
Ability to continue processing over an extended period	Poor	Very good
Ability to remember or retrieve information	Relatively inaccurate	Accurate
Accuracy of work	Makes errors	Makes virtually no errors
Ability to consistently follow instructions	Imperfect	Perfect
Ability to innovate in new situation	Fairly good	Lacking
Ability to learn by trial and error	Fairly good	Lacking

only the information which the program of instructions has made available. A human is best suited to think, reason, and discover; a computer is best adapted to calculate, manipulate, and compare.

The computer can thus extend the power of the human by performing tasks perfectly which humans perform imperfectly and by providing the raw material (data, results of processing, etc.) with which we may reason and discover. This suggests that information processing systems should be designed as human-machine systems in which each is assigned the part for which it is best suited. The applications to be described in the following sections illustrate the ways in which the computer has been used to replace, extend, or enhance human processing.

Recordkeeping

Recordkeeping requirements are an important element in the expenses of almost any organization. These requirements have increased in recent years until about $1 out of every $8 spent for wages and salaries in the United States is used for clerical work. Although the first computers were not intended for the recordkeeping function, the potential in this area was soon recognized, and today recordkeeping applications take up considerably more computer time than any other type of application. Recordkeeping applications are characterized by large numbers of items to be processed with only a small amount of processing required for each item. Some typical examples of recordkeeping applications are payroll, customer accounts, inventory accounting, and production scheduling. A very simple inventory accounting will be described as an example of the recordkeeping use of the computer. Two computer-based approaches to inventory processing will be described—the first is periodic batch processing and the second is immediate processing of each transaction.

Inventory Accounting— Periodic Batch Processing

In inventory accounting, a record is usually kept for each stockkeeping unit (SKU) in inventory, showing the number of units on hand and the cost associated with these units. When there is a receipt or a disbursement, an updating of the SKU record is necessary. Even for a fairly small business, the number of different inventory SKUs will run into the thousands. In the simplest inventory record-keeping system, the record of the past balance on hand for an SKU is read in the computer from a file of SKU records together with the records of transactions affecting the stockkeeping unit, and a new balance is calculated and stored. As part of the updating of the balances, a listing of the current number on hand may be prepared for all stockkeeping units, or the listing may show only items for which there was a transaction (i.e., changes since last listing). The documents, records, and files used are illustrated in Figure 2-1. The illustration is for a simple system of periodic batch processing using magnetic tape for file storage. The flow of processing is diagrammed in Figure 2-2. The general flow is to prepare input (say on punched cards) for all transactions, sort the transactions into the same order as the inventory file, and update each record for which there are transactions. If there are

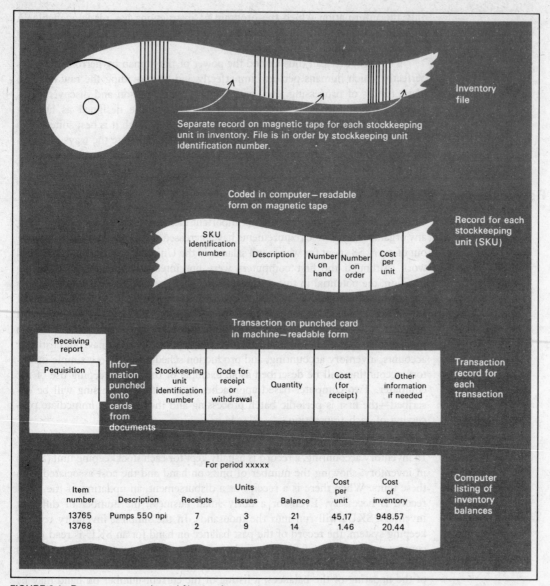

Inventory file

Separate record on magnetic tape for each stockkeeping unit in inventory. File is in order by stockkeeping unit identification number.

Coded in computer—readable form on magnetic tape

Record for each stockkeeping unit (SKU)

SKU identification number	Description	Number on hand	Number on order	Cost per unit

Transaction on punched card in machine—readable form

Transaction record for each transaction

Receiving report

Pequisition

Information punched onto cards from documents

Stockkeeping unit identification number	Code for receipt or withdrawal	Quantity	Cost (for receipt)	Other information if needed

Computer listing of inventory balances

For period xxxxx

Item number	Description	Units Receipts	Units Issues	Balance	Cost per unit	Cost of inventory
13765	Pumps 550 npi	7	3	21	45.17	948.57
13768		2	9	14	1.46	20.44

FIGURE 2-1 Documents, records, and files used in simple inventory accounting application.

no transactions, the record is written on the updated file without change. Most inventory applications which make use of computers are much more complex than this and can include the preparation of a forecast of usage for the item, the calculation of a safety stock requirement, the calculation of an optimal order quantity, and an analysis to detect obsolete and slow-moving items.

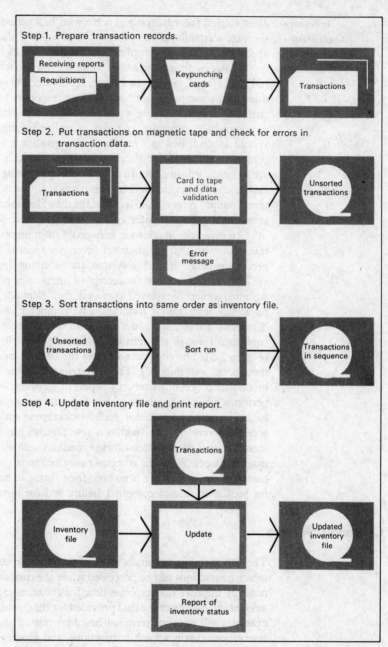

FIGURE 2-2   Steps in simple computer processing procedure for inventory accounting.

Inventory
Accounting—
Immediate
Processing

Most clerical recordkeeping is performed in a periodic processing mode: transactions are accumulated and processed as a batch. This is very satisfactory for some applications, but other applications require or can benefit from immediate processing. An immediate or fast-response system, also referred to as an online-realtime (OLRT) system, consists of a central computer and terminals for input of transactions to the computer and for receiving responses back from the computer. The terminals are provided for every person or machine in the organization having a requirement to originate, retrieve, or utilize information from the computer. A system is described as "realtime" if a request for information is sent to the computer and the result received back very quickly within the time allowed for acting on the information. In other words, processing is performed immediately as each transaction occurs rather than periodically with batches of transactions. The term "online" refers to the fact that the data files, input/output devices, etc., are all connected to the computer either directly or over data communications.

An inventory application may profit from immediate processing of inventory transactions so that the status of inventory records is up-to-date with very little processing delay. In such a system, the receiving department immediately enters via a terminal the record for receipt of items to be placed into inventory. When a customer order is received (say, via the telephone), an order clerk enters the requested order into a terminal. The computer checks the inventory status to determine whether the order can be filled. If inventory is available, the order is confirmed through the terminal to the clerk and by the clerk to the customer (Figure 2-3). The computer reduces the onhand balance because it is sold (even though not yet shipped). The maintenance of the inventory balances by such immediate processing probably is part of an online order entry application which performs other tasks related to entry of customer orders. Note that there must still be an inventory record for each stockkeeping unit, but each record must be accessible very quickly (within a few thousandths of a second). The record is therefore on a direct access storage medium such as a magnetic disk (rather than magnetic tape). Since the computer may be interrogated to obtain the balance on hand for any SKU, there is no need for a listing of balances or transactions except for backup in case of computer failure and for historical analysis.

Customer Service

The use of online terminals and fast-response processing means that many customer transactions can be processed while the customer is being served. This may not only improve the response time for the transaction; it may also improve the amount and quality of the data provided for the customer to make a decision. Three examples will illustrate terminal-based processing to aid customer service—airline reservations, savings bank transactions, and grocery store checkout.

Airline
Reservations

In an airline reservation system a central computer maintains a record of all scheduled flights for several weeks into the future. Each reservation agent has a

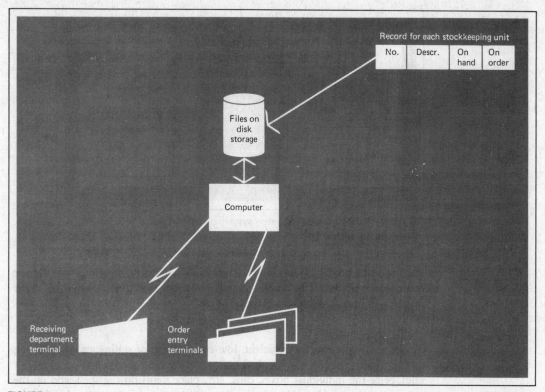

FIGURE 2-3 Immediate processing of inventory transactions.

device for interrogating the computer to determine whether the space that a customer is requesting is available (Figure 2-4). The terminal device is usually a keyboard input and a visual display like a small television screen for output.

If a customer makes a reservation, the computer records this fact in memory and reduces the number of seats available for the flight. The interrogation of the computer and the recording of the reservation occur in a few seconds. If a reservation is not available, alternative flights are displayed on the terminal screen. In many cases, the computer for one airline can interrogate the computer of another airline to make connecting flight reservations.

Savings Bank Transactions In an installation in a savings bank, customer records are maintained on a central computer, and input/output devices are set up at each branch of the institution. Thus, every deposit, withdrawal, payment, etc., is recorded at the time of the transaction, and current customer balances are available at all times at all branches. Savings institutions have an unusually high rate of transactions at pay periods, end of the month, and at interest-earned dates. The online processing allows these peak

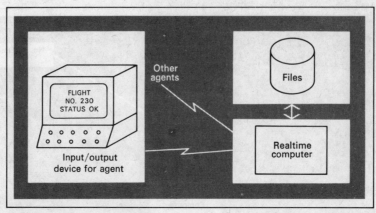

FIGURE 2-4 Online airline reservation system.

loads to be handled with much less delay than when manual retrieval of customer records is required. The system also allows customer-service terminals to be installed in locations such as grocery stores.

Grocery Store Checkout

The supermarket is a very efficient, low-cost method of selling and distributing grocery items. It has a few simple functions: order merchandise (based on rate of sale), price the individual boxes, cans, etc., place items on the shelf, add up the customer order, and bag the order for the customer to carry (or to be placed in the customer's car). The supermarket can be made more efficient if up-to-date rate of sales is available for ordering purposes, if individual items do not have to be marked with price, and if checkout can be speeded up (and be made more accurate). Computer-based checkout systems are now in use. Each item in the store is marked with a bar code which identifies the product by a unique number—the Universal Product Code (Figure 2-5). The price is shown on the shelf for all items, but no individual item is marked for price. At checkout, the product code on each item is in turn placed over a slot containing a beam of light which reads the code. A minicomputer then looks up the current price for the item in computer storage and causes the checkout terminal to print a description of the item, the unit price, the number of items, and the total for the items. An item can be placed on sale (and taken off) merely by changing the price in the computer and the price on the shelf sign. The computer keeps a record of sales by item for reorder purposes.

The advantage to the store is improved inventory control, reduced price-marking expense, reduced checkout expense, and elimination of checkout errors. The advantages to the customer may be lower prices (presumably stores doing this will pass on part of their savings in the form of lower prices), more descriptive data on the checkout listing, and elimination of checkout pricing errors. The disadvantage is the lack of a price on each item.

FIGURE 2-5   Universal Product Code for supermarket checkout—example on a package of gum.

Computer-based Analysis and Processing

The computer can perform any computations that have, in the past, been made by hand or by mechanical calculator. In addition, the stored program used by a computer permits complex-solution procedures to be programmed, and the electronic speed of the computations means that problems which could not be solved because of the time required for manual computation can now be solved in minutes by the computer. Not only the time, but also the cost of computation have been dramatically reduced. A popular large computer system can do computations in 1 minute that would take 100 to 200 years to do manually. Yet the commercial rental cost for using such a system is only about $10 a minute. A man-year of computation, on this basis, costs about 5¢ to 10¢.

The speed and low cost of computations make it possible to provide traditional mathematical and statistical computation at very low cost. These have also resulted in new computer-oriented techniques and in applications not previously feasible. Examples are linear programming, critical path analysis, system simulation, and information retrieval.

Linear Programming   Linear programming is a mathematical method for allocating the resources of a firm to achieve some optimum result (for example, to minimize cost or to maximize profit). The solution to a linear programming problem of any size and complexity involves hundreds of thousands of simple repetitive calculations which would be impractical without a computer. In fact, linear programming methods were developed specifically to take advantage of computer technology. The concepts underlying these methods were known previously but could not be economically utilized because of the volume of calculations involved. Linear programming is used by business firms to find the optimum solution to such problems as the least-cost blend of ingredients for feed (Figure 2-6), the most profitable combination of oil refinery production, and the most economical shipping schedules.

Critical Path Analysis (PERT/CPM)

The scheduling of projects with interdependent activities can become quite complex. Computer programs have been written which analyze activities in order to calculate which are critical to the timely completion of a project and which can take longer than expected without delaying the completion date (have slack). This technique is called PERT, CPM, or critical path scheduling (Figure 2-7).

Systems Simulation

The term "systems simulation" refers to duplicating the essence of a system in a way that allows an investigator to study and work with it. The mathematical or symbolic representation of a system is called the "model." This approach to problem solving is not new. Investigators have frequently made models or representations of reality in order to learn, to test ideas, and to predict the effect of introducing changes. However, the computer has made possible systems studies that heretofore were impractical. Even a modestly scaled systems simulation usually requires more computations than can be efficiently performed by hand.

The sciences use simulation for both physical processes, such as airplane engine performance, and human behavior; business uses it for commercial systems.

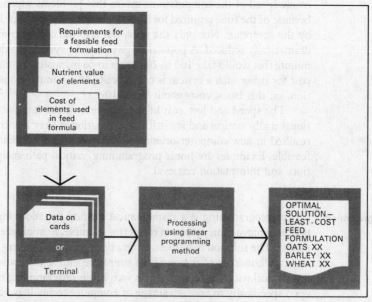

FIGURE 2-6 Linear programming (for least-cost feed formula)

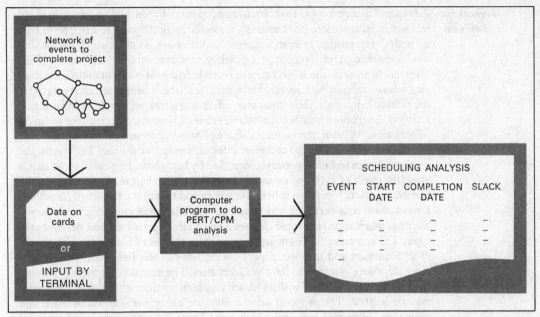

FIGURE 2-7 Critical path analysis by computer.

The simulation approach requires a quantitative description of the system and the programming of the model for computers. The model allows those using it to compress realtime, so that years of operation can be studied in a few minutes. Or the process may be slowed down to study problem areas in detail. Simulation can thus offer a basis for decisions about a new system without the disruptions and the costs associated with trying a system which may fail. To illustrate simulation, consider a business selling hot-water heaters which forecasts its sales as a percentage of new home construction plus a percentage of old homes (some of which need replacement heaters). This could be expressed mathematically as

$$s_1 = ph + gr$$

$$s_2 = s_1 m$$

where s_1 = sales in units, p = percentage of new homes, h = new homes, g = percentage of old homes, r = old homes, s_2 = sales in dollars, and m = average sales price per unit. These simple equations coupled with many others which describe the operation of the business can be programmed on the computer, and the effect on the company of various alternatives can then be studied using this program to perform the necessary computations. There are special languages to assist in writing such planning simulations using either periodic batch processing mode or the interaction at a terminal available with time sharing.

**Information
Retrieval**

Advances in technology have been accompanied by an almost overwhelming increase in information. It is becoming more and more difficult for a person to keep up with developments in even a narrow field. Persons doing research find it very time-consuming and sometimes impossible to make an adequate search of the literature bearing on the subject they are investigating. Millions of dollars are spent each year in duplicating research which has already been completed and reported in the scientific journals. The computer offers a fruitful approach to information retrieval. There are a number of available retrieval systems, especially for technical information. Most of the systems use a key-word approach.

In the approach of the technical information retrieval using key words, the contents of each technical paper are identified by key words. For example, an article about the effect of radiation on metals in the Van Allen belt might be identified by metals, radiation, Van Allen belt, and space. In addition to the key-word identifiers, a short abstract is prepared and stored on secondary storage medium. A person wishing information on a topic chooses a set of identifiers which best describes the topic. The computer is programmed to compare this set of identifiers with the list of all identifiers and to select papers having sets of identifiers containing one or more identifiers common to the topic identifiers. The abstracts for these papers are then printed out, together with an identifying number through which the reference may be located. The retrieval service may use either periodic batch input and output or interactive terminal processing. There are over a hundred retrieval systems which an organization may access for a fee. Examples are psychological abstracts, research in education, United States government research reports issued through the National Technical Information Service (NTIS), and chemistry and chemical engineering abstracts.[1]

Education

The computer has become a key factor in research and analysis by students and faculty. In addition, the computer is being used in the education process itself. Although progress has been slow and costly, the computer will almost certainly be a significant factor in altering the teaching process. Two examples of use of the computer in teaching are computer-assisted programmed learning and decision simulations.

**Computer-assisted
Programmed
Learning**

There are many variations of the concept of programmed learning, but all of them involve short, simple instructional steps and continuous testing. The instruction may be implemented by a book which is arranged into a series of short explanations followed by a quiz question to reinforce the points being made. Or the instruction

---

[1] For a list of 80 such services, see Beatrice Marron, Elizabeth Fong, and Dennis Fife: *A Mechanized Information Systems Catalog,* National Bureau of Standards Technical Note 814, U.S. Government Printing Office, February 1974.

may use a machine which exposes one instructional frame at a time. Both of these methods are single-path instruction methods. The computer allows the use of variable paths. Not all students, in a computer-assisted method, study the same sequence. If a student has grasped a concept (as evidenced by a correct response), he or she proceeds in a direct path to the next step in the material. If a mistake is made at some point, the student is given additional material to explain the topic again. On the basis of the responses, the computer selects the material to be presented. Grading of questions is done instantaneously (Figure 2-8).

The use of computer-assisted instruction (CAI) has tended to be experimental because of the high costs of development of programs and the cost of operating CAI applications. The cost of students using the terminals in CAI has generally been more than $1 per hour. A very competitive price (compared with the lecture method) is less than 50¢ per hour. The use of CAI has, in some applications, been very successful, and therefore this use of computers can be expected to increase.

Decision Simulations

Students in business and economics may gain a good understanding of such topical areas as accounting, finance, and insurance but not have any grasp of the interrelationship of these topical areas and the problems of top management. The decision simulation or management game is a tool for teaching students to integrate what they have learned into a top-management viewpoint. Decision simulations that are complex enough to be effective require a computer for making the necessary computations.

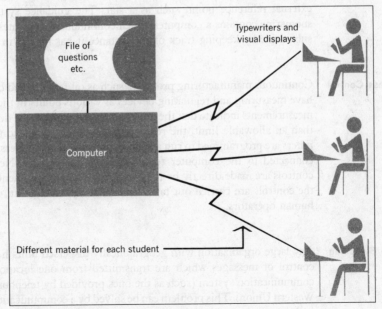

FIGURE 2-8 Computer-aided instruction.

In a decision simulation, several teams represent the management of different companies. Each team must make such management decisions as what to charge for a product, how much to produce, etc. The results of these decisions are calculated by the computer and translated into financial and operating statements which are the basis for evaluation and the making of more decisions.

Guidance and Control

Computers are used in guidance and control systems. In such systems, the computer is connected to measuring devices and controls. The measuring devices furnish data on the process being regulated. The computer then provides data to set or adjust the controls. Since the calculations necessary for these adjustments occur with electronic speed, the measurement and adjustment process is almost continuous. Some examples of computer guidance are missile and nuclear submarine guidance. Examples of computer control are manufacturing process control and message switching. Minicomputers are frequently used for these purposes.

Missile and Submarine Guidance   The large, complex intercontinental missile has a miniaturized but powerful computer inside its guidance portion. The computer accepts information on speed, velocity, etc., and produces data for altering the speed and direction of flight.

Since a nuclear submarine can remain underwater for extended periods, it needs a method for determining its position accurately without the aid of an external reference point, such as a star. The guidance system for the nuclear submarine contains a computer which continuously calculates the position of the submarine by keeping track of the distance it has moved in any direction.

Process Control   Continuous manufacturing processes such as oil refining and chemical production have measuring and regulating devices at various points in the process. When the measurements indicate that the process is deviating from the desired norm by more than an allowable limit, the regulating devices are adjusted (Figure 2-9). Computers are programmed to run a plant in the sense that the measurement devices are connected to the computer for continuous comparison. Necessary changes in controls are made directly by the computer. The measurements and the setting of the controls are carried out faster and more accurately than when performed by human operators.

Message Switching   Any large organization with geographically dispersed units has a problem in the control of messages which are transmitted from one location to another via a communication system (such as the ones provided by telephone companies or by Western Union). This problem can be solved by a communications system in which each location is equipped with a transmitting and receiving terminal linked to a

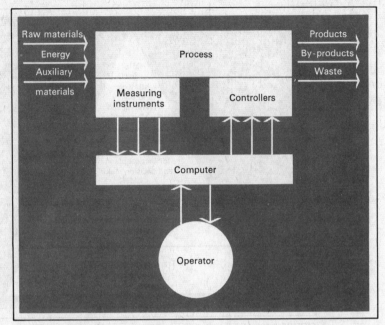

FIGURE 2-9 Diagram of computer process control.

central switching center. The switching center makes the connections between the receiving and sending terminals. Computers are being used to perform the switching function. They also make a record of all messages for reference and do statistical analysis.

Management Information Systems

The early use of computers in organizations tends to concentrate on clerical functions such as payroll accounting and processing of customer accounts. As organizations mature in the use of computers, they emphasize applications which provide information processing support for managerial functions. A system built around this emphasis is often termed a "management information system" or MIS. An MIS utilizes computer hardware and software, manual procedures, management and decision models, and a database to provide information in support of operations management, and decision-making functions in an organization. In terms of the type of information and information processing provided by an MIS, the system may be described as a pyramid structure (Figure 2-10) in which the bottom layer consists of the information for transaction processing, status inquiries, etc.; the next level consists of information resources in support of the day-to-day operations management; the third level consists of information system resources to aid in tactical planning and decision making for management control; and the top

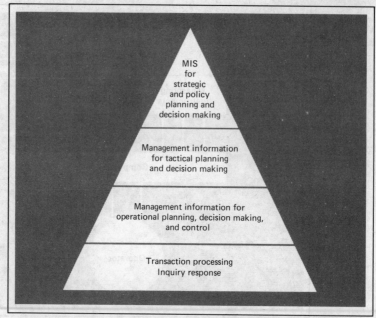

FIGURE 2-10 Management information system. (*Adapted from Robert V. Head, "Management Information Systems: A Critical Appraisal,"* Datamation, *May 1967, p. 23.*)

level consists of information resources in support of the planning and policy making by higher levels of management.

Another way to describe an MIS is the way in which major users of the system will utilize the capabilities provided, as shown below:

User	Uses
Clerical personnel	Handle transactions, process data, and answer inquiries.
First-level managers	Obtain operations data. Assistance with planning, scheduling, identifying out-of-control situations, and making decisions.
Staff specialists	Information for analysis. Assistance with analysis, planning, and reporting.
Management	Regular reports. Special retrieval requests. Special analyses. Special reports. Assistance in identifying problems and opportunities. Assistance in decision-making analysis.

The concept of a management information system is a design objective; implementation will vary considerably among organizations on the basis of the organizational function being served, the information resources available, and the organizational commitment to an MIS.

Other Interesting Uses of Computers

Prediction of Elections

Predictions are based on discovering causal or predictive relationships between variables which can be measured sufficiently in advance of an event or activity to make possible a prediction of the outcome. Computer analysis of election results is possible because the computer can be programmed to carry out complex computations to discover predictive relationships from past election returns and then to apply these predictive formulations to the early returns in an election in order to predict the final outcome. Conceptually, the computer is programmed to do what the shrewd observer does. However, it can do it much more precisely and much faster. The accuracy of the predictions has been excellent. Accurate predictions have been made with as little as 1 percent of the total vote counted. In fact, they have been so accurate that it has been suggested the television networks should delay giving out the results of the computer predictions for national elections for the United States presidency until the polls have closed on the West Coast to avoid influencing the vote there through the prediction of the final outcome.

Medical Diagnosis

Although currently in a very experimental state, computer-assisted medical diagnosis has great potential. In the diagnosis of illness, the physician must note the patient's symptoms and then compare them with the symptoms associated with different illnesses. From this comparison, the physician selects the illness which appears to best explain the patient's condition. The physician may or may not be able to confirm the diagnosis by laboratory tests. This procedure may result in imperfect diagnosis since the matching process which is the basis for the diagnosis depends on the memory of the physician both in detecting all relevant symptoms and in considering all possible illnesses which have such symptoms. The computer application involves having the initial symptoms which were detected by the physician input to a computer, where they are compared with the symptoms and indications associated with all illnesses. The computer can make these comparisons because the specific and detailed information is stored in its memory. The computer memory is then searched to arrive at all possibilities for the diagnosis, together with a description of indicators which should be searched for in order to make a final decision.

Computer Art

There have been two approaches to computer art—one using the symbols of the printer and the other using a graph plotter. For printer art, a program is written to print a series of lines which in total provide a desired visual effect. A graph plotter is an output device which is programmed to draw lines. A stylus with ink is moved over the page under computer control. The pens can be filled with different colored inks to achieve some very interesting effects. Figure 2-11 illustrates the type of computer art that has been produced.

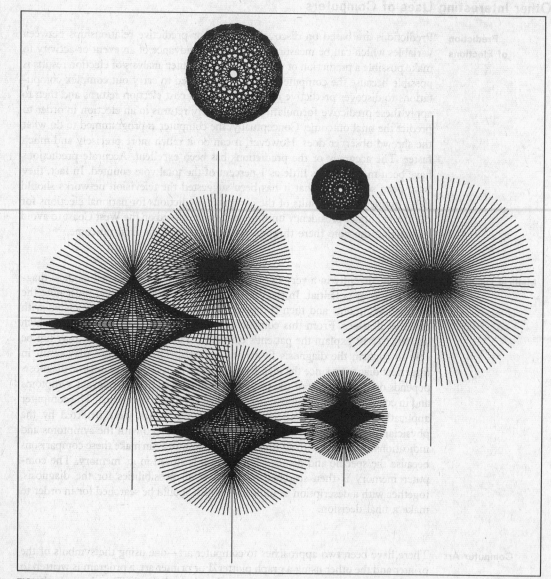

FIGURE 2-11 Computer art. (*Courtesy of Hybrid Computer Laboratory, University of Minnesota.*)

SUMMARY   The computer represents a breakthrough in computation. It extends the capability of humans through its superior speed, accuracy, retrieval capability, confirmability, and ability to follow directions. Humans have unique abilities not found in computers—the ability to innovate and to reason heuristically.

Although originally thought of as being primarily for scientific applications, most computers now in use are in commercial organizations. Routine data processing, such as payroll, sales analysis, inventory control, billing, and accounts receivable, dominates the commercial machines, but new applications are ingenious and exciting. The changes from traditional business information processing systems to customer service online processing and to the concept of a management information system represent a revolution in business systems. The computer has made feasible new techniques such as linear programming, critical path analysis, systems simulation, and information retrieval. Without the computer, these techniques were impractical. Computers are being used as part of the educational process, and guidance and control computers have made possible space exploration and automated factories. This brief description of computer uses has not been exhaustive; rather, it has indicated the types of uses to which computers are being put.

EXERCISES   **1**   Of what advantage are the unique features (speed, stored program, memory) of the electronic computer in the following uses:

(*a*) Payroll   (*d*) Systems simulation
(*b*) Inventory accounting   (*e*) Information retrieval
(*c*) A management information system   (*f*) Process control

2   Outline the logic of accounting for the following recordkeeping applications. What records must be maintained, what transactions recorded, what analyses conducted, and what decisions made?

(*a*) Customer accounts receivable
(*b*) Payroll
(*c*) Sales analysis

3   What are the features associated with:

(*a*) Periodic batch processing?
(*b*) An online, realtime processing application?
(*c*) A management information system?

4   A small businessman has trouble with his cash planning, even though he seems to have a good grasp of his business. He is in constant difficulty with his bank. He has asked you to design a cash model of his business which will inform him of the need for loans under various sales conditions. He gives you the following data as a starter:

(*a*) Cash sales are 40 percent of total sales. Credit sales are collected in total during the following month.
(*b*) Sales are increasing at a rate of 1 percent per month.
(*c*) Cost of sales is 70 percent of selling price. Payment for the goods is made in the month of the sales.
(*d*) Fixed administrative expenses (executive salaries, rent, etc.) are $2000 per month.

Write mathematical equations that describe this information. (These equations are only part of the mathematical model.)

5 In manipulating symbols, a computer often needs to make comparisons and order a list of words, numbers, etc. Assume that the computer interprets a blank as less than any other digit. Special characters are the next highest, then numbers, and finally the alphabetic characters are highest. This is called the collating sequence, and it may vary among different models of computers. Sequence the following list of terms into ascending order (smallest first). A small "b" means a blank.

(a) $15370   (e) DOGbIE
(b) 453700   (f) bCLASS
(c) b15370   (g) CLASSb
(d) DOGGIE

6 Forecasting models on a computer can be much more complex than those using manual computation. Exponential smoothing is a computer-oriented forecasting method similar to a moving average in which unequal weights are given to the data for each past period. The formula is: New forecast = old forecast + alpha (actual for prior period − old forecast for prior period). Alpha is a smoothing constant that can vary from 0 to 1.0, but is usually in the range of from .1 to .2. For computational purposes, the formula can be rearranged as: New forecast = alpha (actual) + (1 − alpha) (old forecast).

(a) Compare exponential smoothing to traditional moving-average methods of forecasting with respect to storage requirements and processing time.

(b) In order to evaluate the simplicity and versatility of exponential smoothing, compute forecasts (rounded to the nearest tenth) using a 6-month moving-average method and using exponential smoothing with an alpha of .2.

Actual data	Six-month moving-average forecast	Exponential smoothing forecast
29		
16		
40 6-month		
36 total = 180		30.5
31		30.6
28	30.0	30.1
32	30.5	30.5
23		
34		
25		

7 Identify a realtime application such as a savings and loan association or airline reservation system. If possible, visit an office where an online terminal is being used for the application. Evaluate the advantages of the realtime processing.

8 What are the characteristics of a processing problem that is suitable and economically justified for computer processing?

9 What are the characteristics of problems that are not suitable for computer processing?

10 What are the general characteristics of a human-machine system using the best capabilities of both human and computer?

PART

THE DEVELOPMENT OF COMPUTER APPLICATIONS AND COMPUTER PROGRAMS

There is a process which has proved effective in the design and development of computer applications and computer programs. Chapter 3 describes this process for both organizational data processing applications and mathematical applications. Chapter 4 explains tools such as layouts, flowcharts, and decision tables that are used in design and development activities. Chapter 5 considers the design of understandable and maintainable computer programs.

CHAPTER 3

THE DEVELOPMENT OF A COMPUTER APPLICATION

A computer application is the use of the computer for a specific task such as processing a payroll or performing statistical computations. Applications can be categorized in a variety of ways. A useful classification of applications is:

Organizational information processing (data processing and MIS)
Mathematical, statistical, and modeling
Information retrieval
Computer-assisted instruction
Data communications
Process control

The basic approach to development and implementation of a computer application is very similar for all types of applications. There are, however, some differences. This chapter describes the development of two major categories—organizational information processing and mathematical, statistical, and modeling applications. Although they have special characteristics, the other four categories of applications named above tend to follow the pattern of development described for organizational information processing.

Organizational information processing applications (often termed "data processing") are characterized by large volumes of transactions and repeated operation over a number of years. Frequently a number of different persons prepare input data and use output from the application. Those who use the output typically do not prepare the input. The format of the documents and reports produced by the data processing application must satisfy a variety of uses and must meet the requirements of internal as well as external recipients (customers, vendors, governmental agencies). The storage requirements for the data files associated with these applications are frequently very large (from a few million to several billion characters). The organizational information processing applications are generally interrelated because of common use of data and the interrelationship of the organizational uses of the output.

Mathematical, statistical, and modeling applications are frequently single jobs or jobs that are repeated somewhat infrequently. The number of transactions to be processed is usually not large (when compared with data processing applications). The user of the application is likely to be involved in preparing (or deciding on) the input. The output is probably used by a few people, and the format of the output is not important so long as it contains the necessary data. Storage requirements are generally fairly small, although there are exceptions. The different applications of this type are generally independent.

The Master Plan for Organizational Information System Applications

Information processing applications in an organization are not usually independent—they are part of an information processing system which processes transactions (such as sales, shipments of goods, etc.) to produce transaction documents and records and provides reports and analyses for management and decision-making purposes. Even though the applications are interrelated, not all applications can be developed at the same time. Priorities must be set. There is therefore a need for a plan which defines an orderly development of the applications needed to meet the organization information processing needs. Such a plan is termed a "master plan" or "master development plan." The master plan defines the processing environment and the development timing for each application. Consideration of development for an organizational application therefore begins with the master plan.

The master plan for an organization's information system is developed by a planning group which is given this responsibility. The work of the planning group will usually be supervised by an information systems steering committee composed of executives whose departments are affected by information processing. When the plan is prepared and approved by the steering/review committee, it is presented to the chief executive or the overall planning committee for the organization (Figure 3-1). The master plan, when approved, becomes part of the overall organizational plan. The master plan generally contains the plan for the next 3 to 5 years, with the current year having the most detail. The plan is updated periodically to reflect changes in the organization, experience with applications in use, and developments in technology. A complete review and updating are performed as part of the organization's planning and budgeting process.

The contents of the information system master development plan will vary among organizations; it is useful for the plan to contain four major sections:

Section of master plan	Contents of section
1 Information system goals and objectives	(a) Organizational objectives affecting the information system (b) External environment affecting the information system (c) Internal organization constraints on information system development (d) Overall objectives for the information system (e) Overall structure of the information system (how the applications fit together to form an information system)
2 Inventory of current capabilities	(a) Inventory of equipment, generalized software, applications, and personnel (b) Analysis of expenses and facilities utilization (c) Status of projects in process (d) Assessment of capabilities
3 Forecast of developments affecting the master plan	(a) Technology forecast relevant to plan (b) Other developments
4 The specific plan	(a) Hardware and software acquisition schedule (b) New application development schedule (c) Old application maintenance (revision) schedule (d) Personnel requirements schedule (e) Financial resources schedule

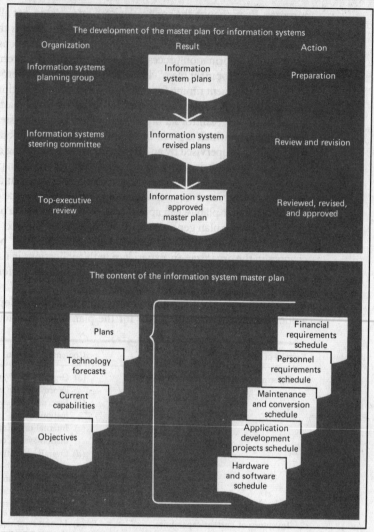

FIGURE 3-1 The information system master plan.

The master plan provides the basis for deciding which application to work on next. It also provides the information system context in which the application will fit. It contains only a general description of the application. The detailed development and implementation of the application follows a sequence of application development procedures (also termed a "development life cycle").

Information System Application Development Life Cycle

The basic idea of the development life cycle is that every application needs to go through essentially the same process to be conceived, developed, and implemented. Information system development involves considerable creativity; the use of the life cycle is the means for obtaining more disciplined creativity by giving structure to a creative process.

The life cycle is important in the planning, management, and control of information system application development. The use of the life cycle concept provides a framework for planning the individual development activities. In order to manage and control the development effort, it is necessary to know what should have been done, what has been done, and what has yet to be accomplished. The phases in the development life cycle provide a basis for this management and control because they define segments of the flow of work which can be identified for managerial purposes and specify the documents to be produced by each phase.

Overview of the Life Cycle

The steps or phases in the life cycle for information system development are described differently by different writers, but the differences are primarily in amount of detail and manner of categorization. There is general agreement on the flow of development steps.

The information system application development cycle has three major stages:

Definition of the application
Physical design
Implementation

In other words, first there is the process which defines the requirements for a feasible cost/effective system. The requirements are then translated into a physical system of forms, procedures, programs, etc., by system design, computer programming, and procedure development. The resulting system is tested and put into operation. No system is perfect, so there is always a need for maintenance changes. To complete the cycle, there should be an audit of the system to evaluate how well it performs and how well it meets cost and performance specifications. The three stages of definition, physical design, and implementation can therefore be divided into smaller steps or phases as follows:

Stage	Phases in development cycle	Comments
Definition	Feasibility assessment	Evaluation of feasibility and cost/benefit of proposed application
	Information analysis	Determination of information needed
Physical design	System design	Design of processing system and preparation of program specifications

	Program development	Coding and debugging of computer programs
	Procedure development	Design of procedures and writing of user instructions
Implementation	Conversion	Final test and conversion
	Operation and maintenance	Day-to-day operation, modification, and maintenance
	Postaudit	Evaluation of results

The information system development cycle is not followed in 1, 2, 3 fashion (Figure 3-2). The process is iterative so that, for example, the review after the system design phase may result in cancellation or continuation, but it may also result in going back to the beginning to prepare a new design.

Each phase in the development cycle results in documentation. The sum of the documentation for the phases is the documentation for the application. The amount of detailed analysis and documentation in each phase will depend on the type of application. For example, a large, complex application will require considerable analysis and documentation at each phase; a report requested by a manager will require little analysis and documentation, but all phases are still present.

Note that the information system development life cycle does not include the equipment selection and procurement cycle. The reason is that the selection and procurement of equipment (except for some specialized equipment) are generally related to many systems rather than a single application. If an application requires equipment selection, this will generally take place during the physical design development stage.

The following percentages provide a rough idea of the allocation of effort (say, man-hours) in the information system development life cycle from inception until the system is operating properly (i.e., excluding operation and maintenance). These percentages will, of course, vary with each project. The ranges shown are indicative of the variations to be expected.

Stage in life cycle	Phase in life cycle	Rough percentage of effort*	Range in percentage of effort*
Definition	Feasibility assessment	10	5–15
	Information analysis	15	10–20
Physical design	System design	20	10–30
	Program development	25	20–40
	Procedure development	10	5–15
Implementation	Conversion	15	10–20
	Operation and maintenance	(not applicable)	
	Postaudit	5	2–6
		100	

*Source: Author's estimates.

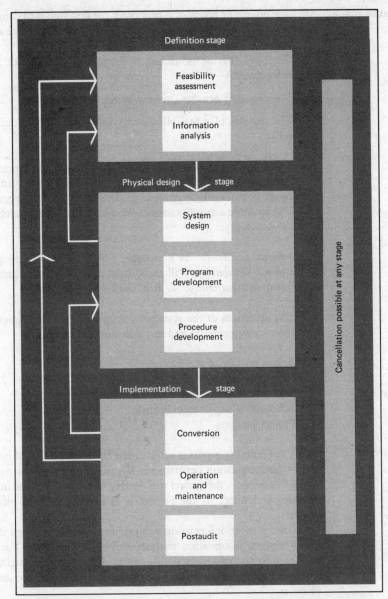

FIGURE 3-2 The information system application development life cycle.

It is instructive to note that upon completion of coding of computer programs (about halfway through program development), the application is probably only about 60 percent complete. For complex systems involving much testing, completion of program instruction coding may mark about the halfway point.

Definition Stage   After the project or problem is proposed, the first step is to define the problem. An analyst is assigned to work with the potential users and prepare a report describing:

> The need for the project (a problem, opportunity for savings, improved performance, etc.)
>
> The expected benefits (in very rough form)
>
> The outlines of a feasibility study (objective, time required, and resources required)

The proposal report is reviewed by the department proposing the project, the information system executive, and the information systems planning committee. If the project definition is approved, the feasibility study is begun.

One or more analysts conduct the feasibility study which is to assess three types of feasibility:

1 *Technical feasibility*   Is it possible with existing technology?
2 *Economic feasibility*   Will the system provide benefits greater than the cost?
3 *Operational feasibility*   Will it work when installed?

The objectives of the system are amplified from the rough objectives in the feasibility study proposal and the following are prepared:

> Rough outline of the system
> Development work plan
> Schedule of resources required for development
> Schedule of expected benefits
> Project budget

The feasibility report is reviewed by the management of information systems and by the requesting department. If it is not part of the master plan (and of significant impact), the project will need to be reviewed by the information systems planning committee. If the project is approved, the next phase is information analysis.

One or more information analysts (or systems analysts if no distinction is made between information analysts and system designers) are assigned to the project. The analysts work with users to define the information requirements in detail and to define the information flow. The results of the information analysis phase are:

1 Layouts of the outputs (reports, transaction documents, terminal output, etc.)
2 Layouts of inputs (transaction input forms, terminal input, etc.)
3 Data definitions for required data items
4 Specifications regarding information such as processing response time, accuracy, frequency of updating, and volume

These specifications complete the definition of what the system is to do; the next step is to design the processing system to produce the results as defined.

Physical Design Stage

The design of the processing system for an application is divided into three phases—system design, program development, and procedure development. Upon completion of this stage of the life cycle, the processing system will be ready for implementation.

The physical design stage begins with the system design. This is the design of the processing procedure (computer and noncomputer) that will produce the reports specified in the information analysis. It designs the equipment usage, the files to be maintained, the processing method, the file access method, and flow of processing. The results of the system design phase are:

1 System flowcharts showing, for example, use of equipment and flow of processing

2 File organization and design

3 A file-building or file-conversion plan

4 Control flowchart showing controls to be implemented at each stage of processing

5 Backup and security provisions

6 A system test plan

7 A hardware/software selection schedule (if required)

The programming and procedure development phases can proceed concurrently. Programmers will be assigned to do the programming; analysts will normally prepare the procedures. The programming phase uses the system specifications from the analysis and system design phases to define the programming tasks. The programs may be obtained by writing and testing new programs or by selecting generalized application programs that are offered for purchase or lease. The result of the programming phase is a set of tested programs that are fully documented.

Procedure development involves the preparation of instructions for users, clerical personnel providing input, control personnel, and operating personnel. The procedure development phase can also include the preparation of training material to be used in implementation.

Implementation Stage

When the programs and procedures are prepared, the conversion phase can begin. Data is collected, files built, and the overall system tested. There are various methods of testing. One is to test the system under simulated conditions; another is to test under actual conditions, operating in parallel with the existing systems and procedures. It is generally considered not good practice to implement a complex system without one of these full system tests.

After all errors and problems that have been detected in the system test are corrected, the system is put into actual operation. Any subsequent errors or minor modifications are handled as maintenance. This is not a trivial activity—about one-third of the analyst/programmer effort is devoted to maintenance of existing programs.

The last phase of the implementation stage is a postaudit. This is a review by an audit task force (composed, for example, of a user representative, an internal auditor, and a data processing representative). The audit group reviews the objectives and cost/benefit representations made in behalf of the project and compares these with actual performance and actual cost/value. It also reviews the operational characteristics of the system to determine if they are satisfactory. The postaudit report is intended to assist in improved management of future projects, improvements in the application under review, or cancellation of the application if it is not functioning properly.

The Development of a Computer-based Application for Mathematics, Statistics, or Modeling

Applications which perform mathematical, statistical, and model processing form a large class of computer usage. This class of usage has sometimes been termed "scientific use." The mathematical applications use the computer to perform computations required by mathematical solution procedures, as for example in the solution of equations. Statistical applications perform the computations to arrive at statistical measures such as mean, standard deviation, and correlation coefficient. Models to be processed by the computer are sets of computer program statements which describe the essential properties of a problem or a process being investigated. For example, a planning model is a set of program statements which compute the values in the various planning equations. A user can change the input data to a model and then rerun the program to investigate the effect of the altered conditions.

Although some of the mathematical, statistical, and model applications may be part of the organizational information system and be specified as applications in the information system master plan, most of these types of applications are in response to the needs of a single user or a class of independent users rather than being required by the information system of an organization. The steps in the application of computer processing to the mathematical, statistical, or modeling problem can be described by the same general life cycle flow as for organizational processing applications, but there are differences in the activities carried on in each phase:

Life cycle phase	Mathematical, statistical, or modeling application
Feasibility assessment	1 Problem identification (and assessment of feasibility of use of computer)
Information analysis	2 Problem (information) analysis to describe input, output, and processing requirements

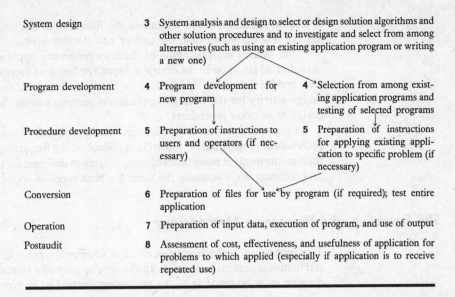

System design	**3**	System analysis and design to select or design solution algorithms and other solution procedures and to investigate and select from among alternatives (such as using an existing application program or writing a new one)		
Program development	**4**	Program development for new program	**4**	Selection from among existing application programs and testing of selected programs
Procedure development	**5**	Preparation of instructions to users and operators (if necessary)	**5**	Preparation of instructions for applying existing application to specific problem (if necessary)
Conversion	**6**	Preparation of files for use by program (if required); test entire application		
Operation	**7**	Preparation of input data, execution of program, and use of output		
Postaudit	**8**	Assessment of cost, effectiveness, and usefulness of application for problems to which applied (especially if application is to receive repeated use)		

Major differences between the life cycle for the data processing applications and the life cycle of the mathematical, statistical, and modeling applications are the reduced emphasis on procedure development, conversion, and postaudit activities for the mathematical, statistical, and modeling applications. In a large percentage of these applications, the life cycle might be described as:

Problem identification
Problem analysis
Solution procedure (algorithm)
Program development (or selection)
Operation

The reduction or elimination of emphasis on procedure development, conversion, and postaudit is a result of the difference between the data processing applications and the scientific applications. The data processing applications require instructions and training for a large number of persons involved with the operation and use of the application. This instruction is required not only when the application is installed but is also used for the training of new and replacement personnel as existing personnel change positions or leave the organization. By way of contrast there may be only one user of the scientific application. If there is repeated use by a variety of users, there will be an increased need for instructions to users. Conversion is generally a small or nonexistent problem for the scientific applications because they do not involve the complex interaction of a number of programs, large data files, and a variety of clerical personnel doing input and making use of the output. Postaudit is a useful practice if there is extensive use of an application.

If it receives a single use or infrequent use, questions of efficiency or effectiveness may be less significant than the cost of new development.

The system analysis phase of the data processing application must devote considerable attention to the design of input, the layout of reports, the structure of files, and the processing approach to be followed. By way of contrast, the system design activity for the scientific applications concentrates on the identification or design of solution procedures.

Program development for a data processing application almost always requires professional programmers. Scientific applications are frequently programmed by the users themselves using programming languages designed for users. The steps in programming are essentially the same for both types of applications.

The Selection of a Processing Methodology

Two processing methods are described in Chapter 2—periodic batch processing and immediate online processing. In the development of a computer application, a decision must be made as to the processing method to be employed.

The Basic Processing Cycle
An application in operation will generally require the performance of six functions (Figure 3-3). These functions will be the basis for the functions in the program design to be explained in Chapter 4.

1 *Data preparation* Activities which capture data and prepare it for input.

2 *Data validation* Checking of data for correctness (also called input-editing). This may occur during data preparation and prior to or during input.

3 *Input* Reading of data from input storage medium or accepting of data from input/output terminal.

4 *Processing* Manipulation of data and performing computational processes.

5 *Normal output* Writing of reports and lists or writing data onto storage for subsequent processing.

6 *Error output* Printing of error messages or writing of error data onto storage for subsequent processing. The error output can occur during data validation, input, or processing.

Alternative Processing Methods
There are two major elements in the different processing methods—time and method of updating the records that are being maintained. The timing is either periodic or immediate; the methods of record updating in files is either serial rewriting of the entire file of records or an updating of each record to be updated in the place in storage occupied by that record. The method of updating of records is related to file organizations. Records may be organized sequentially on the basis of some record key (an identification for a record) or organized nonsequentially.

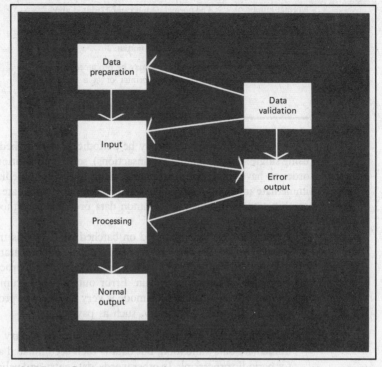

FIGURE 3-3 Basic processing cycle.

The functions associated with an application need not occur in the same time mode. Historically, it has been common to refer to batch (periodic) processing and online (immediate) processing as the two alternatives, but each of the six functions in the flow of processing may be periodic or immediate.

Function	Timing alternatives
Data preparation	The data can be prepared in batches for periodic data entry, or data can be entered immediately via a terminal.
Data validation	Data may be validated immediately at the terminal or by the computer if the terminal is doing direct input.
Input	Input can be individual transactions as they occur, or it can be batches of data at periodic processing intervals.
Processing	The processing can be performed on individual transactions as they occur or on batches of data processed periodically.

Normal output	The normal output can be printed immediately or displayed immediately at a terminal, or output may be written onto storage for later output.
Error output	Error messages may be produced immediately on the printer or at a terminal during processing or may be accumulated for a special error analysis output.

Although each function may be periodic, using batched data, or immediate, using single sets of data items (transactions), some combinations are not feasible. In order to have immediate processing, there must be immediate data preparation, immediate input, immediate data validation, and immediate error output. Three combinations will illustrate common data processing methods.

1   All processing periodic based on batched data. In this traditional batch processing mode (see Chapter 2 for an example), data preparation produces batches of data that are input as a batch, validated as a batch, processed as a batch, and output in an output batch run. Error outputs are accumulated and prepared periodically as a batch. This mode is very efficient for processing which needs to be performed periodically, such as payroll.

2   Immediate data preparation activities with data entry via a terminal and immediate data validation, but data is then accumulated as a batch on storage for periodic processing. In other words, data entry and validation are immediate in order to get validated data in machine-readable form as quickly as possible. This reduces the problems of detecting and correcting data errors but allows the remaining processing to proceed in an efficient batch mode. A variation on this processing approach is inquiry-only processing. Inquiries from user terminals requesting display of data from a file are processed immediately, with the result provided at the user terminal. However, transactions that update or change data in a file are held for periodic batch processing.

3   All functions are immediate for online processing. This is desirable when immediate response is needed using records that are kept up-to-date for each transaction. This is often termed "interactive" processing.

The Development of a Computer Program

A computer is directed by a set of instructions called a program. This section explains the characteristics of a program and describes the steps in preparing a computer program. Subsequent sections summarize the ways an instruction can be coded and identify some important aids to the preparation of computer programs. It is useful to differentiate clearly between system software and application programs. System software consists of programs which facilitate the operation and use of the computer by the application programs. Both types are computer programs and both require the same program development procedure, but the development of system software is an exacting activity generally carried out by specialists. Most system software is developed by the computer manufacturers or by vendors of system software. The emphasis of this text is on the development of application programs rather than system software.

Characteristics of a Computer Program

A program consisting of machine-language steps for directing a computer has three salient features:

1 Each computer instruction specifies the execution of an elementary step or operation in data processing.

2 The sequences of instruction specify what shall be done under all possible conditions during data processing.

3 Instructions can be altered by other instructions as the program is run.

Some examples of program instruction are:

Read a card and store the contents in memory.
Move the contents of one memory location to another memory location.
Add the contents of one memory location to the contents of another.
Print one line of output.

As can be seen by these examples, the computer instructions specify the execution of small, well-defined steps or operations. A program must specify what the computer is to do under all possible conditions. If there is only one possible condition or decision, the program will be a single-path program. If there are alternatives, different program paths must be provided for each of the conditions or alternatives, and a test must be made to determine which condition or alternative is true. This can be illustrated by the conduct of two individuals, Mr. Cautious and Mr. Ordinary, regarding the taking of an umbrella when leaving for work. Mr. Cautious always takes his umbrella just in case it rains. Mr. Ordinary takes his umbrella only if it is raining or cloudy (Figure 3-4).

The decision process of Mr. Ordinary creates two possible sequences of events, whereas the routine of Mr. Cautious is fixed. A computer program may contain both types of sequences. Since the program is a preplanned sequence of instructions to be followed for any and all sets of data relevant to a given problem, all possible conditions must be anticipated, and the sequence of instructions prepared for each. This preplanning of all possible program paths allows the computer to process data at high speed without human intervention. For example, a consumer survey of customer tastes may ask a question, "Do you like the XYZ brand?", and the customer is given three choices—"Yes," "No," and "Not acquainted with XYZ brand." When programming to tally the responses, it is

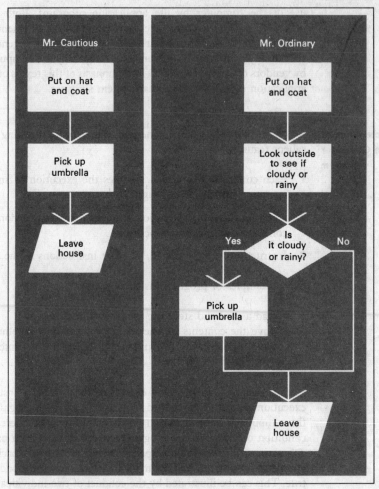

FIGURE 3-4 Short sequence in morning routine of two individuals.

necessary to decide in advance not only how to tally the standard responses, but also what instructions will be followed if the question is not answered or if some other answer is written in.

Steps in Preparing a Computer Program

The preparation of a computer program should have been preceded by system design (solution procedure design). The system design should have provided specifications such as the following:

Reports or analyses to be prepared

Algorithms or solution procedures to be used

Source documents for data collection

Method by which data on source documents will be transcribed to machine-readable form

Computer files to be maintained

Type of file media and file organization to be used

Layout of source document, computer record, computer file, and report

Processing, computer and noncomputer, required

Frequency of processing

Processing approach

Distribution and use of output

The programming of the computer for an application using computer processing follows system design and generally involves five steps.

1	Program planning	Outlining the procedures and logic for the computer processing required for the application
2	Coding	Writing detailed computer instructions using a coding language
3	Assembly or compilation	Translating the computer instruction from the coding language into actual machine language
4	Debugging	Testing the computer instructions to eliminate errors in procedure, logic, and coding
5	Documentation	Preparing and assembling documents which describe the program and its operation

Planning the Program A program of even modest complexity can rarely be written without preplanning. This planning breaks the program (if complex) into smaller modules. A chart may be used to show module relationships. The planning of program flow and logic frequently takes the form of a programming flowchart. In some cases, a decision table is used as an alternative. A set of program flowcharts typically begins with flowcharts showing the overall flow of program steps. This macro or overall flowchart is then supported by one or more levels of detail (micro) program flowcharts. The macro flowchart allows the reader and programmer to keep in mind the overall flow of work, while the micro flowchart has sufficient detail to be useful as a guide in the coding of the computer instructions. The program planning and design tools are described in Chapter 4.

Coding The writing of the actual computer instructions is known as *coding*. Although the computer will accept only instructions written in the absolute or machine-language form, the programmer typically codes in a symbolic coding language more suitable for human use. The symbolic instructions must follow rather rigid rules with respect to format, punctuation, etc. The program of the symbolic coding to machine-language instructions accepted by the computer is done by the assembly or compilation process.

Assembly or Compilation

Assembly is the translation of a program written in symbolic machine-oriented instructions into machine-language instructions. *Compilation* is the term given to the translation or preparation of a machine-language program based on a higher-level procedure-oriented language. The terms are sometimes used interchangeably although they do have slightly different meanings. One *assembles* a program written in BAL (name of a symbolic assembly language), whereas one *compiles* a program written in FORTRAN or COBOL (names of procedure-oriented languages). In both cases, the assembly or compilation process is carried out by a special computer program generally furnished by the manufacturer. The result is a machine-language program which performs the steps represented by the symbolic coding.

Debugging

Rarely does a program run perfectly the first time. There are usually errors in it. The removing of these errors ("bugs") is known as "debugging." Errors in programming can occur from mistakes both in writing the symbolic language and in the logic. Checking for errors should be performed at several stages as follows:

Debugging stage	Description
1 Desk checking	The programmer (and supervisor) review the program before it is released for assembly or compilation. The program is stepped through manually using sample data.
2 Assembly or compilation checking	The translator routine checks to see that all coding rules have been followed. Diagnostic messages are printed out.
3 Program testing using test data	The program is run using data which tests the actions of the program. The test results are compared with precomputed results.
4 Diagnostic procedures	Various procedures are available. For example, a program trace provides a step-by-step printout of the actions of the program, and a memory dump allows the programmer to look at the program and data at a given point in the program.
5 Running during a test period	A program generally needs to run under actual operating conditions for a test period before being accepted.

Documentation

The documentation phase consists of pulling together all the documents associated with the program and assembling them into a run manual and operating instructions. The run manual contains the complete set of documentation for the program. A typical run manual might contain the following: problem description; system flowcharts, layouts of records, files, reports, etc.; program flowcharts and/or decision tables; copy of the symbolic coding; test data used in debugging; program approvals; and record of program changes. The operating instructions used by the computer operator contain all information necessary for the operator.

Coding Computer Instructions

Coding of computer instructions can use different levels of instruction code, ranging from machine-language code to code which is procedure- or problem-oriented, not machine-oriented. These different levels are:

Machine language (absolute)
Symbolic assembly language
Symbolic assembly language with macro instructions
High-level language (procedure- and problem-oriented)

Machine-Language Coding The computer operates with absolute machine-level instructions, and all coding in other languages must be converted to this form. At execution, each machine-level instruction is stored in a set of computer main memory locations. (Data to be used by the program may also be stored in the main storage or may be obtained from secondary storage.) Each computer has its own repertoire of instructions based on the circuitry of the computer. Basically, all digital computers are very similar, but the instructions for one computer will not usually work on another computer of a dissimilar design.

A machine-level computer instruction contains at least two parts—the operation code and the operand. The *operation code* specifies what is to be done, and the *operand* specifies what is to be used to perform the operation. The particular operation code determines how the operand code is to be interpreted. The operand can be:

1 A memory address where a data word is to be stored or retrieved

2 An addressable register (used in processing)

3 The location of an instruction in memory

4 A unit of the computer system such as the card reader, a tape unit, or the printer

5 Literal numbers to be used by the program

The computer stores instructions and data using an internal code based on the two conditions or states of electronic circuitry (to be explained in Chapter 6). The equivalent arithmetic notation is binary (using 0 and 1 to represent the two computer states). Machine-language code is printed using some form of notation in place of binary, such as hexadecimal (also to be explained in Chapter 6).

The machine-language instruction typically contains one or two digits (or the equivalent in binary) for the operation code and four or five digits to identify an operand. Thus, a machine-language instruction may look like 563603, where 56 is, for example, the operation code for addition and 3603 is the address of the memory location where the number to be added is stored. The instruction is, or course, stored in a memory location in a binary representation. Using the hexadecimal operator notation, a machine-level instruction (to add contents of location 1E9 to location 1EF) for the IBM System/370 would appear as follows:

FA6541EF41E9

The corresponding binary representation stored in the computer would be:

111110100110010101000001111011110100000111101001

Symbolic
Assembly-Language
Coding

The machine-language form necessary for machine operation is not well suited to the person who must code the instructions. The reason for this is the problem of keeping track of where everything is stored. Since each instruction and each data word must be given a unique address, writing instructions in absolute code necessitates keeping track of all memory locations. In addition, the numeric memory location identifiers and numeric operation codes are difficult to remember.

Computer manufacturers have met this problem by the use of coding which is symbolic rather than absolute. Mnemonic combinations which suggest the nature of the operation are used in place of numeric operation codes. For example, ADD or A is used as a symbolic operation code for addition instead of a numeric code (such as 12). Each symbolic system has a more or less unique set of mnemonic operation codes. The programmer may also use symbolic addresses for identifying the memory locations used for storage of instructions. The programmer chooses his or her own symbolic addresses, subject only to the naming restrictions of the particular symbolic system. For example, a programmer writing a program to compute a payroll might refer to the memory location by using mnemonics which suggests the nature of the contents of the locations.

Contents	Symbolic address
Gross pay	GROSS
FICA tax rate	FICAR
Cumulative FICA tax	FICAC
Net pay	NET

The symbolic coding might look like the following:

Instruction stored at	INSTRUCTION	
	Operation code	Operand
PAY	ADD	GROSS
	MUL	FICAR

Coding of instructions is usually done on coding paper which assists the programmer in following the correct format. Figure 3-5 illustrates symbolic coding in assembly language.

Since the computer will not operate using mnemonic codes and symbolic addresses, these must be translated into absolute codes and absolute addresses. The translation is done by a set of computer programs referred to as an "assembly system" or assembler. The assembly routine reads the symbolic program from input (say, from punched cards), translates the mnemonic operation codes to machine operation codes, and assigns memory locations for storing instructions and data. The assembly system outputs a machine-language program. The translation from symbolic is one for one; that is, one symbolic instruction results in one machine-language instruction. The assembly routine keeps track of all memory locations used and of all symbolic tags associated with the memory locations. Once

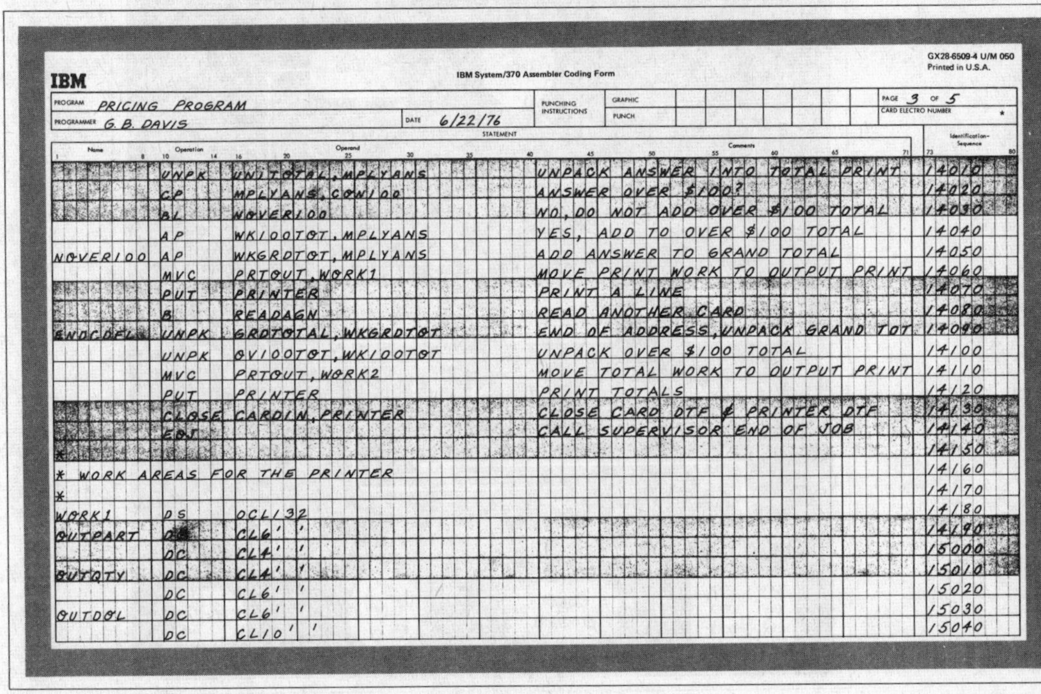

FIGURE 3-5 Sample page of symbolic assembly-language coding.

a memory location is assigned to a particular symbolic address, the same memory location will be assigned to all subsequent uses of that symbolic tag. The process of using a symbolic assembly system is illustrated in Figure 3-6. The translation process includes error diagnostics to detect certain types of coding errors.

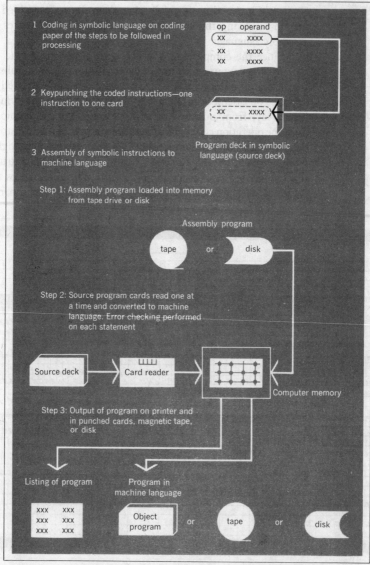

FIGURE 3-6 Preparing a program using a symbolic assembly system.

The advantages of the symbolic coding and assembly program compared with coding directly in machine coding are:

1 Coding is easier, since the programmer can use easy-to-remember mnemonics and symbolic address tags.

2 If a program is changed later or if two programs are combined, machine-language programming would require extensive checking to prevent incompatible memory location use. Programs written in symbolic code are merely reassembled to provide a reassignment of memory locations.

3 The assembly routine provides diagnostic routines to detect errors.

Assembly-language coding is described in more detail in Chapter 15.

Macro Instructions

The use of a symbolic assembly system does not reduce the amount of coding. There is still one symbolic instruction for each machine-language instruction. But many programs have small segments in common. Examples are the steps in reading and writing records, error checking, and scaling values. Since these operations are common to many different programs, it is possible to write short program segments to be included in any program which calls for performing these operations. To accomplish this, an instruction is added to the symbolic system which indicates that the program segment is to be added. When this instruction is used, the assembly system inserts the instruction segment in the machine-language program. An instruction of this type is called a "macro instruction" because one symbolic instruction results in many computer instructions. The macro instruction relieves the programmer of writing repetitious, standard routines and thereby lessens the chance of coding errors. Macros are quite commonly used for programming input and output operations.

High-Level Languages

The logic of using macro instructions can be carried one step further to build a coding language which is machine-independent. The coding language, being machine-independent, can be oriented toward the problem of procedure for which the language will be used. These problem-oriented or procedure-oriented languages are frequently referred to as "high-level languages." There must be a separate compiler for each computer on which the high-level language is to be used. The compiler consists of the translator program and other programs necessary to convert the high-level statements into a machine-language program.

Of the many procedure-oriented languages, the most popular are BASIC, FORTRAN, and COBOL, which are explained in detail in Chapters 16 to 20. The nature of the high-level languages is illustrated by sample lines of coding from FORTRAN and COBOL.

Description of a problem	Language	Coding
$X = \sqrt{\dfrac{A^2 + Y}{2B}}$	FORTRAN	X = SQRT ((A ** 2 + Y)/(2. * B))
Compute net pay by subtracting the total deductions (income tax, FICA tax, etc.) which have already been calculated	COBOL	SUBTRACT DEDUCTIONS FROM GROSS-PAY GIVING NET-PAY.

A high-level language such as FORTRAN or COBOL thus consists of a set of simple rules for writing steps to solve a problem. The compiler program translates these statements and creates a machine-language program (Figure 3-7). The creation of a machine-language (object) computer program by a compiler is a result of translating the high-level coding into program instructions and then combining these instructions with prewritten sets of instructions from a library of such routines provided by the compiler. The compiler thus puts together (compiles) a program from a number of parts and links all the parts together. The high-level language is problem- or procedure-oriented rather than computer-oriented and is therefore much easier to use than symbolic or machine language. Reasonable proficiency in FORTRAN or COBOL can be attained in a small fraction of the time required to develop proficiency in symbolic or machine coding. The advantages of the macro-instruction languages would seem to be so overwhelming as to preclude the use of absolute or symbolic coding, and the trend is for most programming to be in the high-level languages. On the other hand, the translation routine to convert from the language coding to absolute coding must be general enough to handle all possible cases, and, therefore, the resulting program is not so efficient in terms of running time as one which is programmed specifically for the particular problem. The disparity in running time may not be important for one-time scientific problems but may become significant for commercial problems that are run day in and day out. If the inventory-updating run takes 3 hours per day using machine-oriented programming and 4 hours using a high-level language, the difference in running time may preclude the use of the high-level language. Compilers have become so efficient, however, that disparity in running time is frequently not significant.

Aids to Programming

As may be apparent, the success of programming efforts depends not only on the hardware on which the application is to be run, but also on the software aids to programming. Programming aids generally available to users include (in addition to the symbolic assembly systems and compilers already discussed) library routines, program library software, utility programs, program generators, file and database management systems, applications programs, and conversion routines.

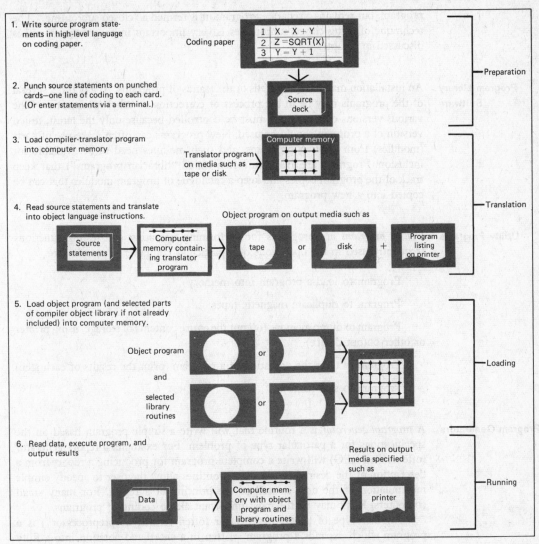

1. Write source program statements in high-level language
   on coding paper.

   Coding paper

1	X = X + Y
2	Z = SQRT(X)
3	Y = Y + 1

2. Punch source statements on punched
   cards—one line of coding to each card.
   (Or enter statements via a terminal.)

   Source
   deck

3. Load compiler-translator program
   into computer memory

   Computer memory

   Translator program
   on media such as
   tape or disk

4. Read source statements and translate
   into object language instructions.

   Source
   statements → Computer
   memory contain-
   ing translator
   program

   Object program on output media such as

   tape or disk + Program
                       listing
                       on printer

5. Load object program (and selected parts
   of compiler object library if not already
   included) into computer memory.

   Object program

   or

   and

   selected
   library
   routines

   or

6. Read data, execute program, and
   output results

   Results on output
   media specified
   such as

   Data → Computer mem-
   ory with object
   program and
   library routines → printer

   Preparation

   Translation

   Loading

   Running

FIGURE 3-7 Preparing an object program from a high-level language program.

Library Routines *Library routines* are program sections which solve a common computational problem. They are written to be spliced into any program being written by a user. Library routines generally include a wide range of mathematical and statistical routines. For example, a routine to calculate the square root of a number is prepared once by the manufacturer or by the user installation and then inserted in a user's program where needed. When the routine is spliced directly into the main program, it is termed an "open subroutine"; when it is attached to the main program, but remains a separate program, it is termed a "closed subroutine." The technique of using closed subroutines is very important in programming and is discussed in Chapter 5.

Program Library Software

An installation may have hundreds or thousands of programs. At any time, several of the programs may be in the process of correction or other modification. The various versions of a program must be controlled because only the latest, tested version of a program should be used. New programs can often make use of parts (modules) from existing programs, and such modules need to be available for inclusion. Programs are available (often called "librarian programs") that keep track of the program copies and keep a catalogue of program modules that can be copied into a new program.

Utility Programs

Utility programs are programs for performing operating and testing functions frequently used in the operations of a particular computer. Examples are:

Program to load a program into memory

Program to duplicate magnetic tapes

Program to dump memory (output the entire contents of storage, using printer or other output device)

Program to trace the operation of a program (print the results of each step)

Program to sort data

Program Generators

A *program generator* is a routine that will write a simple program based on the specifications for a particular type of problem. For example, a report generator (often called RPG) will write a complete program for producing a report from a description of the desired report. RPG routines allow the user to specify simple manipulation of the data as well as the printing of a report. For many small computers, RPG may be the most important aid to coding of programs.

Another type of program generator (often termed a "preprocessor") is a program which expands a program written in a shorthand notation into a fully coded program. For example, a COBOL program generally uses long, descriptive operation and data names for documentation purposes. A programmer may write shortened names and use a preprocessor to expand the coding to the full names.

File and Database Management Systems

A major segment of a program deals with the management of data files. Software termed "file management systems" or "database management systems" is available for file management, relieving the application programmer of many tasks. These file management systems often also contain facilities for easily programming the selection and retrieval of records and preparation of outputs.

Application Packages   These are complete programs which solve problems common to many users. The applications programs are typically ready to use, requiring only a set of data prepared according to the specifications. Examples are linear programming, critical path (PERT) analysis, sales analysis, and inventory simulation. There is also a trend to applications programs that are suitable for a whole industry, such as a complete billing program for electric and gas utilities or an analysis program for brokerage firms.

Conversion Programs   Manufacturers of computers typically provide users with considerable assistance. For customers changing to a new computer from an old one, conversion routines have been written to assist in the process. Since a major problem in conversion is the rewriting of old programs for the new computer, a major difficulty is removed by using a program for the new machine that will accept instructions written for the old. This is done by having the new computer simulate the operation of the old. The simulation program approach to conversion is in contrast to the use of a routine called an "emulator" which interprets instructions for the old computer and executes the corresponding set of instructions on the new computer.

Approaches to Program Job Submission

The contrast between immediate input via terminals and periodic batch input described earlier in the chapter in relation to the timing of processing flow is reflected in two different approaches to the submission of programs. (1) Batch coding and submission and (2) online coding and submission from a terminal.

In batch coding and job submission, a program is coded and punched into cards, job control cards are added to the deck, and the program job deck is left at the computer center to be run along with other jobs of this type. After being run, the output is printed and distributed. Turnaround time between submission can range from less than an hour to several hours.

A terminal may be used to enter the lines of program code and to call for compilation and/or execution. Error messages to the terminal allow immediate correction of errors, resubmission via the terminal, etc. The advantages are quick turnaround and reduced time to make corrections. The disadvantage is the inefficiency of programmers entering coding via a terminal.

A mixed strategy may be used in which programs are first submitted as a batch job (to avoid the entry of large programs via the terminal). The programmer uses a terminal to debug and to make minor changes. When this is completed, a regular batch output is specified, and a program listing is produced on the printer.

SUMMARY   The steps in the development of a computer application follow a similar pattern for all types of applications, but there are differences in emphasis between major application areas such as organizational information processing (data processing) applications and scientific (mathematical, statistical, and modeling) applications. The data processing applications should be defined by a master plan for the information processing system of the organization. Such a plan is developed as part of the planning and budgeting process of the organization. Within the context of the master development plan, each information processing application development follows a development life cycle consisting of a definition stage, a physical design stage, and an implementation stage. These three stages can be further described by eight phases: feasibility assessment, information analysis, system design, program development, procedure development, conversion, operation and maintenance, and postaudit. The organizational use of the applications means there is much emphasis in the life cycle on the design of the input, output, and files and on the preparation of procedures for users.

The scientific applications to perform processing for mathematical, statistical, and modeling problems are not generally part of a master plan. They are most likely to be developed in response to the needs of a researcher or group of researchers. The emphasis of the application development shifts from the design of input, output, and files to the design of processing procedures and solution algorithms. The life cycle for the development of these applications is generally reduced in scope to problem identification, problem analysis, solution procedure design, program selection or development, and operation.

Processing methodology is generally defined as batch or online, but there are a number of variations in the timing of the basic functions of data preparation, data validation, input, processing, normal output, and error output.

A computer program consists of a set of instructions which specify what the computer is to do under all possible conditions. Program development follows the general steps of program planning, coding, assembly or compilation, debugging, and assembly of documentation. The coding of instructions may take several forms—absolute machine-language coding, symbolic assembly-language coding, symbolic coding with macro instructions, and high-level problem- or procedure-oriented language coding. In addition to the coding languages and related translators, the manufacturers of computers and software vendors usually make available software packages which reduce programming effort. Programs may be submitted in batch mode or through a terminal with immediate response.

EXERCISES

1 Why is the master plan important in the development of most organizational information processing applications but not significant for scientific applications?

2 How does programming fit into the development of a data processing application?

3 What parts are logically contained in a master plan?

4 The life cycle for data processing applications has been described differently by different authors. Explain the difference between the life cycle in the chapter and the following two life cycles:

(a) Problem definition   Programming
    Preliminary survey   Programming tests
    Detailed business systems   System tests
    Detailed computer systems   Installation
    Programming specifications

(*b*) Survey   Filemaking
      Systems investigation   Clerical procedures
      Systems design   Systems testing
      Programming   Parallel running

5 What is the life cycle for a scientific application? Show the relationship of this life cycle to the information system application development life cycle.

6 An organization decides to develop a planning model for use by all its 345 branch managers. Which development life cycle is most appropriate? Explain.

7 What is the difference between the following:
(*a*) Assembly and compilation
(*b*) FORTRAN and COBOL
(*c*) Machine-level code and symbolic assembly-language code
(*d*) Emulator and simulator
(*e*) Library routine and applications program

8 Define the following terms:
(*a*) RPG   (*e*) Debugging
(*b*) Macro instruction   (*f*) Desk checking
(*c*) Operand   (*g*) Assembly system
(*d*) Utility routine   (*h*) Library routine

9 How might a programmer use a code-expanding COBOL generator? What would be its value?

10 Why is not all programming done in high-level languages?

CHAPTER

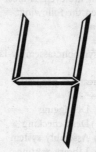

TOOLS FOR USE
IN DESIGN
OF COMPUTER
APPLICATIONS AND
COMPUTER PROGRAMS

Layout Charts

Grid Charts

Flowcharts
Explanation of Symbols
Flowchart Usage Conventions
Guidelines for System Flowcharting
Guidelines for Program Flowcharting
Horizontal Flowcharts

Decision Tables
Format of Tables
Steps in Preparing a Decision Table
Using a Set of Tables
Decision Table Processors
Evaluation of Decision Tables

Summary

Exercises

This chapter describes some of the tools used by systems analysts and computer programmers in analyzing, planning, and designing computer applications and computer programs. The tools are layout charts, grid charts, flowcharts, and decision tables. These tools assist the analysts and programmers in organizing their thinking, describing what must be done, and communicating the design to others. When the application is completed, the various charts are included with the documentation.

Layout Charts

A *layout* is a drawing which shows the format of an input/output record or the placement of data in storage. Preprinted forms are generally used for this purpose. Computer manufacturers make these forms available as part of their service to users of their equipment. They are also available from vendors of forms. The major layout forms in use are card (or terminal input) layout, tape or disk layout, and printer layout. Each of these is described and illustrated.

Each type of input or output card is described by the use of a card layout form (Figure 4-1). The fields on the card are marked off and described by noting the

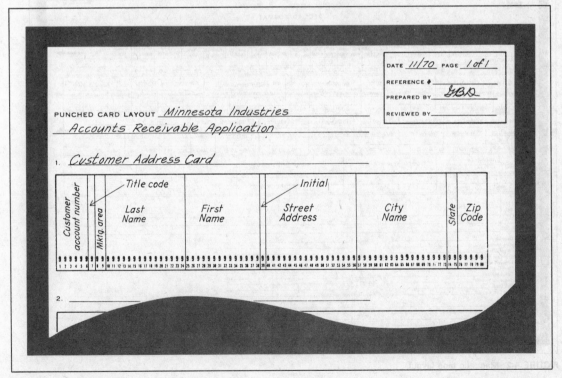

FIGURE 4-1 Card layout.

name of the field, the type of characters (alphabetic, numeric, or alphanumeric), and the location of the decimal point where appropriate. If input is from a terminal, each line of terminal input can be described by a layout form similar to the card layout but containing a larger number of columns.

The *tape layout* shows the format of records written on magnetic tape. It is similar to the card layout except that a card is limited to 80 characters, and a tape record can be as many characters as desired, limited primarily by the main storage space available for holding a tape block during processing (Figure 4-2). A tape layout may also specify tape characteristics such as density and number of records in a block. A disk layout is similar.

The *printer* or *visual display screen layout* assists the programmer in planning the exact placement of data for a printed or displayed output. Headings are shown on the form as well as X's or other notation indicating the data field locations. The vertical spacing of printer paper is often (but not always) controlled by holes in a short paper or plastic tape which is mounted on the printer. When used, this carriage control tape is planned with a form along the side of the printer layout sheet (Figure 4-3).

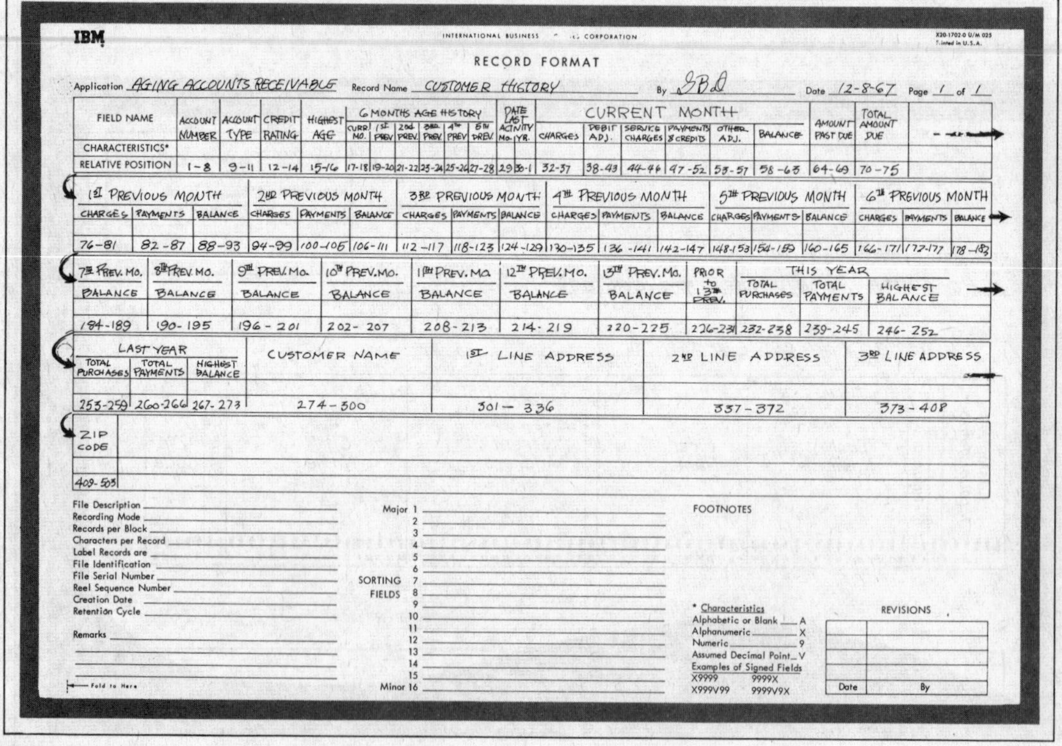
IBM INTERNATIONAL BUSINESS ... CORPORATION X20-1702-0 U/M 025 Printed in U.S.A.

RECORD FORMAT

Application AGING ACCOUNTS RECEIVABLE Record Name CUSTOMER HISTORY By JBD Date 12-8-67 Page 1 of 1

FIELD NAME	ACCOUNT NUMBER	ACCOUNT TYPE	CREDIT RATING	HIGHEST AGE	6 MONTHS AGE HISTORY CURR. MO.	1ST PREV	2ND PREV.	3RD PREV.	4TH PREV	5TH PREV.	DATE LAST ACTIVITY MO.	YR.	CURRENT MONTH CHARGES	DEBIT ADJ.	SERVICE CHARGES	PAYMENTS & CREDITS	OTHER ADJ.	BALANCE	AMOUNT PAST DUE	TOTAL AMOUNT DUE
CHARACTERISTICS*																				
RELATIVE POSITION	1-8	9-11	12-14	15-16	17-18	19-20	21-22	23-24	25-26	27-28	29	30-1	32-37	38-43	44-46	47-52	53-57	58-63	64-69	70-75

1ST PREVIOUS MONTH CHARGES	PAYMENTS	BALANCE	2ND PREVIOUS MONTH CHARGES	PAYMENTS	BALANCE	3RD PREVIOUS MONTH CHARGES	PAYMENTS	BALANCE	4TH PREVIOUS MONTH CHARGES	PAYMENTS	BALANCE	5TH PREVIOUS MONTH CHARGES	PAYMENTS	BALANCE	6TH PREVIOUS MONTH CHARGES	PAYMENTS	BALANCE
76-81	82-87	88-93	94-99	100-105	106-111	112-117	118-123	124-129	130-135	136-141	142-147	148-153	154-159	160-165	166-171	172-177	178-183

7TH PREV. MO. BALANCE	8TH PREV. MO. BALANCE	9TH PREV. MO. BALANCE	10TH PREV. MO. BALANCE	11TH PREV. MO. BALANCE	12TH PREV. MO. BALANCE	13TH PREV. MO. BALANCE	PRIOR to 13TH PREV.	THIS YEAR TOTAL PURCHASES	TOTAL PAYMENTS	HIGHEST BALANCE
184-189	190-195	196-201	202-207	208-213	214-219	220-225	226-231	232-238	239-245	246-252

LAST YEAR TOTAL PURCHASES	TOTAL PAYMENTS	HIGHEST BALANCE	CUSTOMER NAME	1ST LINE ADDRESS	2ND LINE ADDRESS	3RD LINE ADDRESS
253-259	260-266	267-273	274-300	301-336	337-372	373-408

ZIP CODE
409-503

File Description
Recording Mode
Records per Block
Characters per Record
Label Records are
File Identification
File Serial Number
Reel Sequence Number
Creation Date
Retention Cycle

Remarks

Fold to Here

SORTING FIELDS: Major 1, 2, 3, 4, 5, 6, 7, 8, 9, 10, 11, 12, 13, 14, 15, Minor 16

FOOTNOTES

* Characteristics
Alphabetic or Blank A
Alphanumeric X
Numeric 9
Assumed Decimal Point V
Examples of Signed Fields
X9999 9999X
X999V99 9999V9X

REVISIONS

Date	By

FIGURE 4-2 Magnetic tape layout.

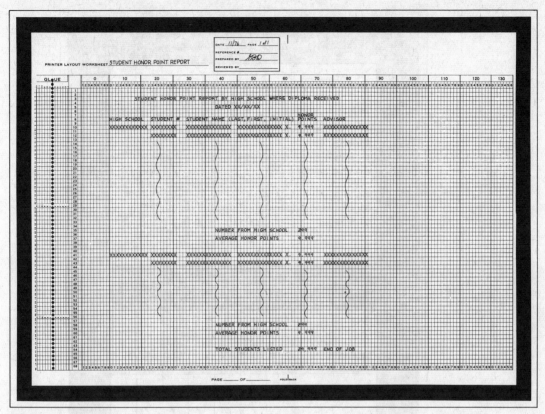

FIGURE 4-3 Printer layout.

Grid Charts

Grid charts are a tabular method of summarizing the connections or relationships between two sets of factors in a matrix format. For example, in planning the organization of a set of interrelated programs which use the same set of data, it may be necessary to summarize which programs use which data items. A grid-chart form is useful for this and similar purposes (Figure 4-4).

A grid-chart analysis is often useful in eliminating unnecessary reports or simplifying reports by eliminating redundant data items. All the data items are listed on the side of the chart; the reports are listed across the top (Figure 4-4). An entry of 1 indicates that the data item appears on the report. By analyzing the redundancies, the systems analyst may be able to reduce the number or complexity of reports.

A grid chart may be applied to the documentation of user procedures. For example, an input procedure which requires different data item input depending on

Grid chart to analyze use of data items by different programs

Data items \ Programs	Sales analysis	Sales forecast	Sales budget	Salesman evaluation	Warehouse analysis	Product evaluation	Other
Customer name				/			
Customer address						/	
Credit code	/						
Territory code	/	/	/	/	(/)		
etc.							

Indicates use of territory code by warehouse analysis

Grid chart to analyze the use of data items for preparation of reports

Data items \ Reports	Attendance report	Foreman's production report	Payroll register	FICA quarterly report	Income tax withheld report	W-2 reports	Other
Employee no.	/	/	/				
Employee name			/	/	/	/	
Employee address						/	
Social Security no.			/	/	/	/	
etc.							

FIGURE 4-4 Grid charts.

the transaction type may use a grid-chart format to summarize these inputs for the user (see Exercise 3).

Flowcharts

Flowcharts are symbolic diagrams of operation sequence, data flow, control flow, and processing logic in information processing. Flowcharts are used both in the design of data processing applications as a means of recording the proposed system design and also as part of the documentation of the completed application. Flow-charts are also useful to those who must review systems (such as auditors) as a concise method to document understanding of an application being reviewed.

The communication function of flowcharts is enhanced if standard symbols are used in drawing the charts. Standard flowchart symbols have been adopted by the American National Standards Institute (ANSI).[1] The symbols have also been adopted internationally by the International Organization for Standardization (ISO).[2] The use of these flowchart standards is voluntary, but they have been widely adopted and their use is therefore encouraged for data processing personnel and others who prepare flowcharts.

Even though the same set of symbols is used for both, it is convenient to distinguish between two types of flowcharts:

1 *System flowchart* This chart describes the sequence of major processing operations (both manual and computer), data flow from and to the files used in processing, and the flow of processing controls.

2 *Program flowchart* This type describes the sequence of operations and logic for a computer program. It is sometimes referred to as a block or logic diagram.

Flowcharts are normally prepared using a flowchart template which is available from computer manufacturers and from independent suppliers of drawing templates. A template is not necessary but does add to the neatness and speed with which a good flowchart can be drawn. Special forms are available to aid in drawing flowcharts. The forms contain predrawn areas in which symbols can be drawn neatly. These forms are a convenience but not absolute requirements.

Various software packages are available to prepare flowcharts from a source program code (computer instructions written in the COBOL, FORTRAN, or assembly languages). The flowcharts prepared by this software tend to be somewhat more detailed than a programmer or an analyst might draw. However, the software provides a useful method of developing a flowchart for those cases in which there is no documentation or documentation is inadequate.

Explanation of Symbols

Figure 4-5 summarizes the 30 standard flowchart symbols; Figure 4-6 provides an example of the use of each of the symbols. There seem to be a large number of symbols to learn. However, there are four basic symbols which are sufficient to describe a data processing system or a program. All other symbols provide additional specificity and clarity.

The general I/O symbol can be used in place of all I/O and storage symbols (except communication link). However, the specialized symbols provide a clearer

[1] The complete American National Standard, X3.5-1970, *Flowchart Symbols and Their Usage in Information Processing,* is available from the American National Standards Institute, Inc., 1430 Broadway, New York, N.Y. 10018.

[2] ISO/R 1028-1969.

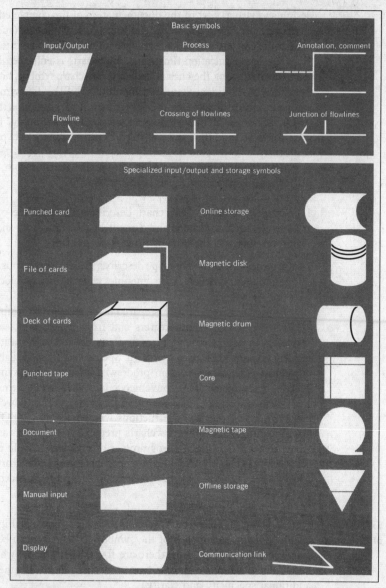

FIGURE 4-5 International (ISO) and American National Standard (ANSI) flowchart symbols for information processing.

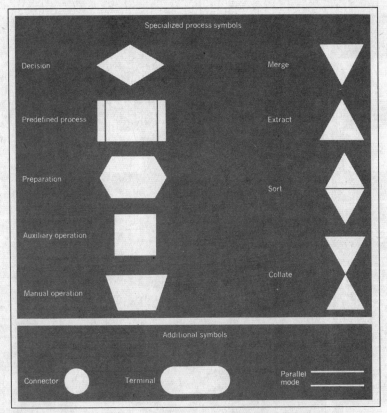

FIGURE 4-5 (*Continued*)

picture of the system. If there is to be output but the exact medium has not been decided, the system is flowcharted with the general I/O symbol; when the output has been decided as printer, then the flowchart is made more specific by drawing the output using the printer symbol. A short description of the document, file, or process is usually written inside the symbol. If additional description or explanatory notes are required, the annotation symbol is used.

Flowchart Usage Conventions

The standard is to draw flowcharts so that they read from left to right and top to bottom. If the flow goes in a reverse direction, arrowheads are used. Arrowheads can, of course, be used in normal flow to increase clarity or readability.

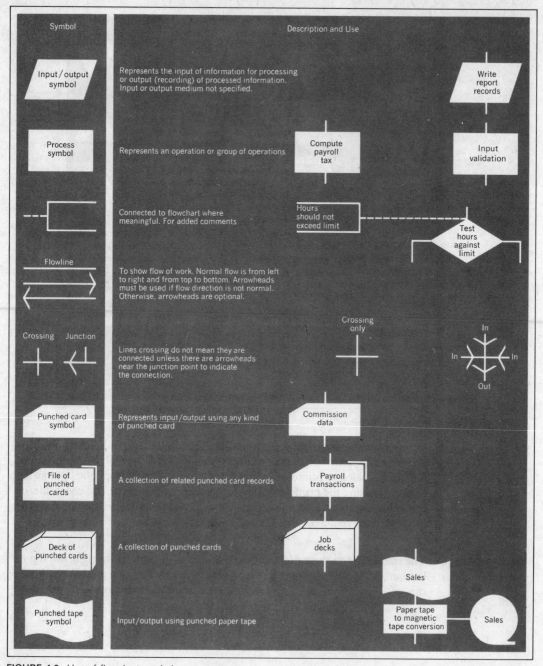

FIGURE 4-6 Use of flowchart symbols.

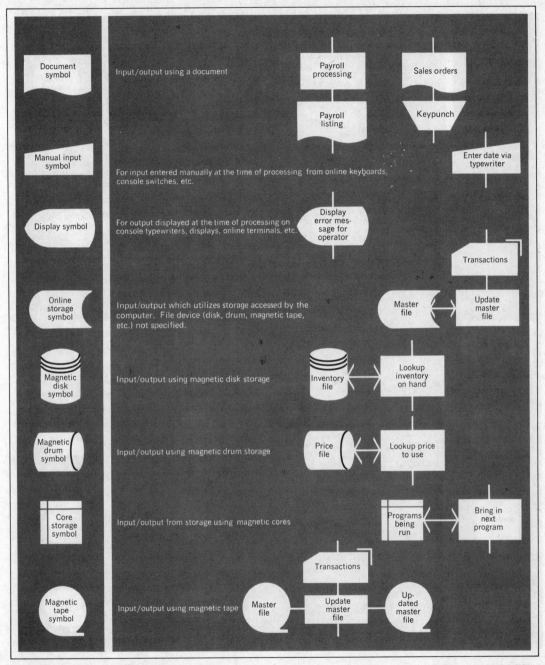

FIGURE 4-6 *(Continued)*

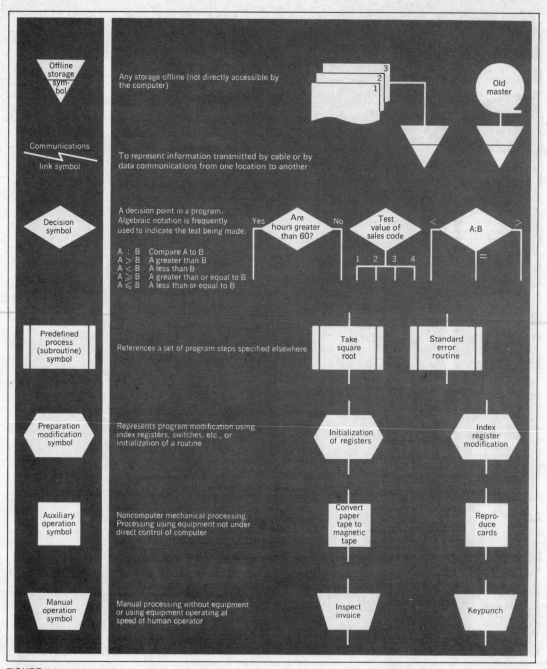

FIGURE 4-6 *(Continued)*

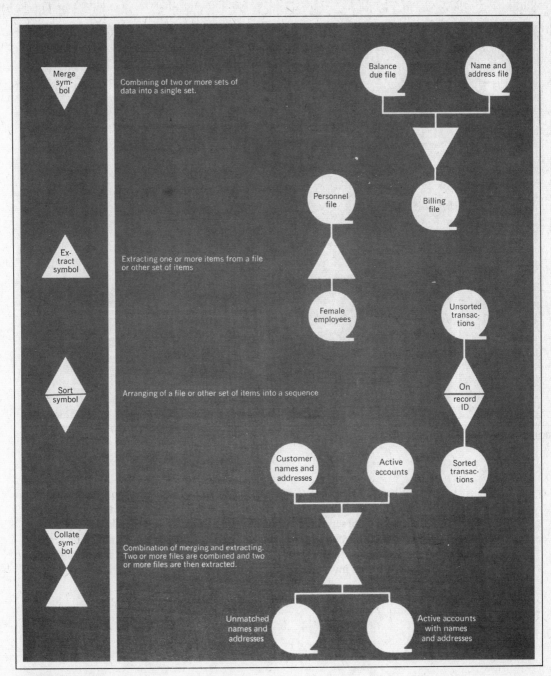

FIGURE 4-6 (Continued)

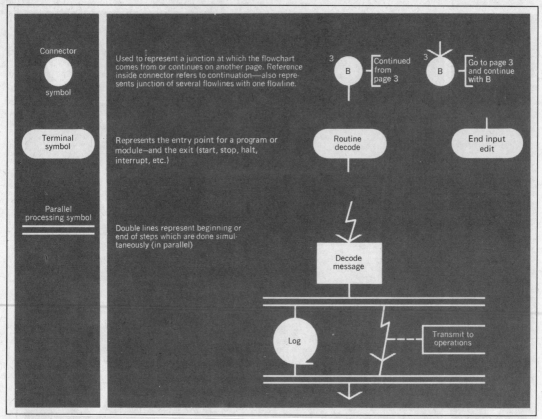

FIGURE 4-6 (*Continued*)

When it is desirable to identify a symbol for the purpose of referencing it, a notation is placed above the symbol to the right or left of the vertical bisector or inside the symbol separated by a stripe. American National Standards for the use of the flowcharts specify a standard use for each. The symbol identifier and striping code can be constituted so as to reflect other information important for the reader, e.g., department involved.

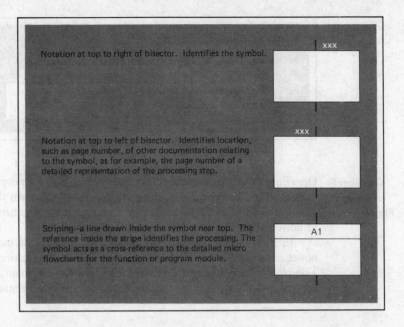

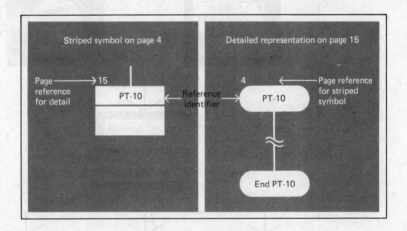

Overlay patterns may be used to show multiple input or output media or files. The front symbol is drawn in full and the other patterns offset behind it (right or left). There may be multiple copies of the same output or different inputs and outputs which are part of a set.

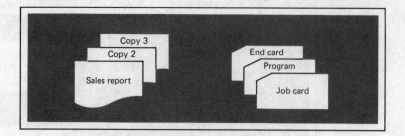

Guidelines for System Flowcharting

Drawing flowcharts is sufficiently creative that no two people will draw them exactly alike. However, following the guidelines for system flowcharting in this section and program flowcharting in the next section will enhance the effective use of flowcharting as an aid to design and documentation.

In the design of a data processing application, it is useful to use system flowcharts to show the flow of data and controls in an application. Figure 4-7 shows a simple system flowchart for one of the major functions in an accounts receivable application—the run which updates the accounts receivable master file. In drawing

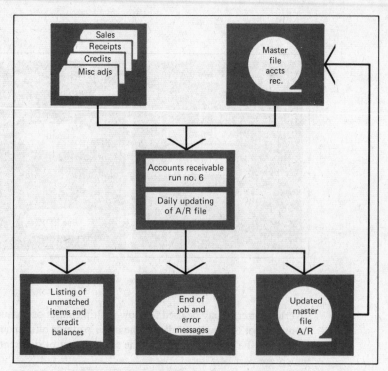

FIGURE 4-7 Simple system flowchart for updating of accounts receivable file.

the system flowchart, the sandwich principle[1] is useful—to have one or more inputs and one or more outputs from a process. The output from one process may be the input to another process (Figure 4-8). When a system flowchart is too large for a single page, it may be divided into a macro chart and several micro charts (one for each process on the macro flowchart). When a system chart must be continued on another page, a clear method of breaking it is to identify the output which will be

[1]The term was coined by Chapin. See Ned Chapin, "Flowcharting with the ANSI Standard: A Tutorial," *Computing Surveys,* June 1970, pp. 119–146.

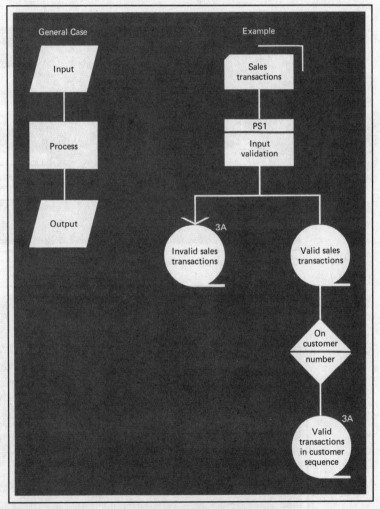

FIGURE 4-8 The sandwich principle in flowcharting.

the input on the next chart with a page and symbol number. Repeat the symbol as an input on the continuation chart with a page and symbol reference back to the flowchart page from which it came. For example, the system flowchart output invalid transactions on page 1 shown in Figure 4-9 is continued on page 2 of the system flowcharts. The flowcharting would repeat the invalid transaction file with a reference.

It is frequently impossible to write suitable explanations in the symbols. One alternative is the use of the annotation symbol. Another alternative is to use an annotation column to the right of the flowchart. Additional comments may be written opposite each symbol (Figure 4-10).

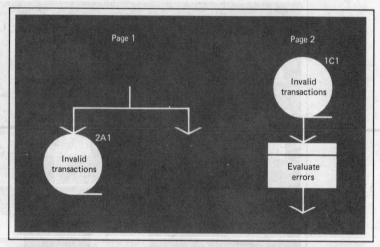

FIGURE 4-9 Breaking a system flowchart.

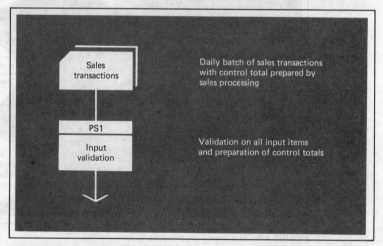

FIGURE 4-10 Use of annotation column.

System charts can be used to show manual processing such as manual procedures to prepare data for computer processing and the manual use of output. For example, the preparation of sales transaction input (shown as input in Figure 4-8) can be diagrammed by a manual procedure system flowchart (Figure 4-11).

Effective error and quality control of a processing application is an important consideration in the design. Although both purposes can be shown on a single system flowchart, it is often useful to draw a separate system control flowchart[1] to identify the flow of controls in an application. Such a control flowchart which

[1] Robert I. Benjamin, *Control of the Information System Development Cycle,* New York, John Wiley & Sons, 1971, pp. 52-53.

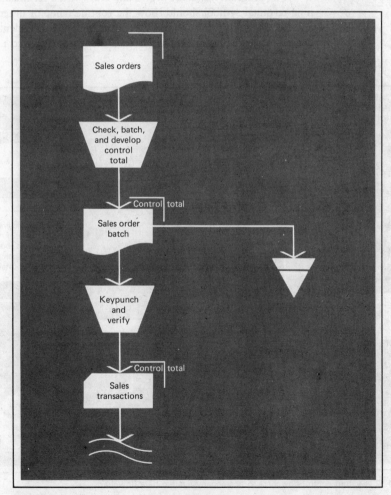

FIGURE 4-11 Flowcharting of manual processes.

accompanies the data flowchart is very useful for reviewers of system design. A copy of the system flowchart for the data flow without any notation is utilized for drawing the control flowchart. The controls associated with each input, transformation, and output of data are written in each box of the control flowchart (Figure 4-12).

Guidelines for Program Flowcharting

The program flowchart (also called a flow diagram or logic diagram) shows the details of the operations or algorithm which transforms the input to the output. A program flowchart may detail the logic of a process symbol in a system flowchart or may detail the logic of a module charted in a higher-level program flowchart by a striped processing symbol (Figure 4-13).

The program flowchart begins and ends with a terminal symbol. The beginning terminal symbol should show the routine name or other identification. The end or exit from the routine is a terminal symbol that identifies the end of the processing or a return to the routine to which the charted module belongs.

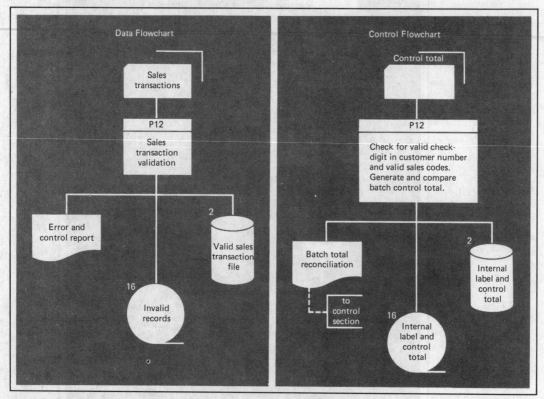

FIGURE 4-12 System control flowchart to accompany system data flowchart.

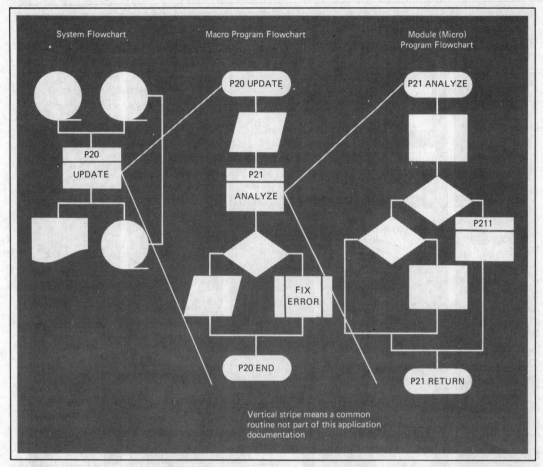

FIGURE 4-13 Relationship of system flowchart, macro program flowchart, and module (micro) program flowchart.

Striping is used in program flowcharts (and system flowcharts as well) to identify processing described in another flowchart. Horizontal striping is used to reference a more detailed flowchart of a module that is described in the same set of flowcharts. In other words, the highest level of flowchart references detailed flowcharts for each major process. Some of the processes at the second level of detail may reference more detailed flowcharts (Figure 4-14). This process is consistent with the modular approach to system and program design explained in Chapter 5. Vertical striping references a routine common to many programs. It is in the routine library, and its flowchart, etc., is found in the library routine documentation. For example, in Figure 4-13, the routine to fix error may be a common routine for all programs.

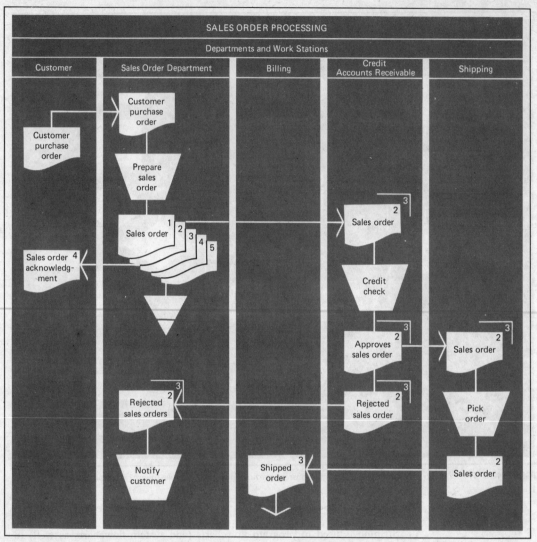

FIGURE 4-14 Horizontal flowchart (partial) of manual system for sales order processing.

Horizontal Flowcharts

The ANSI standard for flowcharts has the flow going from top to bottom and from left to right. Another type of flowchart useful in describing an organizational application is a horizontal flowchart which shows the different organizational units involved in processing (manual and computer) for an application. The flow is between organizational units. The flow described may be documents only or may show operations as well (Figure 4-14).

Decision Tables

Decision tables are a graphic method for describing the logic of decisions. In a tabular format, the decision table lists a set of conditions plus a set of actions and identifies different combinations of decisions which lead to different combinations of actions. These different combinations are termed "rules." The decision table in Figure 4-15 illustrates this tabular format. It is a decision table for use by clerks making a decision on granting of credit at a department store. Rule 2 says to grant credit for an applicant who has not held his or her present job more than 1 year if the applicant has lived in his or her present residence more than 2 years and has a yearly income of more than $7500.

A decision table may be used in place of a flowchart or narrative, or it may be used as a supplement. When applicable, it is a very powerful graphic tool for describing the logic of processing and should be part of the tools of every systems analyst and programmer. A decision table may be used in conjunction with a flowchart. For example, the flowchart may have a section that is more clearly represented by a decision table. As shown below,

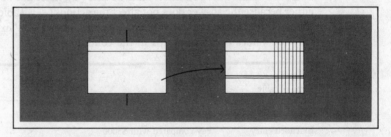

this section is represented by a striped process box in the flowchart which references the decision table. The decision table may be used both for manual procedures and for computer program logic. The decision table can be very useful when collecting data from users on the logic they wish to have applied to a problem

	Credit granting table	1	2	3	4	5	6
Conditions	Held present job more than 1 year	T	F	T	F	F	T
	Lived at present residence more than 2 years	–	T	F	T	F	T
	Yearly income greater than 7,500	T	T	F	F	–	F
Actions	Grant credit	X	X				
	Refuse credit			X	X	X	X
	Refer to credit manager						X

Rule 2 points to column 2.

FIGURE 4-15 Example of decision table.

to organize it into a decision table. It helps to bring out any undefined rules (conditions without specified actions) and is often more understandable to the users than a flowchart. One of the useful applications of decision tables is in the analysis of rules, regulations, and procedures. For example, using decision tables to analyze governmental regulations, French officials discovered 44 classes of persons the regulations excluded from entering France who were supposed to be admissible.

Format of Tables   The decision table is a tabular form divided into four areas (Figure 4-16):

1 Condition stub   3 Action stub
2 Condition entries   4 Action entries

Conditions and actions are connected by an "if . . . then . . ." relationship. The rule can be read, "If the specified set of conditions exists, then perform the indicated actions." The condition stub lists all conditions; the condition entries note the fact that the condition must be met (Y), must not be met (N), or can be either because the answer does not affect the actions (—). Tables with Y, N, and — for condition entries are termed "limited entry" tables. An "extended entry" table may use values or relationships in the condition entries:

Type of table	Condition	Condition entries	
Limited entry	Pay greater than $5000	Y	N
Extended entry	Pay compared with $5000	>	≤

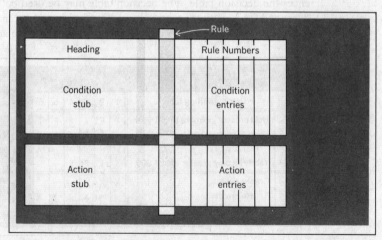

FIGURE 4-16   General form of the decision table.

Since an extended entry table is an extension of a limited entry table, the explanation will concentrate on the latter.

The action stub lists all actions which can follow from the stated conditions. The action entries identify with an X those actions to be taken for a rule. A blank or 0 means the action is not to be taken for that rule.

One of the powerful analytical features of a limited entry decision table is that for a given set of conditions and actions, one can analyze whether or not all the rules have been stated. There are theoretically 2^n rules for n separate conditions. This follows from the number of combinations of the two conditions Y and N. In other words, four conditions would result in 2^4 or 16 rules. A set of eight conditions would require 256 results, which gives a large table. However, in practice the table need not be so large, because many of the rules are redundant. Part of the procedure for developing a decision table should therefore be elimination of unnecessary conditions, testing for completeness, and elimination of redundant (unnecessary) rules.

Steps in Preparing a Decision Table

The steps in preparing a limited entry decision table are:

1 List conditions and actions.
2 Combine conditions which describe both of only two possibilities.
3 Make "yes" or "no" responses (Y or N).
4 Mark actions to be taken for each rule with X.
5 Check for completeness.
6 Combine redundant rules to simplify table.
7 Reorder table for most understandable order of rules.

The explanation will emphasize a systematic procedure for developing a decision table. As analysts or programmers develop some skill, they may be able to arrive more directly at the final table. The beginner should proceed carefully and systematically.

An example will be used to explain and illustrate the procedures. A university has the following criteria for deciding whether to admit students to its graduate school:

Admit a student who has undergraduate grades of B or better, has test scores on the admission test of over 550, and has a grade average of B or better for the past 2 years. Also admit if the overall grade average is less than B but the last 2 years' average is B or better and the test score is over 550. Admit on probation if the overall and 2-year grade averages are B or better but test score is 550 or less. Admit on probation if overall grades are B or better and test score is above 550 but grades during the last 2 years are below B. Also admit on probation if overall grades are less than B average and test score is 550 or less, but grades for past 2 years are B or better. Refuse to admit all others.

The first step is to write down all the conditions and actions.

Conditions **1** Undergraduate grades of B or better
            2 Test scores of over 550
            3 Grade average of B or better during the past 2 years
            4 Test score of 550 or less
            5 Grades less than B during the last 2 years
            6 Overall grade average less than B

Actions **1** Admit
          2 Admit on probation
          3 Do not admit

The second step is to combine conditions which describe the only two possibilities of a single condition. In this case "test scores over 550" and "test scores of 550 or less" can be combined. A single condition "test scores over 550" can represent both because a "no" answer means test score 550 or below. The same reasoning allows the combination of conditions 1 and 6 and also 3 and 5. There are thus only three conditions:

1 Undergraduate grades of B or better
2 Test scores of over 550
3 Grade average of B or better during the past 2 years

Step three is to prepare the "yes" and "no" responses using Y and N for all possible combinations of conditions. Then for each set of conditions mark the action(s) to be taken with an X. The number of rules to be handled in the step is 2^n where n is the number of conditions. In the example, there are three conditions, so there will be 2^3 or 8 rules. The Y's and N's can be inserted in any order, but a systematic method will reduce the effort of filling in the table and reduce the chance of error. Start with the bottom row of the condition entries, and fill in the row starting with Y and then alternating between N and Y. The row above this is filled in by writing two Y's, two N's, two Y's, two N's, etc. The third row from the bottom uses sets of four Y's and four N's. This doubling of the sets of Y's and N's continues until the table is complete. Then analyze each rule and fill in the action entries. Figure 4-17 shows the completed table at this stage.

The next action is to combine rules where there are redundancies. Two rules can be combined into a single rule if all the conditions except one have the same Y and N (or —) condition entries *and* the actions are the same for both. Combine the two rules into one and replace the condition entry of Y and N with a dash (—), which means the condition does not affect the actions below. By use of this procedure, rules 1 and 5 can be combined, as shown. In other words, if grades are B or better in the past 2 years, the student is admitted without regard to overall average. Rules 3 and 7 can be combined, as can 4 and 8 (or alternatively 6 and 8). The resulting table with redundancies removed is shown in Figure 4-17.

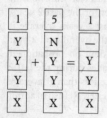

Graduate school admission	1	2	3	4	5	6	7	8
Conditions								
Undergraduate grades of B or better	Y	Y	Y	Y	N	N	N	N
Test score over 550	Y	Y	N	N	Y	Y	N	N
Grades of B or better past 2 years	Y	N	Y	N	Y	N	Y	N
Actions								
Admit to graduate school	X				X			
Admit on probation		X	X				X	
Do not admit				X		X		X

Graduate school admission	1	2	3	4	5
Conditions					
Undergraduate grades of B or better	–	Y	–	–	N
Test score over 550	Y	Y	N	N	Y
Grades of B or better past 2 years	Y	N	Y	N	N
Actions					
Admit to graduate school	X				
Admit on probation		X	X		
Do not admit				X	X

FIGURE 4-17 Decision table for example. Top table is complete table before redundancies. Bottom table is final table with redundancies removed.

The completed table with only five rules must represent the eight possible rules. To check for completeness of the rules, analyze the completed table as follows:

1 Count number of dashes in the condition entries for each rule. The number of rules "represented" by each rule are 2^m where m is the number of dashes. Where there are no dashes, the number represented is 2^0, or 1. A single dash means two rules have been combined ($2^1 = 2$), etc.

2 Sum the number of rules represented by the different rules as computed above.

3 Compare the number of rules represented by the table with the number to be accounted for, which is 2^n ($n = $ number of conditions). If they are equal (and all other features are correct), the table is complete.

In the example, rules 1, 3, and 4 have one dash (2^1 for each, or 6), and rules 2 and 5 have no dashes (2^0 for each, or 2). The sum of 6 plus 2 is equal to 2^3, or 8, rules required by the three conditions. The final table could be rearranged for easier use, but this is not necessary.

Using a Set of Tables

If a problem has many conditions, the decision table may become quite large and difficult to follow. Since the objective of the table is to show the logic of the procedure as clearly and as simply as possible, a large, complex table should be avoided. In most cases a large problem with many conditions can be subdivided into two or more tables. One or more of the actions of the first table will specify that the user should proceed to another table to complete the logic. An action to GO TO another table implies no return; an action to PERFORM another table is used to perform the named table and then return to the next action in the calling table. An example will illustrate this use of more than one table.

> A sales organization is seeking to hire some salesmen and saleswomen having special characteristics. Only unmarried personnel between the ages of 25 and 35 are needed. If male, the salesman is to be over 6 ft in height but less than 200 lb in weight, and not bald. If female, the saleswoman is to be less than 5 ft 4 in. in height and less than 120 lb in weight and is to have shoulder-length hair.

This problem has nine conditions, which would mean a table with 512 rules before reduction. But the problem fits logically into three parts—the overall criteria, male criteria, and female criteria. This suggests that three decision tables should be used—initial screening, male selection, and female selection. The result of this use of three tables is shown in Figure 4-18. All tables have had redundancies removed. Note the third line of the condition stub of the initial screening table. There could have been two conditions, "male" and "female," but, as described previously, there are only two sexes, so naming one is sufficient; a "no" to "male" means female just as clearly as "yes" to "female."

Decision Table Processors

The analysis of the decision tables has followed fairly simple steps, suggesting that the computer might be used in table analysis and that the computer might write instructions to carry out the logic of the rules. This is exactly what has been done. There are decision table processors which will generate computer code from a decision table. The processors also analyze the tables for redundancies, completeness, etc. The processors are used in connection with a programming language such as COBOL, so that part of the program is written in the regular way and part is generated from the decision table.

Evaluation of Decision Tables

The decision table has a number of advantages as a tool for analysis and communication.

1   The table provides a framework for a complete and accurate statement of processing or decision logic.

2   The table is compact and easily understood, thus being very effective for communication between analysts or programmers and others.

3   The table allows mechanization of some programming tasks.

Initial screening	1	2	3	4
Conditions				
Unmarried	Y	Y	Y	N
25 to 35 yrs. in age	Y	Y	N	–
Male = Y; female = N	Y	N	–	–
Actions				
Reject			X	X
Go to male selection table	X			
Go to female selection table		X		

Male selection	1	2	3	4
Conditions				
Over 6 ft. in height	Y	Y	Y	N
Less than 200 lbs. in weight	Y	Y	N	–
Not bald	Y	N	–	–
Actions				
Reject		X	X	X
Accept	X			

Female selection	1	2	3	4
Conditions				
Under 5 ft. 4 in. in height	Y	Y	Y	N
Less than 120 lbs. in weight	Y	Y	N	–
Shoulder length hair	Y	N	–	–
Actions				
Reject		X	X	X
Accept	X			

FIGURE 4-18 Use of a set of decision tables.

The decision table is best for presenting a problem with many conditions; it is not well suited to show the flow of processing where there are few decisions. Decision tables have been used much less frequently than flowcharting. One reason for this is the fact that many applications do not lend themselves to decision tables, but another is the lack of training in their use. On balance, then, the decision table is a very helpful tool for some applications and should therefore be one of the methods that the analyst or programmer can use when appropriate.

SUMMARY   When a computer application is being designed, it is necessary to define explicitly the form and content of input/output documents and files and to describe both the overall flow of work and the processing logic. The tools which are used have been described. These are layout charts, grid charts, flowcharts, and decision tables.

Layout charts are used to describe the form and content of input, files, storage, and output. Examples are card, magnetic tape, and printer layouts. The layouts are usually drawn on printed forms prepared for this purpose.

Flowcharting is the most common method of planning the logic and flow of a computer application. Two types of flowcharts are used—the system flowchart, which describes the flow of documents and major processing tasks, and the program flowchart, which describes the logic of a computer program.

The solution to a problem may be flowcharted in many different ways. There are individual differences in the way a flowchart is prepared in much the same way that there are individual differences in the way different individuals will write a description. The main objective of the flowchart is to communicate the logic and flow of processing in such a way that it is as understandable as possible to the reader. Clarity is enhanced by using standard symbols which have an agreed-upon meaning. Therefore, it is recommended that the ISO or ANSI symbols presented in the chapter be used.

The decision table is used as a supplement or in place of a flowchart, especially for problems with complex sets of conditions and actions. A systematic approach to the development of a limited entry decision table was presented. Although not as widely used as flowcharting, decision tables are a very useful tool for the analyst and programmer.

EXERCISES

1 What is the difference between planning of the application and planning of the program for the application?

2 Using only a knowledge of the meaning of the flowchart symbols, explain what is probably being described by the flowchart segments, which have no description in them, on page 113.

3 Which technique described in the chapter would be used to provide a check in the design process by showing the relationship between data items required for an output document and data items obtained from input documents or storage records?

4 What is the purpose of the card, tape, and printer layouts?

5 Tell in words the contents of a card described by the following card layout.

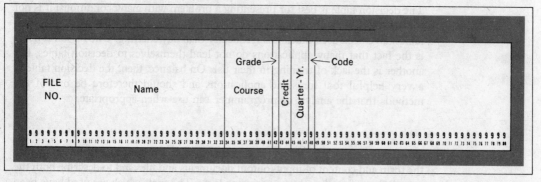

6 Flowchart the following using system flowcharts. Do not show excessive detail.

 (a) A computer run to read cards, write the data on magnetic tape, accumulate a count, and write the count and any error messages on the printer.

 (b) An updating run to update a file on magnetic disk with transactions on punched cards. Error and control messages are written on the printer.

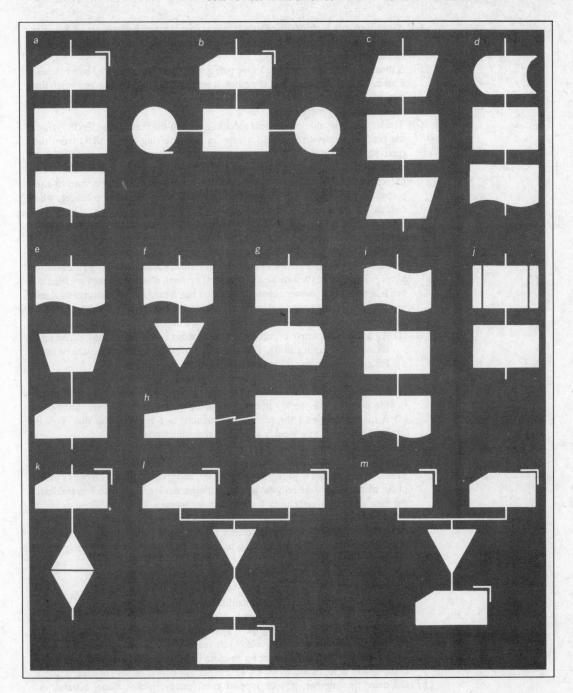

(c) A computer run to print customer statements from a file on magnetic tape. Records in error are copied onto an error file on a magnetic disk. Control totals are written on the printer.

(d) A three-part invoice is prepared. One part is filed, one is accumulated into batches, a batch total is prepared, and the batch is sent to the keypunching and verifying section. The batch is then filed. The punched cards are sent to the computer department for processing.

(e) The accounts-payable department receives a copy of the purchase order (PO) from the purchasing department and a copy of the receiving report (RR) from the receiving department. When invoices are received from vendors, the invoice is matched with the purchase order and the receiving report by a clerk. The clerk prepares a voucher. The accounts-payable supervisor reviews the document and prepares a check. The check is signed and mailed by the office manager, who cancels the documents. The documents are filed.

(f) The cash receipts section of the company opens the mail and prepares remittance advice (a small form for each remittance describing the customer and amount received). The batch of remittance advices for the day are totaled on an adding machine, the total is attached to the batch of remittance advices. These are sent to keypunching where they are keypunched and verified, after which they are filed by batch in a file. The payment cards headed by a batch card with the control total are input to a computer run in which they are sorted by account number, and the control total is checked. The results of the run are:

(1) An audit and control report listing the amount received plus any exceptions found on the input editing. This goes to the accounting department to be used for a general ledger entry and for review of any errors.

(2) A cash receipts journal listing each remittance. This also goes to accounting.

(3) The payment cards which were the input to the run are stored in a temporary file pending the weekly update run, after which time they are destroyed.

(4) A magnetic tape of the receipts is produced as a result of the run. This is held for input to a weekly accounts receivable updating run.

7 Flowchart the following using a program flowchart.

(a) The logic of a computer dating service that matches couples on the basis of similarity of interests with regard to music, art, and sports (a match on one or more of the three), plus same religion and age difference not greater than 5 years older for men and not greater than 1 year older for women.

(b) The logic of computing gross pay. Forty hours or less are at standard pay. Hours over 40 are $1\frac{1}{2}$ times standard pay except Sunday and holiday work, which is at 2 times standard. Sunday and holiday hours are coded separately on the payroll input.

(c) Determine which of four quantities A, B, C, and D is the largest.

(d) $\sum\limits_{i=1}^{100} x_i$ i.e., sum one hundred quantities referred to as $x_1, x_2, \ldots, x_{100}$
Hint: Obtain the sum by adding the x_i's one at a time to an accumulated sum. Set up a test to stop accumulating when you reach 100.

(e) Read a student's numerical score on an exam from a punched card and determine if the grade is to be A, B, C, D, or F. (Set your own limits for each grade.)

(f) Calculate the number of each type of coin (penny, nickel, dime, quarter, or half-dollar) a newsstand vendor should give in change when a person makes a purchase and gives a sum of money as payment. To simplify the problem, assume no purchase or payment amount is in excess of $1.

(*g*) The logic of selecting charge accounts for audit examination. A positive confirmation form requesting the customer to check the balance as reported against his records and report whether or not it is correct will be sent to all accounts which are over $300 and over 60 days old, and to all accounts showing a credit balance greater than $10. A negative confirmation requesting an answer only if there is an error will be sent to all accounts owing less than $300 and over 60 days old, to every tenth account for accounts not over 60 days old, but greater than $200 owing, and to every fiftieth account which is not over 60 days old and has a balance not greater than $200.

(*h*) Hire a prospective employee if he or she is between 21 and 35 years old, does not have long hair, is married male or unmarried female, and has experience in selling or has a grade point average of 3.5 or better.

8 Prepare a decision table for problem 7(*b*), 7(*c*), and 7(*h*).

9 Prepare a set of two decision tables for problem 7(*a*).

10 Fill in the following table, simplify, and analyze completeness:

Reservation procedure	1	2	3	4	5	6	7	8	9	10	11	12	13	14	15	16
Conditions Request for 1st class																
Requested space available																	
Alternate class available																	
Alternate class acceptable																	
Actions Make 1st class reservation																
Make tourist reservation																	
Name on 1st class wait list																	
Name on tourist wait list																	

11 Draw a flowchart to detail the logic shown in the following decision table. The table covers the deductibility of educational expenses on the federal income-tax return.

Educational expenses	1	2	3	4
Conditions				
Education to qualify for employment	Y	N	N	N
Education to maintain or improve skills required in your employment	—	N	Y	N
Education required by your employer or by regulations to retain current employment	—	N	—	Y
Actions				
Educational expenses deductible			X	X
Educational expenses not deductible	X	X		

CHAPTER

5

COMPUTER
PROGRAM
STRUCTURE
AND DESIGN

Objectives of a Structured, Disciplined Approach to Programming
Meeting User Needs
Development on Time within Budget
Error-free Instructions
Error-resistant Operation
Maintainable Code
Portable Code

The Structure of a Computer Program
Modular Design
Basic Modules in a Program

Basic Coding Structures
Simple Sequence
Selection
Repetition
Multiple-Case Selection
Combinations of the Basic Structures
Formatting Programs to Show Coding Structure

Elementary Computer Instructions
Move Instructions
Edit Instructions
Arithmetic Instructions
Transfer-of-Control Instructions
Looping Instructions
Input/Output Instructions
Compiler/Assembler Instructions

Additional Programming Techniques
Programmed Switches
Table Look-up
Subroutines

A Structured, Disciplined Approach to Program Development
Top-down Program Development
Structured Programming
Chief-Programmer Teams
Structured Walk-throughs
Development Support Libraries
HIPO Charts

Documentation of Programs
Summary
Exercises

The purpose of this chapter is to provide insight into the design and structure of computer programs. The chapter describes the modular design of a program, coding structures, types of instructions, and some fundamental coding techniques. These topics are presented within the framework of a disciplined, structured approach to program design and development.

Objectives of a Structured, Disciplined Approach to Programming

During the 5-year period 1970 to 1975, the costs of hardware dropped dramatically—close to one-half as much at the end of the period compared with the beginning. During the same period, the costs of developing programs increased significantly. Control of software performance has become a more important factor than control of hardware performance. The major problems of software performance have been that computer programs frequently:

Do not meet user requirements
Are not produced on time
Cost considerably more than estimated
Contain errors
Are difficult to maintain (to correct or change to meet new requirements)

These difficulties have been observed with such frequency that many organizations have attempted to change the practice of programming to improve software performance. The revised approach can be termed "programming discipline"—well-defined practices, procedures, and control processes. This approach to program design and development has the following objectives:

1 Meeting user needs
2 Development on time within budget
3 Error-free set of instructions
4 Error-resistant operation
5 Maintainable code
6 Portable code

The techniques for achieving these objectives are presented later in the chapter.

Meeting User Needs A program has a purpose, such as to produce a report, prepare a sales invoice, or compute a set of statistics. A program may be elegant, but if it is not used because the potential users find it too complex or too difficult, then it is a failure. A disciplined approach to program design includes a careful analysis of user needs and user involvement in key decisions affecting the practicality of the application.

Development on Time within Budget Estimates of time and cost for programming projects have frequently been substantially in error. Programmer productivity has generally been lower than expected. One objective of a structured, disciplined approach to programming is more accurate estimates, greater productivity, and closer control of the actual time and cost required.

Average productivity in the industry (in 1975) was about eight lines of tested code per day for a programmer using a high-level language such as FORTRAN or COBOL (about 2000 lines per year). Using a more structured approach, installations have achieved dramatic improvements in productivity. One installation boosted productivity to 5000 lines per year, and another expects to achieve an average of 10,000 lines of tested code per programmer per year.

Error-free Instructions

It is generally conceded that all large-scale computer programs contain errors, and it may be impossible to remove every single error from a large set of programs. However, programs may be designed and developed in a way which facilitates detection and correction of errors and thereby achieves virtually error-free instruction coding. There are two approaches to error-free programs. One is a mathematical approach for proving the correctness of a computer program. While promising, the mathematical method is still experimental and not operationally useful. The second approach to error-free instructions is the use of a program structure and programming discipline which supports error-free program design and production. Programming groups with strong quality control procedures have been able to reduce errors in completed, tested programs to an average of one undetected error in 10,000 lines of instructions. This contrasts with a rate of perhaps one error per 100 lines of delivered, tested instructions by programming groups without a disciplined approach to error-free code.

Error-resistant Operation

The erroneous results of a program may be due to program errors or to incorrect input. The program should be designed so that errors will, insofar as possible, be detected during execution of the program. The design features to assist in detecting errors (described further in Chapter 10) are:

1 Input validation
2 Tests of correctness during processing

Input validation is a testing of all input data items to determine whether or not they meet the criteria set for them. For example, data input may be tested for:

Existence of necessary input data items

Data item values within acceptable range

Illogical relationships among input items

Incorrect class of data (e.g., alphabetic characters in a data item field which should be numeric)

Every computer application should perform input validation. This may be accomplished by a separate input validation program (also termed "input editing") or by a separate section of a program, depending on the design of the application and its programs. The input validation will detect all errors which can be found by logic tests; additional errors can be detected by human review of the input data. This human review may be part of the input process, or the input data may be included with the output, and human review for errors can be performed as part of the use of the output.

Tests of correctness during processing generally take the form of reasonableness tests on results and checking the logical relationship of results. For example, the results of payroll processing (say, gross pay for each employee) may be tested for reasonableness, and data items may be tested by crossfooting (e.g., sum of gross pay amounts minus sum of all deductions should equal sum of net pay amounts).

When errors are detected, error messages should be output which clearly identify both the nature of the error and the user responsibility for error correction. The detailed steps in error correction and re-input of the data may be described in the error message or in user documentation for the application.

Maintainable Code
Computer programs change, especially when first placed into use. Programs should be written with the maintenance activity in mind. The structure, coding, and documentation of the program should allow another programmer to understand the logic of the program and to make a change in one part of a program without unknowingly introducing an error in another part of the same program.

Portable Code
A tested program, written in a high-level language, should be transferrable without substantial change to another computer having a compiler for that language. This means that programming which takes advantage of unique machine features should be avoided as should all nonstandard instructions. Straightforward, well-documented instructions are portable with little difficulty; programs with intricate or poorly documented logic are not.

The Structure of a Computer Program

The set of instructions in a computer program will be executed sequentially as written unless an instruction transfers control backward or forward in the programmed sequence. Such transfers are common, and so a computer program can become quite complex (Figure 5-1). The structure presented in this section provides a method for simplifying the design of programs.

Modular Design
Most programs in operational use are too large (in numbers of instructions) to be easily understood if coded as a single sequence of instructions. The method of simplification is to design the program as a set of units often referred to as "blocks"

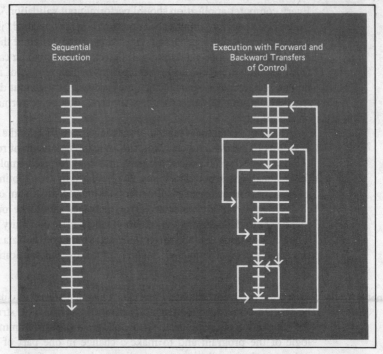

FIGURE 5-1 Impact of forward and backward transfers of control on complexity of programs. (Horizontal lines indicate instructions; vertical lines show processing sequence.)

or "modules." A program module is defined as a part of the program which performs a separate function such as input, input validation, or processing one type of input. A program function may be quite large (in terms of logic and instructions required), so that the function may be further subdivided into logical subfunctions, each of which is defined as a program module. This process of subdivision continues until all modules are of manageable size in terms of complexity of logic and numbers of instructions. A module may therefore consist of only a few instructions; many programmers feel a module should not be more than 50 lines of instruction code (which means it will be contained on one page of printer output). Modular design is useful in managing a large programming project because modules may be assigned to different programmers for coding.

A simple computer program using the modular approach consists of a control module and a number of processing modules. The control module directs the execution of the processing modules (Figure 5-2). A more complex program contains a main control module and a hierarchy of processing modules. The main control module directs the execution of the processing modules. The processing modules invoke other lower-level modules. The control routine can be programmed in a very straightforward manner with no (or few) forward or backward transfers of control. The flow of processing logic is therefore quite clear. This

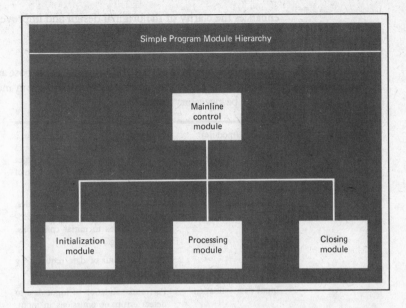

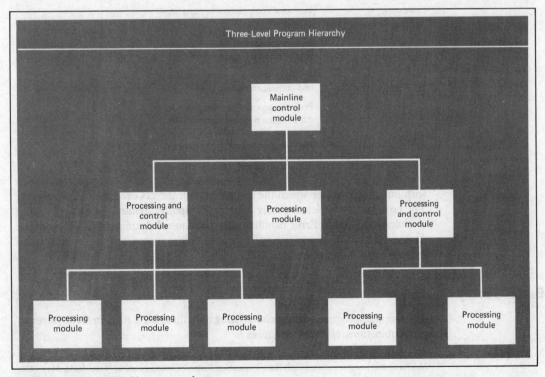

FIGURE 5-2 Modular (block) structure of a program.

enhances the clarity of the original design and improves debugging; it also makes program maintenance easier to accomplish.

Basic Modules in a Program

Although computer programs differ greatly in purpose and processing, it is possible to identify functional modules which will appear in most programs because they tend to be necessary functions.

Function (module)	Description
Main line control	Performs all tests to determine order of processing and directs execution of processing modules.
Initialization	Performs program tasks to open files, set variables to initial values, set program switches to initial conditions, print headings, etc.
Input	Performs input of data required by the program.
Input data validation	Performs validation of input data to detect errors or omissions in input. Edits input.
Processing	Performs computation or data manipulation.
Output	Performs output of data to be provided by the program.
Error handling	Performs analysis of error condition and outputs error messages.
Closing procedure	Performs procedures to end the execution of the program such as rewind and close files, print summary data, and print end-of-program message.

These modules form a logical flow in a program (Figure 5-3). A program begins with initialization after which the control module directs execution of processing. The processing proceeds logically with input, input validation, various processing modules, and output. Error handling may be required during any of the modules. At the conclusion of processing, various closing procedures are performed to complete the program execution.

Basic Coding Structures

All computer programs can be coded using only three logic structures (or patterns) or combinations of these structures.[1]

[1] The proof of this statement is presented in C. Bohm and G. Jacopini, "Flow Diagrams, Turing Machines and Languages with Only Two Formation Rules," *Communications of the ACM,* May 1966, pp. 366–371.

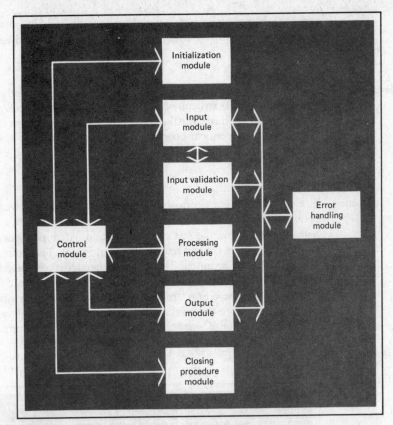

FIGURE 5-3 Basic modules in a computer program.

1 Simple sequence
2 Selection
3 Repetition

The three structures are useful in a disciplined approach to programming because:

1 The program is simplified. Only the three building blocks are used, and there is a single point of entry into the structure and a single point for exit.

2 The three coding structures allow a program to be read from top to bottom making the logic of the program more visible for checking and for maintenance. There is no backtracking.

The ease of coding of programs using the three basic structures and a modular program design depends somewhat on the programming language being applied. Some languages have excellent facilities for this approach; others are somewhat cumbersome. But the technique can be applied with all languages. A fourth structure, the multiple-case selection, is sometimes included as a basic structure, although it is attainable using the sequence, selection, and repetition structures.

Simple Sequence The simple sequence consists of one action followed by another. Logically, it can be termed an AND structure because the first operation is always followed by the second. In other words, the flow of control is to first perform operation A (Figure 5-4) AND then perform operation B. A simple sequence is flowcharted as two process symbols connected by a flowline.

Selection The selection structure consists of a test for a condition followed by two alternative paths for the program to follow. The program selects one of the program control paths depending on the test of the condition. After performing one of the two paths, the program control returns to a single point. This pattern has been termed IF THEN ELSE because the logic can be stated (for condition P and operations C and D): IF P (is true) THEN perform C ELSE perform D (Figure 5-4). A flowchart for the selection structure consists of a decision symbol followed by two paths, each with a process symbol, coming together following the operation symbols. In terms of symbolic logic, the selection structure is an OR pattern because C OR D is executed (but not both).

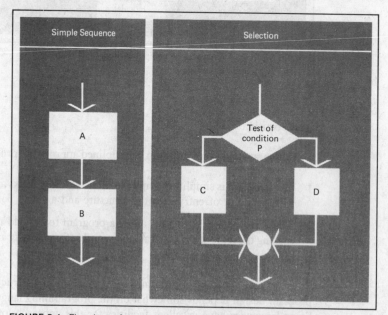

FIGURE 5-4 Flowchart of simple sequence and selection program structures.

Repetition   The repetition structure is also termed a "loop." In a loop, an operation (or set of operations) is repeated until some condition is satisfied. The basic form of repetition is termed DO WHILE (Figure 5-5). In the DO WHILE pattern, the program logic tests a condition; if it is true, the program executes operation E and loops back for another test. If the condition is not true, the repetition ceases. A variation of this same basic pattern is the DO UNTIL. The operation F is performed until the condition is true. The major differences between the loop logic for DO WHILE and DO UNTIL is the location of the test. In DO WHILE, the test occurs before the first execution of the operations; in DO UNTIL, the test occurs after the first execution. In reference to Figure 5-5, if the condition P is not true, the operation E will not be executed for the DO WHILE structure; operation F will be executed once in either case with the DO UNTIL pattern.

Multiple-Case Selection   There are fairly frequent situations in writing programs in which a code or other condition having several values will be tested. Each value of the code or condition results in a specified processing path. This can be coded by nested sets of the basic

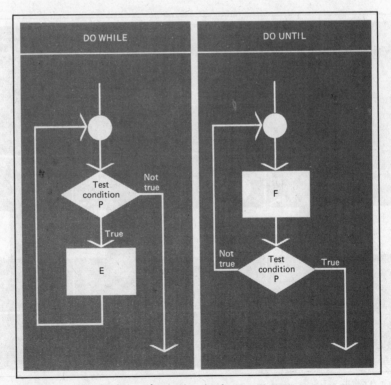

FIGURE 5-5 The two forms of repetition structure.

sequence structure. However, it is often useful to use instructions which provide for a multiple selection. These instructions have names such as CASE, GO TO DEPENDING ON, or COMPUTED GO TO (Figure 5-6).

Combinations of the Basic Structures

One of the objectives of using the three basic structures is to make programs more understandable to those concerned with design, review, and maintenance. It is possible to nest the three simple structures to produce more complex coding while maintaining the simplicity inherent in the three patterns. For example, the logic of the program may involve a selection between two program paths. If one path is chosen, there should be a repetition or loop; if the other is selected, there is a simple sequence. The nesting of the structures is illustrated in Figure 5-7. Note that there is still a single entry/single exit for each structure.

Formatting Programs to Show Coding Structure

The major programming languages provide language facilities for coding the basic logic patterns. Some languages provide better facilities than others, but the basic coding concepts can be used in all programming. The language chapters in the text will apply the concepts.

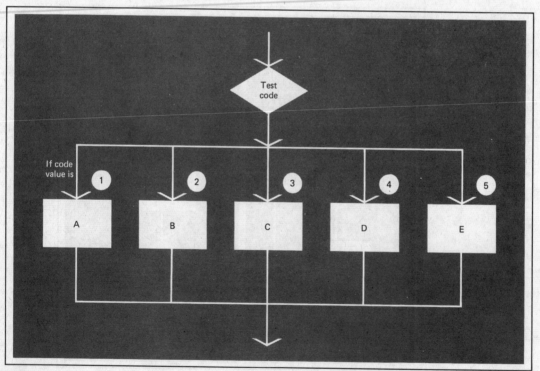

FIGURE 5-6 Multiple selection structure.

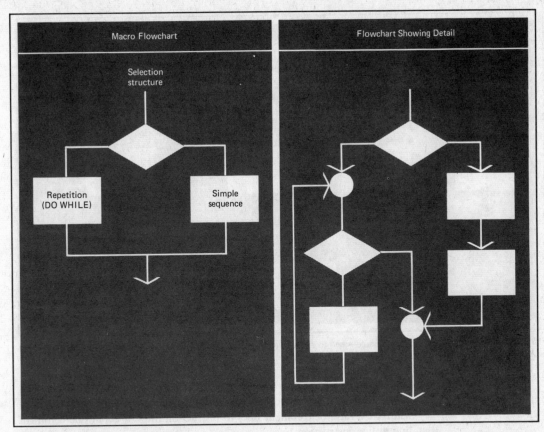

FIGURE 5-7 Nesting of coding structures.

A major factor in writing clear, understandable programs is the use of names, comments, or indentation as a method of showing the program structure. Some guidelines for formatting instruction code are:

1 Each module is identified by a descriptive name. Some programmers also use a code in a module name which shows its relationship to other modules (Figure 5-8). As an example of one possible naming approach, a hierarchical prefix is used to define module relationship. If the main module is identified with A-MAIN-MODULE, the name for an error-handling module might be AE-ERROR-HANDLING; if three submodules are called upon by the error module, these might be labeled AEA, AEB, AEC followed by a descriptive name, e.g., AEA-ERROR-CODE-ANALYSIS.

2 Comments are used in the program to document the logic. Comments are (a) at the beginning of the program to explain the purpose, structure, and flow of the program; (b) at the beginning of each module to explain the purpose of the

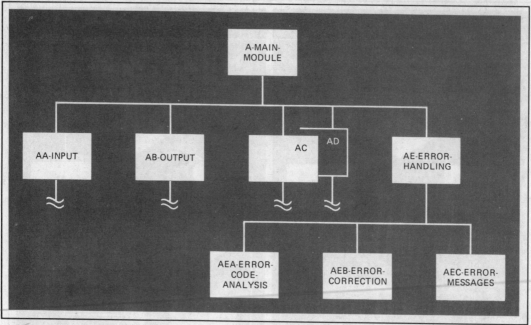

FIGURE 5-8 Use of code at front of module name to show relationship among modules. (Suggested at workshop given by H. Blair Burner, Boeing Computer Services.)

module; and (c) in among the program coding lines to explain coding which may not be clear. Some programmers suggest that well-documented programs will have a ratio of comment lines to instruction lines of about one comment line to five instruction lines.

One suggestion for comments is to consider the program as a book.[1] The program starts with a table of contents listing each module and a very short description of its purpose. Each module (like a chapter in a book) begins with a description of the purpose of the module and the processing logic utilized.

3   Lines of coding are indented to identify logical blocks of code and to show the range of code belonging to program structures. For example, coding might be indented as shown in Figure 5-9. The concept of indentation for clarity of coding receives further illustration in the language chapters.

Elementary Computer Instructions

The instructions available for coding a computer program will depend, in part, on the language being used. However, the nature of a computer program suggests that all languages must have certain instructions. These elementary computer instruc-

[1]Knut Bulow, "Programming in Book Format," *Datamation,* October 1974, pp. 85–86.

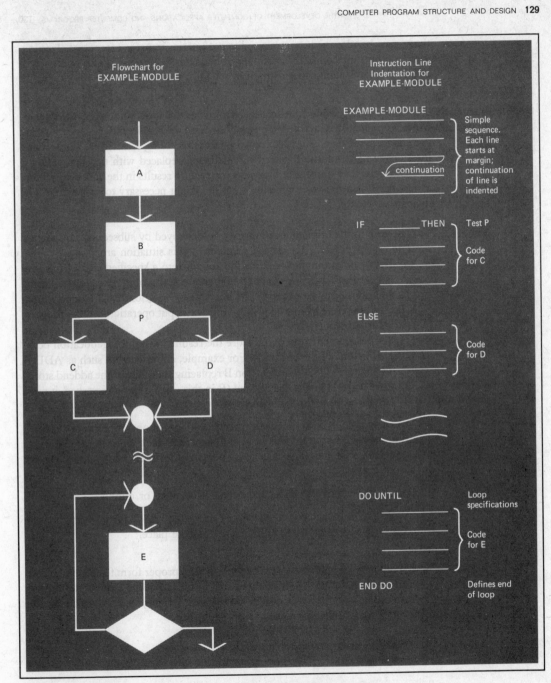

FIGURE 5-9 Indentation of instruction lines to show code structures.

tions may be classified as move, edit, arithmetic, transfer of control, looping, input/output, and compiler/assembler instructions. This general introduction will assist in understanding the instruction set for a specific language.

Move Instructions

The move instructions transfer data from one location in storage to another. Moving might also be termed "copying" because the sending storage locations are not changed; the data codes are copied into the receiving locations. The receiving locations are altered, the former contents being replaced with the new data.

Since the data transfer of the move instruction results in the data being found in identical form in two storage locations, why is it necessary to move data? The major reasons are:

1 The data in the original location may be destroyed by subsequent operations. The move preserves the data. Examples of this situation are:

(a) Data from an input operation is brought into a specified area of memory (sometimes termed an "input buffer area"). Each input operation will bring additional data to occupy the same storage location. Data from an input must therefore be moved prior to the next input operation in order to retain it for subsequent use.

(b) Some arithmetic operations store the results in the storage location occupied by one of the operands. For example, an instruction such as ADD A TO B stores the sum in location B replacing the value of the addend stored there. If the value of the addend (B in this case) is to be preserved, it must be moved prior to the arithmetic.

2 Data may need to be in specified storage locations for operations to be executed using the data. For example, output will generally use a set of storage locations designated as an output area. Data to be output (printed, etc.) is moved to the output area.

3 Data may need to be rearranged before processing or output.

4 In machine-language coding, data may need to be moved from storage into a register which holds data while operations take place.

Edit Instructions

When read into the computer, data may not be in a proper form for computational use. After computation, the data may not be in the form desired for output. Decimal points, commas, etc., need to be inserted. Editing instructions change the form of the data. Examples are:

Changing data coding for a data item
Inserting characters for the output format

Arithmetic Instructions

A computer will have instructions for addition, subtraction, division, and multiplication. In low-level languages, the programmer must provide instructions which scale the operands properly; in high-level languages, scaling is automatic. There are two basic approaches to arithmetic scaling. The first is for the programmer to keep track of the scale factor associated with each number and to write instructions to "line up" the digits in numbers having different scale factors. The other approach is for the computer to keep track of the scale factor and make all necessary adjustments. This is termed "floating point arithmetic."

Computer arithmetic is generally performed using a fixed number of digits (represented by a fixed number of bits, as explained in Chapter 6). The number of digits that can be encoded determines the number of significant digits in the result (the precision). In performing addition, subtraction, and division, it is possible to have overflow or truncation in which some digits are lost because the digits in the result exceed the space for the result. The digits lost through overflow are the leftmost digits in the result; these digits are significant, and therefore it is important for the programmer to detect overflow and to correct for it. Truncation occurs if the rightmost digits cannot all be stored in the space for the fractional result.

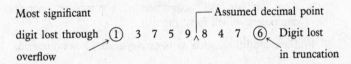

Truncation is less serious than overflow, but programs should normally perform rounding prior to truncating any righthand digits. Some high-level languages do the overflow testing and adjustment or rounding automatically; others require specific coding.

Transfer-of-Control Instructions

The sequence of instructions in a computer program will be executed one after another unless a transfer-of-control instruction breaks the sequence. There are few general types of transfer-of-control instructions.

1 Unconditional transfer
2 Transfer and return
3 Conditional transfer based on comparison
4 Conditional transfer based on absence or existence of a condition

The unconditional transfer of control is called a BRANCH, JUMP, or GO TO instruction. The instruction may be used to branch forward around code not to be executed or backward to a prior instruction. Unconditional transfer-of-control instructions which branch back in a program complicate the program logic; therefore branching backward is generally avoided, where possible.

The transfer and return instructions are used in connection with program modules. The instruction transfers control to call or perform another module. When the called module has been executed, control returns to the instruction in the calling module following the instruction to call or perform.

Conditional transfers are required for the selection coding structure. Comparison is between two data items with the test being for an equality, greater than, or less than condition. Alternative forms such as not equal, greater than, or equal may be used. In some languages, comparisons may be made quite complex by the use of more than one condition in the comparison, for example, IF A IS GREATER THAN B AND A EQUALS D . . . .

Transfer of control based on an absence or existence of a hardware or data condition is required in programming because the existence or absence of a number of conditions is used to decide on the processing path. Examples of such hardware or data conditions are:

1 An interrupt caused by a read, busy, or error condition of processing units or communications units. The interrupt is a hardware feature which causes processing to halt. The program can test the reason for the interrupt in order to decide on the actions to be taken.

2 Arithmetic overflow (an interrupt may occur).

3 The "on" or "off" condition of a computer operator console switch (in computers which have them).

4 Data condition, such as negative, zero, or nonnumeric.

5 End of data file condition.

Some of these condition tests are handled by the operating system and are therefore not the responsibility of the individual program. In some situations, failure to test for a condition may lead to an undetected error. For example, when some languages are used, a failure to program a test for arithmetic overflow may allow undetected overflow to occur with incorrect data resulting.

Looping Instructions

Repetition or looping is a fundamental programming structure. The objective is to use the same set of instructions over and over again rather than to write and store many instructions. Programming languages generally have instructions to code a loop. A loop is generally controlled by a variable which has been or is set to an initial condition. As the loop is executed, the loop control variable may be altered as part of the procedures being executed in the loop, or it may be incremented or decremented by a separate modification. The loop variable is tested to determine whether or not the loop should terminate. The two logic patterns presented earlier are reflected in two alternative arrangements of the loop elements, the loop elements being (Figure 5-10):

1 Initialization of loop control variable
2 Test loop variable for termination of loop
3 If no termination, execute sequence of instructions
4 Modify loop control variable

The instructions for loops provide for setting the initial value of the loop control variable, the modification of the loop control variable, and the test for termination.

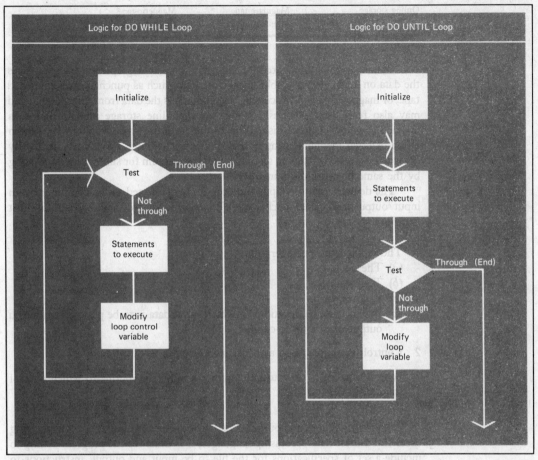

FIGURE 5-10 Detailed logic for two forms of loop.

There is also a program coding method for indicating the range of instructions included in the loop.

Input/Output Instructions   The processing instructions typically operate upon data that is input (read) during processing. When processing is complete, the results are output. There are three major sources of input and three objects for output:

Source	Example for input	Example for output
External storage medium	Punched card	Printed lines Punched cards
A terminal	Typewriter keyboard	Visual display cathode-ray tube (CRT) screen

Online storage	Magnetic tape	Magnetic tape
	Magnetic disk	Magnetic disk

Data is originally prepared for input via some keying operation which places the data on a machine-readable storage medium, such as punched cards, punched tape, or magnetic tape. A processing program reads the data from this medium and may also read data previously stored on an online storage medium (such as magnetic tape or magnetic disk). The output from the processing may be written on an external medium (using a device such as a printer, typewriter, or display device) or may be written on an online storage medium for subsequent processing by the same or other programs.

The devices used for input and output are connected to the computer by an input/output path called a "channel." The instruction for input and output must therefore specify (or imply):

1 The input or output operation
   (*a*) The device
   (*b*) The channel
   (*c*) Read or write
   (*d*) Internal storage locations in which input data is to be put or from which output data is to be copied

2 Control operations such as backspace, rewind, or position

3 Sensing for errors or unusual conditions and error routine to which control should go if detected

The form of input and output construction depends upon the language being used. In business data processing languages, it is usual for the program coding to include a set of specifications for the file to be input and output, instructions to open and close the file for use, and simple instructions to read or write a record from or to the file. The flow of typical instructions for data processing input and output is therefore:

File definition entries	Definitions at beginning of program
OPEN file-name	Open before file is used
GET or READ file-name	Repeated for each record to be read or written
PUT or WRITE file-name or record-name	
CLOSE file-name	Close after last use of file

In the case of some scientific processing languages, the only file definition is a description of the record format. The instructions to read or write specify the device, the data to be input or output, and the format to be used.

Compiler/Assembler Instructions — A program written in a symbolic language must be translated into machine-language instructions. The program may contain some instructions that are instructions to the assembler or compiler which performs the translation. COBOL, for example, provides for compiler instructions which causes the compiler to insert debugging statements. Other instructions will be contained in the job control instructions required for each program to be assembled or compiled.

Additional Programming Techniques

In programming, certain techniques have proved useful. Three of these techniques will be described: programmed switches, table look-up, and subroutines.

Programmed Switches — In programming, a condition may occur in one part of the program which will determine the path the program should take at a later time. In other words, there is a need to program a delayed transfer of control. This can be handled by a programmed switch (also called a "flag"). A switch may be programmed in a number of ways. In high-level languages, a common approach is to set a variable to one of two conditions for the switch to be "on"; the variable is set to a second condition for the switch to be "off." For example, a code of "1" or a literal OFF may be stored in a location to indicate that the switch is off; a code of "2" or the literal ON may be moved to the location to indicate that the switch is on. The switch is tested by a selection coding structure.

Table Look-up — There are many processing situations in which a data item or other factor to be used in a processing must be obtained from a table in storage. In fact, it is considered good programming practice to store tax rates, pay rates, etc., as separate tables rather than including them directly in the program coding. The method of coding should efficiently locate the correct entry in the table for program use. There are many methods of table look-up, but the essence of the methods is to operate upon a given input data item in order to establish a correspondence between the data and the table entry needed. For example, a payroll computation may use a shift-pay differential for the different shifts. The gross pay before shift differential is multiplied by the shift differential factor to give a shift-adjusted gross pay. The shift differentials for five different shifts are stored as five entries in a table. The shift number is used as an index for locating the entry in the table. In many cases, the data is not in suitable form for use as a table index, so that it must be processed further to yield table index numbers.

Subroutines — Even though subroutines were mentioned in connection with program design, the importance of subroutines in programming justifies further discussion. The design of programs as modules or blocks means that a program consists of modules, each defined as performing a separate function. A module may be sections of code within the program and identified only by name as being a separate module, or a module may be a subroutine.

Subroutines are sometimes classed as open or closed. Open subroutines are prewritten sections of code inserted into and made part of the main program. A closed subroutine (the type usually meant by the term) is written so that it may be used independently by any part of the main program or by any program. The subroutine is essentially a program used by another program and can be coded, translated, and debugged independently of the program using it. The usual program procedure is for the main program to CALL the subroutine. The CALL statement describes all data items to be used by the subroutine—data items to be used as input and data items for holding the results to be provided by the subroutine. At the completion of the subroutine processing, control is passed back to the calling program, exiting or returning to the statement following the CALL instruction (Figure 5-11).

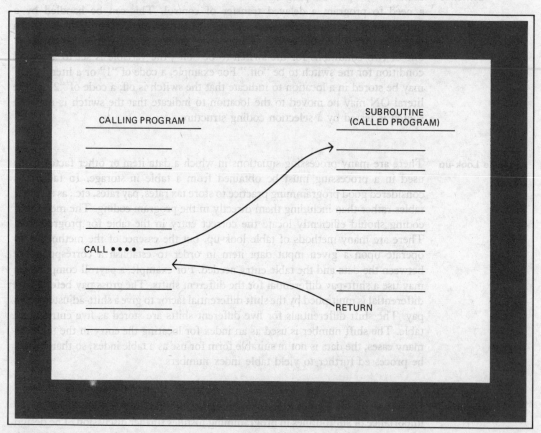

FIGURE 5-11 The use of a subroutine.

A Structured, Disciplined Approach to Program Development

Many of the concepts and approaches presented in this chapter are based on a structured, disciplined approach to program development. Some additional elements have not yet been presented. This section summarizes the elements of an approach to programming that has proved very successful in producing low-error, maintainable programs.

The approach to program development to be described has evolved over 25 years of computer programming. It is sometimes termed "structured programming," but that represents only one element. Although the major software producers have used many of the techniques, IBM pioneered in the synthesis of the elements. The approach was tested during 1970 and 1971 with outstanding success by an IBM team which programmed an online information retrieval system to access data published in *The New York Times*. The system was large (83,000 lines of high-level instruction code). It was developed online over 22 months during 1970 and 1971. Productivity was about five times greater than industry average, and the resulting programs were virtually error-free.

The organizational and structural elements that have produced the improved results for program development are:

1 Top-down program development
2 Structured programming
3 Chief programmer teams
4 Structured walk-throughs
5 Development support libraries
6 Hierarchy plus input-process-output (HIPO) charts

Top-down Program Development

As explained earlier in the chapter, it is useful (and a common practice in programming) to write a program as a set of modules. A hierarchy of modules is normally used with first-level modules controlling the use of second-level modules, second-level modules controlling the execution of third-level modules, etc. Top-down program development is a different approach to the order in which modules are coded and tested.

In a common approach to program development, sometimes termed a "bottom-up procedure," the lowest-level (say level 3) modules are defined, coded, and individually (unit) tested. When all the modules controlled by a higher-level module are ready, the next higher level (say level 2) module is coded and tested. This process continues until the highest-level module (the main routine) is coded. The program can then be tested in total with all interactions among modules being exercised by the testing. The problems in this approach are the lack of integrated testing until the end of the development and the necessity for redesign to correct problems resulting from interfaces (connections) among modules.

An alternative method of program development is a top-down approach. In top-down development, the program is planned as a hierarchy of modules, but programming and testing begins with the top (main) module. When the main module is programmed and tested, second-level modules are then programmed and tested. The testing utilizes both the first- and second-level modules already completed. In other words, at each test the entire program developed to that point is tested. A program unit is coded only after the unit that calls for it to be performed has been coded and tested. How can a module be tested if part of or all its instructions are calls to perform lower-level units (subprogram or subroutine modules) which have not been coded? The answer is the use of a dummy module or stub which contains only one or two statements to identify that the unit is to have been executed by the unit above it. For example, the stub may print the name of the routine. This procedure tests the logic of the next higher level unit.

With Figure 5-12 as a basis for explanation, the steps in top-down development are:

1   Design program. Define a hierarchy of modules or units.

2   The highest-level module (A) is coded completely, and the next level modules (AA, AB, and AC) are coded as dummy modules with only a stub. The highest-level module is tested.

3   Lower-level modules (AA and AB) are coded and stubs inserted for units which they invoke (AAA and AAB for AA and ABA, and ABB for AB). The entire program to that point is tested.

4   Units at a lower level are coded and then tested along with the higher-level modules already coded and tested. The process continues until all units are programmed, integrated, and tested.

The coding and testing of modules proceeds from top to bottom, but it does not have to proceed in parallel for all levels. Some branches of the structure will be developed earlier than others. For example, in Figure 5-12, the module AC remains a stub while AA and AB are coded and tested.

Data for testing the program is developed in an incremental manner. The test data for the highest-level test exercises the main module logic; test data is added at the next level to test the logic of that level, etc. Data-base definitions are written, and data records prepared before the modules requiring the record are coded.

The top-down development approach therefore ensures that the program units are integrated properly. As each lower-level unit is coded and added, the entire, integrated program, as developed to that point, is tested. The higher-level modules which control the logic of the program thus receive the most testing.

Structured Programming   Structured programming is a term applied to a structured approach to the coding of a computer program. The approach generally assumes top-down development and modular hierarchy for a program. Elements generally considered part of structured programming are:

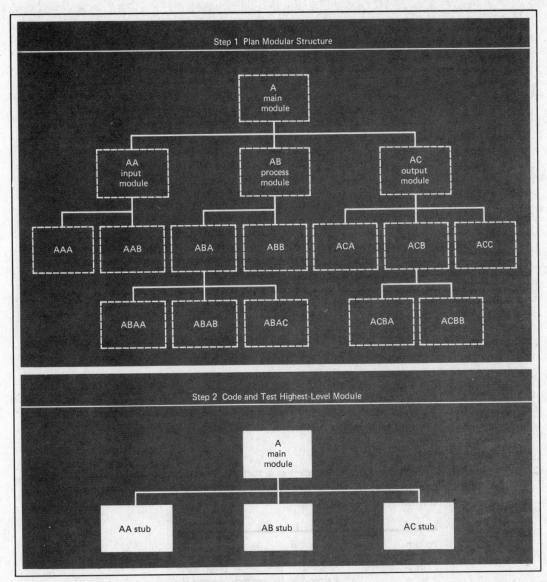

FIGURE 5-12 The top-down approach to program development.

1 Program code uses only the three coding structures of sequence, selection, and repetition (plus the case structure). Forward or backward transfer of control (instructions such as GO TO . . . , BRANCH, . . . , etc.) are not used, or used very sparingly. Structured programming, for this reason, is sometimes referred to as GOTOLESS programming.

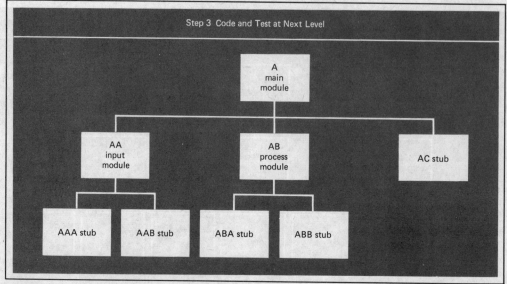

FIGURE 5-12 *(Continued)*

2 Instruction code is indented to reflect the logic of the coding structure. The indentations indicate the beginning and end of coding structures by the same indentation level; functions within the structure are indented further.

3 No module (or unit) of the program shall exceed a stated limit in size. This limit is generally 50 lines of instructions.

Chief-Programmer Teams

The chief-programmer team is a method of organizing and managing the programming of an application. Each programming project is assigned to a team consisting of the following:

Position	Description
Chief programmer	Senior-level professional programmer. Responsible for program design. Has complete technical responsibility for the project. Defines modules to be coded by programmers on the teams and reviews the code written by them. Writes main control routines and other critical code.
Backup programmer	Senior-level programmer. Provides backup for chief programmer and may be given assignment of developing test data for project.

Programmers	Programmers are added to the project as needed. Each is assigned the coding of specific modules which have been defined by the chief programmer.
Librarian	Responsible for semitechnical duties in support of the project such as maintaining the records of the project—documentation, program compilation printouts, test data. Arranges all compilation and testing runs for the programmers on the team.
Others	Specialists may be assigned to the team, as appropriate, for assisting in application design, special coding, etc.

The chief-programmer team concept is a recognition of the need for technical expertise in the leadership of a project, the need for a support function to relieve programmers of clerical duties, and the need for a review of all code by a senior programmer. The leadership and review function of the chief programmer assists in training the programmers in good practice.

Structured Walk-throughs

A structured walk-through is a review of the work of members of a programming team. The review may encompass program design, program instruction code, and documentation. The review is conducted by reviewers (other designers, other members of the team, etc.) selected and invited by the person whose work is being reviewed. The reviewers receive documentation prior to the review meeting. At the meeting, the reviewers comment on the completeness, accuracy, and quality of the work. The developer of the work being reviewed then goes through step by step (walks through) the logic of the work (design, program, documentation, etc.). The walk-through may include a discussion of test data. The reviewers note errors in logic, problems in the design, etc.

The structured walk-through provides a quality control mechanism utilizing the resources of the developer's colleagues. If a proper, open environment is maintained, the structured walk-through not only improves the quality of the product, but also is a method for work improvement by those being reviewed. It is recommended that the review be used only for improving the product, not for management review of individual performance.

Development Support Libraries

The development support library function maintains the records, documents, coded modules, and test data produced by a programming team. Four elements make up the library support function:

Element	Description
A program library stored on the	All modules already developed and latest versions of modules under de-

computer	velopment are stored on a computer file, along with sets of job control statements required for the application.
Software support for library on computer files	The library support software will provide for creating and updating a library for a programming project, retrieving modules for compilation, storing results, and producing listings.
External project documentation	A library of documentation is maintained by the librarian function. It consists of project notebooks containing current listings of all modules, all superseded listings (in order of assembly or compilation), project notes, project documents and reports, etc. Current documentation is thus always available to the project members.
Librarian procedures	The librarian accepts coding or code changes prepared by the programmers; arranges for keypunching, adding of job control cards, and submission for compilation; and updates the computer library and external library for the project.

The librarian support function frees the programmer from many clerical tasks, handling of program decks, submitting jobs, and maintaining the internal and external libraries. It provides for up-to-date, complete records of the project and a complete set of finished and in-progress code at all times.

HIPO Charts HIPO (hierarchy plus input-process-output) charts are a method of planning and documentation of program logic and structure developed by IBM. Often identified with structured programming, the method is useful but not necessary for structured programming. Some programming groups have found HIPO useful, but others have not. A set of HIPO documentation consists of a visual table of contents plus one or more overview diagrams and detail diagrams.

HIPO documentation	Description
Visual table of contents (Figure 5-13)	The visual table of contents is a block diagram showing the hierarchial relationship of program modules. Each module is

further described by HIPO overview and detail diagrams.

Overview diagram
(Figure 5-14)

An overview diagram consists of three major blocks:

1 *Input.* All input requirements are listed (generally files of transactions, master files, and tables).

2 *Process.* The major functions to be performed are listed. Each process will be shown either in another lower-level overview or in a detail diagram.

3 *Output.* All intermediate or final outputs are listed. Examples are files, updated files, reports, and error messages.

Detail diagram
(Figure 5-15)

The detail diagram is the lowest level of the hierarchy. In format, it is the same as an overview diagram except for an extended description section which gives a verbal description of each process shown in the detail diagram and identifies the module name to be used in programming the module.

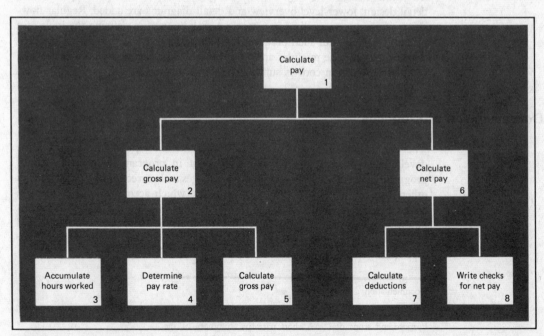

FIGURE 5-13 Visual table of contents. Each block refers to a diagram. (*Courtesy of International Business Machines Corporation.*)

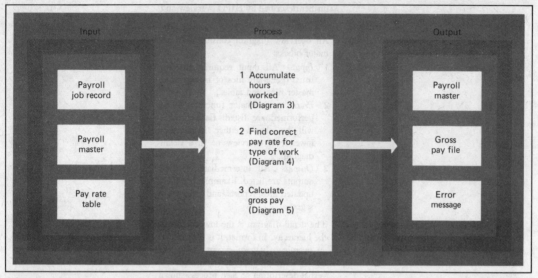

FIGURE 5-14 Overview diagram for block 2 of table of contents (Figure 5-13). (*Courtesy of International Business Machines Corporation.*)

In this approach, the HIPO charts are produced during the development cycle. The initial design uses only overview diagrams; as the development proceeds to detail design, lower-level overview and detail diagrams are added. Regular flow-charts of the type described in Chapter 4 may be used in defining the logic of a program module, but such program logic flowcharts are no included in the final documentation. The modules are small in size and clear in structure so that the program instruction code is sufficient module documentation.

Documentation of Programs

There are essentially two purposes for documentation—the first is to assist in the development process; the second is to assist in program maintenance. Since program maintenance generally involves changes and corrections by programmers other than the developers, the documentation which accompanies a completed, tested program should be clear and complete. The scope of satisfactory documentation may vary considerably depending on the type of application, length and complexity, and language used in coding. However, a minimum documentation for a program should provide for the following:

Documentation element	Description
Purpose and scope of program	A short narrative summary of the purpose and scope of the program.

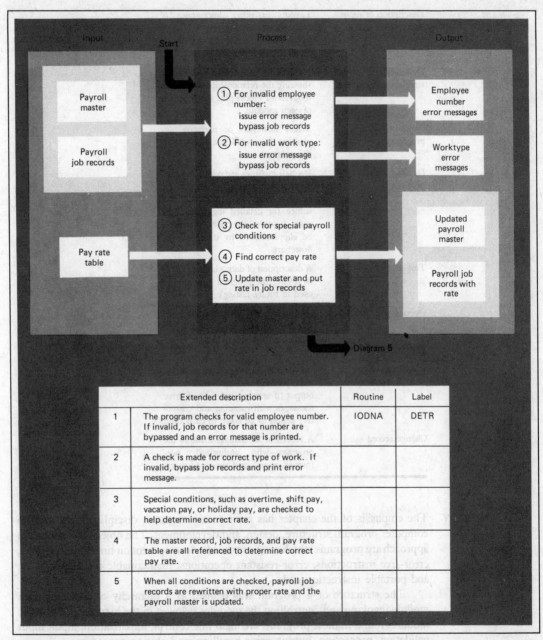

FIGURE 5-15 Detail diagram for block 4 of table of contents (Figure 5-13). (*Courtesy of International Business Machines Corporation.*)

Description of input and output	Layouts or other descriptions of input and output documents. In cases of some files, the program description of the file is sufficient.
Description of structure of program	A diagram of hierarchial listing showing the relationship of program modules or blocks plus a description of each module.
Overall flow of program	Macro flowchart or narrative describing the overall flow of logic for the program.
Detailed logic of program	If small modules are coded in structured format, with ample notes in the program, the computer code will suffice for detailed logic. In some cases, however, the code will need to be supplemented by detailed logic flowcharts.
Test data	A description of data which was used in testing the program (and can be used in future testing).
Operating instructions	Instructions to the operators when running the program. Includes program error messages relevant to operators.
User instructions	Instructions on how to prepare input, to prepare corrections, and to use the output (if appropriate). List of error messages with meaning and corrective action to be taken in each case.
Change record	A record of all changes made to the program—who authorized, performed, tested, and approved them.

SUMMARY   The emphasis of the chapter has been on a structured, disciplined approach to computer program structure, design, and development. The objectives of such an approach are programs which meet user needs, development on time within budget, error-free instructions, error-resistant operations, maintainable instruction code, and portable instruction code.

The structure of a program was defined as a hierarchy of modules, each module invoking and controlling the modules below it in the hierarchy. The basic modules found in most programs are main line control, initialization, input, input validation, processing, output, error handling, and closing procedures.

There are three basic coding structures that can be used to code a program. By using these three structures, the coding is more disciplined and clearer to review and maintain. The structures are simple sequence, selection, and repetition. An additional structure, multiple case selection, is often used. Programs should be formatted to show coding structure. There should be a descriptive name (and comments) at the beginning of each module. Comments are included in the coding where necessary to explain the flow of logic. Lines of coding are indented to identify logical blocks and to show the range of coding structures.

A basic set of computer instructions is found in all languages. These are move, edit, arithmetic, transfer of control, looping, input/output, and compiler/assembler instructions.

Additional programming techniques (over the basic structures) that have proved useful are programmed switches, table look-up, and subroutines. The general ideas are presented in this chapter; the implementation in specific languages is presented in the language chapters.

A structured, disciplined approach to program development was presented. The elements, which may be used singly or in groups, are top-down program development, structured programming, chief-programmer teams, structured walk-throughs, development support libraries, and HIPO charts. The chapter concludes with a discussion of program documentation.

EXERCISES

1 Define:
  (a) Error-resistant operations
  (b) Maintainable code
  (c) Portable code

2 (a) Explain modular design.
  (b) Draw a chart showing the modular hierarchy for a computer program with the following modules:

A	Main line control	AC	Compute pay
AA	Initialize	ACA	Compute regular pay
AB	Read input	ACB	Compute overtime pay
ABA	Validate input data	AD	Report output
ABB	Input error messages	AE	Closing procedures

3 What are the differences in meaning among each set of terms:
  (a) Module, block, or program unit   (c) Branching or transfer of control
  (b) Repetition or looping   (d) Switch or flag

4 Draw a flowchart for a selection structure which performs actions on the IF THEN condition but not on the ELSE condition. Does this still fit the basic structure?

5 (a) Flowchart nested selection structures to select procedures as follows:

Code equal to	Perform procedure
1	ONE
2	TWO
3	THREE
>3	ERROR

(*b*) Show an indentation format for the coding of the above logic.

6 What difference does it make if the structure is DO WHILE or DO UNTIL?

(*a*) Assuming the procedure is to be executed 10 times;

(*b*) Assuming the procedure is to be executed until N > 10 but N is already 15 when the repetition structure is reached.

7 Combine, using a flowchart, a sequence, a selection, and a repetition (DO WHILE) for each branch following the selection.

8 Explain the need for and purpose of each type of elementary computer instructions.

9 Explain for arithmetic:

(*a*) Overflow   (*b*) Precision

10 Flowchart problem 5(*a*) using a case selection structure.

11 How is a programmed switch set, tested, and reset?

12 Why is it better to use a separate tax table that a program can refer to than coding the table in the tax computation program? How is a table accessed using table look-up techniques?

13 How does a closed subroutine differ from prewritten segments of code inserted in a program?

14 A subroutine is coded separately from the programs that will use it. How does the subroutine know what data is to be used when it is invoked by the calling program?

15 Explain the difference between top-down and bottom-up program development. How does it affect the amount of testing for the higher-level modules?

16 How can a module be tested if the modules which it invokes are not yet coded? Explain the use of the stub.

17 Explain structured programming. Why is it called GOTOLESS programming?

18 Define the different job functions in the chief-programmer team method.

19 What might be the responses of a programmer to a structured walk-through?

20 Describe the elements of a development support library.

21 Describe the structure of HIPO charting.

22 Compare the use of macro and micro program flowcharts with HIPO flowcharts.

23 Describe a complete set of documentation for:

(*a*) A small program to calculate the rate of return for an investment. The program will be used by all investment analysts.

(*b*) A large program to do online reservations.

24 A company with a large programming staff reported that they had decided to use three of the six techniques for disciplined program development. Which three do you feel would be most valuable for them?

25 A small company with one programmer asks your advice on introducing the elements of programming discipline. What might they do?

PART

COMPUTER TECHNOLOGY

Part 3 emphasizes computer equipment and the way it operates to store data, perform computation, input or output data, and transmit data over communications facilities. Chapter 6 describes the way the computer represents data and performs arithmetic. Chapter 7 surveys internal operations of the computer and how data can be stored. Chapter 8 explains the equipment and methods by which data is prepared for computer processing, the equipment for input and output, and the facilities for transmitting data between different locations. The equipment for auxiliary storage of data and programs is described in Chapter 9, and an explanation is given of how data is organized for effective processing and retrieval.

CHAPTER

COMPUTER ARITHMETIC AND DATA REPRESENTATION

A computer user can input data, use reports, and even program in a high-level language without understanding anything about computer arithmetic and internal data representation. However, a student desiring a solid understanding of computers will find a modest exposure to these topics very useful. This chapter may therefore be omitted, surveyed, or studied carefully depending on the objectives of the reader. Self-testing quizzes are used in the chapter to aid in learning these topics. The answers to these quizzes are at the end of the chapter.

The Coding of Data for Computer Processing and Storage

The computer operates with devices having only two states—electronic switches which are open or closed, electrical pulses high or not high, magnetized elements having one of two directions of polarities. The two states are represented by 0 and 1. They are called binary (meaning two) digits, a term abbreviated as *bits*. One can think of the computer as moving a string of 0s and 1s through its circuitry and storing strings of 0s and 1s in its memory:

But, the computer needs to be able to represent decimal numbers and alphabetic and special characters. In other words, the computer needs to be able to move and store strings of alphanumeric characters:

Since the computer needs to move and store at least 10 different numeric digits, 26 alphabetic characters, and more than 20 special characters (more than 56 in total) but can represent only 0 and 1, there must be a means for using the binary 0s and 1s to code the alphanumeric characters. There must also be a method for coding numeric data for computation. The use of strings of binary digits is not suitable for human operators, and therefore an operator notation is needed which represents the underlying binary coding. The coding methods will be surveyed before proceeding with explanations of the binary numeral system, the octal and hexadecimal systems, and binary arithmetic.

The Binary Code for Alphanumerics

The way to represent many different characters using only 1s and 0s is to take sets of 1s and 0s and establish a code such that a certain pattern of 0s and 1s represents A, another pattern B, etc. How big will the set of 0s and 1s need to be to represent the alphanumeric characters? There will have to be enough different 1 and 0 combinations to allow a different combination for each of the alphanumeric characters and any other codes needed. For example, a 3-bit set will have eight combinations, as shown below.

Combinations of 0 and 1 with 3 bits

000	100
001	101
010	110
011	111

The number of bits to encode the alphanumerics is at least 6, but for reasons related to the need for more codes, most modern computers use a set of 8 bits. For example, the term 1 − A is coded as follows (an actual code being given only for illustrative purposes):

1		−		A
11110001		01100000		11000001

In other words, the computer moves and stores 1s and 0s (as represented by the two possible states), but sets of the 1s and 0s stand for (code) alphanumerics.

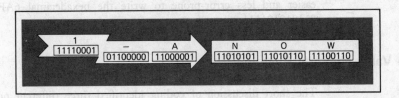

The computer can compare strings of these representations, move them about, rearrange them, and so on.

The Binary Code for Numerics

The coding of each character by a set of 8 bits works for numeric digits as well as for alphabetics. However, for arithmetic processing, 8 bits to represent a number is not efficient, and computers using 8 bits for encoding characters will split the 8 bits into two 4-bit sets for coding numerics. The coding concept is the same as with alphanumerics, with each 4-bit set representing a separate decimal digit. For example, the code for 103 is:

0001	0000	0011

The computer can perform arithmetic on these sets much like arithmetic on decimal numbers. Arithmetic operating on these sets is termed "binary-coded decimal" or "packed-decimal arithmetic."

The use of small sets to encode each digit is not the only method used by a computer to represent a decimal number for arithmetic processing. The second method is to encode numbers by using a long string of binary digits. The strings are actually a very large code. Depending on the computer, the string of bits can be 24, 32, 36, etc., bits in length. For example, the quantity 103 would be coded by a 32-bit binary string as:

00000000000000000000000001100111

Arithmetic performed on such strings is termed "binary arithmetic." In general, it is faster and less complicated for the computer hardware than binary-coded decimal arithmetic.

Operator Notation

The binary codes involving strings of 0s and 1s present no problem when in the computer in their electrical or magnetic representation, but frequently the operator (or programmer) wishes to write down a string of bits (say, for example, a string representing an error code). It is very error-prone and very inefficient to use the string of 1s and 0s. Ponder trying to write down a set of thirty-two 1s and 0s. It is common to write down the string using another related notation. The most common are hexadecimal, in which each set of 4 bits is written with an equivalent hexadecimal character (0 to 9 and A to F), or octal, in which each set of 3 bits is written with an equivalent octal character (characters 1 to 7). As an example, it is easier and less error-prone to write the hexadecimal 6AF than the binary 011010101111.

Place Value Numeral Systems

The short discussion of coding identified three different numeral systems in common use in computer coding or operator notation. These systems are discussed in this section.

Place Value and Absolute Value

The numeral (number) systems to be explained use the concepts of base, absolute value, and a positional value. The base (also called "radix") of the numeral system indicates how many absolute values are used in that system. The positional values are found by raising the base of the numeral system to the power of the position.[1]

---

[1] As a reminder to readers who may have forgotten, the value resulting from raising a number to a power, i.e., the value resulting from exponentiation, is a product of successive multiplications by the number, with the number of multiplications being equal to the exponent. Thus, $3^4 = 3 \times 3 \times 3 \times 3 = 81$. A number to the 0 power is equal to 1. Therefore, $1^0 = 1$, $2^0 = 1$, $3^0 = 1$, etc. A minus exponent represents a fraction. For example, $4^{-3} = (\frac{1}{4})^3 = \frac{1}{64}$.

This is illustrated in Table 6-1 for the decimal system, which has a radix of 10. Note that the positions are numbered to the left of the decimal point starting with 0 and to the right of the decimal starting with -1.

TABLE 6-1 SOME OF THE POSITIONAL VALUES IN THE DECIMAL SYSTEM

Position number	3	2	1	0	Decimal point	-1	-2
Position value (base of 10)	10^3	10^2	10^1	10^0		10^{-1}	10^{-2}
Quantity represented by position value	1000 Thousands	100 Hundreds	10 Tens	1 Units		$\frac{1}{10}$ Tenths	$\frac{1}{100}$ Hundredths

The decimal system has 10 absolute values represented by the digits 0 through 9. Each digit written in the decimal notation is interpreted as having a value equal to the absolute value of the digit (1, 2, 3, etc.) times the position value of the position it occupies. This is illustrated in Figure 6-1 by two examples.

Many numeral systems are possible using different sets of absolute values and different bases. Three of the most important for computers are the binary, the octal, and the hexadecimal systems.

Name	Base	Absolute values
Binary	2	0,1
Octal	8	0,1,2,3,4,5,6,7
Hexadecimal	16	0 through 9,A,B,C,D,E,F

Each of these is discussed in this chapter.

The Binary System The binary system uses the concepts of absolute value and positional value in the same way as the decimal. The difference is that the binary system uses only two absolute values, 0 and 1, and the positional values are powers of 2. Numbers are

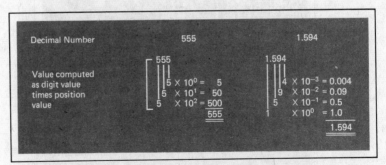

FIGURE 6-1 Absolute value and positional values for two examples with decimal system.

thus expressed in binary notations as a series of 0s and 1s. The two values of binary digits are called "0 bit" and "1 bit." The binary point serves the same purpose as the decimal point. This is illustrated in Table 6-2.

TABLE 6-2 SOME OF THE POSITIONAL VALUES IN THE BINARY SYSTEM

Position	4	3	2	1	0	Binary point	−1	−2	−3	−4
Position value	2^4	2^3	2^2	2^1	2^0		2^{-1}	2^{-2}	2^{-3}	2^{-4}
Quantity represented by position value	16	8	4	2	1		$\frac{1}{2}$	$\frac{1}{4}$	$\frac{1}{8}$	$\frac{1}{16}$

The decimal equivalent of a number written in binary is found by adding the products of the absolute and positional values. For example, the binary 10101011.011 is interpreted as $171\frac{3}{8}$, as shown in Figure 6-2.

Self-testing Quiz #6-1

Before proceeding, test your understanding of the basic concepts of the binary system. Do the following self-testing quizzes—the answers are found at the end of the chapter.

1 What is the decimal equivalent of each of the following binary numbers?
   (a) 1101   (b) 11011   (c) 1.0011   (d) 10.01
2 What is the binary-number equivalent to each of the following decimal numbers?
   (a) 3   (b) 8   (c) 14   (d) 16

The Octal System

The octal system has a base of 8. It therefore uses the absolute values from 0 through 7 and positional values which are powers of 8. This is shown by the octal notation for a group of decimal numbers.

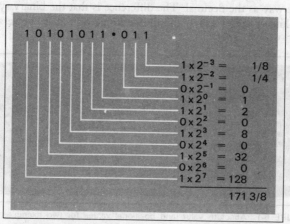

FIGURE 6-2 Example of converting a binary number to the decimal equivalent.

Decimal	Octal	Decimal	Octal
1	1	11	13
2	2	12	14
3	3	13	15
4	4	14	16
5	5	15	17
6	6	16	20
7	7	17	21
8	10	18	22
9	11	19	23
10	12	20	24

The number 224.3 in octal (written 224.3_8) is converted to decimal by taking the absolute values times the position values, as shown below.

$$
\begin{array}{l}
2 \quad 2 \quad 4 \; . \; 3 \\
\qquad\qquad 3 \times 8^{-1} = \quad \tfrac{3}{8} \\
\qquad\quad 4 \times 8^{0} \; = \quad 4 \\
\qquad 2 \times 8^{1} \; = \quad 16 \\
\quad 2 \times 8^{2} \; = \quad \underline{128} \\
\qquad\qquad\qquad\qquad\quad 148\tfrac{3}{8}
\end{array}
$$

Self-testing Quiz #6-2

1 What are the decimal equivalents of the following octal numerals?
(*a*) 10   (*b*) 16   (*c*) 7   (*d*) 70

2 What are the octal equivalents of the following binary numerals?
(*a*) 111   (*b*) 1001

The Hexadecimal System

The hexadecimal system has a base of 16. It uses characters representing the values from 0 to 15 for absolute values and power of 16 for positional values. Because only a single character is allowed for each absolute value in a numeral system, the hexadecimal system uses the characters A through F to represent the values of 10 through 15. (Although one may find many different characters used in mathematics texts, A to F are the accepted characters for computers.)

Decimal	Hexadecimal	Decimal	Hexadecimal
0	0	8	8
1	1	9	9
2	2	10	A
3	3	11	B
4	4	12	C
5	5	13	D
6	6	14	E
7	7	15	F

The hexadecimal $3A1.4_{16}$ is interpreted as the decimal numeral $929\frac{4}{16}$, as shown below.

$$
\begin{array}{l}
3 \quad A \quad 1 \, . \, 4 \\[4pt]
\qquad\qquad 4 \times 16^{-1} \quad = \quad \frac{4}{16} \\[2pt]
\qquad\quad 1 \times 16^{0} \quad = \quad 1 \\[2pt]
\qquad A(10) \times 16^{1} \ = \ 160 \\[2pt]
3 \times 16^{2}(256) = \underline{768} \\[2pt]
\qquad\qquad\qquad\qquad\quad 929\frac{4}{16}
\end{array}
$$

Self-testing
Quiz #6-3

1 What are the decimal equivalents of the following hexadecimal numerals?
   (*a*) F   (*b*) 1E   (*c*) 11B   (*d*) 100   (*e*) 11
2 What are the hexadecimal equivalents of the following binary numerals?
   (*a*) 1111   (*b*) 1000   (*c*) 1101   (*d*) 10001

Converting from One Numeral System to Another

Consider the numeral 111.1. As a decimal numeral it has a value of one hundred eleven and one-tenth. However, if 111.1 is considered a binary numeral, it is equivalent to decimal $7\frac{1}{2}$; if an octal numeral, it is $73\frac{1}{8}$; if a hexadecimal numeral, it is $273\frac{1}{16}$. This section illustrates ways to convert numerals from one of the numeral systems to or from decimal, and ways to convert between binary and the octal or hexadecimal notations.

Conversion to
Decimal by
Summing
Position Values

The method used so far to obtain the decimal equivalent of another numeral system is to sum the different values for each position (absolute value times position value). This process is shown for 111.1 interpreted as binary, octal, and hexadecimal:

$$
\begin{array}{lll}
1 \ 1 \ 1 \, . \, 1_{2} & 1 \ 1 \ 1 \, . \, 1_{8} & 1 \ 1 \ 1 \, . \, 1_{16} \\[4pt]
\quad 1 \times 2^{-1} = \frac{1}{2} & \quad 1 \times 8^{-1} = \frac{1}{8} & \quad 1 \times 16^{-1} = \frac{1}{16} \\[2pt]
\ 1 \times 2^{0} \ = 1 & \ 1 \times 8^{0} \ = 1 & \ 1 \times 16^{0} \ = \ 1 \\[2pt]
1 \times 2^{1} \ = 2 & 1 \times 8^{1} \ = 8 & 1 \times 16^{1} \ = \ 16 \\[2pt]
1 \times 2^{2} \ = \underline{4} & 1 \times 8^{2} \ = \underline{64} & 1 \times 16^{2} \ = \underline{256} \\[2pt]
\qquad\qquad 7\frac{1}{2} & \qquad\qquad 73\frac{1}{8} & \qquad\qquad 273\frac{1}{16}
\end{array}
$$

The above examples contain no zeros, but they follow regular arithmetic rules. The absolute value of zero results in a value of 0 for the position (since the product of the position value and zero is always zero). Note the binary numeral 1000.

$$1 \quad 0 \quad 0 \quad 0._2$$

$$0 \times 2^0 = 0$$
$$0 \times 2^1 = 0$$
$$0 \times 2^2 = 0$$
$$\underline{1 \times 2^3 = 8}$$
$$8$$

The conversion from any numeral system (binary, octal, hexadecimal, etc.) is thus a simple process of finding the decimal equivalent of the digit in each position (absolute value times position value) and summing these. This is somewhat difficult to do quickly, and an alternative approach to conversion to decimal is the multiply-and-add method.

Conversion to Decimal by Multiply-and-Add Method

A decimal equivalent for an absolute value in a position to the left of the point (for binary, octal, hexadecimal, etc.) may be found by taking the absolute value and multiplying it by the base, executing a multiplication for each position to the right of the digit being computed until the point is reached. For example, 1000_2 (binary) and 1000_8 (octal) would be computed as follows:

Binary

1	0	0	0
1	$\times 2$	$\times 2$	$\times 2$

$= 8$

Octal

1	0	0	0
1	$\times 8$	$\times 8$	$\times 8$

$= 512$

This procedure may be combined for all positions to the left of the point as follows: starting with the leftmost nonzero digit, multiply by the base, add the next digit to the right to the product to obtain a sum, multiply this sum by the base, add the next digit, etc., until the point is reached. There is no multiplication following the addition of the position next to the point (the 0 position). For example, 1101_2 (binary) and $103B_{16}$ (hexadecimal) are converted as follows:

	Binary				Hexadecimal			
Product of prior multiplication	—	②	6	12	—	16	256	4144
Number	1	1	0	1	1	0	3	B (11)
Sum	1	3	6	⑬	1	16	259	④⑤⑤
Multiply by base	$\times 2$	$\times 2$	$\times 2$		$\times 16$	$\times 16$	$\times 16$	
Product	②	6	12		16	256	4144	

Answer = 13   Answer = 4155

The method is especially useful in converting binary numerals because it is fairly easy to double and add without resorting to pencil and paper. For binary numerals, the procedure is often called "double dabbling." As an additional binary example, 110111011 is converted by double dabbling to decimal 433 as follows:

Doubling of prior sum		2	6	12	26	54	110	220	442
Binary number to be converted	1	1	0	1	1	1	0	1	1
Sum	1	3	6	13	27	55	110	221	(443)

Note that this could have been done by mentally doubling and adding. The method of arranging product above and sum below the numeral to be converted will be used for showing the answers to the self-testing quiz.

Self-testing Quiz #6-4

1 Using the multiply-and-add method, convert the following binary numerals to decimal numerals:
(a) 1101101   (b) 0111101   (c) 101111   (d) 111000

2 Using the multiply-and-add method, convert the following octal and hexadecimal numerals to decimal:
(a) 123_8 (c) 200_8 (e) 107_{16}
(b) 107_8 (d) 123_{16} (f) $1BE_{16}$

The process of multiplication and addition can be used to convert the numeral to the right of the point. The result of the conversion is a fraction. The numerator of the fraction is obtained by the same process already described of multiplying by the base and adding, starting with the digit to the right of the point. The denominator is obtained by exponentiating the base by the number of digits in the fraction being converted. For example, 0.1001_2 (binary) and 0.17_8 (octal) are converted as follows:

$$0.1001_2 \qquad\qquad 0.17_8$$

	2	4	8			8	
Numerator	1	0	0	1 = 9	1	7	= 15
	1	2	4	9	1	15	

Denominator $2^4 = 2 \times 2 \times 2 \times 2 = 16$ $8^2 = 64$
(4 digits in binary fraction)   (2 digits in octal fraction)

Answers $0.1001_2 = \frac{9}{16}$ $0.17_8 = \frac{15}{64}$

Self-testing Quiz #6-5

Convert the following fractions to decimal:

1 Binary fractions
(a) 0.0101   (b) 0.10001

2 Octal fractions
(a) 0.75   (b) 0.01
3 Hexadecimal fractions
(a) 0.F1   (b) 0.08
4 Mixed numbers
(a) 1101.11_2 (b) $1A.51_{16}$

Conversion from Decimal by Division

The preceding discussion has explained how to convert to decimal from another numeral system. The process of converting decimal numerals to another numeral system is by division for whole numbers. Conversion of decimal fractions is handled differently and is explained later. The procedure is successive division by the base, saving the remainder from each division. The string of remainders is the converted numeral, the first digit of the remainder being next to the point. As an example, the decimal numeral 246 is converted to binary and hexadecimal as follows:

To binary

2	246	Remainder
	123	0
	61	1
	30	1
	15	0
	7	1
	3	1
	1	1
	0	1

Read from bottom

Answer = 11110110

To hexadecimal

16	246	Remainder
	15	6
	0	F (15)

Answer = F6

Self-testing Quiz #6-6

Convert the following decimal numerals:

1 To binary
(a) 186   (b) 109
2 To octal
(a) 186   (b) 95
3 To hexadecimal
(a) 186   (b) 958

Conversion of Decimal Fractions

The conversion of decimal fractions to another numeral system is performed by multiplying the fraction by the new base and saving at each multiplication, the integral digit resulting from the multiplication. This process is continued (multiplying only the fraction remaining) until the fraction becomes zero or until sufficient accuracy has been obtained. The integral digits form the new fraction, reading from top to bottom. As examples, 0.75 and 0.31 will be converted to binary and hexadecimal.

TO BINARY			

EXAMPLE 1		EXAMPLE 2	
Integer	Fraction	Integer	Fraction
—	.75	—.	.31
	×2		×2
1	.50	0	.62
	×2		×2
1	.00	1	.24
			×2
Answer = .11		0	.48
			×2
		0	.96
			×2
		1	.92
			×2
		1	.84
		Answer = .010011...	

TO HEXADECIMAL			

EXAMPLE 1		EXAMPLE 2	
Integer	Fraction	Integer	Fraction
—	.75	—.	.31
	×16		×16
C(12)	.00	4	.96
Answer = .C			×16
		F(15)	.36
		Answer = .4F ...	

Note that .031 decimal did not result in a remainder of zero. Just as a common fraction such as $\frac{1}{3}$ cannot be converted into an exact decimal fraction equivalent (one can write 0.333 . . . but it will never be exact), 0.31 decimal is an example of a decimal fraction that cannot be converted into an exact binary or hexadecimal equivalent. In general, decimal integers can be represented precisely with another base, but most decimal fractions can be represented only approximately. In computation, this can cause slight errors unless care is taken to adjust for it. For example, 0.91 is converted to binary .111010001111 using 12 bits. The conversion back to decimal yields $3,727/4,096 = 0.909912$ (to six digits of accuracy). This example uses a rather small number of bits but illustrates the principle. This fraction can be represented more closely by using a large number of bits, but the number of bits is limited by the design of the computer. The programmer can compensate for this error by adding a very small rounding factor or other similar methods.

Self-testing Quiz #6-7

Convert the following fractions:

1 To binary (to maximum of six places)
   (a) 0.828125 (b) 0.0774

2 To octal (to maximum of two places)
(a) 0.828125 (b) 0.0774
3 To hexadecimal (to maximum of two places)
(a) 0.50 (b) 0.46

Conversion among Binary, Octal, and Hexadecimal

Conversion between binary and octal or binary and hexadecimal may be performed easily by inspection without pencil computation. To convert a binary numeral to octal, begin at the binary point and block off groups of three binary digits. Replace each group of three binary digits with its equivalent octal digit. The digit will range from 0 to 7. To convert from octal to binary, replace each octal digit with the equivalent three binary digits. Use the same process for the fractional portion, starting at the point, adding more 0s if necessary to complete the last set of three. The conversion to and from hexadecimal is identical, except that groups of four binary digits are used and the hexadecimal values range from 0 to F. Examples are the octal and hexadecimal conversions of binary 1111011011011.11011:

Binary	001	111	011	011	011	.	110	110
Octal	1	7	3	3	3	.	6	6

Binary		0001	1110	1101	1011	.	1101	1000
Hexadecimal		1	E	D	B	.	D	8

The ease of conversion to or from hexadecimal (or octal) and binary is the reason that these notations are used to describe the underlying binary numbers. In fact, it is sometimes easier to convert a decimal number to hexadecimal and then to binary than to try to convert it directly to binary from decimal.

Self-testing Quiz #6-8

1 Convert by inspection to binary:
(a) 347.2_8 (b) 347.2_{16} (c) $A71.A_{16}$ (d) 473.4_8
2 Convert by inspection from binary, (1) to hexadecimal and (2) to octal:
(a) 1110110101.11 (c) 1001110100.111
(b) 10000100 (d) 10100100.001

The Flow of Coded Data

The preceding discussion of numeral systems has focused on the representation of numeric quantities, yet much of the processing and storage by computer is alphanumeric data not used in arithmetic computation. The coding of data for computation is usually different than coding for noncomputational data. A description of the flow of coded data will clarify this difference.

Coding of Data on Input and Output

When it first enters the computer (say from punched cards or terminal input), the input data, whether alphabetic, numeric, or special characters, is encoded character by character into a binary character code, one bit set being used for each character. The size of the bit set (usually termed a "byte") is 6 or 8 bits depending on the computer. The most common size is the 8-bit byte (used, for example, by the IBM System/370). The code structure of the byte is divided into two parts—a set of 4 (or 2 in a 6-bit byte) designated as a zone and 4 bits designated as a numeric portion. The zone bits perform the same function as the zone punches on a Hollerith punched card, indicating the group of characters to which the code applies. The specific character in the group is identified by the numeric coding. The set of bits may include error and control bits, but these will not be explained here. Figure 6-3 illustrates the different methods by giving sample codes for the letter A. The examples use codes from two different computers. Note that the numeric portion in each case is 1 for A, but the zone bits are different. This reflects the different design characteristics of the computer. The codes used also define the collating sequence. When sorting data, an A is smaller than a B, and so on,

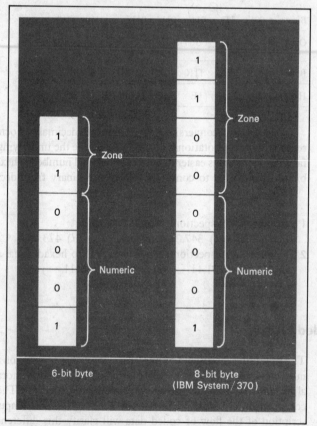

FIGURE 6-3 Sample coding of letter A—parity bit not shown.

but the number 1 may be smaller or larger than an A depending on the zone code for the particular computer.

If the data is not to be manipulated arithmetically, it is stored in this character coding. However, if the number is to be used in arithmetic operations, it must be converted to a binary-coded decimal or binary form. Some computers perform arithmetic on the character-coded format, but the dominant design is for special numeric coding for arithmetic operations.

When data is to be output from the computer to a device such as a printer or a terminal, it must be encoded into a separate character code for each character to be output (including codes for the blank spaces in the output line). Data to be held in storage or written onto magnetic disk or tape may remain in either character code or computational code. The flow of data from input to output is shown in Figure 6-4.

Computational Code   The computational data may be in one of two forms:

1   Binary-coded decimal (BCD) in which each digit is encoded by a set of 4 to 6 bits. The most common method is to encode (pack) two numeric digits in an 8-bit byte. This is termed "packed decimal."

2   Straight binary using a binary string consisting of a fixed set of bits (say 32, 36, or more).

In the binary-coded decimal, the 4-bit positions are interpreted as in straight binary. This coding, often termed "natural binary-coded decimal," is the most common code, but variations of this have also been used.

4-bit-set	Decimal value	4-bit set	Decimal value
0000	0	0101	5
0001	1	0110	6
0010	2	0111	7
0011	3	1000	8
0100	4	1001	9

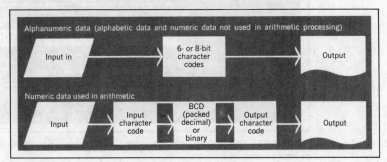

FIGURE 6-4   Flow of coded data in computer processing.

Note that there are bit combinations that are not used. Since only 10 of 16 combinations can be used to represent decimal digits, the remainder are available for other purposes.

The binary string encodes a quantity in the binary-number system. Since a fixed set of bits is used, there will normally be leading 0-bits. However, computation using binary data is faster than that using binary-coded decimal data. Computers such as the IBM System/370 can perform both binary and binary-coded decimal arithmetic, so the choice of coding may depend on the application.

Figure 6-5 illustrates the difference between a binary-coded decimal representation and a straight binary for the number 763. Leading zeros have been dropped from the straight binary in Figure 6-5 (which would otherwise have a total of 32 bits).

Coding Signs and Decimal Points

The sign (positive or negative) of numeric quantities must be represented in order for correct processing to take place. The representation will differ for input/output coding and for the various codes used for arithmetic processing.

Following input, the form of the sign in storage will depend on the way the sign is expressed in the input media. When punched cards are used as the input method, the positive sign is not normally punched. A negative sign may be punched in a separate column in front of the quantity, or it may be expressed as an 11 overpunch on the rightmost digit of the quantity field, as shown by two examples:

1 −4758 (minus sign occupies column)
2 475$\bar{8}$ (minus sign is part of coding for rightmost numeric digit)

The overpunch is most common in commercial processing; scientific and mathematical applications often use the separate minus sign.

When the data card is read, each character (punched one per column) is

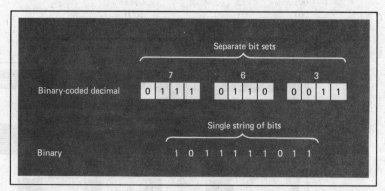

FIGURE 6-5 Comparison of binary-coded decimal and binary representation for decimal number 763.

converted to a character code. The minus sign, occupying a separate card column, is coded by a separate character bit set. The overpunch changes the code of the rightmost character.

For output (say, on the printer), the data must be arranged with a separate character code for each character to be printed. Thus, no matter what method is used for input, the output of −4758 will require that the minus be coded in a separate bit set positioned before the bit sets representing the digits of the quantity.

The conversion of numeric data from character code to the representation for arithmetic processing includes the coding of the sign in the position required for arithmetic. When the methods explained earlier for coding numbers for arithmetic processing are used, the sign is coded as follows:

1 *Binary string* The leftmost bit of the string is the sign bit. For example, +6 would be coded as 0 . . . 00110, while −6 would be coded as 1 . . . 00110. There are variations on this method using the 1s or 2s complement (to be explained) to represent negative numbers.

2 *Binary-coded decimal* The method used with packed decimal is to code the sign using a separate 4-bit set at the right end of the coding. For example, −758 would be coded as (using System/370 codes):

7	5	8	−
0111	0101	1000	1101

Other methods may be used with different coding for BCD, but this is illustrative of the concept.

For data processing applications it is customary not to punch the decimal point for input data. 3.14 and 0.314 are both coded as 314. The programmer keeps track of the decimal point or scaling and writes the program accordingly. In scientific processing, however, decimal points are often punched in the data, and the processing program must then convert it to a data form which has no decimal point. Data for output must be put into individual character codes, and a separate code for the decimal point must be inserted.

An alternative data representation sometimes used (especially in scientific processing) in order to let the computer keep track of the scaling is called *floating point*. The numeric data item is represented by two parts, of which one is the quantity and the other indicates the scaling. This is explained more fully in Chapter 15 (in connection with assembly language programming).

Arithmetic Operations in Binary

Arithmetic operations with decimal numbers depend on several rules which are usually learned at such an early age that the process seems "natural" rather than dependent on a set of rules and tables. For example, we learn to add by memorizing the add table for the decimal system (Figure 6-6). This is a table expressing the

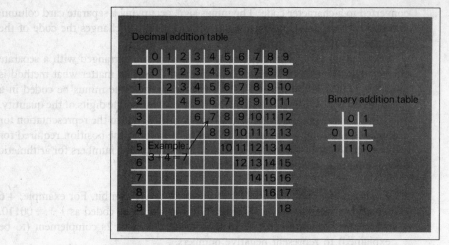

FIGURE 6-6 Addition tables for decimal and binary system.

results of all possible addition combinations of two numbers. Only half the table is needed since it is symmetrical. The sum of two numbers is shown at the intersection of one of the numbers from the row and the other from the column.

Rules for Binary Arithmetic

The rules and add table for binary arithmetic are simpler than for decimal arithmetic. For example, the add table for binary arithmetic (Figure 6-6) consists of only four entries. The table is used in the same way as the decimal add table. Similar tables can be made for multiplication and subtraction.

The computer user or programmer does not usually need to be able to perform binary arithmetic, but some understanding of binary arithmetic is a useful background for understanding computers. In this section, the binary system rules for each of the four basic arithmetic operations of addition, subtraction, multiplication, and division are summarized and illustrated.

EXAMPLES

Rules for binary addition		Binary	Decimal equivalent	Binary	Decimal equivalent
$1 + 1 = 0$	and carry 1 to add to next column	1011	11	1110.01	14.25
		1001	9	11010.11	26.75
$1 + 0 = 1$		10100	20	101001.00	41.00
$0 + 1 = 1$					
$0 + 0 = 0$					

EXAMPLES

Rules for binary subtraction			Binary	Decimal equivalent	Binary	Decimal equivalent
$1 - 1 = 0$						
$1 - 0 = 1$		Minuend	10100	20	101001.00	41.00
$0 - 1 = 1$	with a borrow	Subtrahend	−01001	−9	−011010.11	−26.75
	from the next	Remainder	01011	11	001110.01	14.25
	column of the					
	minuend					
$0 - 0 = 0$						

In subtraction, the borrow reduces the remaining minuend by 1. A borrow will cause a 1 in the next column to the left in the minuend to become 0. If the next column contains a 0, it is changed to a 1, and the succeeding 0s in the minuend are changed to 1s until a 1 can be changed to a 0. For example, 0001 from 1000 will cause a borrow and make the remaining minuend equal to 011. From a computational standpoint, the borrow can also be done by adding a carry to the next column of the subtrahend.

Problem	Step 1	Step 2	Step 3	Step 4
	*1	*11	*011	011
1000	10̸0̸0̸	10̸0̸0̸	10̸0̸0̸	10̸0̸0̸
−0001	−0001	−0001	0001	0001
	1	1	1	0111
	*Carry changes 0 to 1	*Continue changing 0s to 1s	*Until a 1 can be changed to a 0 then proceed with subtraction	

Self-testing Quiz #6-9   Perform the following binary arithmetic.

1   11001
   +10011

2   110111
   +10111

3   101011
   −10010

4   1000
   −111

EXAMPLES

Rules for binary multiplication	Binary	Decimal equivalent	Binary	Decimal equivalent
Copy multiplicand when multiplier digit is 1; do not when it is 0. Shift as in decimal multiplication. Add the resulting binary numbers according to the binary addition rules.	1101	13	101	5
	1100	×12	111	×7
	0	26	101	35
	0	13	101	
	1101	156	101	
	1101		100011	
	10011100			

It may not be obvious how to handle the addition if the result of the multiplication results in columns with more than two 1s. Perhaps the simplest method is to sum each column and write down the resulting binary sum. If the sum is greater than 1, the left-hand digits are placed as carries to the left-hand columns.

Rules for binary division

Start from the left on the dividend.

Perform a series of subtractions in which the divisor is subtracted from the dividend.

If subtraction is possible, put a 1 in the quotient and subtract the divisor from the corresponding digits of the dividend.

If subtraction is not possible (divisor greater than remainder), record a 0 in the quotient.

Bring down the next digit to add to the remainder digits. Proceed as before in a manner similar to long division.

Example of handling of carries in multiplication

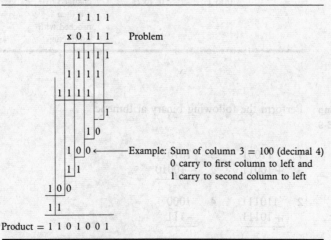

```
          1 1 1 1
      x 0 1 1 1     Problem
        1 1 1 1
      1 1 1 1
    1 1 1 1
            1
          1 0
        1 0 0  ←——— Example: Sum of column 3 = 100 (decimal 4)
        1 1                      0 carry to first column to left and
    1 0 0                        1 carry to second column to left
    1 1

Product = 1 1 0 1 0 0 1
```

EXAMPLE   Binary

	Decimal equivalent

$$0101_\wedge 1$$
$$110\overline{)100001\ 0}$$

		Decimal equivalent
110 ←——— Divisor greater than 100, so put 0 in quotient		30
1000 ←——— Add digit from dividend to group used above		30
110 ←——— Subtraction possible, so put 1 in quotient		30
100 ←——— Remainder from subtraction plus digit from dividend		
110 ←——— Divisor greater, so put 0 in quotient		
1001 ←——— Add digit from dividend to group		
110 ←——— Subtraction possible, so put 1 in quotient		
110 ←——— Perform subtraction, and add digit from dividend to remainder		
110 ←——— Subtraction possible, so put 1 in quotient		
←——— No remainder, so stop		

The decimal equivalent shown at right: $5_\wedge 5$ / $6\overline{)33}$ / 30 / 30 / 30

Self-testing Quiz #6-10

Perform the following binary arithmetic:

1 10111
 ×101

2 1110
 ×111

3 101)1110011

4 111)1100010

Binary Arithmetic Using Complements

One of the problems of the computer hardware designer is to simplify the computer circuitry. Subtraction is usually performed by complementing the number to be subtracted and then adding the complement. This simplifies circuitry because subtraction can make use of the addition circuitry. The complementing process itself is very simple. Since multiplication is basically addition, and division involves subtraction, the change to the complement method of subtraction reduces all computer arithmetic to forms of addition. Negative numbers are usually also handled by complementing.

In the decimal system, also, subtraction may be performed by adding complements. The 9s complement of a decimal number is found by subtracting each digit from 9, and the 10s by adding 1 to the 9s complement.

Number	346	799	192
9s complement	653	200	807
10s complement	654	201	808

The corresponding binary-number complements are the 1s and 2s complements. The 1s complement of a binary number is the number obtained by making each 0 into a 1 and each 1 into a 0. The 2s complement is the 1s complement plus 1.

Binary number   1011   1111   1010

1s complement   0100   0000   0101

2s complement   0101   0001   0110

The rules for complement subtraction of decimal numbers, with the exception of the manner of forming the complement, are the same as for binary numbers.

Rules for complement subtraction—1s complement

Compute the 1s complement of the subtrahend by changing 1s to 0s and all 0s to 1s.

Add the complement to the minuend.

Perform an end-around carry of 1 or 0.

If the end-around carry is 0, the result must be recomplemented and a negative sign attached.

If the end-around carry is 1, no recomplementing is necessary.

EXAMPLE

Problem	Decimal using 9s complement		Binary using 1s complement
14	14		1110
−06	+93		+1001
08	①07	End-around carry of 1	①0111
=	└→1		└→1
	08		1000
	=		
06	06		0110
−14	+85		+0001
−08	⓪91	End-around carry of 0	⓪0111
	└→0		└→0
	91	Recomplement and attach negative sign	0111
	−08		−1000

If the 2s and 10s complements were used in the examples, the end-around carry would be unnecessary, but recomplementing would still be determined by a carry of 0.

Self-testing Quiz #6-11   Perform the following arithmetic using the complements indicated:

1   162 (9s complement)   **2**   345 (9s complement)
          −283   −128

3 358 (10s complement)   **5** 11101 (1s complement)
   − 124   −01011

4 10011 (1s complement)   **6** 10011 (2s complement)
   − 11100   −01001

SUMMARY An elementary grasp of computer codes and binary arithmetic is helpful in understanding computers. When programming or operating a computer, it is necessary to understand the operator notation used by the computer, such as hexadecimal or octal. When data is read into a computer (say, from punched cards), it is encoded and stored in the computer as individual characters, each represented by a 6- or 8-bit set called a byte. Character coding is not, in most computers, suitable for computation. Computational data must be converted to either a binary-coded or packed decimal code for each digit or to a straight binary representation using a fixed-length string of bits. Before printing out computational data, the computer must usually convert back to binary-coded character form. These computer codes are transmitted to the printer where they activate the appropriate print character to print an output readable by humans.

The chapter described concepts of numeral systems using place value and absolute values. The numeral systems most relevant to computers—binary, octal, and hexadecimal—were explained. Conversion between these notations and the decimal system was described. Arithmetic operations in binary were surveyed.

Answers to Self-testing Quizzes

Self-testing **1** (a) 13   (c) $1\frac{3}{16}$
Quiz #6-1   (b) 27   (d) $2\frac{1}{4}$
          2 (a) 11   (c) 1110
              (b) 1000 (d) 10000

Self-testing **1** (a) 8   (c) 7
Quiz #6-2   (b) 14   (d) 56
          2 (a) 7   (b) 11

Self-testing **1** (a) 15   (c) 283   (e) 17
Quiz #6-3   (b) 30   (d) 256
          2 (a) F   (c) D
              (b) 8   (d) 11

Self-testing Quiz #6-4

1 (a)

	2	6	12	26	54	108	
1	1	0	1	1	0	1	= 109
1	3	6	13	27	54	109	

(c)

	2	4	10	22	46	
1	0	1	1	1	1	= 47
1	2	5	11	23	47	

(b)

	2	6	14	30	60	
0	1	1	1	1	0	1	= 61
1	3	7	15	30	61	

(d)

	2	6	14	28	56	
1	1	1	0	0	0	= 56
1	3	7	14	28	56	

2 (a) Octal

8	80	
1	2	3	= 83
Sum 1 | 10 | 83 |

(d) Hexadecimal

16	288	
1	2	3	= 291
Sum 1 | 18 | 291 |

(b) Octal

8	64	
1	0	7	= 71
1	8	71

(e) Hexadecimal

16	256	
1	0	7	= 263
1	16	263

(c) Octal

16	128	
2	0	0	= 128
2	16	128

(f) Hexadecimal

16	432	
1	B(11)	E(14)	= 446
1	27	446

Self-testing Quiz #6-5

1 (a) Numerator

	2	4	
0	1	0	1	= 5
1	2	5

Denominator $2^4 = 16$

Answer $5/16$

(b)

	2	4	8	16	
1	0	0	0	1	= 17
1	2	4	8	17

Denominator $2^5 = 32$

Answer $17/32$

2 (a) Numerator

56	
7	5	= 61
7	61

Denominator $8^2 = 64$

Answer $61/64$

(b)

0	1	= 1

Denominator $8^2 = 64$

Answer $1/64$

3 (*a*) Numerator

	240
F	1	= 241
15	241

(*b*)

0	8	= 8

Denominator $16^2 = 256$

Answer $\dfrac{}{241/256}$

$16^2 = 256$

$\dfrac{}{8/256}$

4 (*a*) Integral portion

	2	6	12
1	1	0	1	= 13
1	3	6	13

(*b*)

	16
1	A	= 26
1	26

Numerator

	2
1	1	= 3
1	3

	80
5	1	= 81
5	81

Denominator $2^2 = 4$

Answer $\dfrac{}{13\ 3/4}$

$16^2 = 256$

$\dfrac{}{26\ 81/256}$

Self-testing Quiz #6-6

1 (*a*)

```
2 | 186
    93  0
    46  1
    23  0
    11  1
     5  1
     2  1
     1  0
     0  1
```
Answer = 10111010

(*b*)

```
2 | 109
    54  1
    27  0
    13  1
     6  1
     3  0
     1  1
     0  1
```
Answer = 1101101

2 (*a*)

```
8 | 186
    23  2
     2  7
     0  2
```
Answer = 272_8

(*b*)

```
8 | 95
    11  7
     1  3
     0  1
```
Answer = 137_8

3 (*a*)

```
16 | 186
     11  A(10)
      0  B(11)
```
Answer = BA_{16}

(*b*)

```
16 | 958
     59  E(14)
      3  B(11)
      0  3
```
Answer = $3BE_{16}$

Self-testing **1** (*a*) 0.828125

Quiz #6-7

$$
\begin{array}{r|l}
 & 0.828125 \\
 & \times 2 \\
\hline
1 & .656250 \\
 & \times 2 \\
\hline
1 & .312500 \\
 & \times 2 \\
\hline
0 & .625000 \\
 & \times 2 \\
\hline
1 & .250000 \\
 & \times 2 \\
\hline
0 & .500000 \\
 & \times 2 \\
\hline
1 & .000000 \\
\end{array}
$$

Answer $= 0.110101_2$ exact

(*b*) 0.0774

$$
\begin{array}{r|l}
 & 0.0774 \\
 & \times 2 \\
\hline
0 & .1548 \\
 & \times 2 \\
\hline
0 & .3096 \\
 & \times 2 \\
\hline
0 & .6192 \\
 & \times 2 \\
\hline
1 & .2384 \\
 & \times 2 \\
\hline
0 & .4768 \\
 & \times 2 \\
\hline
0 & .9536 \\
\end{array}
$$

Answer $= 0.000100_2 +$

2 (*a*) 0.828125

$$
\begin{array}{r|l}
 & 0.828125 \\
 & \times 8 \\
\hline
6 & .625000 \\
 & \times 8 \\
\hline
5 & .000000 \\
\end{array}
$$

Answer $= 0.65_8$ exact

(*b*) 0.0774

$$
\begin{array}{r|l}
 & 0.0774 \\
 & \times 8 \\
\hline
0 & .6192 \\
 & \times 8 \\
\hline
4 & .9536 \\
\end{array}
$$

Answer $= 0.04_8 +$

3 (*a*) 0.50

$$
\begin{array}{r|l}
 & 0.50 \\
 & \times 16 \\
\hline
8 & .00 \\
\end{array}
$$

Answer $= 0.8_{16}$ exact

(*b*) 0.46

$$
\begin{array}{r|l}
 & 0.46 \\
 & \times 16 \\
\hline
7 & .36 \\
 & \times 16 \\
\hline
5 & .76 \\
\end{array}
$$

Answer $= 0.75_{16} +$

Self-testing **1** (*a*) 11100111.010   (*c*) 101001110001.1010

Quiz #6-8   (*b*) 1101000111.0010 (*d*) 100111011.100

    2 (*a*) (1) $3B5.C_{16}$ (*c*) (1) $274.E_{16}$

      (*a*) (2) 1665.6_8 (*c*) (2) 1164.7_8

      (*b*) (1) 84_{16} (*d*) (1) $A4.2_{16}$

      (*b*) (2) 204_8 (*d*) (2) 244.1_8

Self-testing **1** Carries

Quiz #6-9

$$
\begin{array}{r}
1\ 11 \\
11001 \\
+\,10011 \\
\hline
101100 \\
\end{array}
\qquad
\begin{array}{r}
25 \\
+19 \\
\hline
44 \\
\end{array}
$$

3

$$
\begin{array}{r}
0 \\
101011 \\
-\,010010 \\
\hline
011001 \\
\end{array}
\qquad
\begin{array}{r}
43 \\
-18 \\
\hline
25 \\
\end{array}
$$

2

$$
\begin{array}{r}
1\ 111 \\
110111 \\
+\,10111 \\
\hline
1001110 \\
\end{array}
\qquad
\begin{array}{r}
55 \\
+23 \\
\hline
78 \\
\end{array}
$$

4

$$
\begin{array}{r}
0111 \\
10000 \\
-\,111 \\
\hline
01001 \\
\end{array}
\qquad
\begin{array}{r}
16 \\
-7 \\
\hline
9 \\
\end{array}
$$

Self-testing **1**   10111   23   **3** 10111
Quiz #6-10

```
Self-testing   1    10111   23        3  101)1110011
Quiz #6-10           101   ×5                101
                   ─────  ───                ────
                   10111   115               1000
                  101110                      101
                  ──────                      ────
                 1110011                       111
                                               101
                                               ───
                                               101
                                               101
                                               ───

                                              1110
               2    1110   14        4  111)1100010
                     111   ×7                111
                   ─────   ──                ────
                   1110    98                1010
                  1110                        111
                  1110                        ────
                 ───────                       111
                 1100010                       111
                                               ───
```

Self-testing   **1**   Problem   Complement
Quiz #6-11

```
                1    Problem                Complement
                        162                    162
                      −283                     716   (9s)
                                            ⓪ 878

                                 Recomplement  −121


                2       345                    345
                      −128                     871   (9s)
                                            ① 216
                                              ↘1
                                              ───
                                              217
                                              ═══

                3       358                    358
                      −124                     876   (10s)
                                            ① 234   no end around


                4    10011  (19)             10011
                   −11100  (28)              00011   (1s)
                                            ⓪ 10110

                                 Recomplement  −01001


                5    11101  (29)             11101
                   −01011  (11)              10100   (1s)
                                            ① 10001
                                              ↘1
                                              ─────
               End around carry               10010
                                              ═════
```

6   10011   (19)   10011
  $-$01001   (9) $-$10111   (2s)
                                 ① 01010   not end around

EXERCISES   1   Name the position value for each position in the following binary number:
1101111.11101

2   Write the following numbers in binary notation:
(a) 365   (c) 92   (e) 65.31
(b) 444   (d) 917

3   Write the decimal numbers in problem 2 in 4-bit binary-coded decimal notation.

4   Convert the following binary numbers to octal:
(a) 111111111111   (d) 1010101111
(b) 101010101010   (e) 1111100000
(c) 110111001000   (f) 10010001110

5   Convert the binary numbers in problem 4 to hexadecimal.

6   Convert the following octal numbers to binary:
(a) 7755   (c) 5671   (e) 45632   (g) 7
(b) 1234   (d) 15   (f) 65   (h) 6

7   Convert the following binary numbers to decimal, using the multiply-and-add method:
(a) 11100   (c) 1110111   (e) 1101
(b) 10111   (d) 1001   (f) 1101010

8   Convert the following hexadecimal numbers to binary:
(a) FAED   (c) A105   (e) FO
(b) 1239   (d) ABCF

9   Convert the following decimal numbers to octal and to hexadecimal.
(a) 317   (c) 256   (e) 6
(b) 63   (d) 513

10   Do the following binary arithmetic:
(a)   1011   (c) 1011   (e) 1111 ÷ 11
     $+$1001 $\times$11

(b)   11101   (d) 1100   (f) 1101 ÷ 10
     $+$00110 $\times$101

11   Perform the following binary subtractions using regular subtraction and then complement subtraction (with 1s complement):
(a)   1011   (b)   00110   (c) 1011
     $-$1001 $-$11101 $-$11

12   How many characters can be expressed by the following?
(a) 4-bit set   (b) 6-bit byte   (c) 8-bit byte

13   Disregarding arithmetic sign, what is the largest number that can be expressed in binary by a fixed set of 16 bits? If the 16 bits represent 2 bytes, each encoding two packed decimal digits, what is the largest number?

14   How is the arithmetic sign represented in binary and packed decimal coding? How does encoding of the sign affect the quantity that can be represented? Redo Question 13 including coding of the sign.

15 Perform arithmetic in base 8. See example:

Octal: 17   Decimal: 15
       +36   +30
       ─────   ────
        55 (13 − 8 = 5 and 1 to carry)   45

(a)   13   (b)   17   (c)   117
     +26   ×6   −23

16 Given a limited number of binary digits with which to express a fraction, a binary fraction may not be exactly equal to the decimal fraction it represents. In fact, just as the fraction $\frac{1}{3}$ cannot be expressed exactly as a decimal fraction, binary fractions can never exactly equal certain decimal fractions. For the following examples, first convert the decimal fraction to binary and then convert the binary fraction back to a decimal. Use only 6 bits. More would improve accuracy but would be very tiresome for you to do.

(a) .70 (carry this to eight places and note that this will become a repeating sequence)

(b) .750

(c) .24

17 Using the concepts explained in the chapter, interpret the following in terms of the duodecimal system (base 12). Make A = 10 and B = 11.

(a) Convert 16 to duodecimal.

(b) Convert $2A3_{12}$ to decimal.

18 Explain how numeric computational data, read into a computer from punched cards, will be encoded and what other conversions will be necessary in order to perform computations and print and results.

19 Is your mother (or wife, etc.) feeling her age? Why not express her age in a different base! State what base she is using if she says she is 35 but she is really:

(a) 41   (b) 47   (c) 50   (d) 53

CHAPTER 7

INTERNAL OPERATIONS AND STORAGE IN A COMPUTER

A programmer can write programs, an operator can perform his or her duties, and a manager can supervise computer operations—without understanding the internal workings of the computer. However, a general understanding of the internal operations of a computer is a useful background which may help in comprehending how most effectively to program and operate the equipment. This chapter presents a survey of the circuitry, storage, and other internal operating features of computers.

An Overview of the Internal Operation of a Computer

A computer must be able to perform certain fundamental operations internally:

Represent data and instructions
Hold (store) data and instructions
Move the data and instructions
Interpret and execute the commands of the instructions

These internal operations are carried out by the central processing unit (CPU) of the computer. The CPU contains three subunits—the control unit, the processing or arithmetic unit (pronounced a-rith-MET′-ic), and the storage unit. As explained in Chapter 1, these three units plus the input and output subsystems form the elements of a simple computer system (Figure 7-1).

There is no mechanical movement in the central processing unit such as one finds in an adding machine or mechanical calculator. It performs all operations electronically. The operations are directed by a program of instructions in the storage unit in which the data to be operated upon is also held. However, the storage unit is passive in that the data and instructions are merely held there. To be acted upon, the data and instructions must be moved into the control and processing units.

The information held in the storage unit is represented by the two states of the storage medium, for example, the open or closed states of integrated circuits or the

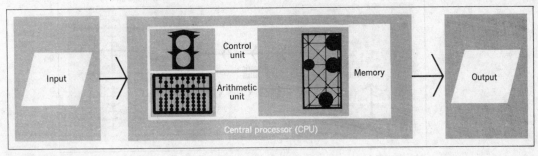

FIGURE 7-1 A computer system.

two magnetized states of ferrite (iron) cores. When data or instructions are moved from storage into the processing or control unit, the information being moved is represented by the two electrical states: pulse and no pulse. While being operated upon in the processing or control units, the data and instructions are held in registers.

The *registers* are devices designed to accept electrical pulse representations, temporarily hold the information by being in a given state, and then release the information in the form of electrical pulses when directed by control circuits. Computer operations, such as comparison and arithmetic, are performed by groups of logic (switching) circuits. This relationship is illustrated in Figure 7-2. It also suggests that much of the computer circuitry is for the purpose of controlling the movement of the electrical pulses. The circuits of the computer are designed to react to two electrical states of pulse and no pulse. Because they are using only two states, the switching logic can be described with Boolean algebra, the arithmetic of logic. The "truth" and "falsity" conditions of the Boolean analysis are identified with "closed" or "open" states in computer circuits which allow an electrical pulse to pass or not pass.

The computer is directed to perform actions by an instruction. The instruction is brought from main storage to the central processing unit and decoded. One part of the instruction specifies what the computer is to do. The other part specifies what the computer is to use in performing the operation (data from storage or a device).

Computer Circuits

The computer operates with electrical pulses. A binary 1 is represented by a sharp voltage pulse; a binary 0 by the lack of the voltage rise. A timing arrangement is used to distinguish the different binary digits being moved.

Pulse train
Binary digit   1   0   1   1   0   0

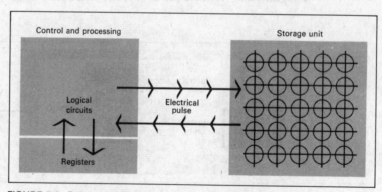

FIGURE 7-2 Relationship between storage and registers.

In order to form the pulses correctly, the computer will have amplifier circuits, which produce pulses of correct amplitude, and shaper circuits, which produce pulses of proper length. In general, the pulses will move through two basic kinds of circuits—switching or logic elements and bit storage elements or flip-flops (explained below). These basic circuits are the building blocks for the registers which hold information being processed and for the other functional units of the computer which encode, decode, accumulate, complement, and compare. The circuits are produced by the techniques of microelectronics.

Circuit Technology

The computer uses the same type of basic components as a television receiver or a radio. Transistors, resistors, diodes, and capacitors are assembled into circuits to control the flow of electric current. Early computers were large and produced substantial heat because they utilized vacuum tubes. The second-generation equipment changed to transistors. The trend in circuit technology has been toward small, fast, and very reliable circuits produced by microelectronic techniques. This same technology produces the circuits for pocket calculators.

Microelectronics is used to produce several entire logic circuits on a single chip. A typical chip might contain hundreds of components in order to form several interconnected circuits. The technology is also used to produce large numbers of memory circuits on a single chip. A typical memory chip might contain circuits to store 2048 bits. In other words, the density of memory circuits tends to be higher than for logic circuits. A chip is very small—say, $\frac{1}{16}$ in. square for a logic chip and $\frac{1}{8}$ in. square for a memory circuit chip (Figure 7-3). The chips are produced on a silicon wafer by a process of photomasking, etching, diffusions, and firings. Two major techniques are bipolar technology and metal-oxide semiconductor (MOS). Both produce miniturized circuitry. The trend in memory circuits is toward MOS.

Logical Circuits

The logical or switching circuits can be described using mathematical logic (also called Boolean algebra). The two states in logic, true and false, are represented by open and closed switches in the electronic equipment. To produce all possible logical functions, only three logical circuits need be used—AND, OR, and NOT (Figure 7-4). The basic circuits are combined in complex groupings to perform the switching for computer operation logic.

The AND gate (also called "AND block") can be thought of as an electronic element into which two (or more) wires enter and one wire exits. The logic statement A AND B is represented by the AND gate; i.e., for a pulse to come out on the exit wire, pulses must be sent into the element on *both* input wires. The truth table for A AND B presents the operating characteristics of the AND gate when 1 is used to represent a pulse and 0 a no-pulse.

The OR gate (also called "OR block" or "mixer") represents the logic statement A OR B. Like the AND gate, it has two (or more) input wires and one output wire. However, the OR gate will allow an output pulse if either or both of the input lines receive an electrical pulse. The truth table A OR B specifies the operating characteristics of the OR gate.

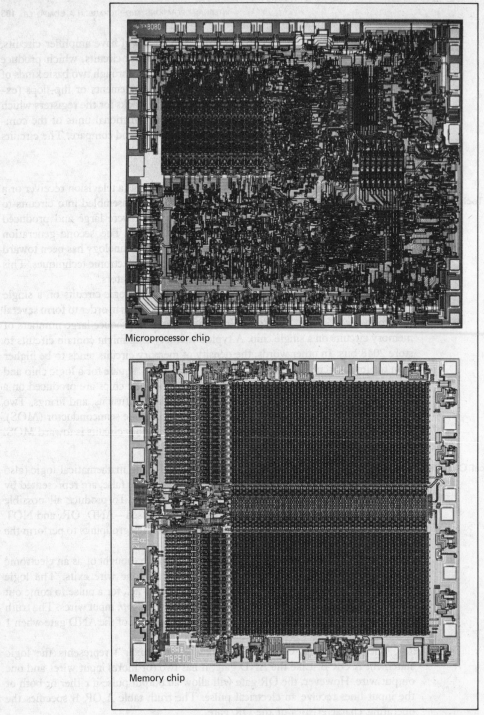

Microprocessor chip

Memory chip

FIGURE 7-3 Photomicrograph of integrated circuit chips used for processing circuitry (top) and for memory (bottom). Note the regularity of the memory circuit compared with the processor circuit. For actual size, see Fig. 1-6. (*Courtesy of Intel Corporation.*)

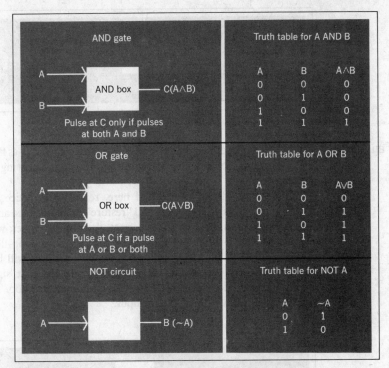

FIGURE 7-4 Logical circuits and corresponding truth tables.

The NOT circuit is very simple—the output is the opposite of the input. There are several common NOT notations; e.g., ~A and $\overline{A}$ are two different ways of writing the opposite of A.

In the design of computers it is desirable to standardize as much as possible. Production is simplified by the use of combinations of standard logic modules. Two common modules are the NAND circuit (NOT AND) and the NOR circuit (NOT OR). The truth tables are not given since the inputs are the same as the AND and OR and the outputs are just the opposite.

Timing or Clock Circuits

It takes time for electrical pulses to reach the proper level for representing a bit, and time for the pulse to travel through the computer. Also, operations in the computer must be performed in an orderly, timed sequence. The control of timing is performed by the use of control signals called "clock pulses" which are emitted from a central device called the "master clock." These timing signals are sent to all the logical components to keep them synchronized.

To illustrate the use of the clock pulse, assume a pulse A which must arrive at a point B at an exact time. By inserting an AND gate and a clock pulse, the pulse at A cannot pass until the clock pulse is also received.

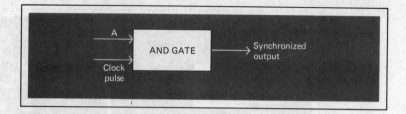

Bit Storage Circuits

Circuits can be used as storage devices. Circuits, referred to as flip-flops, are used in the arithmetic, control, and storage units for remembering bit values during processing.

The term "flip-flop," as used here, refers to a device having two inputs (represented as 0 and 1, or "set" and "restore"), two outputs, and two stable states. When a pulse is applied to the set input, the flip-flop is set; when applied to the restore input, the flip-flop is cleared or restored. If the flip-flop is in one or the other of the two states, the corresponding output signal will be emitted, and the other output will be at the no-signal level. The output signal thus provides information on (stores) the most recent input of the flip-flop. The flip-flop maintains its state until altered by an input.

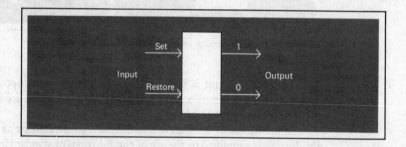

Other bit storage circuits used in developing the basic circuits of the computer are the trigger, or inverter, which is set by a pulse to the state opposite its state before the pulse, and the delay flop which has an output signal but only after a delay. The delay is used to slow down an electrical signal so that the bit represented by the signal appears one cycle later.

Functional Units

The circuits just described—gates, flip-flops, delays, etc.—are combined to form assemblies which perform specified functions necessary to computer operation. Examples of functional units are registers, accumulator, encoder, decoder, complementer, and comparator.

Registers Registers are used to receive, hold, and transfer information used by the processing unit. A register is an assembly of bistable circuits (typically flip-flops). It acts as a temporary memory for the processing unit. There are usually several general registers which perform functions such as accumulate arithmetic results, hold the multiplier for multiplication, and hold the divisor for division. Other registers are an instruction register, which holds the instruction being executed, an address register, which holds the address of a storage location or device, and a storage register, which holds data taken from or being sent to storage. The important registers in the system are frequently connected to small lights on the computer console which display the contents of the registers.

Accumulator An accumulator is an assembly used for addition. The design of the accumulator will depend on whether the computer uses a binary or a binary-coded decimal code and on whether the arithmetic is to be serial (one digit at a time) or parallel (all digits at once). The difference between a binary and a binary-coded decimal accumulator results from the difference in the rules for addition of these two systems. The major difference between serial and parallel arithmetic is in the number of adder units required. Serial addition uses only one 1-digit adder and adds successive pairs of digits one at a time. Parallel addition adds all pairs simultaneously, using a different adder for each pair of digits (Figure 7-5). The serial accumulator is slower than the parallel accumulator but requires less hardware.

The binary half-adder, composed of logic elements, is the basic addition circuit. There are several possible half-adder designs, all of which arrive at the result shown in Figure 7-6. In the half-adder, if there are pulse (1) inputs at A and B (but not both), the sum is 1 (a pulse). When both inputs are 1, the sum is 0, and there is a carry.

The half-adder is incomplete for addition purposes because it does not provide a carry to the next pair of digits to be added. The combination of circuits which correctly adds and carries is called a "full adder." It is essentially two half-adders

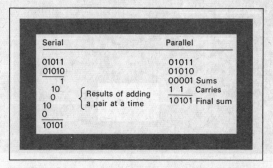

FIGURE 7-5 Comparison of serial and parallel addition.

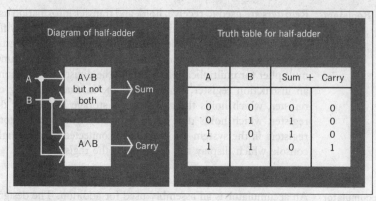

FIGURE 7-6 Half-adder logic.

linked by a delay circuit. The delay flip-flop holds the carry bit and delays it one timing pulse so it can be added to the sum of the next pair of digits which have then entered the adder.

The net effect of the two half-adders and the delay is to produce a sum and carry (if any) from each pair of binary digits and the transmitting of any carry for combining with the next pair to be added. A simplified diagram of a full adder is shown in Figure 7-7.

Encoder, Decoder, Complementer, and Comparator

The encoder translates data from decimal form into binary-coded character form. The decoder, essentially the reverse of an encoder, translates the internal code back into decimal equivalents. In encoding, each input pulse (corresponding to an alphanumeric character) is converted into one or more binary digits.

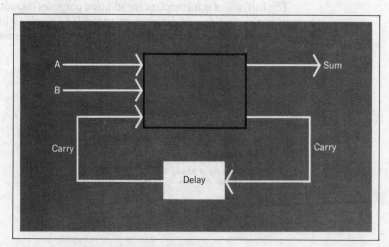

FIGURE 7-7 Simplified diagram of full adder.

Since computer subtraction consists of complementing the subtrahend and then adding, the subtraction operation requires special circuitry to perform complementing. Complementing is quite simple since the 1s complement 1. The inverter circuit performs in this exact manner.

Computer compare instructions form an important element in the modern digital computer. Several methods can be used in designing the comparison assembly. One common method compares pairs (or small groups of bits) until the larger of two quantities has been determined. For example, if 011011 and 010111 are to be compared, the comparison might proceed as shown:

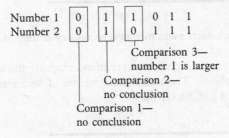

Computer Storage

The operation of the computer requires storage of instructions and data. There is storage in many different parts of the computer system (Figure 7-8). Storage may use different media but is all based on the use of two states to represent a binary digit. The most significant storages in the computer system are:

Storage	Explanation
Primary storage	The main memory which holds "active" programs and data. It uses, in almost all cases, semiconductor or magnetic core storage.
Secondary storage	Auxiliary storage to hold data files and programs not being executed. Lower cost. Generally uses magnetic disk or magnetic tape. Data and programs to be executed are read from secondary storage into primary storage for processing.
Buffer or cache storage	Small storage having very fast access for use in holding very active data. Used mainly with very high speed, large computers. The use is automatic, and the programmer is not usually concerned with it.

Control storage	Called "reloadable control storage" or (if read only) "read-only storage." Contains a computer program (called a "micro-program or microcode") for interpreting computer instructions and converting them to basic operations. Microcode in control storage is essentially a substitute for hardware. The programmer is not usually concerned with it.
Registers	Registers are essentially a form of storage used in processing.

This chapter emphasizes main memory; secondary storage is described in Chapter 8.

Two characteristics significant to primary computer storage are volatility and readout destructability. The major characteristic of secondary storage is access method (discussed in Chapter 8).

Characteristic	Description
Volatility	A storage medium is volatile if stored data is lost when power is removed. Semiconductor storage is volatile; core is not.
Readout destructability	Reading stored data may destroy the recorded data, so it must be restored by a separate operation. This is done automatically by the equipment, and the user is not aware of it. Magnetic core has a destructive readout; semiconductor storage does not.

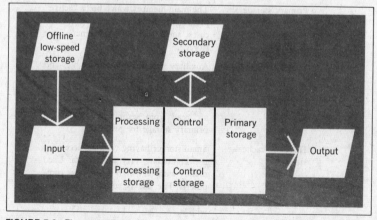

FIGURE 7-8 Elements of a computer system showing different types of storage.

The volatility of the semiconductor memory means that the computer system must make provisions to recover from a power outage by regularly storing important data on nonvolatile storage from which it may be read after the power is restored.

The two most common storage devices for main memory, semiconductors and magnetic core, are explained. Two less used methods of primary storage, thin film and plated wire, are described very briefly.

Semiconductor Storage

A major change in computer technology in the mid-1970s was the change from magnetic core as the dominant primary storage to semiconductors. The semiconductor memory consists of extremely small bit storage circuits (flip-flops) etched on a silicon chip. All the electronic elements to store a bit are placed in such a small area of the chip that a single chip can contain storage for thousands of bits (see Figure 7-3). The individual chips are arranged in groups to form a memory module complete with all interconnections to "plug in" to the computer.

The semiconductor storage operates on the principle of a flip-flop in which the switch is set to a 0 or 1 position by a write command which sets or restores the flip-flop. It remains in the same position until changed. Reading the bit storage consists of measuring the signals from the two possible outputs—one output indicates the switch has been set to 0, the other that it has been set to 1. As mentioned, power is required to maintain the 0 or 1 state. Therefore, stored data is lost whenever power is turned off or interrupted.

Magnetic Core Storage

Magnetic core storage is (and will continue to be) a significant medium for primary storage. A magnetic core is molded from a ferrite (iron) powder into a doughnut shape about the size of the head of a pin. The individual cores are strung on wires to form core planes. Several core planes stacked one on top of another form a core stack (Figure 7-9).

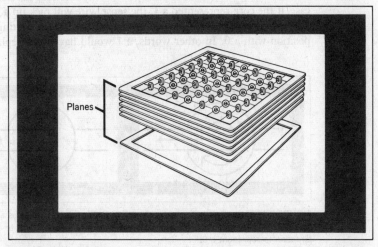

Planes

FIGURE 7-9 Core stack.

One of the experiments commonly carried out in an elementary physics course demonstrates that an iron bar can be magnetized in one of two directions: north-south or south-north. Similarly, a ferrite core can be polarized in two directions. These two directions of polarity form the two states of the core. A core can be placed in either state by the application of a magnetizing force. The direction of polarity will depend on the direction of magnetizing current. The computer designer selects one direction to represent a 0-bit and the other to represent a 1-bit. Once polarized in one direction, a core will retain that polarity until changed.

Figure 7-10 shows a single wire being used to apply current to the core. The typical arrangement uses two wires strung through the core. This arrangement is termed a "coincident-current core memory." One-half of the current required to switch the core from one polarity to another is applied to each of the wires when the core is to be "flipped." The cores are arranged in the planes with the intersection of two wires applying full current to only one core. This arrangement, shown in Figure 7-11, allows the computer to control the state of each individual core. These two wires will write on a selected core, but reading requires more wiring. Although there are several design possibilities, the most common organization of a core memory uses four wires through each core to accomplish reading and writing. In addition to the two wires for applying the magnetizing current, there is an inhibit wire and a sense wire (Figure 7-12).

A core is read by sending a current to polarize the core in a particular direction. If the core is already magnetized in that direction, nothing happens; if it is not, the core changes state. This changing or "flipping" induces a current. The sense wire picks up this current indicating that the core was in the opposite state prior to being changed. For example, if an electrical pulse is sent to write a 0 at a core position and the core is already in the 1 state, the writing of a 0 will flip the core. If a 0 is already there, no change will occur. The "flipping" induces a current which is picked up by the sense wire running through the plane. Only one sense wire is needed for an entire plane, since only one core is sensed at a time. In this case, if the core represented a 1, the sense wire will pick up a current; if a 0, there will be no current. Note, however, that reading by the writing of a 0 left the core position with a 0. In other words, a 1 would have been replaced by a 0 and a 0

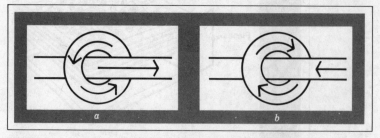

FIGURE 7-10 Two-state representation with ferrite cores. (*a*) Current is applied in one direction to polarize a 1; (*b*) current is reversed and polarity flips to the opposite direction to represent a 0.

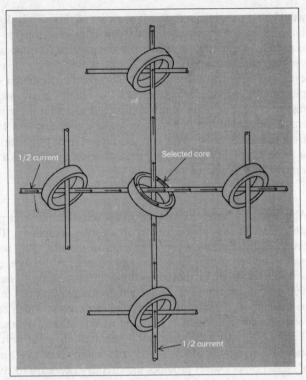

FIGURE 7-11 Selecting a core.

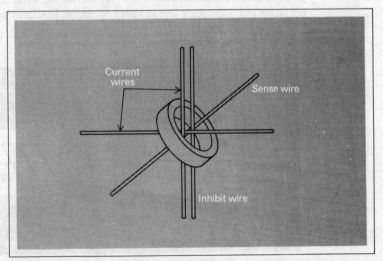

FIGURE 7-12 Closeup of a single core.

would have remained a 0. Reading a core in this way is destructive of the prior information, and to remedy this, the core must be restored to its former state. This is done by attempting to write a 1 at the position (the opposite current from that used to read the core). If no current was sensed during the read cycle, the restore cycle will simultaneously put an inhibit current in the inhibit wire. If the sense wire picked up a current during the read, no inhibit current will be used during the restore cycle. The result of this approach is to inhibit the writing of a 1 if the core was 0 and should therefore remain 0, and the writing of a 1 with no interference from an inhibit current if the core was flipped from 1 to 0 during the read cycle and is to be restored. The necessity to restore after reading is a technological disadvantage of core storage.

Thin-Film and Plated-Wire Storage

Although they have received much less use, thin film and plated wire represent storage technology that is found in existing computers. Thin-film memory is produced by depositing very thin spots of metallic alloy on a ceramic or metal plate. This spot performs in the same manner as the core, except that only two wires are required. A typical thin-film element consists of a rectangle about .025 by .050 in. with a thickness of about 1000 angstroms (.0000004 in.). This rectangle can be thought of as a bar magnet. Applying a current which causes the polarity to rotate but not to flip induces a current which indicates whether a 1 or 0 was stored (Figure 7-13). After the sense field is removed, the polarity is returned to its prior state by a digit pulse which "steers" the polarity back to a 1 or 0 state. An overlay of etched copper wires provides the circuitry necessary to connect the individual elements with the circuits which read and write.

Plated-wire memory or woven-wire memory uses a thin film which is desposited around a fine wire. This wire carries the write current during a write operation and is the sense line in a read operation. Insulated wires are woven across

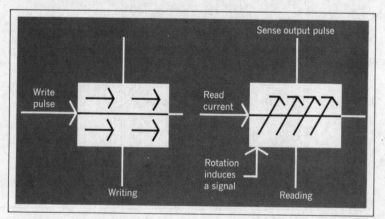

FIGURE 7-13 Thin-film memory.

the plated wire in a fashion similar to weaving cloth. The area where the insulated loop goes around the plated wire (Figure 7-14) forms a bit storage location. Reading is nondestructive.

Storage Addressing

Semiconductors, ferrite cores, and other storage devices are not usable unless data stored there can be retrieved when needed. In order to accomplish retrieval, each storage location has an address which identifies it just as a house address identifies a dwelling. Another comparison is a set of mailboxes in a post office. Each has a unique number which identifies the storage location (Figure 7-15). A person who wishes to store a letter in the box specifies the box number. Likewise, each set of semiconductors in a semiconductor storage or each set of cores in a core storage unit has an address. This address identifies the location so that data may be stored there, and data so stored may be retrieved. The address is a code which identifies the location for the computer circuitry. In other words, the computer circuitry

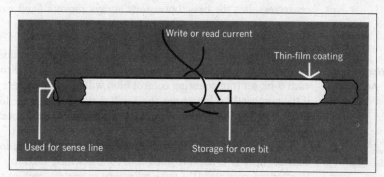

FIGURE 7-14 Plated-wire memory.

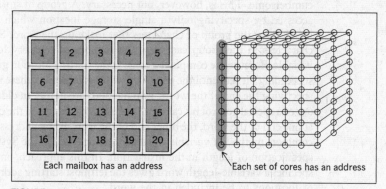

Each mailbox has an address   Each set of cores has an address

FIGURE 7-15 Comparison of mailbox number and core storage address.

associates a separate set of storage devices with each location designation. There is, for example, a set of semiconductors or ferrite cores which is identified by the location 347, another set associated with location 348. Each address refers to a set of storage devices, but how large the set is and what can be stored there depends on the word structure of the particular computer.

A computer word consists of the data which is stored or retrieved when storage to or retrieval from a memory location is specified. There are two basic approaches—fixed-length word and variable-length word. In addition, there is a byte-addressable word structure which combines many of the features of both.

Fixed-Word-Length Addressing

In a fixed-word-length computer, every storage location identified by an address consists of a fixed number of semiconductors, cores, or other storage representations. Some popular word sizes for fixed-word-length machines are 24, 30, 32, 36, 48, and 60 bits. The computer designer makes a choice of word size, and all addresses then reference that number of bits. If the computer is designed with a 48-bit word, each reference to a memory location will access 48 bits. The computer may be able to manipulate parts of words such as small groups of bits which encode characters, but the basic operations always move a fixed word.

Variable-Word-Length Addressing

The variable-word-length or character computer has an address for each set of bits which can encode one character. If it requires 6 bits to encode a character, each 6-bit set (not counting control bits) will have an address assigned to it. Thus, if the number 39 is in storage, the 3 will occupy one storage location having an address, and the 9 will be in another contiguous storage location with a separate address.

If each character is stored in a separate storage location having a separate address, how is a number such as 945823, which takes up six separate storage locations, accessible? If it were necessary to specify each of these six locations in order to access the number stored there, the procedure would become quite cumbersome. This is, however, not necessary. A group of storage locations can be accessed by specifying only a single storage location which defines the starting location for the group of characters that make up the word. Since the number of characters in the group can vary, the number of memory locations accessed is variable. Because the computer begins at the starting location given and picks up all succeeding bit sets until the end of the word is indicated, there must be a method of specifying the end of the word. Two methods are in use, an older method being the use of a special control bit called a "word mark" set to 1 in the code of the character at one end of the word, the other end of the word being addressed. The other, most common, method of variable word addressing (used in the System/370) is explicit specification of length in the instruction. In this approach, any instruction which specifies a variable-length word gives the leftmost starting address plus the number of locations to be included in the word.

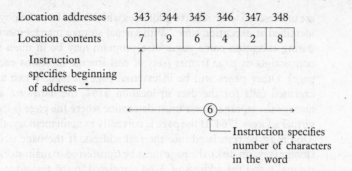

Byte-addressable Combination

Most modern medium- and large-scale computer systems are designed so that fixed and variable words can be used in the same computer. This is done by having a byte-addressable organization. A byte is a group of bits which form a subunit of a computer word. In IBM's System/370, which are byte-addressable computers, each 8-bit byte has an address. Four such bytes make up a 32-bit fixed binary word, the address of which is the address of the first byte. When an instruction references a fixed binary word, the computer automatically stores or retrieves 4 bytes. The computer also has instructions which specify a fixed length of 2 bytes (half-word) and 8 bytes (double word). In addition to these fixed-word-length instructions, there are variable-word-length instructions which specify the first byte of the word and the number of bytes to be included.

Virtual Memory

The virtual storage technique was implemented as early as 1959 (in the Atlas computer at Manchester University, England) and in several computers thereafter, but widespread use across the entire range of computer sizes began in the 1970s. Virtual storage is a method for hardware and software management of application programs (stored in primary and secondary storage), so that an application program need not be restricted in size to the storage space in main memory. In other words, the programmer can write programs as if the computer had practically unlimited main storage (for example, up to 16 million bytes in one computer), even though the main computer storage is only a fraction of that size. Since only a part of the program is active and need be in main storage at any one time, the program is divided into small sections called "pages" (say, 2000 to 4000 bytes in size). A group of pages is sometimes referred to as a "segment." The pages that are active are placed in main memory; the remainder are stored on a direct-access file such as a disk or drum from which they may be loaded as needed.

It is useful to distinguish between the physical (real) storage addresses in main memory and program-generated (virtual) storage addresses. Each instruction and each data item in main storage during program execution is located in a physical storage location, with a real address. In the real storage approach, each program is assigned physical addresses for all instructions and data. In the virtual storage approach, the program has addresses for instructions and data, but these addresses are understood to be relative addresses which will allow the physical locations to be identified at execution time. With virtual storage management, at any given time during execution some pages of a program may be in main storage, possibly in noncontiguous page frames (sets of real storage locations each of which holds a page). Other pages will be in external page storage. When an instruction being executed calls for the data in location 3764, the hardware and software which manage the storage access must determine where the page is located which has the virtual address 3764. If the page is currently in main memory, the virtual address of 3764 must be translated into the real address. If the page is in the external page storage (say, on disk), the page must be transferred to main storage (called "demand paging"), and the address of 3764 translated to the real address in the page. The movement of pages of instructions into main memory, the identification of page location, and the translation of a virtual address to a physical address are performed by hardware and software. Tables which contain the location of pages and main memory addresses for main memory pages are maintained by the operating system. A hardware mechanism (IBM calls it DAT for dynamic address translation) automatically translates each virtual address into a physical address by means of a table look-up procedure.

The operating system monitors page usage; pages not in use are written back to external page storage and pages needed are brought in. Several programs may be in process concurrently so that the paging process may place a significant demand on the central processor and the input/output resources. Under certain conditions, the paging activity becomes so high that little productive work is done. This is termed "thrashing." The software which manages virtual storage monitors page usage and automatically makes changes to eliminate thrashing.

The use of virtual storage has the advantage of eliminating program storage constraints and thereby increasing flexibility of storage use. Virtual storage techniques may improve storage utilization. The disadvantages are the computer resources required to manage the virtual storage. For example, the operating system is larger (requires more storage), the direct-access storage devices must be faster, and additional computer power must be provided to compensate for virtual storage resource use. On balance, virtual storage is a significant development and will tend to be utilized in most medium- and large-scale systems.

Effect of Word Structure on Computer Design

In terms of understanding the difference between computers, the word organization is an important distinction. The differences between fixed-word-length, variable-word-length, and byte-addressable computers are, for the most part, a natural consequence of the different word organizations. In the fixed-word-length computer, every instruction or data word has exactly the same number of bits. All the circuitry is designed to accept this basic block. The variable-word-length computer word can range from one character up to many characters. Computer circuitry cannot therefore be designed to handle a fixed group of bits other than the small number associated with a single character. These two approaches lead to the hardware characteristics (Table 7-1) usually found in computers using these word

TABLE 7-1 HARDWARE CHARACTERISTICS FOR DIFFERENT
WORD-LENGTH DESIGNS

Characteristics	Fixed word length	Variable word length	Mixed byte-addressable
Length of word	Specified	Variable	Both
Registers	Addressable	Storage-to-storage	Both
Arithmetic	Usually binary	Binary-coded decimal	Both
Transfer for data	Parallel	Serial	Both

organizations. One of the important distinctions is the use of addressable registers versus the use of a storage-to-storage approach. This leads to other important differences.

**The Use
of Addressable
Registers**

As explained, a register is a set of storage devices where data or instructions are moved in order to be operated upon. The main storage is passive, merely holding the data and instructions; the register is active storage. A register may be addressable, so that the programmer can write an instruction to load it with the contents of a storage location or to copy its contents into a regular storage location. Or a register may not be addressable, being called into use automatically by the circuitry of the computer.

The use of addressable registers requires a fixed-length word because the register is designed to accept and hold a specified number of bits. When addressable registers are used, data is moved into a register, operated upon, and then moved back to a storage location. The trend in the design of fixed word-length computers is for several addressable registers. For example, IBM's System/370 computers have 16 general-purpose registers for fixed word-length instructions.

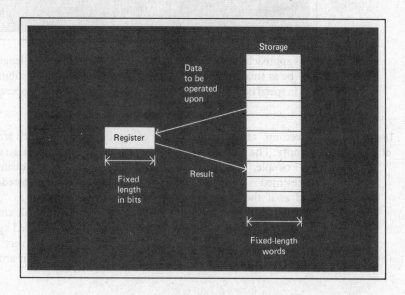

The advantage of a register approach is the speed which can be attained. Data can be transferred from storage to register in parallel, i.e., all bits simultaneously. This is possible because all words contain the same number of bits no matter how small or large the value. If a 32-bit memory location, for example, is storing the number 1, it will have 31 leading 0-bits and one 1-bit. This can be transferred in parallel from storage to a register in exactly the same time as a large number. Once in a register, the arithmetic operations can also be performed in parallel.

Storage-to-Storage Approach

When the word length is variable, transferring the entire word into a register is precluded because the register size cannot be exactly specified. Instead of using an addressable register, the variable-length instructions are executed in a storage-to-storage approach in which a single character or byte is read from storage into a nonaddressable register, operated upon, and the result stored back in a character or byte location. For example, if a 6-digit and a 4-digit number are to be added in a character machine, the addition will be performed serially, a pair of digits at a time. The result will be stored a digit at a time in memory, replacing one of the operands.

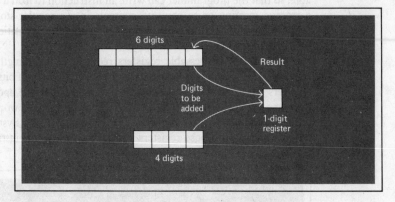

This approach removes the limitation imposed by a fixed-length word. Operands may be as small or as large as necessary. However, this flexibility is achieved at a loss in speed because the storage-to-storage approach must operate in serial fashion.

The Problem of Precision

"Precision" refers to the number of significant digits which are used to express a quantity. The precision for a fixed word-length computer is the size of the word. If, for example, a 32-bit binary word is used, the largest quantity which can be represented is 2,147,483,647. If a larger number is to be stored, two words can be used as if they were a single location. This is known as "double precision." Double-precision hardware is available on many large-scale computers; for small computers, the use of two words for one quantity is handled by program instructions. Another approach to representing very large or very small numbers is explained in Chapter 15 in connection with floating point arithmetic.

Comparing Memory Sizes

In references to a computer, the primary storage is designated in terms of the number of addressable storage locations. Yet an addressable location may range from a large fixed word to a group of bits encoding a single decimal digit. Because of design considerations, memory sizes will usually come in rather odd numbers—multiples of 4096. The term K is used to refer to thousands of addressable locations rounded to the thousands. Thus, 4096 storage locations are termed "4K memory." A 32K memory may actually be 32,768 locations.

Since the storage is described in terms of addressable storage locations and these locations vary widely in their capacity and versatility, the comparison of memory sizes requires some analysis. An initial analysis can be made in terms of the capacity of the storage with respect to alphanumeric characters, decimal digits, and instructions.

Comparing Storage of Alphanumeric Characters

The storage capacity for alphanumeric characters will depend on the number of bytes of storage, each of which encodes one alphanumeric character. This is influenced by the word orientation of the computer.

Word orientation of computer	Method of representing alphanumerics
Binary	Bytes of 6 to 8 bits within a binary word
Binary-coded character	One character per bit set (of, say, 6 bits)
Byte-addressable	One character per byte (8 bits)

As examples, a Control Data Cyber 170 60-bit fixed word-length computer stores 10 alphanumeric characters in each word using 6-bit bytes, the Honeywell 2000 character code uses one location to encode each character, and the byte-oriented UNIVAC 90 series stores one character in each 8-bit byte.

Comparing Storage of Numeric Data

There are two problems in comparing storage of numeric data. The first arises from the difference between encoding numeric data in binary-coded decimal versus binary and the second because of the unused bits in a fixed-word format. In binary-coded decimal encoding of data, each digit is encoded by one bit set, the size of the bit set being 4, 6, 8, or 9 bits, depending on the computer architecture. In packed decimal, an 8-bit byte is divided into two 4-bit sets each of which encodes a digit. However, the sign also requires a separate 4-bit set. In packed decimal, a 9-digit number takes 10-bit sets (5 bytes) in storage. Coding numeric data in binary-coded decimal uses only the storage needed to encode the data words.

Encoding in binary uses a string of binary digits. A binary representation will take roughly 3.36 bits to encode each numeric digit. The maximum size in number of decimal digits which can be represented by a 32-bit computer word, for example, is computed as 31 ÷ 3.36 (31 because 1 bit is reserved for the arithmetic sign), or 9.2. A 32-bit word (31 bits plus sign) can, therefore, encode any number up to and including 2,147,483,647. Coding in binary in a fixed-word computer uses an entire word even if only a single digit is to be stored. There can, therefore, be wasted storage space. However, many binary computer designs allow small binary words (say 8 or 16 bits) for encoding small numbers.

Comparing Storage Space for Instructions

In the simplest case, all instructions are the same size in terms of storage, and one instruction, in a fixed-word-length computer, will occupy one memory location. Although some computers follow this simple approach, most computers have instructions of different length. The IBM System/370, which has a 32-bit word, uses instructions which are 16, 32, and 48 bits (2, 4, or 6 bytes) in length. Another factor complicating comparison of instruction storage is the type of instructions available. The instruction repertoires of different computers vary in power, so that a single instruction in one computer may suffice for what takes several instructions to do in another computer.

The comparison of memory sizes is not a simple matter when all factors are considered properly. In order to make a meaningful comparison, one must know something about the data to be stored, the program to be run, etc. Such an evaluation is beyond the scope of this text, but with the background obtained in these chapters a rough evaluation can be made, and this is usually satisfactory considering the fact that there are many uncertainties in any computer comparison. To illustrate the effect of the three elements to consider in looking at memory size, Table 7-2 gives these measures for three computers having different storage addressing.

Most computer systems can be obtained with a main storage capacity chosen from a large range of possible memory sizes. In the usual case, the storage can be increased by later addition of storage modules. In choosing the size of memory to be installed, one must consider not only the probable necessity for data and

TABLE 7-2 EXAMPLE OF COMPARING MEMORY SIZES

Computer	Orientation	Code	Memory size being compared	MAXIMUM STORAGE IF ALL DEVOTED TO		Addressable locations to encode one instruction
				Alphabetics	Numerics	
IBM System/370	Model 115 small general purpose	Byte-binary	65K	65,536	131,072	2, 4, or 6
Honeywell 2000	Small commercial	BCD	65K	65,536	65,536	1 to 12
UNIVAC 1100/40	Large general purpose	36-bit binary	65K	393,216	393,216	1

program storage but also the storage requirements of the various programming and operating aids described in Chapter 3. Typical primary storage size in computer configurations is increasing in size because of changes in storage technology, reductions in cost, and increased need for storage by system and application software. In the small IBM 1401 computer, 16K was a popular storage size; a comparable storage size for a mid-1975 to 1980 small computer is likely to be 65 to 131K. Many medium-large to large systems have megabyte memories (millions of bytes). The range of storage sizes is indicated by the following primary storage sizes typically available for computers introduced after 1975. In all cases, the storage uses metal oxide semiconductors.

Size of computer	Range of primary storage size
Small	65 to 262K
Medium	131K to 2 megabytes
Large	524K to 6 megabytes
Very large	1 to 12 megabytes

A Computer Operating Cycle

Most computers are designed so that a fixed interval of time is allowed for each operation. A computer which uses fixed time intervals to determine when to initiate the next operation is known as "synchronous." A less common design, the asynchronous computer, initiates the next operation when a signal from the current operation indicates a completion. In both cases, exact timing is necessary to proper operation. The basic timing interval is a pulse emitted by the electronic clock circuits. Since each operation takes a specified number of pulse times, the control circuitry will initiate the proper commands at the correct intervals. The clock time may range from a few microseconds (millionths of seconds) to a few nanoseconds (billionths of seconds).

A frequently mentioned figure in computer timings is storage cycle time. This is the time required to obtain a word from storage. Storage cycle times are in the microsecond or nanosecond range. A typical time to read from a fast semiconductor storage is in the range from 200 to 800 nanoseconds. By way of contrast, the time required to obtain data from secondary storage is measured in thousandths of seconds (milliseconds).

A Basic Cycle   A basic computer cycle can be divided into two parts—the instruction cycle and the execution cycle.

Instruction Cycle   **1**   An instruction is obtained from a main storage location and transferred to the central processor. The instruction is composed of an operation code specifying what is to be done and the address of the data or device to be operated upon (operand).

2 The operation code is transferred to an instruction register and decoded.

3 The address of the operand is transferred to an address register.

4 The address of the next instruction is determined.

Execution Cycle **5** If the operand address refers to information stored in memory, the information is obtained from storage and placed in the storage register.

6 The operation specified by the operation code is performed, using appropriate registers.

The address of the program instruction is found in an instruction counter. This counter is set to the address of the first instruction when the program of instructions is begun. When an instruction is brought from storage, the counter automatically advances to the address of the next instruction. If an instruction occupies one storage location, the counter will advance by 1; if two locations, by 2; etc. This procedure assumes that instructions are stored in sequence in main memory. For many of the instructions, this sequence assumption is correct. The program itself may specify a break in the sequence. In this case, the instruction counter is reset to the instruction address specified.

Speeding Up the The speed of the basic computer cycle may be improved not only by faster
Operating Cycle circuitry but also by hardware features which allow faster storage access, concurrent operations, and look-ahead. Faster primary storage access is obtained by the use of a very high speed buffer (cache) storage. This storage may be quite small, but the trend is toward a size in the range from 8 to 32K. Data items that are in active use by the program are placed in the buffer storage, thereby reducing the data access time. When the program first accesses a data item, it is also loaded into the buffer memory (perhaps along with adjacent data). In most cases, this approach will mean that the very active data will be quickly available in buffer memory. A hardware feature automatically accesses buffer memory instead of regular primary storage for blocks of data items that have been moved there. In other words, the computer software and hardware automatically load and use the buffer storage, so the programmer can ignore it.

The basic cycle of the computer is sequential with one operation following another. It is possible to provide additional hardware, so that certain operations can overlap. For example, many of the operations in the instruction and execution cycle can overlap. Storage of data (from the last operation) and accessing of the storage for the next instruction can be overlapped. In addition to overlapping basic operations, the computer can be designed with several independent processors to handle groups of operations concurrently. This is the concept of distributed processing. As implemented in the central processor, distributed processing is the use of separate processors to handle input and output, instruction processing, and service operations (involving the operator console, system diagnostics, and error-recovery operations). The concurrent use of these three independent processors speeds the overall rate of computer processing. The concept can be extended to more processors.

Look-ahead is a method of reducing instruction and data access time. A set of registers (called a "stack") is loaded with a set of instructions. When the first instruction in the stack is executed, it is dropped from the stack, and the next instruction (following the last one in the stack) is added to the bottom of the stack. This means that the computer can look ahead to the instructions in the stack and put data called for by the instructions in the buffer storage. It can execute small loops (a common operation) very rapidly because the instructions are all contained in the stack.

The Microprogram in the Operating Cycle

The computer has some very fundamental operations which direct the flow of pulses in the circuitry. These basic operations are combined into higher-level operations such as add, move, and compare. This combining of fundamental operations into a higher-level operation can be done by computer circuitry, or it can be programmed into a central processor control program. Because the control program is dealing with low-level operations, it is termed a "microprogram." A combination of wired circuitry and microprogram is also possible. The microprogram is essentially a substitute for additional circuitry. It adds flexibility to a computer because a computer can, by the use of different microprograms, change the instruction available to the programmer.

In the operating cycle, the instruction to be executed is decoded by the microprogram which executes a set of microoperations to execute the instruction. This sequence is slower than wired circuitry, but adds to the number of instructions that a computer can efficiently execute. The microcode can be used to provide programmers with high-level instructions which cannot be cost-justified in the hardware.

The microprogram is contained in a special control storage. This storage was, in some earlier computers, a read-only storage that was loaded at the factory. Current computers use the concept extensively with a reloadable control storage. The smaller computers are likely to have larger control storage because the smaller computers put functions in the microprogram that are wired in the larger computer.

Microprograms are written by specialized programmers and are usually furnished to the installation by the hardware vendor. For example, IBM System/370 microprograms are furnished on diskette (a small floppy disk—described in the next chapter). The microprogram is read by a special disk drive incorporated in the central processing unit.

Alternatives in Computer Design

From this survey of the internal operations and storage of computers, it can be seen that there are several major design alternatives that are of general interest. There are summarized briefly below, with additional comment where there has been no previous discussion.

Characteristic	Discussion
Timing of operations	Computers operate with either synchronous or asynchronous timing. Synchronous timing assigns fixed times to operations; the end of the fixed time for the current operation is the basis for initiating the next operation. Asynchronous timing initiates the next operation after a signal is received that the previous operation is completed. Most computers are synchronous.
Microprogram	Microprograms (also called "stored logic") are used in place of wired circuits to increase the number and variety of instructions that a computer will accept. They are placed in a special control storage.
Transfer of information	Transfer of information is either serial (digit by digit) or parallel (a block or a word at a time). Parallel transfer is faster and is used in most very high speed computers.
Arithmetic circuitry	The basic operation of addition can be performed serially (digit by digit) or in parallel (all digits at once). The parallel mode requires more circuitry than the serial mode but is faster.
Type of numeric representation for arithmetic	Numeric data to be used in arithmetic can be represented internally in binary or binary-coded decimal (packed decimal) form. Both forms may be found in the same computer.
Type of arithmetic processing	Arithmetic may be binary (on pairs of binary strings) or binary-coded decimal (on pairs of bit sets each encoding a digit).
Storage-addressable unit	The addressable unit may be a fixed-length word or a variable-length word. The same computer may be designed to address either fixed- or variable-length words by using a byte-addressable format.
Program addressing	Program addressing may be to real addresses or to virtual addresses (in virtual storage).
Buffer storage	A buffer or cache memory is used to speed instruction and active data access by having the very active elements in a special high-speed storage.
Look-ahead	An instruction stack holds a block of instructions, allowing the computer to look ahead and perform instructions more quickly.
Distributed processors	Independent processing units may be assigned to specific tasks such as operator communication and input/output management.

SUMMARY   The internal operation of the computer is binary, i.e., based on two values or conditions. Examples of the two-valued orientation are:

1   Data is represented in binary or a variation based on binary.

2   Storage in the processing and control units makes use of a bistable (two stable states) device, the flip-flop.

3   Information being moved is encoded by having an electrical pulse represent a binary 1 and a no-pulse a binary 0.

4   The switching circuits are two-valued and can be described using the two-valued arithmetic of Boolean algebra.

The chapter has surveyed the circuits and functional assemblies from which a computer is built, providing a background for understanding how to program and operate a computer.

The characteristics of storage were surveyed, and storage for main memory was described. The dominant form for primary storage is semiconductors, with magnetic core having substantial use. The methods of reading and writing on a core were explained. Thin-film and plated-wire were also reviewed.

The concept of address is a means for identifying storage locations to be used. These addresses can be real or virtual. Storage addresses must be understood in the context of the word structure for the computer being used. The fixed- and variable-word-length organizations are basic alternatives, while a byte-addressable structure is being used to provide both methods in a single computer.

Several important design alternatives have now been presented. These are synchronous versus asynchronous timing, microprogrammed stored logic versus hardware circuitry, parallel versus serial data transfer, parallel versus serial arithmetic, binary versus binary-coded decimal representation and arithmetic, fixed versus variable word length, real versus virtual program addresses, buffer storage, look-ahead instruction stacks, and distributed processors. These alternatives are not independent; once a decision is made as to word, character, or byte addressing, other characteristics are also decided. For example, variable-word-length operations are performed serially, and the arithmetic is binary-coded decimal.

EXERCISES   1   Considered individually, which of the following design alternatives provides for faster operation?
(a) Synchronous versus asynchronous timing
(b) Parallel versus serial data transfer
(c) Parallel versus serial arithmetic
(d) Hardware arithmetic versus microprogrammed arithmetic
(e) Fixed versus variable word length
(f) Binary versus binary-coded decimal arithmetic
(g) Real versus virtual program addressing

2   In the processing unit, data is either being moved or being held in temporary operating storage. How are binary digits represented in these two cases?

3 Give the truth table for:
 (a) A NOR circuit   (b) A NAND circuit
4 Define the following terms:
 (a) Flip-flop   (g) Address
 (b) Register   (h) Double precision
 (c) Encoder   (i) Word (in computer)
 (d) Byte   (j) K (in reference to storage)
 (e) Half-adder   (k) Microprogram
 (f) Clock circuit   (l) Buffer memory
5 Explain the difference between:
 (a) Synchronous and asynchronous timing
 (b) Parallel and serial addition
 (c) Binary and BCD arithmetic
 (d) Real and virtual storage
6 Explain the characteristics (in terms of design alternatives presented in the chapter) that are associated with both variable and fixed word designs. How can both designs be implemented in the same computer?
7 What terms are used to refer to thousandths, millionths, and billionths of a second?
8 Computer memory sizes are usually defined in terms of the number of addressable storage positions. Compare the amount of storage in the following computer memories. Make a general evaluation of the effective memory.
 (a) 40K variable word-length computer
 (b) Fixed word-length (36 binary bits) 32K computer
 (c) Byte-addressable 32K computer
9 How does virtual storage work? Define page, segment, demand paging, page frame, external page storage, and thrashing.
10 Explain how each of the following can store a binary digit. In each case, how is it read?
 (a) Semiconductor   (b) Core   (c) Thin-film
11 Explain the most common method for specifying word length in variable word addressing.
12 What is the difference between using addressable registers and storage-to-storage operations?
13 What is the difference in precision obtainable in a fixed- versus a variable-word structure?
14 How is a buffer storage used?
15 Explain a distributed processing hardware design.
16 Using a rough figure of 3.3 : 1 as the ratio of binary digits needed to encode a digit of a decimal number when using straight binary, approximately how large a number (expressed in decimal digits) can be encoded by (a) 24 bits, (b) 32 bits, (c) 48 bits, and (d) 60 bits?
17 What takes place during the instruction cycle?
18 How is the instruction counter used in obtaining the address of the instruction to be used?
19 A computer instruction may specify "Branch to storage location 1029." What happens to the instruction counter?
20 How is a central processor kept in synchronization?
21 For the computer available to you, determine the following:
 (a) Synchronous or asynchronous
 (b) Storage cycle time

(c) Number of accumulator registers

(d) Serial or parallel addition

(e) Complete add time (for two 5-digit operands if addition is performed serially)

(f) Fixed versus variable-length structure or both (based on byte addressing)

(g) Binary or BCD addition (or both)

(h) Hardware or programmed floating point operations

22 Using the storage address and coding structure for the computer available to you, determine the following for main memory:

(a) Size in addressable units

(b) Number of alphanumeric characters that can be stored if all storage is used for them

(c) Number of instructions that main storage will hold

(d) Number of numeric characters storage can hold

CHAPTER

DATA PREPARATION, INPUT, OUTPUT, AND DATA COMMUNICATIONS

Data Preparation Activities
Recording the Transaction
Transcribing to Machine-readable Form
Data Validation
Conversion to Input Medium
Batching for Input
Alternatives in Data Preparation Design

Offline Data Transcription Devices
Card Punches and Verifiers
Keyboard to Disk, Diskette, or Tape
Magnetic Ink Character Recognition (MICR)
  Encoders

Offline Recording of Data in Machine-readable Form
Optical Character and Optical Mark Encoding
Point-of-Sale Devices
Keyboard to Paper Tape Devices

Terminals
Intelligent and Nonintelligent Terminals
Visual Display Units and Teleprinters
Remote Job Entry Terminals

Transfer of Data between Input/Output Devices and the Computer
Input/Output Cycle
Data Channels

Punched Card Input and Output

Output Devices
Line Printer
Graphic Display Terminal
Graph Plotter
Audio Response
Computer Output Microfilm

Data Communications
Data Transmission
Communications Facilities
Processing Data Communications
Applications of Data Communications

Summary

Exercises

Data to be used in computer processing must be made available in machine-readable form. This may involve data preparation to record and enter data into processing, or an application may make use of secondary storage which holds data that has already been prepared or which holds the results of prior processing that is needed in the current processing. The computer application inputs (reads or accepts) data from devices such as card readers, magnetic tape units, magnetic disk units, or terminals. The results of computer processing are either written onto secondary storage for subsequent use by a computer application or written or displayed in a form that is readable by persons receiving the data. The trend in information processing is to have some applications online, receiving data from remote terminals via data communications facilities and transmitting results back to the remote site to be printed or displayed.

This chapter explains the process and the devices for data preparation, original input, and human-use output. It includes an explanation of data communication operations and facilities. Secondary storage devices are described in the next chapter.

Data Preparation Activities

Data preparation is used to refer to the activities which bring data to the point of input to processing by a computer application. A major part of data preparation is data entry, and that term is often used to refer to the data preparation activities. Five major data preparation activities are:

1   Recording the transaction
2   Transcribing to machine-readable form
3   Validating the data
4   Converting data to input medium
5   Batching for input

There are a number of alternatives in the design of data entry for computer applications. These alternatives affect the manner in which data preparation activities are performed, and some application design alternatives eliminate some data preparation activities.

Recording the Transaction   A transaction is broadly defined as the occurrence of an activity or event (such as a sale, a purchase, enrolling a student, or performing a measurement). Data about the transaction must be recorded in order to provide input to computer processing (for purposes such as sales accounting, purchases recordkeeping, student records, and statistical analysis).

The recording of data during the execution of a transaction can make use of a variety of recording technology. Five major approaches are listed below together with examples of the technology employed. The data entry devices are described later in the chapter.

Approach to transaction recording	Data entry technology
1 Recording on a document for subsequent conversion to machine-readable form	Paper document for conversion by keypunching, keyboard to disk, terminal, etc.
2 Recording on a document in a machine-readable form	Typing document with optically readable typing font or printing characters for reading by optical character reader.
3 Recording with a turnaround document from a previous, related transaction	Document may be in a machine-readable form (punched card or optically readable printing), or it may not be machine-readable and need conversion.
4 Recording which produces both a document and a machine-readable input	Point-of-sale device which produces document (such as cash register tape) and also records transaction on a machine-readable medium (such as magnetic tape, magnetic disk, or paper tape).
5 Recording via a terminal	A visual display terminal or a typewriter terminal.

The first two methods utilize a document to record the data. Careful document design (beyond the scope of this text) is important in reducing the time required for recording data and in reducing recording errors. In the following examples, the use of the boxes for social security numbers reduces the chance that a number with too few or too many digits will be recorded. Asking for a person's name without specifying the order is error-prone. For names such as DAVIS BITTON and HART WILL, which is the last name and which is the first? (One is a historian and the other an accounting professor—the order of both names is first/last.)

Error-prone

Social Security No. _____

Name _____

Better

Social Security Number ☐☐☐-☐☐-☐☐☐☐

Name (please print) ☐☐☐☐☐☐☐☐☐☐☐☐

Last

☐☐☐☐☐☐☐☐☐☐☐

Given Name and Initial

Documents which will be converted by subsequent manual data entry should be designed to aid efficient and error-free entry. For example, data items that are to be entered by keying should be clearly identified (with boxes or small numbers, etc.) and should be on the document in the order in which they are to be entered. Documents to be read by optical scanning should be designed to meet the requirements of the equipment. Background boxes and lines, optical-scanning guide characters, etc., may be necessary.

The use of turnaround documents is a variation on the first two methods. A turnaround document is included with a transaction as a document to be returned as part of the completion of the transaction. It may be machine-readable or may require conversion as does any nonreadable document. For example, a gasoline credit card billing will usually contain an optically readable statement or a punched card portion to be returned with the payment (Figure 8-1). This turnaround document, which represents a record of the payment, is an input to the processing of receipts. No further data input is required to record the payment unless there is a partial payment. The use of turnaround documents is very important in business data processing because much of the data from the transaction is needed for subsequent, related transactions.

In many applications a receipt or other document is prepared by a machine

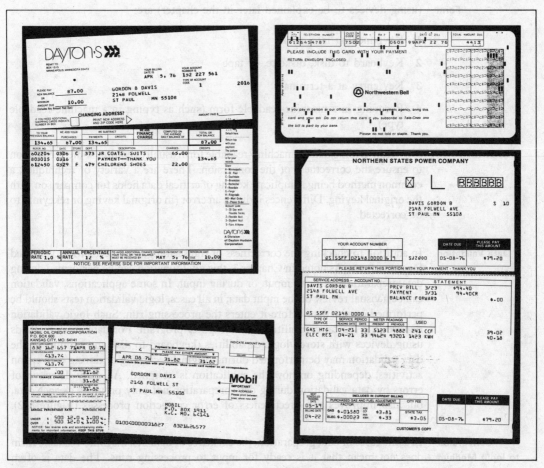

FIGURE 8-1 Examples of turnaround documents used in customer billing.

which can also produce a machine-readable record of the transaction for subsequent processing by the computer. For example, the checkout counter at a discount department store may produce a register tape for the customer and a machine record for sales analysis and inventory accounting.

Computer terminals are being used extensively both to capture data for subsequent processing and to enter data for immediate processing. Terminals can be used for direct entry to the computer or can be used offline with data being accumulated for subsequent input to the computer. The major advantage of terminals is the logic capabilities that are available for assisting the person performing data entry and for validating data while it is being entered.

Transcribing to Machine-readable Form

Transcribing to machine-readable form is required for original documents and turnaround documents that are not machine-readable. The methods of transcribing (using devices to be explained later in the chapter) are:

1 Keypunching into cards

2 Keyboard to disk, diskette, or tape

3 Key entry at a terminal

4 Recoding in a machine-readable form (such as typing in a machine-readable type)

Transcribing data in machine-readable form usually requires some verification to ensure the correctness of the conversion. There are a variety of techniques, a common method being a duplicate keying of critical data fields for comparison with the original keying. Differences indicate an error (in original keying or rekeying) to be corrected.

Data Validation

In addition to checking the correctness of transcribing, data needs to be validated for correctness. As noted in Chapter 3, this vital function can be performed during data preparation, prior to input, or during input. In some applications, validation can be a visual review of the input data; in all cases, logic validation tests should be performed on the data before it enters the processing run. Such logic validation requires the logical capabilities of a computer program. For data entry methods using devices with stored logic capabilities (keyboard to disk and terminals), the data validation may be performed during original recording or during conversion activities, depending on how the application is designed. An early detection of errors by data validation during data preparation not only provides cleaner data, but also improves the effectiveness of error correction processes (Figure 8-2).

Conversion to Input Medium

In some cases of data preparation, the existence of data in a machine-readable form does not mean that it is ready for input to processing runs. The data is often converted to another computer storage medium. In many cases, documents en-

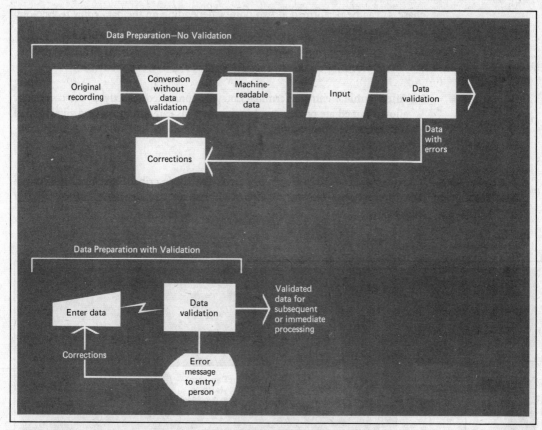

FIGURE 8-2 Examples of data validation during and subsequent to data entry.

coded for optical reading and documents encoded with magnetic ink characters are not input directly into the computer but are read by a special reader which may write the data onto magnetic tape or magnetic disk for subsequent input rather than input directly to processing. Paper tape, small magnetic tape cartridges, and diskettes are sometimes used as input from terminals, but in the typical data processing situation, data on these media requires conversion to a higher-speed input medium such as regular magnetic tape or magnetic disk storage.

Batching for Input   For considerations relating to processing efficiency and control over completeness and correctness of processing, it is frequently desirable to assemble batches of transactions. As explained in Chapter 3, one major approach to processing, periodic processing of batches of data, is referred to as "batch processing." The batching of data, if batch processing is to be performed, occurs during the data preparation phase. It can be performed at two points, depending on the data entry technology being used (Figure 8-3):

1 After recording on documents but prior to conversion activities.

2 After terminal entry. (Terminal entry, if connected directly to the computer, allows immediate processing, but transactions can also be entered and batched for subsequent processing.)

Alternatives in Data Preparation Design The discussion of data preparation activities has described several alternatives in data preparation. Two major sets of alternatives are dependent on the type of processing:

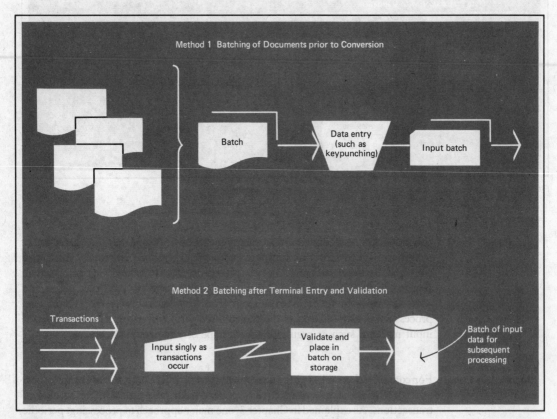

FIGURE 8-3 Point at which batching of transactions may occur for periodic batch processing.

Type of processing	Data entry
1 Immediate online processing	Entry of transactions as they occur via a terminal with validation. No batching, no conversion to machine-readable form, and no conversion to input medium activities.
2 Periodic processing	Alternatives:
	(a) Input via a terminal with validation and batching for subsequent processing.
	(b) Document record with batching before conversion to machine-readable form. Validation dependent on conversion device. Machine-readable records produced by entry or recording device.
	(c) Document in machine-readable form. Conversion to input medium. Validation dependent on conversion device.

The data entry devices to implement these alternatives can be classified into offline devices for converting data originally recorded in a form that was not machine-readable, offline devices for original data recording in machine-readable form, and terminal data entry devices.

Offline Data Transcription Devices

The three devices described in this section are used to transcribe data originally recorded in batches of documents that are not machine-readable to equivalent data in machine-readable form. In addition to the card punch, keyboard to disk, etc., and magnetic ink devices described here, the optical typing method described in the next section can be used in a data transcribing mode.

Card Punches and Verifiers   Although it is being replaced in many new systems, the most commonly used data entry device is still the keydriven card punch. It is estimated that there are about one-half million of these units in service. The majority produce traditional 80-column Hollerith cards, but there are a significant number of keypunches for 96-column cards.

In data entry using keypunches, the keypunch operator is given a batch of documents from which one or more items per document are keypunched into cards. The punching is based on instructions as to how the data is to be entered. After the batch of documents has been keyed, the punched cards and documents are given to a second operator who rekeys the entire set of data for each card or may rekey only important data items. The verifier (or card punch in verifier mode) detects differences between the two punchings. The data for each card for which there is an error is rekeyed and reverified.

There are three generations of keypunches in terms of the technology used (see Appendix 1):

1 The pre-1960 keypunches with a restricted keyboard. The IBM 026 is the major punch of this era.

2 The 1960s keypunch with an expanded keyboard and improved technology. The IBM 029 is the major example.

3 The 1970s keypunch with buffered input before punching. The UNIVAC 1700 and 1800 series and the IBM 129 are examples (Figure 8-4).

The buffered keypunch has a small memory called a "buffer" into which the data is keyed. After all the contents of the card have been entered, the card is punched with data from the buffer. By using two such buffers, the current card contents may be keyed in while the preceding card is being punched. Also, since there is no punching until the entire card contents have been keyed, errors may be corrected in the data still in the buffer. The most recent models of keypunches have added limited processing capabilities for data validation.

An evaluation of the unbuffered and buffered keypunch characteristics suggests that for infrequent use of the keypunch or use of the keypunch by untrained, occasional users, an unbuffered keypunch is satisfactory. But when a modest volume of records is to be transcribed to machine-readable form, a buffered unit should be selected because of the increased speed (say, 50 percent greater).

Keyboard to Disk, Diskette, or Tape

The basic idea of the keyboard to disk, diskette, or magnetic tape devices is to record data on a magnetic medium rather than on punched cards. These devices are generally an alternative or a replacement to card punch and verifier (Figure 8-4). In all cases, these devices offer less noise and greater key entry speeds than is possible in keypunching of cards.

The keyboard to magnetic tape (or keytape) was first introduced in 1964. Although there are existing installations, few new keytape units are being installed because of the superiority of keydisk systems. In keytape units, data is keyed by an operator and recorded on magnetic tape. The magnetic tape allows backspacing, correction, etc. Depending on the model, the magnetic tape can be a regular tape or a cassette. The regular tape can be used directly as input; it is necessary to pool the cassettes and create an input tape.

The key to diskette unit (first introduced by IBM in 1973 as the IBM 3740 data entry system) uses an 8-in.-round floppy or flexible disk to record keyed data (Figure 8-4). The diskette holds a maximum of 1898 records containing up to

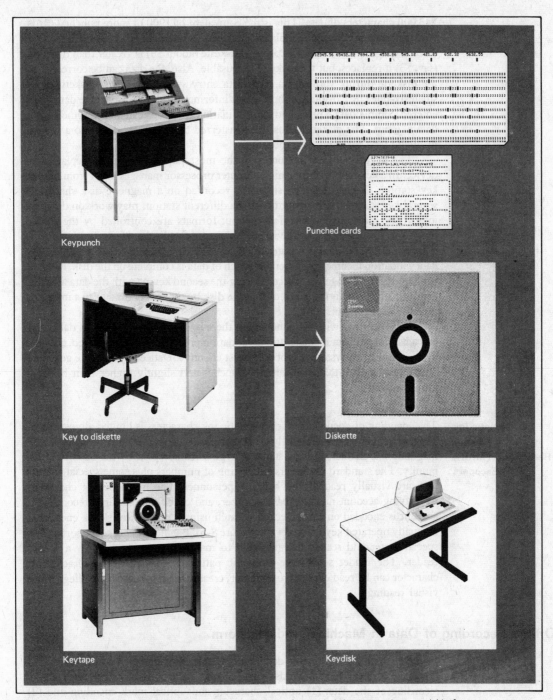

Punched cards

Keypunch

Key to diskette

Diskette

Keytape

Keydisk

FIGURE 8-4 Keyboard data entry equipment for conversion of recorded data to machine-readable form.

243,000 characters of data. This is the equivalent of 1900 or more punched cards. It is permanently housed in a plastic envelope, is quite rugged, and can be mailed since it weighs only 8 oz. The cost of a diskette (about $8) is greater than the cards (say, $3) it replaces, but the diskette is reusable. Also, the data can be corrected on the diskette during verification. The data entry system using the diskette has a small six-line CRT display to show status information and to display the data being entered. Simple data editing and data validation functions can be performed while data is input. The diskettes must be transferred by a separate device to a regular magnetic tape for input to processing.

The keydisk system is currently the most popular keypunch replacement device. In a keydisk system, a minicomputer processor manages input from several key stations. Data from each station is recorded on a magnetic disk shared by several key stations. The operators at the different stations may work on different jobs at the same time; the different input formats are controlled by the shared processor. Each operator has a visual display unit for display of messages, formats, input data, etc. The minicomputer can be used for rather extensive data editing and data validation techniques. When the batch of data is complete on the disk, it can be validated by rekeying data and comparing the second keying with the data fields on the disk. The batch is transferred from the disk by the minicomputer to a magnetic tape for use in input.

In comparison with keypunching, if there is a substantial volume of data entry and a variety of input formats, and if validation procedures can be applied, a shared processor keydisk system is probably most effective. Data entry rates are generally 50 percent greater than standard keypunches and slightly higher than buffered keypunches.

Magnetic Ink Character Recognition (MICR) Encoders

The encoding of documents with magnetic ink characters is limited almost exclusively to banking and especially to turnaround documents such as checks. The magnetic ink characters use a standard type form accepted by the banking community. The standard characters, consisting of numbers plus some special characters, are visually readable by banking personnel. The magnetic ink characters identifying account number, bank number, and check number are precoded; the amount is encoded on each check in a batch using a magnetic disk ink encoder, a manually operated keyboard device (Figure 8-5). Batches of checks are sorted by a special sorter and read and transferred to magnetic tape (or disk) by a special reader. The reader senses the magnetic pattern formed by the characters. A character can be read even if crossed over, creased, or otherwise made illegible for visual reading.

Offline Recording of Data in Machine-readable Form

Many applications require a document that is readable by both humans and machines. Two major methods will produce such a document with a single recording of the data: (1) optical character and optical mark encoding and (2)

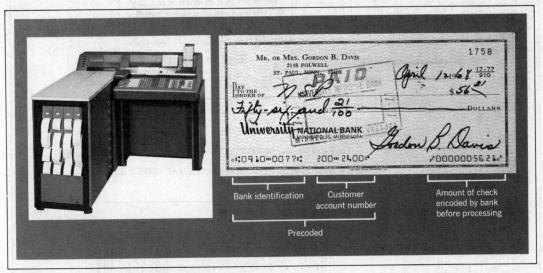

Bank identification

Customer
account number

Amount of check
encoded by bank
before processing

Precoded

FIGURE 8-5 Magnetic ink character recognition equipment.

devices which produce computer-readable data as a by-product of the recording of the transaction and making the necessary transaction document (point-of-sale devices are an example).

Optical Character and Optical Mark Encoding

Encoding for optical character recognition (OCR) at data entry may involve one of three major methods (Figure 8-6):

1   Typing data in a machine-readable type font
2   Handprinting characters
3   Making marks in designated areas on a document

The data encoded in optical characters is read by equipment which either writes the data on magnetic tape for input to processing or inputs directly to a computer.

The typing of data in a machine-readable form may make use of a regular typewriter font, but typically a special optical font is used. The data to be converted to machine-readable form is typed, usually on special input forms which simplify the reading of the data. In fact, forms design is a critical factor in most OCR applications. Readers may be designed to read a single font or multiple fonts.

Handprinting of characters is a limited method of data entry. It requires discipline in handprinting legible characters and is therefore most useful in terms of small amounts of input. For example, a turnaround document may be complete except for partial payments, and these may be handprinted before the document is read (see NSP bill in Figure 8-6). The handprinting must be done in premarked areas, one space being marked for each character.

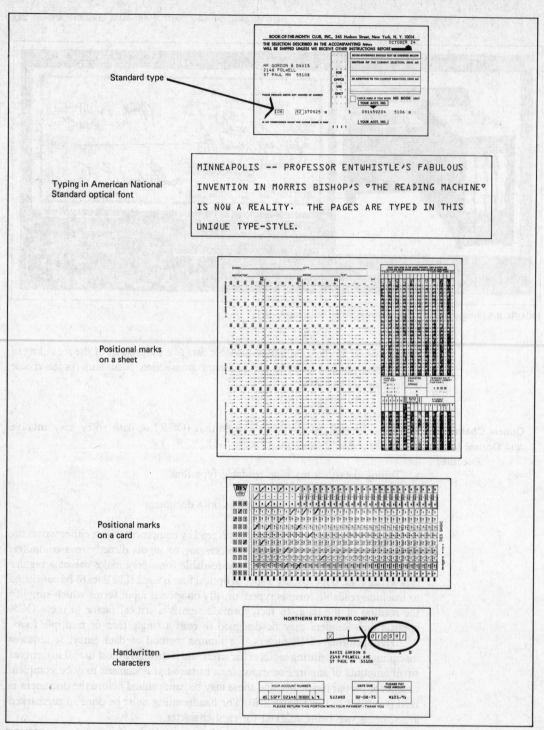

Standard type

Typing in American National Standard optical font

Positional marks on a sheet

Positional marks on a card

Handwritten characters

FIGURE 8-6 Documents which can be read using optical scanning.

Optical mark encoding makes use of predefined areas (say, small squares) which are marked with a slash or other sign to indicate the value selected. These require a relatively simple technology to read compared with optical type font or handwritten characters. The optical mark technique is most appropriate for simple inputs such as answers to multiple-choice examinations or meter readings.

There are multimedia systems available which have optical scanning plus key entry equipment with a visual display unit. Documents are read optically and displayed, and the keyboard is used to add more data or to enter data not readable by the optical scanning. This combination is a significant technological development.

In all optical reading machines, the characters to be read are scanned by some kind of photoelectric device. The photoelectric cells convert the symbols on the document into an analog or digital representation that is analyzed by a recognition unit. The recognition unit matches patterns from the scanner against internally stored reference patterns. Patterns which cannot be identified cause the document to be rejected. There are a number of different methods for recognition. Some of the more common are:

1 *Matrix matching* This method of total character recognition compares individual elements of the scanned character with the elements of all characters which can be identified by the reader. A character is recognized when it matches exactly or quite closely one of the reference patterns. Any type font may be programmed.

2 *Feature or stroke analysis* A character is recognized on the basis of the stroke or line formation of each character. The technique requires a special printing font.

3 *Curve tracing* In this method, especially suited for recognizing handwritten characters which vary in size and shape, a spiraling spot of light follows the outline of a character. Characters are identified by observations as to vertical lines, horizontal lines, etc.

Reading speeds range from, say, 70 to 2400 characters per second. Reader reliability is important. Two measures of reliability are the reject and error rates. The reject rate is the percentage of documents (currently running from 2 to 10 percent) which the reader cannot read. The reject rate can vary considerably depending on the quality control exercised over the form, the recording of the data, etc. The error rate (currently less than 1 percent) is the percentage of documents on which a character has been incorrectly identified. Reentry of characters or data rejected is generally done offline but may use the multimedia keyboard system mentioned earlier.

Optical character recognition equipment is sufficiently expensive that an installation must have a volume range of over, say, 7000 input documents per day which could be read optically (roughly equivalent to the work of six to eight keypunch operators) before such equipment is likely to be economical. Optical mark equipment is fairly low in cost but is generally applicable for simple recording of quantities or questionnaire results. If there is a large volume and the source documents can be made suitable for optical scanning, OCR should be considered. If even parts of each document can be read optically, a multimedia optical reader/keyentry system should be evaluated.

Point-of-Sale Devices

Point-of-sale (POS) devices are used primarily by department stores and supermarkets for data collection while the sale is being entered. The devices have memory and logic processing capabilities. In the case of a department store, the POS device accepts entry of customer account number, product code, etc. The devices accumulate product sales data, customer billing data, etc., and may communicate with a central computer for credit checking. Other data is generally recorded on tape for later input to processing. The supermarket POS systems read product data by scanning a product code printed on every item. The register is connected to a minicomputer which contains prices for all items. The price plus product data is used to produce a register tape for each customer. Sales and inventory data are accumulated by the computer (Figure 8-7).

Point of sale is very useful but adds cost to the recording equipment. The advantages of input validation, automated pricing, credit verification, inventory control, etc., may be sufficient to justify the added cost. The trend is clearly toward use of this type of equipment at point of sale in large supermarkets and large department stores.

Keyboard to Paper Tape Devices

Paper tape is a very limited purpose input/output medium. It is produced as a by-product of input in a variety of business devices such as cash registers, accounting machines, and adding machines. Teletype machines can prepare paper

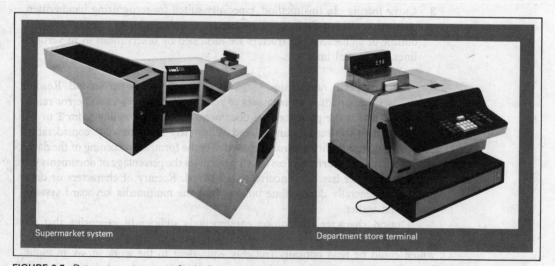

Supermarket system

Department store terminal

FIGURE 8-7 Data entry using point-of-sale devices. (*Courtesy of International Business Machines Corporation.*)

tape while they are in offline mode. The paper tape is then used as a higher than manual speed input for online transmission of data. This medium consists of a paper tape punched with 10 characters per inch (Figure 8-8). Speeds for reading range from 350 to 2000 characters per second (with lower speeds from typewriter attachments). Both eight-channel and five-channel codes are in use. In concept, paper tape can be thought of as being a continuous punched card. This presents advantages such as the fact that no individual record can be lost or put out of sequence because all are on the continuous tape. However, paper tape is more difficult to correct and is less flexible for sorting, etc.

Terminals

Data may be entered into computer processing through terminals. The devices used for terminal data entry can be classified in several ways:

1 Nonintelligent terminals
2 Intelligent (programmable) terminals
3 Remote batch terminal

The terminals can be connected to a computer either directly by cables, if near the computer, or by data communications; or the terminals may be used to accumulate data for subsequent input. The latter option of accumulating data is especially feasible if the terminal has programmable logic and a magnetic recording medium such as diskette or tape cassette. There is a trend toward the use of microprocessors in the terminals (as an alternative to hard-wiring) to implement terminal control for data communications.

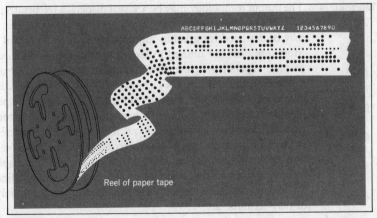

ABCDEFGHIJKLMNOPQRSTUVWXYZ   1234567890

Reel of paper tape

FIGURE 8-8 Punched paper tape using American National Standard code for information interchange (ASCII).

Terminals are rapidly growing as significant elements in data processing configurations. Costs have continued to decrease (cost is about $1000 to $4000 per terminal). It is estimated that there are over 2 million terminals of all types in operation. Terminals are used in connection with data communications to put the input next to the point of origin and to put the output next to the user. This has advantages because data can be validated at entry rather than later and corrections made by the originator. Output can be received directly by the user, reducing the output distribution delay. Terminals allow the computer files to be interrogated at locations remote from the computer. Terminals must be used in immediate processing but can also be used for periodic processing.

Intelligent and Nonintelligent Terminals

The intelligent terminal is also known as a "programmable terminal" or a "logic terminal." The intelligent terminal essentially contains a small computer processor and a fairly small memory. This means that a program can be stored in it to direct the operation of the terminal, validate input, direct communications with a larger computer, etc. Because the intelligent terminal contains a program and can perform many data input validation tasks, it is possible to enter data via an intelligent terminal, validate it for correctness, and then to either transmit the data for immediate processing or record it for subsequent processing. The trend is toward at least some logic in terminals.

A nonintelligent or nonprogrammable terminal must be connected to a computer which accepts data, sends back messages, etc. Input is either processed immediately or stored by the computer for subsequent processing. Teletypes and typewriters used as time-sharing terminals are nonintelligent terminals.

Visual Display Units and Teleprinters

Terminals generally have a keyboard by which to enter data. The terminals may have a magnetic tape cassette (or perhaps a diskette) for recording input or output. The output technology may be a visual display, a teleprinter, or both (Figure 8-9).

Visual display units may be designed for alphanumeric display only, or they may be designed for graphic output as well (to be described later in this chapter). Most terminals are limited to alphanumeric display because of the extra cost of graphic capabilities (several times more expensive). Visual display units are frequently referred to as CRTs because all but a few visual display units utilize the dominant cathode-ray tube technology. Alternative display technologies are light-emitting diodes (LEDs) such as those used in calculators, plasma, and liquid crystal. The most common technique for forming the characters on the CRT screen is the dot matrix. A typical dot matrix consists of 35 dots (seven dots high by five dots wide). The dots required to form a character are displayed. An alternative technique uses a stroke method in which short, straight lines are drawn.

Some capabilities which may be found in the commonly used alphanumeric display terminal are:

1 Control of a cursor which defines where data is to be entered.

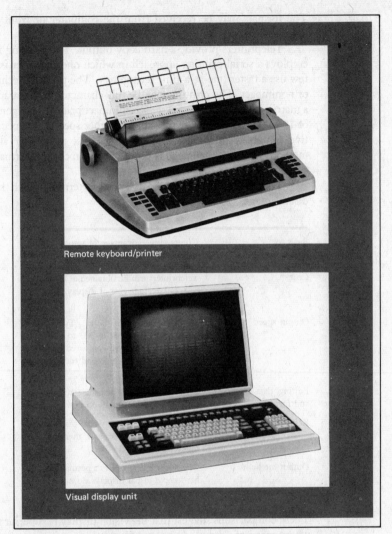

Remote keyboard/printer

Visual display unit

FIGURE 8-9 Alphanumeric terminals.

2 Editing to insert a character in a line, delete a character in a line, and insert or delete a line.

3 Character or field blinking to draw the operator's attention to vital data.

4 Brightness control to highlight some data.

It is common practice to have a format displayed on the screen to guide input (much like a paper form). This requires the format to be protected so that it is not altered by the keyed-in data. Only the filled-in data is transmitted, not the formats.

The formats may be received from the computer or from attached cassettes or diskettes.

Teleprinters provide a hard copy output. The printing mechanism generally employs a serial printing approach in which one character is printed at a time. A few use a faster line-at-a-time technology. The printing technique may be impact or nonimpact. The printing may be full-character or a character image formed by a matrix of dots. Full-character serial impact printing can generally achieve speeds of 10 to 30 characters per second; for higher speeds, it is necessary to use alternative impact technologies such as the matrix printer or alternative nonimpact methods in which the image is produced by an electrothermal (heat) technique on special paper.

The display terminal and teleprinter terminal each have advantages and disadvantages, as noted below:

Basis for comparison	Comparative advantage of visual display unit versus teleprinter
Cost	Teleprinters can be obtained at lower cost, but average cost of display units is dropping.
Output speed	Displays are much faster. Typical visual display output is 300 to 1200 characters per second compared with 10 to 30 characters a second for teleprinters.
Editing, data entry, and formatting	Displays frequently provide extensive capabilities; teleprinters do not.
Reliability	Both are reliable, but visual displays are totally electronic and therefore inherently more reliable.
Output medium	The teleprinter provides a permanent, hard copy; visual displays do not.

These comparisons suggest that the visual display is superior for input or retrieval where speed of output editing and formatting are important, but the teleprinter is superior for applications requiring hard-copy output.

Remote Job Entry Terminals

A remote job entry (RJE) terminal uses a remote batch terminal that groups data into blocks for transmission to a computer. A remote job entry terminal is a remote batch terminal that can initiate (from a remote site) the execution of an application by a computer at another location, transmit the data for the program, and probably receive back and print the results of the application program. The RJE terminal therefore typically consists of a remote console, input device, and output device (Figure 8-10). It has program storage capability to control input communications,

FIGURE 8-10   Remote job entry terminal. (*Courtesy of Data 100 Corporation.*)

output, etc. It may, in fact, be a small computer that can be used as either a job entry terminal or a standalone computer.

Transfer of Data between Input/Output Devices and the Computer

Two major types of input and output can be identified—the input and output from devices directly connected to the computer (often called "peripherals") and input/output from remote devices over data communications facilities. This section describes input and output from peripherals. The peripheral devices are described later in the chapter except for secondary storage peripherals, which are explained in the next chapter.

Input/Output Cycle   An input operation for a peripheral device begins with a program instruction from the central processor which sends a command to the input device to read a record. Reading takes place (frequently by having an input medium such as punched card or magnetic tape move through the input device). Information is read and converted to the code used by the computer system. The coded information is transmitted to the internal storage and stored in memory locations assigned to hold the input record. The data is then available for use by the processing instructions.

An output operation is essentially the reverse of the input procedure. The data to be written is arranged by program instructions in a set of storage locations assigned for this purpose. An instruction to perform output causes the data from the output storage locations to be copied and transmitted to the input/output device which writes it on an output medium.

An input or output device is directed by a control unit. The control unit decodes the input/output command from the central processor and effects operation of the device or devices. Other functions are coding, decoding, and checking of data transmitted between the CPU and the device. The connection between the central processor and the control unit is generally via a channel which is essentially equipment for managing data transfer between the central processor and one or more input/output device control units.

The cycle of activity for an input thus has a sequence approximately as follows (the output cycle is similar):

1 The computer decodes program instructions to read the contents of one block (also called a "physical record"), using a specified input device.

2 A signal is set to the control unit for the device which starts the device in operation. If the device is busy or inoperable, an interrupt or conditional transfer of control is executed, depending on the way the program is written.

3 The device reads the contents of the physical record and encodes it into electrical signals.

4 The control unit codes the data signals and checks them.

5 The data is transmitted to the specified storage locations in main memory via a channel.

6 A signal is transmitted to the central processor that the input operation is completed.

Major input and output design considerations are a result of the difference between input/output speeds and internal processing speeds. To provide a rough understanding of the speed of input/output devices relative to internal speed, a high-speed card reader reads at, say, 1200 cards per minute or 20 cards per second. This is one card every 50,000 microseconds. An average medium-size computer is able to execute from 5000 to 15,000 instructions in the same period of time. The efficiency of the system is therefore increased if the input and output operations can be overlapped or performed simultaneously with computation.

Data Channels Data channels are the method by which the slow input/output operations can be kept from delaying the internal processing. A typical data processing procedure consists of three phases—input, processing, and output. Data is read from one or more devices, the data is processed, and the results are written using one or more output devices. In the absence of any provisions for simultaneous operation of CPU and input/output units, the CPU would be idle a good part of the time (Figure 8-11). By the use of data channels, simultaneous operations by input/output devices and the central processor are allowed (Figure 8-12).

A data channel consists of hardware circuitry which controls the movement of data between the primary storage and the input or output devices. It can be thought

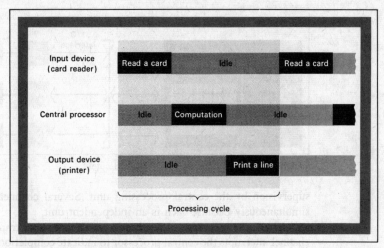

FIGURE 8-11 Processing cycle with no simultaneous operations.

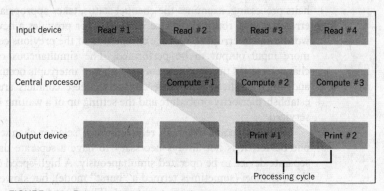

FIGURE 8-12 Processing cycle with simultaneous operations.

of as a separate, small processing unit used only for managing the transfer of data. Each channel has facilities for accepting input/output instructions, addressing input/output devices, obtaining its control information from storage, directing and buffering information transfer, and performing similar functions necessary for an orderly transfer of data. Normally the channel is connected not to an input/output device itself but to the control unit which matches the channel interface (connection) to the internal requirements of the device (Figure 8-13).

The channel is activated by a program instruction which identifies the channel, device, and other data to control the operation. After the CPU has activated the channel and identified the command word, it is free to continue other processing. Once started, the channel will control the quantity and destination of the data transmitted between main storage and the input/output devices without further

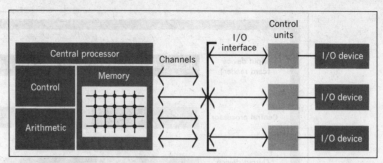

FIGURE 8-13 Use of channels for input and output.

supervision by the central processing unit. Several channels may be operating simultaneously because each is an independent unit.

Channels use an interrupt procedure. When the data transfer is complete, the channel interrupts the central processor to indicate completion of the transfer. The channel will also interrupt processing if an error condition is detected in the input/output device or channel. When the interrupt occurs, the central processor halts processing, examines the channel status, takes appropriate action (such as an error-handling routine) if there is an error, or provides a new channel command word if the interrupt signals the completion of the previous command and there is more input/output to be performed. The simultaneous operation of several channels means the possibility of a number of interrupts occurring simultaneously and other conflicts among the channels. These conflicts are handled by a pre-established priority procedure and the setting up of a waiting line of requests to be serviced.

Although some channels, referred to as "selector channels," can service only one device, it is not always necessary to have a separate data channel for each separate device to be operated simultaneously. A high-speed device will monopolize a channel (sometimes termed a "burst" mode), but slower devices like a card reader or printer can share a channel. The shared channel, frequently called a "multiplexor channel," has a number of subchannels, each of which can sustain an input/output operation. In this mode, sets of data from several devices are interleaved together in the channel. The channel keeps track of these different segments and sends each to its proper destination (Figure 8-14).

The number and capacity of channels supplied with a computer are important elements affecting the capabilities of the computer system. The number of channels is important because this determines the number of devices which can be operated simultaneously. The capacity of a channel is significant because some devices provide a very high rate of data transfer and therefore need a high-capacity channel.

Punched Card Input and Output

Although there is increased use of input, through alternatives such as terminals and keydisk systems, the most common input medium for introducing source data into computer processing is the punched card. Cards are read by a card reader and

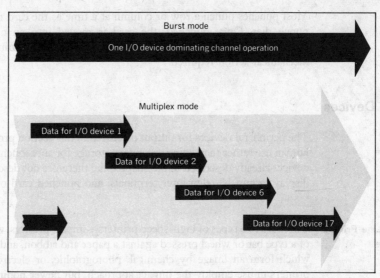

FIGURE 8-14 Modes for channel operation.

punched by a card punch. These two units may be housed in the same cabinet or separately.

The reading of cards requires the following steps:

1 The cards with data punched in them are placed in the read hopper of the card reader.

2 On a command from the computer, a punched card is moved past two separate sensing stations (although some readers use only one).

3 The configurations of punches and no-punches are read by the two stations and are compared to detect read errors.

4 The configuration of punches and no-punches is converted to internal computer code and transmitted to the computer for storage.

5 The card is deposited in an output stacker.

Card readers may use two different methods of sensing the existence of punches—photoelectric cells or wire brushes. In the photoelectric-type reader, punches are detected by photoelectric cells activated by light passing through the punch holes. In the brush-type reader, the card is passed between a wire brush and a metal roller. If there is a punch, the brush makes electrical contact with the roller, thereby sensing a punch. The input/output control systems will normally handle tests for off-normal conditions in the equipment or error conditions and provide operator messages. Examples of these conditions are read error, input hopper out of cards, full output stacker, and card jam.

The punching of cards under computer control requires an online punch.

Most punches punch a row or column at a time as the card moves under a set of punch dies. Once punched, the card is moved into an output stacker. Card punching is normally much slower than card reading because of the additional mechanical action required.

Output Devices

The peripheral devices for output discussed in this section provide final output for human use rather than being secondary storage for subsequent processing. Output devices already described in the chapter and therefore not described here are visual display terminals, teleprinter terminals, and punched card output.

Line Printer   There are two types of high-speed printers—impact printers, which print by means of a type bar or wheel pressed against a paper and ribbon, and nonimpact printers, which form an image by chemical, photographic, or electrostatic means. Most printers in use employ the impact approach, but newer nonimpact printers using electrostatic methods offer an attractive alternative.

Several different impact printing methods are in use; the most common are the chain printer and the printer drum. In the chain printer (Figure 8-15), the print characters are mounted on a chain which moves horizontally in front of the paper. The chain may contain several sets of the print characters. As the character to be

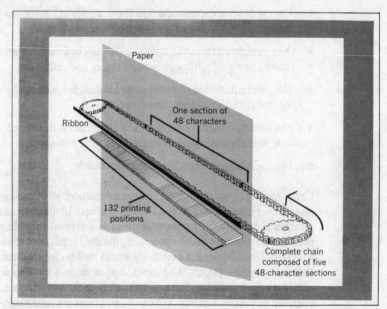

FIGURE 8-15 Print chain.

printed passes in front of each position on the paper where it is to be printed, a magnetically controlled hammer behind the paper presses the paper against the typeface to print the character. Moving one character set of the chain past the paper is thus sufficient to print a line. The entire process for printing a line takes from one-fifth to one-fiftieth of a second, depending on the speed of the printer. The chain is removable, so that more than one type face and set of special characters may be used.

The print drum method uses a metal drum with rows of characters engraved on it. During printing, the drum revolves, moving each row of characters (for example, the row containing A's) past the print hammers. The print hammer for a position is activated when a row of characters to be printed passes, and the hammer presses the paper against the drum to print the character. A somewhat uneven line is sometimes produced by this method.

The vertical spacing of the paper is frequently controlled by a plastic or paper loop on the printer (Figure 8-16), although some printers are controlled completely by program instructions. The loop contains several rows or channels. Punches in these columns designate the positioning of the paper. The tape loop control is activated by a character placed in the first position of the print line. This character is sensed, but not printed, by the printer, and it activates vertical spacing. The

FIGURE 8-16 Tape loop for vertical spacing control. (*Courtesy of International Business Machines Corporation.*)

punched tape loop will position the paper at the top of a page and at different vertical positions on the page (required, for example, by a preprinted form). The tape loop for vertical movement of printer paper is similar in concept to the tab stops for horizontal movement of the carriage on a typewriter.

The very high speed nonimpact printers use electrostatic methods (similar to a Xerox copier) on plain or specially treated paper. The image to be transmitted is prepared in different ways depending on the make—one uses a laser beam, another a set of styli, and a third a character drum and light beam. Some of the printers are for offline only, others for online use. The speeds range from 4000 to 18,000 lines per minute. The process allows forms to be added as a background to the printed output.

Graphic Display Terminal In contrast to the alphanumeric display terminals, a graphic display terminal provides drawings as output on a screen. Almost anything that a graphic artist can draw with lines (straight or curved) can be displayed (Figure 8-17). They are used in interactive design, in presentation of data for business or engineering use, and for pictorial representations. The relatively high cost and specialized nature of the graphic terminals tend to limit their use.

FIGURE 8-17 Graphic display terminal output. (*Courtesy of Tektronix Corporation.*)

Graph Plotter A graph plotter is a device for drawing graphs. Both plots and smooth graphs are possible. A swimsuit manufacturer, for example, uses the graph plotter to draw different size patterns based on the standard pattern of the swimsuit designer. A variety of plotting techniques are used. Figure 8-18 shows the use of the graph plotter for plotting data.

Audio Response A stockbroker, wanting the latest quotation for a security listed by the New York Stock Exchange, dials a special code number. The response is immediate as a voice speaks the quotation over the telephone. The entire transaction is handled by a computer using a voice response unit. The computer interprets the input code number, obtains the data from storage, and transmits the answer to the audio response unit. This unit selects, from a magnetic drum, words and phrases of prerecorded vocabulary which then form a spoken reply. The reply is limited to a relatively small number of words and phrases, but the inquiries and responses can make use of an ordinary telephone. The response unit is suited for applications such as credit inquiry and inventory status where the reply vocabulary can be standardized.

Computer Output Microfilm Computer output microfilm (COM) prepares data on microfilm, either as a roll or as a microfiche. In a common technology the COM device displays data on a CRT screen, and this screen is exposed to microfilm (Figure 8-19). Other methods of exposing the film are also used. At speeds up to 30,000 lines per minute, the rate of recording is faster than printing—about 25 to 50 times faster. The microfilm is small and easily stored. About 2000 frames are stored on a roll. It is read with a microfilm reader. A computer-generated index is used to locate the proper roll or microfiche and to find the right frame. The cost of the microfilm for a page of output is only one-half to one-eighth the cost of a sheet of printer paper. A forms overlay may be used to print headings, lines, etc., to make the output more readable. Additional microfilm copies may be made at very low cost.

The COM equipment is fairly expensive, and so small users who wish to use it take data files to a service center offering COM processing. Costs and processing difficulties are being reduced, so this output method is likely to receive much use by medium and large data processing centers which have applications with extensive printouts needed largely for reference purposes. Such printouts are bulky, take large storage space, and are difficult to access. Archival storage of data files required to meet legal or government regulations is another use.

Data Communications

Data communication is employed to reduce the time required to move data from a point of origin to the computer and from the computer to a point of use. It reduces the time requirements from the hours or days involved in mail or messenger

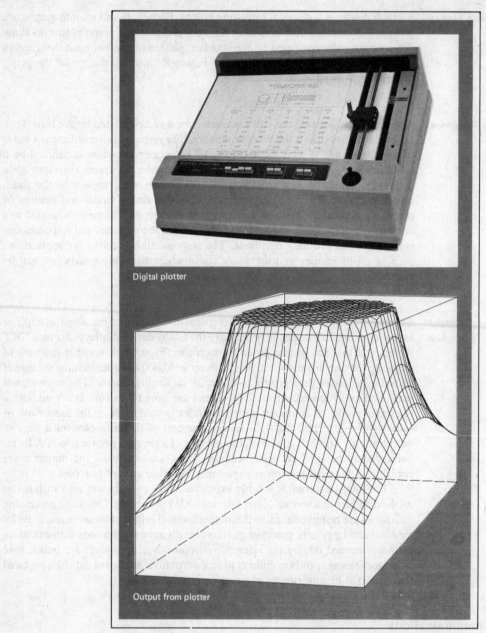

Digital plotter

Output from plotter

FIGURE 8-18 Graph plotter and its output. (*Courtesy of Tektronix Corporation.*)

transportation to the few seconds or minutes for electrical transmission. Data communication should be considered whenever the benefit from this immediate movement of data is expected to exceed the extra cost of the communication.

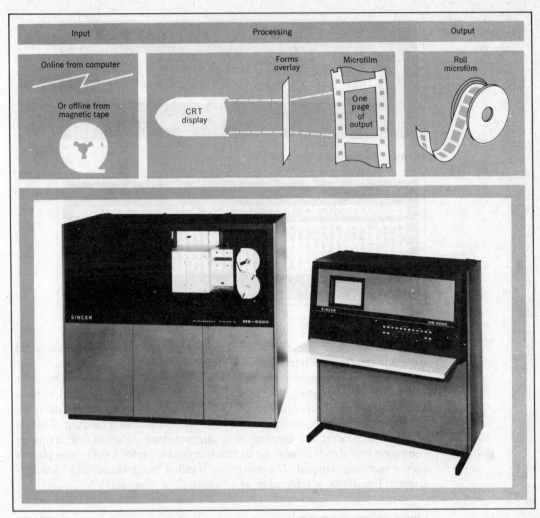

FIGURE 8-19 Computer output microfilm. (*Courtesy of Singer Company.*)

Data Transmission Data is transmitted by an electrical signal or wave form which is defined by the strength of the signal (*amplitude*) and its duration in time (*phase*). The *frequency* of a wave form is the number of times the form is repeated during a specified interval. These three characteristics are diagrammed in Figure 8-20. The signal is an analog or electrical equivalent of the communication input. If the basic shape of a wave form is known, a few measurements at selected time intervals (in other words, a sampling) provide the receiving instrument with enough data to identify the signals. In order to sample during the interval when a bit is transmitted, the receiving terminal must be synchronized with the sending terminal. The standard unit of signaling speed is a "baud," which is one pulse or code element per second.

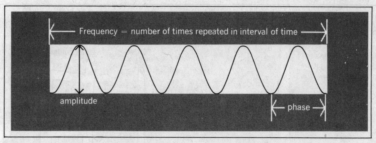

FIGURE 8-20 Diagram of waveform.

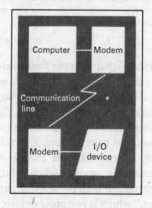

FIGURE 8-21 ASCII code.

The most important code used in data communications is the American Standard Code for Information Interchange (ASCII) (Figure 8-21).

A transmission medium is usually separated into many independent bands or data paths, each consisting of a range of frequencies assigned to it. Band width is an important consideration in data communications. This term refers to the range of frequencies accommodated within a band on a transmission medium. There is a device to convert the constant-level direct-current pulses of the computer equipment into signals suitable for transmission and to perform the reverse process for the receiving terminal. The conversion is called "modulation" and "demodulation." The device is referred to as a "modem" or "data set."

An electrical signal must be repeated or regenerated at intervals along the transmission medium to replenish its strength. The typical analog signal is amplified in whatever shape it is received. In other words, distortions are carried along the line. The newest technology is for a method of regeneration using digital logic which analyzes the signal received and creates a new, clean signal to send along the line. The communications network using this method is called a "digital transmission network." Because of the techniques used, transmission speed and quality are improved. Also, a modem is not required.

Communications Facilities

Some of the types of communications facilities are telephone and telegraph cables, radio, microwave, and satellite. Although under certain circumstances an organization may install its own communications facilities, most communication utilizes the facilities of the public telephone and telegraph companies, the largest of these in the United States being the American Telephone and Telegraph Company (Bell System) and Western Union. There are specialized common carriers which, in certain locations, offer only data communications facilities.

There are three modes of operation for communication facilities—simplex, half duplex, and full duplex.

Mode	Description
Simplex	Communication in only one direction. Used, for example, for a remote device which receives but does not send.
Half duplex	Communications in both directions, but in only one direction at a time.
Full duplex	Communications in both directions at the same time.

Service can be divided into three classes on the basis of band width. Band width determines the maximum transmission speed because the width of a band affects the frequency range that can be accommodated, and a high-frequency state provides for faster communication. The three classes of band width therefore represent three classes of capacity.

Class	Description
Narrow band (low speed)	Communication facilities capable of transmitting data in the range up to 300 bits per second. Typical speeds are 45, 57, 75, and 150 bits per second depending on service used. The Western Union TWX/Telex falls into this class.
Voice grade (medium	Channels used for human voice communications. Speeds range from 600 to 4800 bits

speed)	per second, although some higher speeds can be obtained.
Broad band (high speed)	Communication facilities having a higher band width than voice band width and therefore used for communication involving high data-transfer rates, say, 20,000 to 500,000 bits per second.

The services available to a user from the communications companies include leased lines or public switched lines (the term "lines" commonly refers to all types of communications facilities, even though they may use nonwire methods such as microwave). Leased lines provide users with a specific communications path dedicated to their use only. The switched line (also termed "dial-up"), on the other hand, provides access to the communications network. For the switched line, the path of connections and routing of a message may vary from use to use because the automatic switching equipment in the network selects a path from the many available connections and lines when the connection is dialed. The leased line is more expensive, but its quality is known, and it is available for use at any time. The switched line is less expensive, but it must be connected for each use (through dialing), and the quality of the connection may vary considerably from time to time.

The volume of data transmitted by a single terminal is never high enough to utilize the capacity of a voice-grade line. If several terminals are in use, they can share a single line through the use of a multiplexor. There are various approaches to multiplexing, but essentially the multiplexor divides the line into small segments and arranges the simultaneous transmission of data from a number of devices. A multiplexor at the receiving end reverses the process.

A relatively new concept in data communications services is a value-added network (VAN), also called "packet switching." Users of the service transmit data to a collection point where a minicomputer assembles the data into one or more segments (packets). An address for the destination is attached to each packet. Packets from many users going to diverse locations are transmitted through a high-quality leased line to another minicomputer which transmits each packet to its destination, after stripping off the address, etc., used in the switching. In other words, many users share a high-quality line. The concept can be extended to a network of lines.

Processing Data Communications

The communications carrier provides the transmission facilities. When multiplexors are used, they may be provided either by the carrier or by the user. When the transmitted signal reaches the user, there must be facilities to process it such as line protocol, communications processor, telecommunications access software, and a communications monitor.

The line protocol is associated with line control. If several lines come into a single computer, there are several methods of accepting messages. One method is for the terminal to send when ready and to interrupt the central processor in order for the message to be accepted; the other approach is for the computer to poll the devices (frequently but in turn) to see if there is a message to be accepted. A message generally consists of a heading and a text. The heading defines the terminal, the transaction code, priority, identification of sender, etc. The message has information separators for start of heading, start of the text to be transmitted, end of the text, and end of the transmission. The format of messages, the characters to use as separators, the control character sequence, etc., are the line protocol. There is no single standard line protocol. IBM has proposed a single protocol to be used in all its equipment. The overall communications network design is termed SNA (system network architecture) by IBM; the protocol is called SDLC (synchronous data link control).

Communications processors are small computers which are dedicated to the handling of data communications. They are also termed "front-end processors" because they handle all data communications functions, relieving the central processor of message control activities such as polling, character and message assembly, data code conversion, message editing, error control, message buffering and queuing, and message switching. Such activities can overload the central processor but can be handled by a small, but fast, minicomputer designed for the function. Most systems with significant data communications use a front-end processor.

Software packages, called "telecommunications access methods," are available for sending and receiving messages from terminals, addressing and polling terminals, queuing messages, message logging, system recovery, etc. Acronyms for the IBM packages are BTAM, QTAM, TCAM, and VTAM, with AM standing for access method and T for telecommunications. Other vendors offer similar software.

The management of data communications can become quite complex as the variety of requirements and equipment expands. A specialized software system may be required to handle the data communications and to manage the interface with other software. The data communications software, called a "data communications monitor," is a comprehensive package to manage a wide range of data communications functions.

Applications of Data Communications

Five examples will illustrate the use of data communications in computer processing.

Application	Comments
Data entry	Data is entered for processing via terminals at remote locations. The input data is transmitted (immediately or in a batch during off hours) to the computer over the communications network.
Inquiry processing	Each remote location has an inquiry device connected to the central computer. An example is an online reservation system in which any agent can use a remote device to interrogate the reservation file.

Time sharing

Shared use of a computer by each user having an input/output device connected via communications lines to the central computer, discussed further in Chapter 10.

Data collection

In data collection applications, data from a remote station is transmitted to a central processing facility. An example of data collection with data communications is a system which employs recording devices on the factory floor. When beginning a job, the worker inserts a plastic identification badge and a punched job card into a data collection device in the factory. The data collection device transmits this data to a central computer facility. When the job is completed, the worker repeats the process and keys in the actual number of units produced. By this means, data on the location of each job, job time, and amount produced in the shop is made known immediately to the central computer.

Message switching

An organization which has a number of widely separated locations will normally have a communications network to handle the transmission of messages from one location to one or more other locations. An efficient method of handling this message traffic is to have two-way communication between each remote location and a central message switching center with computer switching. The switching center receives messages, stores them, and transmits them to the designated receiving terminals.

SUMMARY

Data preparation activities (also termed "data entry") record transactions. These activities largely determine the quality of the data that is input to processing.

Data recording can be in a form not readable by machine, in which case the data must be transcribed. The major devices for offline transcription are card punches, keyboard to disk, diskette, or tape, and magnetic ink character encoders. The data may be initially recorded in machine-readable form. Examples are optical character or optical mark encoding, point-of-sales devices, and keyboard to paper tape devices. Data may also be entered via terminals. The data may enter processing immediately or be batched by the terminal or by the computer for subsequent processing. The terminals may be intelligent, performing validation and other functions, or nonintelligent, in which case the computer to which they are attached performs all processing during entry. Terminals are generally of three types: visual display units, teleprinters, and remote batch terminals.

In all but the simplest data processing system, the method for buffering between the input/output unit and the central processor is the data channel which, operating independently of the central processor, manages the transfer of data between the main storage and the input/output device. The data channel is started by an instruction from the central processor, which then proceeds to other processing steps. When the channel detects an error or when it is through with the transfer, it interrupts the central processor.

The chapter discussed two devices in some detail—card reader and line printer. Other input/output devices were discussed in less detail (card punch, graphic terminal, graph plotter, audio response, and computer output microfilm). Input/output devices which are secondary storage, such as magnetic tape and magnetic disk, are discussed in the next chapter.

Data communications are an important element in systems which provide input and output from remote locations. The chapter surveyed data transmission, communication facilities, processing of data communications, and applications of data communications in computer processing.

EXERCISES

1 Define the flow of data preparation activities for the following data entry technology:
   (a) Data is recorded on documents and keypunched. Processing is batch (periodic).
   (b) Data is typed onto machine-readable forms. Processing is batch (periodic).
   (c) Data is recorded on paper documents. Transcription is by online terminals. Processing is batch (periodic).
   (d) Data is entered into an intelligent terminal which transmits data each evening to a central computer where the batch is processed.
   (e) Data is entered via a terminal and processed immediately.
   (f) Data is handwritten on documents and then retyped in optical characters.

2 How are turnaround documents used? Trace the preparation, sending, turnaround, receipt, and processing of a turnaround document in customer billing.

3 Compare keypunches with keydisk devices. Under what conditions would each be suitable?

4 Explain the advantages or disadvantages of paper tape relative to punched cards as input/output media.

5 Define the conditions which suggest the use of:
   (a) MICR encoding   (b) Optical mark encoding   (c) Paper tape

6 A friend borrows one of your checks with MICR coding of account numbers, crosses out your account number, and writes his own. Assuming no further action to make changes, which of the following will happen? Explain.
   (a) Your account will be charged.
   (b) His account will be charged.
   (c) The MICR reader will reject the check.

7 What do the following letters, abbreviations, or acronyms stand for?
   (a) OCR   (c) I/O   (e) CRT   (g) RJE
   (b) MICR   (d) ASCII   (f) COM

8 Describe or explain the following with respect to terminals:
   (a) Difference between intelligent and nonintelligent terminals
   (b) The characteristics for deciding whether to use a visual display or a teleprinter
   (c) Remote batch terminal

9 Compare nonintelligent terminals and keydisk units for entering data for subsequent batch processing.

10 How can an audio response unit deliver a different message to each inquiry (say, inquiries are for current stock quotations)?

11 How does a remote batch terminal fit into the concept of distributed processing?

12 Define the role of each of the following in the input/output cycle:
   (a) Interrupt   (b) Data channel   (c) Device controller

13 Fill in the following table with alternative methods or processes (not all will have three alternatives).

Item	1	2	3
(a) Vertical spacing of paper on printer			

(*b*) Methods of accepting data communications message
(*c*) Printer mechanism for impact printing
(*d*) Sensing of punches on card reader
(*e*) Band widths in data communication
(*f*) Modes of operation for communications facilities
(*g*) Methods of optical character recognition
(*h*) Types of data communications lines

---

14 What difference does band width make for data communications?

15 With respect to data communications, define or explain:

(*a*) Protocol   (*e*) Packet switching
(*b*) Access method   (*f*) Band
(*c*) Communications monitor   (*g*) Interface
(*d*) Multiplexor   (*h*) Front-end computer

16 Diagram and explain the hardware and software for data communications involving:

(*a*) One terminal over a voice-grade line
(*b*) A variety of terminals at different locations

17 Under what conditions is a front-end computer desirable?

18 Describe uses for minicomputers in data preparation, input, output, and data communications.

19 An organization has large volumes of output. Describe how visual display terminals, computer output microfilm, and nonimpact printing may be used in system design to do the output.

20 Describe how a university can use optical and optical mark encoding to process grades.

CHAPTER

SECONDARY STORAGE AND COMPUTER DATA STRUCTURES, FILES, AND DATABASES

Data must be organized in some manner in order for processing to be feasible and efficient. Data items are organized into records. A collection of related records is termed a "file." Files are created when the need for a particular collection of records is recognized. This may necessitate obtaining new data from source documents, or it may involve a selection of records from existing files. A set of logically related data files is called a "database." The creation and maintenance of files and databases is the major factor in the workload of a computer information processing system. These files and databases are stored on secondary storage devices. In this chapter, secondary storage devices, data structures, file organization, file management, databases, and related topics are discussed.

Data Concepts and Data Organization

Data must be organized in order for processing to be feasible and efficient. There are four major levels of data organization: item, record, file, and database. This section describes item, record, and file; the database concept is explained later in the chapter.

Data Items   A *data item* describes some attribute of an object of data processing. For example, if the object of data processing is an employee, a data item may describe the attribute "name." Another data item may describe the attribute "age," a third may describe the attribute "social security number." Data items may form a hierarchical relation among themselves. For example, the attribute "date" is composed of three subitems: year, month, and day. These are termed "elementary items" because they have no subitems into which they can be divided.

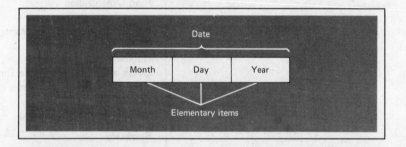

An item is sometimes termed a "field," but a field is the storage space on the physical data processing file medium, whereas the data item is what is stored there. This is most easily seen on a punched card. Sets of columns are defined as fields in which specified data items are punched.

Data items are of either fixed or variable length. For example, names and addresses vary considerably in the number of characters required, but two numeric digits will handle the age of any employee.

Records   Data items which relate to an object of data processing are combined into a record for that object. If the object of processing is a customer, items such as customer number, name, address, balance due, and credit rating form the record for the customer. Other examples are an employee record for payroll processing, a sales order record for sales order processing, and a parts record for parts inventory processing. Each record in the file is identified by a record identifier or record key. An employee account number, employee identification number, and a part number are examples of identifiers that could be record keys.

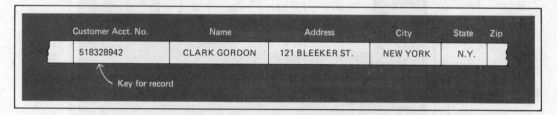

Customer Acct. No.	Name	Address	City	State	Zip
518328942	CLARK GORDON	121 BLEEKER ST.	NEW YORK	N.Y.	

Key for record

Each data item for a record occupies a field on the storage medium. The sum of the storage required by the various record fields is the storage required by the record. Records of a given type may be all the same length (fixed length) or may differ in length (variable length). There are two reasons that records differ in length (Figure 9-1).

1   The size of the fields required differs because the length of the data items varies among records. For example, names differ in length.

2   Some fields will not be present on all records, thereby reducing the size of the record.

In general, it is simpler to program for and to process fixed-length records, but the potential savings in storage space may offset the difficulties of variable-length records.

Where variable-length records are employed, a method is required to specify the length of variable-length fields (if used) and the variable length of the record. Two methods are encountered:

1   A length field is used. For example, a length field may be set as the first item on the variable-length record to specify the length (say, in characters) of the record.

2   A special symbol may be inserted as the last character in a data field or the last character in the record. The computer program reads the field or record until the termination character is sensed, thereby defining the end of the field.

Some records may be divided into two parts—a master portion containing relatively permanent data and detail or trailer portions. For example, an accounts

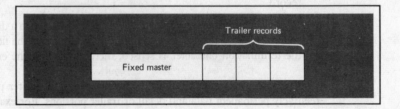

Two Reasons for Variable-Length Record

| Name | Age | Dept. | Rate | Soc. Sec. |

| Name | Age | Dept. | Rate | Soc. Sec. |

Variable length because of variations in item length

| A | B | C | D | E |

| A | C | E |

Variable length because of variation in items included

Two Methods for Specifying Variable Length

Item

| Item length | Name | Item length | Address |

Record

| Record length | |

Use of length field

Item

| Name | * |

Marks end of field or record

Record

| | * |

Use of termination character

FIGURE 9-1 Variable-length records.

receivable system which keeps track of individual invoices might have a master record portion containing fairly permanent customer data, such as name, address, and credit rating, plus several trailer records or repeating records, each containing data on an unpaid invoice.

Trailer records

| Fixed master | | | |

Blocks A *block* is the group of characters that are read or written with each read or write operation on the storage medium. For example, a single punched card is read or written with each operation, so the punched card is a block. A record is a concept related to items which logically belong together; a block relates the physical storage of data. Blocks are, in other words, the smallest unit of data moved from or to a physical file device. A block may contain part of a record, one record, or several records. Although blocks may be of variable length, it is usually convenient to have them of fixed length because the main memory area into which a block is read has to allow for the largest-size block that is going to be read by the application.

Files A collection of related records is called a *file* (also called a *data set*). Examples are a payroll file containing all employee records related to payroll and an accounts receivable file containing all customer records related to accounts receivable processing. Files are created when the need for a particular collection of records is recognized. This may necessitate obtaining new data from source documents, or it may involve a selection of records from existing files and restructuring them into a new file. The creation and maintenance of files is a major factor in the workload of a computer information processing system. Files are kept for a variety of purposes. Four main types are usually identified.

File Type	Purpose	Examples
Master file	Relatively permanent records containing statistical, identificational, and historical information. Used as a source of reference and for retrieval.	Accounts receivable file, personnel file, inventory file
Transaction file (also called "detail file")	Collection of records describing transactions by the organization. Developed as a result of processing the transactions and preparing transaction documents. Used to update a master file.	Sales invoice file, purchase order file, pay rate change file
Report file	Records extracted from data in master files in order to prepare a report.	Report file for taxes withheld, report file for delinquent customer accounts, report file for analysis of employee skills
Sort file	A working file of records to be sequenced. This may be the original or a copy of the transaction file, master file, or report file.	

The record key is used as the basis for sequencing and searching of files. The record key for this purpose can be numeric such as a social security number or alphabetic such as a name. More than one identification field can be used as a key, and therefore the same record may be sequenced on one key for one file and on another key in a second file. For example, a customer file for a department store might be sequenced on account number for processing of sales and customer payments, but by customer name in the file used by accounting personnel responding to customer inquiries.

Information Structures

An information structure defines the relation that data has for the user. For example, the user defines a person's last and first names as having an important relation to each other and the person's address as being related to his or her name. Information structures can be classified as hierarchic or associative (Figure 9-2). The *hierarchic structure* is one in which there is an inferior-superior relation. For example, the invoices in an accounts receivable file belong to a customer (the customer is the owner of the invoices), so the invoice records bear an inferior relation to the record of the customer who is to pay them. Each invoice may have line items which reflect merchandise the customer ordered and received. These line items are in an inferior (belong to) relation to the invoice. This hierarchic relation exists in many parts of the file. On the other hand, the term *associative structure* defines records as related if they have the same value for a data item. Examples are records for employees in the same department which have an associative relation because they all have the same department number, or records for employees which are related because the employees are all women.

In contrast to information structures, the file organization or file structure is the logical formatting of the file for storage purposes. It may be sequential, random, indexed, indexed sequential, etc. The major file organizations are described later in the chapter.

The distinction between physical storage relation and the logical relation among data records is important. The physical storage depends upon the storage medium that is used and the physical relationships that will make processing most efficient. The logical relations exist in the minds of the users and are not necessarily the same as the physical storage. For example, a file of customers for a department store may be physically stored in sequential order by customer account number. But a large number of logical relations can exist among the records in the file. The credit manager may think of the file as consisting of two associative groups: nondelinquent and delinquent customers. A marketing manager may visualize the data in terms of zip code areas where people live (especially if the store uses direct mail or other promotion that can be identified with zip code areas). The task of file organization is to create a file such that any logical relation can be converted into a physical relation for processing.

File Management

File management refers to all activities relating to the creation, updating, and use of files. These activities can be classed as:

1 File creation
2 File processing and maintenance
3 Selection (retrieval)
4 Extraction

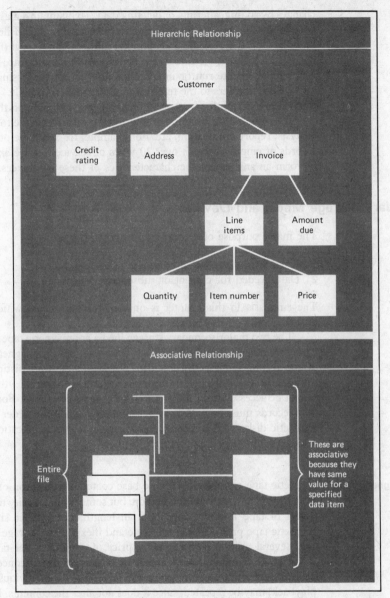

FIGURE 9-2 Information structures.

File creation can refer to the establishing of an entirely new file or the conversion of an existing file in noncomputer form to a computer file medium. The conversion of existing files is one of the difficult problems of converting to a computer system or from one computer system to another.

File maintenance is the updating of a file to reflect the effects of nonperiodic changes by adding, altering, or deleting data. To maintain a master file, new records are added and obsolete or erroneous records are removed. File processing, on the other hand, is the periodic updating of a master file to reflect the effects of current data, often transaction data in a detail file. File maintenance may be performed either in a separate run or in conjunction with file processing runs.

Selection refers to the retrieval of a record from the file. This search process can be very straightforward or quite complex, depending on the file organization.

Extraction is the copying of selected records from a file to form a new file for analysis, report preparation, etc. For example, from the file of all employees, the records of employees with over 20 years of service may be extracted in order to perform an analysis of the characteristics of these employees.

Secondary Storage Media and Devices

The major purpose of secondary storage is to store:

1 Programs or parts of programs not being executed
2 Data needed for current or subsequent processing

The emphasis in this chapter is on the storage of data which is grouped into records, files, and databases.

The two major secondary storage media are magnetic tape and magnetic disk. These are described in some detail. Other media such as magnetic drum, cartridge, extended core, and laser are described briefly. A significant distinction in secondary storage is access. A magnetic tape has serial access so that the nth record on the tape cannot be accessed until the first n-1 items have been read. For example, the first four records must be read one after another (serially) in order to access the fifth. Magnetic disks offer direct access because any storage location can be accessed directly without reading other locations.

Magnetic Tape Magnetic tape consists of a plastic base coated with an iron oxide coating. Tape measuring $\frac{1}{2}$ in. wide is most common, but some high-capacity tapes are 1 in. wide. A reel of tape is normally 2400 ft in length, but smaller sizes are also used. Magnetic tape provides very effective and inexpensive storage. A single tape can store several million characters at a price of about $15 per tape.

The recording of data on magnetic tape is similar in concept to a home tape recorder. Writing (recording) on the tape destroys the previous contents; reading (playback) may be repeated, since it does not alter the contents. For data recording purposes, the tape is divided into channels which run parallel to the edge of the tape. A single character (or part of a word) is encoded on a vertical frame or column. A typical nine-channel tape will contain four numeric bit positions, four zone positions, and the parity position (Figure 9-3). The older, less common seven-channel tape contains two zone positions instead of four. There is a read-write head for each channel.

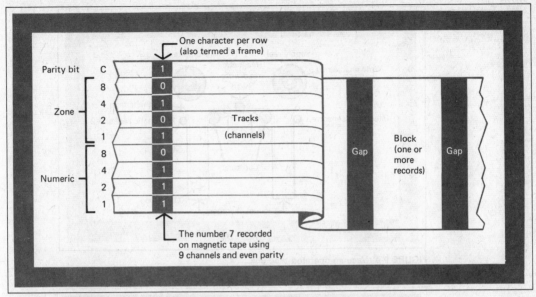

FIGURE 9-3 Recording of data on magnetic tape.

The *tape density* is the number of frames per inch of tape. The common nine-track densities are 800, 1600, and 6250 bits per inch. The older seven-track tapes use 200, 556, or 800 bits per inch. The effective transfer rate is the tape speed in inches per second (75, 125, and 200 are typical) times the density per inch. This is illustrated by a fairly slow, medium, and high speed tape unit:

Ranking	Tape speed, inches per second	Density	Transfer rate, thousands of bits per second
Slow	75	800	60
Medium	125	1600	200
High	200	6250	1250

Increasing the speed and density reduces the time that a frame will be under the read-write head and increases the need for precise positioning and timing. Rewind time is also a factor in tape processing. Tapes written on one model of a tape unit may not be able to be read on another model tape unit because of difference in channels, density, speed, recording method, etc. Where necessary, special tape-to-tape converters are available to handle this task.

Several methods, all quite similar, are used to drive the tape past the read-write heads and to permit starting and stopping the tape quickly. A vacuum-operated tape unit is illustrated in Figure 9-4. Figure 9-5 shows a tape read-write head.

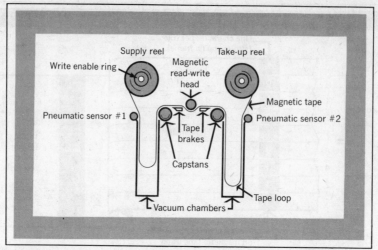

FIGURE 9-4 Vacuum-operated tape unit.

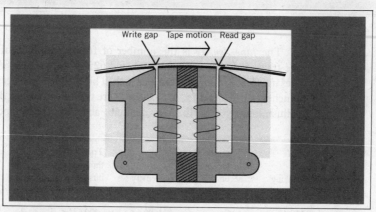

FIGURE 9-5 Two-gap read-write head.

Data records are written on a magnetic tape in a sequence determined by the record key. There is no tape address. When a record is to be found, the tape records are read serially, and the key for the record to be located is compared with the key of each record until there is a match.

Data is physically stored on the tape in blocks. The blocks are separated by an interblock gap. The most common gap length is .6 in. for 800 and 1600 bpi densities and .3 in. for 6250. The tape drive reads a block when a tape read instruction is given. The interblock gap allows the tape drive to detect the end of the block and also to accelerate to the speed required for reading and to decelerate after reading. Some magnetic tape units will read while the tape moves in the reverse direction as well as the forward direction.

The start and stop time associated with the end of a block means that reading time for a file is shortened if the blocks can be made as long as possible. One limit on size is the amount of memory space available for the block when it is read into the main storage. Several records may be put in the same tape block for tape read purposes (Figure 9-6). The capacity of a reel of magnetic tape is increased through blocking because long blocks with many records reduce interblock gaps compared with many short blocks (Figure 9-7).

The first record on a file of magnetic tape records is frequently a header label containing identification information about the file. The OPEN instructions for input files on magnetic tape will cause this header label to be read and perform

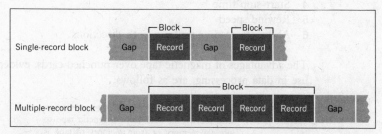

FIGURE 9-6 Blocking of records on magnetic tape.

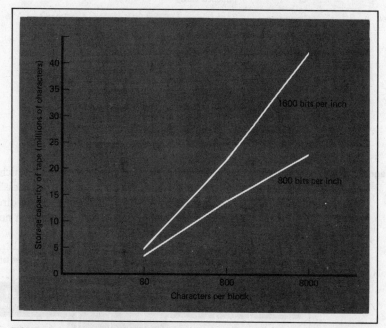

FIGURE 9-7 Storage capacity of magnetic tape as function of density and block size (2400-ft reel and interblock gap of 0.6 in.).

checking to make sure the file is the one called for by the program. When the OPEN instruction is used to open an output file on magnetic tape, it will write a standard header label record. The last record of the file may be a trailer label containing control information such as record count or control totals (Figure 9-8).

In comparison of the performance of tape units, the effective speed and capacity of the units depend on a combination of the following operating characters:

1 Tape density (characters per inch) ⎫
2 Tape speed (inches per second) ⎬ Define transfer rate
3 Size of interblock gap ⎭
4 Start-stop time
5 Rewind speed
6 Ability to read or write in both directions

The advantages of magnetic tape over punched cards, evidenced by its extensive use in data processing, are as follows:

Speed	The transfer of data from magnetic tape to internal memory or from memory to tape is performed at a much higher speed than with punched cards.
Convenience	Tape is more compact than cards and easier to handle.
Capacity	A single tape can hold several million characters. The equivalent of tens of thousands of punched cards may be stored on a reel of tape.
Low cost	A reel of magnetic tape (at about $15) costs less than the punched cards it can replace, and it is reusable.

Magnetic Disk A magnetic disk unit consists of rotating metal disks on which data may be stored. The disk unit is frequently referred to as "random access" or "direct access" storage because any storage position can be read or written directly without having to serially read other records. This direct access, although not strictly random in

FIGURE 9-8 Use of header and trailer labels.

access time, allows processing to be handled on unsequenced input data and without having to process any records not related to the transactions.

A magnetic disk file consists of a stack of disks rotating on a common shaft. There are from 5 to 100 disks measuring $1\frac{1}{2}$ to 3 ft in diameter. In appearance, the disk file suggests a stack of phonograph records (Figure 9-9). The disk units may be classed according to the number of read-write heads (or arms) and the removability of the stack of disks as follows:

1 Heads
   (*a*) Moving head (single head serves more than one track)
   (*b*) Fixed (head per track)
2 Stack
   (*a*) Fixed
   (*b*) Removable (disk pack)

The most common method in terms of numbers of units installed is the moving head with one arm per disk and a removable disk pack.

The access arm for a disk contains two read-write heads—one for the top and one for the underside of the disk. To read or write a record, an access arm must be positioned on the disk over the location to be used. The arm (if a moving head) moves in and out to locate itself in the correct spot. The heads float on a cushion of air 35 μ in. (microinches) from the surface (about one-fifth the height of a smoke particle or one-tenth that of a fingerprint). This closeness requires close alignment to avoid head crashes against the surface.

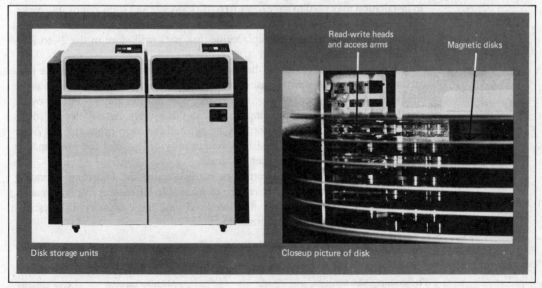

Read-write heads
and access arms

Magnetic disks

Disk storage units

Closeup picture of disk

FIGURE 9-9 Magnetic disk storage. (*Courtesy of International Business Machines Corporation.*)

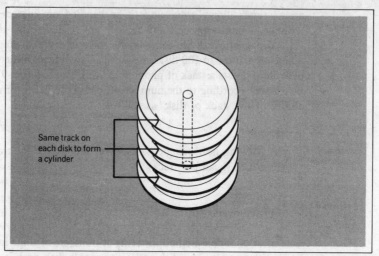

FIGURE 9-10 Accessing of a cylinder using a read-write arm for each disk.

All the arms in a moving-head disk move in and out together. When one arm is positioned over a track on one disk, the other arms are automatically positioned on the same track on all disks. These tracks are termed a "cylinder" (Figure 9-10). Some disk units are available with a read-write head for each recording track, an arrangement that eliminates arm movement altogether. Disk units can have fixed disks or portable, replaceable disk packs. Some system programs and some frequently used files are required to be available virtually all the time. For this reason, an installation may need to have some fixed disk storage and some removable packs. The storage capacity of units varies, but a fixed disk unit may store several hundred million characters, while each replaceable disk pack will store in the 2- to 200-million character range.

A single disk pack does not have sufficient capacity for large online file processing. The trend is toward the use of multiple-pack storage subsystems such as the one illustrated in Figure 9-9 storing between 800 million and 1.6 billion bytes.

Disk technology is also being applied in other ways. Small "floppy" disks about the size of a 45 RPM record are being used for microprograms and other functions. Small single disks are being used to provide low-cost and low-capacity online storage for small computer systems.

When comparing the performance of disk units, the following operating characteristics are important. There are considerable differences in performance, but some figures for commonly used medium- and large-capacity disk systems provide some idea of disk performance.

	PERFORMANCE	
Performance characteristic	Medium capacity	Large capacity
1 Access time, milliseconds	60	30

2	Storage tracks on each disk (also defines number of cylinders	200	400
3	Data transfer rate, bytes per second	312,000	806,000
4	Storage capacity per pack, millions of bytes	29–58	100–200
5	Maximum online storage in a subsystem, millions of bytes	233–466	800–1600

Storage with a capacity of a hundred million characters is capable of holding the written portion of 40 to 50 average textbooks, but due to the storage structures and technical requirements, not all available storage is actually used. The effective capacity is less than the theoretical capacity.

Data is stored in and retrieved from identifiable locations on a disk file. The locations are uniquely identified by an address consisting of disk face, track on the disk face, and perhaps sectors of the track (Figure 9-11). The block for disk reading

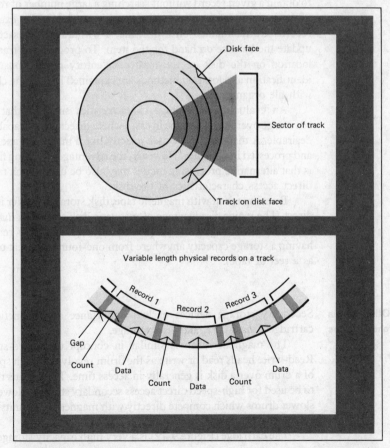

FIGURE 9-11 Disk file addressing.

and writing is typically either a sector, an entire track, or a portion of the track defined by a variable-length record.

The time to access a record in disk storage consists of the seek time and the rotational time.

1 *Seek time* This is the time required to position a movable read-write head over the recording track to be used. If the read-write head is fixed, this time will be zero.

2 *Rotational time* This is the rotational delay to move the storage location underneath the read-write head.

The seek time is much more significant than rotational time. Data on disk files is frequently organized to reduce the seek time.

A major system design and programming consideration with disk storage is the identification of the disk location of a record to be used in processing. In order to obtain a given record without searching a large number of records, some method of determining where a record is stored is needed. If, for example, the inventory records are maintained on a disk file, a withdrawal transaction will be used to update the balance on hand for the item. To process this transaction, the storage location on the disk on the master inventory record must be identified. The identification and location methods are explained later in the chapter in connection with file organization.

An evaluation of storage characteristics suggests that disk files have an advantage over magnetic tape in cases where direct access capabilities are needed or desirable. A disk file can be used exactly like a magnetic tape with records stored and processed in sequence. However, the advantage of having files on magnetic disk is that alternative processing modes may also be used which take advantage of the direct access characteristics of the disk.

By comparison with magnetic tape, disk storage transfer is faster and access is direct. The major disadvantage of magnetic disk storage is that disk files are more expensive than magnetic tape (about 20 times more for removable disk packs having a storage capacity anywhere from one-fourth as great up to about the same as a reel of tape).

Other Media and Devices Secondary storage devices of less importance are magnetic drums, magnetic cartridges, mass core, and laser storage.

The magnetic drum is similar in concept to a fixed-stack magnetic disk. Read-write heads read or write as the drum revolves at high speed. The advantage of a drum over a disk is generally in access time. This means that drums will tend to be used for high-speed direct access secondary storage. However, there are large, slower drums which compete directly with magnetic disk units and head-per-track disks which compete with drums.

The cartridge (Figure 9-12) is a very high capacity storage concept pioneered

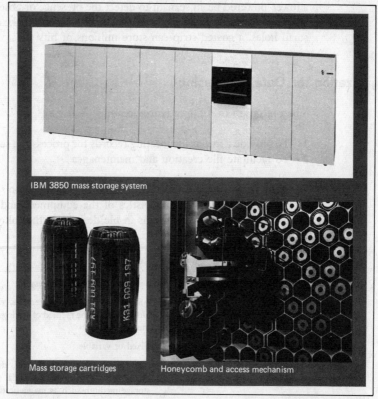

IBM 3850 mass storage system

Mass storage cartridges

Honeycomb and access mechanism

FIGURE 9-12 A cartridge mass storage system. (*Courtesy of International Business Machines Corporation.*)

by IBM (called by IBM the Mass Storage System). Data is stored on small individual rolls of wide magnetic tape housed in small cartridges. The cartridges are stored in cells in a honeycomb-like structure. Any cartridge can be retrieved and ready for use in a few seconds (say, 4 to 8 seconds). Up to 472 billion bytes can be placed online. This is equivalent to 4700 high-capacity disk packs or storage sufficient for more than 200,000 books of average length.

Core storage has many advantages for direct access because there is no movement of the storage medium, thereby eliminating a major source of operating delay and difficulty. However, core is more expensive than other media. Recent developments in fabrication of core storage have resulted in a large-capacity core storage unit for use as secondary storage. At present, use of core storage is limited to large-scale systems having a need for very high speed secondary storage.

Laser storage uses a coated strip as storage medium. A bit may be recorded by having a laser beam burn a tiny hole in the coating or by changing a magnetic field with the laser. For the laser hole technology there can be a hole for representing each bit location. Recording is permanent as with a punched card. To read the card, a lower-powered beam scans it to detect the presence or absence of a bit. Because laser beams can be positioned very accurately and can make and detect extremely small holes, a coated strip can store millions of bits.

File Organization for Data Processing

The objectives of a file organization are:

1 To provide a means for locating records for processing, selection, or extraction
2 To facilitate file creation and maintenance

In attempting to achieve its objectives, the file organization should be designed to take advantage of the characteristics of the equipment and the data processing system. Some key considerations in file design are the following:

Considerations	Comments
File storage access method	Serial access or direct access
File size	Affected by number of records, record size, block size, and the method of storing the data on the file medium
Item design	Fixed or variable
Cost of file media	Cost highest for direct fast access devices such as drum and disk, lowest for serial slow access storage medium such as magnetic tape
File maintenance processing and inquiry requirements	Frequent online updating and retrieval versus periodic processing
Need for a database	Database expands record sizes and increases complexity of file management
File privacy	Security provisions to restrict access and to restrict the making of changes to the file

The file organizations are divided, for the sake of explanation, into organizations used primarily in data processing applications and the list organizations especially applicable for information retrieval. The data processing organizations are sequential, random, indexed random, and indexed sequential.

Sequential File Organization In sequential file organization the records are stored physically in order by the record key. If, for example, the records are for employees and the key is employee payroll number, employee 475 will precede employee 476 on the physical file storage. Sequential file organization is very common because it makes effective use of the least expensive file medium—magnetic tape—and because sequential processing at periodic intervals using a batch of transactions is very efficient. For small data processing systems using punched cards, sequential organization is always used because of the difficulty of alternatives. A disk storage device can be used much like a magnetic tape. The data records are stored sequentially starting at some location so that the first storage location has the first record, the second storage location has the second, etc. If the first location is known, all subsequent locations are filled with data records very much like a magnetic tape. Sequential organization on a disk is often termed SAM for "sequential access method."

When a file is organized sequentially by record key and is accessed serially, there is no need to know specifically where any record is stored, only that it is in order by the sequencing key. Locating any particular record is performed merely by starting at the beginning of the file, reading each record, and comparing its key with the record which is being sought. Efficiency of processing thus requires that all transactions to be processed against a file should be organized in the same order as the file so that the first record on the file to be sought will be found first and the transaction which needs that record will be processed first, the second transaction will find its corresponding record next, etc. In this type of sequential processing using a serial access file, the entire master file is passed through the computer for any type of processing run involving transactions to be processed against the file (Figure 9-13). This is one reason it is desirable to hold transactions until a

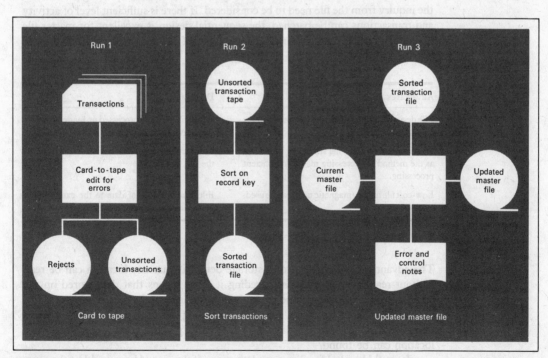

FIGURE 9-13 Runs to update a magnetic tape file from input transactions on punched cards.

reasonable sized batch can be processed. Sequential processing organization is therefore oriented toward periodic batch processing.

The efficiency of sequential organization in locating data required by inquiries depends on the type of inquiry. If the inquiry is for a specific record identified by its key, a serial file such as magnetic tape is searched from the beginning until the record is found. A disk file using sequential organization may search for a specific record by a binary search procedure. This is performed by going to the middle record in the file and comparing the key of that record with the key of the desired record. If the desired record is on the second half of the file, the search continues using only that half. The middle record of the half is examined, and the search then continues with the upper or lower half of that segment. This halving and comparison processing continues until the desired record is located. The binary search is quite efficient. For example, to locate a record with a given key out of 2000 records requires that only 11 records be accessed and compared. All requests involving selection criteria (such as customers living in Falcon Heights having incomes between $10,000 and $15,000) are processed by reading the entire file and checking each record to see if it matches the criteria. Because of the need to pass the entire sequential file to obtain a subset for processing, secondary files are sometimes maintained. The difficulty in using secondary files is in the extra work in updating them.

In evaluation of the sequential file organization, both the updating process and the inquiry from the file need to be considered. If there is sufficient level of activity and transactions can be batched, the sequential design is excellent for master file updating. The advantages and disadvantages of sequential organization when updating master files are the following:

Advantages	Disadvantages
File design is simple—locating a record requires only a sequence key.	Entire file must be processed no matter how low the activity rate.
If activity rate is high, the simplicity of the key as the method for accessing makes for efficient processing.	Transactions must be sorted in the same order as the file.
Low-cost file media (magnetic tape) can be used.	File is always out of date to the extent that a batch has not been processed.

Random File Organization

The advantage of a direct access storage device is that any location can be read without reading the locations preceding it. This means that data stored on the direct access file can be obtained directly if the address of the record is known. The problem of file organization for data processing using direct access storage is therefore how to store the data records so that, given a record key, its storage location can be found.

It would be ideal for direct random access if the record keys could be the same as the identification number for the disk storage locations, but this is almost never the case, and therefore other means must usually be found. Stated another way, the task is to take a set of record keys and map them into a set of disk storage location identifiers. If the record keys ran sequentially with no gaps, this might be a fairly simple matter, but such a condition almost never exists. In addition to gaps, many identification codes are not sequential because they are designed to be significant, such as showing territory or product line.

Because of the infeasibility of making a simple transformation, other methods must be used. The most common arithmetic procedure to transform the record key into a storage address is termed "randomizing" because transformation of the nonsequential numbers to a range of storage addresses is based on the uniform distribution of random digits. If, for example, 100,000 storage locations are to be assigned and the occurrences of the digits 0 to 9 in each position of the storage addresses are tallied, there will be 10,000 1s, 10,000 2s, etc. Therefore, a procedure which takes part of or all the record identification number or record key and produces a random number will generate storage addresses falling somewhat uniformly in the range of the assigned storage identifiers. This procedure is also called "hashing."

The best-known and most frequently used technique for producing addresses by randomizing is division of the key by a positive integer, usually a prime number. The remainder obtained from the division becomes the address locator. The prime-number divisor is usually chosen to be approximately equal to the number of available addresses. There are additional methods, but all attempt to do the same thing—to generate a set of addresses which will map the keys into the storage area as uniformly as possible.

A major difficulty with the randomizing procedure is that some addresses will never be generated, whereas two or more record keys may produce identical disk addresses (synonyms). This is also called a "collision." In that event, one of the records is stored at the generated location with the synonym being stored in an overflow location. The overflow can be handled in one of several ways.

1 The overflow record can be stored in the first available location following the location where it should be found. On any retrieval for which the desired record is not in the location specified, the procedure is to search succeeding locations until it is found.

2 A special data item field in each record points to (identifies) the address of the first overflow record for which the same address was generated. If a third synonym was produced, the overflow address linkage for it is put in the second record, etc. When retrieving a record, the program examines the program at the key-generated address. If it does not have the same key, the program looks at the pointer field and goes to the overflow location for the record.

3 Special overflow areas are used. If the record is not found at the generated address, the program goes to the overflow area which is searched sequentially until the record is found.

Overflow becomes a severe problem if most of the storage locations are used. If, say, 50 percent of the locations are used, overflow is generally not a problem; if 80 percent of the locations are used, overflow will usually become quite large, and this can increase substantially the average number of accesses to locate a record. In this and other disk-addressing methods, it is frequently desirable to have the basic method of obtaining an address refer to a bucket instead of a single record location. A group of records is stored in the bucket, which is then searched sequentially to find the appropriate record. The use of buckets increases storage utilization, and the sequential search of a block or bucket is not typically a substantial hinderance to processing efficiency when compared with the increased use of storage and the reduction in overflow records.

The advantages of the random storage approach arise primarily in situations where the records need to be located randomly and quickly as in online inquiry and online updating. If a random organization file is to be processed sequentially, it would generally need to be copied onto another file and sorted into sequential order. The random approach is often termed "direct access method" or "basic direct access method" (BDAM).

Indexed Random File Organization

Instead of attempting to locate addresses by randomizing, separate indexes may be maintained in which the address of the record being sought is found. Indexes are frequently in order by record key, thereby allowing the index to be searched either sequentially or by a binary search process to locate the address of a record. In some cases, a sequential index is not desirable, and an indexed organization may be created using a tree index.

A tree index consists of the key of a record, a left branch address, and a right branch address. When the file is created, the first record is placed in the first position in each index. The key of the second record to be stored is compared with the first record key. If its key is greater, the right branch of the first record points to the second index address. If it is less, the left branch index address of the first record is set to point to the second address. When the third record is added, it is referenced as being one part of the tree (see Figure 9-14). The result looks much like a tree and is therefore called a "tree structure."

When searching for a record with the tree index, the search starts at the beginning of the file index and by means of a comparison branches through the tree until the desired index is located. The resulting tree search can be reasonably efficient. The storage is efficient since there is a high packing density.

Indexed Sequential File Organization

Indexed sequential file organization is essentially a compromise between sequential access and random access methods. It is often referred to as ISAM for "indexed sequential access method." The records are stored on the disk sequentially by record key so that sequential processing may be performed, but indexes are also maintained to allow direct retrieval based on a key value.

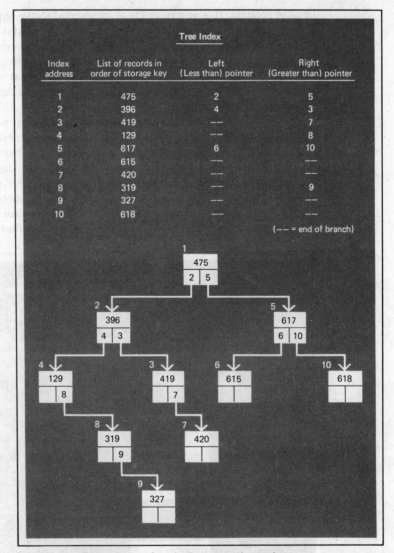

Tree Index

Index address	List of records in order of storage key	Left (Less than) pointer	Right (Greater than) pointer
1	475	2	5
2	396	4	3
3	419	—	7
4	129	—	8
5	617	6	10
6	615	—	—
7	420	—	—
8	319	—	9
9	327	—	—
10	618	—	—

(—— = end of branch)

FIGURE 9-14 Tree indexing of randomly organized records.

In order to directly access a particular record with ISAM, the index is searched and the key is located which then provides the address for access. Note that even though the file is sequential, it can be updated with transactions in random order because the index may be used for directly locating a record for updating. If the file is to be processed sequentially, the index need not be used. In updating the file, the records to be updated are read, updated, and written back in the same location. If a new record is to be inserted in the sequence, completely reordering the file is inconvenient. The record to be inserted is placed in a special overflow area, and a special indicator is placed in the record occupying the location immediately preceding the location where the record will be inserted to indicate the address of the missing record in the sequence. A record that is deleted leaves an empty space. Periodically the file is reorganized to eliminate the overflow addressing and the empty locations.

The indexed sequential organization may be modified slightly to assist in sequential ordering, yet to allow for easy insertions into the file without frequent reorganization. A common method is to arrange records in blocks or buckets with the index referencing the block number. This reduces the size of the index but means that once the block is located the block must be searched sequentially. Since the block is usually small, such a search is not a serious processing impediment. Blocks are organized with extra locations so that the records may be added or deleted from the block without reorganizing the rest of the file (Figure 9-15). It is

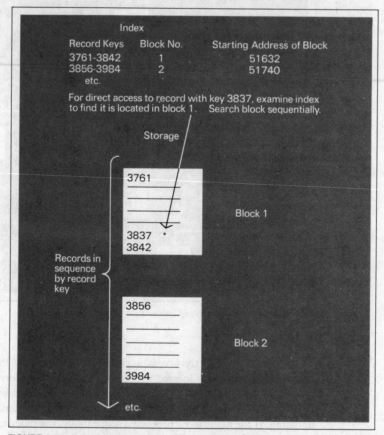

FIGURE 9-15 Indexed sequential organization using blocks.

generally desirable to use special index sequential software to build the file and indexes and to update and reorganize. Such software is available from both the hardware manufacturers and independent software vendors.

Indexed sequential organization is very popular for direct access storage files because it combines the best features of sequential organization with features of direct access by means of the index. Disadvantages are the extra storage requirements caused by the need to allow for insertions to the file, the extra storage for the indexes, the extra processing required in using indexes, and the need to periodically reorder the file.

Selecting a File Organization

In summary, the use of a serial access medium such as magnetic tape for file storage requires sequential organization for efficient processing; direct access media allow sequential, random, indexed random, and indexed sequential organization. The file medium can therefore be a constraint in the organization chosen. The serial access approach to sequential batch processing requires the entire file to be passed, so that by comparison with direct access, it is inefficient to process in the batch-oriented sequential manner if there are few transactions. However, rarely will all records in the file be active. In most files of any size, a 10-percent activity rate (transactions affecting 1 of 10 master records) represents a substantial level of activity. Two major factors in deciding on a file organization are therefore whether processing is to be periodic on batches of data or immediate on single transactions and, if performed on batches of data, the activity rate of updating.

Other considerations in selecting a sequential or nonsequential organization are concurrent processing of files, sorting requirements, and file integrity. One of the processing economies achieved in direct access processing is the concurrent processing of several files. When a sale is recorded, the account receivable can be posted, the inventory withdrawal written, etc., at the same time. In sequential processing using, for example, magnetic tape, this would require several different runs. Nonsequential or random organizations of the file allow processing to be performed on data which is not sequenced. Transactions which update the file or inquiry transactions requiring file access can be handled in random order as the transactions are received.

In processing a transaction against a random organization using a direct access file, the record to be altered is copied from direct access storage, updated, and then written back in the same location (Figure 9-16). This replaces the prior contents of the location. If the updating was in error, the record prior to updating is no longer available. This is in contrast to the approach of creating a whole new file when using serial access and rewriting. Especially in online processing, the direct access file is exposed to the risk of incorrect updating. Special backup and reconstruction must therefore be provided.

Random organization allows for rapid access to a record. However, it requires extra processing time to obtain the address (if address is derived or obtained from an index). Unlike a sequential organization which can fill all locations, the random organizations tend to not use all locations. Randomizing techniques cannot com-

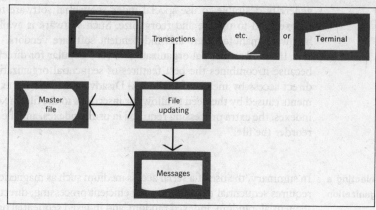

FIGURE 9-16 Direct access processing.

pletely pack the file, and the use of overflow locations increases the average access time. The file must be reorganized periodically to reduce overflow and to eliminate records to be dropped from the file.

The major criteria for selecting among the nonsequential access methods are speed of access (random is usually best), packing of storage (random is worst), ease of meeting processing needs (indexed sequential supports sequential output better than other methods), and level of difficulty and frequency in building and reorganizing the file, given the applications using the files.

List Organizations for Information Retrieval

The problems of access are most severe in information retrieval applications, and an alternative to sequential or random organization is to use some form of list organization. In a list organization, relations among records are established by pointers so that there need be no special physical organization of the file. The use of pointers allows different logic organizations to be established without regard to the actual physical arrangement. A pointer in a record consists of a data item (occupying a field) which gives the address of another record. If the file is on a disk, the pointer to a record is the disk address of that record. There may be many pointers in a record because many different relations may need to be established. List organizations are methods for building structures with the pointers. The most common are simple lists, inverted lists, and ring organizations.

Simple-List Organization   In a simple list an entry in an index points to the first record. The first record in the list points to the second logical record, the second logical record points to the third, etc. The last record in the logical sequence contains a special symbol in the pointer field (Figure 9-17). This is also termed a "threaded list." The sequence of

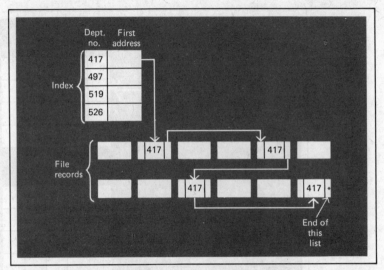

FIGURE 9-17 Simple list.

the physical records is not important because the pointers are specifying the logical relation. For example, in order to establish a logical file involving all employees by department, an index is established with the different department numbers and a corresponding entry into the first employee in the file belonging to that department. If the employees in department 417 are to be read, the search begins with entry for 417 in the department index which has a pointer to the first employee in the department. The first record for department 417 will point to the next record which contains an employee working in department 417, etc. A record can be a part of several logical files because there can be many pointers in the same record.

The updating of a list by inserting a record requires that the pointer of the preceding logical record be changed. If a record has multiple pointers, deletion of the record requires that all pointers be revised. If there are only single, forward pointers, there is no method for going backward in the list to revise the prior pointers. Merely by inserting backward pointers which point to the preceding record, it is possible to insert or delete records easily. This also allows the list to be searched in either direction.

Inverted-List Organization

The list concept of the simple list may be extended. For example, a fairly comprehensive list of characteristics may be established as an index with a pointer to the first record in the file which has that characteristic and with pointers from each such record to the next record having the characteristic. Whereas a sequential file can be thought of as being accessed only through the record key, a full set of characteristics would allow the file to be accessed through any characteristic. The file is then said to be "inverted." In other words, all indexing is by content rather than by record key (Figure 9-18).

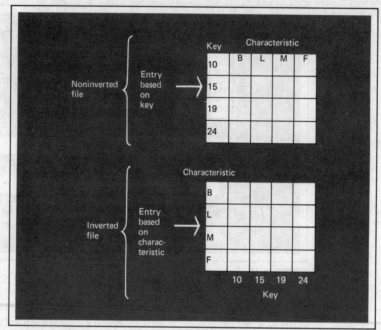

FIGURE 9-18 Inverted file.

The index in an inverted list may be expanded to include a list of all records having a specified characteristic. The pointers are then dropped from the records because the index has the complete list (Figure 9-19). In other words, in a file of personnel at a university all the people born in 1930 will be listed by record identifier following the characteristic "born 1930." This allows searching of the index for the content which is to be found in the file, rather than having to search the file itself. Since the fully inverted file makes every data value available as a basis for search and retrieval, it is excellent for information retrieval applications, especially where the retrieval requirements cannot be specified in advance. The disadvantage is that the index for a fully inverted file will be quite large, and a somewhat modified form is usually the most practical approach for day-to-day use.

A problem in an inverted list is how to efficiently store the list or directory of records containing each characteristic. There is generally no way to determine the length of the list prior to its creation, and the length of the list can change as the data changes. For example, if an attribute in the index is sex—say, male—a company with all male employees would list every single employee record as belonging to this list.

Ring Organization   A ring organization is a list which has pointers going both forward and backward. The first record is an index record which specifies the nature of the ring, and the

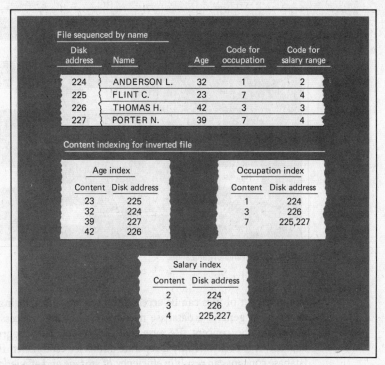

FIGURE 9-19 Use of content indexes for inverted files.

last record in the list points to the first. This allows retrieval to proceed from any record, either backward or forward, until the entire list has been examined.

This is a very useful organization because it provides a facility to retrieve and process all the records in any one ring while branching off at any or each of the records to retrieve and process other records which are logically related. For example, a retrieval request may involve injured employees. When one is found, the next question is, "Who does he or she work with?" This question is answered by taking the pointer for department number and following the list through all employees who are part of that same list until the ring brings the list back to the originating record (Figure 9-20).

Database Concepts and Management

A database is a set of logically related files organized in such a way that access to the data is improved and redundancy is minimized. There can be several databases to reflect several logical groupings of files. The database concept is made operational by a database management system, a software system which performs the functions of creating and updating files, retrieving data, and generating reports. All

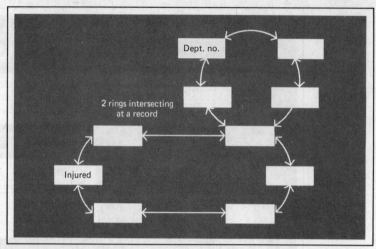

FIGURE 9-20 Ring organization.

data in the set of files can be accessed by any program having the right to use the database. In general a database needs to be on direct access storage in order to implement the concept. Because many different user programs may access the database, it is controlled by a separate authority established for this purpose. The database concept can result in efficiency of storage and efficiency in processing. The efficiency of storage stems from the elimination of redundant files. If each application has its own file, there will be many applications that will be essentially duplicating files. The efficiency of processing arises not only because of the reduction in file storage but also because logically related data items which might otherwise be maintained in separate files are now found in a single file and the processing can take advantage of this fact. A single updating will update an item for all processing applications which use that item, thus reducing the inconsistencies and errors which often occur among separate files. The database reduces the necessity for sorting, comparison, and merging which are often required if separate files are maintained and then merged for interrelated processing. It improves efficiency for retrieval of information because all the files are found logically related in a single place. Two major concepts connected with database are the schema and the database administrator.

Schema The *schema* is a definition of stored data, i.e., it describes the database. Essentially one can think of the schema as a dictionary which describes all the data items in terms of entry type, length, name, etc. The schema is written in a data definition language which describes the data and logical relations between data entities. The schema is thus a comprehensive directory of all data items in the file. It is convenient to have two types of schemas—the conceptual schema which describes the logical structure of the database and an internal schema which defines the physical structure of the database.

In a large database the schema can include a substantial number of items. Any application program will, however, use only a small subset of the items on the database. The subset is described by a user schema or subschema (also termed an "external schema"). The subschema is essentially a description of the items that are to be used in an application program. A programmer writing an application program therefore describes the data which he or she needs by a subschema. The subschema must be compatible with the schema, but it need not be concerned with the physical storage. For example, a schema may have a large record with many fields for each employee. A program requiring only two of the items, say, pay rate and age, defines a subschema for only these two items. The binding of the subschema to the schema is done by the software system and need not concern the application programmer.

The *data manipulation language* (DML) is a language (also called a "database command language") which the programmer uses to transfer data between the program and the database. A DML statement will be a mixture of a host language such as COBOL and special database instructions.

The consequence of the concept of database management and schema/subschema is to remove the database from the control of the individual programmer. All uses of the database must be handled through the database management software. This allows the integrity and security of the database to be under better control than if all programs were allowed to operate directly. Also the individual programmer no longer need be concerned with the physical records. The programmer works with only logical records defined by the user schema.

Database Administrator

The concept of the database which is independent from the application programs and is not available to the application programmers except on a controlled basis means that someone must exercise control. This person is known as a "database administrator." In other words, a function is required to manage and control the database in order to preserve its integrity, maintain its definition, and prevent unauthorized usage or change.

One of the major problems of a database is security. When, for example, there were separate files for different programs, security could be maintained merely by physical security over the files. A program not needing a file would not call for it. In the database approach, a substantial amount of data is collected for use by a variety of programs, some of which are not authorized to access all the data.

The database administrator has responsibility for the database. This means that he or she has responsibility for the schema and exercises validity and access authority for subschemas. The administrator's activities include defining and organizing the database, providing for protection of it, and preparing documentation of it.

**Users and
Suppliers
of the Database**

The persons who are affected by the database are its users and suppliers. The users are those who program applications utilizing the database for persons in the organization who desire information. The suppliers are those who must provide input for storage into the database.

The supplier of the data for the database will find that there is greater emphasis upon integrity of the input data than when only individual applications were involved. The effects of an error can now affect much of the organization, whereas formerly individual files could often be in error without affecting the rest of the organization. For example, the personnel file could be in error without affecting the payroll processing. The measures for data integrity will therefore be measurably strengthened when a database is used and a database administrator enforces the data quality standards.

When individual parts of the organization maintain data files, the amount of quality control over the data is connected with the use to which it is put by that part of the organization. However, with the database and database administrator the level of data integrity must suit organization-wide objectives rather than the needs of an individual organizational unit. In other words, the database is viewed as an organization-wide resource. The centralization of data requires a well-conceived plan governing the development of the database and access to the data. Some users may notice the need for formal security codes and formal procedures for establishing the right to access data.

The users of data will find that the directory issued by the database administrator provides substantially enhanced knowledge of the data resources in the organization. The ability to perform analysis will be considerably improved both by a greater knowledge of data availability and by the retrieval capabilities and report generation capabilities of the database software. These capabilities are generally available to both programmers and nonprogrammers.

The programmer, in using the database, will find that many of the tasks formerly done need not be performed. The data administrator will arrange for such matters as security, backup, and data integrity. All the physical problems of the storage will be separated from the programmer. At the same time, the programmer is restricted in what can be done to the data. The programmer can extract any data for which his or her program has valid security access but cannot alter fields in the data without permission from the data administrator.

**Data Management
Systems**

A data management system enables a user to create and update files; to select, retrieve, and sort data; and to generate reports. Data management systems are an extension of prior concepts in software. In first-generation computers, the programmer was required to write in machine-oriented code, and all functions had to be written for each program. It was soon found that many functions could be generalized and used by all programmers. This was especially true of input/output functions, and so macro instructions were added to assembly languages so that the individual programmer did not have to write the input/output code. Other functions soon became generalized, such as sorting and report generation, and this software is found as part of the generalized software support for a data processing installation. The data management system is an extension of these ideas to the management of the files of an organization. There are two types of data management systems—file management systems and database management systems. The difference between the two is in their scope. The file management system handles individual files, whereas the database management system has the capability for managing an entire database as well as an individual data file.

Two different approaches are used in database management systems. One is the self-contained system which has its own language with which to write programs to retrieve data, etc.; the other is the host language system in which the database management system provides an interface to programs written in a high-level language such as COBOL. Early systems were usually of the self-contained variety, while later systems favor the host language design. Both approaches provide a convenient user inquiry and report preparation capability.

A number of data management systems are available. Each computer manufacturer offers one (generally as extra-cost software); in addition, a number of data management systems are provided by software vendors. Some examples of data management systems in use are:

FILE (DATA) MANAGEMENT		DATABASE MANAGEMENT	
Name	Vendor	Name	Vendor
MARK IV	Informatics MARK IV Systems Co.	TOTAL	Cincom Systems, Inc.
EASYTRIEVE	Pansophic Systems, Inc.	IMS	IBM
DYL-260	Dylakor Software Systems	DL/I	IBM
CULPRIT	Cullinane Corporation	ADABAS	Software AG
SCORE	Programming Methods	System 2000	MRI Systems, Inc.
		IDMS	Cullinane Corporation

Substantial reductions in the time required to program file maintenance and report functions have been reported by installations using data management systems. The newer data management systems continue to improve in generality, flexibility, and quality. These systems are an important element in the trend in processing systems design to greater data independence, more powerful but simpler-to-use languages for data access, and improved operating performance.

Sorting for File Processing

Sorting is an important data processing activity requiring a significant part of the data processing time. Transactions are sorted for three reasons, all related to efficiency:

1 Efficiency in processing
2 Efficiency in distribution of output
3 Efficiency in subsequent retrieval

Transactions may need to be sorted for ease of processing if the processing involves reference to files or involves file updating. Although never required in the absolute sense, sorting of transactions into the same order as the reference or master file is for all practical purposes required for files accessed serially (such as files on magnetic tape). Sorting into the file sequence is sometimes required and often done for improved processing efficiency when the reference or master files are on direct access devices.

Sorting of output for distribution is important both for efficiency and control in distribution. Some examples illustrate this need:

Paychecks are processed in order by employee number but are distributed to each department for issuance. Before the checks are printed, the transaction file is sorted so that the checks are printed in order by department. Control totals and employee counts for control over payroll check distribution are based on departmental employee counts, etc.

Customer statements of amounts due are prepared from a file organized by customer account number. The mailing of the bills requires that they be sorted into zip codes. Before the customer statements are printed, the output file must be sorted by zip codes.

Copies of customer statements are filed for reference purposes on computer output microfilm. Depending on the requirements, this reference output may need to be in customer number order or alphabetical order.

Sort routines are provided as part of the software furnished by the manufacturer, so that individual installations need not write the sort programs. The sort routine is used by specifying the key on which the file is to be sorted, the record length, and similar characteristics. There are a number of different algorithms for sorting. The discussion on sorting will use magnetic tape and simple merge sorting as the example.

There are two steps in merge sorting a tape file. The first is establishing the initial sorting strings, and the second is the merging of these strings into a single, sequenced string. A *string* is a group of records which has been sequenced. The merging process will be explained first.

Two strings sequenced on a key can be merged into a single, sequenced string by looking at the keys of only two records at a time. In other words, no matter how long the two strings, only the next record from each string needs to be in main memory for the sort comparison. This merging of strings is illustrated in Figure 9-21 for two strings of four records.

The two merging strings come from two different input magnetic tape units, and the merged string that results is written on one of two output tapes, alternating

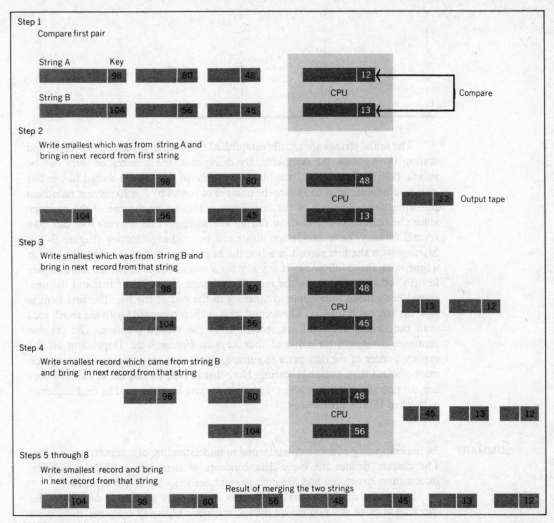

FIGURE 9-21 Merging of two strings.

between the output tapes. When the input tapes have been read, the output tapes become input for the next merge. Suppose there are 15,360 records to be sorted and there are 512 initial strings each 15 records in length; the number of passes, string length, and number of strings are shown below.

Pass number	String length at end of pass	Number of strings on each output tape
1	30	256
2	60	128

3	120	64
4	240	32
5	480	16
6	960	8
7	1920	4
8	3840	2
9	7680	1
10	15,360	1 on final tape

The initial strings are usually established by reading in a group of records and sorting them inside the computer. By doing this, the number of sorts can be substantially reduced. For example, in the case of the 15,000-record file, initial strings of 60 instead of 15 reduce the number of passes by 2, a 20 percent reduction in sorting time. The size of the initial sort is limited by the size of the memory since the records are held there during the sorting. The internal sort can take several forms. The methods are illustrated by exchange sorting (Figure 9-22). Starting with the first record in a list, the key of that record is compared, one at a time, with those following. If any key for a record lower in the list has a higher key (for an ascending sort), the records exchange places in the list, and the new record key is used to continue comparing to the end of the list. The first item is now the largest in the list. The second item is then compared with the third, etc., until the largest key (with its record) is in the second position. The process continues as shown for a list of four keys in Figure 9-22. Depending on the expected order of the data prior to sorting, alternative sorting algorithms may be more efficient than exchange sorting. Note that in tape sorting the key length does not, for practical purposes, affect the length of time for the sort. The final sequence is checked by the final merge.

SUMMARY An understanding of data is fundamental to understanding of computer processing. The chapter defines the basic data concepts of item, record, block, and file. Information structures and file management activities were also explained.

Secondary storage media and devices are used for storage of data files. The characteristics of the two major media, magnetic tape and magnetic disk, were

FIGURE 9-22 Exchange sorting.

described in some detail; other devices and media were surveyed. The distinguishing difference between magnetic tape and magnetic disk is record access. Access to records on magnetic tape is serial; for magnetic disk, it is direct. Most of the advantages and disadvantages stem from this difference.

The organization of files affects both storage requirements and speed of processing. It is convenient to separate the file organizations used primarily in processing applications from the list organizations required for efficient information retrieval. Four data processing organizations were explained—sequential, random, indexed random, and indexed sequential. Three list organizations were described—simple list, inverted list, and ring structure.

A database is a set of logically related files organized to improve access and minimize redundancy. The database is maintained independently of the applications programs. The database is described by various schemas—an overall schema and various user schemas (or subschemas) to define the data for individual applications. A database administrator controls the database and the procedures for access.

Data management software aids in file management and in retrieving data from files. A database management system manages a database. It provides capabilities for creating and updating the database, selecting data, generating reports, etc. It is required for effective implementation of the database concept.

Sorting is a fundamental operation for data processing. In this chapter, a basic approach to sorting was explained using magnetic tape as an example.

EXERCISES

1 Define the following terms:
   - (a) Data item
   - (b) Record
   - (c) File
   - (d) Block
   - (e) Database
   - (f) Information structure
   - (g) Master file
   - (h) Transaction file
   - (i) Sort file
   - (j) Pointer

2 Explain and contrast the following pairs of terms:
   - (a) Item and field
   - (b) Logical files and physical files
   - (c) Record and block
   - (d) Serial access and direct access
   - (e) Fixed length and variable length
   - (f) Hierarchic and associative data relationships

3 Explain how a variable item design affects storage and processing requirements.

4 Take the first name on each page of the telephone book for the first hundred pages and calculate the relative advantage of a variable-length name field over a fixed-length name field. Assume a field size item to indicate length for the variable approach.

5 A processing job involving 2000 records of a maximum length of 300 characters is to be processed once a month. The fields vary in length. Should the item size be fixed or variable? Explain. Would your answer change if there were 20,000 records of 1000 characters maximum and 100 characters minimum?

6 Define each of the following with respect to magnetic tape processing:

(a) Interrecord or interblock gap
(e) Density
(b) Blocking
(f) Transfer rate
(c) Header label
(g) Address
(d) Trailer label
(h) Record key

7 Define each of the following with respect to disk processing:

(a) Track
(e) Stack
(b) Sector
(f) Index
(c) Face
(g) Address
(d) Cylinder

8 What types of storage devices are likely to be used under the following circumstances:

(a) A small retailer using punched card billing forms
(b) A manufacturer interested in up-to-the-minute inventory status information
(c) A large credit-granting agency with need for rapid access for active accounts and slower-speed access to other accounts
(d) A large retailer sending out monthly bills

9 Explain the way a record is located on:

(a) Magnetic tape file
(b) Disk file

10 Compute the number of 80-column punched card records that can be stored on a magnetic tape that is 2400 ft long and uses gaps between blocks as follows:

(a) One record per block:

(1) 800 bytes-per-inch density (.6-in. gap)
(2) 1600 bytes-per-inch density (.6-in. gap)

(b) Ten records per block for both 800 and 1600 bytes per inch.

11 Figure 9-7 is based on nine-channel third-generation equipment. Prepare data on older equipment with a .75-in. gap and densities as follows:

	BLOCK SIZE		
Density	80	800	8000
200			
556			

12 Complete the table of effective transfer rates in characters (bytes per second) for the following (assuming tape speed of 125 inches per second):

	DENSITY (BYTES PER INCH) AND INTERBLOCK GAP (INCHES)		
Block size in characters (bytes)	800/.6	1600/.6	6250/.3
80			
800			
8000			

The basic formula is:

$$\left.\begin{array}{l}\text{Transfer rate}\\\text{(in bytes per}\\\text{second)}\end{array}\right\} = \text{bytes per inch} \times \text{tape speed (in inches per second)}$$

But the effective transfer rate must take into account the gap which requires time to read but has no data. Calculate an effective total of bytes per inch to use in the above formula as follows:

$$\text{Effective bytes per inch} = \frac{\text{block size in bytes}}{(\text{block size/bytes per inch}) + \text{gap (inches)}}$$

13 A company has 190,000 records on magnetic tape, one record per block. Each record is 60 characters. The tape is 2400 ft, the density is 800 bpi, and the interrecord gap is .6 in. By packing 10 records in a block, the number of tapes will be reduced from _____ to _____ (show your computations).

14 Assuming a cost of cards at $1.50 per 1000, a cost of tape at $15, 80-character records, .6-in. interblock gap, and 800-bpi density, calculate the cost of tape storage relative to card storage (assuming full utilization of both and ignoring reusability factors).

15 If a number is multiplied or divided by a prime number such as 17, the resulting digits (especially the middle digits) are relatively random. That is, the occurrence of 0s, 1s, 2s, etc., will be approximately the same in each digit position. How might this fact be used to generate disk addresses from identification numbers?

16 Define the following acronyms:
(a) DASD (c) BDAM (e) IMS
(b) ISAM (d) SAM

17 Explain the logic of a sequential file update run. Why must a sort run have preceded it?

18 Explain the organization of a sequential file. Explain how it is used in:
(a) Updating run
(b) Retrieval request
(c) Preparing report arranged in different sequence

19 Assume the same file is organized sequentially on magnetic tape and also on a disk. How would the search process differ for the two files for obtaining the record of student Jennifer Davis? The file is organized in name sequence.

20 Explain the random file organization.
(a) How is a record located?
(b) How is overflow handled?

21 Explain a tree index. What are the advantages and disadvantages?

22 Prepare a tree index like the one in Figure 9-14 for the following record keys received in the order given:
976 811 894 419 444 519 821 318
709 845 518 240 917 320 200

23 Explain indexed sequential organization. How are blocks used to reduce index size and reorganization needs?

24 Explain what a pointer is and how it is stored in a record.

25 Explain a simple list. Why might it be called a "threaded list" or "knotted list"? Why are forward and backward pointers sometimes used?

26 Explain an inverted file. Why might it be called a "content-indexed file"? Why are pointers not used in the records?

27 A bit index is a string of bit positions, each of which identifies the existence (1-bit) or nonexistence (0-bit) of a value for an attribute. It can be very efficient as an index for a partially inverted file. Construct a bit index for the values for the following three attributes in a partially inverted file of three records.

Record key	Salary class	Sex	Education code
180	1	Male	4
190	2	Male	7
200	1	Female	6

28 Explain a ring organization. How is it used in information retrieval?

29 In a ring structure, an individual Gordon Clark has been found to be part of the ring which identifies sophomores. We wish to find some other characteristics (the record contains several pointers). How is this accomplished?

30 Explain how the files would be processed for the following:

(a) An inquiry to select all male students majoring in mathematics who are 19 years old.
   (1) Using a file organized sequentially
   (2) Using a file organized randomly
   (3) Using an indexed sequential file
   (4) Using a fully inverted file

(b) Select the records for Flint Stanford and Marie Alison, two students on the file. ID numbers are known.
   (1) Using a sequential file
   (2) Using a random file
   (3) Using an indexed sequential file
   (4) Using a fully inverted file

31 What are the characteristics of a database?

32 Explain the difference between the schema and subschema.

33 What are the duties of a database administrator?

34 Explain and contrast file management systems and database management systems.

35 Explain the difference between a host language system and a self-contained data management system.

36 Perform an exchange sort for groups of four of the following numbers and then do a merge sort. Show your strings at each stage.

256	072	296	416
024	288	592	664
096	576	736	656
384	152	888	312
768	134	944	248
536	432	104	984

PART

EFFECTIVE
OPERATION AND
USE OF THE COMPUTER

The first three chapters in Part 4 relate primarily to operations and management of the computer resources of an organization; the last one, Chapter 13, is a summary of current and prospective developments in the entire field of computers. Chapter 10 provides the student with insight into how a computer center operates and describes the alternatives of using an outside computer service center and a time-sharing service. The important areas relating to methods for ensuring accuracy of computer processing and for security of computer resources are described in Chapter 11. A significant management issue is the selection and procurement of new or replacement hardware or software. A commonly used approach is explained in Chapter 12.

CHAPTER

OPERATING AN INHOUSE COMPUTER AND USING OUTSIDE COMPUTER SERVICES

An organization may have an inhouse computer, it may use an outside data processing service organization, or it may use a combination. The decisions and the management of the resulting operations are significant not only because of the expense of the operation or service but also because of the computer operations' role as a service department which accepts input data, performs processing and storage, and provides information. If the function is not well managed, the activities of the entire organization can be impaired.

This chapter discusses both managerial and operating considerations for a computer installation. Students frequently find it difficult to visualize what is happening as the computer operator puts a job into the computer. The section on operating the computer describes how a program is loaded, etc. Another section describes the operating system which manages much of the computer operations. Alternatives to an inhouse computer are explained, both service centers and time sharing.

Structure and Management of Computer Processing in Organizations

The data processing function should be structured and managed according to the same principles used in the rest of the organization. This includes a plan of organization and standards for procedures and performance. The activities in managing the development and running of an application illustrate both the overall flow of work and the management requirements.

Organization Computer processing departments usually follow one of two forms of organization with respect to systems analysis and programmers—the functional or the project organization. These two alternatives are illustrated in Figure 10-1.

The organization charts do not show the location of the computer department in the overall structure. In the most common plan the data processing department reports to the chief financial officer or chief accounting officer, such as financial vice-president, treasurer, or controller. There is, however, a growing tendency to move the data processing executive to a higher position in the organization with a title such as vice-president of management information systems.

As information systems have grown in size and complexity, basic functions of analyst, programmer, operator, and data preparation have been subdivided into further specialties. Some of the major functions which now exist or are beginning to emerge in some organizations are the following:

Position	Description
Information analyst	Works with users to define information requirements. Develops user procedures and instructions. Understands the organization, management, and decision-making functions. Has an ability to work with people.

System designer	Designs computer-based processing system to provide the information specified by the information analyst. This function requires higher technical capability than does that of information analyst. May specialize in area such as data communications.
Systems programmer	Writes specialized software such as operating systems and data management systems. Has technical proficiency in hardware and software.
Application programmer	Designs, codes, tests, and debugs computer programs for applications. Some installations separate programming into commercial or business applications and scientific applications with separate programming groups for the two types.
Maintenance programmer	Works on the maintenance (changes and corrections) of existing programs.
Database administrator	Administers and controls the organization database.
Computer operator	Operates the computer equipment.
Librarian	Stores and issues the computer files on tapes and disks. Files documentation. Maintains record of usage.
Control clerk (also called input/output control clerk)	Records control information and reviews performance of control procedures.
Information systems planner	Plans the future of the information system.

A Master Development Plan

An organization should not develop computer processing applications without an overall plan. As explained in Chapter 3, such a plan is often termed a "master development plan." It describes what the information system will consist of and how it is to be developed. The master development plan provides a framework for all detailed planning of applications, equipment selection, staffing, etc. In general, it contains four major sections (refer back to Figure 3-1).

1 Organizational goals and objectives
2 Inventory of current capabilities
3 Forecast of developments affecting the plan
4 The specific plan

Procedural and Performance Standards

Procedural standards are established by defining clearly and exactly how each job is to be done. This provides each person with a clear description of what is expected and the methods and techniques to be used. The standard methods provide a discipline to the data processing operations, which reduces training difficulties, increases the effectiveness of review and supervision, minimizes the effect of personnel turnover, and provides a basis for performance evaluation. A standard operating procedure manual specifies for all personnel the standard methods to be

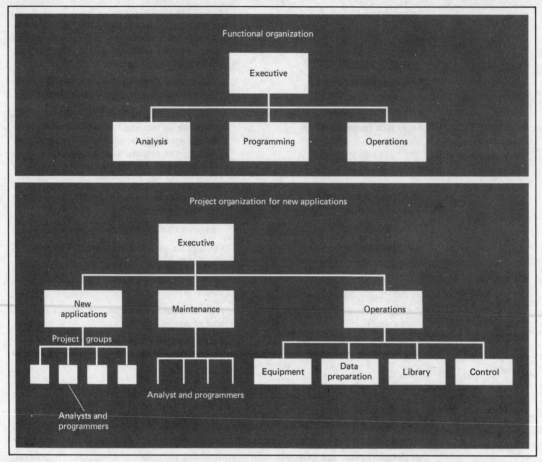

FIGURE 10-1 The basic organizational patterns.

used in that installation. This includes standard procedures for systems analysis, programming, and operating. The manual may also include organization charts and job descriptions.

Performance standards aid in planning, in controlling costs, and in evaluating performance for both equipment and personnel. Equipment standards for each separately operated unit specify the amount of time the equipment should be devoted to setup, production, scheduled maintenance, and unscheduled maintenance. The performance standards for a unit of equipment provide a basis for scheduling work, evaluating operator performance, spotting units to be replaced or repaired, etc.

Performance standards for systems and programming personnel are more difficult to establish than equipment standards because of the problems in estimating a task that has a substantial element of creativity. However, performance estimates can usually be made sufficiently close for management purposes. In one approach to estimation, each assignment is divided into tasks. For example, a programming job may be divided into tasks, and the assignment evaluated in terms of its size and complexity. Preestablished times for size and complexity categories are then applied to arrive at time estimates for performing each individual task using the standard methods for the installation (Figure 10-2). Once a performance standard has been estimated, it provides a basis for scheduling work and evaluating individual progress and performance. This approach is useful for both systems analysis and programming. Equipment operator jobs are machine-paced, and therefore operator scheduling is based on machine standards.

Facilities Management

Many companies have had difficulty in managing their data processing installations. An alternative is the use of facilities management. A firm offering facilities management will take over a company's data processing operation and run it for a fee. By applying standardized management techniques, the facilities management firms appear to achieve substantial savings. The major problem is that of disengagement should the user of facilities management services decide to terminate the arrangement.

Management Activities in Development and Running of an Application

In order to visualize the management of a computer installation, the management activities connected with the development life cycle presented in Chapter 3 will be surveyed.

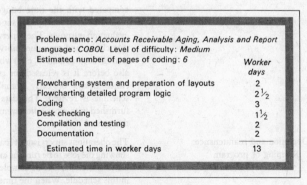

Problem name: *Accounts Receivable Aging, Analysis and Report*
Language: *COBOL* Level of difficulty: *Medium*
Estimated number of pages of coding: *6*

	Worker days
Flowcharting system and preparation of layouts	2
Flowcharting detailed program logic	2½
Coding	3
Desk checking	1½
Compilation and testing	2
Documentation	2
Estimated time in worker days	13

FIGURE 10-2 Estimating programming time.

Steps in life cycle	Management activities
Problem recognition and definition (feasibility assessment)	When the need for a computer application is recognized, a systems analyst is assigned to work on the project. A project name and/or number is assigned for keeping track of time devoted to the project. After a preliminary investigation, the project will be given a time budget for completion of the feasibility phase. The result of this phase will be a feasibility report with cost estimates. If the decision is favorable, the project is placed into the work schedule.

Information analysis and system analysis and design	As work proceeds, the information and systems analysts report the time spent on each element of the job on a time sheet and make an estimate of time to completion. For example, time may be reported by the basic tasks such as the following (or even in more detail):
	
	    Information requirements
	    Application specifications
	    Layout of inputs, reports, and files
	    System flowcharts
	    Development procedures
	
	The supervisor reviews progress based on time reports and time estimates and approves the work when it is completed.

Procedure and program development and conversion	The job is then assigned to a programmer who is given the system analysis specifications, a job number, and a time budget. The job is scheduled as with the systems analysis. The programmers record time by each phase of the job, such as:
	
	    Program planning
	    Coding
	    Desk checking
	    Assembly or compilation
	    Testing
	    Documentation
	    Conversion
	
	The hours are summarized by the clerical staff and compared with the time budget. The job, when completed, is analyzed by the supervisor for programming evaluation purposes. The supervisor reviews the program (for clarity and maintainability of coding, adequacy of testing, documentation, etc.) while it is being written and also before it is released for production use. Based on either delays or early completion, the programmer schedule is revised. The data processing executive is furnished with a periodic summary of program status for managerial review.

Operation and maintenance: Running of program	The operations supervisor prepares a production schedule showing the jobs to be run, the expected running time, and the time each job is to be completed. A new job is inserted in this schedule. When the time arrives for the job to be run, the operator obtains the program and any data files

from the program and file library. Using the operator instructions for the run as a guide, special forms (if any) are obtained, and the program, forms, and data files are loaded into the equipment. The program is then run. The running time is recorded either automatically by the computer or by the operator. The times are summarized by job and by major operating category and reviewed by the data processing management. A record of delays, errors, and other conditions which required corrective action is made and summarized for management review purposes.

Control and distribution of output

The control clerk logs in any control figures prepared when the data was recorded or converted. The control clerk records the computer control totals and checks for any discrepancy. The clerk examines the output for obvious errors and then distributes it according to the instructions in the run manual documentation. Any errors reported by the users are logged in, investigated, and corrected. A report of such errors is made periodically to the data processing management.

Correction and maintenance

Users may decide that there should be a change in the output. Errors may appear that were not detected in the testing. A maintenance programmer is assigned to make the change. The change is planned and approved. After the program changes are made, the programs are retested. The change documentation is added to the application documentation.

Operating the Computer

There are differences in procedures for operating different computers, but there is usually an operator console, instructions must be loaded into memory, there must be a method for starting the program, and there are provisions for specifying successful or unsuccessful terminations.

The Computer Console

The computer console (Figure 10-3) contains a control panel by which the operator monitors the action of the computer. The console may be mounted on the cabinet housing the central processor, or it may be a separate unit. Usually associated with the console is a low-volume input/output device, such as a typewriter or visual display unit. The control panel lights, switches, dials, and the console typewriter or visual display unit are used to:

1 Manually instruct the computer

2 Display the condition and status of the computer equipment and the input/output devices

FIGURE 10-3 Computer console for IBM System 370/145. (*Courtesy of International Business Machines Corporation.*)

3 Display the contents of registers

4 Alter the operation of the equipment

5 Alter the contents of registers or other storage locations

6 Diagnose equipment malfunctions (by maintenance personnel)

The small incandescent lights on the panels of many computer consoles usually display the contents of the various registers. During the running of the program, the lights change too rapidly for the contents to be read. During debugging or when the computer halts, the register contents may be an aid in determining what has happened.

Various lights indicate the operation or condition of important assemblies in the central processor and in peripheral equipment. For example, there may be an overflow light, parity-error indicator, temperature warning light, indicators to display the results of program comparison tests, and lights to indicate off-normal conditions for peripheral equipment. Each item of equipment will have on it a small number of buttons and lights. The buttons are to start, stop, reset, etc., while the lights indicate off-normal conditions. For example, a light on a printer may indicate it is out of paper.

The console typewriter or visual display unit is used by programs or operating systems to send messages to the operator and by the operator to respond. Manual intervention to change the running of a program is frequently handled through the console keyboard.

Loading the Program into Memory

When the source program is assembled or compiled, the result is a machine-language program on some machine-readable medium, such as magnetic tape or magnetic disk. The program is generally stored in a program library. The library may be managed by a software package designed for that purpose. These program library packages are often termed "librarian software."

Each instruction must be stored in memory, so it must be assigned to a separate memory location. This assignment may be absolute, in which case the same instruction will always be put in the same location, or it may be relative, and the specific address is assigned by the load program which is part of the operating system. In relative addressing the assembled or compiled program contains addresses starting at location zero, and the loader adds a constant to arrive at the actual addresses to use.

Instructions will not automatically place themselves in the designated locations. There must be a procedure to take each instruction and place it in the location specified for it. This is accomplished by a load routine in the operating system. The load routine is put into memory in order to read and store the program to be loaded. A load routine may also be part of each program to be loaded. How does the load program get into memory (or the program to load the loader)? One general approach is a "bootstrap" technique. The first instruction entered into memory loads the next one, which loads a third, and so on until a small number of instructions are loaded. These few instructions then load the remaining instructions. A special load button on the console is sometimes available to read the first record into memory to start the bootstrap operation.

Starting the Program

The load program, as its last step, will usually transfer control back to the operating system or perhaps directly to the operating program just loaded and start execution. A message is typed or displayed to the operator to specify that the program has been loaded.

The computer console provides some means for specifying a starting address and transferring control to it. This is necessary in order to allow the operator to start or restart a program at a point other than the beginning. The branching may be done through console switches, dials, or console keyboard.

Successful and Unsuccessful Terminations

Once started, a program may be terminated for one of several reasons.

1 Successful completion
2 Programmed error termination
3 Continuous loop
4 Invalid operation

Successful completion of a program is indicated explicitly by a console message from the program, from the operating system, or from both. Programmed error halts are each associated with a specified console message. By reference to the instructions, the operator can determine the exact reason for the error halt. A program may occasionally get into a continuous loop (executes a sequence of steps over and over again) from which there is no exit. If allowed to continue, the computer would never stop performing the same loops. The reason for this is an error in programming. A loop of this sort may sometimes be spotted by a recurrent pattern on the console lights, but in most cases it is detected because of excessive running time. The expected maximum running time for a program is part of the operator instructions. If the program exceeds this limit, a loop is assumed and the run is aborted. Many computer centers automatically apply limits to small problems written in FORTRAN or similar languages; unless the writer of the program specifies a longer running time, the automatic limit is used. Most recent computers have a clock which can be interrogated by the program for this purpose. A program may also hang up because of an invalid operation or location (usually because of improper instruction modification). For example, a program instruction may send control to a location which contains data. The computer will attempt to use the data as an instruction and, if this is impossible, will halt.

Operating Systems

An *operating system,* also called "OS," "supervisor," "monitor," or "executive," is a set of routines to manage the running of the computer. Operating systems range in complexity from simple systems which manage only basic functions to very complex ones. In general, the more sophisticated the computer system, the more complex the operating system required to manage its use. The philosophy underlying the operating system is that the computer should perform those operator tasks which it can do faster and more accurately and that the computer should be kept operating as continuously and as effectively as possible. For simple, second-generation systems, the operating system was a convenience; for third-generation systems, it is essential to efficient operation.

Managing of Assembly and Compilation Consider the steps, as shown in the table on page 299, required to compile and run a program written in a high-level language such as FORTRAN, both with and without an operating system.

Operator only	Operator and operating system
1 Operator examines program and determines that it is a FORTRAN program.	Operator: Puts program into card reader along with other jobs. Job and control cards are included with each program deck. (Typical job control cards are shown in Figure 10-4.)
2 Operator records start time, operator, and program name on a log.	
3 Operator locates copy of FORTRAN compiler.	
4 Operator loads FORTRAN compiler into storage (manual start).	Operating system automatically:
5 Operator starts FORTRAN compilation (manual start).	1 Determines that program is FORTRAN program to be compiled.
6 At completion, operator examines program printout to see if successful compilation.	2 Loads compiler and starts compilation.
7 If yes, operator loads FORTRAN program into storage (manual start).	3 Checks for successful compilation.

8   Operator determines if all input/output units are properly loaded with input data, cards, paper, tapes, etc.

9   Operator starts execution of program (manual start).

10 At completion, operator decides if it is a successful termination. If so, unloads all input/output media associated with program.

11 Operator writes time of completion on computer log and notes errors or other conditions.

12 Operator examines programs to be run and chooses next one to work on.

4   Loads object program and starts execution.

5   Provides messages to operator regarding any duties he or she may have.

6   Prepares a record of the time taken by the program, records error conditions, and updates operating statistics.

7   At successful completion goes on to next program.

Some of the tasks typically performed by an operating system are given in the following list:

Program loading
Interrupt handling
Scheduling of input/output operations
Operator communications
Job-to-job communications
Job accounting
Job scheduling and management

The scheduling of input/output may include the use of an input/output control system which will perform label verification, assignment of buffer areas in memory

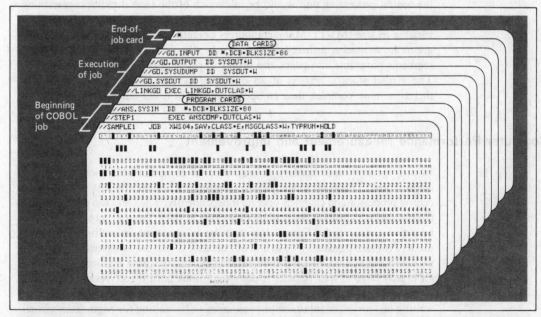

FIGURE 10-4 Job cards for a simple job using Job Control Language (JCL) on IBM System/370 under full operating system (OS) to (1) read a COBOL source program, (2) compile it, (3) execute it using data from the card reader, and (4) print the resulting compilation listing and output on the printer.

for use in input and output, error checking and recovery during input/output operations, etc.

Managing of Scheduling and Multiprogramming

The job scheduling and management activity of the operating system can become quite complex. Their purpose is to provide a steady flow of work to the computer. Scheduling can be divided into two types—sequence scheduling and concurrent scheduling. A sequence-scheduling supervisory program selects the next program to be run on the basis of such factors as time of day, priority rankings of the programs in the job stack, and availability of input data. Only one program is scheduled into memory at a time.

The concurrent-scheduling program not only schedules the sequencing of programs but also directs the concurrent processing of two or more programs. This technique for having the computer handle several programs concurrently is known as "multiprogramming" or "parallel processing." The programs are placed in different sections (partitions) of memory, and the operating system switches control from one to the other. For example, a program to read cards and print their contents may be run concurrently with a program to update a file. The control routine in the operating system first gives control to the read/print program. This initiates a read-a-card instruction. Control is then shifted to the file update program. When the card for the first program has been read, the second program is interrupted and control is passed back to the first program, and so on. Since the read/print routine can proceed no faster than the reader and printer can operate, the central processing unit would be idle much of the time if multiprogramming were not used. The partitions can be fixed in size (sometimes termed MFT) or variable in size (MVT). Many computers operate with virtual storage, i.e., programs are written as if there were unlimited main memory. The operating system segments programs into pages and brings in pages as required during execution. The virtual storage version of an operating system (IBM calls it OS-VS) is therefore more complex than an operating system using only real storage.

Computer Performance Measurement and Improvement

In early-generation computers, measurement of computer utilization was simply elapsed time. This is no longer satisfactory for any but the simplest systems. The central processor and channels operate independently. The CPU can process while the channel is managing the reading or writing of data. Two or more channels can be active concurrently. Several jobs may be in execution in multiprogramming mode. Program pages may be in and out because of the use of virtual storage. But no computer system is completely utilized during the time it is operating. The CPU may have to wait because it cannot continue until it receives data from the channel. The channel may not operate because there are no requests. Jobs may be waiting on storage or input/output resources or be waiting for pages from virtual storage. Computer performance measurement (or computer performance evaluation) determines how well the operating system and application programs are utilizing the hardware for a given job mix, so that corrective action may be taken. Data collection for performance evaluation may be from:

1   Job accounting statistics that are prepared by the operating system [called "system measurement facility" (SMF) by IBM], or a manual job log if there is no automated job accounting

2   Hardware monitor

3   Software monitor

The hardware monitor is a data collection device attached by probes to the circuitry of the computer. It records the occurrence of specified signals by the CPU, memory, and channels. The data is recorded on tape for batch processing. It imposes no load on the computer system and does not interfere with the program. The hardware monitor is best suited for determining hardware component utilization and identifying resource conflicts. Examples of utilization measurements are CPU active (not idle), channel active, program partition active, and operating system active. The cost is fairly high because of special equipment and training in its use.

The software monitor is a high-priority application program or routine inserted into the operating system which collects detailed data on the behavior of the software and operating system during operations by sampling. At established intervals, the monitor routinely interrupts processing and gathers data from internal tables and status registers maintained by the CPU and by the operating system. The data is recorded, say, on magnetic tape, and analyzed. The program requires internal memory space, file space, and some operating time. The measurements have sampling errors. The software monitor is less expensive than hardware. It is suited for determining which jobs are unnecessarily holding onto resources and which jobs must wait for resources.

Experience suggests that the use of monitors can be very productive in improving performance where used properly. But "to put on a monitor to see what we find out" has generally been unsuccessful. The most successful approach is hypothesis-testing where the system is studied and operations analyzed to formulate performance improvement hypotheses. Measurement tools are then used to collect data for testing these improvement ideas.

Another method of performance improvement is optimization of program coding for more efficient execution. The use of certain coding features can vary in execution time, and when programs are executed in a virtual storage environment, coding that requires frequent jumping from page to page can be very inefficient. Yet to go over every program and recode it for efficiency would be very time-consuming and costly. It is not necessary to do so because a small percentage of the coding will be used over and over again, and this small percentage (say, 10 percent) can be examined closely for optimization purposes. In order to collect data on which parts of the code are being used, some compilers provide special measurement instructions; or the user can write some instructions to do this. Users who have analyzed their programs for improvement have been able to achieve substantial savings in running time.

As a rather dramatic example of the impact of performance measurement, a brokerage firm reported a 90 percent reduction in CPU use and a 75 percent reduction in elapsed time after changes following performance evaluation.[1] The firm had an online system for displaying current account information on visual displays. Nightly updating of the database took so long the system was not ready by morning. A software monitor was employed to collect data on program execution and use of resources. A heavy user of CPU time was a library routine for computing the size of data. The use of this routine was eliminated by some relatively minor program coding changes. This reduced the time by half. Other measurements showed waiting time for tape reel mounts. Changes were then made to eliminate this delay.

Using a Service Center for Computer Processing

A data processing service center or service bureau is an organization which provides data processing service to outside clients on a fee basis. There is considerable diversity in the data processing service center industry, but established firms tend to be able to provide a complete data processing service rather than merely renting equipment time. A typical well-established data processing service organization has qualified personnel to analyze customer requirements, write programs, etc., as well as having control over appropriate equipment. Most service centers have standard prewritten software to meet common processing requirements.

A data processing service can be used either in place of manual processing or to supplement an existing internal machine data processing installation. An application which can profitably be turned over to a service center will usually have one or more of the following characteristics:

1   Significant volume of records.

2   Considerable computation.

3   The data must be rearranged in several ways to obtain different tabulations or to perform different computations.

4   The time available for processing is too short for the regular inhouse processing staff, or there are insufficient personnel.

5   The application requires specialized knowledge or special equipment not available inhouse but found in the data processing center.

The service center is an obvious option for a small business or for a business which does not wish to have an inhouse installation. However, even if an organization has

---

[1] "Monitor Cuts CPU Time 90% on Broker's Daily Run," *Computerworld*, May 10, 1976, p. 15.

its own data processing equipment, it may still use a service center for reasons such as the following:

1 Special or periodic overloads

2 Projects requiring specialized handling, specialized knowledge, or special equipment (such as computer output microfilm)

3 Need for experience and assistance in connection with a conversion to new equipment

Types of Service Centers The diversity of service center organizations makes them somewhat difficult to categorize. The following different classifications are useful:

TABLE 10-1 CLASSIFICATION OF DATA PROCESSING SERVICE CENTERS

Ownership	Control of equipment	Frequency of processing	Type of equipment	Processing orientation
Manufacturer	Owner or prime lessee	Batch	Computer	Commercial
Independent	Block time lessee	Remote batch	Time-sharing computer	Scientific
Organization-affiliated		Time sharing	Specialized	Industry specialist
University				Full line

Most of these classifications are easily understood. The control of equipment classification is based on the fact that some service organizations are owners or lessees of their equipment, whereas others use block time (i.e., blocks of computer time) on installations which have excess time.

Periodic batch processing according to a schedule is offered by almost all service centers. Some offer time-shared processing on demand. Remote batch is a compromise between the two. A job is transmitted from a remote device and enters the job stream. It is executed in batch mode without interaction such as frequently occurs in time sharing. The results can be transmitted back to the input/output device at the user installation. Some processing centers are specialists in the type of work they do. For example, a center may specialize in data processing for automobile dealers or in scientific processing for architects. Specialized equipment is required for processing for banks, for processing optically marked tests, etc.

Method of Operation Although the organizational structure for a data processing service center may vary, there tend to be three major functions: sales, consulting/programming, and production.

The sales function is carried on by sales representatives who call upon customers to explain the services offered by the organization. They analyze customer requirements and present proposals for performing services.

The purpose of the consulting and programming function is to perform system analysis and prepare specialized system designs for each customer's unique requirements. If the system is accepted by the client, the service organization also prepares programs.

The production department performs the data processing activity for the firm. This is typically divided into three separate areas: data preparation, quality control, and data processing. The quality-control activity is concerned with controlling customer records and ensuring that the work is done correctly and on time. An account representative or account supervisor in the quality control group is assigned the responsibility for customer contact regarding the data processing.

Another way of describing how a service center operates is to trace the handling of a continuing commercial data processing contract, such as preparation of a payroll or preparation of accounts receivable. The representative who first calls on the customer may work out the solution and make an estimate, especially if the system is relatively uncomplicated and fits standard procedures already developed by the center. If the system is complicated or unique, systems analysts will prepare layouts, system flowcharts, programs, etc. Once the system is agreed upon and programs have been prepared, the client's files are converted to machine-readable form in order to get the system started. These files are then typically (but not always) stored at the service center. Thereafter, documents received from the client are logged in by the data processing center, checked for appropriateness by the control unit, then transcribed to machine-readable form (and verified). The data processing group obtains the master file from the quality-control group, runs the program, and turns the results back to quality control. The account representative examines the master records and the processed reports for completeness and accuracy and returns the master file to the storage area. The completed reports are either picked up by the client or transmitted by messenger service or mail. An error listing accompanies the reports. The client is advised through the error listing or through a call from the account representative as to the procedures to be followed to take care of the errors in the next data processing cycle.

Method of Charging for Service

There are three basic approaches to charging for data processing center services:

1 Fixed price
2 Time and materials at standard rate
3 Cost plus fixed fee or percentage

The fixed fee is preferred in most cases, with the understanding that changes not agreed on in advance can cost extra. It is well suited for standard program packages or for those cases where specifications for the customer's system are firm and few changes are to be anticipated. The fixed-price contract may take the form of a fixed fee, plus a charge for each item processed. There is usually a minimum charge for each processing period for recurring jobs. The minimum reflects the fact that there is an administrative cost associated with each client no matter how small the job.

Charging on the basis of time and materials at a standard rate is suitable where the problem and procedures are well defined but the running time, number of runs, or number of transactions are not known. It is also a useful method of charging in cases where the client's own program is being used. The basis of cost plus fixed fee or percentage is applicable where the problem or procedures are not well defined.

As a general principle, reruns due to erroneous input data or errors caused by the customer are charged to him. Reruns caused by the program being unable to handle conditions which were not excluded when the contract was taken are presumably the responsibility of the service center. In all cases, however, these should be discussed beforehand rather than after the fact.

Using a Time-sharing Service

Time sharing is the concurrent use of a single computer system by many independent users, each user having his or her own programs, each expecting fast response, and each operating independently without an awareness of the use of the facility by others. Time sharing is popular for universities and for certain types of scientific and engineering computation.

Basic Characteristics

Time sharing may be viewed as an extension of multiprogramming in which the computer works on several programs concurrently, going from one to another for the purpose of maximizing the use of the system hardware. Time sharing adds the notion of servicing all programs frequently enough that a user does not become discouraged with the waiting time. The direct access to the computer by many users is the reason that a time-sharing system is also referred to as a multiple-access system.

Time sharing may be used internally within an organization or by a data processing service center. A university, for example, may have a central computer facility with remote terminals at various points on the campus from which many faculty members and students simultaneously make use of the computer. A data processing service center which offers time sharing provides continuous access to the computer.

A time-sharing computer arrangement will typically have the following characteristics:

1 Each user has one or more input/output devices connected to the central computer by communication lines (Figure 10-5). The most common input/output terminal devices are the typewriter and visual display device. The most common communication connection is over the facilities of a telephone company.

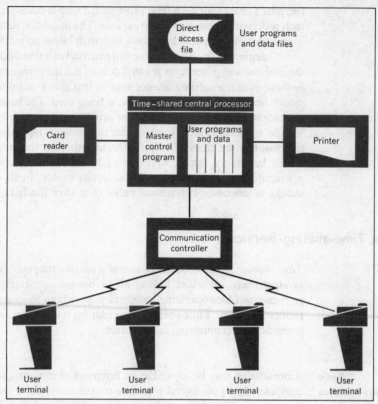

FIGURE 10-5 A time-sharing computer system.

2 Each user acts independently of the others who are connected to the system. Each user sends data and instructions from the terminal, acting as if he or she were the sole user.

3 The central computer accepts the data and instructions arriving simultaneously from many users and, by giving each user a small but frequently repeated segment of computer time, services all users concurrently. For most problems, the computer can send the requested output back almost immediately.

4 The user's data files are maintained at the central computer center. The user instructions to the computer identify the files to be used. The system is designed to prevent one user from making unauthorized access to the files of another user.

5 Each user has a private set of programs, plus access to a set of public programs.

6 The data files, program files, and input/output devices are all directly connected to the computer, so that processing can be performed at random as transactions occur or requests are made.

Time sharing may make use of a computer which does only time sharing, or time sharing may be provided by a part of the computer resources dedicated to that activity, the remainder being available for regular processing. The latter arrangement is sometimes called a time-sharing option (TSO). In either case, the operating system must have special routines for managing the sharing of the computer memory and processing time.

Methods for Sharing a Computer

In time sharing, the computations associated with a problem typically are not run continuously until the answer is obtained, because this might mean that a program requiring a long running time would cause an excessive delay for other users. Instead, each user is given a small amount of computer time with such frequency that the access appears to be continuous.

In implementing this sharing arrangement, there are two problems: sharing the main memory and sharing the central processor. Sharing the main memory is a problem since there is a limit on the size of storage, such that all the program sharing the processor cannot be in memory at once. Sharing the central processor presents difficulties because the computer must switch between programs, giving each a share of the time so that no program is noticeably delayed.

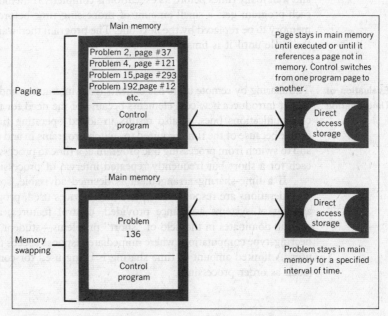

FIGURE 10-6 Methods for sharing main memory in time sharing.

There are many schemes for sharing the main memory (Figure 10-6). These may be classified as (1) paging and (2) memory swapping. In paging, each program is broken into small sets of instructions. These pages may range from a fairly small number of instructions to quite a large segment of a program. For example, one large scientific system uses pages of 1000 computer words, while another business-oriented service uses pages of only 64 words. When a program is to be run, a single page (or a small number of pages) is brought into memory and executed. Any reference by this page to another page in the program will necessitate bringing that page into memory. The previous page is no longer needed, and its memory space can be released. Pages from many programs may be in memory simultaneously, thereby allowing the computer to switch between programs.

In the memory-swapping approach, the entire program is moved in or out of main memory. Only one program is in memory at a time, and it is allowed only a very short residence before it is rolled out in favor of the next program. Both alternatives require a sophisticated program to supervise the operation and high-speed transfer rate from secondary storage.

If pages from many programs are in memory at the same time, the computer shares the processing time among them. Two methods may be used for deciding when to switch between them. One method is to switch at the end of a very short time slice. Each program gets its slice of time if it can use it. This is very useful in scientific processing where the time for any one problem is not known. The other method is to switch each time the program being executed has to wait for a direct access file reference or for an input/output operation. A program may thus execute and wait many times before its execution is complete. If memory swapping is used, each program gets a small amount of processing time before being moved from memory to be replaced by the next one. The program then waits its turn, repeating the cycle until it is finished.

An Evaluation of Time Sharing

The sharing by remote users has benefits from interaction and immediate processing. It introduces new cost elements because of the need for terminal devices and communications lines. It also results in added operating time at the computer center because of the time required to switch programs in and out of main memory and to switch from processing one program at a time to processing many programs, each for a short but frequently repeated interval of processing time.

If a time-sharing arrangement is deemed advisable, some of the selection considerations are response time, terminal devices used, programming language, amount of systems assistance provided, control features, and stability. Time sharing dominates in the field of "short" problems—student, research, and engineering-type computations where immediate response speeds the other work of the user. A limited amount of time sharing is being used for commercial processing (such as order processing).

SUMMARY   The management of the data processing organization can make effective use of traditional management methods. These include job descriptions, organization charts, a master development plan, standard procedures, and performance standards. Where a company does not wish to be involved in day-to-day management, operations may be turned over to a facilities management firm.

The operation of the computer is under the direction of the operating system. The operator makes use of the computer console and the console typewriter or visual display unit to communicate with the computer. The operator does not have to load the individual programs into the computer; this is usually done by the operating system on the basis of job instructions and job control cards.

The complexity of operations when a computer is doing multiprogramming, using virtual storage, etc., makes it difficult to evaluate operating performance and to know how to make changes for improved efficiency. Performance measurement improvement methods include the use of job statistics, hardware monitors, and software monitors to collect data by which performance improvement hypotheses may be tested.

An inhouse computer is not the only alternative. A user may consider a data processing service organization. Almost all such organizations offer batch processing service; a smaller number offer time-shared use of a computer. Because of the unique characteristics of time sharing, an organization with an inhouse computer may still make use of outside time-shared computing.

EXERCISES
1   Define the following terms:
    (*a*) Facilities management   (*e*) Multiprogramming
    (*b*) Loader   (*f*) Paging
    (*c*) Bootstrap technique   (*g*) Memory swapping
    (*d*) Operating system
2   Explain the difference between the duties of a systems programmer, an applications programmer, and a maintenance programmer.
3   Explain the difference between an information analyst and a system designer.
4   Define the general content of a master development plan.
5   What can the operator learn from the console lights?
6   What are the advantages and disadvantages in using facilities management firms?
7   How is a program loaded? How does it get started? What causes it to stop?
8   What are the advantages of the use of performance standards?
9   Why should an installation adopt standard procedures?
10   What is the purpose of job control cards?
11   Why would an operating system with variable partitions for multiprogramming be more complex than one with fixed partitions? Why would virtual storage make the operating system more complex?
12   Explain the difference between hardware and software monitors.
13   The data processing manager feels that monitors should be used to "see if anything pops out." Contrast this with the hypothesis approach and explain why the proposal

by the DP manager is not likely to be effective.

14 Why might a company with an inhouse computer use a service center?

15 A service center went into bankruptcy. What happens to the client files at the service center?

16 A data processing service center offers a payroll service—preparation of checks, tax reports, analyses, etc. What method are they likely to use in charging for the service?

17 List advantages and disadvantages of time sharing for
(*a*) Scientific processing   (*b*) Commercial data processing

18 What event might make a time-sharing user aware of other users?

19 What is the difference between paging and swapping for time sharing?

20 What must the operating system do to operate in time-sharing mode?

21 One company reported dramatic savings from transferring some jobs from time sharing to batch. Why were these savings possible?

CHAPTER

11

QUALITY CONTROL AND SECURITY IN COMPUTER PROCESSING

Computer data processing removes many traditional procedures for the detection and control of errors. A clerk doing data processing by hand or using a calculating device which produces a visible record will scan the results of his or her work and will question answers which appear to be unreasonable or not "right." In the computer installation, computations are performed at electronic speed, and intermediate results are stored in the computer in a form which cannot be scanned visually. Metal disks, metal drums, and plastic tape hold the files in which records are stored. Since the data stored on the magnetic surfaces cannot be read without a machine conversion, questions arise about the state of various records and the accuracy of computations made by the machine. How does a person know, for example, that the results of a statistical computation are correct or that the accounts-receivable file contains the data it should? A related question which applies to files where there are no visible records is the extent to which the concern should protect itself against the destruction of the records either through an accident or through malfunctioning equipment. There is also the problem of internal control. In data processing by hand or by mechanical equipment, there is typically a sufficiently large staff involved in processing any given set of figures so that the division of work and the various cross-checking procedures provide considerable control against inaccuracy and fraud. The computer staff, on the other hand, is small and has under its control the computations and records which previously were divided among large staffs of clerical personnel.

Too often, computer centers operate with a higher error rate than is necessary because management does not insist upon a lower error frequency. Error control is not without cost, and a manager needs to understand the method for error control and the attendant problems in order to evaluate the value of tighter control against its cost.

This chapter describes the methods for quality control over computer data processing. The emphasis of the chapter is upon controls in a data processing environment rather than controls for one-time scientific or engineering problems. However, one section of the chapter discusses quality control for one-time computational problems.

An Overview of Quality Control in Data Processing

The control over the quality of computer data processing should be established not just by having a correct program but by a series of controls which are applied at each stage of processing. The flow of processing is shown in Figure 11-1. Error detection and control procedures can be applied at each of the activities in the flow:

> Data recording
> Data transmittal to data processing
> Data preparation for processing
> Input to processing
> Processing

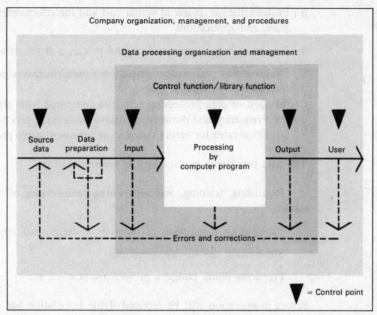

FIGURE 11-1   The control framework for computer processing.

Files and programs
Output
Distribution of output
Output use

Control procedures for these different control points are described in the chapter. Not all will be applicable to each application. The designer of an application must choose the appropriate methods from the available techniques. These techniques are applied in an organizational framework—both the overall organizational controls and the specific organization of the data processing equipment.

Organization for Data Processing Control   The data processing organization exists within a larger organizational framework. As such, data processing should be subject to standard organizational controls. Significant control is exercised by top management, data processing management, and the control function and library function within data processing.

Top management has the overall responsibility for data processing. This consists of:

1   Authorization of major changes or additions to hardware and acquisition of purchased software
2   Authorization of major applications to be put on the computer system

3 Postinstallation review of actual cost and the effectiveness of hardware, software, and applications

4 Review of organization and control practices of the data processing function

5 Evaluation of performance based on a performance plan or standard of performance. This will include
  (*a*) Cost of data processing activities compared with planned cost
  (*b*) Frequency and duration of delays in meeting processing schedules
  (*c*) Error rates for errors detected at various control points

The data processing management is responsible for:

Recruiting, training, and supervising performance of data processing personnel

Supervising completion of projects to design and implement applications

Supervising day-to-day operations

Preparing plans, budgets, project justification, etc.

Errors in operation will be reduced if the installation has standard procedures which are followed by all personnel. This will include standard programming practices, standard operating procedures, and standard control procedures.

The control function in a data processing installation consists of activities which monitor the processing and ensure that no data is lost or mishandled during processing. In small installations, the control activities may be performed by the data processing manager and a clerk; in large installations, there will be a separate staff. The duties of the control function will include:

1 Logging in batches of input data and recording control information

2 Recording progress of work through the department

3 Reconciling control totals produced at various stages of processing

4 Scrutinizing console log and/or preparation and analysis of control reports from system performance data

5 Supervising distribution of output

6 Liaison with users regarding errors, logging correction requests, and recording corrections made

7 Maintaining error log and preparing error report

A librarian function in the operations part of the organization maintains control over data files and programs. The librarian is responsible for storing magnetic tapes, disk packs, card decks, etc., on which the data files and programs are stored. The librarian may also be in charge of the documentation records. Data files and programs are issued to computer operators on the basis of the schedule of jobs to be run. They are returned to the librarian after the job has been completed. One of the duties of the librarian is to record the condition of magnetic tape with respect to read-write errors encountered, unusable portion of tape, etc. The librarian may also be responsible for offsite storage of backup files and backup copies of programs.

Building Error Control into Applications	Error control in a computer application begins with the application design and is aided by quality control procedures during the development process. The design should provide for adequate input validation, for control comparisons and control outputs during processing, for data in the outputs that will aid users in detecting errors, and for an audit trail to trace the processing performed. The development process should produce error-free, maintainable programs. Suggested approaches which aid in this objective are top-down modular design, chief programmer team, structured programming, structured walkthroughs, and a comprehensive test plan for checking the application. Special care should be taken to prepare instructions and procedures for handling and correcting errors detected during processing.
Conceptual Basis for Control Techniques	Redundancy is the basis for control techniques. *Redundancy* has a precise definition in communication theory, but for the purposes of this discussion can be defined more broadly as an extra element in a code, an operation, etc., which would not be necessary except for the need for error control. In general, as redundancy is increased, error detection is improved. However, there is a cost associated with redundancy, and too much redundancy can reduce system effectiveness. For example, one check bit in a code is quite good at detecting most transmission errors. Two redundant code elements improve the error-detection rate and allow some automatic correction of errors. But the extra error detection and error correction are obtained at the price of increased transmission time, extra circuitry, etc. The check bits themselves introduce possible errors in transmitting them, performing the checks, etc. The extra check bits are redundant in that they would not be necessary if transmission were 100 percent correct.

The concept of redundancy in error control will be observed in most of the controls described in the chapter. Redundancy does not, however, provide automatic error control; error-control procedures must be designed to use the redundant elements to detect errors. For example, a check bit does not detect an error in transmitting a code. This is done by circuitry which uses the check bit. Examples of redundant elements which are explained in the chapter are:

Parity or check bit
Read after write check
Check digit
Hole count
Two read stations

Control total
Hash total
Key verification
Echo check

Evaluating Error Controls

The major error-control procedures to be presented in this chapter provide for protection against almost any type of error. Despite the availability of these methods, one still hears about payroll checks being written for $1 million instead of $100. In these cases, elementary control features have not been used. On the other hand, error controls, like all other controls, require an expenditure of resources. Programmed controls require programming effort; they also take up valuable storage. In other words, controls need to be part of the data processing system, but they can be expensive; therefore, before implementing a control, the designer should evaluate its merits by asking such questions as

1 How frequently might this error occur?
2 What are the monetary consequences of the error?
3 What are the nonmonetary consequences of the error?
4 What is the cost of detecting these errors?
5 If the error is missed at this point, will it be detected later?
6 What are the consequences of late rather than early detection?

Control over Data Preparation and Input

The flow of control in data processing starts with data preparation and moves to input procedures, processing, output, and distribution of output to users. Data preparation and input are the weakest links in the chain of data processing. The input data for processing may be in error for one of four general reasons: (1) It may be incorrectly recorded at the point of inception; (2) it may be incorrectly converted to machine-readable form; (3) it may be incorrectly read or otherwise entered into the computer; or (4) it may be lost in handling. Controls should therefore be established at the point of data creation and conversion to machine-readable form, at the point the data enters the computer, and at points when the data is handled, moved, or transmitted in the organization. Table 11-1 presents an inventory of methods which the system designed can use in order to achieve the level of error control required for an application.

Procedural Controls and Data Review

Standard clerical practices and well-designed data forms impose procedural controls on the creation of data. For example, if a part number is to be written on a document, boxes may be printed which contain the exact number of spaces required for the part number. Any clerk writing a part number containing less or more digits than the quantity required will notice the error. For example, bad and

TABLE 11-1 METHODS FOR INPUT DATA ERROR CONTROL

At point data is created and converted to machine-readable form	At point data is first put into the computer	At points data is handled, moved, or transmitted
Procedural controls	File label	Transmittal controls
Data review	(internal)	Route slip
Verification	Tests for validity:	Control total
Check digit	Code	External file labels
Input echo	Character	
Terminal validity checks	Field	
	Transaction	
	Combination of fields	
	Missing data	
	Check digit	
	Sequence	
	Limit or reasonableness test	
	Control total	

good document designs (from an error-control standpoint) for collecting a social security number are shown below:

Bad   Social security number _____
Good Social security number ☐☐☐ - ☐☐ - ☐☐☐☐

Where direct input terminals are used, templates over the keys, identification cards, and other procedural aids help to reduce input errors. Turnaround documents (described in Chapter 9) reduce data entry errors because the data to be entered is prepared by a prior computer operation.

Some installations make a review examination of data (especially codes which identify part number, product, etc.) before it is converted to machine-readable form. This checking may be performed in connection with the addition of information, or it may be an entirely separate step.

Verification of Conversion to Machine-readable Form

When data is punched into cards or keyed onto tape or disk, the accuracy of the data conversion can be tested by mechanically verifying the keypunching operation. For keypunching of cards, this may require two separate keydriven machines (a card punch and a verifier) or a single machine which can operate in both punch and verify modes. The data is first punched by a keypunch operator. The punched cards and original data are then given to a verifier operator who inserts the punched card in the verifier and rekeys the punches using the original source documents. The verifier does not punch, but instead compares the data keyed into the verifier with the punches already in the card. If they are the same, the punched card is presumed to be correct. A common indication that this check has been performed is for the verifier to place a notch at the end of the card or over the column containing the difference. Similar verification is used with a keydisk or keytape device where data is keyed and recorded directly on a magnetic disk or tape. The same device is used (at separate times) both to record data and to verify it. The verification process includes the correction of errors.

Verification is a duplicate operation and therefore doubles the cost of data conversion. Various methods are used to reduce the amount of verifying. One method is to verify only part of the data. Some data fields are not critical, and an error will not affect further processing. Examples are descriptive fields containing vendor name, part description, etc. which, under most circumstances, are not critical. The use of prepunched cards, prepunched stubs, and duplication of constant data during keypunching may allow verification to be restricted to the variable information added by the card punch. A second approach used with statistical data is to verify only if the keying error rate is above an acceptable level. Each operator's work is checked on a sample basis. If the error rate is acceptable, no verification is made; if not, there is complete verification. Other control procedures to be explained may be substituted for verification, e.g., a check digit on an account number or a batch control total.

Check Digit In most applications involving an identification number, it may be verified for accuracy by a check digit. A check digit is determined by performing some arithmetic operation on the number. The arithmetic operation is performed in such a way that the typical errors encountered in transcribing a number will be detected. There are many possible procedures. For example, a simple check digit procedure might be as follows:

1 Start with a number without the check digit.

2 Multiply each digit by the weight assigned to the digit position. Examples are $1 - 2 - 1 - 2, \ldots$, and $1 - 3 - 5 - 7 \ldots$.

3 Sum the individual digits in the resulting products plus the digits not multiplied.

4 Divide the sum-of-digits by the modulus and save the remainder.

5 Subtract the remainder from the modulus to give the check digit.

6 Add check digit to number (at end or elsewhere).

The most common modulus is 10; the next most common is 11. As an example, assume the number 47648, modulus 10, and weights of 1 - 3 - 5 - 7 - 9:

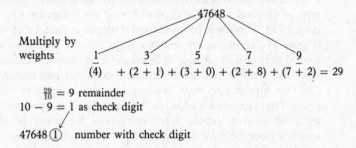

Multiply by
weights

$$(4) + (2 + 1) + (3 + 0) + (2 + 8) + (7 + 2) = 29$$

$\frac{29}{10} = 9$ remainder

$10 - 9 = 1$ as check digit

47648 ① number with check digit

Note that check digit procedures are not completely error proof. For example, if weights of 1 - 2 - 1 - 2 were used, 47846 and 47678 would yield the same check digit. It is, however, unlikely that transpositions of this form will occur. The check digit does not guard against assignment of an incorrect but valid code, for example, the assignment of the wrong but valid identification code to a customer.

The checking of the code number for the check digit may be performed by either a data preparation or data entry device such as a keypunch, keydisk, or intelligent terminal, or it may be programmed into the computer. The use of the check digit as part of the preparation device or terminal has the advantage that an incorrect code is detected before it enters the computer process. A data item checked by a check digit does not normally need to be verified. Examples of uses are charge account numbers, employee pay numbers, and bank account numbers.

Input Echo and Terminal Validity Checks

When data is input via a terminal (either offline or online), the data being input can be displayed in a manner that will facilitate visual review and verification of input. For example, the input data can be formatted to aid in the review (with labels, separation into data items, lining up decimal positions, etc.). Also, codes and abbreviations can be expanded to identify the meaning of the code. If input is code 47 for $\frac{1}{2}$-in. strapping tape, the terminal might display CODE 47 1/2 INCH STRAPPING TAPE.

As previously mentioned, intelligent terminals can be programmed to perform validity checks on input data. Nonintelligent terminals can transmit to a computer which may perform validity tests as part of the process of data acceptance from the terminal. The types of validity tests that can be made are described later in the chapter. In either case, when errors are detected, an error message may be displayed and an immediate correction made.

Input Validation

Before data is used in updating computer files or other computer processing, it is usually tested for errors to the extent possible or appropriate in the light of the consequences of input errors. A separate input validation run or input editing run may be used, or the checking may be performed at the time of processing. Input validation is usually performed even if the data was validated at an input terminal. If errors are detected, the erroneous transaction or the record found to contain an error is shunted aside, rather than having the computer stop in order to make corrections. There will be some control output at the time of the input validation (Figure 11-2). A complete analysis of the rejected transactions may be prepared immediately or subsequently. The erroneous records will usually be written on an error file. Items which are rejected are corrected and reentered at a later run.

One approach to error handling is a circulating error file or error log. All rejected transactions are added to the error file. Those responsible for corrections are given an error report. When corrections are made, the error transaction is removed from the error file. As a result, there is a file of uncorrected transactions which is subject to review. If an error is not corrected, managerial action may be taken. An error log in which rejected transactions are recorded and then checked off when corrections are made is also used to prevent duplicate corrections.

Error controls at the point data is entered into the computer are file labels and tests for validity. Control totals are used at this point, but these totals are such a basic procedure and useful in movement controls as well that they are described separately.

A file label is a record at the beginning and also possibly the end of the file which contains identification and control information. These records are used to ensure that the proper transaction file or master file is used and that the entire file

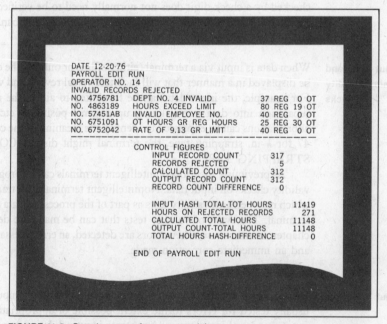

```
DATE 12-20-76
PAYROLL EDIT RUN
OPERATOR NO. 14
INVALID RECORDS REJECTED
NO. 4756781   DEPT NO. 4 INVALID        37 REG   0 OT
NO. 4863189   HOURS EXCEED LIMIT        80 REG  19 OT
NO. 57451AB   INVALID EMPLOYEE NO.      40 REG   0 OT
NO. 6751091   OT HOURS GR REG HOURS     25 REG  30 OT
NO. 6752042   RATE OF 9.13 GR LIMIT     40 REG   0 OT
─────────────────────────────────────────────────────
              CONTROL FIGURES
              INPUT RECORD COUNT        317
              RECORDS REJECTED            5
              CALCULATED COUNT          312
              OUTPUT RECORD COUNT       312
              RECORD COUNT DIFFERENCE     0

              INPUT HASH TOTAL-TOT HOURS      11419
              HOURS ON REJECTED RECORDS         271
              CALCULATED TOTAL HOURS          11148
              OUTPUT COUNT-TOTAL HOURS        11148
              TOTAL HOURS HASH-DIFFERENCE         0

END OF PAYROLL EDIT RUN
```

FIGURE 11-2 Sample output from input validation run.

has been processed. The label at the beginning is the header label which identifies the file. It is considered good practice to label all files with header labels. Typical contents are

> Name of file
> Creation date
> Purge data
> Identification number
> Reel number (for magnetic tape)

The trailer label is the last record and summarizes the file. When used, the trailer label contents normally include

> Record count
> Control totals for one or more fields
> End-of-file or end-of-reel code

The data can be subjected to programmed tests by the computer in the input validation run or by a programmable terminal at data entry to establish that it is within the limits established for valid data. Some examples of validation which can be done are:

1 *Valid code* If there are only a limited number of valid codes, say, for coding expenses, the code being read may be checked to see if it is one of the valid codes.

2 *Valid character* If only certain characters are allowed in a data field, the computer can test the field to determine that no invalid characters are used.

3 *Valid field size, sign, and composition* If a code number should be a specified number of digits in length, the computer may be programmed to test that the field size is as specified. If the sign of the field must always be positive or must always be negative, then a test may be made to ensure that there is not an incorrect sign. If the field should contain only numerics or only alphabetics, then a test may be made to determine that the field does indeed contain a proper composition of characters.

4 *Valid transaction* There is typically a relatively small number of valid transactions which are processed with a particular file. There is a limited number, for example, of transaction codes which can apply to accounts receivable file updating. As part of input error control, the transaction code can be tested for validity.

5 *Valid combinations of fields* In addition to each of the individual fields being tested, combinations may be tested for validity. For example, if a sales representative code may be associated with only a few territory codes, this can be checked.

6 *Missing data* The program may check the data fields to make sure that all data fields necessary to code a transaction have data in them.

7 *Check digit* The check digit is verified on identification fields having this control feature.

8 *Sequence* In batch sequential processing the data to be processed must be arranged in a sequence which is the same as the sequence of the file. Both the master file and the transaction file may be tested to ensure that they are in proper sequence, ascending or descending as the case may be. The sequence check can also be used to account for all documents, if these are numbered sequentially.

9 *Limit or reasonableness* This is a basic test for data processing accuracy. Input data should usually fall within certain limits. For example, hours worked should not be less than zero and should not be more than, say, 50 hours. The upper limit may be established from the experience of the particular firm. Input data may be compared against this limit to ensure that no input error has occurred or at least no input error exceeding certain preestablished limits. Examples are:

(*a*) The total amount of a customer order may be compared with the customer average order amount. If this order exceeds, say, three times the amount of the average order, then an exception notice may be printed.

(*b*) A material receipt which exceeds two times the economic order quantity established for the particular item might be subject to question.

(*c*) A receiving report amount may be compared with the amount requested on the purchase order. If there is more than a small percentage variance, then there is an assumption of an error in the input data.

(*d*) In a utility billing, consumption is checked against prior periods to detect possible errors or trouble in the customer's installation.

Control Totals Control totals are a basic method of error control to determine whether all items in a batch have been received and processed. The control total procedure requires that a control figure be developed by some previous processing and that the current data processing recompute this amount, comparing the resultant total with the previous total. Control totals are normally obtained for batches of data. The batches are kept to a reasonable size, so that errors can be easily isolated. For example, the sales slips to be processed by computer are first added on an adding machine to arrive at a control total for the sales in the batch. A control total for payroll might be the number of employees for which checks should be prepared. Control figures may be financial totals, hash totals, or document or record counts.

Financial totals These are totals such as sales, payroll amounts, and inventory dollar amounts which are normally added together in order to provide financial summaries.

Hash totals These are totals of data fields which are typically not added. The total has meaning only as a control and is not used in any other way in data processing. To determine that all inventory items are processed, a control total might be developed of the inventory item numbers, and this control would be compared with the sum of the item numbers obtained during the processing run.

Document or record count In many cases, rather than obtaining a financial total or hash total, it may be sufficient merely to obtain a count to ensure that all documents or records have been received and processed.

Control totals prepared prior to computer processing are furnished to computer processing as an input data item. The computer is then programmed to accumulate control totals internally and make a comparison. A message confirming the comparison should be printed out even if the comparison did not disclose an error. These messages are then subject to review by the control clerk (Figure 11-3).

When processing is performed online as transactions occur, there is no batch control because the transactions are not batched. However, it is possible to apply the batch concept. Transactions are accumulated during a period such as a day. Batch totals are also accumulated for various groupings of transactions (logical batches). At the end of the period, logical batch totals are available for checking against other counts or physical data collected by operations. The transactions may be sorted and printed as a logical batch listing. For example, there may be a listing of transactions by terminal or by salesperson (Figure 11-4).

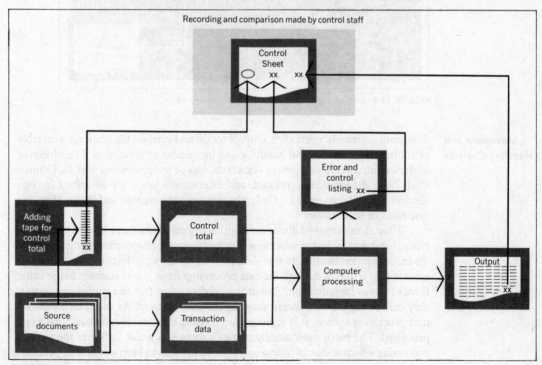

FIGURE 11-3 Use of control totals.

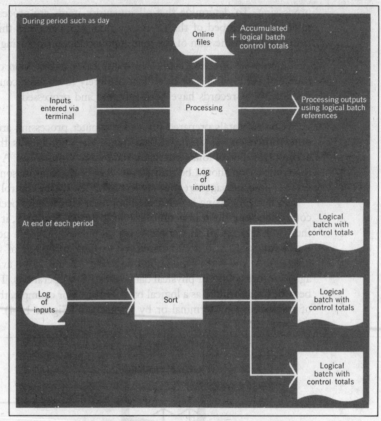

During period such as day

Online files

Accumulated + logical batch control totals

Inputs entered via terminal

Processing

Processing outputs using logical batch references

Log of inputs

At end of each period

Log of inputs

Sort

Logical batch with control totals

Logical batch with control totals

Logical batch with control totals

FIGURE 11-4 Use of logical batches in online processing.

Movement and Handling Controls

Transmittal controls, route slips, control totals, and external file labels are examples of controls over the internal handling and movement of input data. The objective of these controls is to prevent (or detect) the loss or nonprocessing of data. Control totals have already been explained, and external file labels are described in connection with file safeguards. Only the transmittal controls and route slips are discussed in this section.

When data is moved about through an organization, there is always a possibility that it may be lost or otherwise diverted from the proper processing channels. To ensure proper identification of data as it moves through the company, and more especially as it moves through the data processing steps, it is customary to use some form of status identification. As batches of data enter the data processing center, they may be logged on a listing showing the data received. As each batch passes a data processing station, it is registered, recording the fact that the batch has been processed. The batch itself usually carries a route slip which indicates the path of processing which it should follow and provides spaces to keep a record of processing performed. After data documents have been processed, they are canceled by marking or perforating to prevent accidental or deliberate reprocessing.

Control over Processing

Control over processing makes use of programmed controls. The processing should provide a processing trail which is suitable both for internal needs and as an audit trail for audits of the organization.

Programmed Control over Processing

The types of program controls which test the computer processing are the limit or reasonableness test, the crossfooting or crosstesting check, and control figures.

As with input data, a control over processing can be exercised by program steps which test the results of processing by comparing them with predetermined limits or by comparison with flexible limits which test the reasonableness of the results. In a payroll application, the net pay can be checked against an upper limit, an amount such that any paycheck exceeding the limit is probably in error. In a billing operation for a relatively homogeneous product, such as steel bars and plates, the weight of the shipment may be divided into the billing in order to develop a price per pound. If the price per pound exceeds the average by more than a predetermined percentage, a message will be written for subsequent follow-up to determine if the billing is in error.

It is frequently possible to check computer data processing in a manner similar to the manual method of crossfooting. Individual items are totaled independently, and then a crossfooting total developed from the totals. For example, in a payroll application, the totals are developed for gross pay, for each of the deduction items, and for the net pay. The total for net pay is then obtained independently by taking the total for gross pay and deducting the totals for each of the deduction items. If this crossfooting does not yield identical figures, then there has been some error in the program of processing.

Control figures developed in a manner similar to the input control totals can be used for testing the data processing within the machine. For example, the number of items to be invoiced in a billing run may be used as a control total and compared with the number of items billed on invoices.

The Processing Trail

The processing trail (or audit trail) consists of references, intermediate printouts, listings, etc., which document the flow of processing such that

1 Any transaction can be traced to the accounts in which it is aggregated and the report totals of which it is a part.

2 Any total in a report or in an account can be explored and traced back to the detailed transactions from which it was aggregated.

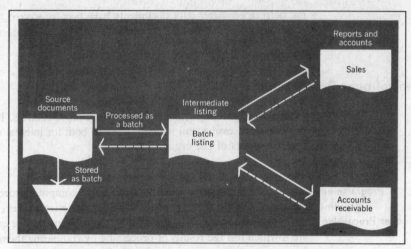

FIGURE 11-5 Processing trails.

Two examples will illustrate the concept of the processing trail.

Assume a credit sale which is to be traced to the accounts receivable record and to its inclusion in the sales figure. The sales invoices are probably batched and given a batch number. As part of the processing, the sales for the batch would be added to the sales total, and each individual sale would be added to the appropriate customer accounts receivable account. The batch itself might be listed. Any source sales transaction can be traced first to a transaction listing with a batch number and then to the recording of sales totals. The sales can also be traced via the batch reference to each sales entry in the accounts receivable detail file. The reverse procedure in this case is quite simple. The accounts receivable and sales entries have batch references which point to a transaction listing and to the batch of transaction documents (Figure 11-5).

The provisions for a processing trail may take several forms, but in all cases, there must be a means for tracing from the source document forward to the final aggregation and back from the aggregation to the source document. For batch processing, this is done by such references as batch number, document number, date of processing batch, etc. When processing is performed online on individual transactions rather than on batches of data, each transaction is identified by a unique identifier which is input or is assigned by the computer. Logical batches (stored for access or printed) form another basis for an online audit trail (refer back to Figure 11-4). References in records which point to the updating transaction use the unique identifier for the transaction and/or the reference to the logical batch.

Control over Output and Distribution

Before being distributed, the output from computer processing should be checked in two ways:

1 Comparing of control totals on output with previously prepared control total (balancing to input controls)

2 Screening to spot obvious errors

The distribution of output should be controlled to ensure that only those authorized receive it. Part of the control documentation for an application is the distribution list.

Persons receiving the output are an important error-detection control point, and provisions should be made in the system design for error feedback from recipients of output.

Hardware Features for Control over Equipment Malfunctions

Computer hardware consists of both mechanical parts (such as card reader transport) and electronic elements. The electronic portion is very reliable; the mechanical portion is somewhat less error-free. Both need periodic maintenance. The

TABLE 11-2 METHODS FOR ERROR DETECTION IN COMPUTER HARDWARE

Method of error detection	Description	Example
Redundant code character	Extra bit in coding of data. The number of 1-bits is summed. The parity bit is the 1-bit or 0-bit which makes the sum of 1-bits equal to an odd number (if odd parity).	Parity check bit
Duplicate process	Same operation is performed twice and the results compared.	Two read stations for card reader
Echo check	Signal sent to device to perform an operation; device returns a signal verifying that equipment was activated.	Printer echo check (Are print wheels in proper position?)
Validity check	Only certain results are correct.	Validity check on codes received from card reader
Equipment check	Test that equipment is operable.	Testing of photoelectric cells on card reader using them

Parity check bit example:

C	1 ← Check bit
B	0
A	0
8	0
4	0
2	1
1	1

6-bit code with parity bit

Number 3

error-control methods used with hardware are summarized together with one or more examples in Table 11-2.

Computer Installation Security

A data processing installation should establish and follow procedures which safeguard the hardware, programs, and data files from loss or destruction. If loss or destruction does occur, advance provisions should have been made for reconstruction and recovery. Security involves physical safeguards, procedural controls, a retention and reconstruction plan, and insurance.

Physical Safeguards   The physical safeguards may be classified as fire protection, access security, protection, and off-premises storage. The National Fire Protection Association calls for housing the computer in a noncombustible environment, storage of vital records in storage cabinets having a class C rating (1 hour at 1700°F), separate air-conditioning and power controls readily available in an emergency, and a fire extinguishing system. A sprinkler system can damage the equipment, so a Halon gas extinguishing system is preferred.

The computer room houses both expensive equipment and vital records. Some records may be confidential, and so access to the computer center should be restricted to those having a legitimate need to be there. The access security may be a key, a badge-activated lock, a guard, etc. Such access security provisions should be supported by personnel practices to screen applicants to avoid security risks, to recover keys and badges upon termination of employment, etc.

In the case of terminals which provide access to computing resources and/or to the organization database, there must be special safeguards. Unauthorized use of the computer is a misuse of organizational assets. In most organizations, there is confidential information in the files which should be restricted—salary data, for example. Security should be especially strong for changes by a terminal user of data in the master files. There is no method of completely restricting access, because any safeguards which are programmed can be changed through programming. The terminal use restrictions can be quite effective, however, by setting up provisions such as the following:

1 A "lockword" or "password" which the user must provide in order for file access to be accomplished. The passwords may provide varying degrees of access. For example, a password may identify a user as time sharing only, access only, or access and update.

2 A catalog of eligible users which is checked before access.

3 Scrambled data fields for confidential information. The data field is unscrambled for users who establish a need to know through a password. Other

users who may accidentally obtain access get only meaningless data. This cryptography approach to coding of confidential data may also be used to prevent data being sent over communication lines from being "tapped" by an unauthorized person.

Off-premises storage is used to provide a further safeguard for essential data processing records. Space can be rented in a secure, fireproof location, or another storage location in the same company can be used.

Procedural Controls Procedural controls can be used in the management of a computer center in order to minimize the possibility that an operator error will result in the destruction of a data or program file. Some common methods are external labels, magnetic tape file protection rings, and library procedures.

Files should be clearly labeled so that the operator will know the file contents. Punched card files are usually labeled on the top of the deck by the use of a felt marking pen. File name, identification, and date are commonly written. The first and last cards are also labeled. Magnetic tape reels and disk packs are labeled with a paper label attached to the tape reel or disk pack.

A physical safeguard used to prevent writing on a magnetic tape and destroying information prior to the release date for the tape is a removable plastic or metal ring, the absence of which will prevent writing on the tape.

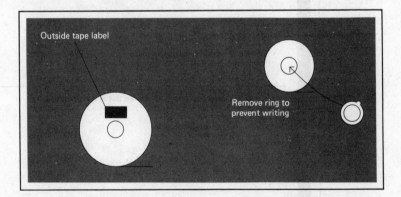

Library procedures provide for recordkeeping to maintain a log of the use to which tape reels and disks have been put and for a systematic method to store tapes and packs that allows them to be easily located or replaced in the storage racks.

Programs should be protected against loss by documentation which is updated when changes are made. A copy of the documentation and all updating changes should be stored off-premises along with data files and copies of the programs. Programs should be protected against undocumented changes by a change approval and documentation procedure. After a program has been approved and put in use, there will be a need for program changes. These should be approved by the program manager or data processing manager. A record of the change should be prepared and filed with the run manual for the program (Figure 11-6). The changes should be carefully tested.

The program change record is useful in keeping documentation current. It is very time-consuming to correct all documentation each time a program change is made. Instead, a change record is included with the documentation. The original

<table>
<tr><td colspan="2" align="center">DATA PROCESSING PROGRAM CHANGE RECORD</td></tr>
<tr><td>Program name or description</td><td>Change number _____

Date
change effective _____</td></tr>
<tr><td colspan="2">Program number</td></tr>
<tr><td colspan="2">Change initiated by _____ Date _____
Change request approved by _____ Date _____</td></tr>
<tr><td colspan="2">Description of purpose or reason for change</td></tr>
<tr><td colspan="2">Description of changes made (and effect on this and other programs)</td></tr>
<tr><td colspan="2">Change made by _____ Date _____
Change tested by _____ Date _____
Change posted to run manual _____ Date _____
Change posted to operator instructions _____ Date _____
Review of changes _____ Date _____</td></tr>
</table>

FIGURE 11-6 Program change notice.

documentation, plus the change records, form the current documentation.

The source program in machine-readable form used in making changes should be safeguarded by the librarian and issued only upon authorization. Some organizations use program library management software which performs program updating and automatically provides a record of all changes and data needed for reconstruction if the change is to be removed.

Retention and Reconstruction Plan

The retention plan of a data processing department provides a means for record or file reconstruction. Source documents are retained at least until the computer file has been proved and balanced with its controls. However, other considerations may require a longer storage period for these documents. Important master files should be reproduced and a copy maintained in secure storage, preferably off premises.

A retention plan for magnetic tape is generally accomplished by the use of the son-father-grandfather concept. The files retained under this concept on, for example, a Wednesday (assuming daily processing) would be

Wednesday's file	(Son)
Tuesday's file	(Father)
Monday's file	(Grandfather)

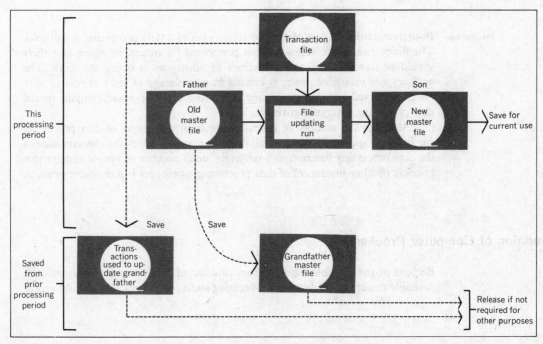

FIGURE 11-7 Son-father-grandfather concept for retention of magnetic tape files.

If, during processing on Thursday, the Wednesday tape were destroyed, Tuesday's tape would be processed again with Wednesday's transactions to recreate Wednesday's master tape. If no other processing or retention considerations require keeping the tape longer, the old grandfather can be released when a new one is produced (Figure 11-7).

Disk file processing, unlike magnetic tape, does not automatically produce a duplicate, updated copy of the file. To provide for reconstruction, the disk must be duplicated before processing to provide a reference point and all transactions saved until the next reference file copy is made. The reference copy can be put onto another disk or a magnetic tape.

Computer security requires not only a retention plan but also a contingency plan. This will cover disruptions such as fire, bomb threats, etc., and will define the procedures for reconstruction in the event of loss of a file or destruction of equipment. The plan will include backup physical facilities through either the manufacturer, a service center, or another user. It may include special programs to facilitate reconstructing of files. As an example of the problem, a recent news item reported a wildcat strike by bus drivers who had not been paid at the appointed hour. The reason for the delay was the bankruptcy of the service bureau which processed the payroll. The files and programs were not transferrable to another service bureau, and the payroll had to be prepared by hand. The manual processing was too slow to meet the deadline.

Insurance   Insurance should be part of the protection plan of a data processing installation. The major risk is fire unless work is performed for others, in which case there should be liability insurance for errors or omissions in doing the work. The ordinary fire insurance policy is limited in its coverage of risks associated with losses connected with data processing. Therefore, many organizations take special data processing insurance coverage.

Although the number of losses arising from dishonesty of data processing employees is apparently quite small, the risks associated with the concentration of the data processing function in a relatively small number of people suggest that bonding (fidelity insurance) of data processing employees is a desirable practice.

Auditing of Computer Processing

Because of the possible damage from undetected and uncorrected errors, it is desirable to have some computer processing audit procedures. These audit procedures may be performed by the control section and by an internal audit group. Investigations should be made on a regular basis of conditions which suggest possible errors. Examples of such investigations are:

1 Investigation of all limit violations, such as payroll checks which exceed the maximum allowable.

2 Investigation of discrepancy between computer records and physical count, such as the difference between the physical inventory counts and the perpetual record maintained through the computer.

3 Investigation of items which change radically for no apparent reason, such as an expense which has been fairly constant and then changes without apparent cause.

4 Investigation of items where statistical analysis indicates a change from normal relationships. For example, the gross profit percentage in a business will tend to be constant and can therefore be used as a standard for comparison with data produced by the computer.

As a part of the regular auditing by the internal and external auditors, there should be a review of the processing control organization and practices and tests to determine compliance. Independent tests should also be made on data files to check the quality of records.

The concentration of processing in a small number of files and few personnel increases the possible damage from malicious destruction and also increases the possibility of certain types of computer-based fraud. The dangers from fraud are probably overemphasized, but they do exist. The protection against such fraud rests primarily on proper control practices, but auditing can assist in identifying risk and detecting possible fraud. The audit can also review and test security provisions and practices.

Quality Control for Computational Programs

The emphasis so far in the chapter has been on quality control over business data processing. The one-time nature of scientific or statistical processing does not require the full range of controls. However, it introduces new problems of quality assurance for the computational programs—in the statistical software used and in the individual programs.

In the case of statistical software furnished by the manufacturer or by software houses for general use, the packages tend to be good. However, there may be errors in them. For example, a statistical package used for several years at a university was found to have an error in one of its routines. This was detected when the same problem was run using this routine and a similar routine on another computer. A routine may work well in most cases but not handle conditions such as negative numbers, etc. The problem of arithmetic precision may cause different statistical packages to yield slightly different results. The user of a statistical package may find it so convenient to obtain output that the necessary thought of its applicability may be overpowered by the availability. On balance, a user of statistical packages should exercise care in selecting the package to use (and understanding what it does) and should perform reasonableness tests on the results.

Quality control over user-written computational programs can be improved if steps such as the following are taken:

1 Test all conditions in the program with special attention to negative and zero data if these are not expected. Test the program with data values at each breakpoint and at the breakpoints plus one and minus one. If, for example, processing is different for data having a value less than 100 (i.e., 100 is the breakpoint), tests should be made on data values 99, 100, and 101.

2 Print out all input data as part of the output of the program.

3 Print out intermediate results if this can be meaningful in evaluating the resulting computations. For example, an iterative procedure which is converging to an answer may tally the number of iterations and print every nth result.

SUMMARY A major problem with computer data processing systems is control over the quality of the processing. The responsibility for quality extends from top management down to the control function in the data processing department. Top management should require adequate justification before approving projects and should follow with reviews of performance. The data processing department should be organized to provide for division of responsibility and a clear assignment of duties, including the control function and library function. Documentation and other desirable management practices should be included.

The control over data entry and input is very important because most errors occur at this point in the processing. The equipment, on the other hand, is very reliable and, in general, has adequate controls. Programmed controls over processing can detect some program errors. The programs themselves should be controlled to prevent unauthorized changes. Also, a protection plan for computer files, programs, and program documentation should be part of the operations of a computer installation.

This chapter has surveyed the major techniques and major considerations associated with the different control points. Adequate controls have a cost associated with them. Therefore, data processing management should understand control practices and evaluate their use on the basis of the cost of the control versus the consequences of an error being undetected at that point in the data processing cycle.

EXERCISES

1 Explain the concept of redundancy and how it applies to error detection.

2 A systems analyst made the discovery that double-entry accounting has a large amount of redundancy. He stated that his "system" would eliminate this and use only single entry. Evaluate this from the point of view of error control.

3 In a well-known fraud, a computer programmer working for a service bureau wrote a program for a bank which listed all overdrawn checking accounts. This same programmer was sometimes assigned as a night operator to run the job. One evening, he inserted a patch to have the computer ignore his account number if it were overdrawn. He then proceeded to overdraw his account. What control features would have prevented or detected the fraud?

4 Examine the following two check-digit procedures to determine the relative merits of each. Apply the procedures to the number 37657123 and evaluate the probability of simple transpositions giving the same check digit.
Method 1: See textbook
Method 2: Same as method 1, except that the weights are $1 - 2 - 1 - 2 \dots$

5 Write down any 10 six-digit numbers. Test each of them to determine if you have a valid account number, assuming the last digit is a check digit and the method is the one presented in the text.

6 Both inside and outside recipients of output are important elements in the control framework. Evaluate the effectiveness of customers as control elements in detecting *and* reporting errors. What other nonprocessing considerations are relevant in deciding to depend on customers to detect and report errors?

7 What is the purpose of the control function? What are the duties which might be assigned?

8 How might an error in keypunching of input data get past the verification process?

9 What is the purpose of input data validation?

10 What validation might be used to detect the following input data errors:
(a) Transcription error creating wrong customer account number
(b) Pricing error—wrong price used
(c) Quantity written as number of pounds but issued in tons, not pounds
(d) Wrong plant coded in shipment instructions—plant does not stock item
(e) Seven-digit salesperson code used instead of eight-digit product code
(f) No price entered

11 A computer at the University of Waterloo was held "hostage" by a group of campus dissidents occupying a campus building. When the police finally began to clear the building, the dissidents "killed" the hostage. At Fresno State College, a student threw an incendiary device through the glass window and into the computer room. The computer was completely destroyed. Assume that you are the director of computer services for a university and outline steps you should take to safeguard your computer facilities. Assume that the computer is used for both academic purposes and university data processing.

12 The internal auditor for a large mutual fund made a check of computer room security during the evening and found that there was a period of one-half hour when no employee was present. The room was wide open. Other than malicious destruction, what was at risk?

13 A large credit-card company has the following procedure for handling customer complaints about billings. An indicator is set in the customer record, and the customer receives a notice with the next billing stating that "Your communication has been received. Please pay undisputed amount." The complaint is turned over to an

investigator who may or may not get to it. However, the computer is programmed to start dunning the customer starting 1 month from the first notice. Describe how this procedure might be improved.

14 Evaluate, using the criteria given in the chapter, the merits of controls to:
  (a) Prevent item quantities on purchase orders prepared by the computer from exceeding certain limits
  (b) Prevent shipping-order errors
  (c) Prevent billing errors
  (d) Prevent sales-analysis errors
  (e) Prevent overpayment of wages to an employee

15 The master payroll file on magnetic tape was inadvertently written over by another processing run.
  (a) What elementary operating control procedure was not used?
  (b) How can the installation recreate the master file?

16 Why is a hash total used?

17 What errors will a parity bit procedure detect? Which will it not detect?

18 An agent specializing in industrial espionage offers the sales data from any sales office of a competitor. The competition transmits the data over communications lines. You inform the competitor and suggest protective measures. What might these measures be?

19 How is an input echo used in detecting and correcting errors?

20 Define possible duties of internal auditing with respect to computer processing.

CHAPTER

ACQUISITION OF COMPUTER HARDWARE AND SOFTWARE

Acquisition of computer hardware and software is an important topic not only because large expenditures may be involved but also because the computer can alter the operation and management of an organization. Computer hardware and software that do not meet the needs of the organization represent a loss of the expenditures made and, usually more important, may result in significant loss due to the disruption of the organization. No major acquisition of hardware or software should be undertaken without adequate investigation and careful planning of the implementation.

Evaluating hardware or software systems is a complex task and one which cannot adequately be described in a single short chapter. On the other hand, the overview of this chapter should assist the student in understanding the factors involved in evaluating the desirability of computer hardware or software acquisitions, in selecting a specific system, and in the installation of the selected system.

Criteria for Evaluation

The fundamental criterion in a business organization for deciding whether to install a new computer system, replace an existing computer, obtain a software package, or implement a new application is whether the system will help to produce greater profits. For a nonprofit or government organization, the criterion is whether the computer will result in either reduced operating costs or significantly improved ability to provide service to customers, clients, or the public.

The benefits can be classified into three categories:

1 *Cost displacement* This would include all decreased operating costs through reductions in personnel, reductions in space utilization, etc.

2 *Operation efficiencies* This would include the benefits arising from better information. Examples are reduced inventory (reduced costs for carrying inventory), improved scheduling of production (less idle time), and reduction in billing time (faster collections).

3 *New methods* The computer produces benefits from new methods of operation and management. For example, an immediate response system allows new methods of order entry, production scheduling, management analysis, etc.

4 *Intangible benefits* This includes items for which the benefits are difficult to quantify, such as improved service (improved responsiveness to inquiries and improved delivery time), more timely analyses for planning and control, and improved analysis for decision making.

In the early days of computer usage, most computers were justified on the basis of direct clerical cost displacement. It should be noted that, in a large percentage of cases, these cost reductions were not achieved. Today, the emphasis is on increasing profits through the use of the computer. The latter criterion is more nebulous than direct cost reductions but should not be ignored. There are also other considerations, such as the fact that some businesses could not return to manual processing even if they wished; the large clerical staffs which the computers replaced may no longer be available. The processing of checks, for example, is now so completely computerized that it would be virtually impossible for a bank in a large city to process checks manually.

Studies have shown that companies with aggressive and alert managements tend to be extensive users of computers. However, these facts are not sufficient to justify a computer or a move to acquire a more sophisticated model.

Cost Characteristics of Computer Installations

It is difficult to make general statements about cost characteristics because the costs may vary considerably from installation to installation. Nevertheless, it is useful to describe general tendencies in terms of percentages of total costs. The first breakdown is in terms of percentage of total expenditures devoted to the major objects of expenditure (objects for which expenditures are made, such as personnel or hardware).

Object of expenditure	Percent of total cost*
Personnel	60
Equipment and equipment maintenance	25
Supplies	5
Building and overhead	10

*Author's estimates.

Note that supplies and equipment and equipment maintenance are only 30 percent of total expenditures, whereas personnel are double the equipment and supplies cost. The trend has been for the equipment costs to decrease as a percentage of total expenditures and for the personnel costs to increase. This trend is likely to continue. The supplies figure is surprisingly high because, although paper, cards, etc., are inexpensive, the computer system makes use of massive quantities.

The object of expenditure indicates what the expenditures purchase. Another very meaningful breakdown of the same costs is to show the functions or purposes for which they are spent. For this division, four major functions are identified: development of new applications, maintenance on old applications, operations (running current applications), and administration. In other words, these are the reasons why personnel were hired, equipment installed, etc. In the beginning of a new installation, the percentages would be much higher for new applications. These figures show the breakdown for a continuing installation in operation for some time.

Expenditure by function	Percent of total cost*
New applications (investigating, designing, planning, and implementing)	20
Maintenance to correct and update existing applications	10
Operations (data preparation, data entry, and execution of existing applications)	65
Administration	5

*Author's estimates.

Two-thirds of an installation's expenditures go for current operations to run existing applications. About one-third goes for developing new applications and maintaining old ones. The relationship between new applications and maintenance of old ones is important because it emphasizes the fact that to keep a computer application in use requires a continuing expenditure. Changes will be made, it will need to be updated to become consistent with some other system, some latent errors will need to be corrected. This maintenance expenditure is significant, representing half as much as is spent on developing new applications.

There is a substantial start-up cost to get a completely new system (as opposed to a replacement system) selected, installed, tested, and ready to run. Making a general statement is difficult, but start-up costs may equal one-half to one whole year's expected operating costs after installation.

Guidelines for Success in Using a Computer

Some computer installations have been very successful; others have been plagued by trouble. What is the difference? Equipment problems are rarely to blame for the troubles of a computer installation. Failure of the manufacturer to deliver software on schedule or failure of the software to meet specifications may be quite disruptive, but the major elements of success are within the company. These are:

1 Top management participation and support

2 Adequate planning and control

3 Adequate consideration of human problems caused by the introduction of the computer and a program of action to handle the problems

Top management participation and support are necessary conditions for success. Since the installation of a computer can be disruptive to the organization, the entire organization must understand that top management is solidly behind the new system. Lower levels of management will tend to support what is clearly being supported by top management. The top management also needs to be involved in deciding on the broad outlines of the new system. The design, as far as top management is concerned, must be "our design" and "our system," not "your design" and "your system."

The installation of a new or replacement computer system extends over a long period of time. If it is not properly planned and controlled, the different activities will not be achieved on time, and the parts of the system will not mesh correctly. The planning and control of the steps in installing a computer system should utilize standard management techniques. This means that responsibility should be defined, criteria and objectives should be specified, schedules and deadlines should be established, work assignments should be made, and procedures should be established for spotting deviations from this plan.

Installing a new computer data processing system in a proper manner requires many months of preparation prior to the moving in of the equipment. As a rough guide, installing a batch-oriented medium-scale data processing system in an organization which has not had a computer before requires from 12 to 24 months from the point that the decision is made to investigate the feasibility of the computer system until the system is running satisfactorily with the first applications. Figure 12-1 gives a reasonable approximation of minimum times. However,

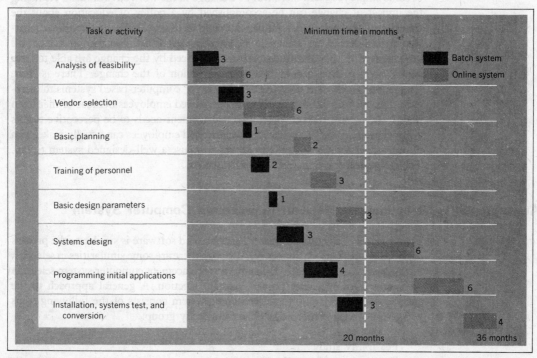

FIGURE 12-1 Minimum times for implementing a new medium-scale computer data processing system.

the total elapsed time may, in some cases, be reduced by performing some tasks simultaneously, rather than one after another. Assuming that the decision has been made to install a computer, the total elapsed time until the system is operating is not likely to be less than 9 months for a batch system and 18 months for a complex online system. Where replacement computers are to be selected and installed, the time required is dependent on such variables as the transferrability of the old applications to the new system. A reasonable estimate for the time between the decision to replace and its implementation might be two-thirds of the original time estimates between decision and implementation.

Small business-oriented computer systems can frequently be installed in a much shorter period of time than the more complex systems because the vendors provide prewritten applications which are modified only slightly for each user. The use of the "canned" application packages allows installation of a small business computer and operation of its basic applications in, say, 3 months after vendor selection.

In the matter of human problems caused by the introduction of computers, some form of resistance to the change by both clerical and supervisory personnel is the rule rather than the exception. A computer system (or a substantial change to a more sophisticated system) will cause changes in the organization. Jobs will be eliminated, there will be a change (reduction or increase) in the status and prestige of some employees, and there will be a change in the work environment. Reducing the impact of change can be accomplished by a policy of education about the change, the reasons for it, and the nature of the change, plus a policy of participation in considering the change. It is generally agreed that resistance to change will be decreased to the extent that persons influenced by the change are able to have some "say" in the planning and implementation of the change. There is some inclination on the part of systems designers for computer-based systems to disregard the opinions and suggestions of experienced employees because of their own zeal in the use of the computer. The management needs to be perceptive to this type of problem and recognize that experienced employees can usually make even a mediocre computer system work and can cause a well-designed system to fail. Their cooperation is therefore vital to success.

An Approach to Selection of a New or Replacement Computer System

The process of selecting computer hardware and software is similar to the process of selecting production machinery. Although there are some similarities in selection methods, it will be useful to discuss new or replacement computer system selection separately from specific software package selection. A general approach to the analysis of the desirability of a computer system consists of the following steps which are carried out or supervised by a study group:

Feasibility study
Preparation of manual of specifications

Obtaining of equipment proposals
Selection

The first three steps are described in this section of the chapter; selection of the computer equipment is the subject of the next section.

The Study Group   A recommended approach to computers is to form a committee or task group to direct the evaluation study. For most organizations, the committee should consist of middle-management personnel who represent the principal functions of the business, plus an executive from the systems function. One of the major problems in systems design is understanding the requirements of the different portions of the organization. The use of middle-management personnel who are reasonably high in the organization and can speak authoritatively about the requirements of their functions gives authority and scope to the work of the group. They can also be freed from part of their responsibilities in order to allow adequate time for this assignment. Although the members of the study group do not have to be technically proficient, they should have a reasonable overall understanding of data processing. A short training course for the committee may therefore be desirable. The task group must be provided with technical staff support. For an organization with a computer installation that is studying the value of a new or expanded system, the staff support can come from the data processing systems staff. For an organization without prior experience, the use of outside consultants is frequently advisable. If used, consultants should work with, guide, assist, and otherwise aid the study group by providing the experience and technical expertise which the committee may not have. It is not usually advisable to turn the entire evaluation process over to outside consultants without having them work with an internal group.

The Feasibility   The purpose of the feasibility study is to investigate the present system, evaluate
Study   the possible application of new or revised computer-based methods (and also noncomputer methods), select a tentative system, evaluate the cost and effectiveness of the proposed system, evaluate the impact of the proposed system on existing personnel, and ascertain the need for new personnel.

To define an improved information system, the study group must understand the information requirements of the organization. This understanding may be obtained by the dual process of examining the existing data processing system to determine what is currently being done and of investigating through interviews and analysis what information needs to be provided that is not being furnished by the existing system. Data on the cost of operating the current system needs to be collected in order to make a cost-benefit analysis for a new system.

The data collection procedure consists of interviews with personnel who prepare and who use information. This leads to analyses of system objectives, of decision processes, and of necessary information for processing and decision purposes. The information analysis will include preparation, movement, use, and storage of documents, reports, files, records, and data items. The result of the data collection will be:

1 Description of events which lead to data processing and the response time and accuracy needed by the system user.

2 Samples of all input, output, and file documents.

3 Description of use of information and the processing performed by each person receiving or issuing documents.

4 Information and document flow within the organization.

5 Description of all files. The description includes the use, rate of growth, inquiry rate (why and by whom), and frequency of updating (if a master file).

From this documentation of events, documents, information flow, and files, a description of the existing system can be organized and new systems laid out. Techniques for the system design are system flowcharting, grid charts, networks, specification sheets, layouts, etc.

When conducting interviews, the staff of the study group should seek to discover the information and data processing requirements not satisfied by the current system and to find out what information is needed. In this phase, it should be recognized that many persons do not know what they need or can use. Some analysis is then required to help the user perceive what information would be useful.

From the information obtained in the feasibility study, the study group formulates one or more tentative systems, then makes rough estimates of their cost and their ability to meet system objectives. From these tentative systems, one of which should usually be a modified version of the present system, a system is selected as the best solution and is then analyzed further in terms of personnel impact, cost benefit, and suitability in terms of the needs to be met. Care should be taken to design the system to take advantage of the special capabilities of the new or replacement computer rather than merely computerizing or speeding up an existing system.

The personnel impact portion of the feasibility study assembles data on the impact on company personnel of the proposed system. Rough plans are formulated for orienting, training, counseling, and adjusting the work force to the computer system. Estimates are made of the cost of the adjustment.

The cost-benefit study summarizes the benefits to be expected from the computer, the expected cost, and expected savings. A useful approach is to separate the tangible, measurable benefits from the intangible. The tangible benefits are used to estimate an expected savings and rate of return. The intangible benefits may also have benefits assigned to them; they are used in a judgmental decision process after the tangible benefits have been evaluated. Table 12-1 shows a summarized analysis. This would be supported by an analysis showing more detail. The figures are rough because specific equipment has not yet been selected. For the purposes of an

TABLE 12-1 PRELIMINARY COST-BENEFIT ANALYSIS FOR
COMPUTER SYSTEM

Estimated initial cost of a new computer system	
Cost of site preparation	$xx
Analysis and programming of basic applications	xx
Cost of training, file conversion, parallel operations, etc.	xx
Total one-time costs	$xx
Estimated annual operating costs	
Computer and related equipment rental or amortization	
and maintenance	$xx
Software rental	xx
Program maintenance	xx
Operating personnel	xx
Space charges, supplies, power, etc.	xx
Total operating costs	$xx
Annual savings from displaced costs plus value of operation efficiencies and new methods less annual operating costs	$xx
Rate of return (rate at which present value of savings equals present value of one-time costs)	xx%
Intangible benefits (list)	

investment analysis, the life of a system is probably about five to eight years. Six years is probably a satisfactory compromise unless added facts are available which dictate otherwise.

The results of the feasibility study together with the recommendations of the study groups are summarized and presented for top management approval. If the project is approved, the next step is to prepare a manual of specifications for use in procurement.

**Manual of
Specifications**

The *manual of specifications* is a statement of requirements which defines specifically what is to be accomplished by the proposed computer. It is a fairly detailed document. Most of the data needed for it is collected in the feasibility study. The document serves both as a summary of the proposed system for internal purposes and as a statement for use in inviting equipment proposals from vendors of data processing equipment. The system specifications will usually include the elements listed in Table 12-2.

The underlying concept for the manual of specifications is that the company should define its requirements and that the vendor proposals will be measured against these specifications. However, the rather complete specifications of the system requirements should not be used to discourage innovative suggestions by the vendors. The manufacturer preparing a proposal should be allowed to suggest alternative or improved methods for achieving stated objectives.

TABLE 12-2 ELEMENTS IN A MANUAL OF
SPECIFICATIONS FOR SYSTEM PROCUREMENT

1 Introduction
 (a) Description of organization
 (b) Summary of requirements
 (c) Current equipment
 (d) Selection process (criteria to be used, form of responses, etc.)
 (e) Acceptance tests

2 System requirements
 (a) Hardware features required
 (b) Software required
  (1) Compilers (FORTRAN, COBOL, RPG, etc.)
  (2) Utility packages (e.g., sort routine)
  (3) Application packages (e.g., linear programming, payroll
   processing)
  (4) Operating system
 (c) Support required
  (1) System designers provided by vendor
  (2) Backup facilities
  (3) Test time and facilities
 (d) Constraints
  (1) Planned delivery date for equipment and software
  (2) Time constraints on processing
 (e) Desirable features not required to meet specifications
 (f) Capability for future growth

3 Major applications (for each, the following)
 (a) System description
 (b) File description including current size and growth rate
 (c) Input data specifications and volume of input
 (d) System flowcharts for each run and run descriptions giving
  (1) Frequency of processing
  (2) Volume of transactions
  (3) Suggested method of processing

Obtaining On the basis of a preliminary screening, four or five vendors may be invited to
Equipment submit proposals. Each vendor is provided with a copy of the manual of specifica-
Proposals tions and the rules for submitting proposals. There may be follow-up interviews
with vendors to clarify any misunderstandings or uncertainties in the specifications.

 When the proposals are ready, the manufacturer's representative is usually
provided with an opportunity for a presentation to the study group. At this
meeting, he or she will summarize the proposal and answer questions. The
manufacturer's proposal should normally contain the points listed in Table 12-3.

Deciding on the Computer System

The manual of specifications plus the manufacturer's proposals provide input for
the decision process on equipment selection. The need for a systematic alternative
has prompted the use of ranking methods. There are a number of methods for

TABLE 12-3 OUTLINE OF INFORMATION NORMALLY FOUND IN A MANUFACTURER'S PROPOSAL

1 Proposed equipment configuration
  (a) Equipment units
  (b) Equipment operating characteristics and specifications
  (c) Options or alternative configurations
  (d) Ability of the system to expand (modularity)
  (e) Special requirements as to site and other installation costs

2 Cost of proposed configuration
  (a) Rental and purchase price by unit
  (b) Extra shift rental
  (c) Maintenance contract if a unit is purchased
  (d) Software rental

3 Availability of specified software and special software packages

4 Systems support
  (a) Systems analysis included; cost for added services
  (b) Programming services included; cost for added services
  (c) Customer maintenance engineer availability
  (d) Customer education support and schedule of rates

5 Terms
  (a) Acceptance of specified delivery date or proposed alternative delivery date
  (b) Payment terms
  (c) Lease-purchase and other options
  (d) Amount of test time to be provided

6 System performance for specified applications
  (a) Changes in design if different from that specified in requirements
  (b) Timings (how long each application takes)
  (c) Changes in timings using optional equipment

7 Other information

evaluating throughput for evaluation purposes; the major methods are discussed below.

When a vendor is selected, an order is placed. The contract with the manufacturer is usually based on a standard contract form. However, there are still many points for negotiation. For example, the assistance to be provided by the manufacturer—number of systems analysts who will assist in implementing the system or number of hours of free test time—may vary from installation to installation depending on the negotiations. Now that equipment costs are firm, a final cost analysis can be prepared.

Ranking of Equipment Proposals   The evaluation may be simple if only one manufacturer can satisfy specifications; but in general, several manufacturers will respond with proposals worthy of consideration. Since there are a number of considerations, both quantitative and subjective, one method is to rank each manufacturer by a point system. For each criterion for evaluation, a possible number of points are assigned, and then each manufacturer is rated by assigning part of or all the possible points. A summary for such an analysis is given in Table 12-4. There is a supporting analysis for each of the summary criteria. For example, software evaluation might include such sub-criteria as

Operating system evaluation
COBOL evaluation
FORTRAN evaluation
Report generator evaluation
Data management system evaluation
Storage requirements
Other software evaluation

Evaluation criteria will receive various weights from different users. The major questions are whether the proposed equipment will perform the job in the time allowed, its relative cost, and whether it has sufficient flexibility to expand as more applications are added. A system should allow for growth—in file size, in number and scope of applications, and in volume of transactions. Most systems can provide for growth by the addition of equipment options. For example, a stripped-down, minimum-memory-size computer may have its power increased by adding faster input/output units, more storage, or special instruction packages. A compatible family of computers allows the user to move from one computer in the

TABLE 12-4 SUMMARY SHEET FOR POINT-RANKING METHOD OF COMPUTER EVALUATION

		PROPOSALS		
Criteria for evaluation	Possible points	A	B	C
1 System performance (42 percent)				
(a) Hardware performance	60	60	41	42
(b) Software performance	60	39	43	31
(c) Expansion capabilities	55	41	48	30
2 Vendor capabilities (25 percent)				
(a) Vendor performance	40	25	32	21
(b) Maintenance and backup	20	14	18	13
(c) Installation support	20	12	18	12
(d) Staff preference	25	15	20	5
3 Cost (33 percent)				
(a) Rental price	50	35	23	40
(b) Terms for extended use	20	17	5	18
(c) Ongoing educational cost	25	21	9	17
(d) Maintenance and backup cost	20	15	10	14
(e) One-time system and education cost	20	18	11	14
Total points	415	312	278	257

family to a larger size without reprogramming. It is necessary to evaluate not only the existing software but also the probability of promised software being available when expected.

In evaluating hardware and software, it is frequently desirable to program and run a test problem to try out the effectiveness of the software and to evaluate the operating problems. The manufacturer will usually provide time for testing. Frequently, an order must be placed before any test machine is available. But the practice in the industry is to use the initial sales order as a basis for scheduling machine delivery. When the delivery time is close (say, 6 months), the order is firmed. Thus, there is usually sufficient time to evaluate by test runs the equipment which may not have been available when the initial order was placed.

In evaluation of equipment, the alternative of a mixed system should be considered. Several firms offer plug-in compatible peripherals (say, a tape unit or a disk unit) which have higher performance at a lower cost than the manufacturer's units. The main disadvantage of these independent peripherals is in the added management problems of dealing with more than one vendor and related questions of responsibility for equipment-caused failures.

Comparing Throughput Performance

The study group should make an analysis of the applications timings furnished by the manufacturer and conduct an independent analysis of the computer capabilities. There is no foolproof method for selecting the best computer system; there are too many uncertainties. However, a combination of the stated system times for the applications contained in the specifications and independent evaluation of throughput provide a reasonably good basis for decision.

If the programs have not yet been written, how can a valid time estimate be made? For some computer runs using utility packages such as the sort routine, the times can be estimated with a high degree of precision. Some jobs are input/output bound, so that as long as the computational steps stay within the bounds of the input/output times, these times can be used. Other routines can be evaluated by estimating number of instructions required and multiplying by an average time per instruction. The proposal should be checked to ensure that all estimating procedures are specified. The time estimates should include handling and setup time where required and should show the timing for each unit of the configuration for each run; these times should be summarized by day. Such a summary shows the peak requirements, since some runs are daily, others weekly or monthly, and provides an estimate of the peak load of the system.

There should also be some independent evaluation of the manufacturer's times. This can be performed using data from computer information services and by specially constructed kernel or benchmark problems. The information and analysis services available for this purpose range from a computerized analysis (which makes independent timings for a specified list of computers and compares them for decision-making purposes) to comparisons based on instruction times or standard benchmark problems.

In using evaluation techniques, it should be kept in mind that the real criterion for measuring system performance is throughput. The comparisons that are made are in lieu of the complete throughput analysis, which cannot be made in advance because all programs would have to be written and running. The following frequently used methods of comparison are listed together with comments on their effectiveness:

Comparison techniques	Comments
Memory cycle time	Extremely gross measure. Unreliable because systems differ in hardware organization, overlapping of operations, etc.
Add time	Extremely gross measure. Perhaps useful when comparing computers with same hardware organization.
Instruction times	Very gross measure since the frequency of instruction use must be considered.
Instruction mix times (average for a mix of instructions)	An average instruction time based on the expected frequency with which each instruction is used for different types of applications. Gross measure, but better than unweighted instruction time. At best, it is a measure of raw internal computing power.
Kernel problem	Sample problems are coded with the system's own instructions and time. Especially useful for standardized mathematical applications. Gives a measure of internal performance. Does not reflect the input/output, multiprogramming, operating system, etc.
Standard benchmark problems	Standard problems of a type normally performed. The problem is coded, and time to perform the standard task is estimated or measured by running it. Standard benchmark problems usually reflect the type of jobs done but are not a sample of the complete processing system as it will operate.
Simulation	The characteristics of the proposed system are compared with the characteristics of available computers, and the performance of the different systems are simulated by a computer program.

Converting to a Computer System

Rarely is a computer delivered shortly after the order is signed. Usually there is a lapse of several months. Within the limits of possible delivery dates, the installation date should be planned at the customer's convenience rather than at the manufacturer's. The conversion to a new or replacement computer is a major project and should therefore be carefully scheduled and coordinated. The conversion must be supervised, preferably by the new data processing manager (if a new system) or by the current manager (if a replacement computer). The installations may be assisted by the study group. Some of the preparatory activities are site preparation, training, preparation of initial applications, file conversion, and cutover to the new system.

Site Preparation and Training

A medium- or large-scale computer will usually require some special site preparation. The manufacturer will provide complete specifications for the electrical, space, air-conditioning, and other needs of the equipment, and a site-planning engineer from the vendor will usually be available for assisting in site planning. This planning may include physical security and provisions for an uninterrupted power supply.

Initial training of staff in programming and using the equipment will typically be available from the manufacturer. The amount, type, and cost of training should be agreed upon when the contract is negotiated. Manuals and other instructional materials are normally available from the vendor.

Preparation of Initial Applications and Cutover

The initial applications to be run on the computer should be written and debugged prior to delivery of the equipment. In other words, when the computer is working and turned over to the organization, the first applications should be programmed, debugged, and ready to run. As part of the agreement to rent or purchase the equipment, the user should have negotiated with the computer manufacturer for a certain number of hours of time on that model computer at the manufacturer's test facilities. Additional time may of course be purchased. This provides the customer with computer time to assemble or compile, debug, and test programs prior to the installation data. The customer's personnel can also gain experience in operating the equipment. Testing is also required with application packages or systems (such as standard accounts receivable application) obtained from the vendor, but the preparation and testing time may be substantially reduced.

Prior to the beginning of processing, all master files must be prepared. For a completely new installation, this will normally involve extensive conversion of data to punched cards or keydisk and then to the computer file storage medium. This must be done with care and with a substantial amount of control and checking, so that the initial file is correct. If the conversion is from one model computer to another, the old files possibly may be run on the new equipment without change. If not, a conversion program may be necessary, or special equipment such as a tape-to-tape converter may be used.

When converting from one computer system to another, various methods or combinations are used to ease the problem of rewriting programs.

Method	Explanation
Emulation	An extra-cost feature, it is usually implemented by a microprogram (in a special storage) which executes the instructions of the old computer on

	the new one by interpreting each old instruction into its equivalent in the new instructions. Programs do not run as fast under emulation as when they are rewritten in the language of the new computer.
Simulation	Does the same function as the emulator except that it is a regular program which interprets each instruction and executes the equivalent instructions in the new machine. Generally slower than emulation.
Conversion routines	Routines which produce source programs for the new computer from the source program for the old system. Used both for symbolic languages and for making required changes for various high-level languages, such as FORTRAN or COBOL.

During the start-up for a new system, unforeseen difficulties may arise in the processing programs. Also it is often difficult to obtain a proper cutoff. For these reasons, it is usually a good idea to run both old and new systems in parallel until the new system is found to be operating satisfactorily (say, 2 to 4 weeks). A cutoff point is then established, the files are updated to the cutoff point, and all transactions initiated after that point are recorded using only the new system.

The specifications used to solicit vendor proposals should have included equipment acceptance criteria. The sales or rental contract with the vendor should also state explicitly the conditions for acceptance of the equipment. Several criteria may be used such as percentage of downtime for repairs, performance of hardware and operating system on benchmark problems, software performance in compilation, etc. These acceptance tests should be run successfully before the equipment is accepted.

Computer user organizations may be a useful source of information for the user. These organizations are operated by the participating users of the same equipment but are supported by manufacturers. The groups share information, pressure the manufacturer, establish standards, etc.

Postinstallation Review

In preparing for a computer system, cost and benefit estimates are made. But it often happens that the cost savings are not realized and the benefits are not as great as projected. A computer system disturbs existing jobs and procedures, and, frequently, the personnel will duplicate the work of the computer because they do not trust the new system or do not understand the new procedures.

A postinstallation review is a desirable procedure to detect unrealized benefits, cost reductions not made, and lack of adherence to the new system. Measures may then be taken to improve performance. If there are substantial deviations in cost or performance by the computer processing group, they should be reviewed in order to appraise the cause and to assess possible courses of action. Plans for a postinstallation review probably improve the planning and estimating performed in deciding on the computer. If it is known that there will be a follow-up, estimates and plans are likely to be made more carefully than if such an appraisal is not anticipated.

Financing Use of Computer Equipment

There are three major approaches to financing the use of computer equipment— rent or lease from a manufacturer, purchase or lease from an independent leasing firm. The terms which can be negotiated under each of these methods will depend on the manufacturer, the leasing agent, and the negotiating strength of the user.

Rental or Term-Lease from the Manufacturer

Rental or fixed-term lease is the most common financing method. There is a rental or lease price which includes maintenance for using each piece of equipment and, depending on the manufacturer, a rental price for each software system. Manufacturers differ in the rental agreements they offer, but a common approach calls for a base rental for 176 hours of actual use per month. This represents one 8-hour shift per day for the average month of 22 working days. Hours above 176 are charged at a lower rate (a common percentage is 10 percent of the implied hourly rate for the first 176 hours). The trend in computer rentals is to reduce the second- and third-shift rental charges. The use of computers on a rental agreement can usually be canceled by the user on fairly short notice, say, 1 to 3 months. Most manufacturers offer a reduced rental rate for users who sign a long-term lease (2 to 5 years) for the equipment. For example, the basic rate may be reduced and extra use charges may be eliminated. Users can also rent with options to purchase.

The major advantages of renting or leasing are the absence of a large capital outlay, the assumption by the manufacturer of all maintenance, and the removal of the risk of obsolescence for the user. The latter risk is not entirely removed, since a user has large amounts invested in special site preparation, training, programming, and other costs which are lost if the computer must be replaced by one of another manufacturer. The major disadvantages of rental or fixed-term lease is the higher total cost. The manufacturers have tended to base rentals on 5-year life, but computers being installed are likely to be used longer than this—probably closer to 8 or 9 years.

Purchase of Equipment

The major incentive for purchase is the savings to be had over the life of the equipment. There is also a tax advantage because of the investment credit provisions of income tax law. The purchaser assumes a risk with respect to the reliability of the equipment, amount of maintenance, and obsolescence.

If the equipment is purchased, separate arrangements must be made for maintenance. Several possible arrangements are:

1 Maintain equipment using own personnel

2 Purchase a complete parts and labor maintenance agreement from the manufacturer

3 Pay for maintenance personnel on an hourly rate when needed, and pay for parts as used

The maintenance risk varies for different units in the computer configuration. For example, central processors are very reliable, while disk files or magnetic tape units, because of the precision required in their moving parts, are more likely to require frequent maintenance. Therefore, some installations will purchase part of their equipment and rent the rest.

One consideration in a maintenance program is the need for a continuing relationship with the manufacturer. As weak points are discovered or improvements are found desirable, the manufacturer usually makes field changes in the equipment. Since these occur throughout the life of the equipment, a purchaser will want to be aware of them so that a decision can be made as to whether they should be made.

An impediment to purchase is the risk of obsolescence. The possibility of outgrowing a system can be guarded against by acquiring a system with growth possibilities, both in the basic system and in available options for adding equipment.

When the risk of obsolescence has been considered, the decision of purchase or rental becomes a standard problem in capital expenditure analysis. A rough rule of thumb frequently cited is that a computer installation with a useful life of more than 5 years should be purchased rather than rented. However, a specific analysis should be made.

Third-Party Leasing of Computers

A company which has examined the obsolescence and reliability problems and has concluded that purchase is the best alternative may not have funds available, or may find that using the funds for purchasing computers will restrict future sources of funds. Under these circumstances, the possibility of leasing from an independent leasing company should be examined.

A third-party lease typically provides for the purchase by a leasing company of the specific equipment configuration desired by the user. The leasing company then leases it to the user. Lease agreements vary, but usually they have provisions such as the following:

1 User agrees to lease for a minimum period, say, 5 years, with purchase and trade-in options.

2 The lease payment includes a maintenance contract and other charges.

3 There is no additional charge for second- or third-shift operations (except perhaps some additional maintenance charges).

4 After the minimum period, the lease charges drop to a lower rate.

5 If the lease is terminated before the minimum period is up, there is a termination charge.

Acquisition of Software Packages

As explained in earlier chapters, there are two general types of software: system software and application software. System software consists of programs or sets of programs to support the efficient use of the computer. Examples are operating systems, database management systems, job accounting systems, and compilers. Application software refers to programs or sets of programs that perform a specific processing application. Examples are accounts receivable, inventory control, and statistical analysis.

Traditionally, system software was provided by the hardware vendor and application software was prepared by the user. Software was, during the early years of computing, included as part of the hardware, without extra cost. Most (but not all) manufacturers now price it separately. There is therefore an incentive for the user to evaluate alternative software packages.

The acquisition of independent (proprietary) system software instead of system software from the hardware vendor is generally based on improved efficiency, enhanced capabilities, or lower cost of the proprietary software. About half of all proprietary software in use is system software.

The acquisition of proprietary applications packages is an alternative to user development of the application programs. The application can be implemented more quickly and frequently at a lower cost. However, the package may not exactly meet the needs of the user. A small computer user may not be able to justify application development costs to make the application exactly what is needed; a larger user is more likely to do so. Because of the lower cost, reduced risk (because the package exists for testing), and reduced implementation time, software packages should always be considered as an alternative to inhouse development.

Sources of Software Packages The main sources of proprietary software packages, both system software and application software, are the following:

Source	Comments
Hardware vendor	Traditional source of system software. Many have variety of application packages.
Software house	Companies which specialize in development of software.
Software brokers	Companies which market software devel-

oped by others. Software package quality tends to vary considerably from this source because the software has such a variety of development environments.

User groups
: User groups have traditionally exchanged software. However, there is no support for the packages which are exchanged and documentation is generally inadequate.

A user in search of potential packages for evaluation should inquire of the hardware vendor. In addition, a search may be made using reference sources for software. The most comprehensive source is the *ICP Software Directory,* a listing of proprietary software packages. Other useful sources are analytical services such as *Datapro* and *Auerbach Software Reports* and the computer magazines which carry news and advertising about software packages.

Evaluating a Software Package

A necessary precondition to software package evaluation is a determination of requirements. The problem to be solved should be defined, the basic processing functions specified (inputs, processing, and outputs), and requirements for interface with the operating system and other applications identified. The requirements can be used in requesting vendors to present their packages for consideration. On the basis of the requirements, many of the potential packages can be eliminated, leaving only a small number for detailed evaluation.

In the evaluation, a formal point method may be used similar to the one proposed for hardware. Or a less formal method may use a series of analyses which will clarify the differences among the packages. The following are useful steps. The sources of data are the package vendor, package documentation, current users of the package, and rating services.

1 Compare functional capabilities of package with the requirements that have been developed.

2 Evaluate any hardware constraints in using the package on the computer system. Storage requirements and equipment usage are examples.

3 Evaluate software problems in using the package. Will the operating system, compilers, etc., interface properly with the package?

4 Evaluate computer operating characteristics such as throughput timing, ease of installation, ease of operating. How good are the operating instructions?

5 Evaluate use characteristics such as input requirements, report formats, controls, audit trails, error detection and error handling, and special forms. How good are the user instructions?

6 Evaluate the maintainability of the package. How well is it documented for

maintenance? Is it written in a disciplined form that is easily maintained? Is it coded in a standard language? Who will maintain the package?

7 Evaluate the flexibility of the package in meeting changing needs and growth.

Users of packages report considerable differences in quality, especially as reflected in documentation for users, operators, and maintenance programmers. The investigation of package characteristics is therefore essential to successful acquisition and use.

Packages which still appear viable after the preceding investigation should be demonstrated in some manner. Perhaps the best approach is to use benchmark tests at one's own installation. Some packages are not large enough to justify the expense of benchmarking and may be demonstrated at another installation, or a trial use period for the most likely package may be used as a method of final evaluation.

Contract negotiations for software packages are important. They should cover points such as guarantee period, return privileges if the package is not satisfactory, penalties for late delivery, support by vendor in installation and maintenance, agreed upon modifications, list of deliverables, and performance standards the package must meet.

SUMMARY In evaluating the acquisition of new or replacement computer systems, there are some cases in which industry practices or competitive pressures require computerization. In most cases, the decision is based on cost and benefit. The costs can be determined with reasonable accuracy; benefits require considerable estimation.

A major change in the cost characteristics of computer installations has been a reduction in the relative importance of equipment costs as a percentage of total cost. This is now on the order of 25 percent and continuing to decrease.

Success in computer selection and installation seems to depend on the participation and support of top management, adequate planning and control, and adequate steps to alleviate the human problems caused by the dislocation resulting from the computer system.

An approach to investigation of new or replacement systems described in the chapter includes a study group which conducts a feasibility study and, if the decision is to proceed, prepares a manual of specifications for the system. This is used for obtaining and evaluating equipment proposals. The decision on the computer equipment can be systematized by the ranking method of assigning weights to various evaluation criteria and assigning points to each manufacturer for each criteria. The evaluation of throughput is the most complex evaluation, and various methods may be used. These range from very simple comparisons to complex simulations.

Converting to a new computer system also requires careful planning and scheduling. A period of parallel operation is needed to make sure the system is debugged. At the end of an initial period of operation, a postinstallation review is essential to assess performance compared with plans.

The methods of financing the use of computers were also discussed in the chapter. These are rental, purchase, or lease from an outside vendor. There are advantages and disadvantages to each. The majority of users still rent or lease from the manufacturer, but there is a perceptible trend toward purchase.

The acquisition of software packages, either system software or application software, is of increasing importance because there is a trend toward increased use of packaged software. The general approach to software acquisition is to develop a statement of requirements, conduct a search for suitable candidates, and then evaluate the packages using data from the vendor, current users, evaluative services which report on packages, and results of demonstrations. Packages differ considerably in quality, and therefore a careful evaluation is necessary.

EXERCISES

1 An executive in a company with a successful computer installation was called by a friend, an executive in another organization, who asked if he might come and have a chat. He stated, "We are getting our computer in a couple of months and are looking for ideas on how to use it." Evaluate the position of the company making the inquiry.

2 What criteria can be used to evaluate the following proposals:
   (a) Proposal to obtain a computer primarily for payroll processing now being done by a large number of clerks.
   (b) Proposal to obtain a computer primarily for production scheduling and inventory control. It would replace clerks using manual methods and would also allow the use of advanced techniques.
   (c) Proposal to obtain a small scientific computer for linear programming applications.
   (d) Proposal to put remote inquiry stations at all sales offices. Sales representatives would be able to make direct inquiries about status of inventory, items scheduled into production shipments, etc.

3 What is the advantage of a middle-management study group committee?

4 Under what circumstances is it appropriate to rely on manufacturers' representatives?

5 What is the manual of specifications?

6 What should be included in a run description?

7 Why is a new system run parallel with the old one? What problems does this create?

8 Assume you are asked to advise the financial vice-president of a distributing company in the following situation. The company built a new warehouse with automated handling equipment. The system relies on a computer to process data in a way not previously done. The company was told that this processing was feasible. It is now 2 months until the new warehouse will be ready. No programs have been written, and the manufacturer says that a larger machine will be required. What should he do?

9 Why would a company buy peripherals from another vendor?

10 In 1969, IBM unbundled—i.e., it started charging extra for most software, systems engineers, and customer education, which had formerly been provided without charge. Rentals were reduced slightly. Evaluate the effect of this decision on:
   (a) An existing installation that was renting
   (b) An existing installation that had a purchased machine
   (c) An independent software company
   (d) A competing manufacturer which did not unbundle

11 A new computer system has been installed. A program written in the predecessor

machine language is to be run once a month. Evaluate the relative merits of emulation, simulation, and conversion routines.

12 How can a vendor estimate times for runs which are not yet written?

13 Suggest the applicability of the various methods of comparing computer performance for the following situations:

(a) Comparing two models in the same family of computers

(b) Comparing two computers with similar word organization

(c) Comparing several computers for use on a wide range of scientific problems

(d) Comparing several computers for rather standard data processing tasks—mostly sorting, file updates, and reports

(e) Comparing several computers for all-round use

14 What major methods of ownership and financing use of a computer are employed? Under what conditions is each method appropriate?

15 In the postinstallation review it is found that the monthly cost displacement savings that were predicted did not materialize to the extent planned and these savings will never offset the conversion costs. What action should be taken? Explain.

16 What should the company do to be ready to use the computer when it arrives?

17 How can resistance to the introduction of a computer be reduced?

18 Compare the typical reasons for lease or purchase of proprietary system software and the reasons for lease or purchase of proprietary application software.

19 What are the sources of package software? Evaluate the general quality of products attainable from each source.

20 Explain an approach to evaluation of software packages.

CHAPTER 13

CURRENT AND PROSPECTIVE DEVELOPMENTS IN COMPUTER HARDWARE, SOFTWARE, AND APPLICATIONS

The field of computers is changing so rapidly that it is difficult to speak authoritatively of future developments because these are being so quickly translated into current use. Therefore, the distinction will not always be clear as to what is currently being done and what is going to be done soon. This chapter provides a point at which these developments can be discussed. Some of these developments are already being implemented, while others are unknown to actual installations. Some developments will be only mentioned to make the reader aware of them; others will be discussed in more detail.

Articles describing future developments in computer systems frequently refer to the "fourth generation," but the term is generally undefined. There has been general agreement on first-, second-, and third-generation equipment, the distinction being based primarily on circuitry. The first generation was marked by tubes, the second by transistors, and the third by microcircuitry. It is not yet clear what the distinguishing characteristics of a fourth generation might be. IBM's System/370 was introduced 5 years after the first installation of the System/360. However, it is an improved and enhanced system rather than one that is radically different. The use of semiconductor memories is a new development, but it does not seem to be a change of the magnitude that occurred between the first- and second- or second- and third-generation equipment. Micrologic is an important element in the new computers, but the idea has been implemented for several years. Large-scale integration provides faster, denser circuitry, but is an extension of third-generation microcircuitry. In essence, there is no agreement on what a fourth generation means, or whether it has yet arrived. This chapter, therefore, avoids that terminology.

Developments in Computer Hardware

There has been a clear and continuous trend in hardware toward reduced size, reduced cost, increased speed, and an improved cost/performance ratio. This trend is likely to continue. At the same time, users are finding it valuable to have greatly improved capabilities to support more complex processing requirements. The result is that users have more hardware in more complex configurations.

Circuitry The past size reduction in circuitry has been dramatic. An integrated circuit the size of the letter "O" contains elements that required several cubic feet of space in first-generation tube circuits and several cubic inches of circuit boards in second-generation equipment. Current large-scale integration (LSI) technology provides 1000 to 2000 circuits on a chip, and further increases in density are forecast.

Circuit speed has increased many times, and cost has been reduced to a fraction of that in early computers. This trend to faster, lower-cost circuitry will continue. For example, IBM reports devices performing binary switching in less than 10 picoseconds ($1/10^{12}$). This is more than a thousand times faster than currently available circuits. The device, called a Josephson junction, uses only 1/10,000 as much electric power as a transistor.

Very low cost microcomputers or computers on a chip have made it feasible to place computer logic in peripheral devices, terminals, etc. This trend is expected to continue.

Processor Design

The design of the central processor is being influenced by the availability of low-cost circuits, by the need for flexible design, and by the need for improved performance for certain activities. The low cost of circuitry means that many functions performed by software may be included in the hardware. The need for flexible design is accomplished by stored logic in a control storage. A computer with stored logic capabilities may be microprogrammed to accept instructions for any other computer. New functions can be added to the equipment by means of changes in the microprogram (also called "firmware"), whereas adding new hardware functions might be impossible, and attempting to execute them using software might be too slow and cumbersome.

Several small processors can be included in the processor design to handle separate functions. There can be a small processor for input/output channel control, a processor for data communications control, a database processor, etc. The concept of multiple processors can be extended to multiple arithmetic processors to achieve an array or pipeline processor which can simultaneously process entire arrays of data, an ability valuable in high-volume computation applications such as weather forecasting.

Data Capture, Data Preparation, and Data Input Devices

Data capture, preparation, and input are still major problems in computer processing. The trend is clearly toward the replacement of keypunches with keydisk systems and for various methods of direct entry. The trend in terminals for data capture and data preparation is the inclusion of some logical capabilities (intelligence) so that data may be validated while it is being recorded at the terminal. The terminals frequently include devices to read coded documents, such as various optical codes.

An interesting development to watch is voice recognition equipment. It has had limited use but appears to have high potential in certain applications, especially where the person doing the input has both hands busy and is required to provide only simple input. Current equipment can recognize a small number of words (say, 20 to 40 words). Since there are individual differences in speech, the equipment is "trained" to recognize a set of spoken words as pronounced by each individual using the system.

Output Devices

In general, there is a trend toward a greater variety of output devices. Audio output and computer graphics are receiving increased use. The increased volume of data to be output is being handled by the use of visual display devices (instead of typewriters) at terminals, nonimpact printers, and computer output microfilm. The nonimpact printers provide very high speed output. Various technologies are employed; a significant one is the use of a laser beam to write the characters on a rotating drum that is electrostatically charged. The drum prints on paper in much the manner as an electrostatic (say, Xerox brand) copier. Examples of maximum printing speeds are 13,000 lines per minute offered by one manufacturer and 21,000 by another. This contrasts with 1000 to 2000 lines per minute for high-speed impact printers. Computer output microfilm (COM) also achieves high-speed output that takes much less storage volume than paper output. The major constraint to the general use of laser printers and COM is the high cost of the devices, and so they are justified only for large-volume users.

Storage Devices Semiconductor memory has replaced core memory as the major storage technology for main memory. There has been substantial improvement in magnetic storage density, and so magnetic tape and magnetic disk still dominate secondary storage. These magnetic storage devices are expected to be improved further with increased densities and lower cost. However, current and prospective developments suggest that alternative higher-density, lower-cost storage may become available. Two alternatives that appear promising are holographic storage and magnetic bubble memory.

There are two forms of holographic storage—mechanically driven and optical. In the mechanically driven type, data bits are stored by a laser beam (a very tiny, concentrated beam of light) which records a 1-bit by burning the coating on a tape or film. The recording is permanent in the same way as a punched card. The spot is read by a laser beam of lesser power which detects the existence or absence of a hole. Each hole is very small so that, in one existing device, 13 million bits can be recorded per square inch. This method is in use, but major problems are the mechanical movements to position the beam and the nonerasable character. The optical holographic methods are in a more experimental state. A laser beam is passed through an array of light valves to produce a binary pattern of darkness and light. The pattern can theoretically be very large, say, 100,000 bits. This pattern is stored on a light-sensitive material such as thermoplastics, or on ferroelectric crystals. The stored data is read by directing a laser beam to the desired hologram, and an image of the page of light patterns is sensed and analyzed into 0 and 1 bits. If practical optical memories become available, they would provide high-density storage of very large capacity at low cost.

A newer approach to computer storage technology is a magnetic bubble memory. The technology is based on tiny magnetic domains or "bubbles" that appear in certain kinds of crystalline materials under the control of magnetic and electrical fields. The presence of a bubble signifies a 1-bit, the absence a 0-bit. A train of bubbles can be shifted from cell to cell in a shift register to read the storage. Storage density is very high, about 1 million to 100 million bits per square inch.

Data Communications Facilities Virtually all computer systems have the capability for remote input and output via data communications facilities. The demand for data communications has grown very rapidly, and future growth in demand is expected to be high. Trends in data communications are higher speed, greater reliability, and lower cost. These results can be achieved by special digital networks based on electronic switching. Such networks are in operation and can be expected to increase in scope and use.

System Configuration

Trends in system configurations reflect a shift toward the computer as a utility which is designed to service remote users with both interactive computing and terminal-directed batch processing. Two trends to support the computer utility are multiprocessor configurations at central sites servicing a large number of users and dispersed or distributed systems.

Large, centralized systems providing interactive processing are tending toward the use of more than one processor, with the processors dividing the tasks. There are efficiency considerations supporting such configurations, but perhaps more important is the need for the reliability which can be obtained in a multiprocessor system.

An alternative trend in large systems is to disperse the processing capability. Remote sites are provided with minicomputers to perform much of the processing and to maintain local data files. Only selected tasks are transmitted to a larger, central computer which also maintains the organization-wide database.

The concept of the computer network can be extended to networks in which the computer system for one organization is interconnected with the computer system of another organization. An example is the computer for an airline reservation system being able to make reservations on an interconnecting line by directly communicating with the computer for that airline.

Developments in Computer Software

Hardware improvements have been spectacular and rapid; software improvement has been much slower and generally delivered less than promised. Current and prospective developments are for simplified operation and improved performance for system software and for greater use of leased or purchased application software.

The trend in computer systems is to a network of CPUs, input/output processors, and communication processors with the scheduling and allocation of resources under the control of the operating system. The operating system provides automatic management of files, data communication, and input/output. The trend is for the operating system to be internally more complex, but less complex for the user. The trend is also to design hardware facilities that will make the operating system more efficient.

Improved performance of software is being achieved not only in increased throughput but also in reduction of errors. The emphasis on programming discipline (as described in the text) is resulting in a marked reduction in errors in software.

The use of purchased (or leased) application software is expected to continue. The supply of well-written, well-documented, and flexible application packages has substantially increased the attractiveness of using such packages. The trend in small computers is for the vendor to provide a large selection of such packages as part of the support for the system.

Developments in Information Systems

The use of computers is extending into a wide variety of applications ranging from space flight to computer-assisted surgery. A major area of development is in the use of computers by organizations to support management and decision making. Such information systems are so large that researchers have proposed automation of many of the system-building functions.

Management Information Systems

An organization has transactions that it must process in order to carry out its day-to-day activities. The payroll must be prepared, sales and payments on account must be posted: these and others are data processing activities and might be termed clerical in nature; they follow rather standard procedures. The computer is useful for these clerical data processing tasks, but a management information system performs other tasks as well and is more than a data processing system. It is an information processing system applying the power of the computer to provide information for management and decision making.

A management information system (or MIS), as the term is generally understood, is an integrated, man/machine system for providing information to support the operations, management, and decision-making functions in an organization. The system utilizes computer hardware and software, manual procedures, management and decision models, and a database.[1] Chapter 2 describes the pyramid nature of an MIS and the way an MIS affects different users.

When an MIS system is in use, there is a systematic collection and storage of data not previously obtained. More online entry and retrieval devices may be utilized. There is an increased availability of current, accurate information for all levels of personnel. Reports, responses to information requests, analysis, planning, and decision making receive improved processing and information support. The implementation of such systems is one of the most challenging areas in the application of computers. It is anticipated that the development and refinement of systems based on the MIS concept will continue to be a major objective of organizations using computers.

Automation of Information System Design

Programming has received most of the attention in terms of improving system-building performance by automating various programming tasks, use of facilitating software in programming, modularization, etc. The analysis and design of infor-

---

[1] For a comprehensive discussion, see Gordon B. Davis, *Management Information Systems: Conceptual Foundations, Structure, and Development,* New York: McGraw-Hill, 1974.

mation systems are more difficult and more crucial tasks. Some work has been performed to systematize and automate this process; considerably more needs to be done.

Methods have been proposed for quantitatively describing system requirements, so that algorithms can be applied to the design process. The next step is to automate the system-building task. Major elements in the approach being followed by a major research project[1] are indicative of the kind of research activity to be expected:

1 Development of a problem statement to describe requirements of an information processing system completely and unambiguously.

2 Development of computer programs to analyze information system problem statements for errors and to produce output analyzed in a form useful for physical design of information processing system.

3 Development of algorithms to design optimal information processing system and for reorganizing of data.

Impact of Computers on Organizations and Individuals

Computers are already present at all levels of organizations. An individual in an organization making extensive use of computers cannot remain unaffected by changes in information processing systems. A significant change expected in such organizations is in organizational structure. The effect on the individual is in such areas as job content, reduction in allowable individual behavior, and privacy. The structure of the computer industry raises societal, economic power issues.

Impact on Structure of Organizations

In the speculation as to the impact of computers on the organizational power and status structure, most attention has been concentrated on the middle-management level. The reasoning is that computers provide top management with a greater span of control and that many of the judgmental decisions usually handled by middle management will be programmed into the computer. Therefore, less middle management will be required, and its power and status will decline.

However, one might argue that most of the time of middle-management personnel is spent on tasks which are motivational or which require unstructured decision making or judgmental reasoning. Therefore, although some decisions may be taken from them and central planning may further restrict their range of decision making, all other middle-management functions will remain. The problems of managing people are still critical and are not computerized. Furthermore, the frequency of change may make it more difficult than was thought to routinize many middle-management decisions.

[1] ISDOS project at the University of Michigan. See Daniel Teichroew and Hasan Sayani, "Automation of Systems Building," *Datamation*, August 15, 1971, p. 25-30.

The question of whether complex computer systems will cause organizations to centralize operations that have been decentralized is not yet answered. In a decentralized organization, planning and decision making at the individual plant or other facility are delegated to the local manager. In a centralized organization, all important decisions are made by a central staff at the headquarters. It is clear that some individual decisions are being centralized—an example is centralized inventory control, in which a computer system keeping track of all inventory at all locations is usually able to make better decisions than the individual managers. On the other hand, the economic and managerial considerations which have prompted some organizations to decentralize are still strong. Examples are the need for local response to changing conditions and enhanced motivation.

On balance, however, it seems quite clear that the computer has already had some impact on organization and management and will have greater impact as more complex computer-based information and control systems are implemented. It is likely that the most successful systems will be ones that divide tasks between the worker and the computer (a man-machine system) rather than fully automated systems. In a task-division system, the decisions by computer are structured, routine decisions, the decisions made by the worker are the unstructured, difficult ones. And even computer decisions will need to be monitored. It would take an executive with an excess of faith in computer programs (written by mere mortal programmers) to let important decisions be handled automatically by a computer without human review.

Quality of Individual Life

Computers have created interesting and challenging new jobs and have eliminated many fairly routine clerical tasks. On the other hand, some computer-based jobs are quite routine, such as keypunching or key-entry of data. Automated systems provide users with increased processing and data retrieval capabilities, yet the systems tend to require that users be regimented to a fairly rigid discipline with regard to input, etc.

The use of computers in systems with which individuals must deal, e.g., billing and payroll, often results in a sense of frustration and alienation. It took the author 1 year to get a simple billing error straightened out with a credit card organization. Repeated notes requesting adjustment were ignored. Computerized notices were automatically generated which became increasingly threatening, and finally led to the author sending a letter to the president before human intervention was achieved. Although this system had obvious weaknesses in terms of dealing with individuals, it is not atypical. Such experiences often mark the computer as the villain in a society in which systems are frequently designed to treat the individual as an object of automated processing rather than as someone for which processing is required.

Although the fears of computer surveillance have perhaps been overemphasized, there is little question but that the computer has introduced a new dimension in the conflict between the desire by segments of society to have information and the desire of individuals to have privacy and to restrict public information to a minimum. With many manual files, it was impossible from a practical standpoint to interchange data. Files degraded fairly quickly because of misfiling, etc. File access was limited by cost and speed of access. Computers, by contrast, make it possible for government and private organizations to interchange data about individuals quickly and cheaply.

Legislation defining the responsibilities of governmental agencies maintaining files on individuals and defining the rights and remedies of individuals with respect to such files has been passed by the federal government of the United States, by most states of the United States, and by many of the Western, industrialized nations. Legislation regulating nongovernmental data files is pending but has generally not been implemented.

Competitive Structure of Computer Industry

The computer industry presents a problem to the United States economic-social system. Unlike many countries which encourage monopolies, the United States views concentrations of economic power as inconsistent with the political system, and the policy of the government under the antitrust laws is to promote competition by "breaking up" giant companies which dominate an industry. The computer industry is under continuous scrutiny in this regard because IBM dominates, with about 70 percent of the market. Most of the remainder of the business is divided among five companies having United States market shares of from 3 to 7 percent (Honeywell Information Systems, Inc., Univac Division of Sperry Rand Corp., Burroughs Corp., The National Cash Register Co., and Control Data Corporation). There is then another set of companies with even smaller shares of the total market. The issue of competition is also found outside the United States. The number of independent computer mainframe manufacturers in Europe has declined to only two; Japanese computer manufacturers have flourished only through government intervention.

IBM has been very profitable; its competitors have not. This is not because of lack of economic power. The computer divisions of some large, powerful companies (General Electric Co. and RCA Corporation) were not able to obtain profitability. Yet IBM does not quote unduly low prices. In the industry, there is agreement that IBM provides a price umbrella under which the other companies have a chance of making a profit. The economics of scale in hardware and software favor IBM (to develop a compiler for one machine costs the same as for 10,000), but IBM's sales are usually made on the basis of marketing skill and level of support (such as software) rather than on the basis of hardware price. Should IBM be "broken up" into independent, smaller companies? The answer is not obvious, and the debate will likely continue for some time. An antitrust suit to legally decide the issue is in progress.

SUMMARY

Barring some dramatic new hardware change, there seems to be no major element which signals a change from third- to fourth-generation equipment. However, circuitry is becoming smaller, faster, and less expensive. More logic is being placed in peripheral units and terminals, circuitry is being used in place of software, and specialized processors are being used to handle specific functions in a processing system.

The changes in input devices are generally toward increase in "intelligence" in terminals. Some new devices such as voice recognition are coming into use. Relatively new devices to speed output are computer output microfilm and non-impact, electrostatic printers. Traditional storage devices continue to improve. New devices to watch are holographic optical storage and magnetic bubble memory. Data communications will continue to improve through the use of specialized data communication networks.

The trend in computer system configurations is toward either centralized multiprocessor systems or a distributed processing network of small computers. Developments in computer software suggest simplified user operation and improved performance for system software and greater use of leased or purchased application software.

One of the major areas of development in organizational use of computers is the design and implementation of management information systems which support management and decision-making functions in an organization. Because organizational information processing systems are difficult and time-consuming to design and implement, major research efforts are being devoted to the automation of at least part of the process of system design and building.

The computer is having a continuing and increasing impact on organizations and individuals. Although organization structure has not been dramatically changed, there are perceptible changes in organizational behavior. The quality of individual life is affected by changes in job content and by computer system responsiveness to human problems and to changes in privacy. This dominance of the computer industry is a matter of concern to those who believe in competition. The computer, like most technological innovations, can be both good and bad for individuals. On balance, there is probably little question that computers are beneficial to society. Yet, there is a need to improve the rules for those situations in which the individual deals with a computer-based system.

EXERCISES
1 Prepare a report on a hardware development. Examples are:
    (*a*) Microprocessor   (*d*) Use of laser beams in storage devices
    (*b*) Holographic memory   (*e*) Digital data communications networks
    (*c*) Bubble memory
2 Prepare a report on a computer use or computer industry development such as:
    (*a*) Privacy and the computer
    (*b*) Automated information processing system design
    (*c*) The IBM antitrust action
3 Investigate and report on the use of:
    (*a*) Microprocessors
    (*b*) Minicomputers in distributed processing networks serving remote locations
    (*c*) Specialized processors

4 What are the elements of an MIS? How does each support the management use of computers?

5 Why should an honest man need to worry about computer dossiers?

6 Assume that the price of a personal computer is in the same price range as a color television set.

   (a) What would it be useful for if it were a small unit the size of an adding machine with limited input, output, and storage?

   (b) What would it be useful for if it could be connected via the telephone to a large computer?

   (c) How would it change the usage if the home computer had a typewriter keyboard and alphanumeric input and output?

PART 5

COMPUTER PROGRAMMING LANGUAGES

The purpose of Part 5 is to provide specific instruction in computer programming languages. Chapter 14 is an overview of high-level programming languages, thereby giving guidance in selecting a language for a specific purpose. Chapter 15 explains common features of machine-oriented assembly languages with IBM System/370 Assembly Language used for illustrative examples. The remaining chapters explain the instructions to write complete, executable programs in the three most widely used programming languages: BASIC, FORTRAN, and COBOL. BASIC is a simple language and is most commonly employed by occasional users who program from terminals in time-sharing mode. FORTRAN is used for writing programs to do algebraic or formula-type processing. COBOL is the dominant language for writing programs to do data processing tasks commonly required for organizational information systems. FORTRAN and COBOL are rich in features, and the explanations span two chapters for each of these languages. The first of the two chapters describes the elementary features of the language and provides a good introduction for the student who does not desire extensive coverage; the second chapter for FORTRAN or COBOL covers additional language elements and advanced features. The language instruction emphasizes a disciplined approach to writing understandable, maintainable programs.

CHAPTER

14

SELECTING A LANGUAGE FOR COMPUTER PROGRAMMING

Given a specific algorithm or procedure to be processed by a computer, how shall the processing or solution procedures be programmed? There are many possibilities. The time and effort for programming may vary considerably depending on the language used. Beginning students frequently do not appreciate the variety of languages and programming aids that can be used. The purpose of this chapter is to describe the types of languages and software packages that are generally available. The discussion covers only high-level languages and software packages. Machine-level assembly language coding is discussed in Chapter 15.

Considerations in Selecting a Language

In selecting a language, there are a large number of considerations. Some of the major ones are noted below along with comments.

Selection consideration	Comments
Type of problem	There are languages especially designed for specific types of problems. These are described later in the chapter.
Skill level of programmer	Certain languages are designed for the occasional programmer; others are for the professional programmer.
Terminal or offline program entry	Some languages are well suited for entry via a terminal.
Complexity of problem	Some languages are designed for simple problems; other are better able to handle complex problems (but the languages are more complex). Some languages have versions which optimize coding to reduce either compiling time or execution time.
Portability	If a program is to be used at more than one installation and perhaps on more than one computer, a standard language in common use should be selected.
Availability	A language that is available and well supported by an installation is preferred to a language that must be purchased or is not well supported.
Availability of consulting	There will usually be a need for consultation regarding a program if the programmer is unfamiliar or inexperienced in the language. The availability of such support for use of a language is a significant plus factor for a language.
General purpose versus specialized	Languages may be general purpose and very versatile or specific and restricted. The general-purpose language, when learned, has wide applicability. The specialized package, while more applicable to one problem, has little transferability to other problems.

Language versus package	A language is generally used to describe procedures, a package (such as a statistical package) is generally programmed by specifications and procedural statements.

In general, the beginning user should select well-supported, widely used languages and packages in preference to little-used but specialized languages. Simple languages with high consulting support are favored over complex languages rich in esoteric features. The beginner should not fail to consider alternatives such as statistical packages and callable subroutines.

The Operation of a Compiler

As explained in Chapter 3, a high-level language is a language that is designed to describe the problem, the desired results, or the procedures of problem solution to be followed. The program written in a high-level language must be translated into machine-language statements. The software to do this is termed a "compiler."

There are two types of high-level languages to be described in this chapter. The first group are procedure-oriented. They are used to describe the procedures to be followed to solve a problem or perform processing. Examples are BASIC, FORTRAN, and COBOL (the languages described in detail in Chapters 16 to 20). Other software packages for solving problems are programmed by the use of specifications which describe the data and the result to be obtained. They are more problem-oriented than procedure-oriented. Examples are the statistical packages. The explanation of translation procedures and operation of a compiler will emphasize use of the procedure-oriented language, but the principles of translation are similar.

Development of High-Level Languages   The idea of high-level languages is attributed to Grace Hopper, head of programming for UNIVAC. Her work led to two early languages—FLOWMATIC and MATHMATIC, which reflect the development of the two major types of languages—algebraic and commercial. Since high-level languages are oriented toward the procedures by which problems are solved, it is logical to have one language which is designed for problems formulated in mathematical terms and another designed for commercial data processing problems. The development of high-level languages has been rapid and has led to a proliferation of languages. Each language consists of a set of words and symbols, plus a set of rules for using this vocabulary to define problem-solving procedures. The words, symbols, and rules are intended to allow the computer user to clearly state the procedures needed to solve a problem. The vocabulary of the language is therefore similar to the language used in mathematics and/or data processing.

If each computer manufacturer or large user were to develop a separate high-level language, an important benefit available with problem-oriented languages would not be realized. This advantage is a standard language which can be translated by all computers. With such standardization of high-level languages, a program written by persons having access to one computer can be used by persons having the use of an entirely different computer. This portability is possible because the language itself is designed for expressing solutions to problems and is essentially independent of the particular computer on which the problem will be run. Each computer must, however, have its own individual programs to do translation of the high-level coding into a machine-level program.

The use of a common, standardized language has developed in two ways— first, by the prior establishment of specifications for a common language (examples are COBOL and ALGOL), and second, by the evolution of a widely used language to a standard form (such as FORTRAN). The three major high-level languages, FORTRAN, COBOL, and BASIC, have been standardized by the American National Standards Institute (ANSI). The use of these three languages in this text is based on ANSI standards.

Translation Procedure	To implement a high-level language using the compiler concept requires three elements—specifications for the language; a translator routine to interpret statements written in the language and convert them to appropriate machine-language instructions; and a library of subroutines which can be compiled into the machine-language program.

The source program, written in a specific language, must follow the rules for that language. These rules specify the form, structure, and terms used in writing instructions. Certain words, sometimes called "reserved words," have precisely defined operational meanings when used in source program statements. The specifications essentially describe a limited-purpose language. One has to learn both operation words and symbols, which are like a foreign-language vocabulary, rules of grammar for using the vocabulary, and punctuation symbols to produce statements. In addition to words and symbols, the language provides for names chosen by the programmer to designate the storage locations where input data items, results obtained during processing, etc., are stored.

The use of language specifications is illustrated by the following statements using two common procedure-oriented languages to specify the computation $x = a - b - c$.

Language	Statement
FORTRAN	X = A − B − C
COBOL	SUBTRACT B AND C FROM A GIVING X.

In both cases, X, A, B, and C are names assigned by the programmer. In the FORTRAN statements, the minus sign is interpreted by the translator program as meaning subtraction. In the COBOL statement, the words SUBTRACT, AND,

FROM, and GIVING have specified meanings the same or similar to those associated with the terms in ordinary English.

The translator, sometimes called the "processor," is a computer program which reads the source language statements one at a time and prepares a number of machine-language instructions to perform the operations specified or implied by each source statement. Typically, the preparation of a set of instructions does not involve the compiler writing all the required machine-level steps. In many cases, the compiler merely writes linkage instructions so that the object program can make use of subroutines provided by the compiler library of subroutines. For example, a FORTRAN statement to solve the problem $x = \sqrt{y}$ is written as $X = SQRT(Y)$. The translator interprets the different symbols and letters and then generates instructions to obtain the value of a variable designated as Y from a storage location, to transfer this value to a prewritten library subroutine which calculates the square root, to return control back to the main program, and to store the results of the square-root computation in a memory location associated with the variable name X.

The prewritten subroutines are contained in the compiler library. The object language statements generated by the computer are an incomplete program until they are combined with the appropriate routines from the library. Two approaches are used. In one method, all subroutines needed by the object program are written out with the rest of the object program. In the other approach, the library routines are added when the object program which includes the subroutine linkages is loaded for execution.

The process of translating a source statement so as to compile a program requires that the computer program identify:

1   The memory location associated with each quantity used in the program
2   The operations to be performed
3   The proper order for processing

The translator keeps a table for identifying names that refer to data items (and related storage locations) and a table of words and symbols that describe operations. The computer can compare each symbol, name, or other word in a source statement with those in the tables and thereby identify its meaning. The proper order of processing is specified by the rules of the language.

The design of a translator routine will vary with the computer on which it will be used. A typical sequence of actions a translator routine might follow are:

1   The source statement is read character by character until a complete variable name, operation word, or operation symbol has been detected.

2   A comparison is made of the variable name, operation word, or operation symbol with tables of these symbols until an identification is made.

3   The combination of variable names and operation identifiers is translated into an ordered sequence of actions based on the order rules of the language and form of the statement.

4 The translator writes the machine-language statements onto the output medium to be used. The instructions are either operating instructions or linkages to subroutines.

As an example, suppose that the translator reads a statement such as $X = A + B - 3.5$. It compares X with a list of identifiers, and finds that X has been assigned to a location such as 3407, so it sets up the final instruction as "store result in location 3407." The locations for A and B are found from the same list as being perhaps 3804 and 3812. A value of 3.5 is stored in a table of constants to be used by the program, say, in location 2412. The translator also identifies the plus and minus by comparing these characters with a list in storage. The compiler now constructs a sequence of instructions to:

1 Add contents of locations 3804 and 3812 and hold results in a temporary location.

2 Subtract contents of location 2412 from temporary location used to store $A + B$.

3 Store results of step 2 in location 3407.

These three steps may involve many instructions because of arithmetic scaling considerations, error checking, etc.

Types of High-Level Programming Languages

There are a large number of high-level languages. Some are fairly specialized; others are quite general in scope. Some are primarily for use by those doing their own programming; others are for use by trained programmers. A useful categorization for this chapter is by the orientation of the language.

1 Algebraic formula-type processing
2 Business data processing
3 String and list processing
4 Multipurpose processing
5 Simulation
6 Specialized applications

Each of these categories is discussed in order to provide a general understanding of the types of languages available.

Algebraic Languages The algebraic languages are oriented toward the computational procedures for solving mathematical and statistical problems or problems which can be expressed in terms of formulas or numerical solution procedures (called algorithms). These problems are often termed "scientific" as opposed to data processing problems. Examples of problems for which this type of language is suited are statistical analysis of data, solution of sets of equations, and cash flow analysis for a firm.

The algebraic languages have good facilities for expressing formulas, for describing computational procedures, and for doing common mathematical functions. These facilities are illustrated here together with some examples of statements in an algebraic language which execute solution procedures. On the other hand, the algebraic languages have rather poor facilities for describing complex input or output, for manipulation of nonnumeric data, and for handling of files, because these capabilities are not generally important in scientific processing.

EXAMPLES

Language Facility	Sample Algebraic Language Statements
Express formulas.	
Solve formula for x	
where $x = \sqrt{\dfrac{(a + b)}{d}}$	$X = \text{SQRT } ((A + B)/D)$
Describe computational procedure.	
Sum one hundred quantities	
$S = \displaystyle\sum_{i=1}^{100} X_i$	$\begin{aligned}&\text{DO} \quad 100 \; I = 1{,}100\\ &\qquad S = S + X(I)\\ &100 \quad \text{CONTINUE}\end{aligned}$

The most common algebraic languages and their acronyms are:

Acronym	Meaning or Type of Orientation
FORTRAN	Formula Translator
BASIC	Beginners All-purpose Symbolic Instruction Code
PL/1	Programming Language, Version 1
ALGOL	Algorithmic Language
APL	A Programming Language

All the algebraic languages are very similar; having learned one of them, a user will find it quite easy to understand the others. A common characteristic of the algebraic languages is an emphasis on the users being able to write their own programs using the language rather than having to depend on a professional programmer.

FORTRAN is by far the most commonly used algebraic language and is described in detail in Chapters 17 and 18. BASIC was developed as a language for time-sharing purposes. Widely used, it is oriented toward simple problems and terminal operation. BASIC is easily learned and is well suited to the novice or occasional user. It is explained fully in Chapter 16. PL/1, ALGOL, and APL are not explained in detail in this text; they are described and illustrated later in the chapter. PL/1 is a general-purpose language, but the programmer can treat it as an algebraic language, disregarding the other facilities.

Data Processing Languages

Often termed "business" or "commercial processing languages" to distinguish them from algebraic languages, the data processing languages emphasize the language capabilities for describing data processing procedures in information processing applications. These applications usually involve files, considerable manipulation of nonnumeric data, high volume of input and output, and arrangement of data on output documents. The processing procedures do not usually require extensive mathematical manipulation. Some common problems for which this type of language is suited are processing of payroll, inventory, and accounts receivable.

COBOL is the major language in this category. It is described fully in Chapters 19 and 20. PL/1 has facilities for commercial processing, and so it is an alternative to COBOL. Another alternative to COBOL is RPG, or Report Program Generator. It is an important language for small computers not having sufficient capabilities for COBOL and is therefore described in this chapter.

String and List Processing Languages

A string is a sequence of characters; for example, a sentence is a string. These languages are important in the handling of text material. A linguist desiring to search for word usage could make use of a string processing language, as could a writer using the computer to edit text. The major types of operations are searching for patterns, replacing one pattern by another, and inserting and deleting characters in the string. The languages might also be described as symbol manipulation languages. The following examples will illustrate:

A researcher wishes to count the number of times the term "sin," "saint," and "sinner" are used in a religious text.

A text of a technical report stored on computer magnetic tape is to be printed, but first the text is to be updated. All references to "United States of America Standards Institute" are to be replaced by "American National Standards Institute."

References are to be searched for titles with the words "computer" and "auditing."

The most important of the string manipulation languages is SNOBOL. It has gone through several versions, the most recent being SNOBOL4. "Text editors" are software packages which perform string processing functions.

A set of data items can be sequenced by putting them in physical order in storage. Another method is to attach a data item to each data element which specifies where the next item in the sequence is stored. This item, termed a "pointer," allows the data elements to be stored in any order; the pointers provide the means for processing in a given order. This arrangement is termed a "list." Examples of list processing languages designed for this purpose are IPL and LISP; they are quite specialized.

Multipurpose Languages

Why should a programmer need to learn a separate language for algebraic procedures, for data processing, and for string processing? Separate languages have some advantages, but since there is overlap among languages, a multipurpose language would appear to have advantages.

One of the earliest multipurpose languages was JOVIAL, developed as a language for military command and control applications. The most important of the multipurpose languages is PL/1. Another general-purpose language receiving academic use is PASCAL.

Simulation Languages

Simulations may be written in algebraic or multipurpose languages. However, a computer program to simulate operations involving queues can become quite complex and difficult for the programmer to handle. For example, a simulation of the operation of a job shop will involve many processing stations (machines) and many waiting lines of jobs waiting to be processed. Simulation languages have been developed to assist in describing simulation procedures (and especially queue discipline) for computer processing. The most common are GPSS (General-Purpose System Simulator), originally developed by IBM, and SIMSCRIPT, originally developed by Rand Corporation.

Specialized Application Languages

The list of languages could become quite long, but many of them are very specialized and not of general interest; others have received too little use to be of interest except to the specialist or perhaps the historian. Two examples will illustrate the very specialized languages:

Language	Purpose
APT (Automatically Programmed Tools)	To write programs to control machine tools.
COGO (COordinate GeOmetry)	To assist civil engineers in doing computations needed in surveying.

A Short Survey of Selected Languages

The three most used languages, BASIC, FORTRAN, and COBOL, are described in detail in succeeding chapters. This section provides a short introduction to four important languages which receive a significant amount of use.

The APL Language   Often termed Iverson's language after K. E. Iverson, APL (A Programming Language) is perhaps the most sophisticated of the modern programming languages. It is primarily a time-sharing language. The structure of the language and the available commands appear to be very effective in assisting users to develop and program problem-solving algorithms. The language is especially powerful in defining the processing of arrays of numbers and text-type data. Two features of APL that are different from other algebraic languages are an expanded character set for writing expressions and the fact that statements are executed from right to left without a precedence rule (although the factors inside parentheses are executed first). Some examples follow:

Symbol	Meaning	Example	Result
$\lceil$	Maximum	$5\lceil 8$	8
$\lfloor$	Minimum	$5\lfloor 8$	5
$\div$	Divide	$5 \div 2$	2.5
$*$	Power	$3*2$	9
$\times$	Times	4×5	20
$\leq$	Not greater	$4 \leq 5$	1 (1 for yes, 0 for no)
ρ	Size (number) of members of an array	ρA	10 (if array A has 10 members)

TABLE 14-1 SIMPLE APL PROGRAM TO COMPUTE MEAN OF AN ARRAY

APL program	Comments
∇ MEAN	Name by which this program is identified
[1] 'ENTER NUMBERS'	Print message to user
[2] X←☐	Request input of set of data items called by an array or vector named X
[3] A←(+/X)÷ρX	Compute the mean (average) of all data items called X and assign to variable named A
[4] 'MEAN IS EQUAL TO'	Print heading
[5] A	Print mean
∇	End-of-program-symbol

In a terminal which does not have these symbols, alternative symbols are used.

A simple example of an APL program to compute the mean of an array will illustrate the language (Table 14-1). The key sentence to compute the mean [3] is a useful illustration. The elements of the sentence are:

ρX   Number of quantities in array, i.e., the number of quantities that are being summed.

+/X   Sum all values in an array X.

A←   Assign result to variable A.

Since $(+/X)$ is enclosed in parentheses, the summation is done first. Working then from right to left, the sum is divided by the number of quantities summed and the result is assigned to A. Even in this simple example, the power of a language with simple vector commands is apparent. Users of APL are very enthusiastic, and its applications are expected to grow.

The PL/1 Language

PL/1 (Programming Language, Version 1) is designed as a general-purpose language, combining the major features of both COBOL and FORTRAN and introducing features not found in either. It was introduced by IBM in 1960 in conjunction with the IBM System/360 series. The language has facilities for the realtime programmer and the systems programmer in addition to the traditional commercial and scientific programming features.

The PL/1 language is divided into modules or subsets for different applications and different levels of complexity. A programmer using one subset need not even know about the other modules. If the programmer does not state a choice among the various alternative specifications, the compiler automatically chooses a default interpretation. In each case, the default specification is the one most likely to be required by the programmer who is not using the advanced features.

Advocates point to advantages for PL/1 over FORTRAN and COBOL, but the economics of programming and program maintenance are such that many installations prefer to stay with existing languages rather than switch to a new language, even if it has new features. PL/1 has to date had only modest success against FORTRAN and COBOL, and apparently these two languages will expand to include the best of PL/1, rather than PL/1 becoming a dominant language.

PL/1 allows the programmer considerable freedom. For example, there are no special indentations or reserved columns on the coding sheet—a free format is used. This makes it easy to apply the concept of structured programming that indentation should show program structure. The language is very supportive of the block structure required for structured programming.

A PL/1 program is constructed from program elements. The basic program element is the statement. Statements are combined into large elements—the procedure or block. A statement in PL/1 is a string of characters terminated by a semicolon. A block begins with a procedure name and ends with the statement END procedure-name. Variable names may be up to 31 characters in length. A break character _ is used to provide a meaningful multiword name. In addition to the usual arithmetic operators of $+$, $-$, $*$, $/$ and $**$, there are the following:

Comparison operators		Bit-string (Boolean) operators	
$>$	greater than	¬	NOT
$>=$	greater than or equal	&	AND
$<$	less than	|	OR
$<=$	less than or equal		
¬$=$	not equal to		

Some typical PL/1 statements are:

```
A = B**2;
X = Y/3 + 5;
IF HOURS > 40
    CALL OVERTIME;
ELSE
    GROSS_PAY = HOURS*RATE;
```

Data in PL/1 can be either numeric or string. String data consists of a group of characters or bits. Data can be grouped into arrays and in structures (hierarchies). A DECLARE statement is used to specify the array or structure attribute of the data. For example, a 2 × 3 matrix referred to as X is defined by the statement:

DECLARE X(2, 3);

A payroll record with the structure shown below

Payroll

Name			Hours
Last	Middle	First	

could be defined by the statement:

```
DECLARE 1 PAYROLL,
        2 NAME
            3 LAST CHARACTER(15),
            3 MIDDLE CHARACTER(15),
            3 FIRST CHARACTER(15),
        2 HOURS FIXED DECIMAL(2);
```

The numbers 1, 2, and 3 correspond to level numbers.

The programmer has considerable flexibility in input and output. Input/output is either record input/output, which consists of discrete records, or stream input/output, which is a continuous stream of characters. The input/output for records uses READ and WRITE statements, while stream input/output uses GET and PUT statements. The sample programs use the GET and PUT statements. Three methods of designating the form of the data are data-directed, list-directed, and edit-directed. For example, assume data names of HOURS and RATE (hours worked and rate of pay) to be read from cards:

Method	Form of data on card	Explanation
Data-directed	HOURS=42, RATE=4.253;	Each data item is written with its data name.

List-directed	42,4.253;	The items are listed in order and separated by a space or commas.
Edit-directed	424253	The items are listed in order. The form of the data is defined by a format list.

Other important features of PL/1 are specifications by which the programmer can direct the computer to work on more than one procedure concurrently, as in multiprogramming. There is a sort verb by which the programmer can specify the file to be sorted, the sort key, and the order. Storage allocation is also very flexible.

Two simple examples written in PL/1 do not illustrate the power or versatility of the language but do show its general form. Figure 14-1 shows a simple program to compute gross pay. Figure 14-2 is a sample program to prepare a mathematical table.

The RPG Language

Report Program Generator (RPG) is a language in which the programmer writes the specifications for the problem and the compiler generates a program. RPG is offered by several manufacturers, but it is not standardized. This explanation is based on RPG for the IBM System/3 and System/370. RPG is well suited for the types of problems usually run on a small computer, so that it is an important programming aid for computers of this class. In fact, for small-business computers, it is the dominant language.

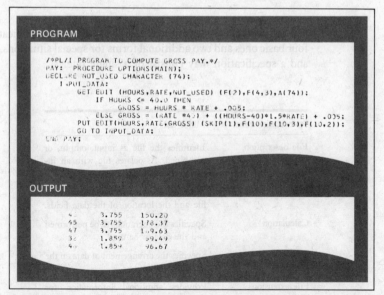

```
PROGRAM

/*PL/1 PROGRAM TO COMPUTE GROSS PAY.*/
PAY:  PROCEDURE OPTIONS(MAIN);
DECLARE NOT_USED CHARACTER (74);
    INPUT_DATA:
        GET EDIT (HOURS,RATE,NOT_USED) (F(2),F(4,3),A(74));
            IF HOURS <= 40.0 THEN
                GROSS = HOURS * RATE + .005;
            ELSE GROSS = (RATE *40) + ((HOURS-40)*1.5*RATE) + .005;
        PUT EDIT(HOURS,RATE,GROSS) (SKIP(1),F(10),F(10,3),F(10,2));
        GO TO INPUT_DATA;
END PAY;
```

```
OUTPUT

    40   3.755   150.20
    45   3.755   178.37
    47   3.755   199.63
    32   1.859    59.49
    40   1.859    96.67
```

FIGURE 14-1 PL/1 program to compute gross pay and sample edit-directed output from program.

PROGRAM

```
/*PL/I PROGRAM TO PREPARE TABLE OF SQUARES AND SQUARE ROOTS.*/
TABLE:  PROCEDURE OPTIONS(MAIN);
    PUT EDIT (' NUMBER SQUARE SQUARE ROOT') (PAGE,A(26));
    DO I = 1 TO 10;
    X = SQRT(I);
    J = I**2;
    PUT EDIT(I,J,X)(SKIP(1),F(5),F(7),F(14,5));
    END;
END TABLE;
```

OUTPUT

```
NUMBER SQUARE SQUARE ROOT
  1     1       1.00000
  2     4       1.41421
  3     9       1.73205
  4    16       2.00000
  5    25       2.23607
  6    36       2.44949
  7    49       2.64575
  8    64       2.82843
  9    81       3.00000
 10   100       3.16228
```

FIGURE 14-2 PL/1 program to prepare table of squares, square roots, and sample edit-directed output from program using exponent form.

A problem is programmed in RPG by filling out specification forms. There are four basic ones and two additional forms for special situations. Not all are required, and a specification may consist of a single line.

Specification form	Major use
File description	Identifies the file as input, output, or combined. Associates file with an input/output device.
Input	Describes the records contained on the file and the location of the data fields.
Calculation	Specifies the operations to be performed and the data to be used.
Output	Specifies the arrangement of data on the output medium.
File extension	Provides additional information for chaining, using tables, and using direct access files.

Line counter	Specifies line control if report is to be written on tape or disk for subsequent printing.

The RPG specifications provide all information for the program. Each specification is punched into a card. The set of specification cards is read by the RPG compiler, and an object program is generated.

The sample program will use a simple gross pay computation (already presented in PL/1). Some headings will be used on the printed output. The input for the program is hours (columns 1–2) and rate (columns 3–6) on a punched card. The calculations are straight time for 40 or less hours and time-and-a-half for all hours over 40. The output is in the form shown in Figure 14-3.

The sample specification sheets are given in Figure 14-3. The file of cards containing the hours and rates is called the PDATA file. The input data fields are called HOURS and RATE. The output file is called REPORT. The result of the computations is GROSS for gross pay.

The file description form defines PDATA as an input file (1) to be read from the card reader. REPORT is defined as an output file (0) on the printer.

The input specification sheet for PDATA defines the data fields as columns 1 and 2 for HOURS, with no decimal position, and columns 3 to 6 for RATE, with the decimal position three places from the right.

The first action on the calculation sheet is the test to find out whether hours exceed 40. If they do, control proceeds to the line marked with 21; if hours do not exceed 40, control goes to N21 (NOT 21). 21 is an arbitrary designation. For over 40 hours, the computations prepare an amount TEMP2 which is a revised hour figure giving overtime credit. The H means to round the result.

The output specification of the report first defines the heading line and then the form and position of the variables on the detail line. The edit word ' ,$0. ' defines a dollar sign and decimal location in the output.

The ALGOL Language

ALGOL (ALGOrithmic Language) is an algebraic language similar to the algebraic features in PL/1. It is quite popular in Europe but has never achieved substantial use in the United States. ALGOL is well suited for structured programming because of its block structure. Each procedure is named, and the end of procedures are defined explicitly by the END command. Figure 14-4 illustrates a simple ALGOL program to compute a table (same problem as the PL/1 program in Figure 14-2).

Subroutine Packages

When developing and writing programs in languages such as FORTRAN or PL/1, the programmer should take advantage of statistical and mathematical routines which can be called by the user program. The programmer codes in FORTRAN or

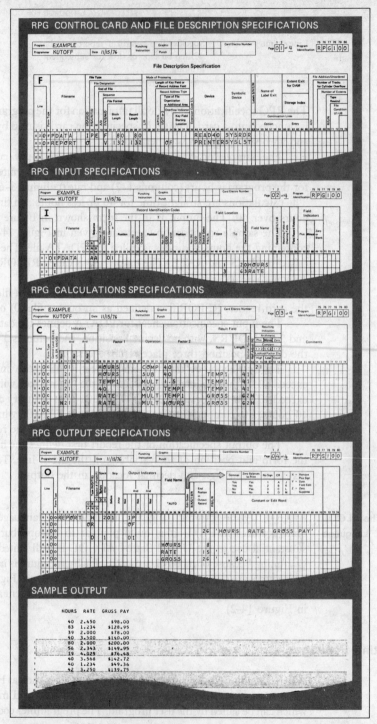

FIGURE 14-3 RPG specification sheets for program to compute gross pay and sample output from program.

```
'BEGIN'
   'REAL'B;
   'INTEGER' I,X;
   OUTPUT (61,'('↑'('NUMBER SQUARE SQUARE ROOT')',/')');
   'FOR' I:= 1 'STEP' 1 'UNTIL' 10 'DO'
      'BEGIN'
         X:= I↑2;
         B:= SQRT(I);
         OUTPUT (61,'('/4ZD,BBBBBBZZD,BBBBD.DDD')',I,X,B);
   'END';
'END'
```

FIGURE 14-4 Simple ALGOL program to compute table of squares and square roots.

PL/1 and includes a CALL for the subroutine desired. Most large installations and university computer centers have extensive libraries of such routines. The two most common libraries are SSP and IMSL.

SSP (Scientific Subroutine Package) This set of over 200 mathematical and statistical routines is provided by IBM in FORTRAN or PL/1 and is available on most IBM equipment and some non-IBM equipment. A manual is available from the IBM Corporation.

IMSL FORTRAN Subroutines A set of about 200 FORTRAN callable subroutines has been developed and is maintained by International Mathematics and Statistical Libraries, Inc. A manual is available from IMSL. A computing center with this set of subroutines will have documentation available to users.

Some examples of the subroutines available in these packages illustrate their capabilities:

Major category	Example
Analysis of experimental data	Covariance analysis test
Basic statistics	Calculate means, standard deviation, and correlation coefficients
Eigen analysis	Eigenvalues and eigenvectors of a symmetric matrix
Random numbers	Generate normal deviates
Nonparametric statistics	Kendall's test for correlation
Sampling	Simple random sampling with continuous data
Vector-matrix arithmetic	Transpose product of a matrix

Other subroutine packages are also available. For example, IBM has a package of subroutines designed for forecasting called the Forecasting And Modeling System (FAMS).

Statistical Packages

It is rarely necessary for an investigator to code a computer program to do statistical analysis because prewritten computer programs are available for almost all statistical analysis. The statistical programs are self-contained sets of programs which perform statistical analysis based on user specifications. The user must define the form of the input data and specify the computational options desired. No knowledge of computer programming is required (although it may be helpful).

A few of the most common general-purpose packages and sets of routines are listed (in approximate order of use) to provide some idea of the options available. Manuals are listed, but later editions may be available. There are also a number of less used or specialized packages and routines that may be supported by a particular installation.

SPSS (Statistical Package for the Social Sciences) A comprehensive program for processing common to the social sciences, it is maintained by the National Opinion Research Center, University of Chicago. A manual is available: Norman H. Nie, et al., *Statistical Package for the Social Sciences,* 2d ed., McGraw-Hill, New York, 1975, 675 pages.

BMDP AND BMD (Biomedical Computer Programs)[1] Assembled and maintained by the Health Sciences Computer Facility at the University of California at Los Angeles, the newer BMDP contains 26 programs while BMD contains over 50 programs. These have wide use. Good user documentation is provided in the BMD and BMDP manuals: *BMD Biomedical Computer Programs,* University of California Press, 1973, 773 pages; *BMDP Biomedical Computer Programs,* University of California Press, 1975.

OMNITAB II This is a large, unified set of computer routines developed by the National Bureau of Standards to do statistical and numerical analysis. It is available from the National Technical Information Service (NTIS), 5285 Port Royal Road, Springfield, Virginia 22161. A manual is available: *OMNITAB II Users Reference Manual,* U.S. Government Printing Office, Oct. 1971, 253 pages.

Figure 14-5 is a sample of specification input and resultant output for an SPSS program. The data consists of 70 pairs of data items for monthly gross income and amounts contributed to the Consolidated Fund drive. The specifications call for descriptive statistics and a scattergram (in which two extreme values were eliminated).

---

[1]For a comparison of BMD and BMDP programs, see James W. Frane, "The BMD and BMDP Series of Statistical Programs," *Communications of the ACM,* October 1976, pp. 570–576.

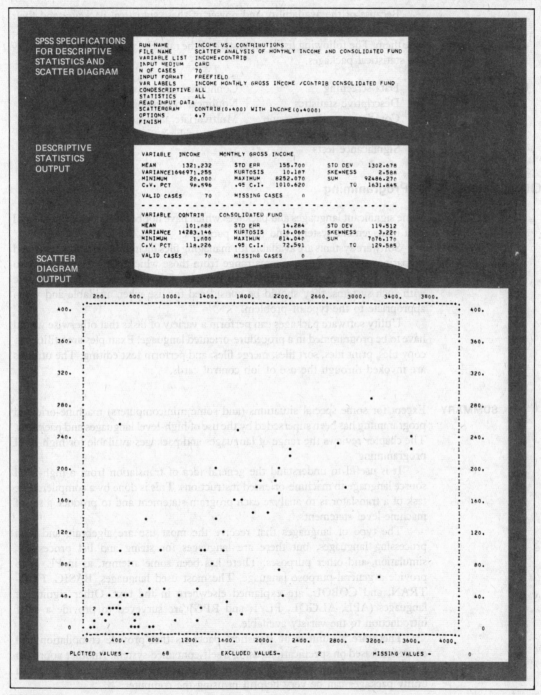

FIGURE 14-5 Example of specification input to SPSS statistical package and resulting outputs.

Because of the availability and power of these statistical packages and their ease of use, any student or researcher requiring statistical analysis should investigate them. The following list is suggestive of the range of processing performed by the statistical packages.

Data screening	Confidence intervals
Descriptive statistics	Nonlinear regression
Correlation and regression	Multivariate analysis
Analysis of variance	Factor analysis
Significance tests	

Other Packages for Programming

Some significant languages and packages which have not been discussed are file and data management systems and utility packages.

Software systems are available for managing files including extracting data and preparing reports. These systems range from those which manage single files to complex database management systems. Because of the language facilities available with such systems, they should be considered for use when available and when appropriate to the type of problem.

Utility software packages can perform a variety of tasks that otherwise would have to be programmed in a procedure-oriented language. Examples are utilities to copy files, print files, sort files, merge files, and perform text editing. The utilities are invoked through the use of job control cards.

SUMMARY Except for some special situations (and some minicomputers) machine-oriented programming has been superseded by the use of high-level languages and packages. The chapter reviews the range of languages and packages available for high-level programming.

It is useful to understand the general idea of translation from a high-level source language to machine-oriented instructions. This is done by a compiler. The task of a translator is to analyze each program statement and to produce a set of machine-level statements.

The type of languages that receive the most use are algebraic and data processing languages, but there are languages for string and list processing, simulation, and other purposes. There has been some attempt, as in PL/1, to provide a general-purpose language. The most used languages, BASIC, FORTRAN, and COBOL, are explained elsewhere in the text. Other significant languages (APL, ALGOL, PL/1, and RPG) are surveyed to provide a brief introduction to the variety available.

There are a number of statistical packages that provide compilation and execution based on specifications using a self-contained system. Another approach is to use subroutine packages which are obtained by call statements. These and utility packages can be very helpful in using the computer.

EXERCISES

1 Apply the considerations in selecting a language to each of the following situations.
 (a) A once-a-year analysis of distribution of salaries
 (b) A statistical processing performed now and then by market research
 (c) Payroll processing performed weekly
 (d) A mathematical formulation to be run only once
 (e) A simulation expected to take 600 hours of computer time

2 Describe the steps in using a high-level language for processing the solution of a problem.

3 How does a compiler translate a source program and produce an object program?

4 What is an algebraic language? How does it differ from a data processing language? Identify the orientation of the following languages: BASIC, FORTRAN, COBOL, PL/1, RPG, and GPSS.

5 Why should there be special languages for string processing and simulation? Be specific as to the exact type of processing that the language handles.

6 Define the orientation, the status of use, and the type of problem which is suited for APL, PL/1, ALGOL, and RPG.

7 Identify the following statements as APL, PL/1, or other language.
 (a) X = Y**2
 (b) X = Y**2;
 (c) COMPUTE X = Y**2.
 (d) A←(x/y)÷ρy
 (e) C = A + B
 (f) C = A + B;
 (g) IF GROSS-PAY>300 THEN GO TO ERROR_1;
 (h) ∇NEW

8 PL/1 is so large and complex that the occasional user cannot learn it all. Yet it is said to be a replacement for FORTRAN, which can certainly be used by the nonprofessional programmer. How is the solution to this problem approached in PL/1?

9 Describe the purpose of each of the specification sheets used in the RPG version illustrated in the text.

10 A student has a set of data to be analyzed. Describe the merits of writing a complete, new program, using a statistical package, or using a subroutine in a program.

11 A computer center has several statistical packages available including OUROWN and SPSS. Assuming OUROWN is more efficient in execution than SPSS, which should be used by:
 (a) A researcher who will share the results with colleagues?
 (b) A student running a short, one-time job?
 (c) The English department for evaluating each instructor each quarter?

12 How can one be sure that a subroutine or package is providing correct results?

13 Programmers argue about the merits of PL/1 versus FORTRAN. What are the considerations that have inhibited a change to PL/1?

CHAPTER

15

MACHINE-ORIENTED SYMBOLIC ASSEMBLY LANGUAGE

The purpose of this chapter is to provide an understanding of the coding of programs using a symbolic assembly language. Symbolic assembly languages are machine-oriented, and most assembly language instructions are merely a symbolic equivalent of a machine-level instruction. Therefore, some understanding of programming at this level is useful in comprehending the field of computers and computer processing.

The chapter is aimed at a general understanding rather than a specific skill in coding programs in symbolic assembly language. Example coding is given using the symbolic assembly language for the IBM System/370, but these examples will be insufficient for developing coding skill in that language. The fundamental System/370 instructions are used in the illustrations, but many 370 instructions are not covered. If the reader desires to write programs in a specific assembly language, the chapter may be profitably used as a general introduction to programming with assembly-type languages. A manufacturer's manual for the language (or other manual designed for the language) can then be used for the detailed coding rules.

The symbolic assembly languages for the IBM System/370 and System/360 are, for all practical purposes, identical. The chapter refers to System/370, but the reference could read "System/360 and System/370." The IBM System/370 assembly language is referred to as "assembler" or "BAL" for Basic Assembly Language. In the cases when the chapter is used as a basis for a general understanding of assembly language coding, it is useful to do some simple coding using the System/370 instructions described in the example coding of the chapter. To assist in this approach, there are a number of self-testing exercises at the end of the chapter for which answers are given. After each section do the related self-testing exercises. These will add to your understanding and will provide some testing of your comprehension of the material in that section.

Assembly Language Instructions

As explained in Chapter 5, a computer must have certain types of instructions. These can be described generally as:

> Move data
> Arithmetic
> Transfer of control (also called branching)
> Editing
> Input/output
> Looping, subroutine linkage, and other program modification
> Assembler specifications

There are assembly language instructions for each of these. Each of the symbolic assembly instructions is the direct equivalent of a machine-level instruction except for symbolic input and output instructions and assembler specifications. The general approach in symbolic assembly-level programming is to code the input and output using macro instructions which are converted by the assembler to a set of machine-level instructions. An added set of instructions required for coding programs are instructions which direct the assembler (the software which translates the assembly-language code into machine instructions).

Format of a Machine-oriented Instruction

In general, a computer instruction will specify or imply four elements:

1 The operation to be performed

2 The operands (registers, storage locations, channels, input/output devices, etc.) to be used

3 Location operand where results will be put (e.g., in a register or a storage location)

4 The location of the next instruction

The general format of an instruction is operation code plus operands. The operation code determines how the operands are to be interpreted. Different operation codes require different types of operands. The following are examples of operation, operation operand(s), and location operand for the result:

Operation	Register, storage location, or device to be used	Register or storage location to hold or obtain result
Add	Contents of register or storage location	A receiving register or receiving storage location
Move	Contents of a register or storage location	A receiving register or storage location
Read (a card)	The card reader	Specified or implied locations in storage where card contents are stored

After an instruction is executed, the next instruction must be located. Two methods are used—sequential location and explicit specification. Instructions are normally stored sequentially, so that the location of the next instruction is understood to be the next in the sequence unless there is a transfer of control instruction which breaks the sequence.

The source of the four specifications required for a machine-level instruction can be summarized:

Specification	Source
Operation to be performed	Operation code
Operands to be used	One or more specified

| Locations for storage of results | Defined or implied by instruction |
| Location of next instruction | Next instruction in stored sequence or else specified by instruction operand |

The instructions may also contain codes to specify index register modification, indirect addressing, and base register displacement. The specifications are explained in the chapter.

Effect of Hardware Design on Instruction Format

The form of the instruction and coding of operations are affected by the underlying hardware design. As explained in Chapter 7, it is useful to classify the designs as:

> Word-oriented
> Character-oriented
> Combination

It has become quite common to combine both word-oriented and character-oriented instructions in the same computer.

In the word-oriented or fixed-word-length computer, all processing uses addressable registers, each of which holds a fixed-length word, i.e., specific number of bits (such as 32, 36, 60). The bits in the register can encode a single numeric quantity, a floating point quantity (with characteristic and fraction in the word), a set of characters (using subdivisions of 6 to 8 bits in the word), or a binary code in which each bit is significant. The essential point is that all data for processing is moved into a register from storage, processed in the register, and stored back in a storage location. Each storage location is therefore designed to hold the same number of bits as the registers (a fixed-length word).

In the character-oriented computer, each storage position encoding a character (or perhaps two numeric digits) is addressable. Instructions specify variable-length operands (variable-word length). Processing uses single character registers in a storage-to-storage method.

The computer which has both register and character instructions (as typified by the IBM System/370) uses storage addresses for each storage location that can encode a character (an 8-bit byte storage location). These byte storage locations are utilized in the System/370 as storage references by the different instruction types but interpreted differently:

1 *Register instructions* The first byte of the storage locations making up the word is addressed. The register instruction obtains and uses the number of bytes required by the register. Thus, a regular full-word register instruction will automatically utilize four 8-bit bytes because register length is 32 bits. A typical instruction will specify an operation plus a register and a set of storage locations storing a word.

2 *Character instructions* The first byte storage location for each of two operands

is specified. The number of bytes to be included in each of the operands is also specified (or implied) by the instruction. A typical character instruction will have an operation code plus two storage operands, one of which is used for storage of the result. Character instructions are of two types:

(a) Character instructions using data (alphabetic, numeric, etc.) coded one character per 8-bit byte.

(b) Packed decimal instructions which operate on sets of bytes, each of which encodes two numeric digits (by a 4-bit binary-coded decimal code). The sign for the numeric quantity occupies one digit position. The quantity 76532 would be coded as follows:

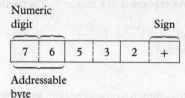

Numeric digit

Sign

Addressable byte

The use of pairs of digit codes means that a leading zero will be part of the data if the numeric digits do not fill the first digit position.

The formats of the IBM System/370 instructions are based on whether the instruction is a register instruction or a character (storage-to-storage) instruction plus the type of operands used. The instructions differ in length because of the necessity for different specifications. There is an operation code in each case plus operands as follows:

IBM designation	Bytes to code machine instruction	Explanation
RR	1	Register operand to register operand
RX	2	Storage operand to register operand
RS	2	Register operand to storage operand
SI	2	Immediate operand (data in part of instruction) to storage
SS	3	Storage-to-storage with variable word (field) length operands

Coding Rules for Assembly Language

Each assembly language has rules for coding. There is a similarity because of the necessity for most functions to be available in all languages. Special coding paper is often available to assist the programmer in following the coding rules. As typified by the IBM System/370, the coding rules cover the format of an instruction line plus compiler-directing instructions to name and define storage locations, define values to be stored in locations, and define the beginning and end of programs. Coding should be written so as to be maintainable by others. A page of System/370 symbolic coding in Figure 15-1 illustrates assembly coding.

Format of an Instruction Line

Coding paper for convenience in coding in System/370 assembly language is shown in Figure 15-1. The columns are for convenience since the assembler allows free-form coding. Instruction elements may be in any column but must be in the right order, separated by one or more blanks, or in the case of operands, separated by commas. Comments can (and should) follow on the same line. A complete line of comment has an asterisk in column 1. The sequence field is for programmer convenience in numbering statements.

The general format of an instruction is:

Label (*name*)   Assigned to instruction line (not required unless line is referenced by a transfer of control).

Operation code   A one- to five-character mnemonic such as L for load, ST for store.

Operands   These can be symbolic names for storage locations (up to eight characters), numbers for registers (or symbolic names assigned to them), or a literal.

References to variable-length words may include a length in bytes enclosed in parentheses. If the name has been defined as a given length, the use of the name implies the length without explicit specification.

Instructions may use relative coding in which the operand address is specified by being relative (+, −, *, and /) to some known address.

Operand coding	Explanation
ALPHA+8	Operand address is 8 bytes greater than address assigned to ALPHA
BETA−16	Operand address is 16 bytes less than address of BETA
*+32	Operand address is 36 bytes beyond address of current instruction (leading * means address of instruction itself)

Instructions may specify index registers and base registers in parentheses following the operands. This use is explained later in the chapter.

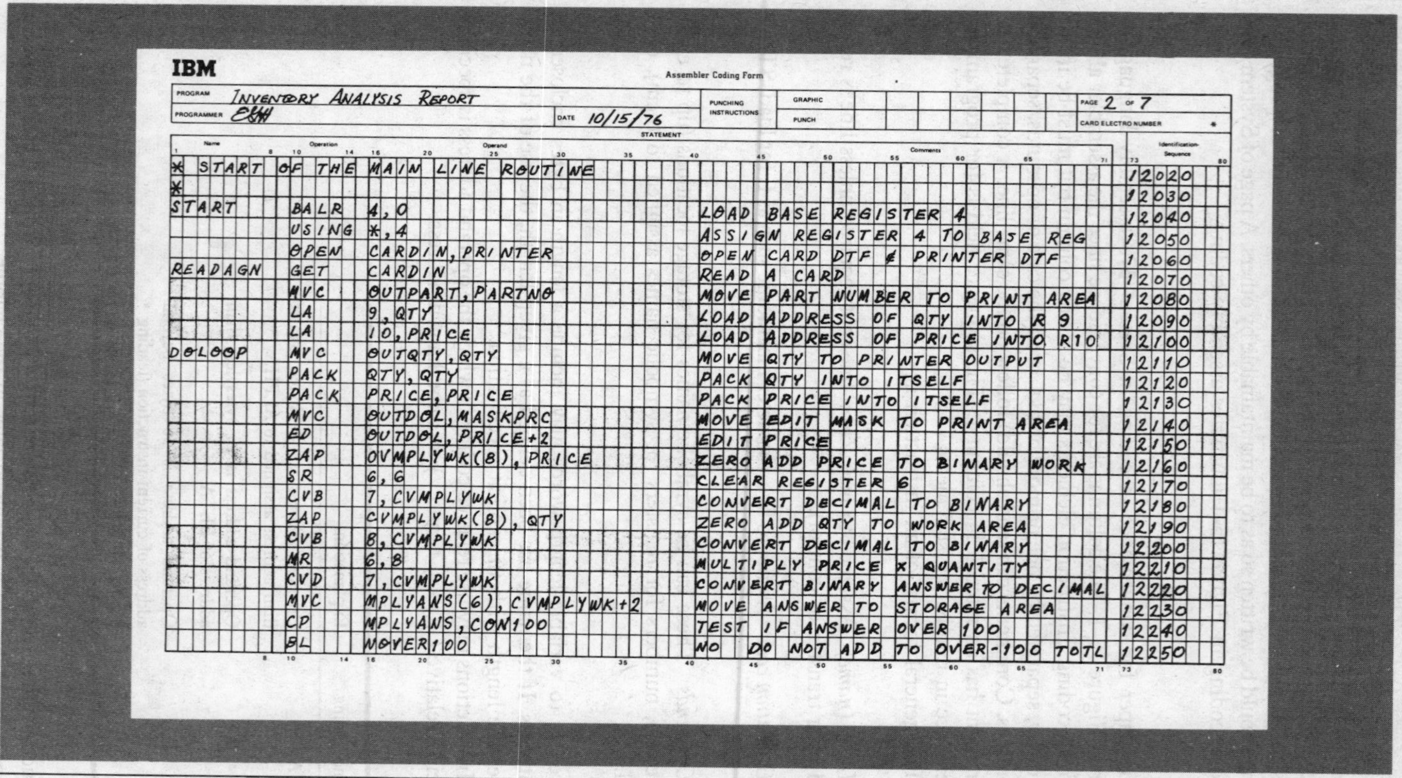

Assembler Coding Form

IBM — Assembler Coding Form
PROGRAM: INVENTORY ANALYSIS REPORT
PROGRAMMER: ESW
DATE: 10/15/76
PAGE 2 of 7

Name	Operation	Operand	Comments	Identification-Sequence
*		START OF THE MAIN LINE ROUTINE		
*				
START	BALR	4,0	LOAD BASE REGISTER 4	12020
	USING	*,4	ASSIGN REGISTER 4 TO BASE REG	12030
	OPEN	CARDIN,PRINTER	OPEN CARD DTF & PRINTER DTF	12040
READAGN	GET	CARDIN	READ A CARD	12050
	MVC	OUTPART,PARTNO	MOVE PART NUMBER TO PRINT AREA	12060
	LA	9,QTY	LOAD ADDRESS OF QTY INTO R 9	12070
	LA	10,PRICE	LOAD ADDRESS OF PRICE INTO R10	12080
DOLOOP	MVC	OUTQTY,QTY	MOVE QTY TO PRINTER OUTPUT	12090
	PACK	QTY,QTY	PACK QTY INTO ITSELF	12100
	PACK	PRICE,PRICE	PACK PRICE INTO ITSELF	12110
	MVC	OUTDOL,MASKPRC	MOVE EDIT MASK TO PRINT AREA	12120
	ED	OUTDOL,PRICE+2	EDIT PRICE	12130
	ZAP	OVMPLYWK(8),PRICE	ZERO ADD PRICE TO BINARY WORK	12140
	SR	6,6	CLEAR REGISTER 6	12150
	CVB	7,CVMPLYWK	CONVERT DECIMAL TO BINARY	12160
	ZAP	CVMPLYWK(8),QTY	ZERO ADD QTY TO WORK AREA	12170
	CVB	8,CVMPLYWK	CONVERT DECIMAL TO BINARY	12180
	MR	6,8	MULTIPLY PRICE X QUANTITY	12190
	CVD	7,CVMPLYWK	CONVERT BINARY ANSWER TO DECIMAL	12200
	MVC	MPLYANS(6),CVMPLYWK+2	MOVE ANSWER TO STORAGE AREA	12210
	CP	MPLYANS,CON100	TEST IF ANSWER OVER 100	12220
	BL	MOVER100	DO NOT ADD TO OVER-100 TOTL	12230

FIGURE 15-1 Example page of symbolic assembly language coding for IBM System/370 (using special coding paper).

400

Assembler-directing Instructions

A few of the major assembler-directing instructions are explained. All data storage locations to be referenced by the program must be defined by an assembler-directing instruction:

Name   DS specification

The specification uses a repeat number, a symbol for type of operand (CL for character, F for fullword, H for halfword, and D for a doubleword operand) followed by the length in bytes in the case of CLs.

Name	Operation	Operand	Explanation
ALPHA	DS	CL20	Assigns name ALPHA to 20-byte field
GAMMA	DS	2F	Assign name GAMMA to the first of two words and reserves a second word following GAMMA

Constants needed by the program may be assigned a name by a DC assembler instruction. In the typical case, the specification is written as:

Name   DC   type, the constant enclosed in quotation marks

There are a number of types of constants; three will be used in the chapter—CL for characters, F for fullword, and P for packed decimal constant. Examples are:

RATE	DC	F'3175'	A constant that is the binary equivalent of 3175 is stored in a location assigned the name RATE
NAME1	DC	CL'DATE'	The characters encoding the word DATE are stored in five bytes assigned the name NAME1

Constants may be coded as part of the instruction by an = sign followed by the type code and the literal enclosed in quotes. For example, an instruction to add the constant 5 (in binary) to the contents of register 5 might read:

A   3,=F'5'   ADD 5 TO REGISTER 3

There are a number of other assembler instructions that will not be explained. Two that are used in all programs are START (as first executable statement) and END (as last statement in program).

The IBM System/370 instructions (as with most computers) are not assigned absolute locations. The locations are all relative to a base point established by a base register which modifies every address to make it within the range where the program and data are stored. The base register is assigned, dropped, etc., by special instructions that are not described in the chapter.

**Programming
Discipline in
Assembly Language**

Coding a symbolic assembly language program in such a way that it is error-free and maintainable is more difficult than with higher-level languages. However, the concepts of programming discipline still apply. A symbolic program may be designed and written in a modular fashion. This may involve both physical modules written as subroutines and logical blocks of code that are not physically separate. Programming techniques with logic that is not readily apparent should be avoided. Comments should be added to the lines of code and extra comments added to define and explain logical blocks of code. Indentation may be used to emphasize the range of loops. Comments should clearly explain conditions causing transfer of control. Before proceeding, question 1 in the self-testing quizzes at the end of the chapter may be used to test your understanding.

Move Instructions

As explained in Chapter 5, the purpose of the move instructions is to transfer data from one location in storage to another storage location. Moving can also be termed "copying" because the sending location is not changed; it is merely copied into the receiving location. The receiving location is altered, being replaced with the new data.

Move instructions are basically of two types—register transfer instructions for computers which use addressable registers and storage-to-storage transfer instructions for computers with character-addressable storage. Both types are discussed in this section. The need to clear or zero storage locations is also explained.

**Data Transfer
Using Registers**

For a fixed-word computer, the register serves as an intermediate storage in the transfer of data between two storage locations. The amount of data transferred is usually a computer word. There are two basic transfer instructions—the first one loads the register (copies the contents of a memory location into a register) and the second puts the register contents in a storage location. The instructions specify or imply three things: (1) the operation (load or store), (2) the register, and (3) the memory location to be used. If a symbolic instruction mnemonic of L for load and ST for store is used, the instructions might appear as follows:

```
L     6,PAYAMT
ST    6,NEWPAY
```

where L and ST signify load and store, 6 refers to register 6, and PAYAMT and NEWPAY are symbolic names for the storage locations from which data is to be loaded and which data is to be stored. Because "load" and "store" are copy instructions, a load and store sequence will result in the same data being found in two separate storage locations, plus the register, as shown on the next page.

In addition to the basic load and store instructions for data transfer with registers, there may be variations such as a register-to-register transfer or a

Description of instruction	CONTENTS OF		
	Register 8	Memory locations	
		1006	1007
Contents before instruction (X's are unknown data)	XXXXXXX	9643001	XXXXXXX
Load register 8 with contents of 1006 (L 8,1006)	9643001	9643001	XXXXXXX
Store contents of register 8 in 1007 (ST 8,1007)	9643001	9643001	9643001

multiple-register load or store in which a single instruction will load consecutive memory locations into consecutive registers (or the reverse as a store instruction). There may be instructions to load or store half a word or to load or store a double word (using two consecutive memory locations and two registers).

Storage-to-Storage Move

In contrast to the fixed-word approach of registers, a storage-to-storage transfer usually involves a variable word containing from one to a large number of characters. A move instruction will copy a number of characters from one series of locations in storage to another. Since each bit set for encoding a character is addressable, the move instruction must specify the set of locations from which the data is to be moved and the set of locations to which it is to be copied. There are two methods for specifying the set of locations (the number of adjacent locations).

The most common method for variable word addressing, typified by the IBM/370 character instructions, specifies the leftmost location of the field, and the instruction gives the number of character positions to be transferred. In the case of a data transfer from 963-966 to 968-971, the sending field will have an address of 963 and a length of 4. The receiving field begins at 968, and no length specification is required. The coded instruction for the System/370 might be MVC 968(4), 963, where MVC is the mnemonic for "move characters." The instruction might also be written using symbolic names. MVC RATE,NEWRT would move the contents of the locations identified with RATE to the locations identified with NEWRT.

Filling a Register or Storage Location with Zeros

The programmer does not need to zero out the previous contents of a memory location before storing new data at that location. The storing of data in a location automatically destroys the previous contents. There are, however, several occasions for zeroing ("clearing") a location. One of these is when a memory location will be used to tally a count or accumulate a sum in an add-to-prior-sum fashion. The location must be cleared to zero for the same reason that an adding-machine operator totals the adding machine before beginning to add.

The clearing operation can take several forms. If a "clear register" instruction is available in a computer using addressable registers, this will fill a register with zeros. To clear a memory location, the register contents are stored there. If a clear register instruction is not available, an alternative, such as subtract the register contents from itself, accomplishes the same purpose. In a storage-to-storage logic, a field of zeros is moved into the location to be zeroed. Frequently, combination instructions are available to zero and perform an operation—such as zero and add. Question 2 of the self-testing quizzes may be used to test your understanding of the move instructions.

Arithmetic Instructions

The arithmetic instructions at the machine-level are quite simple and easy to understand. There are instructions to add, subtract, multiply, and divide. The programming of arithmetic is, however, complicated by keeping track of the decimal point (scaling), by considerations of precision, and by the possibility of overflow.

Scaling The decimal point is not part of the data word for arithmetic processing. Integral digits (1, 7, 95) and fractional digits (.1, .7, .095) are all alike to the computer circuits. It is necessary, however, to keep track of the scaling (decimal point location) of a number for reasons such as these:

1 To be able to locate and insert the decimal point in the printed output

2 To line up numbers being added or subtracted, so that digits with like positional values are paired

3 To prevent or control arithmetic overflow in which the result of an addition, subtraction, or division is greater than the capacity of the register or field where the result is to be stored

4 To be able to locate the decimal point in the result of a multiplication or division in order to preserve the significant digits

Two methods are available for keeping track of the decimal point—the fixed decimal system and the floating decimal point system. The floating point system can be implemented either as a hardware feature or by software using a series of program steps. Floating point arithmetic is explained later in this chapter. Most data processing problems coded in assembly language are run using the fixed decimal system in which the computer circuitry operates on fixed, assumed decimal points, and the programmer must keep track of the actual decimal point locations.

In a fixed decimal system, the programmer may use rules which involve counting the number of digits before and after the decimal point of the operands. From this count, the decimal point may be calculated for the results (or the scale factor method to be discussed later in the chapter may be used).

The computer performs arithmetic either in binary, in binary-coded decimal (packed decimal), or in both. The binary-coded decimal is, for purposes of scaling, rounding, etc., the same as decimal arithmetic, since the computer encodes each decimal digit using a separate set of bits.

In a computer using decimal arithmetic, the programmer can line up decimal points for arithmetic by shifting. $\boxed{36750_\wedge}$ is turned into $\boxed{03675_\wedge}$ by shifting one place to the right. If the computer uses a fixed binary word, the lining up of decimal points can be accomplished by multiplying or dividing by powers of 10. For example, if 24 and 2.4 (both identical in storage) are to be added, the 24 might be multiplied by 10 to give a number which is understood to be 24.0 even though the computer treats it as 240. The number 24 (11000) multiplied by 10 (1010) gives 240 (11110000).

Before scaling		After scaling	
$\boxed{0000011000}$ = 24		$\boxed{0011110000}$	24.0
$\boxed{0000011000}$ = 2.4		$\boxed{0000011000}$	2.4
		$\boxed{0100001000}$	26.4 (sum)

Arithmetic Precision

In the register approach to processing using fixed-length words, the processing uses storage locations (words) which contain a set number of bits. A 32-bit word can represent a number as large as 2,147,483,647, but what happens if the number to be represented is larger? Two approaches are taken. In the first, some of the low-order digits at the right are dropped in order to allow more significant digits to be added at the left. The programmer keeps track of the lost digit positions and when the number is printed out, prints some zeros for these positions. In other words, the exact digits are lost, but the scaling is preserved and is represented by zeros or other notation. The number of digits the computer can retain is the precision.

A second approach is to use two computer words together to achieve a double precision. This is done usually with special routines, but some computers provide for double-precision arithmetic as part of the instruction repertoire. The double words are stored in adjacent memory locations, one containing the most significant digits and the other the least significant digits of the number.

Addition and Subtraction

The instructions to add or subtract must specify the memory locations of the two operands (augend and addend) and the location where the result (sum) is to be stored. The data words to be added or subtracted must be arranged so that the corresponding units, tens, etc., positions are paired. This may be thought of as lining up the decimal (or binary) points, even though there are no decimal or binary points in the data words.

For example, assume two quantities, A (497.65) and B (1.3760), are stored in two separate storage locations. If a command were given to add them without considering the calculated position of the decimal points, the answer would be incorrect.

Manual arithmetic	Incorrect computer	Correct computer
A 497.65	A 4976500	A 4976500
B 1.3760	B 1376000	B 0013760
A + B 499.0260	A + B 6353500	A + B 4990260

The instructions to perform arithmetic will differ depending on whether the arithmetic is performed on fixed words by registers or by a storage-to-storage approach on individual digits. The register method will typically use three instructions to load the augend into a register, add the addend, and store the sum back in a memory location. If the assumed decimal or binary points are not already lined up, the scaling of the fixed words may be adjusted by either shifting (to be explained later in the chapter), multiplying, or dividing. For example, the following System/370 instructions add REGPAY and OTPAY and store the sum in TOTPAY (assuming REGPAY and OTPAY have the same scaling):

```
L     2,REGPAY
A     2,OTPAY
ST    2,TOTPAY
```

The storage-to-storage method for addition and subtraction will typically require only a single instruction to execute an addition or subtraction. An additional instruction is sometimes necessary in order to have the results stored where desired. Since storage-to-storage arithmetic can address a specified set of characters in storage, the operands are not of a fixed length. The programmer can add together two 2-digit numbers, a 20- and a 30-digit number, etc. The result is put directly in storage, so that the result field must be large enough to receive it. The usual instruction for addition is to add the contents of one of the specified operands to the contents of the other. This "add-to-one-of-operands" logic means that the contents of one of the operands will be automatically replaced by the result field, thereby destroying the data in that operand. If that operand should not be destroyed, it must be copied prior to execution of the instruction. If there is a specific location where the result is to be stored, one of the factors is moved into this location and the other factor added to it. If the fields to be added are of unequal length, the operand fields to be used for the result field must be the larger of the two because addition will cease when all the digits in the smallest operand have been processed.

For the purpose of examples of storage-to-storage addition and subtraction, assume character-storage addressing (as typified by the IBM System/370). The

System/370 uses an address for each pair of decimal digits. The operand is addressed by the leftmost storage location. The sign is stored in the last digit position of the set of bytes making up the operand. The first operand in the arithmetic instruction is the receiving field. Assume storage as follows:

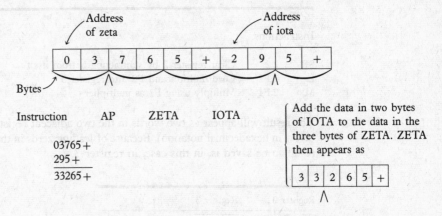

| Instruction | AP | ZETA | IOTA |

03765+
295+
———
33265+

Add the data in two bytes of IOTA to the data in the three bytes of ZETA. ZETA then appears as

Multiplication

The instructions to multiply specify the multiplier and multiplicand. The maximum number of significant digits in the result is equal to the sum of the number of digits in the multiplier and multiplicand. The minimum number is one less than the maximum, as shown by the examples below.

Maximum	Minimum
781 (3)	321 (3)
68 (2)	25 (2)
52108 (5)	8025 (4)

This means that, for a fixed word-length computer using registers, the resulting product will occupy two registers. In a variable word-length computer, the product will occupy a number of adjacent storage locations equal, at a maximum, to the number of digits in the multiplicand and multiplier.

The IBM System/370 multiplication instructions require the use of two adjacent registers; the first register is cleared, the second is loaded with the multiplicand, and the multiply instruction references the first register plus the multiplier (in storage). The result will appear in the two adjacent registers (replacing the multiplicand, etc.). As an example, assume the following two factors in storage (binary words expressed in hexadecimal notation), using registers 2 and 3 for the computation:

	Symbolic name	Contents	Decimal value
Multiplier	location F1	+00000118	280
Multiplicand	location F2	+00000431	1073

Instructions:

SR	2,2	Clear register 2 by subtracting it from itself
L	3,F2	Load multiplicand F2 into register 3
M	2,F1	Multiply using F1 as multiplier

The result will appear as two words in the two adjacent registers 2 and 3 (shown below in hexadecimal notation). Because of leading zeros in the factors, the entire result to be saved is, in this case, in register 3.

Register 2	Register 3	
00000000	00049598	= 300440 in decimal

The variable-length instructions develop the answer in a product field set up for this purpose by the programmer. The steps in programming and multiplication are typically:

1 Move the multiplicand into the product area.

2 Execute multiply instruction using product area and multiplier field as operands.

The result is found in the product area. For example, using IBM System/370 packed decimal instructions, a field NIX containing 00625+ (3 bytes) is multiplied by a field called JIX containing 025+ (2 bytes), and the result found in location KIX (5 bytes) is 000015625+.

ZAP	KIX,NIX	Move contents of location NIX to KIX and zero out rest of KIX (zero and add packed decimal).
MP	KIX,JIX	Multiply packed decimal contents of KIX (which contains copy of multiplicand) by contents of JIX, which is the multiplier. Result is located in KIX, writing over the previous contents.

Scaling in multiplication follows the rule that the number of digits to the right of the decimal location in the product is the sum of the number of places to the right of the decimal position in the multiplier and multiplicand. The number of places to the left of the decimal is equal to the number of places to the left in the multiplier and multiplicand, except that the first digit in the product area may be zero.

EXAMPLES	SCALING				SCALING	
	Left	Right			Left	Right
$110_\wedge 01$	3	2		$2011_\wedge 2$	4	1
$\times 91_\wedge 31$	2	2		$3_\wedge 14$	1	2
$10045_\wedge 6131$	5	4		$06315_\wedge 168$	5	3

While this approach to scaling is satisfactory for simple problems or hand computations, it is not always so, and the scale-factor method or floating point arithmetic explained later in the chapter is used.

Division   The instructions to divide must specify a divisor and a dividend. The locations of the two results, the quotient and the remainder, are specified by the instructions for the computer being programmed. The size in digits of the quotient and remainder is usually limited to the size of a computer word register in a fixed-word computer using registers. When using character (packed decimal) instructions, the quotient size is generally equal to the number of digits in the dividend, and the remainder is equal in size to the number of digits in the divisor. The remainder, as in manual arithmetic, is the numerator of a fraction which has the divisor as the denominator.

$$\begin{array}{r} 007 \quad \text{Quotient} \\ \text{Divisor} \quad 14\overline{)100} \quad \text{Dividend} \\ 02/14 = \text{Remainder} \end{array}$$

The IBM System/370 fixed-word divide instructions use two adjacent registers. The first register of the pair is cleared, the second register is loaded with the dividend, and the divide instruction references the first register and the storage location of the divisor. Assume a dividend in a location called COST containing a 32-bit binary word equal to 300440 (+00049598 in hexadecimal notation) and a divisor of 1073 (+00000436 in hexadecimal notation) located in UNITS. The instructions to divide COST by UNITS to arrive at unit cost are:

```
L    3,COST     Load dividend
SR   2,2        Clear other register used in division
D    2,UNITS    Divide by contents of location UNITS
```

The result of the division will be (hexadecimal):

Register 2	Register 3
00000000	00000118
Remainder	Quotient (unit cost) = 280 in decimal

The IBM System/370 decimal instructions using variable word-length logic are similar in concept to the decimal multiply sequence. A storage area is specified that will hold both the quotient and the remainder. The first step is to move the dividend into this divide area and zero out the remaining locations. The next instruction is "divide," with the operands being the divide area and the location of the divisor. Both the quotient and remainder appear in the divide area. For example, if the contents of GRADES is to be divided by the contents of CREDIT using DVSN as a divide area, the following instructions will be used:

Symbolic name	Contents (decimal)	Length in bytes
GRADES	10300+	3
CREDIT	072+	2
DVSN	unknown	5

Coding		Contents of DVSN
ZAP	DVSN,GRADES Load dividend (GRADES) into divide area and zero out rest of area (DVSN)	0000010300+
DP	DVSN,CREDIT Divide by contents of CREDIT	00143+004+ Quotient Remainder

The scaling rules for division differ depending on whether the arithmetic division is character or word and whether the word is interpreted as integers or as a fraction. In the example, 103.00 was divided by 72 to give 1.43 as a result. If further precision were needed, the dividend would be made larger.

Overflow Overflow describes a size error condition in which the storage locations which are assigned to hold a result are not large enough to hold all the digits. Overflow generally refers to loss of digits at the left end of a group of digits. These are the most significant digits. If digits at the right end of a group are not to be stored for some reason, either truncation or rounding can occur. In truncation, the digits are merely dropped, whereas in rounding, the rightmost digit that is retained is increased by 1 if the digit dropped is 6 or greater.

Most significant digit lost through overflow → ① | 7 | 9 | 6 | 5 | 4 | 3 | 7 | 4 | ② ← Digits lost in truncation or rounding

Arithmetic overflow occurs in addition, subtraction, and in some types of division operations:

1 In addition, overflow occurs when the sum of the most significant (leftmost) digits in the accumulator register or accumulator field exceeds 9.

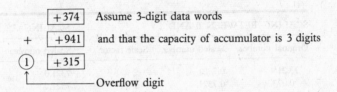

	+374	Assume 3-digit data words
+	+941	and that the capacity of accumulator is 3 digits
①	+315	

└─── Overflow digit

2 In subtraction, overflow occurs when the remainder exceeds the number of digits in the accumulator. This can occur only if one of the quantities is negative.

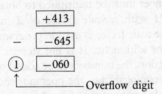

	+413
−	−645
①	−060

└─── Overflow digit

3 Overflow will occur in division in the special case of a register computer which treats all words as being fractions. Overflow will occur in such a computer whenever the dividend is greater in absolute value than the divisor, since this will result in a number greater than .9. This does not apply to the IBM System/370 computer.

Overflow creates a problem because the overflow digit is usually lost. The existence of overflow is usually signaled by some sort of error indicator or error interruption. If the overflow indicator or interrupt shows overflow during addition or subtraction, it is a relatively simple matter to shift the number and replace the digit that has been lost, because the lost digit will always be 1. Overflow in division is more difficult, and the remedy does not necessarily follow automatically, as in addition and subtraction. In some computers, the programmer writing in assembly language must program tests for overflow and write routines to make adjustments; in others, there is an automatic procedure involving an interrupt handling routine in the programs which operate the system.

The Scale-Factor Method

The assembly language programmer must keep track of the decimal point, yet the various rules for scaling results of an arithmetic operation (locating the position of the decimal point) are sometimes ambiguous and difficult to implement. The scale-factor method is an alternative approach. This method involves converting all numbers used in computation to a common base, such as whole numbers or fractions. The programmer records the number of places the decimal point had to be shifted to the right or left when the number was converted to the common basis. This number (+ for places shifted to left and − for shift to right) is the scale factor.

SCALING BETWEEN 0 AND 1			SCALING AS INTEGRAL NUMBER	
Original number	Scaled number	Scale factor	Scaled number	Scale factor
73.21	0.7321	2	7321.0	−2
0.07321	0.7321	−1	7321.0	−5
0.007321	0.7321	−2	7321.0	−6
7321.0	0.7321	4	7321.0	0

Any common basis may be used. The scale factor represents the power of 10 by which the scaled number must be multiplied to obtain the number as originally scaled. Thus, 0.7321 with a scale factor of 2 means 0.7321×10^2 or $0.7321 \times 100 = 73.21$. The scale factor is used in programming in order to know how to position the data for arithmetic. It is not stored.

For addition or subtraction, the numbers to be added or subtracted must have the same scale factor. To accomplish this, the operands should be adjusted to the largest scale factor. The scale factor of the sum or remainder will be the same as the scale factor of the operands.

Original number	Scaled number	Scale factor	Scaled numbers for addition	Scale factor
149.21	0.149210	3	0.149210	3
1.213	0.121300	1	0.001213	3
49.20	0.492000	2	0.049200	3
				=
		Result of addition	0.199623	3
		or	199.623	

The scale-factor method for keeping track of the decimal point in multiplication involves multiplying the two-scaled numbers and adding the two-scale factors. The product is scaled by the new scale factor.

EXAMPLE   Multiply 3.475 by 412.64

Scaled number	Scale factor
0.3475	1
$\times$0.41254	$+3$
0.143392400	4
$0.143392400 \times 10^4 = 1433.92400$	

When the scale-factor method is used for keeping track of the decimal point in division, the scaled divisor is divided into the scaled dividend, and the quotient has a scale factor formed by subtracting the scale factor of the divisor from the scale factor of the dividend.

EXAMPLE   Divide 370.36 by 15.76

$$.235 \times 10^2 = 23.5$$
$$0.1576\overline{)0.0370360}$$

Scale $\uparrow$ $\uparrow$
factors   (2)   (4) $4 - 2$ = scale factor of 2 for quotient

Floating Point Arithmetic   The task of keeping track of scaling is not too difficult for the uncomplicated data processing typical of business applications. But for complicated scientific problems, it becomes much more troublesome. The reader may have noticed that the scale-factor method of scaling depends on rather simple rules. Therefore, it is possible for the computer to develop and keep track of its own scale factors. Arithmetic in which the computer does this is called "floating point arithmetic."

In floating point arithmetic, the computer program converts all numbers to be used by the program to a form consisting of a fraction (or mantissa) and an exponent (or characteristic). The *exponent* is the power of 10 (or other radix) required to change the mantissa back to the original form. It corresponds to the scale factor in the scale-factor method. The *mantissa* may be expressed in many forms. The scientific or normal form has one place to the left of the decimal (absolute value greater than 1 but less than 10). The standard form of the mantissa for 12.41 is therefore 1.241 with an exponent of 1. Some computers use a form in which the mantissa is always less than 1 (a fraction).

In computer computation, it is desirable to avoid a negative exponent. Therefore, the exponent is frequently written in an excess form, such as excess-128, in which 128 is added to the exponent. In excess-128 notation, an exponent of 00 is equivalent to 10^{-128}, and an exponent of 256 is equivalent to 10^{+127}. The same principles can be used for a notation with different limits and different radices.

In floating point arithmetic, the combination of fraction and exponent is stored in memory as a single data word. In order to perform arithmetic using two floating point words, the words are first separated into the two elements. Arithmetic is performed on the mantissas to obtain the result, then arithmetic is performed on the characteristics to obtain the exponent for the result. The fraction and exponent for the result are then combined into a data word and stored in memory.

Floating point arithmetic may be implemented by either hardware or software. The larger System/370 computers have floating point hardware instructions. Programming is performed as with other instructions, except that the scaling can be completely ignored because the floating point instructions keep track of the scale factor and automatically adjust for it.

Question 3 in the self-testing quizzes, covering the preceding arithmetic section, can now be used for evaluating understanding of the section.

Transfer of Control Instructions

A computer program is a sequence of steps. The program executes the instructions one after another in the order they are found in memory unless a transfer of control instruction breaks the sequence. This break in the sequence, often called "branching," is necessary because the computer program must usually provide not one but many possible program paths. One of these paths is selected during the running of the program on the basis of the results obtained to that point, or on some other condition. This is the selection structure explained in Chapter 5. For example, the path a program is to follow may depend on whether a numerical result is positive, zero, or negative. This is programmed as a test of the number followed by three different sets of instructions to handle the three outcomes (Figure 15-2). When programming this example, there must be a transfer of control to specify which of the three sequences of instructions will be used. When one of these sequences has been used, there must be a branching from the sequence up to the coding which is common to all processing. There are three general types of transfer of control instructions:

1 Unconditional transfer
2 Conditional transfer based on comparison
3 Conditional transfer based on absence or existence of a condition

Unconditional Transfer

Normally, the program instructions are stored in consecutive locations and executed sequentially. An instruction counter keeps track of the location of the next instruction. However, there are occasions in programming when a straight sequence of instructions cannot be maintained. The jump or branch instruction provides for an unconditional transfer of control. This directs the processor to find the next instruction at a location other than the next location established by the instruction counter. The branching does not depend on a comparison or test of condition. An example of the use of unconditional transfer of control is branching to the main line flow after performing an alternative sequence of instructions as shown in Figure 15-2. An example of an unconditional branching instruction is:

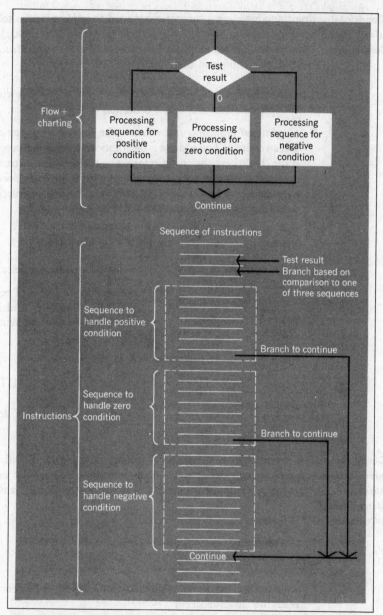

FIGURE 15-2 Programming of three alternative program paths.

B NEXT

where NEXT is the label for the next instruction to be executed.

Conditional Transfer Based on Comparison

Branching based on a comparison is used to implement the selection structure. It involves the comparison of two data words or data fields. The result of the comparison determines the path the program takes. The instructions for branching based on a comparison usually require two instructions:

1 *Compare instruction*   The instruction compares two data words (either numeric or alphanumeric) and sets a condition code or indicator.

2 *Conditional branching instruction* . The instruction specifies a condition code and an address. The address is the location to which the program should branch if the condition code or indicator set by the compare instruction is equal to the specified code in the instruction or one of a group of specified codes. If not equal, the program does not branch. The branch instruction mnemonic will usually include the condition. For example:

BH	Branch on high	BE	Branch on equal
BL	Branch on low	BNH	Branch not high

An example of a pair of register instructions in symbolic coding is:

C	3,PAY	Compare the contents of register 3 with contents of location PAY and set condition code
BH	FUNNY	Branch if the register contents were greater than PAY

An example of storage-to-storage instructions is:

CL	PAY,LIMIT	Compare PAY with LIMIT and set condition code
BL	OKAY	Branch to OKAY if PAY less than LIMIT

Conditional Transfer Based on Absence or Existence of a Condition

The conditions on which the branching is based are usually a data condition, overflow from arithmetic, and equipment status. Examples of conditions which might be tested and thus be the basis for a conditional transfer of control are:

1 Whether a data word is zero, positive, or negative

2 Overflow

3 The "on" or "off" condition of a console switch

4 The condition of an input/output unit, i.e., whether it is busy and therefore not ready for an instruction

5 The existence of various type of errors during processing (such as a read error)

These conditions usually set a condition or error indicator which is specified by the instruction as the reason for branching to occur. If the condition code or indicator is not set, i.e., the condition has not occurred, the conditional branching will not be performed. If the programmer does not write the conditional branching test, the condition will not be acted upon. For example, each arithmetic operation in the System/370 sets a condition code that can be tested. If there is no branching instruction, the condition code is ignored; a branch instruction such as

BZ ISZERO

will test the condition code and transfer control to the specified location if the arithmetic result were zero.

Interrupts   Many computers have provisions for automatic transfer of control if certain conditions occur, rather than relying on the programmer to insert conditional branching instructions to test for them. The interrupt, or "trap," transfers control to a fixed location when a condition such as overflow, parity error, or input/output device needing attention is detected. In addition, the interrupt process provides a record of the instruction to which control should go after the interrupt is handled, codes describing the reason for the interrupt, and various other status information.

When an interrupt occurs, control is transferred to a specified location from which there is a transfer of control to a routine to interpret the cause of the interrupt and take appropriate action. The interrupt-handling routine is usually a part of the software provided by the manufacturer in the operating system, so that the programmer does not need to write it. After the error message or other action has been taken, the computer transfers control back to the next instruction following the one during which the interrupt occurred. In essence, an interrupt system provides an automatic transfer of control based on a condition with the action to be taken being determined by an analysis of the interrupt code.

Use question 4 in the self-testing quizzes to evaluate understanding of the transfer-of-control material.

Editing

When read into the computer, data sometimes may not be in a proper form for computational use. After computation, the data is not usually in the form desired for output—no commas separate the thousands or millions, and there is no decimal point. The purpose of the editing instructions is to rearrange data words, alter individual digits or bits, convert from external form to internal processing form, and set up the data in a suitable form for printing or punching. The editing instructions, for discussion purposes, are divided into four major types—shifting, logical or bit alteration, data conversion, and output editing.

Shifting   Shift instructions are used in fixed word-length computers to rearrange digits in a word. For example, in a 10-digit fixed-length word, 0763497621, the programmer may wish to use only the third through the seventh digits, i.e., the word to be used is 0000063497. Shift instructions provide for the rearranging and eliminations required to assemble the word into the desired form. Such instructions are not necessary in a variable word-length computer because by varying the address and length specification, the desired digits can be obtained. Shifting can also be used for multiplication or division. For example, shifting a binary number in a register one place to the left is equivalent to multiplication by 2.

Shift instructions use one or two registers and typically provide for several variations:

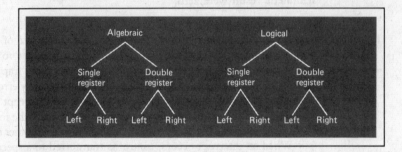

The difference between an algebraic shift and a logical shift is the treatment of the sign bit. In the algebraic shift, the sign is not part of any shifting; in the logical shift, the sign bit moves as a regular bit. In a binary computer, a word of, say, 32 bits will consist of a sign bit as the first bit and 31 data bits. If the word holds character codes, the word will be divided into bytes (say, four 8-bit bytes), each of which encodes one alphanumeric character. The sign bit is, in this case, used as a data code bit. When shifting, the sign bit will need to move, whereas in the binary word, shifting bits into the sign position would not be appropriate. Other coding, such as Boolean codes, may also use the sign bit as a regular data bit.

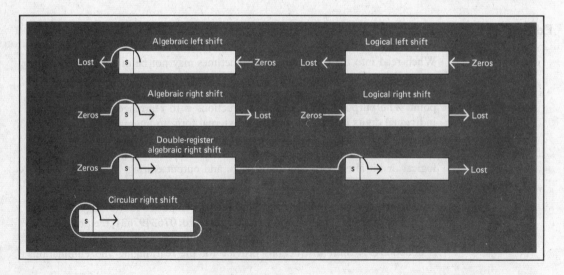

The shift may be either left or right. When shifting occurs, zero bits enter the vacated spaces, and digits shifted out are lost. If, however, a double-register shift is used, digits pushed out of the first register of the pair will enter the second register, causing a shift of its contents. A variation is a circular shift in which the digits pushed out at the end (say, the right end) of a register reenter the other end (left end).

To illustrate the use of shifting, assume a fixed-length word in the form

(hexadecimal)

7	6	5	7	8	4	8	9

Load word into register 1

76578489

Shift two hexadecimal places to left

57848900

Shift four hexadecimal places to right

00005784

Logical or Bit Alteration

The bit instructions, frequently referred to as "filtering" or "masking," operate on a word to alter the bits. The bit instructions use two words—the word with the bits to be altered and the control word (called a "mask") which determines how the first word is to be altered. Each of the bits is operated upon independently of the other bits in the word. The matching of each data bit with a corresponding bit in the control word determines the state of the data bits after the instruction is executed.

The instructions for bit manipulation will usually provide for logical AND, logical OR, and logical exclusive OR. The results of these operations are:

Instruction	Result word will have a 1-bit if:
AND	Both data bit and mask bit are 1
OR	Either or both data bit or mask are 1
Exclusive OR	Either (but not both) data bit or mask bit is 1

Otherwise the result bit will be zero. For example, the table of outcomes for an AND operation is:

AND

Data	Mask	Result
0	0	0
0	1	0
1	0	0
1	1	1

These instructions can be used to erase bits in the data word, to add bits to the data word, or to combine two data words. Using the same example as with shifting, assume a data word (hexadecimal) 76578489 as a code. Digits 4, 5, 7, and 9 are needed; the other portions are to be erased. By combining the data word using AND with a mask consisting of 000FF0FF (remember F in hexadecimal is 1111), the result will save the desired bits and erase the others. In the figure below, all 32 bits are shown:

Data word	0111	0110	0101	0111	1000	0100	1000	1001
Mask word	0000	0000	0000	1111	1111	0000	1111	1111
Result (AND)	0000	0000	0000	0111	1000	0000	1000	1001

Data Conversion

In binary computers and in some character computers, data in the input/output code is not suitable for arithmetic computation. When the data is read into the computer, it is in a character code. It must be converted to binary or to a packed decimal before it can be used in arithmetic. When data is to be output, it must be converted to character coding. Typical instructions will convert from character coding to binary and from binary to character. The IBM System/370, for example, uses binary or packed decimal for computation and an 8-bit character coding for input and output. There are two pairs of instructions:

1 Pack (PACK) converts from character coding to packed decimal. Convert to binary (CVB) converts from packed decimal coding to fixed-word binary coding.

2 Convert to decimal (CDV) converts from binary word to packed decimal coding. Unpack (UNPK) converts from packed decimal to character coding.

Some computers using binary-coded character for computation do not need the instructions to convert to or from binary or to pack and unpack.

Output Editing

In order to make meaningful printed output, leading zeros need to be suppressed (replaced with blanks), commas need to be inserted to separate groups of digits, a period needs to be inserted to mark the decimal point, and other characters need to be inserted, such as * or $. This editing can be performed by shifting, masking, inserting, etc., but most computers have special editing instructions to simplify this task.

The usual procedure for editing uses two fields—(1) the field to be edited and (2) a pattern field containing symbols which control the editing. The edited result replaces the pattern field. The programmer defines the pattern field as a word to be stored as part of the program. A simple editing instruction is used to illustrate this concept. Similar instructions are found in most computers. The IBM/System 370 uses special codes for each pattern character, but these codes are not used in the examples in order not to obscure the concept.

EXAMPLE 1   A data field consisting of the digits 937421 is to be printed out as $9374.21. A pattern or control field is stored in the computer in the form $dddd.dd where d stands for a digit location. The instruction is given to move the characters in in the data field to the control field and edit. This causes the two to be combined, and the result stored in place of the control field.

Data field	937421
Control field	$dddd.dd
Result field	$9374.21

EXAMPLE 2   A data word in the form 0000194 is to be printed out as 1.94. The edit word is 0ddddd.dd. The leading zero specifies the leading zeros are to be suppressed, i.e., replaced by blanks, so that the result will be printed as 1.94.

Answer question 5 in the self-testing quizzes to test understanding of editing.

Input/Output Instructions

Input/output programming ranges considerably in complexity depending on the complexity and versatility of the computer system. Programming may be handled at the symbolic level using three different approaches:

1   Symbolic machine-level instructions
2   Macro instructions
3   Input/output control system (IOCS)

The symbolic machine-level programming is used for simple input/output situations or where the input/output for the computer is quite simple. The latter condition usually applies to computers with restricted input/output capabilities. The macro instruction approach is a simplification for programming I/O.

The IOCS is an extension of the macro instruction concept. It was developed to reduce the complexity of input/output programming and at the same time to provide an efficient and well-controlled management of the input/output functions. Input/output control routines are usually part of the routines under the operating system. The programmer writes input/output definitions and macro instructions. The assembly routine prepares the necessary machine-level instructions plus the linkages to the input/output control routine.

In the input/output control system approach to programming of input and output as typified by the IBM System/370, each file to be read is described in a file definition. The type of file (input, output, or both), the device to be used, the record form (fixed, blocked, or unblocked), the storage area name, etc., are examples of the information included in the file definition. Figure 15-3 is an example of a file definition for records to be read from punched cards.

The file is opened before use and closed following its last use. A macro

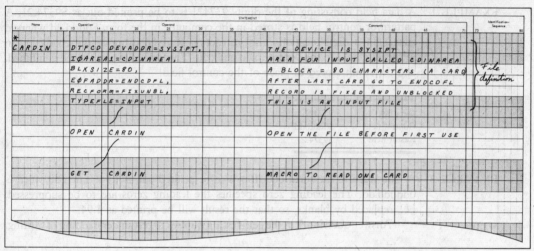

The coding form shows the following entries:

```
*
CARDIN    DTFCD  DEVADDR=SYSIPT,           THE DEVICE IS SYSIPT
          IOAREA1=CDINAREA,               AREA FOR INPUT CALLED CDINAREA
          BLKSIZE=80,                     A BLOCK = 80 CHARACTERS (A CARD)  } File
          EOFADDR=ENDCDFL,                AFTER LAST CARD GO TO ENDCDFL       definition
          RECFORM=FIXUNBL,                RECORD IS FIXED AND UNBLOCKED
          TYPEFLE=INPUT                   THIS IS AN INPUT FILE

          OPEN   CARDIN                   OPEN THE FILE BEFORE FIRST USE

          GET    CARDIN                   MACRO TO READ ONE CARD
```

FIGURE 15-3 File definition for a card input.

"OPEN file name" handles the reading and checking of header labels and performs other checking and housekeeping to get the device on which the file is found ready to operate. The "CLOSE file name" macro performs housekeeping. Control is programmed by a control macro (commonly CNTRL) which specifies the file name and control codes.

In using macros for input and output, the input macro (GET is a common command) makes available one logical record from the physical record. The output macro (PUT) places a logical record into position to be written. Suppose, for example, that a physical record, such as a block on magnetic tape, contains 10 logical records. The first use of the GET input macro will cause the reading of the entire block of records and the moving of the first record into position for use by the program. The next use of the GET macro will move the second record into the location where the record is to be used. A second physical record is not read because it is not yet necessary.

In summary, a sequence of macros used for all files (cards, printed output, magnetic tape, etc.) might be as follows:

File definition entries	
OPEN file name	Write once before file is used
GET file name	
GET file name	Repeated for each logical record to be obtained

PUT file name $\quad\Big\}\quad$ Repeated for each logical record to be written

CLOSE file name $\}$ $\quad$ After last use of the file

Answer question 6 in the self-testing quizzes at the end of the chapter.

Looping

The technique of looping is basic to programming. It implements the repetition structure described in Chapter 5. The objective of a loop is to use the same set of instructions over and over again, rather than having to write and store many instructions. This can be illustrated by a program segment which sums 100 quantities stored in locations 1000 to 1398 (each word is a fixed length of four bytes). Assuming the use of addressable arithmetic registers, the straight-line coding to sum 100 numbers requires 101 separate instructions. The first instruction is a "load accumulator register," the next 99 are "add to accumulator register" instructions, and the final instruction is a "store the register used as the accumulator." Given the first data location as 1000, and IBM System/370 symbolic operation codes of L for load accumulator (use register 2), A for add to the accumulator register, and ST for store accumulator register, the coding would be as follows (remember that each data word covers four bytes):

Symbolic coding		Absolute address of word being used	Contents of accumulator (register 2)
L	2,DATA	1000	Contents of four bytes addressed by location 1000
A	2,DATA + 4	1004	Contents of 1000 + 1004
A	2,DATA + 8	1008	Contents of 1000 + 1004 + 1008
A	2,DATA + 396	1396	Contents of 1000 + 1004 + 1008 + $\cdots$ + 1396
ST	2,SUM		

In terms of speed of execution the straight-line coding cannot be improved, but it requires coding (and storing) 101 instructions. Since the only change in each of the add instructions is an increment of 0004 in the address portion, a loop is indicated.

The programming of a loop involves the modification of some elements in a set of instructions, so that the same instructions may be repeated. In the above example of summing 100 numbers, the same addition instructions could be used for all 99 additions after the load instruction if the addition instruction could be modified with each repetition to change the storage address by 4. This change may be made by altering the instruction as if it were data, but this is rarely done because computers are almost always designed with index registers for this purpose.

Index Registers
Index registers are registers which can be used for purposes such as address modification and as loop counters (to keep track of number of repetitions of a loop). This discussion focuses on the use of index registers to modify the instruction address. In some computers, these are separate registers designed for use only as index registers; in other computers (such as IBM System/360 and System/370), 15 of the 16 general registers can be used as index registers. The four low-order bytes of the eight in the register form the index register (the other four being ignored).

Recall from the discussion in Chapter 7 that an instruction to be executed is moved out of storage into special registers for decoding—the operation code into an operation register and the operand address into an address register. The index register addition (or subtraction) to alter the address occurs during the instruction cycle after the instruction has been copied from its storage location into the address register but prior to its execution, so that the instruction in storage is not altered by the index register modification. Nor does the modification alter the contents of the index register.

In the following example, assuming the instruction specifies the addition of the contents of location 1000 to the contents of an accumulator register, the actual execution, under the index register modification shown, would result in the contents of location 1004 being used rather than 1000.

Address from instruction	03E8	Contents of address register holding operand address prior to index register modification (hexadecimal 03E8 = 1000)
	0004	Contents of index register
Address to be used (effective address)	03EC	Contents of address register holding operand address after index register modification completed (hexadecimal 03EC = 1004)

Index register modification is specified by the use of a code in the instruction. In symbolic coding, the use of an index register is usually specified by a separate code identifying the index register to be used. As an example, the System/370 symbolic coding specifies the register in parentheses following the symbolic data name being referenced.

A 2,DATA(3)	Add to general register 2 (used as an accumulator) the contents of a storage location obtained by taking location DATA and modifying it by adding the contents of general register 3 (used as an index register).

To program the use of index registers, there must be instructions for loading an index register with an initial value, for incrementing or decrementing its contents, and for testing its contents. In addition to these basic index register instructions there may be special instructions which perform a sequence of instructions useful in programming techniques such as looping. In the case of the IBM System/370, the regular register instructions to clear, add increment, compare, etc., may be used in index register operations.

Coding a Loop

There are two basic forms for coding a loop—the DO WHILE form and DO UNTIL form. Both were described in Chapter 5. The main difference is the location in the loop of the test for termination. The DO WHILE is illustrated here. Generally, the programmer (or the installation) will choose one of the patterns and use it in all programs in order to simplify program maintenance. The instructions available with the computer may influence the pattern chosen. For example, some computers have special instructions to simplify coding of the increment-test logic of the DO UNTIL loop. The general steps in the DO WHILE loop are the following.

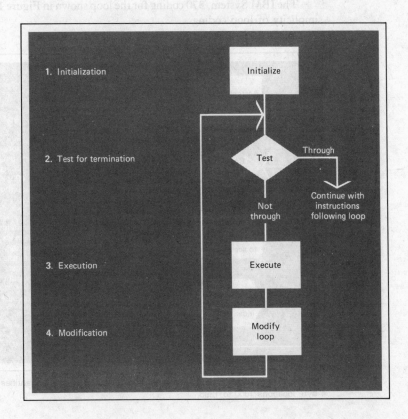

1. Initialization   Initialize

2. Test for termination   Test   Through

     Continue with instructions following loop

     Not through

3. Execution   Execute

4. Modification   Modify loop

The general steps in the DO WHILE loop are coded as follows:

1 *Initialization*
   (*a*) Set index register to initial value, such as 0 or 1.
   (*b*) Perform other initialization such as clear accumulator location if add-to-accumulator logic is used.

2 *Test index register* to see if the loop has been executed the required number of times.

3 *Execution* Instructions to be modified are coded with the number of the index register to be used.

4 *Increment index register*

A loop may use an index register as a loop counter but not modify instruction addresses. The logic for such a loop is identical except for the coding of address modification. Figure 15-4 shows a flowchart for index-register modification for the problem of summing 100 quantities each stored in a 4-byte location numbered from 1000 to 1396.

The IBM System/370 coding for the loop shown in Figure 15-4 illustrates the simplicity of loop coding.

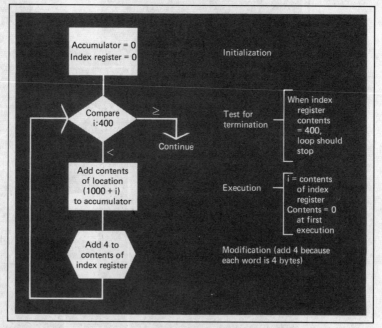

FIGURE 15-4 Loop using index register modification to add 100 quantities stored in 4-byte locations 1000 to 1396.

SR	2,2	Clear register 2 being used to accumulate the sum
SR	3,3	Clear register 3 being used as index register
BEGIN C	3,=F'400'	Compare contents of index register 3 to 400 (=F'400' defines the constant 400 for comparison)
BNL	ENDIT	If comparison showed index register 3 equal or higher than 400 (not low), branch to ENDIT; otherwise continue
A	2,DATA(3)	Add (DATA + contents of index register 3) to accumulated sum in register 2
A	3,=F'4'	Increment index register 3 by 4
B	BEGIN	Branch back to beginning of loop
ENDIT ST	2,SUM	When loop is complete, store the sum in register 2 in the location called SUM

In writing the code, the range of loops should be clearly marked by labels on the lines of code (BEGIN, ENDIT, etc.), by comment lines, and by indentation.

The above example used the simplest System/370 instructions. There are several additional instructions to simplify loop coding. For example, a single instruction is available to increment, compare, and branch (or not branch). Another instruction automatically does the operations to increment, test, and branch for the execution of a loop a defined number of times.

Before continuing, do the self-testing quizzes in question 7 and check your answer.

Other Program Modification Techniques

There are a number of additional program modification techniques that may be used. Some common methods used in assembly language programming are switches, table look-up, indirect addressing, and subroutines. These techniques should be used carefully and in a disciplined fashion, so that the resulting programs can be easily maintained.

As far as the computer is concerned, an instruction stored in memory is not different from a data item. Consider the possible contents of two locations in storage, location 376 and location 740, each of which holds 16 bits. The bit representations stored in these two locations may be identical, but they can mean entirely different things.

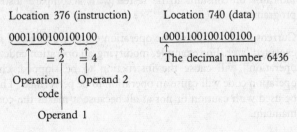

Location 376 (instruction)

Location 740 (data)

The instruction (for IBM System/370) is interpreted as "compare the contents of two registers (2 and 4)." Suppose by some error that the data in location 740 was used as an instruction; the result would be identical with the use of the instruction in location 376. Since they are the same, location 740 can be an instruction and location 376 can be data. Suppose that the computer adds the contents of data location 644, which contains 000000000000001, to the contents of data 740 and stores the results back in the same location. The data storage location will then hold the number 6437. Suppose the same operation is performed on the instruction stored at location 376. The result will be an altered instruction which in this case states: "Compare the contents of registers 2 and 5 (rather than 2 and 4)." It follows that any part of the instruction can be altered by performing arithmetic operations (add, subtract, multiply, erase, etc.). For example, adding the contents of a location in the form 0000000100000000 to the contents of 376 will alter the operation code of the instruction to make it say, "Add (rather than compare) the contents of the two registers."

The fact that an instruction may be operated upon in the same way as data often suggests unusual coding to modify an instruction and thereby achieve a result with less coding. Such unusual methods should generally be avoided because they are error-prone and make program maintenance more difficult. The use of index registers in modification techniques is preferred because the instruction itself in storage is not altered. If the program must be restarted, the instructions need not be restored to the initial condition.

**Programmed
Switches**

Some computers have hardware switches that can be tested by the program. Another type of switch is the programmed switch which is a technique for programming a delayed transfer of control. When an analysis at one point in a program establishes the branching that is to take place later in the program, the programmed switch may be used to handle the delayed selection. In some cases, the original test can be repeated, but it may be more efficient to use a switch technique. In other cases, the original information is no longer available. Several techniques may be used, and some computers have instructions which facilitate programming switches. Some of these techniques are:

1 Loading a factor into an index register which is used to modify a later sequence.

2 Setting an indicator or storing a constant in a storage location, the value of indicator or constant to be tested with a compare instruction later in the program.

3 Current modification of the operation code or address of an instruction to be executed later. For example, modifying an operation code to the code for "no operation" will cause the instruction to be skipped; changing to another operation code will cause an operation to be performed. This technique should be used with caution or not at all because it makes the code more difficult to maintain.

A single example (Figure 15-5) will illustrate the switch concept in programming. Records containing the physical characteristics of a sample of American males over 21 years of age are processed. At one step in the processing, it is necessary to find out which height class each man is in. Later in the program, the records of all men with heights between 6 ft and 6 ft 1 in. or 5 ft and 5 ft 1 in. are to be written on a magnetic tape. During the height-determination process, a switch is set which will cause the program to branch to a write tape sequence if the man is

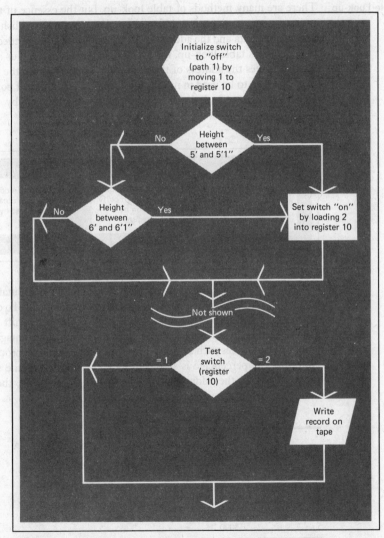

FIGURE 15-5 Illustration of use of programmed switch (using a register to hold switch data).

in one of the specified height classes. The setting of the switch may use any of the techniques mentioned; assume that it uses an index register. Setting the switch to an initial "off" position (path 1) is performed by loading a 1 into the index register. Setting the switch to the write position involves loading a 2 into the index register (say, register 10). The register contents are examined later in the program to see which path should be followed.

Table Look-up There are many methods of table look-up, but the essence of these methods is to operate upon a given input data item in order to establish a correspondence between the data and the address of the memory location needed for processing. In direct address table look-up, for example, a base address, plus some element from the data, gives the address of the item to be obtained from the table. The element from the data to be used in modifying the address should (if possible) be placed in an index register and the instruction then be modified by the index register contents.

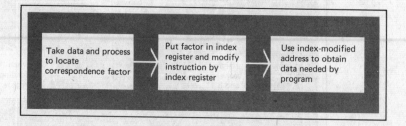

An example of direct address table look-up is the computation of a payroll in which there is a shift-pay differential for the different shifts. To determine the shift differential, it is necessary to multiply the pay before the shift differential by the shift-differential percentage. If the shift-differential percentages are stored in a table with addresses such as the following, a simple look-up procedure can be used. Note that the percentage is stored in location [3070 + 4 (the shift number)]. In order to obtain the address of the factor from the table, the shift number is multiplied by 4 and added to a base address of 3070.

Shift worked	Memory location of shift percentage
1	3074
2	3078
3	3082
4	3086
5	3090

The steps in using the technique in this situation are:

1 Calculate pay at base rate.

2 Obtain the shift number.

3 Multiply the shift number by 4 and place result in index register.

4 Modify the multiply-by-shift-differential instruction by index register so that the address for the multiplier refers to the location of the proper percentage. The address of the shift-differential percentage in the instruction to multiply has the operand address in the form of 3070.

5 Execute the multiply instruction.

Indirect Addressing   Indirect addressing is not available with the IBM System/370 but is a feature that is often found in computers. In indirect addressing, the instruction address refers not to the address of the operand but to an address whose contents are the operand address. To illustrate, assume that location 3458 contains 004762; then direct and indirect addressing will be interpreted as follows for an "add to accumulator register" instruction ADD 3458.

Direct addressing	Indirect addressing
ADD 3458 means to add the quantity found at location 3458 (the quantity 004762) to the contents of the accumulator register.	ADD 3458 means to ADD the quantity found at the location specified by the contents of 3458. In other words, the instruction to be executed is ADD the contents of location 4762.

When available, indirect addressing is implemented by a special code in the instruction. Multilevel indirect addressing is usually possible; i.e., the address referenced by the contents of the first address may also be an indirect address, the contents of that location in turn may be an indirect address, and so on.

The value of indirect addressing lies in the capability for modification of a large number of common address references by a single change. This process may be compared with a family which moves frequently and changes its telephone number. Rather than informing everyone of their new number each time they move, they have everyone call a single number which has a recorded message specifying the current telephone number. By merely changing the contents of this message, all callers are informed of the altered location. In terms of programming, all sequences of instructions in a program which reference the same, changeable address may be modified by having the instructions reference, with indirect addressing, a location which contains the address to be used.

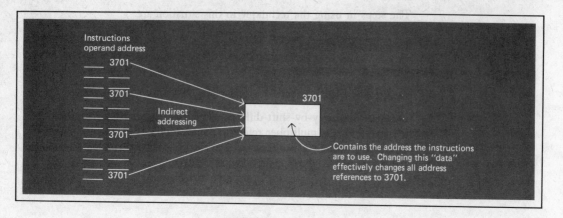

Instructions
operand address

_____ 3701

_____
_____
_____ 3701

_____

_____
Indirect
addressing

3701

_____
_____ 3701

_____

_____
_____ 3701

Contains the address the instructions
are to use. Changing this "data"
effectively changes all address
references to 3701.

Subroutines   A *subroutine* is essentially a program within a program. The main program transfers control to the subroutine which accepts the necessary data, performs its function, and returns control back to the point in the main program from which it came. The subroutine may be written as a separate program and may be assembled and tested separately. The technique may be used to reduce program complexity by coding as subroutines the major modules of a large program. Since the subroutine is to be used by the main program, there must be provisions for transferring control to (entering) the subroutine and for returning to the main program. If the subroutine needs data, there must be a means for identifying its location and result obtained by the subroutine (Figure 15-6). The linkages can be coded in symbolic assembly language either by the use of regular instructions or by the use of special linkage instructions which simplify the programming. There are many variations in technique, and a programmer (or perhaps an entire programming group) will usually settle on a standard technique in order to make it easier to review the coding at a later date. Some possible methods of subroutine linkage in assembly-level programming are:

Linkage required	Method of coding
Transfer from main program to starting address of subroutine.	Use of either a regular branch instruction or a special subroutine branch instruction.
Set up data to be used by subroutine.	The data may be stored in locations which have a specified relationship to the calling or reentry address; the data may be put into specified registers or storage locations; or the addresses of the data may be stored for reference by the subroutine.
Make results from subroutine available to main program.	Same as for data.
Set up reentry address to which control should return after the subroutine.	A reentry address is stored in a register or a specified storage location.

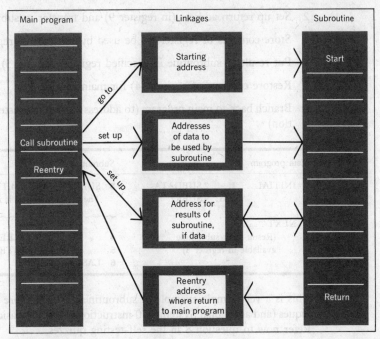

FIGURE 15-6 Linkages in use of subroutines.

In addition to the linkages, it may sometimes be necessary to save (by storing) all register contents before beginning the subroutine and to restore them before reentry to the main program. For example, a main program might detect an error, transfer to an error subroutine for correction, and then return to the main routine to continue processing. The specific method of performing the subroutine linkages is determined by the instructions and features of the computer being programmed and the preferences of the programming installation. In order to get an idea of the possible methods, a simple procedure using index register and the instructions for the IBM System/370 will be explained. The main program, before it transfers control, loads an index register (or storage locations) with the data for use by the subroutine. A special transfer instruction (BAL) specifies the subroutine address and a register in which the return address will be automatically loaded. The subroutine will usually begin by storing the contents of the registers to be used by the subroutine. The result of processing is stored in a specified register or storage location. At the end of the subroutine, the saved register contents are restored and control is returned to the main routine by transferring control to an address stored in a register by the transfer instruction (BR means transfer unconditionally to the location stored in the register included in the instructions). In the example, the subroutine linkages are identified by number as follows:

1 Set up data to be used by subroutine (in register 2)

2 Set up return address (in register 9) and transfer to subroutine

3 Store contents of registers to be used by subroutine (register 4)

4 Put result of subroutine in specified register (register 3)

5 Restore contents of register (4) for main routine

6 Branch back to main program (to address stored in register 9 by BAL instruction)

Main program			Subroutine		
1 INITIAL	L	2,SUBDATA	**3** SUBR1	ST	4,TEMP
2	BAL	9,SUBR1	The data to be used is in register 2, not shown.		
NEXT					
(Result from subroutine			**4**	L	3,RESULT
available in register 3)			**5**	L	4,TEMP
			6 LAST	BR	9

This is a very simple example of subroutine linkage. There are additional techniques (and additional System/370 instructions), but the basic ideas are the same. Refer now to question 8 in the self-testing quizzes.

SUMMARY   The chapter provides a survey of programming using a symbolic assembly language. The System/370 instructions are used in chapter examples, but these are chosen to illustrate the types of instructions that are available and the way instructions are coded rather than being a complete description of System/370 instructions. Emphasis in the chapter is on basic instructions; many complex instructions which simplify programming are not described or are mentioned only briefly.

The general format of an instruction is the same for all computers: operating code and operands. The location of operation results and location of the next instruction are either specified or implied. The hardware design affects the instruction format for a given computer. Two major formats are register instructions for fixed-word processing and character (or decimal) instructions to process variable-length operands in a storage-to-storage fashion. The coding rules differ among assembly languages, but there is a strong similarity. Instructions are coded using mnemonic operation codes and symbolic names for operands. The language provides facilities for naming data storage locations and for defining constants to be used in processing. To emphasize and communicate program logic, the coding rules allow comments and usually allow indentation.

The basic instruction repertoire for a computer includes instructions to move data, to perform arithmetic, to transfer control, and to edit data words or fields. A major problem in programming arithmetic operations is the necessity for keeping track of the location of the decimal point. The programmer can use a method such as the scale-factor method to calculate and remember the scaling of data words.

The computer can also be used to calculate the scale factor and keep track of the location of the decimal point. This is called floating point arithmetic and may be implemented either by special hardware features or by software programs.

Input and output instructions are generally coded using macro instructions which relate to an input/output control system for the computer. Looping can be coded in a variety of ways, but index registers are generally used. Index registers are a powerful method of instruction modification useful in other coding techniques as well. The chapter explained the use of the program modification techniques of switches, table look-up, indirect addressing, and subroutines.

Self-testing Quiz

The answers follow the set of questions. Assume the IBM System/370 instructions in the text examples.
1 Assembly language coding rules:
   (a) If a quantity is assigned a storage address name of GROSS, how could the location 12 bytes from GROSS be addressed?
   (b) Define a name HEADING to a 15-byte field in storage.
   (c) Define a name QUARTER for a constant of 25 stored as a full binary word.
2 Move instructions:
   (a) Move the contents of location ALPHA to location BETA. Use register 3.
   (b) Move the contents of location ALPHA to D1, D2, D3, and D4. Use register 6.
   (c) Move the contents of character field ALPHA to field BETA.
   (d) Move the contents of packed-decimal variable-length operand ALPHA to D1, D2, D3, and D4.
3 Arithmetic instructions:
   (a) Add ZETA to BETA and store the result in SUM1. Use register 3.
   (b) Add ALPHA to itself, subtract DATA1, and store the result in EX12. Use register 4.
   (c) Add the packed-decimal quantity RATE1 to RATESUM.
   (d) Multiply HOURS X RATE and store results in GPAY. } Fixed words; use
   (e) Divide SUMS by CUST and store the quotient in AVES. } registers 2 and 3.
   (f) Divide NUTS by BOLTS. Assume NUTS is 3 bytes, BOLTS is 2 bytes, and the divide area called DAREA is 5 bytes in length.
   (g) Multiply packed-decimal DATAX (03765+) by DATAY (024+). Use MULTAREA as a product area.
   (h) Add a constant 5 to COUNTER (a full binary word). Use register 6.
   (i) Clear register 7 by subtracting its contents from itself.
   (j) Using the scale-factor method,
      (1) Multiply 56.02 by 3.5.
      (2) Divide 203.45 by 1.4.
      (3) Add 83.04 and 8.304.
4 Transfer of control:
   (a) Compare packed decimal fields GPAY and NPAY and branch to ERROR1 if NPAY greater than GPAY.
   (b) Compare (using register 3) the contents of SALE with 5000 (a literal) and branch to OVER if SALES is greater.

(c) Using register instructions, branch to NOKAY if SALES are less than MINI-MUM.

(d) Branch to ZEROR if the result of an arithmetic operation is zero.

5 Editing:

(a) The following instructions operate upon a quantity called CODE (hexadecimal value 37658321).

L	2,CODE	Load CODE into register 2
N	2,=X′000FF0FF′	AND operation using a mask word (in hexadecimal)
ST	2,CODEN	

What will be the result of CODEN?

(b) DATA1 has packed decimal data in the form 0037652+. Assuming a pattern word of 0dddd,ddd, what will be the result of an edit command?

(c) Data on an input card is 753. It is read as a 3-byte set of characters. What instructions convert it to a binary word?

6 Input and output:

(a) What is the result of GET if the entire record is on a punched card?

(b) What is the result of PUT if the output record is a line on the printer?

7 Looping and index register modification:

(a) Assuming the following instruction format and an instruction to add the contents of TABLE1 to register 3 with TABLE1 being modified by the contents of register 8.

OP CODE	REGISTER	OPERAND	INDEX REGISTER
A	3,	TABLE1	(8)

(1) If index register 8 is zero and TABLE1 refers to storage location 1936, what will the instruction do?

(2) If index register 8 has a contents of 4, what will the instruction do?

(3) After executing the instruction in the previous question, what does the instruction look like in storage?

(4) If the programmer wishes the next execution of the instruction to be "add the contents of TABLE1 + 8, i.e., 1944, to register 3," what type of instruction(s) will make this modification?

(b) Given the following symbolic instructions, arrange them in a DO WHILE loop logic to sum every other number in a set of 200 fixed word-length data items (4 bytes each) and store the sum in SUM. Index register modification is used. (BNL means branch if not low, i.e., $\geq$.)

INCR	A	9,=F′8′	Add to index register
CONT	ST	2,SUM	Store result in sum
BEGIN	SR	2,2	Set accumulator register to 0
COMPR	C	9,=F′800′	Compare index-register contents to 800
	SR	9,9	Set index register to 0
	BNL	CONT	Branch out of loop if index register $\geq$ 800
ADDIT	A	2,DATAX(9)	Add DATAX + i when i = value of index register specified in ( )
	B	COMPR	Return to beginning of loop

(c) Change the loop instructions in (b) to a DO UNTIL loop—add, increment, and then test. Use BL (branch if low) instead of BNL.

8 Other modification techniques:

(a) Assume that the machine-level operation code of an unconditional branch is 00. If the computer were referred to a data location containing all zeros, as the address of the next instruction, what would happen?

(b) An instruction is stored in a location with symbolic address NEXT1, and a constant of 4 is stored in symbolic location FOUR. What will be the effect of the following sequence of instructions?

```
L    2,    NEXT1
A    2,    FOUR
ST   2,    NEXT1
```

(c) What is the effect of the following sequence of instructions (not System/370) if the instructions marked * use indirect addressing? Assume storage location 4731 contains 4755, 4755 contains 4757.

```
LDA    4757    Load accumulator register
ADD*   4755    Add to accumulator register
STO*   4731    Store contents of accumulator register
```

Answers to Self-testing Quizzes

1 (a) GROSS + 12

(b) HEADING   DS   CL15

(c) QUARTER   DC   F'25'

2 (a) L   3,ALPHA
      ST   3,BETA

(b) L   6,D1
    ST   6,D2 ⎫
    ST   6,D3 ⎪ Since the operation is a copy, the contents
    ST   6,D4 ⎬ may be stored (copied) more than once.
    ST   6,D5 ⎭

(c) MVC   BETA,ALPHA

(d) MVC   D1,ALPHA
     MVC   D2,ALPHA
     MVC   D3,ALPHA
     MVC   D4,ALPHA

3 (a) L   3,BETA
     A   3,ZETA
     ST   3,SUM1

(b) L   4,ALPHA
    A   4,ALPHA
    S   4,DATA1
    ST   4,EX12

(c) AP   RATESUM,RATE1

(*d*) SR   2,2   Clear register 2

     L   3,HOURS   Load multiplicand

     M   2,RATE   Multiply by RATE

     ST   3,GPAY   Store result in GPAY

(*e*) L   3,SUMS   Load dividend

     SR   2,2   Clear register 2

     D   2,CUST   Divide ALPHA by BETA

     ST   3,AVES   Store quotient

(*f*) ZAP   DAREA,NUTS   Move NUTS into divide area and

     DP   DAREA,BOLTS   zero rest of field

(*g*) ZAP   MULTAREA,DATAX

     DP   MULTAREA,DATAY

(*h*) L   6,COUNTER

     A   6,=F'5'

     ST   6,COUNTER

(*i*) SR   7,7

(*j*) (1) .5602   2

       .35   1

       ‾‾‾‾‾   ‾

       .196070   3 = 196.07

    (2)   .1467 = 146.7

     .14$\overline{)}$.020345

      ↑   ↑

      (1)   (4)   4 − 1 = 3

    (3) .83040   2

       .08304   2

       ‾‾‾‾‾   ‾

       .91344   2 = 91.344

4 (*a*) CL   NPAY,GPAY

     BH   ERROR1

  (*b*) L   3,SALE

     C   3,=F'5000'

     BH   OVER

  (*c*) L   3,SALES

     C   3,MINIMUM

     BL   NOKAY

  (*d*) BZ   ZEROR   following arithmetic instruction

5 (*a*) (hexadecimal) 00058021

  (*b*) 37,652

  (*c*) PACK converts it to a 2-byte packed decimal quantity | 7 | 5 | 3 | + |. CVB converts it to a 32-bit binary word.

6 (*a*) A punched card will be read and the contents will be made available to the program.

  (*b*) A line of output will be printed.

7 (*a*) (1) It will execute A 3,TABLE1, i.e., add contents of location 1936 to register 3.

    (2) It will execute A 3,TABLE1 + 4, i.e., add contents of location 1940 to register 3.

    (3) It is the same A 3,TABLE1(8) because index register modification occurs during the instruction cycle after the instruction has been copied from storage. The instruction in storage is not affected.

    (4) By adding 4 to the contents of index register 8, the instruction when executed will automatically execute TABLE1 + 8.

(b)	BEGIN	SR	2,2
		SR	9,9
	COMPR	C	9,=F'800'
		BNL	CONT
	ADDIT	A	2,DATAX(9)
	INCR	A	9,=F'8'
		B	COMPR
	CONT	ST	2,SUM
(c)	BEGIN	SR	2,2
		SR	9,9
	ADDIT	A	2,DATAX(9)
	INCR	A	9,=F'8'
		C	9,=F'800'
		BL	ADDIT
	CONT	ST	2,SUM

8 (a) The computer will attempt to use the data as if it were an instruction. This means it will branch to location zero since 00 in the data word is interpreted as branch and the location address portion of the data word being used as an instruction is zero.

(b) The instruction located at NEXT1 will be altered to increase the operand address by 4. If the instruction at NEXT1 were A 3,DATAX, it will now be A 3,DATAX+4. If the operand address in machine code for DATAX were 3762, this machine address will now be 3766.

(c) Instructions actually executed are:

$$
\left.\begin{array}{ll}
\text{LDA} & 4757 \\
\text{ADD} & 4757 \\
\text{STO} & 4755
\end{array}\right\} \quad \text{i.e., add (4757) to itself and store sum in 4755.}
$$

EXERCISES

1 What are the reasons for the following types of instructions:
(a) Unconditional transfer of control   (d) Move
(b) Suppress leading zeros   (e) Shifting
(c) Clear register

2 What is the difference in format between a register instruction and a character (storage-to-storage) instruction?

3 If four bytes stored at DATA3 are to be copied into DATA4, explain how it would be possible to use either a register or storage-to-storage move.

4 Define the following terms:
(a) Scale factor   (e) Packing
(b) Overflow   (f) Precision
(c) Floating point   (g) Characteristic
(d) Radix

5 Why does the programmer have to keep track of the decimal point (scaling) in fixed point arithmetic?

6 Using the scale-factor method, calculate the decimal point in the result of each of the following:
(a) 92.43×317.64 (d) $4530.1 - 176$
(b) $.00943 \div .012$ (e) $.007 \times .003$
(c) $4530 + 1.76$

7 Describe the difference between the register instruction and the character instructions to:
(*a*) Add and subtract   (*b*) Multiply

8 Describe the computational steps the computer must perform when using floating point arithmetic.

9 Assuming an excess-50 notation for floating point and a "between 0 and 1" scaling of the fraction, interpret the following:
(*a*) 4847650   (*b*) 5039500   (*c*) 5370591

10 Branching usually requires two machine instructions. Why? What are they?

11 Explain branching based on the following:
(*a*) Arithmetic result (such as zero)   (*b*) An interrupt

12 Assuming a 10-digit fixed word-length computer (not IBM System/370) with left destructive shift and right circular shift, show the left shifts and right shifts required to make the following changes. The X's are unknown digits.

Original	Changed to
(*a*) OXXXXXOO	OOOXXXXX
(*b*) XXXOOXXX	OOXXXXXX
(*c*) XXXXXOOO	OOOXXXXX

13 Using a hexadecimal notation, what will be the result of the following logical instructions?

Operation	Data word	Mask word
(*a*) AND	3741	FFFF
(*b*) AND	2148	OOFF
(*c*) OR	1930	FO11
(*d*) OR	1028	OOOO
(*e*) Exclusive OR	5510	FO4O

14 How does the output pattern or control word simplify output editing?

15 What is the value of index registers in programming loops?

16 Explain the difference between straight-line coding and looping with respect to (1) the number of instructions in the program and (2) the number of instructions executed.

17 What is a switch in programming? How may a programmed switch be used?

18 What conditions must exist for the direct address table look-up method to be used?

19 If the argument (factor) for table look-up were put in an index register, how might the index register be used in table look-up operations?

20 What are the distinguishing features of a closed subroutine?

21 What is the reason for using subroutines?

22 What linkages are necessary between a subroutine and the main routine?

CHAPTER 16

THE BASIC PROGRAMMING LANGUAGE

BASIC (Beginners All-purpose Symbolic Instruction Code) is an algebraic programming language developed at Dartmouth College in the mid-1960s by John Kemeny and Thomas Kurtz. It was designed to make using the computer easier for students. It also has features which simplify the design of a compiler that translates a program in BASIC into machine code. The language has received most of its use in connection with time sharing. There is a proposed American National Standard for the BASIC language. The ANS BASIC is minimal BASIC, but implementors have usually included additional features. These additional features are often termed "extended BASIC." The extended features tend to be less standard than minimal BASIC.

To assist in self-study of BASIC, there are self-testing quizzes in the chapter. The answers are at the end of the chapter.

Introduction to BASIC

Overview The major application of BASIC is in time sharing in which the programmer-user has a typewriter input and output terminal such as a Teletype. Some terminals use a visual display screen for output. Programs are typed and transmitted line by line to the computer. After the program is received, it is compiled and executed, and the results are typed on the typewriter or displayed on the screen. The terminal may also have a punched paper input and output. This allows a program to be prepared offline (without being connected to the computer) by being punched into a paper tape. The punched paper tape is then transmitted to the computer, saving online connection time. BASIC is available on some computers for regular batch compilation (using punched card input), but this use of BASIC is much less common than its use as a time-sharing language.

Figure 16-1 shows the printout resulting from a programmer writing a simple program at a terminal connected to a time-sharing computer and having it executed. The programmer responses are underlined or otherwise noted. A glance at the program reveals that the language is very straightforward. There are statements to READ, PRINT, do computation, define input data, etc.

Coding, Compilation, and Execution of BASIC Programs A BASIC program consists of a number of lines of coding, each of which must have a line number. The line number may have from one to five digits. There are no provisions for continuing one line of coding onto the next. In general, a line is limited to 72 characters. If a line of coding is too long, it must be split into two separate lines.

The statements in a BASIC program are numbered in increasing order from

OK	Better	
1 -----	10 -----	
2 -----	20 -----	Allows insertion of a statement
3 -----	30 -----	numbered 11, 12, etc.
4 -----	40 -----	

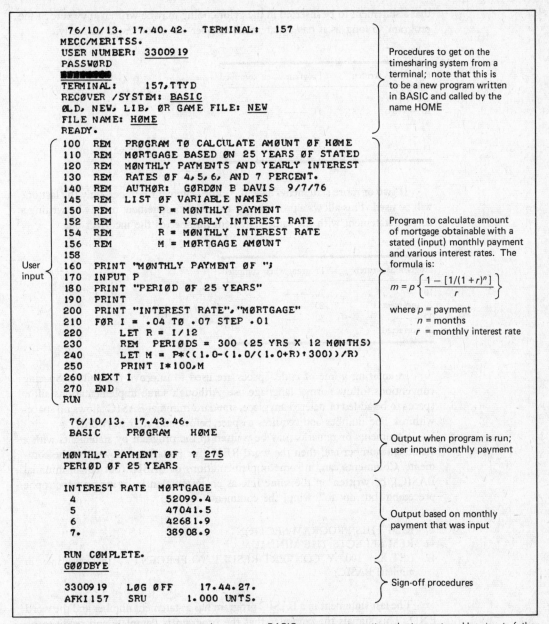

```
      76/10/13.  17.40.42.   TERMINAL:   157
MECC/MERITSS.
USER NUMBER: 330099 19
PASSWØRD
████████
TERMINAL:      157, TTYD
RECØVER /SYSTEM: BASIC
ØLD, NEW, LIB, ØR GAME FILE: NEW
FILE NAME: HØME
READY.
```

Procedures to get on the timesharing system from a terminal; note that this is to be a new program written in BASIC and called by the name HOME

```
      100   REM   PRØGRAM TØ CALCULATE AMØUNT ØF HØME
      110   REM   MØRTGAGE BASED ØN 25 YEARS ØF STATED
      120   REM   MØNTHLY PAYMENTS AND YEARLY INTEREST
      130   REM   RATES ØF 4,5,6, AND 7 PERCENT.
      140   REM   AUTHØR:  GØRDØN B DAVIS  9/7/76
      145   REM   LIST ØF VARIABLE NAMES
      150   REM       P = MØNTHLY PAYMENT
      152   REM       I = YEARLY INTEREST RATE
      154   REM       R = MØNTHLY INTEREST RATE
      156   REM       M = MØRTGAGE AMØUNT
      158
User  160   PRINT "MØNTHLY PAYMENT ØF ";
input 170   INPUT P
      180   PRINT "PERIØD ØF 25 YEARS"
      190   PRINT
      200   PRINT "INTEREST RATE", "MØRTGAGE"
      210   FØR I = .04 TØ .07 STEP .01
      220       LET R = I/12
      230       REM  PERIØDS = 300 (25 YRS X 12 MØNTHS)
      240       LET M = P*((1.0-(1.0/(1.0+R)↑300))/R)
      250       PRINT I*100,M
      260   NEXT I
      270   END
      RUN
```

Program to calculate amount of mortgage obtainable with a stated (input) monthly payment and various interest rates. The formula is:

$$m = p \left\{ \frac{1 - [1/(1 + r)^n]}{r} \right\}$$

where p = payment
  n = months
  r = monthly interest rate

```
      76/10/13.  17.43.46.
      BASIC    PRØGRAM    HØME

MØNTHLY PAYMENT ØF   ? 275
PERIØD ØF 25 YEARS
```

Output when program is run; user inputs monthly payment

```
INTEREST RATE    MØRTGAGE
     4              52099.4
     5              47041.5
     6              42681.9
     7.             38908.9

RUN CØMPLETE.
GØØDBYE

330099 19   LØG ØFF    17.44.27.
AFKI 157    SRU        1.000 UNTS.
```

Output based on monthly payment that was input

Sign-off procedures

FIGURE 16-1 Printout of steps in entering and executing a BASIC program using a time-sharing system. User inputs (other than program) are underscored.

the first statement to the last. There may be missing numbers; in fact, it is a good idea to number so that statements may be inserted if found later to be necessary. The statements are rearranged in increasing order during compilation. This means that a statement to be inserted in the prior coding may be written anywhere in the program so long as it has a statement number which orders it correctly.

Program as written	Program when compiled
10 -----	10 -----
20 -----	11 -----
30 -----	20 -----
40 -----	30 -----
11 -----	40 -----

If two or more statements have the same statement number, only the last one will be used. This allows a programmer to correct a statement merely by writing a correct statement with the same statement number as the incorrect one.

Program as written	Program when compiled
10 -----	10 -----
20 incorrect	20 -----
30 -----	30 -----
20 corrected	

In entering a line of code, spaces are used to improve readability. Spacing conventions follow normal language use. Although some implementations allow spaces to be added or deleted anyplace, standard minimal BASIC allows no spaces within a line number and requires a space before and after keywords.

Comments or remarks may be written in the program by statements with a statement number and then the word REM (for remarks) followed by the comments. Comments can, in some implementations of BASIC (but not in minimal BASIC), be written on the same line as an instruction by using an apostrophe preceding (but not following) the comment.

```
40   REM THIS PROGRAM SECTION
41   REM SELECTS THE MINIMUM.
42   LET X = 100 * Y 'CONVERT RESULT TO PERCENT      (not available in
     minimal BASIC)
```

The last statement in a BASIC program has a statement number and the word END. This signals the compiler that the program is complete and ready to be compiled. Execution of a BASIC program in time-sharing mode is signaled by the word RUN (with no statement number).

If BASIC is being compiled from a card deck in batch mode, regular job control cards must be used. Each computer system has unique job cards, and so the programmer must determine these for the computer being used. Generally, there is one or more job control card at the beginning of the program to specify that the program is written in BASIC, etc., and one or more at the end of the program.

Programming Discipline and Structured Programming in BASIC

A general introduction to programming discipline and structured design was presented in Chapter 5. Many of the ideas can be applied in writing BASIC programs; others are difficult to implement in the BASIC language. BASIC was designed for the occasional user writing fairly short computational problems. The emphasis was on ease of programming rather than on easily maintainable code. Many of the problems written in BASIC are expected to be discarded after a single use. The teaching of BASIC has therefore tended to ignore programming discipline.

Even though BASIC programs may be of short duration (but many are not), the quality of the program is likely to be enhanced if simple structural and documentation rules are followed. The rules are illustrated in the chapter.

1 Include comments (using the REM sentence) at the beginning of the program to give the program a descriptive name, to state the author and date written, and to explain the purpose of the program. Describe each variable in the program. For example:

```
10  REM   CONVERSION PROGRAM TO CONVERT FAHRENHEIT
11  REM       TEMPERATURE TO CENTIGRADE TEMPERATURE.
12  REM   AUTHOR-G. B. DAVIS 9-29-76.
13  REM   INPUT IS TEMPERATURE IN FAHRENHEIT.
14  REM   OUTPUT IS FAHRENHEIT INPUT AND
15  REM       CORRESPONDING CENTIGRADE TEMPERATURE.
16  REM       RESULT ROUNDED TO NEAREST TENTH DEGREE.
17  REM   PROGRAM REPEATS UNTIL INPUT OF 99.
18  REM   PROGRAM VARIABLES—
19  REM       F = FAHRENHEIT TEMPERATURE
20  REM       C = CENTIGRADE TEMPERATURE
```

2 Blank lines (or a REM statement number with all blanks or asterisks) may be used to emphasize logical blocks of code. A blank line is coded by a statement number and a space before carriage return.

3 Use indentation to show the range of loops and to define subroutines and other logical blocks of code.

4 Use comments (REM or same line comments) to explain the purpose of statements likely to be difficult to understand. Use especially with GO TO and GOSUB statements.

5 Write logical blocks of code as subroutines if this simplifies the program. The mainline control block executes a subroutine by an instruction called GOSUB (to be explained later in the chapter).

Variable Names A BASIC program can refer to a number, an array of numbers, a string of characters, or an array of characters by a name. Names are used because the value is not known when the program is written; i.e., it will be input or it will be calculated by the program. The rules for forming names for these three purposes are:

Purpose of name	Naming rules
To refer to a number	Single alphabetic character or single alphabetic character followed by a single numeric digit. Examples are A, B, A1, B3.
To refer to an array of numbers	Single alphabetic character followed by parentheses enclosing subscripts (to be explained later in the chapter). Examples are A(5), B(3,7), C(6).
To refer to a string of characters	Single alphabetic character plus a dollar sign. Examples are A$, B$, and X$.
To refer to an array of strings	A single alphabetic character followed by a dollar sign. It is always accompanied by subscript(s) in parentheses (to be explained later in chapter). Examples are A$(1), B$(1,2), C$(Z,1).

The use of a name to refer to a numeric quantity is a common mathematical procedure; less common is the use of a name to refer to a string of characters. A string is a sequence of alphabetic, numeric, and special characters. The characters may be manipulated but not be used arithmetically. Examples of strings are ABC123 and MY NAME IS. The maximum length of a string that is referenced by a string name will vary with the implementation of BASIC. The ANS minimal BASIC standard is 18 characters.

Writing Statements to Perform Arithmetic

The following is an arithmetic statement in BASIC:

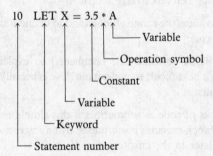

10 LET X = 3.5 * A

- Variable
- Operation symbol
- Constant
- Variable
- Keyword
- Statement number

The statement says: Let the current value stored in a memory location called X be replaced by the result of the multiplication of 3.5 and the current value stored in a location called A.

Numeric Constants and Variables

Some numbers in a BASIC statement are written as numerical quantities. These are termed "constants." A numeric constant may be an integer (written with or without a decimal point) or a decimal quantity written with a decimal point. Commas *cannot* be used to separate thousands, millions, etc. A minus is used in front of a negative quantity; a + sign is optional. A constant without a + sign is considered positive. The numeric constant can have six digits (or more in some implementations of BASIC).

An exponent form may be used. It is especially helpful for writing very large or very small numbers. The significant digits (at least six) are followed by E and an exponent which specifies that the decimal point should be moved to the right (for an exponent with a plus sign or no sign) or to the left (for an exponent with a negative sign). The maximum exponent may vary for different implementations; the ANS minimal BASIC limit is ± 38.

The following are valid BASIC constants:

-4	4.	3.5E+4	(interpreted as 35000)
$+4$	5.5	3.5E-4	(interpreted as .00035)
4	9.1754	3.5E1	(interpreted as 35)

Variables are names assigned to qualities which can vary during the program. As explained, variable names for numeric quantities are either a single alphabetic letter or a single letter followed by a single numeric digit. The maximum precision obtainable from a numeric variable is at least six digits (although it is common to have a precision of eight or more digits for an integer quantity and six or more significant digits for a decimal quantity).

Operation Symbols and Mathematical Functions

The symbols used to indicate operations in BASIC are the following:

+	Addition
−	Subtraction
/	Division
*	Multiplication
↑ or ∧	Exponentiation

The use of the / for division allows the statement to be on the same line. $\frac{A}{B}$ is expressed as A/B. Multiplication uses the asterisk to avoid confusion. Multiplication cannot be implied. For example, *ab* in a mathematical formula would mean $a \times b$. In BASIC, it must be written explicitly as A*B. However, a minus sign in front of a variable implies multiplication by -1. For example, $-A$ is equivalent to

−1*A. Most implementations of BASIC use ↑ for exponentiation; the proposed ANSI standard calls for ∧ as the symbol. This text will use ↑ because it is the symbol in general use.

There are mathematical functions which are frequently used in programming. The coding to perform these functions is contained in the compiler. To use these functions, the programmer merely codes the 3-letter function name followed by the value or expression (in parentheses) to be used by the function.

The most common functions provided by BASIC (and required for ANS minimal BASIC) are the following. The argument is represented by X.

SQR(X)	Square root
ABS(X)	Absolute value
LOG(X)	Log to base e (natural log)
EXP(X)	Exponentiate e
INT(X)	Take integer portion
RND	Random number
SIN(X)	Sine
COS(X)	Cosine
TAN(X)	Tangent
ATN(X)	Arctangent
SGN(X)	Determine sign

For example, the function to take the square root is called SQR. The argument or value for which the square root is to be taken can be a constant, a variable, or an arithmetic expression which must be solved to obtain the value to be used.

SQR (35)	Take square root of 35
SQR (A)	Take square root of current value of variable A
SQR (A + B)	Take square root value of (A + B)

Most of the functions fit the common mathematical usage. However, INT, RND, and SGN need some further explanation.

INT(X)   Supply the largest integer not greater than the argument quantity (X in this case). This means that the function will give the integer portion of a positive number and the next integer value for a fractional negative quantity. For example, if X = 3.75, the instruction LET Y = INT(X) will store 3 at Y. If X = −3.75, the result would be −4.

RND   Provide a random number with a value between 0 and 1. There is no argument. LET A = RND places a random number in A.

SGN(X)   Examine sign of argument. Result is +1 if positive, 0 if zero, and −1 if negative. If X = −12, the result of LET Y = SGN(X) is −1 stored in Y.

Arithmetic Expressions and Replacement Statements

An arithmetic expression is written using a combination of variables, constants, operation symbols, and functions. A replacement statement is of the form LET v = e, where v is a variable name and e is an expression. The value resulting from the arithmetic expression is assigned to the variable name and replaces prior contents of the memory location associated with the variable name. The = sign means replace or assign rather than equality. For example, LET B = B + 1 is not an equality but a valid replacement statement. It means that 1.0 plus the current value of B will be the new value of B. Many compilers allow the word LET to be omitted.

The order in which operations are performed follows normal mathematical rules. These can be described as the parenthesis rule and the order rule.

1 Parenthesis rule. Computations inside parentheses are performed first. If there are parentheses inside parentheses, the inside pair is performed first.

2 Order rule. In the absence of parentheses, computations are performed in the following order:
   (a) Exponentiation
   (b) Multiplication and division
   (c) Addition and subtraction

If the sentence contains computations on the same level, they are performed from left to right. For example, X = A/B*C is interpreted as

$$X = \frac{A}{B} C$$

Examples of replacement statements illustrate these rules.

BASIC	Formula
10 LET A = SQR(X) + Y/2.5 + B	$a = x^{1/2} + \dfrac{y}{2.5} + b$
20 LET X + A*(B + C)	$x = a(b + c)$
30 LET X + A*B + C	$x = ab + c$
40 LET Y = SQR (ABS(A/(B + C)))	$y = \sqrt{\left\| \dfrac{a}{b + c} \right\|}$
50 LET R = B↑1/3	$r = \dfrac{b^1}{3}$
60 LET R = B↑(1/3)	$r = b^{1/3}$

Note that parentheses must be used in some cases to specify the correct order of processing. In other cases, parentheses are optional but should be used for documentation. For example, LET X = A/B*C can be written LET X = (A/B)*C. The two are equivalent, but the second is explicit and is therefore less likely to be misunderstood by the original programmer or by subsequent users of the documentation.

Self-testing Quiz— 1 Indicate if valid or invalid and if valid, why.
BASIC #1   (a) Variable names   VALID   INVALID   IF VALID, WHY?

          (1) B
          (2) B9
          (3) 1B
          (4) RB
          (5) R$
          (6) R$1

    (b) Expressions
          (1) AB
          (2) A + B↑3
          (3) A1*SQR(A1)
          (4) −B

  2 Write formulas for the following BASIC statements.
    (a) 10   LET A = SQR (G↑3)
    (b) 20   LET B = 3*Y/X + W*1.3
    (c) 30   LET C = 3.1417 + (X + 3)/4
    (d) 40   LET D = Z↑2/5*W
  3 Write BASIC statements for the following formulas.

    (a) $a = \dfrac{bc}{d}$

    (b) $b = \sqrt{xy}$

    (c) $c = \sqrt{x/y}$

    (d) $d = 2xy$

    (e) $e = 3|yz|$ (| | means absolute value)

  4 The following statements have no parentheses. Rewrite them with explicit parentheses.
    (a) LET A = X↑2*3*Y + Z
    (b) LET B = X↑Y+R↑Y/2
    (c) LET C = SQR(A/R+X)
    (d) LET D = X+Y/S+R
  5 What is the value of A for each of the following:
    (a) LET A = INT(B) if B = −2.1
    (b) LET A = INT(C) if C = 3.9
    (c) LET A = ABS(D) if D = −15.4
    (d) LET A = ABS(E) if E = 16.1
    (e) LET A = SQR(F) if F = 25.0

Input and Output

Input and output in BASIC are very simple and fairly inflexible. Provisions to call for data are included with the program, to call for data to be input from the terminal during execution, and to print the results in a standard manner with headings if desired.

Input and Output Instructions

There are four input/output instructions:

READ list	Read data from data block in the program
DATA values	Defines data to be called for by the READ statement
PRINT list	Types data, headings, and labels
INPUT list	Accepts data from the user terminal

where list is a sequence of variable names separated by commas.

Note that data for use by the program can be programmed as input from the terminal by means of the INPUT statement or can be programmed by the READ and DATA statements. The READ statement requires all data to be used by the program to be listed in DATA statements. Numeric data items must be separated by commas. String data items are enclosed in quotation marks if they contain commas or leading spaces; otherwise the quotation marks are optional and a comma separates items. The data specified by DATA statements is stored as a string of data items in the computer memory. The program maintains a pointer to identify the next data item to be used. When the first READ statement is executed, it takes as many data items from the string as there are variable names in the list. The next READ statement executed takes the next data items, etc. For example:

```
10   READ A,B,C
20   DATA 5,16,12
10   READ A$,B$,C$
20   DATA THE,END,",E.G.,"
```

The first READ will take the data items 5, 16, and 12 and assign them to the variables A, B, and C. The execution of the second READ causes THE to be stored as the current value of A$, END as the current value of B$, and ,E.G., as the value of C$.

```
10   READ X,Y
20   DATA 5.4,7.61,3.75
```

This READ example will take the first two values and assign them to X and Y. A later execution of a READ statement will obtain the remaining value from the DATA list.

DATA statements are used in the same order as they appear in the program (based on their statement number). Therefore, the READ form of input requires that the DATA statement(s) list the values to be used in the order they will be called for by the program. Most programmers put DATA statements together at the end (or beginning) of the program for convenience. When the data in the DATA statements has all been used, the program will halt if another READ is attempted. However, the programmer can start over at the beginning of the data string by the use of the statement RESTORE. RESTORE moves the pointer back to the beginning of the list. In some BASICs, RESTORE* restores only the numeric pointer and RESTORE$ restores the pointer for string variables only.

The INPUT statement is used when data needs to be entered during execution of the program. INPUT causes a ? to be displayed by the terminal, and then the program waits for input of the data called for by the input statement. When the data is typed in and the terminal RETURN key is pressed, the program continues. For example, the statement

INPUT A,B

will print ? and then wait for the values for A and B to be input. The rules for the reading and input of data are summarized.

RULES FOR READ AND INPUT

1 All items listed in DATA statements are formed into a data string in the order they appear in the program.

2 Each use of a READ takes the specified number of quantities from the string.

3 When the data string is exhausted, an attempt to read will cause the program to terminate.

4 The use of the RESTORE statement will cause the program to start over at the beginning of the data string.

5 The use of INPUT causes a ? to be printed or displayed at the terminal and the program to wait until the user types in the data called for by the INPUT statement.

The PRINT statement can be used to skip a line (print a blank line), print labels or headings, and print the value of variables. The statement is written as PRINT followed by the list of output items separated by commas or semicolons. If there is no list of items, a blank line will appear. Each PRINT statement begins a new line (with some exceptions to be explained). Examples illustrate this usage:

```
10   PRINT "THESE ARE ANSWERS"
20   PRINT
30   PRINT A,B
```

The result of the three PRINT statements is shown (if A = 4.1715 and B = 5.2).

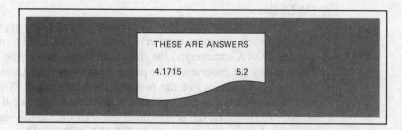

```
THESE ARE ANSWERS

4.1715        5.2
```

In BASIC, the programmer has little control over the format of the data. The page is divided into five zones or fields (generally 15 characters in size). The variables are printed in the zones, five to a line in the order specified in the PRINT statement. The forms of the data fields are determined by the compiler. It provides as much precision as possible. Therefore, data items might be printed as integers (4), as decimal number with fractional part (3.1417), or using the exponent format (7.86598E + 10). The number of digits in the printed output will depend on the implementation of BASIC being used. As a minimum, there will be at least six significant digits (for quantities having more than six digits). If the particular implementation allows n significant digits (n being at least six), then the rules for output can be stated as follows:

1 Integer quantities with no more than n digits will be printed as integers. For more than n digits, the exponent form will be used and only the first n significant digits will be printed.

2 Decimal quantities with an integer and fractional part will be rounded to n digits until further rounding would drop an integer digit. The quantity is then presented in exponent form.

3 Decimal quantities with only a fractional part will be presented in exponent form if there are leading zeros and more than n digits in the fractional quantity. The leading zeros are dropped in the exponent form. Trailing zeros may be added to show n significant digits in the output.

Number to output	Printed as	Comments
76549	76549	
483765421	4.83765E + 8	Too many digits, so exponent form
5.876	5.876	
61.37254	61.3725	Rounding and dropping of excess digits in fraction
.0000000025	2.50000E − 9	Too many digits and leading zeros, so exponent form used

The PRINT statement can contain variables, expressions, and literal data (enclosed in quotation marks). Expressions are evaluated, and only the result is printed. Literal data is printed starting at the next data zone.

EXAMPLES

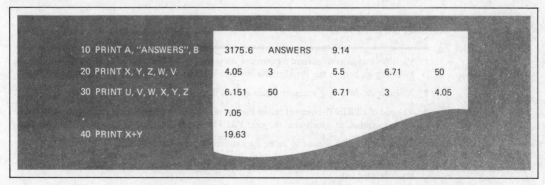

```
10 PRINT A, "ANSWERS", B      3175.6    ANSWERS    9.14

20 PRINT X, Y, Z, W, V        4.05      3          5.5      6.71     50

30 PRINT U, V, W, X, Y, Z     6.151     50         6.71     3        4.05

                              7.05

40 PRINT X+Y                  19.63
```

If the PRINT statement has less than five variables, printing starts with the left zone, and then unused positions are left blank. If the PRINT statement has more than five variables, the first five are printed on the first line and the rest on the lines following, see example on page 453. It is possible to position output starting at a specific column by means of the TAB function. PRINT TAB(N);A will position the output of A starting at the Nth column. If N = 16, the value of A will start at column 16. If the argument of TAB has a fractional part, it will be rounded rather than truncated.

The use of a semicolon instead of a comma causes the output to ignore the output zones and place only one space before the next output. For example,

10   PRINT "X=", B, "Y=", C

with commas will cause an output of (if B = 4.5 and C = .6)

X=   4.5   Y=   .6

10   PRINT "X=";B;"Y=";C with semicolons will print

X= 4.5 Y= .6

A comma or semicolon following the last item in the READ list suppresses the line spacing. In other words, it will cause the next item to be printed to appear on the same line (if there is space). For example,

10   PRINT "VALUE OF PAYMENT =";
20   INPUT P

will cause an output of

VALUE OF PAYMENT = ?

This example illustrates a program design concept. Whenever input is required from the terminal, there should be a message describing to the user the data to be input.

RULES FOR PRINT

1 Variables and labels separated by commas are printed in five zones in the order listed. A comma following an item in the list signals a move to the next print zone for the next item.

2 A semicolon following a numeric data entry will space the next item one space.

3 The end of a PRINT statement causes the line to terminate except when a comma or semicolon is the last symbol, in which case the next PRINT statement is a continuation on the same line.

4 The TAB function is used to locate data starting at a specific column.

5 Expressions may be written in the PRINT statement. They are evaluated (result calculated) and the result printed out.

6 A literal enclosed in quote marks is printed exactly as it appears.

7 The format of the data is automatically defined by the compiler.

    (*a*) The implementation of BASIC will specify the number of significant digits to be printed. It will be at least six.

    (*b*) Trailing zeros are not printed in the fractional portion except in the exponent form.

    (*c*) If the entire integer part of the quantity cannot be printed in six digits (or more depending on implementation), the quantity is printed using the exponent form.

    (*d*) Exact integers are printed without the decimal.

EXAMPLE PROGRAM

Enough BASIC features have now been presented to write a complete program. Figure 16-2 illustrates a program using the statements that have been explained. Note the use of the PRINT statement to tell the user what data to compute and the form of the data.

String Variables in Output

The PRINT statement provides for literal output by enclosing the literal in quotes. String variables can also be used (with most compilers). The string of output characters is defined by either a replacement statement or an INPUT statement. For example, if C$ is to have the value MY NAME IS and D$ is to have the value JAN DEGROSS, they could be defined by any of the following:

PROGRAM

```
100  REM   PROGRAM TO CALCULATE COMPOUND AMOUNT OF $1.00
110  REM   FOR N YEARS AT I PERCENT COMPOUNDED QUARTERLY.
120  REM       N = NUMBER OF YEARS
130  REM       I = INTEREST RATE AS INPUT
140  REM       J = INTEREST RATE AS DECIMAL
150  REM       A = PRESENT VALUE OF $1.00
160  REM   *************************************************
200  PRINT "INPUT YEARS, PERCENT INTEREST"
210  INPUT N,I
220  LET J = I/100
240  LET A = (1+J/4)↑(N*4)
250  PRINT
260  PRINT "COMPOUND AMOUNT OF $1.00 IN";N;"YEARS AT";
270  PRINT I;"PERCENT IS";A
280  END
```

OUTPUT

```
INPUT YEARS, PERCENT INTEREST
? 5,7

COMPOUND AMOUNT OF $1.00 IN 5 YEARS AT 7 PERCENT IS 1.41478
```

FIGURE 16-2 BASIC program to compute compound amount to which $1.00 will accumulate if interest is compounded quarterly. Number of years and rate of interest are input. The formula is $[1 + (i/4)]^{4n}$, where i is the yearly interest rate and n is the number of years.

20 DATA MY NAME IS , JAN DEGROSS, or DATA "MY NAME IS", "JAN DEGROSS"

---

10 INPUT C$,D$
? MY NAME IS ,JAN DEGROSS

When the data is to be printed, the string name is used in the PRINT statement. Rules for spacing with commas and semicolons apply. 10 PRINT C$;D$ will cause an output of

MY NAME IS JAN DEGROSS

10 LET C$ = "MY NAME IS"
20 LET D$ = "JAN DEGROSS"

---

10 READ C$,D$

1 Write PRINT statements to provide the following headings on output:

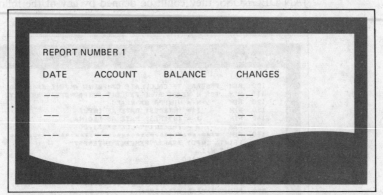

```
REPORT NUMBER 1

DATE      ACCOUNT     BALANCE      CHANGES
__          __          __          __

__          __          __          __

__          __          __          __
```

2 Write PRINT statements to provide the following output lines (where xxx = numeric data):

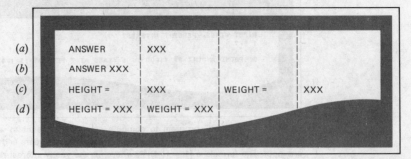

```
(a)   ANSWER       XXX

(b)   ANSWER XXX

(c)   HEIGHT =     XXX         WEIGHT =    XXX

(d)   HEIGHT = XXX   WEIGHT = XXX
```

3 Provide data for the two READ statements

```
10  READ A,B
20  READ X
```

4 (*a*) Write statements to obtain the first name (string) and age in years from the user at the terminal.

(*b*) Write statements to output the first name and age in the following *output* format:

name IS nn YEARS

5 Print the string variable M$ (containing REPORT OF VIOLATIONS) starting at column 21.

6 Write a complete BASIC program to read credits for each of two courses taken and the grades for the two courses as a numeric value (A = 4, B = 3, etc.). Compute the grade-point average and print it with a descriptive heading. The answers to the quiz will give a sample against which you can check yours, but write your own. If possible, compile and run it. *Hint:* Write two or three REM lines at the beginning of the program as documentation. The last line must be the END statement.

Control Statements

Transfer of Control   Transfer of control or branching provides the program with the capability for selecting different program instructions depending on the data at the point of transfer. For example, if a program is computing gross pay for employees who receive overtime at $1\frac{1}{2}$ times the regular rate for hours over 40, there may be two program branches—one branch for up to 40 hours and another branch for overtime. A sample branch segment and flowchart are shown in Figure 16-3.

There are two types of transfer of control; there is a BASIC statement for each. "s" refers to a statement number.

1 Unconditional transfer of control   GO TO s
2 Conditional transfer of control   IF condition THEN s

The unconditional transfer specifies the statement number to which control transfers (is executed next). The conditional specifies where control should go if the condition is satisfied. If the condition is not satisfied, the program continues with the next statement in the sequence. The conditions use the following relational symbols:

=	Equals
<	Less than
<=	Less than or equal
>	Greater than
>=	Greater than or equal
<>	Not equal to

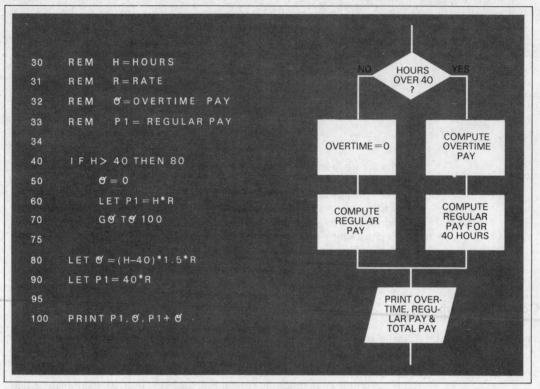

```
30      REM    H=HOURS

31      REM    R=RATE

32      REM    O=OVERTIME  PAY

33      REM    P1= REGULAR PAY

34

40      IF H> 40 THEN 80

50         O = 0

60         LET P1=H*R

70         GO TO 100

75

80      LET O =(H-40)*1.5*R

90      LET P1= 40*R

95

100     PRINT P1, O, P1+ O
```

FIGURE 16-3 Flowchart and program segment—two program branches.

Both individual variables and expressions may be compared for deciding on a transfer of control. Strings may also be compared. Examples are:

10   IF X > Y THEN 50 (Go to statement 50 if the value of X is greater than Y)
10   IF SQR (M) + 5.4 < = 2 THEN 40
10   IF A$ > B$ THEN 70

A STOP statement is available. It is not necessary to use STOP to have the program terminate. If the program is out of data or has reached the END statement, it will stop. In some cases, however, using STOP to specify termination at a point other than the end of the program statements will be convenient. Note that END is the last statement, and, therefore, there is only one in a program. It is valid to GO TO an END statement. STOP statements may appear more than once.

CONTROL STATEMENTS

GO TO s   or   GOTO s
IF expression relation expression THEN s
STOP
END

1 Write statements for the following:

    (a) Branch unconditionally to statement 75.

    (b) Branch to 60 if A is less than B^2.

    (c) Branch to 90 if A + B is not equal to Z.

    (d) Branch to 100 if the string A$ is less than or equal to the string C$.

2 Write a complete program to evaluate a quiz show winner's decision. He has won either $25,000 cash or $200 a month for 15 years (180 months). The question is which he should take assuming an interest rate of 6 percent ($\frac{1}{2}$ percent a month). Print a message with the decision. The decision is to accept the annuity ($200 a month) if the present value of the payments is greater than $25,000. The formula for computing the present value is:

$$200 \left(\frac{1 - \dfrac{1}{(1 + i)^n}}{i} \right)$$

where i = interest rate (per month)

         n = number of periods (months in this case)

Loops

Loops are a programming technique for repeating the execution of a set of instructions. The technique is frequently used in connection with subscripted variables. The BASIC language has instructions to define subscripted variables and to perform looping.

Subscripted Variables

A collection of items (quantities or strings) which can be classed together can be identified by a single name, and individual items in the collection (called an "array") can then be referenced by the name of the collection plus the position of the item in the array. For example, a list of sales might be called S. The third item (the amount of the third sale) would be identified as S(3). The ith item would be S(i). Mathematical notation uses a lowered number, but because the terminal or card punch is used, the subscript is written as a number enclosed in parentheses.

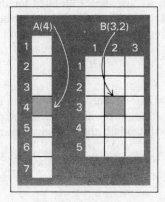

FIGURE 16-4 Arrays.

A list, such as the one described, is a one-dimensional array and can be visualized as a column of entries. A two-dimensional array, called a "matrix," provides for twofold classification. Individual entries are defined by a row number and a column number. Figure 16-4 illustrates these forms.

BASIC uses a single alphabetic character to designate an array. The subscripts can be constants, variables, or expressions. In all cases, the result must be an integer quantity. If a variable used as a subscript refers to a mixed quantity having both a whole part and a fractional part, the fractional part will be dropped (after rounding). It is better programming to explicitly drop the fractional part by the use of the function INT (which truncates). The following are all valid subscripted variables.

1   A (I,J)
2   A (24,13)
3   A (3)
4   A (5*I)
5   A (INT (R))
6   A (5*I − B + C)

Since the number of cells in an array will vary among arrays, the BASIC compiler must receive data on the amount of memory to set aside for the entries. BASIC handles this in two ways.

1   Automatic assignment of 11 cells for each dimension for subscripts running from 0 through 10 (11 cells for single dimension array and 11×11 or 121 for a two-dimensional matrix).

2   The use of the DIM statement which defines the maximum size for each dimension of the array. For example, 10 DIM X(100) sets aside 101 cells of storage for a list which can go from X(0) to X(100).

In either case, whether the automatic assignment or the DIM statement is used, it is not necessary to use all the storage spaces allocated for the list or array. For example, in many problems, the 0 column and 0 row may be ignored because it may be more convenient to number subscripts starting with 1. The DIM statements are generally placed in a group at the beginning of the program.

Loop Instructions   A *loop* executes a set of instructions a number of times, each time altering one or more variables so that each execution is different from the preceding one. The effect of looping is to reduce substantially the number of instructions required to code a program.

The BASIC instructions for looping consist of a FOR . . . TO . . . STEP instruction and a NEXT instruction. The FOR instruction is used at the beginning of a loop to establish the loop conditions; the NEXT instruction defines the end of the loop. The general form of the instructions are:

FOR   unsubscripted variable = expression TO expression STEP expression
NEXT   unsubscripted variable

Some examples will illustrate the formats.

```
10  FOR I = 1 TO 15 STEP 1   {STEP can be omitted if it is 1;
    . . .                     {compiler assumes STEP is 1
    . . .
50  NEXT I
10  FOR I = X TO Y + Z STEP R
    . . .
    . . .
50  NEXT I
```

As examples of how the loop is used, assume an array A with 50 entries. For examples after Example 1, all statements are the same except statement 50, so only this statement is given.

EXAMPLE 1   Sum the elements of the array and store the sum in S.

```
10  DIM A(50)
    . . .
    . . .
40  S = 0                    { S is set to 0 before the loop
50  FOR I = 1 TO 50 STEP 1   { because of the "add to" logic at
60      S = S + A(I)         { statement 60.
70  NEXT I
```

EXAMPLE 2   Sum every other element of the array.

```
50  FOR I = 1 TO 50 STEP 2
```

EXAMPLE 3   Sum every R*th* element starting with the T*th* element and going up to and including the $(R + L)th$ element.

```
50  FOR I = T TO R + L STEP R
```

Loops can be written inside loops. For example, assume a matrix B for which the elements are to be summed. The matrix has 20 rows and 15 columns. The 0 row and column will not be used.

```
10  DIM B(20,15)
    . . .
    . . .
20  S = 0
```

```
30  FOR I = 1 TO 20          ⎫
40      FOR J = 1 TO 15   ⎫  ⎪
50          S = S + B(I,J) ⎬ Inner  ⎬ Outer
60      NEXT J            ⎭  loop ⎪ loop
70  NEXT I                    ⎭
```

When loops are written inside loops, the inner loop is executed until satisfied, the outer loop is then incremented, and the inner loop starts over. In the above example, the elements will be summed across a row: (1,1), (1,2), (1,3), . . . (1,15), (2,1), (2,2), . . . (20,15).

In coding BASIC programs, it is desirable to use indentation to visually show the range of a loop. The FOR . . . TO statement which begins the loop and the NEXT statement which ends the loop are indented to the same point. The statements inside the loop are indented (say, four spaces).

```
FOR
    STATEMENT
    STATEMENT
    ETC
NEXT
```

In the above example of nested loops, the inner loop is indented to show its relationship to the outer loop.

RULES FOR SUBSCRIPTED VARIABLES AND LOOPS

Subscripted variable name has single alphabetic character.
Subscripts are separated by commas and enclosed in parentheses.
One or two subscripts may be used.
Subscripts may be constants, variables, or expressions.
Subscripts must have positive integer values.
Subscripts from 0 to 10 are implied for each dimension of a variable used with subscripts. Additional elements require a DIM statement.
DIM letter (integer, integer) dimensions an array.
The loop instructions are:
  FOR variable = expression TO expression STEP expression
  NEXT variable name
  Loop variable name must be unsubscripted variable.
  STEP may be omitted; compiler assumes step of 1. (STEP may be decimal fraction or negative, but be careful if using loop variable as subscript.)

Self-testing Quiz—
BASIC #4

1 Write a program segment to find the largest number in an N entry array called X. Put the largest one in B. If two are equal, choose either. The maximum size of the array is 50.

2 Write a program segment to print out every other entry in a K entry array called D. The maximum size of the array is 100.

3 Sum all the entries in a 10 × 10 array called D. Store the result in S. Use indentation to show structure.

Additional Features

The additional features explained in this section are important features that are generally available in BASIC. All except the matrix instructions are included in minimal BASIC.

Functions   BASIC provides functions such as SQR (square root), but it is frequently desirable for programmers to write their own function or subroutine. This allows a routine to be written once and then used several times in a program.

A single statement function is written as a statement preceded by the word DEF. The DEF defines the statement as a function. It must occupy only one line, may not use other user-defined functions, and may not use subscripted variables. The name of the function returning a numerical result is three letters starting with FN. A string function (if implemented) has the name FN$ plus a single alphabetic character.

Writing a statement function is useful only if the function will be used in two or more places in the program. For example, assume a program needs to compute $\sqrt{X^3 + 5}$ several times in a program. The definition would be written as:

10   DEF FNS (X) = SQR (X↑3) + 5

To use the function, the programmer writes a statement with the argument to be used in place of X in the statement

10   Y = FNS (25)   Y = 130
10   Y = FNS (Z + 3)   If Z = 12, Y = 63.09

The rules for single-statement functions are summarized as:

RULES FOR FUNCTIONS
_____

The form of a user function definition is
  DEF FNa (list) = e   for a numeric result
  DEF FN$a ( ) = e   for a string result (not part of minimal BASIC)
where a is any alphabetic character
     list is the function variables separated by commas
     e is an expression

Restrictions
  Definition may occupy only one line
  Definition may not include other user functions
  Definition may not use subscripted variables
_____

Subroutines and   A program may be coded in modular fashion with subprograms or subroutines by
Modular Programs   the use of the GOSUB statement. The subroutine is not named (as in most languages); instead, its starting point is defined by a transfer of control statement.

GOSUB s where s = statement number

The statement number named in the GOSUB statement is the starting statement of the subroutine; the ending statement is a RETURN. The program goes back to the statement following the GOSUB statement. This essentially allows the programmer to exit from the main program flow, execute a set of statements, and return to the main flow. The subroutine may, therefore, be entered from many points in the program. The transfer to the subroutine does not transfer any variables. All variables used in the subroutine must be defined before transfer to the routine and have the same name as the corresponding variables in the subroutine. The general flow for a simple modular program is shown in Figure 16-5. The rules for subroutines are summarized below.

RULES FOR SUBROUTINES

The subroutine is written as a set of statements ended by a statement in the form:

RETURN

To use the set of statements, the program has a statement in the form:

GOSUB s

where s is the statement number which begins the set of subroutine statements

Matrix Instructions One of the powerful features of extended BASIC is the availability of matrix instructions. These are summarized below:

MATRIX INSTRUCTIONS

MAT	INPUT	Accept input of matrix elements (enter row at each input?)
MAT	READ	Read all matrix elements from data block
MAT	PRINT	Print the matrix
MAT	+	Matrix addition
MAT	−	Matrix subtraction
MAT	*	Matrix multiplication
MAT	( )*	Scalar multiplication
MAT	INV	Matrix inverse
MAT	TRN	Matrix transpose
MAT	ZER	Matrix of all zeros
MAT	CON	Matrix of all 1s
MAT	IDN	Identity matrix

For example, MAT C = A + B, where A, B, and C are matrices.

The matrix instructions simplify the writing of instructions to manipulate matrices. In general, matrix input and output is row by row. A semicolon following a matrix print will cause minimum spacing so that more than five elements will appear on a line. For example, if a 5 × 5 matrix is to be printed out, the program segments, both those not using and those using the MAT instructions, are:

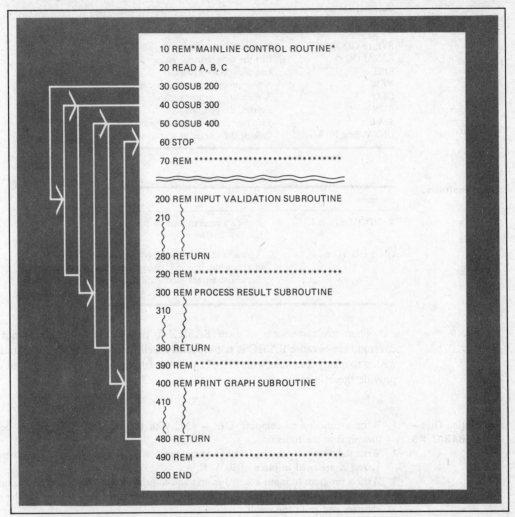

```
10 REM*MAINLINE CONTROL ROUTINE*

20 READ A, B, C

30 GOSUB 200

40 GOSUB 300

50 GOSUB 400

60 STOP

70 REM ******************************
```

```
200 REM INPUT VALIDATION SUBROUTINE

210

280 RETURN

290 REM ******************************

300 REM PROCESS RESULT SUBROUTINE

310

380 RETURN

390 REM ******************************

400 REM PRINT GRAPH SUBROUTINE

410

480 RETURN

490 REM ******************************

500 END
```

FIGURE 16-5 Use of subroutines in BASIC.

Without matrix instructions	With matrix instructions
10 FOR I = 1 TO 5 PRINT A(I,1), A(I,2), A(I,3), A(I,4), A(I,5) 30 NEXT I	20 MAT PRINT A

System Instructions   It is generally necessary to have a system manual for the implementation of BASIC being used. However, certain system commands are commonly used:

Command	Purpose
BYE or GOODBYE	Terminates use of system
CATALOG	List the time-sharing catalog
LIST	List the specified program
NEW	A new program is being written
OLD	A previously written program is to be used
RUN	Execute the program
SAVE	Save (store) the current program (file)
UNSAVE or PURGE	Cancels the storage of a program

Other Instructions

Statement	Purpose
RANDOMIZE	Provide a random start for the random function RND
ON n GO TO s_1, s_2, . . .	A transfer of control based on the value of a variable. If n = 1, control goes to the first statement number; if 2, to the second, etc.

There are statements in some BASICs to process files. These will not be covered here because BASIC is not especially well designed for files. If a student wishes to manipulate files with BASIC, the manual for the BASIC being used will provide these instructions.

Self-testing Quiz—BASIC #5

1 Write a function to compute $\sqrt{B^2 - 4AC}$ with the value of B, A, and C being furnished to the function.
2 Write statements to use the function from Question 1 to obtain an answer R when Z, Y, and X are used in place of B, A, C.
3 Write a program to input a 2 × 3 matrix and to print it out. Use matrix instructions.
4 Write a program to input a matrix A (2 × 2) and a matrix B (2 × 2). Add the two matrices and print the result.
5 Write a subroutine to find the largest of three numbers A, B, C.
6 Write a statement to use the subroutine in Question 5.
7 Write a complete program to prepare a table of compound amounts of $1 at 8 percent for 10 years, compounded yearly. Print appropriate headings.

Summary of BASIC

Variable names
For numeric quantities, the first character of name must be alphabetic. If used, second character must be numeric.

String quantity
Alphabetic character followed by $.

Array name
Single alphabetic character for numeric array; single alphabetic characters plus $
for string value array.

Operations
Add   +
Subtract   −
Multiply   *
Divide   /
Exponentiate ↑ or ∧

Relations
Less than   <
Equal   =
Greater than   >
Less than or equal   <=
Not equal   <>
Greater than or equal >=

Functions (ANS minimal BASIC)
ABS   Absolute value
ATN   Arctangent
COS   Cosine
EXP   Exponentiate e
INT   Integer portion
LOG   Log to base *e*
RND   Random number
SGN   Sign of argument: +1 for +, 0 for 0, −1 for negative
SIN   Sine
SQR   Square root
TAN   Tangent

Replacement
LET v = e   Computes and assigns value

Input and output
READ   Read data from data block defined by DATA statements
DATA   Define data for use by READ statements
INPUT   Calls for and accepts data from typewriter during execution
RESTORE   Restart use of data block at beginning
PRINT   Print numbers or literals
PRINT TAB( )   Position output line and print

Control
GO TO s   Go to statement number s

IF condition THEN s	If condition is true, go to statement s; else continue
ON v GO TO s^1, s^2, . . .	Variable GO TO depending on value of v
FOR v = 1 TO t STEP r	Loop instruction; i = initial value, t = termination value, and r = step at each increment (can be omitted if 1)
NEXT v	End of loop; increment v
STOP	Stop execution
END	End of program statements

Others

DIM	Define size of arrays
REM	Remark line to document program logic
RANDOMIZE	Provide random start for RND function
DEF	Define a function
GOSUB s	Perform a subroutine
RETURN	Return from a subroutine
MAT	Matrix operation

Answers to Self-testing Quizzes

BASIC #1 **1** (*a*) (1) Valid
 (2) Valid
 (3) Invalid—must start with alphabetic letter
 (4) Invalid—second character can only be numeric digit
 (5) Valid—for a string
 (6) Invalid—no digit in name of string (although this is allowed in some implementations)
 (*b*) (1) Invalid—needs to be A*B
 (2) Valid
 (3) Valid
 (4) Valid—same as −1*B

2 (*a*) $a = \sqrt{g^3}$ or $g^{3/2}$
 (*b*) $b = 3y/x + 1.3w$
 (*c*) $c = 3.1417 + [(x + 3)/4]$
 (*d*) $d = (z^2/5)w$

3 (*a*) 10   LET A = B*C/D
 (*b*) 20   LET B = SQR(X*Y)
 (*c*) 30   LET C = SQR(X/Y)
 (*d*) 40   LET D = 2*X*Y
 (*e*) 50   LET E = 3*ABS(Y*Z)

4 (*a*) LET A = ((X↑2)*(3*Y)) + Z
 (*b*) LET B = (X↑Y) + ((R↑Y)/2)
 (*c*) LET C = SQR((A/R) + X)
 (*d*) LET D = X + (Y/S) + R

5   (a) −3
    (b) 3
    (c) 15.4
    (d) 16.1
    (e) 5.0

BASIC #2 **1** 10 PRINT "REPORT NUMBER 1"
            20 PRINT
            30 PRINT "DATE", "ACCOUNT", "BALANCE", "CHANGES"
     2 (a) 10 PRINT "ANSWER", X
        (b) 10 PRINT "ANSWER";X
        (c) 10 PRINT "HEIGHT =", X1, "WEIGHT =", X2
        (d) 10 PRINT "HEIGHT ="; X1; "WEIGHT ="; X2
     3 30 DATA 10.5, 3, 7.6 (Two separate DATA statements could also be used.)
     4 (a) 10 PRINT "INPUT FIRST NAME FOLLOWED BY COMMA AND
                    AGE IN YEARS"
             20 INPUT N$, A
        (b) 10 PRINT N$; "IS"; A; "YEARS"
     5 10 PRINT TAB(21); M$
     6 10 REM GRADE PROGRAM
            20 REM AUTHOR G. B. DAVIS 6-15-75
            30 REM C1, C2 = CREDITS; G1, G2 = GRADES ON SCALE A=4
            40 REM ************************
            50 DATA 3,4,4,2
            60 READ C1, C2, G1, G2
            70 LET A = ((C1*G1) + (C2*G2))/(C1 + C2)
            80 PRINT "GRADE POINT IS"; A
            90 END

BASIC #3 **1** (a) 10 GO TO 75 or GOTO 75
        (b) 10 IF A<B↑2 THEN 60
        (c) 10 IF A+B<>Z THEN 90
        (d) 10 IF A$<=C$ THEN 100
     2 10 REM QUIZ PRIZE DECISION
            20 REM AUTHOR GORDON B. DAVIS 9-7-76
            30 REM P = PRESENT VALUE OF MONTHLY ANNUITY
            35 REM *********************
            40 LET P = 200*((1 − (1/1.005↑180))/.005)
            50 IF P > 25000 THEN 80
            60 PRINT "ANNUITY IS $"; P; "ACCEPT CASH"
            70 GO TO 90
            80 PRINT "ANNUITY IS $"; P; "ACCEPT ANNUITY"
            90 END

BASIC #4 **1** 10 DIM X(50)
              . . .
            20 B = 0

```
          30   FOR I = 1 TO N
          40       IF X(I) < = B THEN 60
          50       B = X(I)
          60   NEXT I
     2    10   DIM D(100)
               . . .
          20   FOR I = 1 TO K STEP 2
          30       PRINT D(I)
          40   NEXT I
     3    10   S = 0
          20   FOR I = 1 TO 10
          30       FOR J = 1 TO 10
          40           S = S + D(I,J)
          50       NEXT J
          60   NEXT I
```

BASIC #5
```
     1   DEF FND(B,A,C) = SQR (B↑2 − 4*A*C)
     2   LET R = FND(Z,Y,X)
     3   10   DIM A(2,3)
          20   MAT INPUT A
          30   MAT PRINT A
          40   END
     4   10   DIM A(2,2), B(2,2), C(2,2)
          20   MAT INPUT A
          30   MAT INPUT B
          40   MAT C = A + B
          50   MAT PRINT C
          60   END
     5   100   REM SUBROUTINE TO FIND LARGEST OF THREE NUMBERS
         110   REM ************************************************************
         120   LET B1 = A
         130   IF B < = B1 THEN 150
         140   LET B1 = B
         150   IF C < = B1 THEN 170
         160   LET B1 = C
         170   RETURN
         180   REM ************************************************************
     6   GOSUB  100
     7   10   REM COMPOUND INTEREST TABLE PROBLEM
         20   PRINT "COMPOUND INTEREST TABLE AT 8 PERCENT"
         30   PRINT
         40   PRINT
         50   PRINT "PERIOD", "COMPOUND AMOUNT OF $1.00"
         60   PRINT
         70   FOR I = 1 TO 10
         80       LET A = (1 + .08)↑I
         90       PRINT I,A
        100   NEXT I
        110   END
```

EXERCISES 1 Write one or more BASIC statements to perform each of the following:

(a) Read A,B,C from a data block.

(b) Define five data items, 3, 7, 6.4, 5.5, and 4.3, plus six data items of 1.5.

(c) Print a heading "THIS IS IT" starting at column 27.

(d) Define a string variable THIS IS IT in a DATA statement and print the string.

(e) Print A in the first zone and B in the third zone.

(f) Transfer control to statement 50 if A is greater than B.

(g) If K is 1, go to statement 140; if 2 go to statement 190; if 3 to 230.

(h) Add 1 to I if I is less than 6; otherwise continue.

(i) Execute I = I + 4.1317 10 times.

(j) Print a 2 × 4 matrix.

   (1) Not using MAT instructions

   (2) Using MAT instructions

(k) Dimension an array A for 100 cells.

(l) Dimension a 2 × 8 array called M.

(m) Accept input of X from terminal.

(n) Define a function to calculate $X^3 + 4$.

2 Write complete programs to do the following:

(a) Calculate a 12-month moving average covering 20 months.

(b) Add to problem 2(a) the average using exponential smoothing where each new value is $(1 - A)*(old\ value) + A*latest\ observation$. Use an alpha value (A) of .1.

(c) Compute a list of present values for 10 years. The formula is

$$P = \frac{Amount}{(1 + i)^n}$$

Use i of 15 percent, amount of 1.00, and n of 10 periods.

(d) Add to problem 2(c) by making a table

Years	Rate		
	05	10	15
1	—	—	—
2	—	—	—
⋮	⋮	⋮	⋮
10	—	—	—

(e) A bank provides, for each mortgage holder, a list showing the amount of each payment that is interest and the amount that is repayment of principle. Write the program to calculate the required payment. The formula is

$$R = l\left(1 - \frac{i}{(1 + i)^n}\right)$$

where R is payment, l is loan amount, i is interest rate, and n is number of periods. Prepare a table of principal and interest for each payment. Print a sample output for 10 periods monthly interest rate of .0075 and loan of $3000.

(f) Given any amount of a restaurant check up to $5 and any amount tendered up to

$5, find the number and denomination of currency and coin to return as change. Print "PAY MORE" if not enough is tendered.

(g) Calculate the mean and standard deviation for an array of N numbers where N is input followed by input of the array.

(h) Add to problem 2(g) numbers not from input but generated by the RND function. Make the numbers have a mean of 10. (*Hint:* Multiply each RND result by 20 since RND gives numbers with mean of .5.) Run the problem twice.

(i) Add to problem 2(h) the random start feature of RANDOMIZE. Run twice.

(j) Convert any given decimal number to another number system and print the result. Use one of the following:
   (1) Binary
   (2) Duodecimal (base 12)
   (3) Octal
   (4) Hexadecimal

(k) Print the outline of an evergreen tree. *Hint:* Use the PRINT TAB statement.

(l) Compute the rate of return for an investment. See the example flowchart for this computation in Figure 18-12 near the end of Chapter 18.

CHAPTER

17

FORTRAN—
ELEMENTARY
FEATURES

Introduction to FORTRAN

FORTRAN (an acronym for FORmula TRANslator) is the most widely employed algebraic language and is available for use on almost all computers. Although not limited to mathematical problems, it is especially useful for problems which can be stated in terms of formulas or arithmetic procedures. This covers a wide range of problems. For example, FORTRAN is suitable for such diverse problems as analysis of sales statistics in a business and analysis of structural stress for designing a building.

Development of FORTRAN

FORTRAN was developed originally by IBM in conjunction with some major users. First announced in 1957, it has been implemented by most computer manufacturers for almost all computers. FORTRAN has changed and evolved. New features have been added as the need has been perceived or as equipment capabilities have allowed. This evolutionary process resulted, during the development period, in several FORTRANs of increasing complexity. These were referred to as FORTRANSIT, FORTRAN, FORTRAN II, and FORTRAN IV. Each new version made a few changes to the basic instructions and included additional features. In 1966, a voluntary FORTRAN standard, American National Standard (ANS) FORTRAN, was adopted. The ANS specifications described Basic FORTRAN as a subset of the full FORTRAN. The International Standards Organization defined three levels of FORTRAN, with the second level being between ANS Basic FORTRAN and the top level, full FORTRAN.

In 1977, a revised FORTRAN standard was proposed. The 1977 proposal adds features to the previous 1966 standard FORTRAN, clarifies some ambiguities, and makes a few minor changes. The new standard also defines two different levels for FORTRAN implementation, subset FORTRAN and full FORTRAN. Subset FORTRAN is a compatible subset of the higher level full FORTRAN. This text is based on the 1977 proposed standard, although differences between the new standard and the old will be noted since many compilers may not accept the added 1977 features. The features in this chapter include only the features found in subset FORTRAN; Chapter 18 includes high-level features. The chapters concentrate on the most used features; some advanced features are therefore described in less detail.

Standard FORTRAN is preferred in all cases because of considerations of maintainability and portability, even though a particular installation may have some useful, but nonstandard, features. There are some student-oriented FORTRANs which provide very useful diagnostics. They are generally standard except that they may have some restrictions with respect to a few features. The most common of these is termed WATFOR or WATFIV (for University of Waterloo FORTRAN FOUR or FIVE).

How to Study FORTRAN

Learning FORTRAN is like learning a special-purpose language. There are rules of construction and vocabulary to learn, and one becomes proficient by doing rather than by much reading. To be effective, FORTRAN study must include practice in using the rules to write statements. Since the rules must be followed exactly, the way to acquire working familiarity is to read an explanation and follow the reading by working problems. Chapters 17 and 18 are arranged with short self-testing quizzes following each section of explanation. The answers to the quizzes are found at the end of each chapter.

Flowcharting all but the simplest exercises is strongly recommended. The drawing of a clear flowchart helps in providing for all possible conditions and provides documentation for the program. At first, students tend to have difficulty thinking of problems in terms of the logic of the required procedures; preparing a flow diagram assists in laying out a problem in procedural terms.

It is very helpful to write and actually run several FORTRAN programs. Experience with students learning FORTRAN has shown that the steps required to get a program to run solidify understanding of the language and clear up points which seem hard to grasp.

Overview of FORTRAN

FORTRAN is a language for instructing a computer, but the language is machine-independent. In other words, the programmer writing FORTRAN does not need to know the details of the computer's operation. The language is procedure-oriented. It is well suited for instructing the computer in a problem-solving procedure. The language consists of a vocabulary of symbols and words and a grammar of rules for writing procedural instructions. The symbols, words, and rules utilize many common mathematical and English-language conventions so that the language is easy to learn and to understand. The rules are, however, precise and should be followed with care. The basic instructions to the computer to carry out problem-solving procedures may be classified as follows:

Type of statement	Purpose
Input/output	To direct the computer to obtain data from a specified input device and to output data using a specified output device
Assignment	To perform arithmetic, logical, or character processing using data from the program or data read into memory by an input statement and to assign results to a variable name
Control	To control the order in which the program is to be executed or to cause a set of one or more statements to be executed a specified number of times
Specification	To direct the compiler in the translation and program-building process

The nature of a FORTRAN program is illustrated by a short example. This sample program directs the computer to read three values called A, B, and C from a punched card, to sum the three quantities, to take the square root of the sum, to print the square root, and then to come to a halt.

FORTRAN statement	Type of statement
READ (1, 900) A, B, C 900 FORMAT (3F10.2)	Input/output
X = A+B+C Y = SQRT (X)	Arithmetic assignment
WRITE (3, 900) X, Y	Input/output
STOP	Control
END	Specification (to compiler)

The simplicity, formula orientation, and English-like character of the language are shown by the example. To write FORTRAN requires mastering the set of symbols, words, and rules which constitute the language.

Preparing a Program in FORTRAN

As with any computer programming effort, preparation for programming in FORTRAN requires problem analysis to understand what must be accomplished. The next step is to define clearly the procedures to be followed in the problem solution. Flowcharting is very useful because of its suitability for describing the procedures and also because the flowchart is valuable documentation for the program. (See Chapter 4 for a complete description of flowchart symbols and other aids, such as card and printer layouts.)

The flowchart for the FORTRAN example is shown in Figure 17-1. Another useful approach to program logic design is to write a series of statements in English

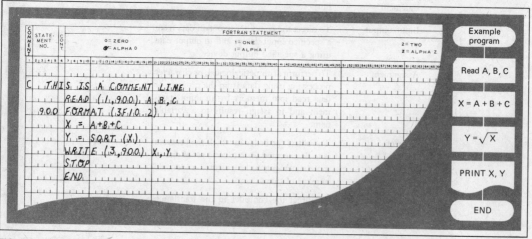

FIGURE 17-1 Coding sheet and flowchart for simple program to sum three numbers and take square root of the sum.

(a pseudocode) to describe the flow of processing. These statements form an English-language equivalent of the computer program statements. For example, the pseudocode statements for the very simple program in Figure 17-1 might read:

Read three values from a card.
Sum the three quantities and take the square root of the sum.
Print the sum and the square root.

When the program flowchart and/or pseudocode statements have been prepared, the next step is to code the FORTRAN statements, using FORTRAN coding paper. The coding form typically has 72 columns on it, although some forms have 80 columns. The short sample program presented earlier is written on a FORTRAN coding form in Figure 17-1. The columns are used as follows:

Column	How used
1	Comments and special options. C (or C or * in new standard) in column 1 indicates that what follows on the line is not translated. The line is printed as part of the program listing and is therefore used for explanatory comments in the program listing.
2–5	Statement reference number. Must be right-justified (extra spaces to left).
6	If a FORTRAN statement is too long for one line, it may be continued on the next line by putting a nonzero digit in column 6 of the continuation line (or lines). Column 6 of the initial line being continued may have a blank or a 0.
7–72	FORTRAN statement.
73–80	Each statement will be punched onto one card. A punched card has 80 columns. The last eight columns either are not used or are used for identification. They are not translated. When statements are entered via a terminal, the 73–80 convention may not apply.

In coding FORTRAN statements, certain conventions will reduce the possibility of error when the lines of coding are punched into cards or entered at a terminal:

1 Use the FORTRAN coding paper. Each space on the coding form corresponds to a column on a punched card, so that one character is written in each space. This reduces errors in keypunching.

2 Code only in printed capital letters. A keypunch does not have lowercase letters, and the printed capitals are easier to read.

3 Clearly differentiate between numbers and letters which are similar. The letter O and the zero are the biggest problems, but S and 5, Z and 2, and I and 1 are often confused. Various methods are used for differentiating, such as underlining or slashing either the letter or the number. It is very common for FOR-TRAN programmers to slash the alphabetic O. The American National Standard coding convention (shown below) is to put a line through the letters Z and to add a loop to O, leaving the related numbers as they are usually written. The standard method is illustrated in Figure 17.1 on page 476.

Letter	Number
O̶	0
Z̶	2
I	1
S	5

4 FORTRAN statements may be punched on any standard card punch. However, it is useful to understand the code differences between key punches (see Appendix 1). The IBM Model 29 cardpunch for programs to be run on an IBM System/370 has the FORTRAN characters on the keyboard. If a Model 26 cardpunch is used, it may not have a FORTRAN (scientific) character set. The proper punches may still be put into the cards, but the printing at the top of the card will show a different character.

FORTRAN is available on most time-sharing services in which the user enters a program from a terminal. However, the most common practice is to punch the program into cards, and this procedure is assumed in the text. When coding a line of FORTRAN, the statement itself can begin anywhere in columns 7 through 72. It does not have to start at column 7. Spaces may be used in the line of coding to improve readability. The compiler ignores spaces before or after operation symbols and before or after the variable names and other operands. Thus, $K = A + B + C$ is equivalent to $K=A+B+C$.

Programming Discipline in FORTRAN

The concepts of programming discipline or good programming style presented in Chapter 5 apply to FORTRAN. However, FORTRAN is not a block-structured language, so that it is difficult, cumbersome, and usually impossible to code FORTRAN without the use of the GO TO statement.

FORTRAN programs can be written using subroutines and function subprograms (to be explained), but this is cumbersome for small programs. An alternative approach for small programs or even within modules is the use of pseudoblocks, i.e., not blocks in the sense of a block-structured program but logical blocks of actions or documentation within a FORTRAN program. The need for a clear program structure increases with the size of the programs. The use of logical blocks may seem excessive structure and documentation for a very small program. However, the approach will be used for even the simplest example programs in the text because developing good programming practices from the start is important. The approach is also valuable for the documentation provided.

The characteristics of good programming style for FORTRAN can be divided into good form and layout for the program and good practice in the selection and use of program statements. The guides to form and layout are presented in Figure 17-2 and illustrated in Figure 17-3 except for statement indentation, to be ex-

---

FIGURE 17-2 GUIDES FOR FORTRAN PROGRAM FORM AND LAYOUT

1 A FORTRAN program or subroutine is organized into a set of logical units or program blocks each of which consists of a group of FORTRAN comments and statements. FORTRAN is not well designed for a block structure, so these are not blocks in the same sense as with other languages but might be termed pseudoblocks.

2 Each block is visually defined in the program by comment lines. The following procedure is recommended:
(a) Blocks are separated by two blank lines (C or * in column 1 and rest of line blank).
(b) Each block begins with a solid line of asterisks.
(c) The second line of the block (following the solid asterisks) begins with C* (or **) in columns 1 and 2 and ends with asterisks in columns 71 and 72. The block is named or described in this line. The identification can include the block number.
(d) Additional lines describing the block contain **or C* in columns 1 and 2 and ** in columns 71 and 72 with description beginning at column 4.
(e) The block description is followed by a solid line of asterisks.

3 Comments are used within blocks prior to statements that need explanation. The inside-block comments have a C or * in column 1. Actual comments begin in column 31 with an asterisk followed by the comment up to column 72.

4 The normal flow of a FORTRAN program is:

Identification block (comments only)
Description-of-variable-names block (comments only)
Dimension-declaration-and-initialize block ⎫
Input block   ⎪
Validate-input-data block   ⎬ May be combined or expanded
Process block(s)   ⎪
Normal-outputs block(s)   ⎪
Error-outputs block(s)   ⎭

5 The identification block contains the program name, author and date programmed, short description of purpose (what program does), limitations of program (such as limits on range of input values handled, number of variables, etc.).

6 The description-of-variable-names block lists and describes each variable name used in the program. Each line begins with ** or C*. The programmer may choose to list them in order of occurrence and then (as part of debugging) rearrange them alphabetically for final documentation. Variable names should be as descriptive as possible.

7 Statements within the program are numbered sequentially with gaps of 10 (to allow insertions). Each processing or input/output block begins with a new series; e.g., the first block begins with 100, the second block begins with 200. FORMAT statements are numbered with a separate series (say, 900 or 9000 and gaps of 5 or 10).

8 FORMAT statements may be in a FORMAT statement block at the end (or beginning) of the program or following each input or output statement. The position next to the input/output statement is preferred by this text unless the same FORMATs are used by a number of I/O statements.

9 Program indentation should be used to visually define the logic. This will be most useful with DO loop (described in Chapter 18).

```
C************************************         ← Line of asterisks before
C* PROGRAM NAME                      **
C* PROGRAM DESCRIPTION....           **
C* AUTHOR. ALISON M. DAVIS           **
C* DATE WRITTEN. 2/16/76             **
C************************************         ← and after block
C                                              description
C
C************************************
C* LIST OF VARIABLE NAMES            **       ← Each line of comments
C* ALPHA-DESCRIPTION....             **          inside block description
C* BETA-DESCRIPTION....              **          begins with C* (or **)
C************************************            and ends in columns
C                                                71-72 with **.
C
C************************************
C* DIMENSION-AND-INITIALIZE.         **
C************************************
      DIMENSION ALPHA(100)
      BETA=0
      ETC..............
C
C
C************************************
C* BLOCK 100 INPUT AND VALIDATION    **       ← Each processing block
C* DESCRIBES THE PROCESSING...       **          begins with a new
C************************************            number series, e.g.,
  100 READ (1,900)ALPHA,BETA                     100, 200, etc.
  900 FORMAT(100F10.0,F8.0)
      IF(BETA .GT. 50.0) GO TO 300
      ETC..............
C
C
C************************************
C* BLOCK 200 PROCESS DATA            **
C* DESCRIPTION OF PROCESSING...      **
C************************************
  200 X = ALPHA(1) + BETA
      Y = SQRT(X)
      ETC..............
C                                            ← Two blank cards visually
C                                              separate blocks [C (or *)
C************************************           in column 1]
C* BLOCK 300 OUTPUT-NORMAL AND ERROR **
C************************************
  300 WRITE (3,910) BETA,X,Y
  910 FORMAT(F10.0,5X,F10.2,3X,F5.2)
      ETC..............
      STOP
      END
```

FIGURE 17-3 Outline of program form and layout.

plained in connection with control statements. These suggestions reflect basic concepts of form; nevertheless, there can be considerable variation in program style while still achieving the basic objectives of clear, maintainable programs.

The basic structure of a FORTRAN program is:

Program identification
List of variables   }   comments only
Program statements

The program statements can be grouped into pseudoblocks for program documentation purposes. Some typical blocks which are found are:

Initialization (including dimension and declaration)

Input
Input validation $\Big\}$ or Input and input validation

Process

Normal output
Error output $\Big\}$ or Output-normal and error

Note that a small program may combine these blocks; a large program may have many more. The meaning and purpose of each of these parts of a program are explained in the chapter. Good practice in the selection and use of program statements is explained in connection with the description of FORTRAN statements.

Submitting FORTRAN Programs for Compilation and Execution

The general steps in performing a FORTRAN program can be summarized as the following:

1 Problem recognition and definition

2 Selection of solution procedures (algorithms) and data structures

3 Specification of program structure and logic for each part (by flowcharts, diagrams, and pseudocode)

4 Coding of FORTRAN statements

5 Source deck preparation
   (a) Punching of FORTRAN statements into punched cards—one line of coding into one card (source program deck)
   (b) Preparation of data (for example, punching into punched cards)

6 Compilation and debugging
   (a) Submission of job (the job consists of job control cards, source program deck, and data deck)
   (b) Debugging using compilation listing from the computer

7 Execution after all errors have been removed

8 Completion of documentation

The submission of jobs to be run requires, on most computers, a knowledge of the job control cards required by that computer. Since these are different for different computers, they cannot be provided by this text. You must obtain specific information on job control cards for the computer you are using. As an example of common practice, Figure 17-4 shows the deck structure for a FORTRAN job. Job control cards are generally required for the following purposes:

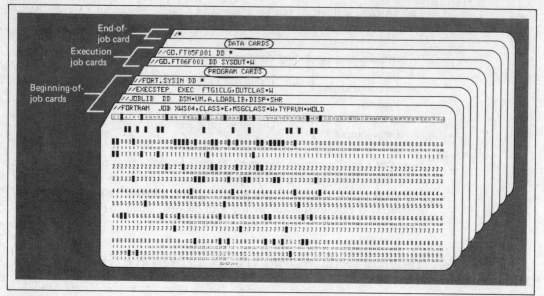

FIGURE 17-4 Job control cards for FORTRAN job on IBM System/370.

1 Identifying the job (probably the first card)
2 Identifying the end of the FORTRAN source program deck
3 Identifying the end of the data
4 Identifying the end of the job

Other purposes are to identify the language, specify execution, give messages to the operator, assign input/output units, etc.

Writing Statements to Perform Arithmetic

When a mathematical formula is written, three specifications are either expressed or implied.

1 The quantities to be operated upon. If a quantity can vary from problem to problem, it is designated by a symbol such as y, x, b, and a. If the quantity is fixed, it is written as a numeric constant such as 3.71 or 44.791.

2 The operations to be performed. These are indicated by symbols such as $\sqrt{\ }$, $+$, $-$, $/$, and $\times$, or by notational positions such as the raised number to indicate an exponent.

3 The order in which operations are to be performed. Parentheses are used to remove ambiguity about the order of operations.

To illustrate these specifications, a simple equation such as $x = \sqrt{y^2 + bd}$ states that the quantity associated with the symbol y is to be exponentiated, the quantities b and d are to be multiplied, and then the product of b and d is to be added to y^2. The square root of the resulting sum is taken, and the answer is associated with the variable x.

FORTRAN is a language for writing formula-type problems, and therefore FORTRAN also provides for the three specifications given in a mathematical formula. Some forms of mathematical notation are not suitable for FORTRAN because they cannot be punched on a card or entered in most terminals. The punched card, for example, does not allow for such notations as the raised exponent, the divisor below the expression to be divided, and the square root sign. Alternative notation suitable for computer input must be used by FORTRAN. The methods used by FORTRAN may be summarized as:

Specification	How provided in FORTRAN
Quantities to be operated upon	Variable names and constants
Operations to be performed	Operation symbols and function names
Order of operation	Order rule and parentheses

Constants and Variables

Constants and variables are used in FORTRAN in the same sense as in mathematical notation. A quantity which is not known or which can vary in different problems is a *variable* and is assigned a variable name. The name refers to a computer storage location where the data is stored. This name may be a single symbol, such as A, X, or Y, or it may be a descriptive name, such as ALPHA, BETA, or RATE. If, however, the quantity in the mathematical expression is fixed, then the number itself may be written. In FORTRAN, a number written in an arithmetic expression is called a *constant*. Thus, if a variable is used in formulating a problem-solving procedure, a variable name is used in FORTRAN; if a constant is used in the solution procedure, a constant is written in the corresponding FORTRAN statement. At this point, there is a direct correspondence between the symbol used in the formula to denote a variable and the variable name in FORTRAN and between the constant used in the formula and the constant in FORTRAN. In certain instances in FORTRAN, it is necessary to be more precise than the mathematical notation. In hand computation, many things are understood and do not need to be expressed, but a computer program proceeds *exactly* as instructed without judgment about whether the computation is meaningful. FORTRAN rules separate constants and variables into types—the two most important being integer and real types.

An *integer quantity* (sometimes called a "fixed point quantity") is one which has no fractional parts. It contains only whole numbers. The numbers 3, 19, and 475 are integer quantities. Integer variables and integer constants are required in certain cases where the quantity cannot assume a fractional value. For example, a set of statements can be executed only an integer number of times; in a list of numbers, the position in the list must be a whole number. The use of a number which could have a fractional part would not make sense in cases such as these.

Most computations can result in an answer having a fractional part. *Real quantities* can have, but do not require, a nonzero fractional part. The numbers 7.1, 3.1417, 99.01, and 81.0 are real quantities (also called "floating point quantities"). It is good programming practice to write a zero following the point for real numbers without a fractional part (4.0 instead of 4.). This reduces keying errors.

FORTRAN has specific rules for differentiating between variable names for real quantities and variable names for integer quantities and between real constants and integer constants.

RULES FOR SYMBOLIC VARIABLE NAMES

Purpose of variable name
To associate a symbolic name with a quantity which is not known or can vary.

Rules for forming
1 First character must be alphabetic.
2 No special characters are allowed (i.e., the names can contain only letters and numbers).
3 The total number of characters must not exceed six.

Integer variable names
Starts with one of the letters I, J, K, L, M, or N.

Real variable names
Starts with one of the letters other than I, J, K, L, M, or N. In other words, names starting with A through H and P through Z are real variable names.

A TYPE statement may be used to alter the first letter convention for selected variables; an IMPLICIT statement may be used to alter the type designation of a given first letter (to be explained in Chapter 18).

EXAMPLES

Variable name	Valid (V) or invalid (I)	If valid, integer (I) or real (R)	If invalid, why
X	V	R	
X123	V	R	
XY	V	R	
ALPHA	V	R	
BETA − 3	I		(−) is special character
$134	I		$ is special character
X19.1	I		(.) is special character
NUTS	V	I	
MOTHERS	I		Too many characters
MOM	V	I	
RATE	V	R	
1455A	I		Does not start with alphabetic character
M O	I		Blank is special character

RULES FOR CONSTANTS

Purpose of constant
To write a specific number in the program. Two types are used—integer (fixed point) and real (floating point).

General rules for forming constants
1 The decimal digits 0 through 9 are used to form a constant.
2 A minus sign must be used for a negative constant. A plus sign is optional; an unsigned constant is considered positive.
3 The size of a constant is limited to either a maximum number of digits or a maximum magnitude. There is a considerable range in allowable sizes for different computers.

Rules for forming an integer constant
1 A constant *without* a decimal point.
2 Size limit ranging from 6 to about 10 digits. Most processors accept 6 or more.

Rules for forming a real constant
1 A constant *with* a decimal point.
2 All processors accept real constants with up to eight digits. Most processors accept more digits.

Use of exponent-form real constant
If the quantity to be represented is larger or smaller than the limit can express, a special exponent form is used. The form consists of a number with a decimal point in it followed by the letter E and a signed integer exponent. A positive exponent means the actual decimal point should be moved the number of places to the right specified by the integer. A minus exponent moves the decimal point to the left. This corresponds to scientific exponent notation. The limits of the exponent vary with different computers, but all accept E forms with a magnitude between 10^{38} and 10^{-38}.

EXAMPLES

Constant	Valid (V) or invalid (I)	If valid, integer (I) or real (R)	If invalid, why
123	V	I	
123.	V	R	
123.0	V	R	
12 3	I		No imbedded blanks allowed
123.E + 13	V	R (exponent form)	
123.E − 13	V	R (exponent form)	
3.141769984376432	I		Too many digits
987.4E + 299	I		Exponent too large

As indicated by the rules for constants and variables, different FORTRAN processors may have different limits for the number of characters in a variable name, the number of characters in a constant, and the size of the exponent in the E form. If a program is to be written for running on only one processor, the limits of that processor can be followed. Otherwise, using the minimum specifications will ensure compatibility with all FORTRAN compilers.

The different arithmetic types—integer and real—are handled differently by the computer. Integers are an exact binary-code representation of the decimal system integers, but the size of the quantity is limited and no fractional part is retained. The floating point quantities are carried in the computer in a normalized floating point form in which the computer word has two parts—the significant digits (or mantissa) and the exponent (or characteristic) by which to convert the significant digits to the actual number. The process of storing decimal fractions as binary fractions may yield very small differences of the same type as found when the common fraction $\frac{1}{3}$ is converted to a decimal fraction. The mechanics of floating point arithmetic are carried out automatically and need not concern the FORTRAN programmer. The number of significant digits in the result of a computation is limited. Eight is a common limit, although there are many compilers which exceed this and some compilers which allow the precision to be specified.

Self-testing Quiz— FORTRAN #1

Fill in the following table for constants and variables. If a form is invalid for most implementations but may be valid for some, note this difference.

		Valid or invalid	If valid, constant or variable	Integer or real	If invalid, why
1	FATHERS				
2	DAD − 0				
3	FICA				
4	INTR				
5	F145				
6	ABLE				
7	X − 14				
8	19E25				
9	18.47				
10	19876.45110				
11	98				
12	19875694315				

Operation Symbols and Intrinsic Functions

The manner in which FORTRAN provides for variable names and constants has been defined. The next step is to explain the manner in which mathematical operations are specified. FORTRAN defines an expression in the mathematical sense as a variable or as one or more constants and variables connected by operation symbols.

OPERATION SYMBOLS

Symbol	Stands for	Example
+	Addition	A + B
−	Subtraction	A − B
/	Division	A/B
*	Multiplication	A*B
**	Exponentiation	A**3

In addition to these five operation symbols, FORTRAN provides prewritten program modules that perform common mathematical functions. They are termed "intrinsic functions." The intrinsic functions are specified by writing the function name and putting the argument (expression to be operated upon) inside a set of parentheses. This is illustrated by four common intrinsic functions:

SQRT	Take square root of the expression
ABS	Take absolute value of the expression
EXP	Exponentiate e to the power represented by the expression
AMAX1	Take largest value from list in expression

EXAMPLES

Problem	FORTRAN expression
$x = \sqrt{y}$	X = SQRT (Y)
$x = \sqrt{y + b}$	X = SQRT (Y + B)
$x = |y - b|$	X = ABS (Y − B)
$x = e^{y+b}$	X = EXP (Y + B)
$x = \max(a,b,c)$	X = AMAX1 (A,B,C)

The expression for a function can include another function. As an example, X = SQRT (ABS (Y − 7)) takes the square root of the absolute value of (Y − 7).

The FORTRAN standard specifies a generic name for each function plus specific names which identify the type (integer, real, etc.) of the arguments. If the generic name is used, the compiler examines the type of the arguments and selects the correct function type. In other words, either the generic or type specific function name may be used. In the older 1966 FORTRAN, only the specific names were used, so the specific names are preferred for the sake of FORTRAN portability. A few commonly used functions are summarized in Table 17-1; additional functions are explained in Chapter 18.

There is a set of trigonometric functions (Table 17-2). The argument is real (stated in radians of an angle); the result is real.

Forming Arithmetic Expressions and Arithmetic Assignment Statements

An arithmetic assignment (replacement) statement is of the general form $v = e$ where v stands for a variable name and e stands for an arithmetic expression. The expression consists of one or more variable names and/or constants connected by operation symbols. The form $v = e$ does not necessarily mean that v is equal to e. It directs the computer to replace the previous value of the variable on the left side of the equals sign with the results of the expression on the right. Or, in other words, it assigns the value of the expression on the right to the variable name on the left of the equals sign. Thus, the statement X = X + 1.0 means that the value of X is incremented by the constant 1.0, and this new value is stored at X. If X is referred to later in the program, the new value is the one made available. Because the computer executes the expression on the right side of the equals sign and then stores the result at the location of the variable on the left, having anything but a variable name to the left of the equals sign is illegal.

TABLE 17-1 SELECTED FORTRAN INTRINSIC FUNCTIONS

Generic name	Specific name	Type of argument	Type of function result	Function performed on expression
ABS	IABS	Integer	Integer	Take absolute value
	ABS	Real	Real	
MAX	MAX0	Integer	Integer	Take largest value from list
	AMAX1	Real	Real	
MIN	MIN0	Integer	Integer	Take smallest value from list
	AMIN1	Real	Real	
SQRT	SQRT	Real	Real	Take square root
EXP	EXP	Real	Real	Exponentiate e to power represented by expression
LOG	ALOG	Real	Real	Take natural log (to base e)
LOG10	ALOG10	Real	Real	Take log to base 10
REAL	FLOAT	Integer	Real	Convert from integer to real type
INT	IFIX	Real	Integer	Convert from real to integer (truncating fractional part)

TABLE 17-2 TRIGONOMETRIC FUNCTIONS IN FORTRAN

SIMPLE TRIGONOMETRIC		ARC FUNCTIONS		HYPERBOLIC FUNCTIONS	
Name	Function	Name	Function	Name	Function
SIN	Sine	ASIN	Arcsine	SINH	Hyperbolic sine
COS	Cosine	ACOS	Arccosine	COSH	Hyperbolic cosine
TAN	Tangent	ATAN	Arctangent	TANH	Hyperbolic tangent

In a mathematical expression, there is an accepted notational form which specifies the order in which the operations are to be performed. For example, $X + \dfrac{Y}{Z}$ is not the same as $\dfrac{X + Y}{Z}$. In the first instance, Y is divided by Z, and the result is added to X; in the second, X is added to Y, and the result is divided by Z. In some cases, the order of operation is not important because operations are commutative. Thus, $X = A + B + C - D$ can be performed in any order, and the results will be identical. Mathematical notation also uses parentheses to specify the order of computation, although it is possible to have notational systems which do not use parentheses.

FORTRAN uses both a precedence or order rule and a parentheses rule to specify the way an arithmetic expression is to be handled. The *parentheses rule* is that operations will be performed in the innermost set of parentheses first (using the order rule where appropriate) and then in the next set, etc., until all operations inside parentheses have been performed. Then the remaining operations in the expression are carried out according to the precedence rule.

The *precedence rule* is that, in the absence of parentheses to indicate order, all exponentiation will be performed first, all multiplication and division next, and all addition and subtraction last. Where the precedence of operations is the same, such as multiplication and division, the operations will be performed in order from left to right.

	FORTRAN	Formula
EXAMPLES	X = A + B/C − D**2	$x = a + \dfrac{b}{c} - d^2$
	X = (A + B)/(C + D)	$x = \dfrac{a + b}{c + d}$
	X = (A + B)/C + D	$x = \dfrac{a + b}{c} + d$
	X = A*B*C + 1.5	$x = abc + 1.5$
	X = (A*B*C) + 1.5	$x = abc + 1.5$
	X = (A*B)*(C + 1.5)	$x = (ab)(c + 1.5)$
	X = A**2 + 1.0	$x = a^2 + 1$
	X = A**(Z + 1.0)	$x = a^{z+1}$

Parentheses should be used freely. If unnecessary, they do no harm, and they improve the maintainability of the program. It is better to be explicit by using parentheses than to rely on the order rules. Parentheses are also used in order to avoid having two operation symbols together. It is illegal to write A + −B where the minus is a sign relating to B. Using parentheses to separate the two operation symbols makes the expression valid: A + (−B). Parentheses are always used in pairs. A common error in writing FORTRAN is to forget the closing side of the pair.

The rules for forming arithmetic expressions and statements can now be summarized. The student should pay particular attention to the precedence rules.

RULES FOR FORMING ARITHMETIC STATEMENTS

1 The general form of an arithmetic statement is $v = e$, where v stands for any variable name and e stands for an arithmetic expression.

2 The portion of the arithmetic statement to the left of the equals sign is a variable name. It must not contain arithmetic operations.

3 The equals sign means "assign as the value of the variable on the left the result of the expression on the right." It is not an equality sign in the mathematical sense.

4 Two operation symbols may not be used next to each other.

5 Spaces may be used whenever desired to improve readability. The compiler ignores them.

6 Parentheses are used to specify order of operation and to avoid the two-operation symbol restriction. Operations inside parentheses are performed first. Parentheses must always be used in pairs.

7 In the absence of parentheses, the precedence rule for performing arithmetic operations specifies the order. Within one of the precedence levels, the operations are performed from left to right. The precedence rule is:

First—exponentiation
Second—multiplication and division
Third—addition and subtraction

Integer and Real Data in Arithmetic Expressions

Since the data types integer and real have different characteristics with respect to a fractional part, mixing them in an expression must be used with caution. If the expression has only integer-type variables and constants, the expression is integer and integer arithmetic will be used. If only real variables are used, real arithmetic will be applied. Exponents do not change the type of an expression, so a real expression may have an integer exponent without mixing the types. If the expression mixes types of variables or constants, the compiler automatically introduces a function (FLOAT or IFIX) to convert to one type, the type being the type of the result. (A warning message may also be produced in the program listing.) For example,

Expression	Converted to
X = A + B	No conversion—already a real expression
I = K + L	No conversion—already an integer expression
X = A + K	X = A + FLOAT(K)
I = K + A	I = K + IFIX(A)

The use of a real exponent for an integer variable is not allowed: (I**A); the compiler in that case converts the variable rather than the exponent: (FLOAT(I)**A).

Data types are converted across the equals sign. If the types are different, the result of the expression on the right is converted to the type of the expression on the left of the equals sign. Thus, I = X + Y will convert the sum of X and Y to an integer result called J. Any fractional part from X + Y is lost.

The FORTRAN programmer should be careful in using integer division because the fractional result is lost (truncated, not rounded), as illustrated by the following examples:

Arithmetic statement	Result
I = 3.1417	I = 3
J = 7/3	J = 2

If M = 4, N = 5 then:

X = N/M	X = 1.0 because 5/4 was truncated to 1 and then converted to a floating point 1.0
JIX = M/N	JIX = 0 because 4/5 will result in no whole numbers

It is not good programming practice to have the compiler make changes in types because it obscures the conversion process for the reader of the program. Since conversion of real to integer results in the loss of the fractional part, the programmer may not perceive the consequences of a mixed-type expression. If the program explicitly codes FLOAT or IFIX, the logic is clearer to the programmer when debugging and to those who must maintain the program.

The FORTRAN programmer should also keep in mind the fact that an integer number has an exact representation in the computer, whereas a real number may have a binary representation that is very close but not exact because some decimal fractions cannot be represented exactly in binary (see Chapter 6). This slightly inexact representation does not normally cause an error except when conversions from real to integer are involved. For example, assume KMONT = 12 in the following expression:

IDAY = INT(2.6*FLOAT(KMONT)−0.2)

The answer should be 31 but may be 30. The result of 2.6 * 12.0 − 0.2 is represented in the computer (in binary) as 30.99999. . . . If the result were to be printed out, it would be 31 because the compiler would make the small rounding adjustment required before printing. However, in internal processing, the truncation function is performed before any rounding adjustment; it merely drops the fractional part. Such difficulties as the above happen very seldom in programming, but the student should be aware of the possibility. The program can, in such cases, be written to include a small rounding factor.

RULES FOR INTEGER AND REAL TYPES IN EXPRESSIONS

1 If data types are mixed in the expression, variables or constants that are of a type different from the result type will be converted by fixing or floating. Good programming practice is to explicitly code these FLOAT and IFIX conversions. Alternative generic junction names for conversion are REAL and INT.

2 In the statement $a = b$, if a is of a different type than b, the results of b will be translated to the type of a. If the conversion is from real to integer, the fractional part of the expression result will be truncated.

3 Fractional parts from division of integer variables are truncated.

4 The forms of exponentiation are
   (a) Integer expression with integer exponent
   (b) Real expression with real exponent
   (c) Real expression with integer exponent
   The exponent may be any arithmetic expression meeting these type restrictions.

5 The expression containing an integer expression to real exponent is converted by floating the integer expression.

Self-testing Quiz—
FORTRAN #2

1

Expression or statement	Valid, invalid, or mixed type	If invalid or mixed, why
(a) A**2+1		
(b) A**(2+1)		
(c) A**(B+C/D)		
(d) A/B+D/3		
(e) IX+JX+4		
(f) KX = A+BI		
(g) FUN = SQRT (A + AXEL/BETA)		
(h) X = (A+B)/((C+D)*E*I)		
(i) X+Y = Z*ALPHA		
(j) J = I**A		
(k) X = A**I		

2 If A = 3.0, B = 2.5, I = 3, and J = 2, what will be the result of the following statements?

(a) X = A/B   (c) KIX = J/I
(b) K = I/J   (d) NIX = I+2/J

3 Write the FORTRAN statements for the following formulas:

(a) $X = \sqrt{\dfrac{a+b}{4}}$ (e) $Y = \log_e x$

(b) $X = \sqrt[3]{\dfrac{a}{b}} + 2$ (f) $r^2 = x^2 + y^2$ (find r)

(c) $Y = e^x$ (g) Volume of sphere $= \dfrac{4}{3}\pi r^3$ (using 3.1417 as value of π)

(d) $X = 2i^3 + ab/d$

4 Write the formulas for the following FORTRAN statements:

(a) PV = A/(1.0+AI)**N   (d) Y = EXP(−X**2)
(b) AREA = 3.1417*R**2   (e) RHO = A*COS(THETA)
(c) DISCR = B**2−4.0*A*C   (f) X = A+B/C**D*E*F+1.0

5 Write the following FORTRAN statements, eliminating unnecessary parentheses:

Formula	
(a) $x = \dfrac{a+b}{ef}$	X = (A + B)/(E * F)
(b) $x = abc + 1$	X = (A*B*C) + 1.0
(c) $x = \left(\dfrac{ab}{c}\right)d$	X = ((A*B)/C)*D

Elementary Input and Output

FORTRAN provides for the use of several input/output (I/O) devices. The devices typically available are:

Input	Output
Card reader	Printer
Magnetic tape unit	Magnetic tape unit
Disk storage unit	Disk storage unit
Console typewriter	Console typewriter
	Card punch
Terminal (typewriter or visual display unit)	Terminal (typewriter or visual display unit)

In this chapter, only the elementary input/output instructions using the card reader, card punch, and printer are presented. The magnetic tape and magnetic disk instructions are presented in Chapter 18. Since they are similar in purpose and form to the input/output instructions explained here, no difficulty should be encountered in learning to program additional input/output devices that may be available.

Input/Output Instructions

In the basic FORTRAN, obtaining data from an input device and writing data on an output device involve a pair of statements. The pair consists of the input/output command and the FORMAT statement. The input/output statement specifies what is to be done, what unit is to be used, and what variables are involved. The FORMAT statement specifies the form of the data being read in or written out.

Since the input or output operation involves the pair of statements, provision must be made for specifying the FORMAT statement to be used with a given input/output statement. This identification is accomplished by assigning a unique statement number to the FORMAT statement and then including this statement number in the input or output statement.

The FORMAT statement describes the form of the data to be read, printed, punched, etc., so that the input or output statement need specify only the variables involved, the order in which they are to appear, and the equipment to be used. The input/output statement specifies the variables by listing the variable names in the order in which they are to be used. There are two basic input/output instructions—READ (u,f) list and WRITE (u,f) list, when f refers to the FORMAT statement reference number and u refers to the designation for the input/output unit.

The unit designation is an integer constant or an integer variable. Both of the following are correct forms:

READ (1,905)A,B,C
READ (NREAD,905)A,B,C

There are no standard unit designations; they differ among manufacturers and even different compilers of the same manufacturer. If this is so, how can a program written for one computer be run on another without substantial change? Two methods can be used. The first is to use an integer variable name for the unit and define its value either by a statement in the program (one statement change would change all designators) or by reading the value of the variable.

$$NREAD = 60 \qquad \text{If } 60 = \text{unit designation for card reader.}$$

$$\vdots$$

READ (NREAD,905)A,B,C

The second (and more common) method is to specify the unit designation by means of a job control card. In other words, the job control card allows the programmer to use any integer number in the program and specify to the system that it designates a card reader, etc. In this text, a card reader is designated by the integer 1 and a printer by 3.

An alternate form of the input and output statement is included in both the full 1966 and the new FORTRAN standard (but not subset FORTRAN) and is provided in most implementations. The form eliminates the unit designation. READ means read from the standard device (generally card reader), and PRINT means to output using the printer.

Unit designation form	Name designation form
READ (1,905)A,B	READ 905,A,B
WRITE (3,910)A,B	PRINT 910,A,B

Additional input and output features (including input and output without formats) are described in Chapter 18.

INPUT/OUTPUT INSTRUCTIONS

Symbols used in description

u = unit designation (integer variable or integer constant) for input/output unit. Unit designations differ among implementations.

f = statement number of format statement to be used with the input or output instruction.

list = list of variables which are to be read, printed, punched, etc., in the order in which they are to be used. The variable names are separated by commas.

Form of instructions

READ (u, f) list

Reads from an input unit the quantities associated with the listed variable names and puts them into storage for use by the program.

WRITE (u, f) list

Writes variables using an output unit. Form of output varies with output unit and FORMAT statement.

Alternate forms of unit designation (not always implemented)

READ f, list

Reads from a punched card the quantities associated with the listed variable names and puts them into memory.

PRINT f, list

Prints a line of output using the quantities represented by the list of variable names.

| EXAMPLES | READ (1,905)A,B,C⎫ | Read from the card reader with variable names A, B, and C. |
| | *READ 905,A,B,C ⎭ | Read according to the FORMAT specified by statement 905. |

WRITE (3,910)I,BETA⎫   Write on printer the quantities assigned to variable names I and
*PRINT 910,I,BETA ⎭   BETA. Use format specified by statement 910.

*Full FORTRAN

In summary, the basic input/output instructions for FORTRAN require only four elements: the command word (READ, WRITE), the input/output unit designation, the FORMAT statement reference number, and the list of variable names in the order they are to be read, printed, punched, etc.

The FORMAT Statement

The purpose of the FORMAT statement is to describe the form of the data being read or written. The FORMAT statement for all input/output media is the same. In fact, a single FORMAT statement can be used to define data to be read from a card reader, to be punched into cards, or to be printed on the printer as long as the form of the data is the same in all cases. The FORMAT statement does not have to appear next to the input/output statement using it. The statement number is sufficient identification, so that the FORMAT statement can be written before or after the input/output command using it. Some programmers put a FORMAT statement next to the first input/output statement referencing it; others group all FORMAT statements together at the beginning or end of the program. A convention used in this text is to number FORMAT statements beginning with 900 and to place each one next to the statement which references it.

In order to describe the form of the data for input/output, three elements must be specified or implied:

1 *Type of editing* This can specify real, integer, real with exponent (or other types to be explained later).

2 *Field size* This is the number of columns on punched cards or printer paper, or character positions on other storage media, that are to be made available for storing the quantity. The quantity need not occupy all the field, but cannot occupy more columns or positions than specified as being available.

3 *Location of decimal point* This is expressed as the number of places from the right. This specification is eliminated from the FORMAT statement for integer quantities (because it has no meaning).

The FORMAT statement consists of the statement number, then the word FORMAT followed by specifications separated by commas. Each specification consists of three parts. The first part is a single-letter edit descriptor as follows:

Letter	Type of quantity
F	Real
E	Exponent form of real
I	Integer

The next part of the FORMAT statement is the field size in numbers of spaces or columns. This is the maximum number of character spaces or columns the quantity is to occupy. If the number takes less than the field size (for output), the number is right-justified (number starts at right side of field), and the unused positions to the left are blank. The field size is limited by the size of the media being used. A punched card has only 80 columns, and printer paper has about 132 spaces, depending on the printer being used. I8 in a FORMAT statement says that the variable being formatted is an integer variable and occupies eight spaces or less. The field size for output should allow for the sign of the quantity. For real output, the size should provide space for a decimal point. An X specification means a field is to be skipped and not processed. The number of positions to be skipped are written, followed by X. 13X means that the next field of 13 positions is to be skipped.

The third part of the FORMAT statement, used with E and F fields, is the location of the decimal point in the field. The general form of the F and E field specifications is Fw.d and Ew.d, where w is the field width and d is the number of positions in the field to the right of the decimal. In a field of 10, a specification of F10.3 will position the decimal in the fourth position from the right.

The field specification is used in input in a slightly different way than in output. The use in output will be discussed first, and then the differences will be noted.

In output, the computer positions the data in the field by means of the decimal point position. The integer digits are positioned to the left of the decimal point, and the fractional digits are positioned to the right. 0 for d (number of integer places) in the F form will position a decimal at the right. Integer numbers are right-justified. Two conditions can occur—in one the digits exceed the positions available, in the other the number of digits is less than the number of positions available.

1 Digits exceed positions available.

(*a*) The condition when the number of integer digits exceeds the integer field to the left of the decimal is called "overflow." This will result in a field of asterisks to indicate overflow. For example, 67943.2 to be printed with a FORMAT statement of F8.4 will cause overflow as shown, and the output will be a field of asterisks (or other overflow error indications).

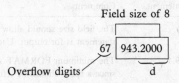

Field size of 8

67 | 943.2000

Overflow digits   d

(*b*) If the number of fractional digits exceeds the fractional field size (specified by d portion of specification), the excess digits will be truncated after rounding (but be careful here). No error indication occurs. For example, 7.6543 printed with F8.2 would print 7.65. The 43 would be truncated and lost.

2 Digits do not fill field.

(*a*) If digits in integer portion do not fill all positions, the unused positions to the left are filled with blanks.
Examples (b's stand for blanks)
98.5 and F10.1 = bbbbbb98.5
145 and I6 = bbb145
Since the unused places to the left are filled with blanks, larger than necessary field size is one way that spaces can be inserted in output.

(*b*) If fractional digits do not fill the fractional portion of the field, the remaining positions are filled with zeros. This applies, of course, only to floating point fields.

EXAMPLES   347.56 and F10.5 = b347.56000
347.56 and F10.3 = bbb347.560
675 and I8 = bbbbb675

It is necessary to leave a space for negative quantity when a minus sign is to be printed. It is good practice to always allow for a sign in the output field. The number of digits to be written out in an F field is therefore two less than the field width (allowing for the sign and the decimal point).

In many printers, the first character position on the line is used to specify carriage control for vertical spacing of the output. It is therefore good practice to format data so that the first space on the line is blank (no carriage action) except where a specific spacing is to be performed.

The problem of truncation and overflow means that, where the result has any unknown range of magnitude, the E form is to be preferred. An E specification can be written so that it will always show the maximum number of significant digits in the result. This is done by making the field size seven positions larger than the number of significant digits obtained from the compiler. For example, with eight significant digits, E15.8 will print all significant digits, plus the exponent to convert to the actual form.

EXAMPLES	Data	FORMAT statement	Comments
	19	I3	The field size should allow for a sign if the FORMAT statement is for output. Use actual field size for input.
	493.7652	F9.4	The minimum FORMAT specification for printing is 9, since a space should be left for the sign.
	−0.131E+13	E10.3	Format should allow for sign (minus or blank), zero, decimal point, and four places for the exponent. The exponent is in the form ±Enn, ±0nn, or ±nnn. This means the field size is at least 7 more than number of significant digits to be written out.

The FORMAT statement is treated differently with a READ punched-card statement than with a WRITE statement in two cases. First, no provision need be made for an input sign unless it occupies a column by being punched. If values are negative, the sign must be punched in the input (as a leading −), but if all values are positive, no sign is needed. (The commercial convention of an overpunch to show a negative number is not used by FORTRAN.) The second difference is in the decimal point. A decimal point punched in the data takes precedence over the decimal location specification of the FORMAT statement. The advantage in punching the actual decimal point is that the real number may then appear anywhere in the specified field. If the decimal is not punched, the real number (and all integer values) must be right-justified because the decimal point for an input variable without a decimal punched in it is counted from the right side of the field just as if any unfilled positions on the right side of the field were filled with zeros. An F specification for input will accept data in decimal format, or in an exponent format. For example, 4537.6, 0.45376E+04, or 0.45376+04 can all be read by an F specification.

The basic approach to input and output has now been explained. The next section of this chapter explains how to put headings and other notes on the output from the program. In Chapter 18, additional input/output methods and specifications are explained, including ways to read or write more than one record using a single instruction. For the present, one instruction is assumed to read, write, punch, etc., one card or one printed line.

FORMAT STATEMENT

General form

s FORMAT (list of specifications separated by commas) where s is a statement number

Form of specifications

Fw.d   Real variable
Ew.d   Exponent form   w stands for field size
Iw   Integer variable   d stands for number of decimal positions to right of decimal
wX   Skip field

Fitting data to field size

1   Data is justified to the right in the field, except in the case of data being input in which a punched decimal position overrides a FORMAT-specified decimal position.

2   If integer positions of result are greater than field size, an overflow error condition results and a field of asterisks is output.

3   If significant digits in fractional portion exceed number of positions in field to right of decimal point, the quantity to remain is rounded and the excess digits are truncated.

4   Using the E form can ensure maximum accuracy without truncation or overflow. The d portion should be the same as the number of significant digits with the field width 7 higher. For example, E15.8 will ensure maximum accuracy if the maximum number of significant digits is 8.

The following examples illustrate the FORMAT rules:

1   In output, the field size should allow a space for the sign, and real numbers must also allow a space for a decimal point, as shown by the following table:

Form of variable	To be printed or punched as	FORTRAN FORMAT statement
XXX$_\wedge$XXX	XXX.	F5.0
XXXXXX0000000$_\wedge$	0.XXXXXE+12	E12.5
−XXXXX	−XXXXX	I6
−XX$_\wedge$XXXXXX	−XX.XX	F6.2
X	X	I2

2   The following data is packed on a punched card without spaces between. Variable names are assigned as shown. No decimal points are punched, but the proper scaling is shown by the carets.

   X   Y1   YJ   YK   KIX

9$_\wedge$8 7 8 9$_\wedge$4 1$_\wedge$0 9 4 8 6 7 6 5 4$_\wedge$8 8

The statement to read these variables would be as follows: (Note that no allowance is made for a sign or a decimal point in the input field size because none appears in the data.)

     READ (1,900)X,Y1,YJ,YK,KIX
900   FORMAT (F2.1,F4.1,F4.3,F6.0,I2)

3   In Example 2, statements to read only X and YK would be:

     READ (1,900)X,YK
900   FORMAT (F2.1,8X,F6.0)

4 For E FORMAT input from cards, the punching of the E is optional. The following are all valid, assuming the same quantity:

XXXXX.XE12
XXXXX.X + 12
.XXXXXX + 17

Note that the exponent changed when the decimal point was moved.

5 An output in exponent form using E15.8 may appear (depending on the compiler) as $\pm$0.XXXXXXXXEyy, $\pm$0.XXXXXXXX$\pm$yyy, or $\pm$0.XXXXXXXX$\pm$0yy.

Self-testing Quiz—
FORTRAN #3

1 Read the following data from a punched card. The data is referenced by the variable names ALPHA, BETA, IOTA, and JIX.

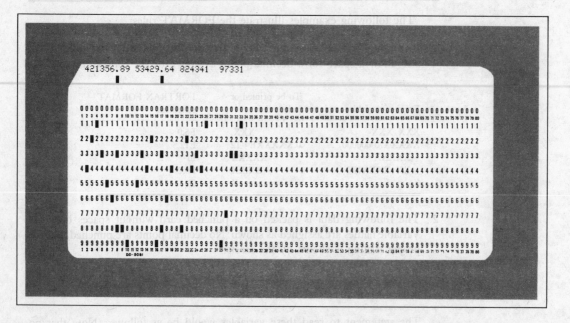

Note that the sizes of the fields, including blank spaces at the left, are:

Variable	Field size	Columns
ALPHA	10	1–10
BETA	9	11–19
IOTA	7	20–26
JIX	7	27–33

2 Print the above variables in reverse order. Leave two spaces between ALPHA and BETA, not counting the sign position. Do not use the X to skip spaces.

3 Print the variables IOTA and BETA. Do not print the fractional portion of BETA. Do not use a field size larger than absolutely necessary, but provide 10 spaces (not counting the space allowed for a sign) on either side and between the quantities.

4 What will be the result of the following set of WRITE and FORMAT statements if X = 1.0375 and IYEAR = 95?

```
        WRITE (3,900) IYEAR,X
900     FORMAT (I10,F10.2)
```

5 What is the minimum specification for printing or punching the following variables? (Remember to allow for decimal point and sign.) X's stand for nonzero integers.

Form of variable	To be printed as	FORTRAN FORMAT statement
(a) XXXX∧XXXX	XXXX.XX	
(b) XXXX∧0000	XXXX.0	
(c) −XX∧XXXXXX	−XX.XXXXXX	
(d) ∧XXXXXXXX	.XXX	
(e) XXXX	XXXX	
(f) −XXXXXXX0000000∧	−0.XXXXXXXXE + 14	

6 Write a complete FORTRAN program, punch it or enter via a terminal, and run it for the following problem: In the year 1626, Peter Minuit purchased Manhattan Island from the Indians for $24 worth of beads, cloth, and trinkets. Suppose the Indians had taken $24 cash and invested it; how much would they have in 1976 (the Bicentennial year), assuming interest is compounded quarterly? Do the following for the problem:

(a) Prepare a program description block and a list of variables block using comment lines.

(b) Use a single input-process-output block to code the processing.

    (1) Read the annual interest rate from a punched card. Punch the decimal. For example, use 6 percent, which will be .06.

    (2) Compute the accumulated amount using the formula $a = 24.0 \, (1 + i/4)^{4n}$ where i is the annual interest rate and n is the number of years.

    (3) Print out the interest rate used and the result twice, using both F (say, F13.0) and E edit descriptors (say, E16.8).

    (4) The last two statement lines are STOP and END (to be explained in the next section).

Code the FORTRAN statements and compare your program with the sample program in the answers to the Self-testing Quiz. Make necessary corrections. Include the data card and job control cards. Compile, debug, and execute the program. If your answer differs from the result shown in Figure 17-9 (in the answers), explain the difference.

Providing
Descriptive Labels
and Headings
on Output

It is frequently desirable to provide descriptive labels and headings on output (primarily printed output). A program to compute the variance and standard deviation of an array of numbers might have an output such as the following:

THE VARIANCE IS	XXXXXX.XX
THE STANDARD DEVIATION IS	XXX.XX
THE NUMBER OF OBSERVATIONS IS	XXX

The descriptive character output illustrated above is sometimes termed "Hollerith output." FORMAT specifications permit any combination of letters, numbers, and special characters on a line of output. There are essentially four methods for providing headings and other character output.

1 H edit descriptor in the FORMAT statement
2 Apostrophe edit descriptors in the FORMAT statement
3 A set of characters in list-directed output
4 Character data stored internally and referenced by variable names

Only the first two are explained in this chapter; the last two are described in Chapter 18. The H edit descriptor is the traditional method but tends to be error-prone. The apostrophe method is therefore preferred (but may not be available on older implementations of FORTRAN).

The use of the H edit descriptor for character output is quite simple. It involves writing out the output exactly as it is to appear (including blanks) and then counting the number of character positions occupied. The number of positions is followed by an H to indicate that the specified number of positions following is not to be translated, but is to be transferred exactly as written to the output line. For example, to print THE ANSWER IS which takes up 13 spaces, the H specification of the FORMAT statement would be 13HTHE ANSWER IS. As noted previously, standard FORTRAN specifies that the first character on the output line for a printer is not printed but is used for printer carriage control (explained in Chapter 18). A blank in the first position of the print line will not cause any special line control. Therefore, Hollerith fields, which begin at the left on the line, should have the first space blank (unless the character is a line-control character).

The H specification may be placed in with a list, or it may be the sole output of the WRITE (or PRINT) statement. For example, if the answer is the variable Z which has a specification of F10.2, the set of WRITE and FORMAT statements to print THE ANSWER ISbb±XXXXXX.XX will be (b stands for a blank):

```
        WRITE (3,900)Z
900  FORMAT (16H THE ANSWER IS    ,F10.2)
```

Note that the H specification provides for two spaces after IS. The blanks could also have been provided by making the field size for Z two spaces wider. Since the number is right-justified, the extra two spaces would have appeared at the left. The Hollerith line starts at the left side of the page, so the first position is blank. A heading such as ANALYSIS PROGRAM, to be centered on a page with 132 printing spaces, would be written with a WRITE statement having no variable list, as follows:

```
      WRITE (3,900) [or PRINT 900]
900   FORMAT (58X, 16HANALYSIS PROGRAM)
```

Note that it was easier to skip the 58 spaces to the center than to include these in the H specification. The separating comma in the FORMAT statement, necessary with E, F, and I formats, is optional with the X and H forms.

The apostrophe method encloses the characters to be output in apostrophes. If the field to be output contains an apostrophe, two consecutive apostrophes are used.

EXAMPLES	Statements	Output
	WRITE (3,900)	
	900 FORMAT (' NOW IS THE TIME.')	NOW IS THE TIME.
	WRITE (3,910)	
	910 FORMAT (' I CAN''T DO IT.')	I CAN'T DO IT.

Self-testing Quiz—
FORTRAN #4

Write a set of PRINT and FORMAT statements to provide the following lines of output. Write each using both the H and apostrophe edit descriptors. A page is assumed to have 132 spaces. Remember that the first space on the line should be blank.

1 $\longleftrightarrow^{25}$ THE TOLERANCE IS CALCULATED ATbbXXX.XX

2 $\longleftrightarrow^{10}$ AMOUNT OF SAVINGS IS $ XXX.XX

3 NUMBER IS XXXX
4 THE END.

5 $\longleftrightarrow^{5}$ ITEM $\longleftrightarrow^{10}$ AMOUNT

6 Write a complete program (including a description block and a list of variables block). A bank offers continuous compounding at 6 percent annual interest. However, interest is actually paid quarterly. If the savings account is closed prior to the quarter-end, no interest is paid for that quarter. The bank's competitor offers quarterly compounding, also at an annual rate of 6 percent. The difference is not huge, but continuous compounding does provide some additional income to the investor. Given an amount to invest and the number of quarters the investment will remain in the bank, compute the amount of interest earned under both methods and the compound amount under continuous interest. Print out a message similar to the following example output (try an investment of $1000 for 15 years or 60 quarters at 6 percent per year):

IF YOU INVEST $ XXXXX.XX TODAY AT XX.XX PERCENT

AND LEAVE IT FOR XX QUARTERS COMPOUNDED CONTINUOUSLY

YOU WILL EARN $XXXXX.XX INTEREST

AND RECEIVE BACK A TOTAL OF $XXXXX.XX

YOU RECEIVE $XXX.XX MORE USING CONTINUOUS

COMPOUNDING THAN QUARTERLY COMPOUNDING.

The following formulas can be used:

$$c = pe^{ni}$$

where c = compound amount with continuous compounding
  p = amount invested
  n = number of periods (quarters in this case)
  i = interest per period (quarterly interest or .06/4 for the suggested data for this problem)
  e = exponential (use the EXP function)

$$a = p(1 + i)^n$$

where a = compound amount with periodic compounding p, i, and n as above

The interest in both cases is the compound amount (c or a) minus the investment p. The above output requires six FORMAT statements; a method of using a single FORMAT statement for multiple line output is explained in Chapter 18.

Control Statements

FORTRAN statements in a program are executed sequentially. In order to alter the sequence of execution, a control statement is used. This can be either an unconditional transfer (GO TO) or a conditional transfer. It is frequently desirable to be able to transfer control on the basis of the value of a variable or the results of some computation. Four statements are available for this purpose in FORTRAN:

1 Computed GO TO
2 Logical IF
3 Arithmetic IF
4 Assigned GO TO (Chapter 18)

STOP, PAUSE, and END control statements are also discussed in this section.

GO TO Statement   When the sequence of execution is to be broken, control must go to some statement other than the next one. The identification by which a statement is referenced is the statement label (statement number). A statement label is an integer number of from one to five digits. The statement label is placed in columns 1 to 5 of the coding form as a reference number for the statement which follows on the line. Since the statement numbers are for reference, they do not need any particular sequence, but it is good programming practice to put them in a sequence and to have a unique sequence for each program block. Any statement which will be referenced in the program must have a statement number. Otherwise, a statement number is optional.

The unconditional transfer-of-control statement in FORTRAN is

GO TO n (or GOTO n)

where n is a statement label. When this statement is encountered, the next statement to be executed will be the one numbered by n. After statement n is executed, control continues with the statements following n. Because excessive use of GO TOs may make a program difficult to debug and to maintain, they should be used with care.

Computed   The computed GO TO statement transfers control to one of several possible
GO TO Statement   statements based on the integer value of an expression:

GO TO $(s_1, s_2, s_3, \ldots, s_n)$, integer value of expression

In the definition, the s's refer to statement numbers. If the integer value of the expression is 1, control will go to the first statement number listed; if the variable value is 2, control will go to the second, etc. The comma following the right parenthesis was required in the old standard but is now optional. Some other compilers require an integer variable for the expression, but the newer compilers will perform truncation if a real variable or real expression is used. The number of statement numbers in the list may be limited in some processors; in others, there is no fixed limit. If the variable value is negative, 0, or greater than the number of statement labels, control passes to the next statement.

An example will illustrate the use of the GO TO statement. A program to analyze the distribution of amount of sales by invoice may set up the following four categories (it is assumed that no sale exceeds $2999):

Less than $500
$500 to $999
$1000 to $1999
$2000 to $2999

The sales are punched on a card in the form XXXX.XX. A partial program and flowchart are shown in Figure 17-5.

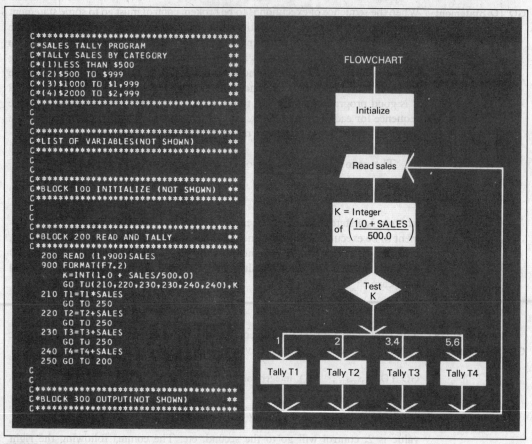

```
C*************************************
C*SALES TALLY PROGRAM              **
C*TALLY SALES BY CATEGORY          **
C*(1)LESS THAN $500                **
C*(2)$500 TO $999                  **
C*(3)$1000 TO $1,999               **
C*(4)$2000 TO $2,999               **
C*************************************
C
C
C*************************************
C*LIST OF VARIABLES(NOT SHOWN)     **
C*************************************
C
C
C*************************************
C*BLOCK 100 INITIALIZE (NOT SHOWN) **
C*************************************
C
C
C*************************************
C*BLOCK 200 READ AND TALLY         **
C*************************************
      200 READ (1,900)SALES
      900 FORMAT(F7.2)
          K=INT(1.0 + SALES/500.0)
          GO TO(210,220,230,230,240,240),K
      210 T1=T1+SALES
          GO TO 250
      220 T2=T2+SALES
          GO TO 250
      230 T3=T3+SALES
          GO TO 250
      240 T4=T4+SALES
      250 GO TO 200
C
C
C*************************************
C*BLOCK 300 OUTPUT(NOT SHOWN)      **
C*************************************
```

FLOWCHART

Initialize

Read sales

$$K = \text{Integer of } \left(\frac{1.0 + SALES}{500.0} \right)$$

Test K

| 1 | 2 | 3,4 | 5,6 |

Tally T1   Tally T2   Tally T3   Tally T4

FIGURE 17-5 Partial program and flowchart for sales-tally problem.

The program in Figure·17-5 does not provide any way to stop the program. The program will terminate when there are no more input cards and the operating system detects the end-of-job card.

The sales-tally program can be used to illustrate some good programming practices. The GO TO (in the newer FORTRAN standard) could have been written as:

GO TO (. . . .) 1.0 + SALES/500.0

It was written in two steps for clarity in the example. Also, the INT (or IFIX) function which takes the integer portion of the result is redundant because there will be truncation across the equals sign to the integer variable K. However, using an explicit function even when redundant is recommended because it makes the operation clearer and reduces the chance for error in understanding and maintaining the program.

There must be GO TOs following each tally instruction. Note that all of the GO TOs are forward to a single statement at the end of the group which transfers back to begin with a new card. This is usually easier to follow than with frequent backward transfers.

The sales-tally program also illustrates the need in programming for initializing variables which are to be used as accumulators. In this case, T1, T2, T3, and T4 must be set to zero before use. The reason for this zeroing is the form of the accumulator statement which adds the specified variable to the previous contents of the accumulating variable to form a new subtotal.

T1 = T1 + SALES

T1 represents the subtotal to which the sales in class 1 should be added. The first time the statement is executed, the subtotal should be zero. The only way to ensure this is to clear it by a statement to put zeros in the accumulator variable. For example, a statement T1 = 0 will set the variable T1 to zero. This procedure is analogous to clearing an adding machine by pressing "total" before adding a set of numbers.

Logical IF Statement

There are two IF statements: the logical or relational IF statement and the arithmetic IF statement. For clarity of programming, the logical IF is always preferred even in cases where two logical IF statements are required to do the same test as a single arithmetic IF. The new FORTRAN standard contains FORTRAN features that greatly enhance the basic IF statement. These enhancements are explained in Chapter 18.

The general form of the logical IF statement is

IF (e) st

where e = a logical (relational) expression and st is almost any executable statement. In a simple case, the logical expression consists of two arithmetic expressions (which may be only variable names) separated by a relational operator. If the relation is true, the statement following is executed; if false, control passes to the statement following the logical IF statement.

The relational operators are

Operator	Representing
.LT.	Less than
.LE.	Less than or equal to
.EQ.	Equal to
.NE.	Not equal to
.GT.	Greater than
.GE.	Greater than or equal to

Note that a period precedes and follows the operators to differentiate them from variable names. Examples of logical IF statements are

IF (A .GT. B) GO TO 3
IF (SQRT (X) .LE. 5.0) X = 10.0

If control is to go to 150 if A is negative, 160 if A is zero, and 140 if A is positive, two logical IF statements are required:

IF (A .LT. 0) GO TO 150
IF (A .EQ. 0) GO TO 160
140〜〜〜〜〜〜(A is positive)

If two or more relational expressions are to be compared, the logical operators .AND. and .OR. may be used. .NOT. is used to indicate negation (opposite) of the relation. The 1977 FORTRAN adds XOR and EQV logical operations. XOR is for the logical exclusive OR which results in a true condition when one or the other but not both expressions are true. EQV is logical equivalence. When ANDs and ORs are used in the same expression, the parenthesis rule (inside parentheses first) and an order rule can be applied. In the absence of parentheses, the order or precedence rules are applied:

1 Arithmetic operations (using the precedence rule for them)
2 NOT
3 AND
4 OR and XOR
5 EQV

Operations having the same precedence are executed from left to right.

Example	Explanation
IF (PAY .GT. 45.0 .AND. AGE .LE. 17.0) TALLY = TALLY + 1.0	Add 1 to TALLY only if both PAY .GT. 45 and AGE .LE. 17 are true.
IF (HRS. .GE. 60.0 .OR. OT .EQ. 10) GO TO 10	Transfer control to statement 10 if either of the relational statements is true.
IF (HRS. .LE. 60 .AND. HRS. .GT. 0 .OR. CODE = 1.0) GO TO 200	Transfer to 200 if HRS. are less than or equal to 60 and are greater than zero or transfer to 200 if CODE = 1.0.
IF (.NOT. (CODE .EQ. 1)) GO TO 300	Transfer to 300 if CODE is not equal to 1 (could have been coded simpler).

The logical IF statement can be used to explicitly provide for the end of a program. In the sales-tally program, the program kept reading cards until all cards were exhausted, at which point an attempted read caused the operating system to terminate the job. An explicit method of termination is to place a code in a special last card following all data and to test each card for the code. For example, a sales value of 9999999 might be used in the termination data card. Following the READ statement, sales would be tested as follows:

IF   (SALES .EQ. 9999999.) GO TO 300
     (where 300 is output to be performed after all data has been processed).

Another method of specifying the action to be taken when the end of the data has been reached is the END control item in the input statement. This may not be available in some older FORTRANs. When available, it is very useful. The form of the item is END = s where s is the statement to which control should go when the data has all been read. As an example, assume the read statement below is to be executed until there are no more data cards, at which time control is to go to statement 400.

READ (1,900,END = 400) A,B,C

In writing tests of equality and in other statements, the programmer must be aware of the consequences of the two types of data representation. The integer representation is exact, and therefore it is valid to test for equality on integers. A test for equality on a real quantity developed through computation and a real constant may not show equality even though they are apparently the same because of slight rounding and conversion differences. If it appears that such differences can arise, the program should be written to allow for them. If processing should stop when a variable ANSR is 45.0 (or more), the program should be written: IF(ANSR.GE.45.0)STOP rather than IF(ANSR.EQ.45.0)STOP.

Arithmetic   The form of the arithmetic IF statement for conditional transfer of control is:
IF Statement

IF (expression) s_1,s_2,s_3

where the expression may be a variable name or arithmetic expression. If the expression, when evaluated, is negative, i.e., less than zero, control goes to the first statement label listed; if zero, to the second statement number; and if positive, to the third. The statement labels are separated by commas.

The arithmetic IF statement is versatile because most tests can be made to fit the less-than, equal-to, and greater-than trichotomy. However, it tends to be error-prone in reading programs, so the logical IF is preferred for program clarity. The statement A:B (compare A with B), which is flowcharted with a decision symbol, is programmed with an arithmetic IF statement as follows:

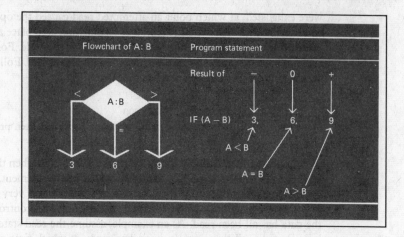

The following examples will illustrate the versatility of the IF statements ($>$ means greater than, $<$ means less than, $\geq$ means greater than or equal to, $\leq$ means less than or equal to):

Condition and transfer	Arithmetic IF statement	Logical IF statement
1 $X>6$, go to 17; $X\leq6$, go to 98	IF $(X-6.0)98,98,17$	IF (X.GT.6)GO TO 17 IF (X.LE.6)GO TO 98
2 INDEX ≤98, go to 2; INDEX >98, go to 4	IF (INDEX -98)2,2,4	IF (INDEX.LE.98)GO TO 2 IF (INDEX.GT.98)GO TO 4
3 If the absolute value of $(X^3-39)>158$, go to 17; otherwise go to 12.	IF (ABS(X**3 -39.0) -158.0)12,12,17	IF ((ABS(X**3 -39.0)) .GT.158.0)GO TO 17 GO TO 12

The logical IF alternative illustrates a programming practice. In the third example, if the expression is not true (does not go to 17), then it is by default sent to 12. In the first two examples, the test is repeated (even though not necessary) because it makes the logic completely specified. Either approach may be used, but keep in mind the value of some redundant code for clarity of program logic.

The STOP, PAUSE, and END Statements

STOP, PAUSE, and END are control statements that may be conveniently discussed at this time.

The STOP and PAUSE statements are identical except for the fact that a STOP statement brings the program execution to a final halt, while a PAUSE statement brings the program to a temporary halt such that performing the start or run procedure will continue the program at the next statement following the PAUSE. Thus, both statements bring the program to a halt, but the PAUSE is restartable, and the STOP is not. STOP does not physically stop the computer, but terminates the program and turns control of the computer back to the operating system (that set of computer routines which directs the operation of the computer system).

STOP AND PAUSE STATEMENTS

STOP } PAUSE}	Basic forms
STOP n } PAUSE n }	n is the integer number displayed when the statement is executed. It is limited to four octal digits in Basic FORTRAN and five octal digits in full FORTRAN.

A program may have many STOP and PAUSE statements in it, and it is useful to know which one of these statements has caused the computer program to halt. An integer number written following the STOP or PAUSE statement will be displayed on the printer when that statement is executed.

A STOP statement is frequently used as the statement to which control is transferred if a condition which ought never to occur does occur. For example, suppose a variable X is to be tested to see if it is zero or positive. If zero, control goes to statement 198; if positive, to statement 300. If X should never be negative, what should the programmer do? The statement might be written IF (X .LE. 0) GO TO 98 using the reasoning that X cannot be negative. However, a prudent course is to code an error message or a STOP statement as the point to which control is transferred if this illegal condition should occur.

IF (X .LT.0) STOP 20

The code of 20 indicates the reason for the program stopping before successful execution.

The END statement is a compiler-directing statement and is not translated. It is the signal to the compiler routine that there are no more statements to be processed. It must therefore appear as the last statement of each routine compiled as a separate program.

SUMMARY OF CONTROL STATEMENTS

Notation
s stands for a statement number.
$s_1, s_2, \ldots, s_m$ stands for a series of m statement numbers.

Unconditional transfer
GO TO s   Transfers control unconditionally to s.

Conditional transfer
GO TO $(s_1, s_2, s_3, \ldots, s_m)$,i   Transfers control to s_1 if value of variable i is 1; to s_2, if value is
                                     2, etc.

IF (e) st	Executes statement st if relation expression e is true; otherwise continues with next statement.

IF (expression) s_1, s_2, s_3

If result of expression inside parentheses is:	Control goes to:
− (negative)	s_1
0 (zero)	s_2
+ (positive)	s_3

Enhancements to IF statements are presented in Chapter 18.

Other control statements

STOP or STOP n	Stops program without provision for restarting. STOP n displays n when stop occurs.
PAUSE or PAUSE n	Halts program; operator must take action to start up where stopped.
END	Signals compiler that there are no more statements in the program to compile. Last physical statement in program.

Self-testing Quiz—
FORTRAN #5

Write program segments to perform the operations indicated.

1 If a customer class is 1, transfer control to statement 100; if 2, to 200, etc., up to statement 700 if the value of the class is 7. CLASS is the name of the variable.

2 If the square root of $X^2 + Y^2$ is less than 100.0, the answer (ANSWR) is to be 12X. If greater than or equal to 100.0, the value of ANSWR is to be X^2. Print the answer in a field of 10 with two decimal positions.

3 Find the largest quantity represented by three variables—ALPHA, BETA, and GAMMA. Call the largest quantity BIG. If two are equal, either value may be used. (*a*) First write statements without using AMAX1 function and then (*b*) write statements using the function.

4 Two variables, NIX and KIX, should be unequal. Find the largest in absolute value (without regard to sign). Print out the largest. If they are equal, bring the computer to a temporary halt and display 98 on the display device. Assume a maximum of six significant digits in the result. After printing, terminate the program.

5 Find out if $-550 \leq X \leq 1000$. If X falls within these limits (between -550 and $+1000$), print out YES. If not, print out NO. Then halt the computer. (*a*) Use a logical IF and then (*b*) an arithmetic IF.

6 Write logical IF statements to test whether A is greater than B and greater than C or if A is less than D and equal to E. If so, transfer control to statement 110. If false, go to statement 130.

7 Rewrite the Manhattan purchase program presented in Self-testing Quiz #3, Question 6, to include input validation which rejects (with an error message) a negative or zero rate or a rate greater than 15 percent.

Suggestions for Writing Programs

At this point the basic elements of FORTRAN have been presented. Input, output, arithmetic, and control allow almost any problem to be solved with the simple statements provided thus far. However, it is the addition of subscripted variables, the DO, subroutines, etc., that makes FORTRAN such a powerful and useful language. These are presented in Chapter 18. Since all the basic elements to write a program are now available, this section discusses some suggestions for the novice programmer and presents some short, illustrative programs.

Suggestions for the FORTRAN Programmer

1 Analyze the problem and flowchart or sketch the program using a pseudocode before beginning to write statements.

2 Use FORTRAN coding paper. This will aid in keeping the standard form and make it easier to keypunch. FORTRAN coding paper is available from all major computer manufacturers and suppliers of forms.

3 Use the pseudoblock structure to divide the program into logical segments and include an identification block and a list of variables block.

4 Use comments freely. Suggested format is to begin the inside-block comments in column 31.

5 Validate input data to make sure it falls within the limits assumed for the program. Provide suitable error messages and correct or reject bad data.

6 Print out input data as a check against incorrect input. Doing this is also useful for understanding the results.

7 Use parentheses to avoid ambiguity. Do not rely upon unfamiliar precedence rules.

8 Avoid the arithmetic IF in favor of the logical IF.

9 Code for clarity, not efficiency.

10 When setting up conditional transfers, provide explicit error stops or error messages for instances when conditions which should never occur actually do occur.

11 Check for incorrect logic following a basic IF. Remember that unless the action of the IF is to transfer control, the statement following the IF will be executed in both true and false cases. For example,

```
IF (A .GT. B) BIG = A
BIG = B
```

The program makes BIG = A if A is greater than B and then passes control to the next statement which makes BIG = B. In other words, the logic works only for B greater than A. Some new FORTRAN enhancements provide improved, alternative coding for this situation (to be presented in Chapter 18).

12 If available (some older compilers may not allow it), use the apostrophe method for character output. Use of the H edit descriptor in a Hollerith field is error-prone. It is worth the trouble to double-check H fields.

13 A program of any consequence should be checked out by running it with comprehensive test data for which the results are known.

Illustrative Programs The three programs that follow are quite simple but illustrate the elements presented in the chapter. The cost of running the sample problems was 7¢ each using the University of Minnesota Control Data Cyber computer.

The first sample program is to read a Fahrenheit temperature from a card where it is punched in columns 1-6 in the form XXX.X and to convert it to centigrade. The formula for this conversion is

$$c = \tfrac{5}{9}(f - 32)$$

After each card is read and the computation is made, the result is to be printed as FAHRENHEIT IS XXX.X AND CENTIGRADE IS XX.X. The program is illustrated in Figure 17-6. The Fahrenheit-to-centigrade program is complete and

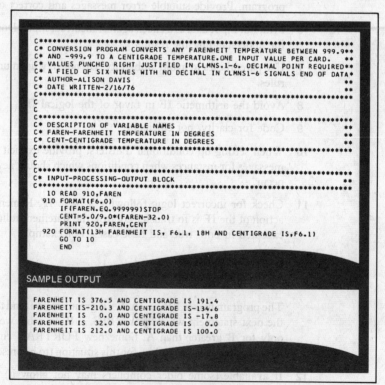

```
C************************************************************************
C* CONVERSION PROGRAM CONVERTS ANY FARENHEIT TEMPERATURE BETWEEN 999.9**
C* AND -999.9 TO A CENTIGRADE TEMPERATURE.ONE INPUT VALUE PER CARD.   **
C* VALUES PUNCHED RIGHT JUSTIFIED IN CLMNS.1-6. DECIMAL POINT REQUIRED**
C* A FIELD OF SIX NINES WITH NO DECIMAL IN CLMNS1-6 SIGNALS END OF DATA*
C* AUTHOR-ALISON DAVIS                                                **
C* DATE WRITTEN-2/16/76                                               **
C************************************************************************
C
C
C* DESCRIPTION OF VARIABLE NAMES                                      **
C* FAREN-FARENHEIT TEMPERATURE IN DEGREES                             **
C* CENT-CENTIGRADE TEMPERATURE IN DEGREES                             **
C************************************************************************
C
C
C************************************************************************
C* INPUT-PROCESSING-OUTPUT BLOCK                                      **
C************************************************************************
   10 READ 910,FAREN
  910 FORMAT(F6.0)
      IF(FAREN.EQ.999999)STOP
      CENT=5.0/9.0*(FAREN-32.0)
      PRINT 920,FAREN,CENT
  920 FORMAT(13H FARENHEIT IS, F6.1, 18H AND CENTIGRADE IS,F6.1)
      GO TO 10
      END
```

SAMPLE OUTPUT

```
FARENHEIT IS 376.5 AND CENTIGRADE IS 191.4
FARENHEIT IS-210.3 AND CENTIGRADE IS-134.6
FARENHEIT IS   0.0 AND CENTIGRADE IS -17.8
FARENHEIT IS  32.0 AND CENTIGRADE IS   0.0
FARENHEIT IS 212.0 AND CENTIGRADE IS 100.0
```

FIGURE 17-6 Program to convert Fahrenheit temperature to centigrade with sample output.

will run. There is no limit on data cards. The program will process until a temperature input of 999999 is read.

The second sample problem is to compute *n* factorial (n!). Factorial *n* is equal to the product of the positive integers from 1 to *n*. For example, factorial $4 = 1 \times 2 \times 3 \times 4 = 24$. By definition, $0! = 1$. The program is to read *n* (called VALUE in the FORTRAN program) from a card and compute n! (called FACTRL in the FORTRAN program). The result is to be printed in E form to preserve maximum accuracy (which is assumed to be eight places). The program is shown in Figure 17-7. When testing the program, keep in mind that factorials can become very large: $3! = 6$ but $25! = 0.15511210E+25$.

The third sample problem is that of a contestant on a television quiz program

```
C*******************************************************************
C* FACTORIAL PROGRAM CALCULATES THE FACTORIAL OF ANY NON-NEGATIVE  **
C* INTEGER LESS THAN 100.  NEGATIVE INPUT VALUES YIELD ERROR MESSAGES.**
C* MAXIMUM 2 DIGIT INPUT,RIGHT-JUSTIFIED COLS 1-2. NO DECIMAL REQUIRED**
C* AUTHOR-ALISON DAVIS                                             **
C* DATE WRITTEN 2/16/76                                            **
C*******************************************************************
C
C
C*******************************************************************
C* DESCRIPTION OF VARIABLE NAMES
C* VALUE-THE NUMBER FOR WHICH THE FACTORIAL IS BEING COMPUTED      **
C* FACTRL-THE FACTORIAL OF THE NUMBER                              **
C* COUNTR-A COUNTER WHICH IS INTIALIZED AT ONE AND INCREMENTED BY ONE **
C*         UNTIL THE VALUE OF THE COUNTER EQUALS VALUE OF THE NUMBER. **
C*******************************************************************
C
C
C*******************************************************************
C* BLOCK 100-INITIALIZATION,INPUT,AND INPUT VALIDATION             **
C* TEST FOR INVALID NEGATIVE INPUT. SET COUNTER AND FACTORIAL AT ONE. **
C*******************************************************************
      100 READ 905,VALUE
      905 FORMAT(F2.0)
          FACTRL=1.0
          COUNTR=1.0
          IF(VALUE.LT.0)GO TO 300
          IF(VALUE.GT.0)GO TO 200
C                               *THE NUMBER IS 0 SO FACTORIAL IS ONE.
          FACTRL=1
          GO TO 310
C
C
C*******************************************************************
C* BLOCK 200-PROCESS BLOCK FOR NUMBERS GREATER THAN ZERO           **
C* REPEAT MULTIPLICATION UNTIL THE COUNTER EQUALS THE NUMBER.      **
C*******************************************************************
      200 FACTRL=FACTRL*COUNTR
          IF(COUNTR.GE.VALUE)GO TO 310
          COUNTR=COUNTR+1.0
          GO TU 200
C
C
C*******************************************************************
C* BLOCK 300-OUTPUT BLOCK (ERROR AND NORMAL)                       **
C*******************************************************************
      300 PRINT 910,VALUE
      910 FORMAT(F6.0,50H THE NUMBER IS NEGATIVE SO FACTORIAL IS UNDEFINED.)
          STOP
      310 PRINT 915,VALUE,FACTRL
      915 FORMAT(13H FACTORIAL OF,F6.0,5X,E15.8)
          STOP
          END
```

FIGURE 17-7 Program to compute factorial *n*.

who is offered the choice of $25,000 immediately or $200 a month for 15 years. He thinks he can earn an average of 6 percent on money. The problem is to compare the present value of the $200 a month at 6 percent with the immediate prize of $25,000 cash to select the better of the two alternatives. The program for solving this problem is shown in Figure 17-8. The present value is found using 180 months and a monthly interest rate of 0.005 (i.e., 0.06 for the year ÷ 12 months).

Self-testing Quiz—
FORTRAN #6

1 Flowchart and write a complete program to compute the economic order quantity using the formula:

$$EOQ = \sqrt{\frac{2ac_o}{c_u i}}$$

where a = annual sales in units (read from card)
c_o = cost of placing order (given as $4)
c_u = cost per unit (read from card)
i = cost of carrying inventory expressed as percentage (given as 0.20)

```
C******************************************************************
C* EVALUATION PROGRAM EVALUATES WHETHER IT IS BETTER TO ACCEPT AN  **
C* ANNUITY OF $200 A MONTH FOR 180 MONTHS(ASSUMING 6% INTEREST-OR 1/2%**
C* PER MONTH) OR TO ACCEPT $25,000 IN CASH.NO INPUT NECESSARY.     **
C* AUTHOR-ALISON DAVIS                                             **
C* DATE WRITTEN-2/16/76                                            **
C******************************************************************
C
C
C******************************************************************
C* DESCRIPTION OF VARIABLE NAMES                                   **
C* VALAN-VALUE OF ANNUITY                                          **
C******************************************************************
C
C
C******************************************************************
C* PROCESS-OUTPUT BLOCK                                            **
C* VALUE OF ANNUITY IS CALCULATED AND COMPARED TO $25,000.         **
C******************************************************************
      VALAN=200.0*((1.0-(1.0/(1.0+.005)**180))/.005)
      IF(VALAN.LE.25000)GO TO 20
   10 PRINT 910,VALAN
  910 FORMAT(21H VALUE OF ANNUITY IS ,F10.2,15H ACCEPT ANNUITY)
      STOP
   20 PRINT 920,VALAN
  920 FORMAT(21H VALUE OF ANNUITY IS ,F10.2,15H ACCEPT $25,000)
      STOP
      END



      VALUE OF ANNUITY IS   23697.32 ACCEPT $25,000
```

FIGURE 17-8 Program to evaluate whether it is better to accept annuity of $200 per month for 180 months or $25,000 cash, assuming an interest rate of 6 percent ($\frac{1}{2}$ percent per month).

If *EOQ* is less than 1 month's average usage, 1 month's usage is used as the *EOQ*. Print the results.

2 Flowchart and write a complete program to tally all employees not subject to further FICA (social security) deduction because their earnings equal or exceed the limit (say, $14,100). There are 1000 employees, with the amounts for each employee punched on a card in the form XXXXX.XX in columns 48–55. Count the cards to make sure that 1000 employees have been processed. (Use 10 employees instead of 1000 to make testing easier.) Evaluate the error-proneness of the program. Under what conditions will it fail?

Answers to Self-testing Quizzes

FORTRAN #1

Valid or invalid	If valid, constant or variable	Integer or real	If invalid, why
1 Invalid			Too many characters
2 Invalid	—	—	No special character allowed
3 Valid	Variable	Real	
4 Valid	Variable	Integer	
5 Valid	Variable	Real	
6 Valid	Variable	Real	
7 Invalid			Special character (−) not allowed.
8 Invalid (May be allowed in some FORTRAN implementations but not standard)			Decimal point missing. Exponent should be signed. Correct is 19.E + 25.
9 Valid	Constant	Real	
10 Invalid (For most implementations)			Too large
11 Valid	Constant	Integer	
12 Invalid (For most implementations)			Too large

FORTRAN #2

Valid, invalid, or mixed type	If invalid or mixed, why
1 (*a*) Mixed (to be converted)	Will be converted to A**2 + 1.0
(*b*) Valid (integer arithmetic for integer exponent is valid)	
(*c*) Valid real type	
(*d*) Mixed (to be converted)	Converts to A/B + D/3.0
(*e*) Valid integer type	
(*f*) Mixed (valid) converts result to integer type	
(*g*) Valid real type	
(*h*) Mixed (to be converted)	Better to code as X = (A + B)/((C + D)*E*FLOAT(I))
(*i*) Invalid	Expression (X + Y) to left of equals sign not allowed.

(*j*) Mixed   Integer may not have real exponent, so conversion to J-FLOAT(I)**A

(*k*) Valid   Integer exponent allowed

---

2 (*a*) 1.2   (*b*) 1   (*c*) 0   (*d*) 4

3 (*a*) X = SQRT ((A+B)/4.0) Do not forget that the constant 4 should be real.

(*b*) X = (A/B+2.0)**(1./3.). Exponentiating to the $\frac{1}{3}$ power is the same as taking the cube root. Note the exponent must be real or it would turn out to be zero. The parentheses around the exponent are necessary. Why?

(*c*) Y = EXP(X)

(*d*) X = 2.0*XI**3+(A*B)/D Note that the I in the formula is renamed to fit FORTRAN. Otherwise, a mixed-type expression would result.

(*e*) Y = ALOG(X)

(*f*) R = SQRT(X**2+Y**2) Note that the square root of the right side was taken since no expression is allowed on the left side.

(*g*) V = (4.0/3.0)*(3.1417*R**3)

4 (*a*) $p = \dfrac{a}{(1+i)^n}$ (*d*) $y = e^{-x^2}$

(*b*) $a = \pi r^2$ or $3.1417r^2$ (*e*) $\rho = A \cos \theta$

(*c*) $d = b^2 - 4ac$ (*f*) $x = a + \left(\dfrac{b}{c^d}\right)ef + 1.0$

5 (*a*) All are necessary.   (*b*) A*B*C+1.0   (*c*) A*B/C*D

FORTRAN #3 **1**   READ (1,910) ALPHA, BETA, IOTA, JIX
900 FORMAT (F10.2,F9.2,I7,I7)

2   WRITE (3,900) JIX, IOTA, BETA, ALPHA
900 FORMAT (I7,I7,F9.2,F12.2) Leave first position on line blank.
WRITE (3,905) IOTA, BETA
905 FORMAT (10X,I7,10X,F7.0)
The result will be:

---10---- 824341 ----10----- 53429.

4 The result will be (with b standing for a blank space): bbbbbbbb95bbbbbb1.04

5 (*a*) F8.2   (*c*) F10.6   (*e*) I5
(*b*) F7.1   (*d*) F5.3   (*f*) E15.8

6 See Figure 17-9. The program was run on three different computers. One of the computers gave a slightly smaller result (27,058,163,712 versus 27,081,355,025). The difference is explained by the method used for exponentiation and by the difference in word sizes. The result for the computer with a small word size is more affected by rounding and truncation.

FORTRAN #4 **1**   WRITE (3,921) TOLER
921 FORMAT (25X,30HTHE TOLERANCE IS CALCULATED AT, F8.2)
921 FORMAT (25X 'THE TOLERANCE IS CALCULATED AT',F8.2)

```
C************************************************************
C* MANHATTAN ISLAND PROGRAM                                **
C* CALCULATES THE AMOUNT THAT THE $24 INVESTED IN 1626 TO PURCHASE **
C* MANHATTAN ISLAND WOULD BE WORTH IN 1976(THE BICENTENNIAL YEAR) IF **
C* INTEREST WERE COMPOUNDED QUARTERLY.INPUT INTEREST RATE WITH DECIMAL**
C* PUNCHED IN COLUMNS1-3, EXAMPLE:6 PERCENT IS INPUT AS .06 **
C* AUTHOR-ALISON DAVIS                                     **
C* DATE WRITTEN-2/18/76                                    **
C************************************************************
C
C
C************************************************************
C* DESCRIPTION OF VARIABLE NAMES                           **
C* RATE-INTEREST RATE                                      **
C* AMOUNT-WORTH OF $24 INVESTMENT IN 1976                  **
C************************************************************
C
C
C************************************************************
C* INPUT-PROCESS-OUTPUT BLOCK                              **
C************************************************************
      READ(1,900) RATE
  900 FORMAT (F3.2)
      AMOUNT=24.0 * (1.0 + RATE / 4.0) ** (4.0*350.0)
      WRITE(3,910) RATE,AMOUNT,AMOUNT
  910 FORMAT(F5.2,F13.0,E16.8)
      STOP
      END
```

SAMPLE OUTPUT

```
.06 27081355025.  2.70813550E+10
```

FIGURE 17-9 Example program for Manhattan Island problem (question 6, self-testing quiz 17-3).

2   WRITE (3,922) SAVIN
   922   FORMAT (10X,22HAMOUNT OF SAVINGS IS $, F7.2)
   922   FORMAT (10X, 'AMOUNT OF SAVINGS IS $',F7.2)
3   WRITE (3,923) NMBER
   923   FORMAT (10H NUMBER IS, I5)
   923   FORMAT (' NUMBER IS',I5)
4   WRITE (3,924)
   924   FORMAT (9H THE END.)
   924   FORMAT (' THE END')
5   WRITE (3,925)
   925   FORMAT (5X, 4HITEM, 10X, 6HAMOUNT)
   925   FORMAT (5X,'ITEM',10X'AMOUNT')
6 See Figure 17-10 on page 520.

FORTRAN #5 **1** GO TO (100, 200, 300, 400, 500, 600, 700), CLASS
On older compilers the variable has to be integer, e.g., written as IFIX(CLASS) or INT(CLASS).

```
C********************************************************************
C* CONTINUOUS INTEREST PROGRAM                                     **
C* CALCULATES INTEREST EARNED AND AMOUNT RETURNED FROM AN AMOUNT   **
C* INVESTED WITH CONTINUOUS COMPOUNDING. ALSO CALCULATES DIFFERENCE**
C* EARNED FOR CONTINUOUS COMPARED TO QUARTERLY COMPOUNDING.        **
C* INPUT CARD. AMOUNT INVESTED IN COLS 1-10(F10.2), YEARLY INTEREST**
C* RATE AS A DECIMAL IN COLS 11-15 (F5.3),AND NUMBER OF QUARTERS   **
C* INVESTED IN COLS 16-18(F3.0).                                   **
C* AUTHOR. GORDON B DAVIS                                          **
C* DATE WRITTEN. 2/26/76                                           **
C********************************************************************
C
C
C********************************************************************
C* DESCRIPTION OF VARIABLE NAMES                                   **
C* CONT-INTEREST EARNED WITH CONTINUOUS COMPOUNDING.               **
C* DIFFR-DIFFERENCE BETWEEN AMT. RETURNED WITH CONTINUOUS COMPOUNDING **
C*      AND AMT. RETURNED WITH QUARTERLY COMPOUNDING(RCONT-RQUAR). **
C* PRINC-AMOUNT INVESTED                                           **
C* QRATE-QUARTERLY INTEREST RATE                                   **
C* RATE-YEARLY INTEREST RATE                                       **
C* RCONT-PRINCIPAL PLUS INTEREST WITH CONTINUOUS COMPOUNDING       **
C* RQUAR-PRINCIPAL PLUS INTEREST WITH QUARTERLY COMPOUNDING        **
C* XNUMB-NUMBER OF QUARTERS.                                       **
C********************************************************************
C
C
C********************************************************************
C* BLOCK 100  READ AND PROCESS                                     **
C********************************************************************
  100 READ (1,900) PRINC,RATE,XNUMB
  900 FORMAT (F10.2,F5.3,F3.0)
      QRATE = RATE/4.0
      RCONT = PRINC * EXP(XNUMB*QRATE)
      RQUAR = PRINC * (1.0+QRATE)**XNUMB
      CONT = RCONT-PRINC
      DIFFR = RCONT - RQUAR
C
C
C********************************************************************
C* BLOCK 200  NORMAL OUTPUT                                        **
C********************************************************************
  200 RATE = RATE * 100.0
      WRITE (3,910)PRINC,RATE
  910 FORMAT(16H IF YOU INVEST $ ,F8.2,10H TODAY AT ,F5.2,8H PERCENT)
      WRITE (3,920)XNUMB
  920 FORMAT(18H AND LEAVE IT FOR ,F3.0,33H QUARTERS COMPOUNDED CONTINUO
     -USLY)
      WRITE (3,930)CONT
  930 FORMAT(16H YOU WILL EARN $ ,F8.2,9H INTEREST)
      WRITE (3,940)RCONT
  940 FORMAT(31H AND RECEIVE BACK A TOTAL OF $ ,F8.2)
      WRITE (3,950)DIFFR
  950 FORMAT(14H YOU RECEIVE $ ,F6.2,22H MORE USING CONTINUOUS )
      WRITE (3,960)
  960 FORMAT(41H COMPOUNDING THAN QUARTERLY COMPOUNDING. )
      STOP
      END
```

SAMPLE OUTPUT

```
IF YOU INVEST $ 1000.00 TODAY AT  6.00 PERCENT
AND LEAVE IT FOR 60. QUARTERS COMPOUNDED CONTINUOUSLY
YOU WILL EARN $ 1459.60 INTEREST
AND RECEIVE BACK A TOTAL OF $ 2459.60
YOU RECEIVE $ 16.47 MORE USING CONTINUOUS
COMPOUNDING THAN QUARTERLY COMPOUNDING.
```

FIGURE 17-10 Example program for interest comparison problem (question 6, self-testing quiz 17-4).

2 Alternative *a* (logical IF):

```
     IF ((SQRT(X**2+Y**2).LT.100.0)ANSWR=12.0*X
     IF ((SQRT(X**2+Y**2).GE.100.0)ANSWR=X**2
     WRITE (3,900)ANSWR
900  FORMAT (F10.2)
```

Alternative *b* (with arithmetic IF)

```
     IF (SQRT(X**2+Y**2)-100.0)110,120,120
110  ANSWR = 12.0**
     GO TO 130
120  ANSWR = X**2
130  WRITE (3,900) ANSWR
```

3 (*a*)
```
     BIG = ALPHA
     IF (BETA.GE.BIG)BIG=BETA
     IF (GAMMA.GE.BIG)BIG=GAMMA
```
   (*b*)
```
     BIG = AMAX1(ALPHA,BETA,GAMMA)
```

4
```
     IF (NIX.EQ.KIX)PAUSE 98
     LARGE = NIX
     IF (ABS(KIX).GT.ABS(LARGE))LARGE = KIX
     WRITE (3,910) LARGE
910  FORMAT (I7)
     STOP
```

5 (*a*) Logical IF

```
     IF (X.GE.-550.0.OR.X.LE.1000.0)WRITE(3,900)
900  FORMAT (4H YES)
     IF (X.LT.-550.0.OR.X.GT.1000.0)WRITE(3,910)
910  FORMAT (3H NO)
     STOP
```

   (*b*) Arithmetic IF

```
     IF (X+550.0)110,110,100
100  IF (X-1000.0)120,120,110
110  WRITE (3,910)
910  FORMAT (3H NO)
     GO TO 130
120  WRITE (3,920)
920  FORMAT (4H YES)
130  STOP
```

6
```
     IF ((A .GT. B .AND. A .GT. C) .OR. (A .LT. D .AND. A .EQ. E)) GO TO 110
130  _____
```

7 See Figure 17-11 on page 522.

FORTRAN #6 Only the input-process-output block is shown (see flowchart on page 523).

1
```
     C  PROGRAM TO CALCULATE ECONOMIC
     C  ORDER QUANTITY
        READ (1,900) A,CUNIT
900     FORMAT (F10.0,F6.2)
        EOQ = SQRT (2.0*A*4.0/(CUNIT*.20))
        IF (EOQ.LT.(A/12.0))EOQ = A/12.0
        WRITE (3,910)A,CUNIT,EOQ
```

```
C**********************************************************************
C* MANHATTAN ISLAND PROGRAM                                          **
C* CALCULATES THE AMOUNT THAT THE $24 INVESTED IN 1626 TO PURCHASE   **
C* MANHATTAN ISLAND WOULD BE WORTH IN 1976(THE BICENTENNIAL YEAR) IF **
C* INTEREST WERE COMPOUNDED QUARTERLY.INPUT INTEREST RATE WITH DECIMAL**
C* PUNCHED IN CLMNS.1-3. EXAMPLE-6 PERCENT IS INPUT AS .06. INPUT THAT**
C* IS ZERO, NEGATIVE, OR GREATER THAN .15 RESULTS IN ERROR MESSAGES  **
C* AUTHOR-ALISON DAVIS                                               **
C* DATE WRITTEN-2/18/76                                              **
C**********************************************************************
C
C
C**********************************************************************
C* DESCRIPTION OF VARIABLE NAMES                                     **
C* RATE-INTEREST RATE                                               **
C* AMONT-WORTH OF $24 INVESTMENT IN 1976                            **
C**********************************************************************
C
C
C**********************************************************************
C* INPUT-INPUT VALIDATION-PROCESS BLOCK                              **
C**********************************************************************
      READ(1,900) RATE
  900 FORMAT (F3.2)
      IF(RATE.LE.0.OR.RATE.GT..15)GO TO 110
      AMONT=24.0 * (1.0 + RATE / 4.0) ** (4.0*350.0)
C
C
C**********************************************************************
C* OUTPUT-NORMAL AND ERROR                                           **
C**********************************************************************
      WRITE(3,910) RATE,AMONT,AMONT
  910 FORMAT (12H THE RATE IS,F5.2,16H AND AMOUNTS ARE,F13.0,E16.8)
      STOP
  110 WRITE(3,920)
  920 FORMAT(40H ERROR-NEGATIVE,ZERO,OR TOO LARGE INPUT.)
      STOP
      END
```

SAMPLE OUTPUT

```
THE RATE IS 0.06 AND AMOUNTS ARE 27081355025.  2.70813550E+10
```

FIGURE 17-11 Example program for Manhattan Island problem with input validation (question 7, self-testing quiz 17-5).

```
  910   FORMAT (14H FOR USAGE OF ,F10.0,2X,11HAND COST OF
        ,F6.2,2X,7HEOQ IS ,F10.0)
        STOP
        END
2   C   PROGRAM TO TALLY EMPLOYEES NOT
    C   SUBJECT TO FICA TAX
        NTOTAL = 0
        TALLY = 0
  100   READ (1,900) WAGES
  900   FORMAT (47X,F8.2)
        IF (WAGES.GE.14100.)TALLY = TALLY + 1.0
        NTOTAL = NTOTAL + 1
        IF (NTOTAL.LT.1000)GO TO 100
        WRITE (3,910)TALLY,NTOTAL
```

(See flowchart on page 524.)

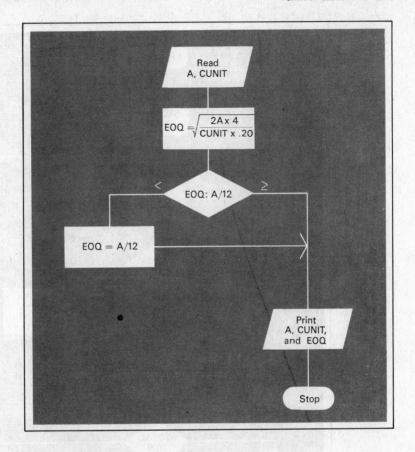

910 FORMAT (F10.0,I10)
     STOP
     END

The program logic requires that there be at least 1000 cards. If there is an error and there are not 1000, the program will abort with no output. For error control, the READ statement might be coded.

100 READ(1,900,END=150) WAGES

Statement 150 is inserted as the next to last statement in the program. It prints an error message and the value of TALLY and NTOTAL to that point.

EXERCISES

1 What is the purpose of a C in column 1 of the FORTRAN coding?
2 What is the purpose of column 6 in the FORTRAN coding?
3 What is the purpose of the variable name in FORTRAN?
4 What is the difference between a variable and a constant?
5 In mathematical notation, AB means $A \times B$. What does AB stand for in FORTRAN?

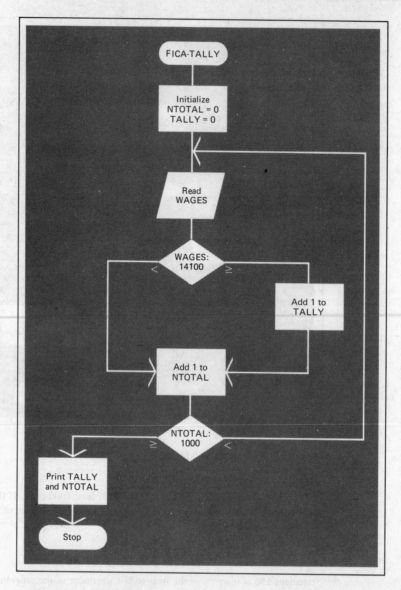

6 What is the source program, and what is an object program?

7 How does the compiler routine know when the entire program to be compiled has been read?

8 What are the precedence rules for arithmetic operations, relational operations, and both types of operations when included in a logical IF?

9 Fill in the following table:

	Valid or invalid	IF VALID,		If invalid, why
		Constant or variable	Integer or real	

(a) MAN
(b) WOMAN
(c) X − 19
(d) RATE
(e) I
(f) OUTPUT
(g) 9FOUR
(h) DOLL
(i) 18.97
(j) BETA
(k) J19
(l) 134.1E19
(m) 1.9E-20

10 What are the allowable forms for exponentiation?

11 Write the FORTRAN expressions for the following:

(a) X^a (c) X^{i+1} (e) $X^{1/3}$ (g) $X^{i/j}$

(b) X^i (d) e^x (f) X^{-4} (h) $\dfrac{1}{X^2}$

12 What is the result of each of the following statements, given the stated values for the variables?

(a) X = Y + Z/A ⎫
(b) IX = Y + Z/A ⎬ Y = 3.0, Z = 4.5, A = 2.0
(c) I = J/K
(d) I = L/J + K ⎬ J = 3, K = 9, L = 10
(e) I = J + L/K − L ⎭

13 Write the formulas, given the following FORTRAN statements:

(a) Y = SQRT (X**2 + 2.0)/(1.0 − X**N)
(b) X = THETA + SIN (THETA)
(c) Y = 1.0/X
(d) E = ((A**2 + B**2)**(1./2.))/A
(e) X = A**B*C + D*E/F*G**2

14 Write the FORTRAN statement to solve the formula for each of the following:

(a) $j = \sqrt{v}$
(b) $a = |x + y|$ where $|\ |$ means the absolute value.
(c) $x = a(-b)/c(-d)$

(d) $s = \dfrac{p}{q} + \dfrac{3r}{s}$

15 What difference may be encountered between the minimum specifications for reading 1237.59 from a card and the minimum specifications for printing or punching this same number?

16 Write program statements for the following formulas—read the necessary variables from cards, perform the arithmetic operation, and then print the input variables plus the result. Assume in all cases that a field of 10 is sufficient and 2 decimal places are desired.

(a) $\dfrac{e+f}{2}$

(b) $\dfrac{-b+\sqrt{b^2-4ac}}{2a}$

(c) $\dfrac{xy}{\sqrt{x^2y^2}}$

17 Complete the following table using minimum FORMAT specification:

Data as found on card	Format to read	Desired printing	Format for printing
(a) XXX.XXX		XXX.XXX	
(b) XXX		XXX.0	
(c) .XXXXE+17		0.XXXXE+17	
(d) −.XXXXE+5		−XXXX0.	
(e)	F5.2		F5.1

18 Write sets of WRITE and FORMAT statements to make the following outputs. Leave first position on line blank in all cases.

(a) $\xleftarrow{\text{52 spaces}}$ ANALYSIS PROGRAM

(b) CHI SQUARE TEST IS XX.XX

(c) PART NO. $\xleftarrow{\text{20 spaces}}$ QUANTITY $\xleftarrow{\text{10 spaces}}$ AMOUNT

(d) PROGRAM DATA IS INCORRECT.

19 Write a program segment to find the value of COST when COST is a step function of volume.

If VOL is between 0 and 100	COST = 200 + .3xVOL
If VOL is over 100 but not over 1000	COST = 300 + .3xVOL
If VOL is over 1000 but not over 5000	COST = 350 + .25xVOL

20 Flowchart, write, and execute a complete program for each of the following problems. Code the program in good form using input validation for input data.

(a) Write a general program (see the third example program) to accept any proposition of an immediate sum versus an annuity. The formula to find the present value of an annuity is

$$P\left(\frac{1-(1+i)^{-n}}{i}\right)$$

where P = annuity per period

$\quad i$ = interest rate per period

$\quad n$ = number of periods.

(b) Prepare a table showing the period, balance, interest earned, and cumulative interest earned if a sum of money is left to accumulate for N years in a savings institution which pays $5\frac{1}{2}$ percent a year compounded annually. Read the amount and N from a card in the forms XXXX.XX and XX. The formula to find the amount is $P(1 + i)^n$, where i is the interest rate per period.

(c) Write a complete program for an inventory valuation. In valuing inventory purposes, many business firms use the rule of "cost or market, whichever is lower." Read in pairs of cost figures (cost and market) from cards and prepare the following analysis. Number the values as they are printed.

INVENTORY

Number	Cost	Market	Value for inventory
1	XX.XX	XX.XX	XX.XX
2			
⋮			
n			
Total	XXX.XX	XXX.XX	XXX.XX

(d) A common method of forecasting used with computers is exponential smoothing. Starting with the last forecast, the new forecast consists of the old forecast plus a percentage of the difference between the old forecast and the actual amount. In terms of a formula:

New forecast = old forecast + alpha(actual − old forecast)

Using the following actual data, punched one per card, prepare the report shown. Use 35.0 as the old forecast to start the forecasting process. Compare ALPHA of .15 and .5. Use data of 37, 31, 32, 34, 35, 36, 31.

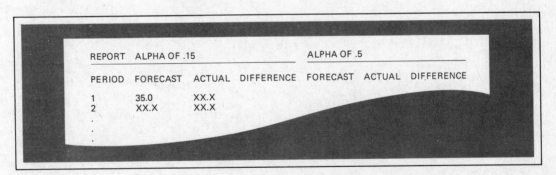

REPORT	ALPHA OF .15			ALPHA OF .5		
PERIOD	FORECAST	ACTUAL	DIFFERENCE	FORECAST	ACTUAL	DIFFERENCE
1	35.0	XX.X				
2	XX.X	XX.X				

(e) Given any amount of a restaurant check up to $25.00 and any amount tendered up to $40.00, find the number and denomination of paper money and coins to return as change. If not enough is tendered, print out PAY MORE.

(*f*) Mr. Jones of the ABC Company started the year in fine shape. His company made widgets—just what the customer wanted. He made them for $0.75 each, sold them for $1.00. He kept a 30-day supply in inventory, paid his bills promptly, and billed his customers 30-day net. The sales manager predicted a steady increase of 500 widgets each month starting with sales of 1000 in January. When Jones realized that the cumulative profit for the first 4 months was going to be $1750, he left on April 29 for a Florida vacation. Suddenly he got a phone call from his treasurer: "Come home! We need money!" The performance of the company is summarized below. Note that production and inventory are priced at 75¢.

Month	Sales	Profit	Prod $	END OF MONTH		
				Cash	Receivables	Inventory
Dec.				$ 875	$1000	$ 750
Jan.	$1000	$250	$ 750	1125	1000	750
Feb.	1500	375	1500	625	1500	1125
Mar.	2000	500	1875	250	2000	1500
Apr.	2500	625	2250	0	2500	1875

Write a program to prepare the forecast from January to December (number the months 1 to 12).

CHAPTER

FORTRAN—
ADDITIONAL
FEATURES

This chapter, continuing the description of FORTRAN, presents additional features and extensions of the basic features described in Chapter 17.

Subscripted Variables

Subscripts provide a notation which simplifies the programming of many problems especially repetition structures such as program loops. Before presenting the FORTRAN notation for subscripts, it may be helpful to review the need for subscripts.

Arrays, Vectors, and Matrices

A list of quantities which can be classed together can be thought of as a one-dimensional array. A quantity in the list is identified by a name given to the entire list, plus a subscript which refers to the position in the list occupied by the quantity. For example, sales by customers would form a single-dimension array as shown in Figure 18-1.

If S is used to denote sales, the sales to customer 3 can be identified as an array element S_3, to customer 4 as S_4, etc. Mathematical notation uses a lowered number as a subscript.

A two-dimensional array, or rectangular array (often called a "matrix"), provides a twofold classification. For example, a classification of females by height and weight would result in a rectangular array. A single name can be used to refer to the matrix, and when any particular element or classification in the array is referred to, the name is used with a subscript. By convention, the row is always written first and the column second. For example, if F is used to refer to the twofold classification of females, $F_{3,4}$ refers to the number of those who are in weight class 3 and height class 4, as illustrated in Figure 18-2.

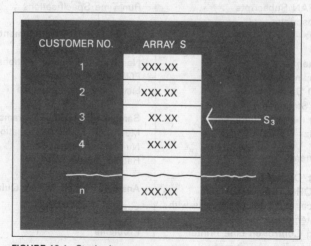

FIGURE 18-1 Single-dimension array

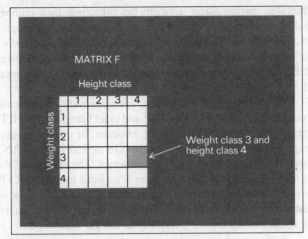

FIGURE 18-2 Two-dimensional array.

A threefold classification uses three subscripts. The first subscript refers to the row, the second to the column, and the third to the level. For example, a classification by weight, height, and age will result in the three-dimensional array shown in Figure 18-3.

If the entire classification by weight, height, and age is termed C, persons falling into weight class 2, height class 4, and age class 1 are identified as $C_{2,4,1}$. The classifications are listed as subscripts in order by row, column, and level.

In short, subscripts are used to identify one out of a related set of items. All items in an array have the same name because they are all in the same category. The subscript identifies the array element within the array.

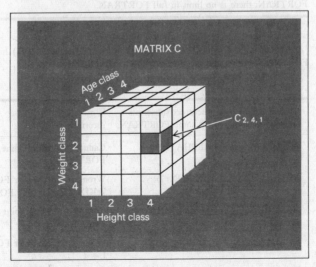

FIGURE 18-3 Three-dimensional array.

Form of FORTRAN
Subscripts

Standard mathematical notation for subscripts uses numbers or letters written below the level of the symbol to which they apply. Since neither the keypunch nor the printer in a computer system is equipped to handle lowered characters, subscripts are represented in FORTRAN enclosed in parentheses immediately following the name. The previous array examples would appear in FORTRAN as S(3), F(3,4), and C(2,4,1).

Subscripts must be integer, since positions in an array can only be whole numbers. In Subset FORTRAN[1] and older versions of FORTRAN, subscripts can be only integer variables, integer constants, or integer expressions. Floating point expressions are allowed for subscripts in the full FORTRAN, but only the integer portion of the result is used as a subscript. The number of subscripts is limited to three in Subset FORTRAN; there is no limit in full FORTRAN. The subscripts are separated by commas. In some older FORTRANs (but not the new standard) the arithmetic expressions are limited to multiplication, subtraction, and addition, in the following forms, where k is an integer constant and i is an integer variable:

Addition or subtraction	$i \pm k$
Multiplication	$k * i$
Combinations	$k * i \pm k'$

THE GENERAL FORM OF SUBSCRIPTS

$s(I_1)$
$s(I_2)$
$s(I_1, I_2, I_3)$

s = any subscripted variable name (integer, or real)
I = expressions allowed as subscripts (limited to integer expressions in Subset FORTRAN)

Subscripts are separated by commas. The number of subscripts is limited to three in Subset FORTRAN; there is no limit in full FORTRAN.

---

[1] As explained in Chapter 17, the new FORTRAN standard (1977) has two versions: the full FORTRAN version and the limited Subset FORTRAN version.

EXAMPLES

Correct subscripts	Incorrect subscripts for some FORTRANs	Why might be incorrect
ALPHA (9)	ALPHA (X)	Cannot be floating point in Subset FORTRAN
BETA (1,7)	JIX (KIX*7)	Wrong form for older FORTRANs; should be 7*KIX. OK for 1977 FORTRAN.
IOTA (I,J,K)	X(NIX, YIX)	Cannot be floating point in Subset FORTRAN
GAMMA (M,3)	SALES (1+I,J)	Wrong form for older FORTRANs; should be I + 1

X (KIX, JIX, 7)	CLASS (I,J,K,L)	Too many subscripts for Subset FORTRAN
Y (7*KIX,8)		
Z (NIX + 3,JIX)		

The Use of Subscripts

Each time the program translating the FORTRAN source statement to an object language encounters a variable name, it assigns a memory location to it. A subscripted variable name presents a problem because the number of memory locations to be assigned to it is not always apparent from the program. In fact, the number may vary, depending on the problem being run. To allow the compiler to assign the correct number of memory locations for a subscripted variable, the programmer must specify the maximum size of the subscripts, i.e., the maximum size of the array. The statement for doing this is the DIMENSION statement. This may appear any place in the program before the first use of the subscripted variable. However, it is usually good practice to put all DIMENSION statements at the beginning of the program in a DIMENSION-AND-INITIALIZE block. The standard full FORTRAN allows dimensions to be expressed as lower and upper bounds (but this is a rather advanced feature).

BASIC FORM FOR DIMENSION FOR SUBSCRIPTED VARIABLES

DIMENSION $s(k)$, $s(k_1,k_2)$, $s(k_1,k_2,k_3)$, $s(k_1,k_2, \ldots , k_n)$

If more than one variable is dimensioned, the variables are separated by commas.

s = any subscripted variable name
k_1,k_2,k_3 = the maximum number of rows, columns, and levels

ADDED DIMENSION FORM FOR FULL FORTRAN

DIMENSION $s(k_1:k_2, k_3:k_4, \ldots , k_n:k_m)$

In subscript $k_1:k_2$, k_1 is the lower bound and k_2 is the upper bound. k_2 must be larger than k_1 but can be negative. The dimension is computed as $k_2 - k_1 + 1$.

Examples of DIMENSION statements are:

DIMENSION A(100)
DIMENSION A(100), B(50), C(10,10)
DIMENSION NIX(10, 10, 5), KIX(50, 10)
DIMENSION A(2:50) [In full FORTRAN]

Care should be taken not to dimension larger than will be necessary for the maximum set of data. A DIMENSION X(100, 100, 100) calls for 100 × 100 × 100 memory locations. Although valid in form, this requirement for 1 million memory locations exceeds the internal capacity allowed for most problems.

When a dimensional variable name is used in an executable statement, it must always be used with a subscript to identify which location is desired. The only exception to this rule is a specialized input/output situation in which a variable name without a subscript references the entire array (to be explained later).

Two short sample problems will illustrate two types of uses for the subscripted variable.

The first problem is a program to tally the number of students whose grade-point averages fall into each of five categories. The subscripted variable will be called "TALLY." TALLY has five categories:

Category	Grade point
TALLY(1)	0.0 to 0.99
TALLY(2)	1.0 to 1.99
TALLY(3)	2.0 to 2.99
TALLY(4)	3.0 to 3.99
TALLY(5)	4.0

The program should read a card with the grade-point average for a student given on it. This variable, called GPA, is in the form X.XX. A GPA of 9.99 terminates the reading of cards and causes the tallies to be printed. After reading the input, the next step is to determine which category the student's grades are in and to add 1 to the tally for that category (Figure 18-4). Note that the data itself is used to provide the subscript category by which it is classified. The statement $I = INT(GPA + 1.0)$ thus provides the proper integer for the tally statement.

```
C*****************************************************************************
C* DIMENSION AND INITIALIZE                                                **
C* FIVE TALLY VARIABLES FOR GRADE POINT CATEGORIES                         **
C*****************************************************************************
      DIMENSION TALLY(5)
      TALLY(1)= 0
      TALLY(2)= 0
      TALLY(3)= 0
      TALLY(4)= 0
      TALLY(5)= 0
C
C
C*****************************************************************************
C* BLOCK 100 READ AND TALLY BY GPA CATEGORY                                **
C* (VALIDATION OF  INPUT DATA  NOT SHOWN)                                  **
C*****************************************************************************
  100 READ(1,900)GPA
      IF(GPA.GE.  9.99) GO TO 300
  900 FORMAT(F5.2)
      I= INT(GPA +1.0)
      TALLY(I) = TALLY(I)+ 1.0
      GO TO 100
C
C
C*****************************************************************************
C* BLOCK 300 OUTPUT (NOT SHOWN)                                            **
C*****************************************************************************
      END
```

FIGURE 18-4 Program segment for tally grade-point problem.

(The INT function is redundant but clarifies the logic.) IFIX could have been used instead of INT as the function name.

The second problem is to sum 100 quantities called X that are stored in memory as subscripted variables. An IF statement is used to terminate a simple loop, as shown in Figure 18-5. If subscripts were not available, the program to add 100 numbers would require statements listing all 100 variable names.

Self-testing Quiz—
FORTRAN #7

1 State whether the following statements or expressions are valid, and if invalid for some FORTRANs, state why.

Statement or expression	Valid for all	FORTRANs for which invalid and why
(a) DIMENSION C (100), NIX (100)		
(b) A (14,NIX,X)		
(c) A (JIX*KIX)		
(d) ALPHA (10, 10, 5)		
(e) DIMENSION ALPHA (100), BETA (100,10)		
(f) GAMMA (A + 5.0)		
(g) DELTAS (5 − I)		

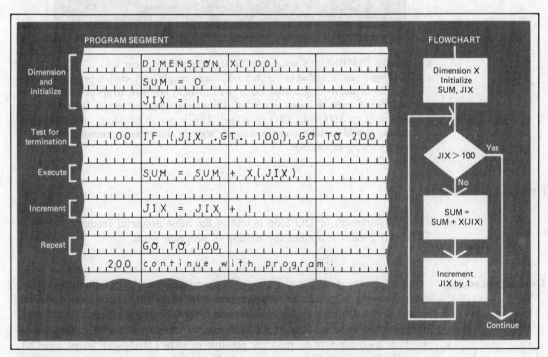

FIGURE 18-5 Program segment to sum quantities stored as subscripted variables.

2 Write the DIMENSION statements for the following arrays:
(*a*) An array of 100 sample observations
(*b*) A two-dimensional array to classify persons by sex and by 1 of 10 occupations
(*c*) An array to classify business firms by 1 of 8 size groups, 1 of 15 types of business groups, and 1 of 5 location classes
(*d*) Four arrays A, B, C, and D, each having 15 entries
3 Give the subscripted variable names by which the following matrix array elements are identified.

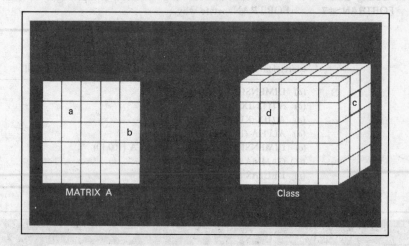

4 Give the DIMENSION statements for the arrays in Problem 3.
5 Using logic similar to that in Figure 18-5, write a simple but complete program to read five pairs of numbers from five cards (F10.2,F10.2) into two arrays A and B. Then multiply the arrays to create an array C. Print array elements from A, B, and C, a set to a line [e.g., A(1), B(1), C(1) on a line]. This is not an efficiently coded program because, as will be seen, there are simpler ways to code these operations, but it is a useful learning experience.

The DO Statement

The DO statement or DO loop is one of the most powerful features of FOR-TRAN. It greatly simplifies the writing of program loops.

Concept of Looping Looping is repetition based on program modification. A set of one or more instructions is executed a number of times, each time altering one or more variables in the set, so that each execution is different from the preceding one. The effect of looping is to reduce substantially the number of instructions required for a program. Two types of looping are possible in FORTRAN—IF loops and DO loops. Both accomplish the same purpose, but DO loops are simpler to write. It is useful to understand IF loops, however, both because they can be used when the restrictions on DO loops make the DO type not feasible and because they illustrate the requirements for a loop. See Figure 18-5 and the answer to Self-testing Quiz #7, Problem 5 (Figure 18-13) for examples of simple IF loops.

An IF loop requires the following steps for the DO WHILE logic presented in Chapter 5.

1 Initialize to the first value the loop control variable being modified.

2 Test to see if the loop control variable has exceeded the limit. If limit is exceeded, branch out of loop; if not exceeded, continue with next statement in program.

3 Execute the set of statements.

4 Modify the loop control variable.

5 Branch back to beginning of loop.

The logic of the loop can be altered slightly by the location of the test. Note, in the loop logic above, that if the initial value is greater than the limit, the loop will not be executed at all. By placing the test last in the sequence, the loop with initial value greater than the limit will execute at least once (DO UNTIL logic).

A program segment to sum the quantities identified by odd-numbered subscripts (1, 3, 5, . . .) in an array of 210 numbers will illustrate the IF loop procedure. The array is called DELTA and is assumed to have already been placed in memory.

Program		Comment	
Previous statements			
	SUM = 0	Initialize accumulator variable.	Initialize.
	K = 1	Initialize control variable.	
100	IF (K.GT.210)GO TO 200	Test control variable against limit; if limit is exceeded, exit from loop.	Test for termination. Continue or branch out.
	SUM = SUM + DELTA(K)	Statement to be executed.	Execute.
	K = K + 2	Increment control variable.	Modify and return to beginning of loop.
	GO TO 100		
200	Next statement after loop		

Note that the program can be altered to start with the tenth variable merely by changing the initial value of the control variable; the program can be altered to sum every third value by changing the value of the increment to 3, and changing the test constant to another value would alter the times the loop would be executed.

Form of the
DO Statement

The DO statement is a repetition command which simplifies the writing of loops. It automatically initializes the loop variable, passes control to the statements to be executed, modifies the loop variable, and tests to see if the variable exceeds the limit.

The DO loop begins with a DO statement which defines the statement to be included in the loop, the variable which controls the loop, the termination value for the loop variable, and the increment. The end of the loop is a CONTINUE statement. A loop can usually end on a statement other than CONTINUE, but the use of CONTINUE for all loop terminations adds clarity to the program structure. The statements between the DO and the CONTINUE statements are indented (say, four spaces) to visually show the range of the loop. For example:

```
    DO 150 I = 1,10,2
        C(I) = A(I)*B(I)
        WRITE(3,900) A(I), B(I), C(I)
150 CONTINUE
```

The example DO statement says that the statements between the DO statement and the statement with a label of 150 should be executed repeatedly based on a loop variable called I. The value of I starts at 1 and increments by 2 each time through the loop. The loop is repeated as long as I is less than or equal to 10. The general form of the DO is summarized below.

THE DO STATEMENT

DO s i = m_1, m_2, m_3

s = the statement label (number) of the last statement in the loop (the terminal statement).

i = the index or control variable which in Subset FORTRAN and older FORTRANs must be an integer variable.

For Subset FORTRAN and older FORTRANs, an m must be either an integer or an integer constant. In full FORTRAN, any real expression may be used.

m_1 = the initial parameter, i.e., the initial value of the loop variable.

m_2 = the terminal parameter, i.e., the limit for the loop variable.

If m_3 = 1, then
DO s i = m_1, m_2

m_3 = the incrementation parameter, i.e., the increment value by which the loop variable is to be modified. If m_3 is not stated, it is assumed to be 1.

In the older 1966 FORTRAN, a comma between s and i is an error; in the newer standard, a comma between s and i is optional; for example, DO s,i = m_1, m_2, m_3.

In flowcharting a DO loop, the programmer can write the flow diagram in terms of the DO loop statement itself. The terminal statement number, control variable, initial value, terminal value, and incrementation value are specified within a processing symbol. A dotted line may be used to visually define the range of the DO loop as shown in Figure 18-6 on page 540.

Use of the DO Statement   Several illustrations will explain the way the DO statement is used.

EXAMPLE 1   Write a DO loop to execute the same processing as the IF loop example, i.e., to sum the variables with odd-numbered subscripts between 1 and 210.

Program segment	Flowchart

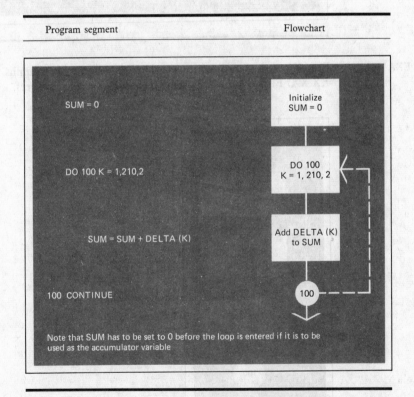

SUM = 0

DO 100 K = 1,210,2

SUM = SUM + DELTA (K)

100 CONTINUE

Note that SUM has to be set to 0 before the loop is entered if it is to be used as the accumulator variable

EXAMPLE 2   Multiply two arrays A and B, with N entries in each, to form a new array C.

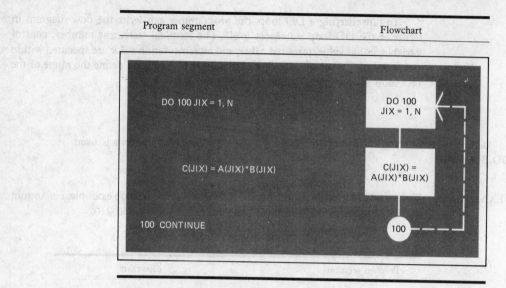

Program segment	Flowchart

DO 100 JIX = 1, N

DO 100
JIX = 1, N

C(JIX) = A(JIX)*B(JIX)

C(JIX) =
A(JIX)*B(JIX)

100 CONTINUE

100

EXAMPLE 3   Read K punched cards with a variable X in each card in columns 1–10 in the form XX.XX. Find the arithmetic mean (average) of the numbers.

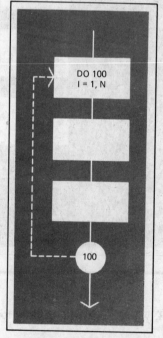

DO 100
I = 1, N

100

FIGURE 18-6 Flowcharting a DO loop.

Program segment	Flowchart

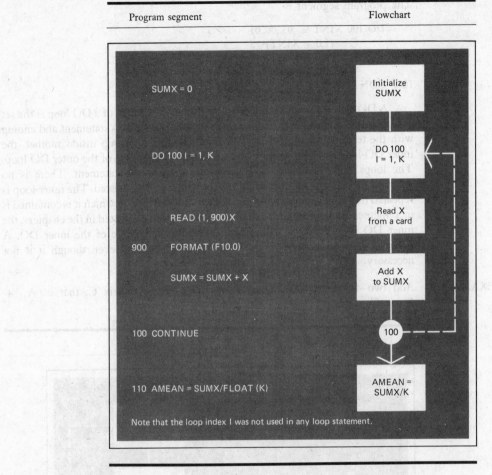

Program segment	Flowchart
SUMX = 0	Initialize SUMX
DO 100 I = 1, K	DO 100 I = 1, K
READ (1, 900)X	Read X from a card
900 FORMAT (F10.0)	
SUMX = SUMX + X	Add X to SUMX
100 CONTINUE	100
110 AMEAN = SUMX/FLOAT (K)	AMEAN = SUMX/K

Note that the loop index I was not used in any loop statement.

EXAMPLE 4   If the compiler being used accepts the newer full standard FORTRAN, a loop may be written with real expressions. Write a DO loop to prepare a table of compound amounts for a principal sum of 1000 for 5 years at 3, 4, 5, and 6 percent. Formula is $P(1 + i)^n$ where P is 1000, i is .03, .02, etc., and n is 5. In other words, the table will appear as:

Percent	Compound amount
3	1159.27
4	1216.65
5	1276.28
6	1338.23

The program segment is

```
DO 100 XINT = .03,.06,.01
    C = (1.0 + XINT)**5
    INTR = XINT*100.0
    WRITE (3,900)INTR,C
100  CONTINUE
```

A DO loop can contain DO loops within it. The range of a DO loop is the set of statements starting with the statement following the DO statement and ending with the termination statement. When nesting one DO loop inside another, the inner DO loop must be entirely contained within the range of the outer DO loop. The loops may, however, have the same termination statement. There is no specified limit to the number of DO loops which may be nested. The inner loop is repeated the specified number of times each time the loop in which it is contained is incremented. Following the rules for program design presented in the chapters, the inner DO is indented to show the relationship and range of the inner DO. A separate CONTINUE is used for each loop for clarity even though it is not necessary.

EXAMPLE 5 Add two 4×6 matrices called A and B to form matrix C; that is, $A_{11} + B_{11} = C_{11}$, etc.

Program segment	Flowchart

The order in which the program will perform the computation is defined by the DOs. The J values go through a cycle from 1 to 6 each time I changes by 1. Thus the computations will be:

$$C(1, 1) = A(1, 1) + B(1, 1)$$
$$C(1, 2) = A(1, 2) + B(1, 2)$$
$$C(1, 3) = A(1, 3) + B(1, 3)$$

$\qquad\qquad\qquad\qquad\qquad\qquad$ $\left[\begin{array}{l} \text{I is set to 1} \\ \text{J loops from 1 to 6} \end{array}\right.$

$$C(2, 1) = A(2, 1) + B(2, 1)$$
$$C(2, 2) = A(2, 2) + B(2, 2)$$

$\qquad\qquad\qquad\qquad\qquad\qquad$ $\left[\begin{array}{l} \text{I is set to 2} \\ \text{J loops from 1 to 6 again} \end{array}\right.$

$$C(4, 5) = A(4, 5) + B(4, 5)$$
$$C(4, 6) = A(4, 6) + B(4, 6)$$

$\qquad\qquad\qquad\qquad\qquad\qquad$ $\left[\begin{array}{l} \text{I is set to 4} \\ \text{J loops from 1 to 6 for the fourth time} \end{array}\right.$

EXAMPLE 6 A company manufactures three types of wooden widgets—economy, standard, and super. Varying amounts of wood, hardware, and labor go into each widget. These specifications are given by matrix SPEC. The cost of each element is given by column vector COST. The amount of production is given by row vector VOL. A FORTRAN program is to find unit cost (UCOST) for each type of widget and to find total cost for the production (TCOST). The program segment is shown in Figure 18-7.

Although stated in terms of matrix multiplication, this problem illustrates the concept of setting up arrays to make FORTRAN coding simple. The problem would have had the same coding if there were 100 products and 50 cost elements. Essentially, any list or array of quantities which can fit in a single classification should probably be subscripted and handled as an array.

Rules for Using the DO Statement

A DO loop is initialized by the execution of the DO statement, and the loop makes a normal exit after it has been executed the requisite number of times. The termination statement (the CONTINUE if the pattern described here is followed) must be executed in order for the incrementation and testing action of the loop mechanism to be activated. It is possible to transfer out of the loop range, execute other statements, and then return to the loop. The rules are given below:

RULES FOR DO LOOPS

1 Older FORTRANs require that an executable statement should be used as the first statement following the DO statement. This excludes DIMENSION, FORMAT, etc., from following immediately after the DO statement.

2 A DO statement's parameters should not be altered by statements within the range of the DO. This includes the values for i, m_1, m_2, and m_3 as previously defined for the DO statement.

3 The control variable can be used as a variable inside the range of the DO loops (but it is not required). If an exit other than a normal exit is made from the loop, the current value of the control variable is available for use outside the loop. After a normal exit, it is not available.

4 DO loops should be entered through the DO statement. Never transfer from a statement outside the range of a DO to the inside of the range. An inner DO can transfer into the range of the outer DO because the inner DO is already in the range.

5 The iteration count for the loop is established as the integer value from INT $((m_2 - m_1 + m_3)/m_3)$. If negative, the count is zero. A count of zero means the loop will not be executed at all (Older FORTRANs execute the loop once.)

The last rule regarding the iteration count means that a DO statement DO 100 I = 4, 3 will not be executed at all (processing will continue with the statement following the CONTINUE for the loop). In some older FORTRANs, the loop would execute once. In other words, the current FORTRAN standard requires a DO WHILE repetition structure; older FORTRANs followed a DO UNTIL. This may affect portability of programs, and so the prudent programmer will code in a way that the program will operate properly no matter which logic the computer follows.

In writing loops, questions of efficiency arise. A computation can often be performed outside the loop once and then provide for the inner loop computation, thereby reducing processing time. However, such efficient coding should be carefully used because it tends to make the program logic less clear. As an example, assume a program to produce a table of interest rates (for $1.00) using the formula

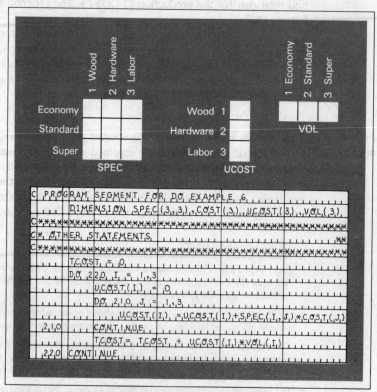

FIGURE 18-7 Program segment for DO Example 6.

$A = 1.0(1 + i)^n$ where i (the interest rate called XI) and n are the number of periods. Since $1 + i$ is the same for each computation, it can be computed once outside the loop for efficiency. But unless the tables are very large, the efficiency is not significant enough to justify loss of clarity.

Clear coding of loop	More efficient
	FACTR = 1.0 + XI
DO 100 I = 1,N	DO 100 I = 1,N
A = (1.0 + XI)**I	A = FACTR**I
(other statements)	(other statements)
100 CONTINUE	100 CONTINUE

Self-testing Quiz—
FORTRAN #8

1 Complete the table:

DO statement	Is it always, sometimes, or never valid	If always invalid or if invalid for Subset or for older FORTRANs, explain why
(a) DO NIX I = 1,7		
(b) DO 7,I = 1,NIX		
(c) DO 999 MIX = 1,J,K		
(d) DO 8 JANE = JOE, + 7		
(e) DO 9 K = 10,8		
(f) DO 88 LUCK = 7,7		
(g) DO 13 ILL = 7,15,3		
(h) DO 45 I = 1, N − 1		
(i) DO 20 X = 1,10,2		

2 At the completion of the following program loops, what will be the value of K, L, and M?

```
        M = 0
        DO   101   I = 1,10
            K = I
            DO  100 J = 1,5
                L = J
                M = M + 1
100         CONTINUE
101     CONTINUE
```

3 How many times will the loops defined by the following DO statements be executed? Note where common pre-1977 practice may differ from the standard. Which statements are not allowed by Subset FORTRAN?
(a) DO 3 I = 5,5

(*b*) DO 3 I = 5,1
(*c*) DO 3 I = 1,5
(*d*) DO 3 I = 1,5,3
(*e*) DO 3 A = .1,.5,.2
(*f*) DO 3 A = .03,.30,.05

4 In what order will the following program segment print out the subscripted variables from a three-dimensional array?

```
      DO 120 I = 1,2
          DO 110 J = 1,2
              DO 100 K = 1,2
                  WRITE (3,900) ARRAY (I,J,K)
100               CONTINUE
110           CONTINUE
120   CONTINUE
```

5 What will the following program segment do?

```
      DO 150 I = 1,30
          SUM = 0
          SUM = SUM + A(I)*B(I)
150   CONTINUE
```

6 Which of the following DO loop nests are valid?

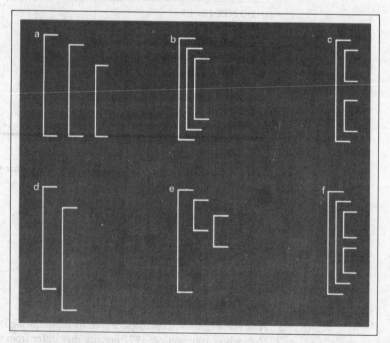

7 Write a program segment to sum the products from multiplying the elements in array LIX by the corresponding elements in array MIX. There are N entries in each.

8 Write a program segment to find the largest number of an N-entry array called X. Put the largest one in BIG.

9 Write a program segment to print out every other entry in a K-entry array called DAD, starting with the second entry.

10 Write a program segment to shift the values in an array A so that A(1) = A(2), A(2) = A(3), etc. A(N) should contain original value of A(1). Be careful with A(1).

11 Write a program segment to shift the values in a 25-entry array called ALPHA so that A(2) = A(1), A(3) = A(2), etc., and A(1) = A(25). Be sure to check your logic carefully.

Block IF Statements

A major change in the 1977 FORTRAN Standard is the addition of the capability to conditionally execute groups of statements. This capability allows FORTRAN programs to be more block-structured and to eliminate many GO TO statements that are considered undesirable in structured programming. This is a significant change in FORTRAN and a major enhancement of the language. Whenever programs must be portable for use on computers without the block IF, these features should not be used; otherwise, the use of these features will improve FORTRAN program clarity. Since this capability is not yet generally available, the example programs will not use the block IF features.

BLOCK IF STATEMENT

IF (condition) THEN
  statements for IF block
ELSE
  statements for ELSE block
END IF
	All statements between the condition and the ELSE are executed if the condition is true; statements between ELSE and END IF are executed if the condition is not true. The ELSE and ELSE block statements may be omitted.

ELSE IF (condition) THEN	IF statements may be nested by use of the ELSE IF. . .THEN statement

The use of the block IF can be illustrated by example. Refer back to the program to compute the factorial of a number in Figure 17-7 on page 515. Block 100 and 200 could be coded more clearly with a block IF. The recoding of the program also takes advantage of the 1977 FORTRAN feature of real variables as DO loop variables and apostrophe specification of Hollerith output. There were five GO TOs in the original version of the program. There is only one GO TO in the revised version.

EXAMPLE
```
C* BLOCK 100 ** INPUT, INPUT VALIDATION, AND
C*              ** FACTORIAL FOR ZERO.
  100 READ 905,VALUE
  905 FORMAT (F2.0)
      FACTRL = 1.0
```

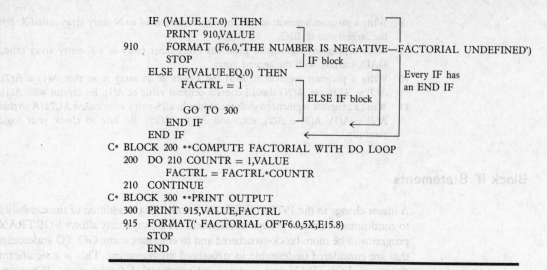

```
         IF (VALUE.LT.0) THEN
             PRINT 910,VALUE
910          FORMAT (F6.0,'THE NUMBER IS NEGATIVE—FACTORIAL UNDEFINED')
             STOP
         ELSE IF(VALUE.EQ.0) THEN
             FACTRL = 1

             GO TO 300
         END IF
         END IF
C* BLOCK 200 **COMPUTE FACTORIAL WITH DO LOOP
200   DO 210 COUNTR = 1,VALUE
         FACTRL = FACTRL*COUNTR
210   CONTINUE
C* BLOCK 300 **PRINT OUTPUT
300   PRINT 915,VALUE,FACTRL
915   FORMAT(' FACTORIAL OF'F6.0,5X,E15.8)
      STOP
      END
```

As a second example, if a code number is equal to 1 or 2, pay is computed as $3.75 \times$ regular hours and overtime is set to zero. If the code is 3, pay is $4.15 \times$ regular hours and overtime is $1.5 \times 4.15 \times$ hours over 40. If code is more than 3, print ERROR IN CODE.

EXAMPLE

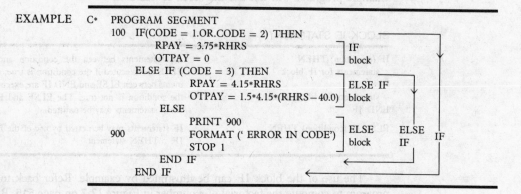

```
C*  PROGRAM SEGMENT
100   IF(CODE = 1.OR.CODE = 2) THEN
         RPAY = 3.75*RHRS
         OTPAY = 0
      ELSE IF (CODE = 3) THEN
         RPAY = 4.15*RHRS
         OTPAY = 1.5*4.15*(RHRS – 40.0)
      ELSE
         PRINT 900
900      FORMAT (' ERROR IN CODE')
         STOP 1
      END IF
      END IF
```

Additional Input/Output Features

If only the basic input/output statements are used, frequently several statements are required to input and output data, and the control that can be exercised over the line spacing is minimal. This section explains additional input/output features which simplify the writing of certain types of input/output procedures.

Repetition of Format Specifications

When several variables for input or output have the same specification, a single specification can be repeated by placing an integer number in front of it. For example, 7F10.3 means that the F10.3 specification is to be used seven times. The repetition number is not used with H fields.

By enclosing a set of specifications in parentheses and placing an integer number in front of the set, the set will be repeated the number of times indicated. 3(F10.0, I3) is the same as (F10.0, I3, F10.0, I3, F10.0, I3).

Enclosing a set of specifications in parentheses without a number to indicate repetition implies that the set of specifications will be repeated, using a new record for each repeat, until the list of variables in the input-output statement has been taken care of. The effect of the unmodified group in parentheses is discussed in detail later. The following examples illustrate the repeat feature. The repeat will stop when the list of variables to be used is exhausted. The program uses only as much of a FORMAT as is needed.

Examples of FORMAT repeat are:

Format	Effect
(I3, 7F10.0)	I3 and repeat F10.0 up to seven times.
5(I3, F10.0)	Repeat (I3, F10.0) five times.
(I3, 5(F10.0, I2))	I3 and repeat (F10.0, I2) five times.
(7I2, 3(F10.0, I3))	Repeat I2 seven times, and then repeat (F10.0, I3) three times.

Handling Physical and Logical Records with FORMAT Statements

In the preceding chapter, one FORMAT statement was assumed for each line of output, each card read, etc. FORTRAN allows considerably more versatility in input and output. Lines, cards, etc., may be skipped, and a single FORMAT statement may be used for more than one line of output.

The concepts of a physical record and a logical record are important in understanding how to use FORMAT specifications effectively. A *physical record* is a unit from which data can be read or on which data can be written. Examples are a punched card and a line on the printer paper. A *logical record* consists of items of data which logically belong together. They may occupy less than one physical record, exactly one physical record, or more than one physical record.

The slash / is used in a FORMAT statement to terminate the current physical record. The closing right parenthesis of the FORMAT statement also terminates the current physical record. Using more than one slash causes unit records to be skipped. The slash can be written anywhere in the FORMAT statement. Examples are:

FORMAT (//, 3F10.0)
FORMAT (I2, /, F10.0)
FORMAT (I2, F10.0, /)

Since the right, closing parenthesis also terminates a physical record (and therefore can be thought of as a slash), rules can be formulated for the effect of slashes.

USE OF SLASHES IN FORMAT

1 N slashes at the beginning or end of a FORMAT causes n physical (unit) records to be skipped.

2 A slash in the middle of a FORMAT will cause the current record to be terminated, and a new physical record will be brought into use (starting at the beginning of the new record).

3 More than one slash in the middle of a FORMAT will cause n − 1 records to be skipped.

4 Commas before and after the slashes in the FORMAT specifications are optional.

Examples of the use of slashes are:

FORMAT (with read)	Effect
F(10.0/I3)	Reads two cards; the first card has a variable specification of F10.0, the second uses I3.
(3F10.0/)	Reads a card with three F10.0 values, then skips a card.
(///F6.3)	Skips three cards and uses F6.3 for variable on fourth.

FORMAT (with print)	Effect
(F10.0/)	Prints a line with F10.0 and then skips one line.
(3F10.0,/,I3) Commas optional	Prints three F10.0 values on a line, skips to next line, and prints an I3 value.
(F10.0,///)	Prints F10.0, then skips three lines.

What happens if the number of variables in the input/output list is different from the number of specifications in the FORMAT statement? The effects can be summarized as:

Condition	Effect	Example
More specifications than variables in the list.	Extra specifications are ignored.	READ(1,900)A,B,C 900 FORMAT(5F10.0)
More variables than specifications.	When specifications are exhausted (i.e., the right parenthesis of the FORMAT is reached), a new record is brought into use, and the FORMAT specifications are repeated.	WRITE(3,900)A,B,C 900 FORMAT(2F10.0) Writes output on two lines with A and B on first line and C on second line.

What happens if the FORMAT specifications call for a total of field widths which are greater than one physical record? The first record is used in total, and another record is brought into use for the remainder. For example, if a 160-character line is specified as being written on 132-character printer paper, the line will have the first 132 characters on the first line and the remaining characters at the beginning of the next line.

It has already been explained that the rightmost parenthesis in the FORMAT acts to terminate the current physical record. When the end of the FORMAT is reached without exhausting the list of variables, the record is terminated, a new record is brought into use, and the FORMAT specification is repeated. However, the program goes back to the most recent left parenthesis in the FORMAT (a specification in parentheses) and begins at that point for the repeating of the specifications. For example, the following format

READ (1,900)J,A,B,C,

—————————————Most recent left parenthesis

900   FORMAT (I6, (F10.0))

will read J and A from the first card. The list is not exhausted, so the specifications must be repeated with a new punched card. Because of the rule just mentioned, only F10.0 is repeated, not the entire specification. Since the list is still not exhausted, F10.0 is again repeated with a new card. In other words, the example reads from three cards: J and A on card 1, B on card 2, and C on card 3. These rules allow considerable flexibility in input or output. The following examples for FORMAT (and a write statement) illustrate the rules:

(I3/(F10.0))	Prints I3 values on one line, goes to next line, and prints an F10.0 value. If more variables, it continues printing one F10.0 to a line.
(I2/(3F10.0))	Prints I2 on one line, then prints three F10.0s per line until list is exhausted.
	I2
	F10.0 F10.0 F10.0
	F10.0 F10.0 F10.0

Vertical Spacing Control on Line Printer

On line printers running under FORTRAN, the first column on the line is not printed; the position is used for vertical spacing control of the printer. The output is written to keep column 1 blank unless spacing control is desired. If spacing control is required, a numeric character is assigned to the first position by an appropriate FORMAT statement. The easiest way is to have a one-character Hollerith field. The space-control characters are:

Character	Vertical spacing before printing
Blank	One line
0	Two lines
1	To first line of next page
+	No advance

For example, a FORMAT (1H1) or FORMAT ('1') will space to the next page.

Horizontal Positioning

The use of extra spaces in a specification causes blanks to be inserted in a line. The nX specification causes n positions to be skipped (and filled with blanks). In full 1977 FORTRAN, the X may be signed to move the output back rather than forward ($-nX$ repositions in a backwards direction). This would allow a field to be reread. A Tc specification is a tabulating specification which positions the input or output device at the *cth* character position. For example, writing a FORMAT (T50, 'REPORT OF SALES') will output the heading starting at position 50 on the line.

Implied DO Loops in Input/Output

Several methods have been presented for reading or writing subscripted variables. Each variable may, for example, be named in the list of variables.

READ (1,900) A(1,1), A(1,2), A(2,1), A(2,2)

This method is cumbersome if many variables are to be read.

A second method is to read in the subscripts at the same time as the variable, thus avoiding the listing of the subscripts in the input/output statement. Input data items to be used as subscripts must appear before the variables to which they apply.

READ (1,900) I, J, A(I,J)

As each card is read by the above statement, the first two values specify the subscript location to which the third value is to be assigned. This might be a useful method if the data items are in random sequences and each data record contains the subscripts as well as the quantity to be stored.

A third method for reading or writing subscripted variables is to include the statement in a DO loop. If the statement is a READ instruction, the order in which the subscripted-variable values appear on the data cards must correspond to the order implied by the DO loop. Each time the DO loop goes through the cycle, a READ command is executed.

DO loop		Order of data values
	DO 150 I = 1,N	A(1)
	READ (1,900) A (I)	A(2)
900	FORMAT (F10.0)	.
150	CONTINUE	.
		.
		A(n)
	DO 150 I = 1,N	A(1,1)
	DO 140 J = 1,3	A(1,2)
	READ (1,900) A (I,J)	A(1,3)
140	CONTINUE	A(2,1)
150	CONTINUE	.
		.
		A(n,3)

Each of these methods for reading or writing subscripted variables has disadvantages or limitations. The listing method is cumbersome, the specification of subscripts in the data card involves extra data input unless there are special reasons for it, and the DO loop is limited by the fact that each loop initiates a repeat of the input/output command. A very useful extended feature is a form of input/output statement called an "implied DO loop." The form of the statement is similar to that of the DO loop. In fact, as many as three implied loops may be nested. The form is shown by the following examples:

READ (1,3) (A(I), I = 1,N)
READ (1,3) ((A(I,J), J = 1,N), I = 1,N)

Note that each of the loop parameter specifications is enclosed in parentheses. Note also the placement of the commas.

In addition to the fact that it is a shorter form, the advantage of the implied DO loop over the regular DO loop is that the resulting variables are treated as a single list so that input or output from physical records is entirely under FORMAT control. For example, READ (1,900) (A(I),I = 1,N) will read the variable from the cards differently, depending on the FORMAT.

FORMAT	READ instruction reads
FORMAT (F10.0)	One variable per card
FORMAT (8F10.0)	Eight values per card
FORMAT (40F10.0)	Five cards with eight values on each (assuming 80 columns available for data)
FORMAT (2F10.0/F10.0)	Two variables on first card, one variable on second card, two variables on third card, etc.

Nested loops are possible. The outer loop is put last, and the innermost DO (the one which changes most rapidly) is next to the variable. The loops should be listed so that they match the arrangement of the data.

Implied DO loop	Order in which variables are read
READ (1,900) (A(I), I = 1,N)	A(1), A(2), A(3), . . ., A(N)
READ (1,900) ((A(I,J), I = 1,N), J = 1,N)	A(1,1), A(2,1), A(3,1), . . ., A(N,N)
READ (1,900) ((A(I,J), J = 1,N), I = 1,N)	A(1,1), A(1,2), A(1,3), . . ., A(N,N)
READ (1,900) (((A(I,J,K), I = 1,N), J = 1,N), K = 1,N)	A(1,1,1), A(2,1,1), A(3,1,1), . . ., A(N,N,N)

An instruction for an entire array to be read, printed, punched, etc., can be merely the array name without subscripts or DO loops, etc. The DIMENSION statement will already have specified both the fact that it is a subscripted-variable name and the size of the array. This form can be used only when the entire array is desired in natural order, i.e., in column order. This command is analogous to the implied DO where the column order (row varies most rapidly) is specified. The FORMAT reacts as if the entire array were listed. Thus, the FORMAT will specify not only field size but also the quantity of the variable values to be found on each card (for input) or line (for output). For example, if ALPHA is dimensioned as ALPHA(100), READ(1,900) ALPHA will read all 100 values according to FORMAT 900.

It is also possible in the current standard FORTRAN to define part of an array to be output in much the same manner as an implied DO loop. This is termed an "array block item." Where a_1 and a_2 are array element names:

$a_1:a_2$ Write all array elements from a_1 to and including a_2

$a_1:$ Write all elements from beginning of array up to and including a_1

$:a_2$ Write from a_2 to end of array

EXAMPLES	WRITE(3,900) ALPHA(5):ALPHA(10)	Write ALPHA(5) through ALPHA(10)
	WRITE(3,900) ALPHA(5):	Write from ALPHA(1) through ALPHA(5)

DATA Statement   In many programs, there are variables which should be set to an initial value. This may be accomplished by input of data as the first step in the program, by assignment statements, or by a DATA statement. The DATA statement provides initial values for variables, arrays, and array elements. The form of the DATA statement is:

DATA nlist/clist/,nlist/clist/

nlist is a list of variable names, array names, or array element names.

clist is a list of the values to be assigned. A value can be repeated by using an integer and asterisk in front of the constant, the integer specifying number of repetitions of the constant.

EXAMPLES   DATA A,B,C/5.0,3.5,4.9/ assigns 5.0 to A, 3.5 to B, and 4.9 to C.
DATA A,B,C(3)/3*10.0/ assigns 10.0 to A, 10.0 to B, and 10.0 to C(3). DATA ALPHA/50*0/ places zeros in all 50 elements of array ALPHA. The nlist (in full FORTRAN but not in Subset) can be an implied DO statement. For example, if the elements from 10 to 20 in a 50-element array BETA are to be initialized to 5.0, the DATA statement can be written as:

DATA (BETA(I), I = 10,20)/11*5.0/

The DATA statement is usually placed at the beginning of the program in the initialization block. It is a useful statement, especially when an entire array or a number of variables used as accumulators are set to zero. For example, to set TALLY1, TALLY2, and a 100-element array GAMMA to zero can be performed using assignment statements and a DO loop or a DATA statement.

Method without DATA statement	With DATA statement
TALLY1 = 0	
TALLY2 = 0	
DO 150 I = 1,100	DATA TALLY1, TALLY2, GAMMA/102*0/
GAMMA (I) = 0	
150 CONTINUE	

List-directed READ and WRITE

The new full FORTRAN (but not Subset) allows list-directed input and output. Some older compilers also allow it. In this form of input and output, there is no FORMAT statement. On input, the data items to be read are listed in the READ statement which has no FORMAT statement label; the values to be read appear in the order specified by the input list, separated by blanks or commas. For example, to read A,B, and I,J using list-directed input, the READ statement and an input data card would be as follows:

        READ (1) A,B,I,J   where (1) specifies card reader
or READ,A,B,I,J   where card reader is implied

The data would appear as:

    125.0,13.765,15,12   } Each data item separated by a comma

or   125.0   13.765   15   12   } Each data item separated by one or more spaces

The data item values for list-directed input are separated by commas and/or spaces. A repeated value can be shown by a repeat number (2) plus an asterisk followed by the value. The same value 495.2 for three variables for A, B, and C might therefore appear as:

READ(1)A,B,C

3*495.2

If no value is to be input, this can be expressed by successive commas or by n* with no value. For example, a READ(1)ARRAY where array is dimensioned as 25 but only values for 5 and 7 are to be inserted might be input as:

4*76.1,,13.9,18*

      └Skip value

In the previous example, a slash could be used to show the termination of the input of data; the effect is to insert null values in the rest of the items in the list.

4*,76.1,,13.9,/

List-directed input is very useful. It is especially helpful when data is input from a terminal because spacing is more difficult to control.

On output, the data is displayed or printed in I or (E or F) format depending on whether the name identifies an integer or real value. The compiler will select E or F editing on the basic of the value of the data. The output will be separated by spaces (or commas).

Expressions in Output List

A feature of the new full ANS FORTRAN not found in older FORTRANs or in Subset is the use of expressions in the output list. The expression is evaluated and the result printed. Examples illustrate this feature.

WRITE (3,900) 3, A, A**2
900   FORMAT (I5,F10.0)

If $A = 4$, the output will be

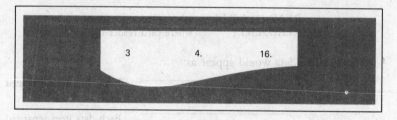

3   4.   16.

or in list-directed output

WRITE (3) 3, A, A**2

in which case the output is formatted by the compiler.

Self-testing Quiz— FORTRAN #9

1   What is the effect of each of the following FORMAT specifications?
   (a) (F6.0)   (g) (F10.0//(F10.0))
   (b) (3I2,4F10.0, 3E15.8)   (h) (///F10.0)
   (c) 4(I3, F10.0)   (i) (F10.0, 5/)
   (d) (I2, (I3))   (j) (1H1)
   (e) (I7, (F10.0))   (k) (T40,F10.2,'ONE')
   (f) (I5/F10.0)   (l) ('1')

2   What will each of the following program segments do?

(a)   DIMENSION A(10,10)
        READ (1,900) A
900 FORMAT (F10.0)

(b)   DIMENSION B(5,5)
        READ (1,910) ((B(I,J),J = 1,5),I = 1,5)
910 FORMAT (8F10.0)

(c)   DIMENSION C(6,6)
        READ (1,920) (C(1,J),J = 1,6)
920 FORMAT (6F10.0)

(d)   DO 130 K = 1,3   or READ (1,930)(((X(I,J,K),I = 1,
          DO 120 J = 1,N   N),J = 1,N),K = 1,3)
             DO 110 I = 1,N
                READ (1,930) X(I,J,K)
930   FORMAT (F10.0)
110   CONTINUE
120   CONTINUE
130 CONTINUE

(e)   READ (1,940) J, Y(2,J)
940 FORMAT (I2,F10.0)

(f)   DIMENSION KIX (4,4)
        PRINT (3,950) KIX
950 FORMAT (4I10//)

3 Use the DATA statement to initialize A to 40.1, B to 3.7, C and D to 1.0, and all elements in a 100-element array BETA to zero.

4 Use an implied loop in DATA statement to initialize to 2.0 every other element between 15 and 49 in an array called ARRAY.

5 How does the computer distinguish among data items in a list-directed input?

6 Write a statement to read the following input without a FORMAT statement:
762.42   1800.   14   18   5*6.0

7 Write a statement to output the square root of A without a FORMAT.

Character String Input and Output

Alphanumeric character strings can be input, manipulated, and output by FORTRAN statements. Using H or apostrophe editing in FORMATs to output character strings has already been explained. This section explains how to read, manipulate, and output character data.

Defining a Character String

The character data (also called Hollerith data) can be alphabetic, numeric characters not to be used in numeric computation, and special characters. Character data is stored in the computer and therefore can be referenced by a name. The character string GBD can be referred to by ANAME just as the data 147.6 can be referred to as AVALUE. Each character in the character string occupies one character storage unit. The length of a character data item is the number of character positions (including imbedded blanks) in the string. For example, 'I WILL' occupies six positions. Character data can be defined as a constant in the program. The character string is enclosed in apostrophes. For example, ANAME = 'G. B. DAVIS' stores the name in 11 character positions. Any reference to ANAME will obtain the string of characters. In older FORTRANs, such constants were written using an H; for example, ANAME = 11HG. B. DAVIS.

Variable names assigned to character strings do not have any special first letter as do integer names. A variable name is identified with a character string by a character assignment statement:

ASTRING = 'NOW IS TIME'

or by a CHARACTER type statement. This can be used for individual variable names or for character arrays. A length specification is required unless the length is 1.

EXAMPLES		
	CHARACTER *10 ANAME,BNAME,R	Defines all variables in list as length 10.
	CHARACTER A*10,B*6	Defines A as character variable name with length 10; B is length 6.
	CHARACTER ARRAY*6	Defines each element in ARRAY as holding a 6-position character string. ARRAY is dimensioned elsewhere.
or	CHARACTER ARRAY(10)*6	Dimensions 10-element character array of length 6 for each element.

A character substring is a continuous portion of a character string. It has a name and may be assigned values and referenced. The substring name is followed by the character identification for the first and last characters to be included, separated by a colon. For example, the characters stored in positions 8 to 10 of character variable ALPHA are assigned a substring name BETA by the following:

BETA(ALPHA(8:10))

Expressions (the integer value) can be used to specify the limits of the substring. For example,

BETA(ALPHA(3.0*B:Y/Z))

Input of a Character String

A character string may be input in several ways:

1 The A edit descriptor
2 List-directed character input
3 DATA statement

The A edit descriptor specifies the number of characters to be read from the input and stored in the positions identified with a character variable name. The form is An, where n is the number of characters. The characters to be read can include blanks. For example, if the 10-character data strings for NAME1 and NAME2 are being read from a punched card, the READ and FORMAT might be as follows (NAME1 and NAME2 would already have been defined as CHARACTER types):

```
      READ(1,900) NAME1, NAME2
900   FORMAT(A10,A10)
```

In list-directed character input, the characters are enclosed in apostrophes. When the input data is not as large as the storage, the data is left-justified, and the rest of the storage positions are filled with blanks; if the storage is too small, the leftmost input characters are lost.

The DATA statement to initialize character data uses the character constant form of enclosing in apostrophes. The names must have been defined as CHARACTER type. For example:

DATA ANAME/'FLINT STANFORD'/

In older FORTRANs the form of the DATA statement uses an H, for example,

DATA ANAME/14HFLINT STANFORD/

Manipulation and Output of Character Strings

The manipulation of character data may use any of the relational operators. There is a means for linking together character strings (concatenation).

Character strings or substrings can be combined or linked by the concatenation operator //. For example, if A and B are defined as a CHARACTER type and contain 'NOW' and ' IS' the statement:

X = A//B

will produce a string X with the value 'NOW IS'. Character constants may be used. For example,

X = 'NOW'//B

will also yield X of 'NOW IS'.

Character strings may be compared using the relational operators. For example, two names may be compared to see if they are identical. If so, processing should go to statement 500.

IF(NAME1.EQ.NAME2)GO TO 500

If the strings being compared are of unequal length, the logic assumes the shorter one has trailing blanks to make them equal.

A character constant may be used in the comparison. For example, a test to see if an input is the word END (and if so, GO TO 600) would read:

IF(WORD.EQ.'END')GO TO 600

In older FORTRANs the statement might be IF(WORD.EQ.3HEND)GO TO 600.

For output of character data, the program may use A edit specifications with FORMAT statement, or output may be list-directed, in which case the output will be printed with no spaces, commas, or apostrophes between two successive character outputs. In A editing, an A field size greater than the character variable length will result in leading blanks in the output field; an A field too small for the string will truncate the rightmost characters for output.

Self-testing Quiz—
FORTRAN #10

1 Define ANAME and LNAME as character variable names of length 10.
2 Define a five-element character array BARRAY of length 6.
3 Compare a character variable LNAME with the constant CLARK. If equal, go to 600.
4 Define a substring ABREV as characters 1 to 3 of LNAME.
5 Concatenate ABREV and the constant ABC to form CBREV.
6 Read ten 8-character names in fields of 8 from a card and store in a 10-element array NAMES.
7 Initialize a character variable FNAME with AARON.
8 An 11-character field MISSISSIPPI is to be printed using a specification of A6. What will be printed?
9 Write statements to read an employee's name from a punched card (columns 1–15) and print it as the heading for an analysis of the employee's performance. The name should be printed starting at column 45.

File Access Methods and Use of Secondary Storage in FORTRAN

FORTRAN has the two basic READ and WRITE instructions. Using different input/output units requires only that the unit designation be changed for the unit to be employed in the program. For example, to input or output at a typewriter or visual display unit instead of a card reader or printer requires only a change in the unit designation. In the case of secondary storage on magnetic tape or disk files, additional instructions are available for operations that are frequently required.

File Access
Methods

Before describing file access methods, it is useful to understand the existence of both formatted and unformatted records.

Formatted records consist of internal representation defined by the FORMAT used to write the record. An unformatted record (written without a FORMAT) is generally stored in a form that is most efficient to the computer being used, for example, in binary for numeric data rather than in binary-coded character for each numeric digit. The choice of unformatted read or write is therefore based on efficiency considerations.

The file access methods available in full Standard FORTRAN are sequential, stream, and direct access. In Subset FORTRAN, stream access is not included, and there are severe limitations on direct access.

1 *Sequential access* Records are read in serial fashion in the same order they were written. The records may be formatted or unformatted, but all are the same. List-directed input is not allowed. This can be implemented on tape or disk storage.

2 *Stream access* List-directed output (compiler-directed formatting) and list-directed input must be used. The program treats the variables to be read or written as a stream of data without a concept of logical or physical records. Either tape or disk storage is allowed.

3 *Direct access* This can be implemented only on direct access storage such as disk. Records may be read or written in any order. Each record must have a unique positive integer identifier called a "record number," specified when the record is first written. The records are stored in order by record number. The records are either all formatted or all unformatted. Direct access input/output statements must be used to write or read. All records have the same length. List-directed input or output cannot be used.

In sequential and stream (but not direct access) files, the last record of the file may be an endfile record. This record is used only to signal the end of the file. The existence of the endfile record may be tested by the END = s specifier in the READ or WRITE statement.

READ(6,900,END = 300)

Auxiliary Input/Output Statements

The statements which are useful when auxiliary storage is utilized are the control information list in the READ or WRITE statement, the OPEN and CLOSE statements, and file positioning statements. An INQUIRE statement will also be explained. These features are rather specialized, so the section is a brief overview intended to alert the reader to the kind of capabilities that are available.

The control information list is used as part of the READ or WRITE statement to specify unit to be used, FORMAT, and directives for change of execution sequence. The form is a three- or four-letter identifier followed by an equals sign and a unit, statement, or record number. The five specifiers are:

UNIT = unit number of device
FMT = format statement label
REC = record number for direct access
ERR = statement label to which control goes if there is an I/O error
END = statement label to go to if end of file

The alphabetic identifier is not required for unit or format. The following are identical:

READ(1,900)ALPHA
READ(UNIT=1, FMT=900) ALPHA

The specifier REC defines the variable name (or other expression) that identifies the integer value of the record in a direct access file. If the record number is defined by IRECNO and control should go to 600 in the event of error, the READ would be:

READ(1,900,REC=IRECNO,ERR=600)
or   READ(UNIT=1, FMT=900, REC=etc.)

The END specifier is used only with a sequential or stream access file, not with a direct access file.

The OPEN statement is used to connect an existing file to a unit or create a new file and connect it to the unit. The CLOSE statement terminates the connection of a file with a unit.

THE OPEN STATEMENT

OPEN(olist)

The olist is a list of specifiers for the features of the file, the unit number always being required, others being optional:

UNIT   = unit number (UNIT = is optional)
ERR   = statement label for transfer if error
NAME   = name of the file
STATUS = OLD, NEW, SCRATCH, or UNKNOWN
ACCESS = SEQUENTIAL, STREAM, or DIRECT
FORM   = FORMATTED or UNFORMATTED (for direct access file; if not specified, it is unformatted)
RECL   = record length for a direct access file (required)
MAXREC = maximum record length
BLANK   = NULL or ZERO to specify handling of blanks

A new direct access unformatted file might be opened by the following:

OPEN(12,ERR=600,NAME=SAMPLE,STATUS=NEW,ACCESS=DIRECT,RECL=200)

THE CLOSE STATEMENT

CLOSE(clist)

where the clist is:

UNIT   = unit number(UNIT=is optional)
ERR   = statement label
STATUS = KEEP or DELETE

If a file on unit 8 is to be released, the CLOSE might read:

CLOSE(8,STATUS = DELETE)

Since all the specifiers for an existing file are stored with the file, it is often necessary to obtain information about it. This is done by the INQUIRY statement. This will not be explained because if it is required, the programmer should consult the implementor manual. One example will illustrate its use.

INQUIRY (6,FORM = FRM, RECL = ILENGTH)

Upon execution, FRM will contain the characters FORMATTED or UN-FORMATTED, and ILENGTH will contain the length of the records in the file.

File positioning statements are used to backspace, write an end-of-file record, or rewind. There are two forms:

FILE POSITIONING STATEMENTS

BACKSPACE unit or BACKSPACE(alist)
ENDFILE unit or ENDFILE(alist)
REWIND unit or REWIND(alist)

where alist is:

UNIT = unit number (UNIT = is optional)
ERR = statement label

As an example of BACKSPACE, the following causes unit 6 to backspace one record.

BACKSPACE 6 or BACKSPACE(UNIT = 6)

As an example of ENDFILE, the statement to write an end-of-file record at the end of a sequential file on tape unit 6 would be:

ENDFILE 6 or ENDFILE(UNIT = 6)

Self-testing Quiz—
FORTRAN #11

1 Complete the table:

Access method	Order records read	File medium	Use of list-directed I/O	Use of end-of-file record
Sequential	Same order as written	Tape or disk	Not allowed	Yes
Stream				
Direct				

2 Write the statements to OPEN and to read PAYNO and PAYRTE from a new direct access file called PAY on unit 8. The record number is IRNO, the error routine label is 600, and the record length is 250. Close the file after use.

3 Write the statements to OPEN a formatted sequential file on tape unit 9 and to write a record composed of COURSE and GRADES. Backspace and read the record just written and print it. Close the file. The name of the file is STUDNT.

Subprograms

A *subprogram* is a program which is used by a main program. (The main program may have an optional statement PROGRAM name as its first statement.) Subprograms simplify programming because a single routine is used for all occurrences of a computational procedure, with only the data changing. Subprograms also simplify debugging because they can be tested separately. The programmer can use intrinsic subprograms which are part of the FORTRAN system, or special-purpose subprograms can be written. These programmer-written subprograms take four forms:

1 A statement function which is defined by a single statement in the main program. It is used in a statement.

2 A function subprogram is written as a separate program which returns a value to the main program. It is used by writing its name in an expression.

3 A separate program termed a "subroutine." It is called upon by a separate CALL statement.

4 A block data subprogram.

The specifications for the first three types of subprograms are outlined in Table 18-1. The block data subprogram is explained later in the section.

Statement Function   A statement function is defined by a single statement. The definition appears in the program after specification statements but before the first executable statement; the definition is not an executable statement. After being defined, the function may be written in an expression in the same manner as the mathematical functions described previously, such as SQRT and ABS.

The statement function is defined by writing the name chosen for the function. The name is followed by the list of defining (dummy) arguments separated by commas and enclosed in parentheses. The name is formed in the same way as a variable name (begins with I-N for integer, etc.). The name with its dummy arguments is set equal to an expression which uses the dummy variables in it. This statement only defines the function; it is not executed.

In order to use the function that has been defined, the name of the function is written in an expression with the actual variable names to be employed written in place of the dummy variables. The actual variables are listed in the same order and have the same type as the dummy variables. The program will make the computation defined by the function using the values of the actual variables in the calling

TABLE 18-1 SPECIFICATIONS FOR STATEMENT FUNCTION AND SUBPROGRAMS

	Statement function	FUNCTION subprogram	SUBROUTINE subprogram
Where defined	Internally defined in a single statement in the program using it	Externally defined in a separately compiled independent program	Externally defined in a separately compiled independent program
How defined	$f(x_1, x_2, \ldots, x_n) = e$ (should not be given a statement number) f = function name e = expression $x_1, x_2, \ldots, x_n$ = dummy arguments of the function	FUNCTION $f(x_1, x_2, \ldots, x_n)$ Program steps $f = e$ (name defined in program) RETURN (at each logical exit from program) END	SUBROUTINE $f(x_1, x_2, \ldots, x_n)$ Program steps RETURN (at each logical exit from program) END
How named	Same as variable name	Same as variable name. Type of name changed by a type specification in front of word FUNCTION	Same as variable name, except the name of subroutine has no type significance
How called into use	Appearance of name in an expression $v = \ldots f(a_1, a_2, \ldots, a_n) \ldots$ $a_1, a_2, \ldots, a_n$ = actual calling arguments of the function	Appearance of name in an expression $v = \ldots f(a_1, a_2, \ldots, a_n) \ldots$ Dummy arguments can also return values.	CALL statement CALL $f(a_1, a_2, \ldots, a_n)$ or CALL f
Number of outputs	One	One. Dummy arguments can also return values.	Any number
Restrictions on form of calling argument	Type, number, and order of calling arguments must agree with the dummy arguments of the definition; must have at least one argument; arguments may include subscripted variables or expression	Type, number, and order of calling arguments must agree with the dummy arguments of the definition; argument may be a variable name, subscripted variable, array name, expression, or external procedure; must have at least one argument	Same as function subprogram except that it need not have an argument

list. The resulting value will be put into the statement being executed as the value of the function. For example:

Defining statement   DESCF (B,A,C) = (B**2 − 4.0*A*C)
Using the function   X = BETA + DESCF (ALPHA,Y,Z)

The effect of the function is the insertion of the function into the statement using the calling variables in place of the dummy variables. In the example, this means that the statement to be executed will perform the following computation:

X = BETA + (ALPHA**2 − 4.0*Y*Z)

Function Subprogram   The disadvantage of the arithmetic statement function is that it can be only one statement in length. The function subprogram eliminates this restriction, and other restrictions as well (see Table 18-1). Although used in the same way as the arithmetic function in writing program statements, it is defined quite differently.

The function subprogram is written as a separate program and may be compiled separately. However, it must be included with the main program when the main program is to be run. When the function is used, the main program transfers to the subprogram to perform computations and then returns to the main program with a single value—the result of the computation using the values specified by the function. The dummy variables may also be used to return values.

The defining of the function in the subprogram takes the form of the word FUNCTION followed by the function name, followed by the dummy variables of the argument separated by commas and enclosed in parentheses. The beginning letter of the name indicates the type of the result unless a type specification is used.

FUNCTION $f(x_1,x_2, \ldots ,x_n)$ or type FUNCTION $f(x_1,x_2, \ldots ,x_n)$

---

f = e   (In other words, the name of the function must be defined in the program.)
RETURN
END

Examples of function naming are:

FUNCTION DOIT(A,B,I)
INTEGER FUNCTION ALPHA(A,B,I,J) which means result will be an integer value.

The RETURN statement is put at the logical end (or ends if more than one logical end) of the program. It signals that control is to return to the program from which the transfer to the subprogram was made. The END statement is required as the last statement because this is a separate program for compiling purposes. The END statement includes the RETURN, so no RETURN is needed before END (except in older FORTRANs, which require RETURN before END). As noted, the function name must be defined in the function program.

The function subprogram is used in writing program statements exactly the way the statement function is used. The list of arguments, specified when the function name is used, will replace the dummy variables in the definition.

For example, a program may, at several points, need to calculate the economic lot size. The economic order quantity (EOQ) is calculated from the formula:

$$\sqrt{\frac{24VS}{AC}}$$

where V = average monthly usage in units
S = setup or order cost
A = carrying cost expressed as a decimal
C = variable cost per unit

The EOQ is the quantity calculated by the formula except that, for this program, it must not be less than 1 month's average usage or more than 12 months' average usage. If it exceeds these limits, the EOQ is set equal to the limit. The difference (DIFF) between the calculated EOQ and the limits is to be computed. The function subprogram is shown in Figure 18-8.

In order to make use of the EOQ formula program in a statement, it is necessary only to write EOQ (a_1,a_2,a_3,a_4,a_5), where the a's stand for floating point arguments (variables or constants) used in place of the V, S, A, C, and DIFF of the subprogram. For example, ORDER = SPECL + EOQ(X,Y,C1,C2,Z) will return the EOQ value when X, Y, C1, C2, and Z are used as factors. It will then be added to SPECL and stored in the variable ORDER. The value associated with Z will be the value of DIFF in the subprogram.

Subroutine A function subroutine always returns a single value to the program statement where it is used. The subroutine subprogram removes this restriction. The subroutine may have arguments, but it does not require them. It does not automatically return a value to the main program.

As noted in Table 18-1, the subroutine is a separate program which is defined by the word SUBROUTINE followed by a name and arguments, if arguments are required. The name has no type significance.

SUBROUTINE $f(x_1,x_2, \ldots ,x_n)$
_____
_____
_____

RETURN
_____
_____

END

The argument of the subroutine may include an array as well as single variables. If an array is used, it must be dimensioned in the subroutine.

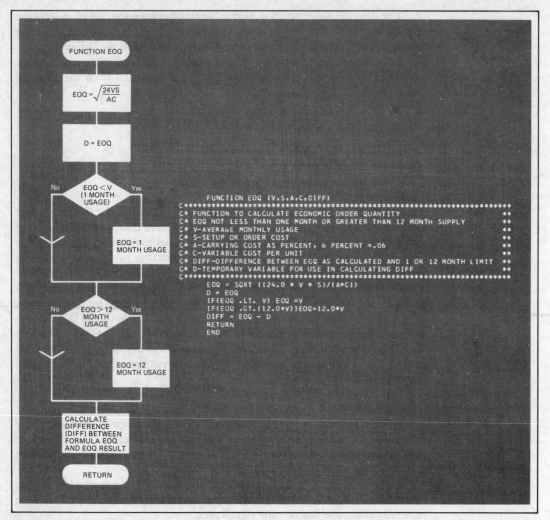

FIGURE 18-8 Function subprogram to calculate economic order quantity.

The subroutine is used by writing a CALL statement. If an argument is needed, the actual variables to be used are listed in the same order and type as the definition arguments. A subroutine can itself call other subroutines.

    CALL f(a$_1$, a$_2$, . . . , a$_n$)
or   CALL f

For example, a program requires the ordering of several arrays in descending sequence by magnitude from the largest to the smallest value. The arrays are all one-dimensional, and the number of quantities in an array range from 10 to 100.

The subroutine is written so that one of the arguments is the array name and the other is the number of entries. The subroutine program shown in Figure 18-9 is dimensioned to handle the largest array.

Note that the subroutine is general and will work for an array of 100 or less entries. The quantities are arranged by successive comparisons, shifting the larger values to the front until the array is ordered. A program needing to order an L-element array called GRADES merely writes the following statement:

CALL ORDER (L, GRADES)

After the array GRADES is ordered, control is returned to the statement following the CALL. Note that the L in the actual argument is not the same as the L in the subroutine. These are considered to be entirely different because the programs are compiled separately.

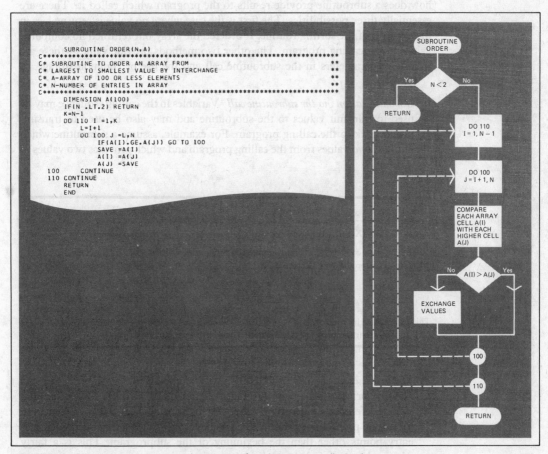

```
       SUBROUTINE ORDER(N,A)
C**********************************************************************
C* SUBROUTINE TO ORDER AN ARRAY FROM                                **
C* LARGEST TO SMALLEST VALUE BY INTERCHANGE                         **
C* A-ARRAY OF 100 OR LESS ELEMENTS                                  **
C* N-NUMBER OF ENTRIES IN ARRAY                                     **
C**********************************************************************
       DIMENSION A(100)
       IF(N .LT.2) RETURN
       K=N-1
       DO 110 I =1,K
          L=I+1
          DO 100 J =L,N
             IF(A(I).GE.A(J)) GO TO 100
             SAVE =A(I)
             A(I) =A(J)
             A(J) =SAVE
100       CONTINUE
110    CONTINUE
       RETURN
       END
```

FIGURE 18-9 Subroutine program to order an array from largest to smallest value.

In flowcharting programs with subroutines, the subroutine program or module symbol is used to indicate a subroutine CALL.

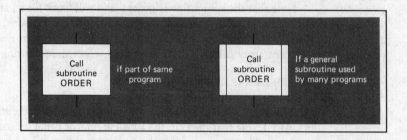

If a subroutine does not automatically return a value to the calling program, how does a subroutine provide results to the program which called it? There are essentially three possibilities. The first is the case where no value is returned, as in the example of the sorting routine. It ordered the array but returned no computed values to the calling program. The other two methods provide values—these are the use of parameters in the subroutine call and the use of common storage.

1 *Communication via the subroutine call* Variables in the calling sequence may be used to transmit values to the subroutine and may also be used to transmit results back to the calling program. For example, assume a subroutine which requires two values from the calling program and which provides two values as a result.

Calling program	Subroutine
CALL COMP (X,Y,A1,A2)	SUBROUTINE COMP (A,B,C,D)
A1 and A2 now contain quantities computed by subroutine (identified in subroutine as C and D).	C = _____
	D =
	END

This means that the subroutine is not limited in the number of values which may be communicated back to the calling program by this method. These values may include arrays.

2 *Communication via COMMON* As will be explained, the programmer can identify variables as being in a storage area called COMMON. This means that storage references in the subroutine refer to the same locations as references in the calling program. An additional statement, the ENTRY statement, identifies entry points other than the beginning of the subprogram. This is a fairly advanced feature for a complex program.

The COMMON and EQUIVALENCE Declarations

A variable name used in a subprogram is not related to the same variable name used in the main program. The two variables are assigned to different memory locations, and computations affecting one do not affect the other. There are, however, many instances in which it is convenient and desirable to have a variable name in both programs (usually the same name, but they may be different names) refer to the same quantity in the same memory location. This is accomplished by the use of the COMMON declaration.

COMMON $v_1, v_2, \ldots, v_n$

where v is a variable name or array name common to more than one program. An array name in common defines the entire array, so that no argument is used for the array name.

A COMMON declaration listing the variable or array names in the same order must be included in each subprogram having these common elements. If a variable in the subprogram is the same as a variable in the main program but has a different name, putting the two variables in the same position in the list will result in their using the same memory location. If the variable and array names in the COMMON declaration are the same, the easiest way to proceed is to duplicate the COMMON card. Of course, any arrays included in the COMMON declaration must be dimensioned the same way by the different programs.

EXAMPLES

Main program COMMON A,B,C ⎫
Subprogram COMMON A,B,C ⎭   A,B,C in main program references same data as A,B,C in subprogram

Main program COMMON X,Y,Z ⎫
Subprogram COMMON A,B,C ⎭   X,Y,Z in main program references same data storage locations as A,B,C in subprogram

---

The use of COMMON allows communication among independent program units. Instead of a list of variable names in the subroutine definition and subroutine CALL which specify data to be used and data names for results, the data required for processing and the results to be stored may be placed in COMMON. Experienced FORTRAN programmers are able to manipulate the storage assignments by means of COMMON declarations.

The EQUIVALENCE statement is used in a program to indicate that two variables are to use the same memory location. The reason for using this statement may be that, due to an error, two different names have been written for the same item. Or the reason may be to conserve memory space. Two or more variables used at different points in the program may be assigned to the same memory location if the earlier variable's values do not have to be preserved. Using the same name for all the variables would also cause them to share the memory location, but this may not be consistent with the naming scheme, etc., being used. Other reasons may also arise in individual programs. Two entire arrays of equal dimension may be equivalenced. An entry from an array may be equivalenced to a nonsubscripted variable. Two arrays may be overlapped in whole or in part, but two individual array entries may not be equivalenced.

$$\text{EQUIVALENCE } (v_1, v_2, \ldots, v_n)$$

where all the variable names listed inside each set of parentheses are to be assigned to the same memory location.

EXAMPLES	
EQUIVALENCE (X,Y)	X and Y are to be assigned to the same memory location.
EQUIVALENCE (A(3),X)	X and A(3) are to reference the same location.
EQUIVALENCE (I,J),(R,S) Incorrect-EQUIVALENCE (A(3),B(9))	I and J are the same, and R and S are the same. This is incorrect because two subscripted variables cannot be equivalenced.

The COMMON and EQUIVALENCE declarations should appear in the program ahead of any statements using the variables which they declare. A recommended order for these declarations (if any of the variables to be equivalenced are in COMMON) is

1 DIMENSION
2 COMMON
3 EQUIVALENCE

EXAMPLES
DIMENSION A(100),B(100)
COMMON A,B
EQUIVALENCE (A,B)

These three statements indicate that the two arrays A and B, with 100 elements in each, are to occupy the same memory locations and that this is in the memory area reserved for COMMON.

The preceding use of COMMON is termed "blank COMMON" to distinguish it from named common blocks. In other words, blocks of COMMON may be given names. This allows common units used by only part of the subprograms to be defined as common without defining them in all program units. The form is to have the block name enclosed in slashes precede the variable names in named common.

EXAMPLES
COMMON /A/X,Y,Z /B/M,N,F   Means block A contains X,Y,Z and block B
contains M,N,F

It was noted that variables not in COMMON (in a subprogram) are lost when control is returned to the calling program. It is possible to save all the data from the subprogram by the SAVE statement.

SAVE program unit name	Saves all variables in a unit such as a subroutine, e.g., SAVE SUBA
SAVE variable or array names or common block names within slashes	Saves named items

**Block Data
Subprogram**

The purpose of the block data subprogram is to provide initial values for variables and array elements in named common. A block data subprogram is not executed. It begins with the BLOCK DATA statement:

BLOCK DATA symbolic name

The BLOCK DATA statement is followed by statements which define data (which has been specified in a named common block) such as DIMENSION, COMMON, EQUIVALENCE, DATA, and TYPE statements. The last statement is END.

    The reason for the block data subprogram is that named common is used by several program units, and so no local program unit can have the data initialization. The block data subprogram defines initialization at the global level of the entire set of programs and subprograms. An example of a block data subprogram is the following:

BLOCK DATA BD1
DATA ALPHA /50*0/BETA/1.0/
END

**Self-testing Quiz—
FORTRAN #12**

1 Identify statements *a* through *e* in terms of subprograms and functions. The statements are considered to be part of a single program.

    (a) X(A,B) = (A**2 + B**2)**(1./3.)   (d) CALL CALC (ALPHA, BETA)

    (b) Y = X(C,R)   (e) SUBROUTINE CALC(X,Z)

    (c) ALPHA = RBD (Y)   Z = X**2

2 What do the following programs do?

```
C   MAIN PROGRAM                    FUNCTION SUM(X)
    DIMENSION ARRAY (100)           DIMENSION X(100)
    READ (1,900)A                   SUM = 0
900 FORMAT (10F8.0)                 DO 100 I = 1,100
    ANS = SQRT (SUM(A))                 SUM = SUM + X(I)
    WRITE (3,900) ANS           100 CONTINUE
    STOP                            RETURN (optional)
    END                             END
```

3 In a program, there is a statement Y = X**2 + (a function written by the programmer). What are the differences between a statement function and a function subprogram which would dictate the use of one or the other in this case?

4 Write a subroutine that will interchange rows and columns of square matrices. The subroutine should handle matrices from 2 × 2 to 20 × 20. Name the routine MOVE (remember that the name of the subroutine does not indicate mode).

5 If, with reference to Problem 4, the matrix to be rearranged is called ALPHA and is KIX × KIX in size, what is the statement to perform the move?

6 Write a function subprogram to find the positive, real root (if it exists) of a quadratic equation. The *a* term is always positive for this problem. The formula is:

$$\text{ROOT} = \frac{-b + \sqrt{b^2 - 4ac}}{2a}$$

If there are no real, positive roots, make the answer equal 0.

7 Illustrate the use of the function subprogram written for Problem 6.

8 Two subprograms and a main program all refer to the same set of three variables called X, IOTA, and CHI and to an array called SILLY by the two subprograms and DILLY by the main program. Write three statements to declare these variables as COMMON.

9 Write a program to read n (say, 10) data items in F10.2 fields and print the input. Write a subroutine to order the data items from smallest to largest. Call this subroutine and then print out the ordered array. For a small array, interchange sorting is satisfactory. In interchange sorting, the first variable is compared with each of the other variables. If the value being compared is smaller, the two are interchanged. This continues through the array. The result is the smallest value in cell 1. The same procedure is followed for cell 2, etc. See Figure 18-9 for large-to-small sort logic.

Additional Features of Standard FORTRAN

The features of FORTRAN presented thus far include those which have received the most use. There are additional features a programmer will want to use as he or she becomes more proficient.

Additional Data Types and Type Statements

Integer, real, and Hollerith data types are the most common, but full FORTRAN allows three additional types—double-precision, complex, and logical.

1 Double-precision data items are real types which occupy twice the storage and provide approximately double the precision of real variables.

2 Complex data variables are represented by an ordered pair of real data—one representing the real part and one the imaginary part of a complex number.

3 Logical data variables assume only the values of true or false.

There are special functions to handle the double-precision and complex data types. In general, the name is the same as for real variables but with a D prefixing double-precision functions and a C prefixing complex functions (where complex functions make sense). For example, the SQRT real function is DSQRT for double-precision and CSQRT for complex data types. A complex data constant is written as an ordered pair inside parentheses, for example, (3.5, 4.1).

Also, certain variables may need to be specified as double-precision, complex, or logical. This is done with the type declaration using DOUBLE PRECISION, COMPLEX, or LOGICAL. For example:

COMPLEX ALPHA   makes ALPHA refer to a complex variable.

An IMPLICIT statement is provided for the programmer to define an initial letter or letters for a variable name to refer to a given data type. The character-first letter definition also defines the length. By example:

IMPLICIT INTEGER (A,B), REAL (L−N) CHARACTER (X∗10, Y∗5), COMPLEX (C,D)

The PARAMETER statement is used to give a constant a symbolic name. By example:

PARAMETER FIVE = 5, RATE = 4.3, HEADING = 'PAYROLL REPORT'

The constant name can be used in any statement to refer to the constant. For example, IF (X.GT.FIVE)--.

Additional FORMAT Edit Descriptors The edit descriptors explained so far are (w = field length in characters, d = number of positions to right of decimal, n = integer constant):

Iw	For integer input/output
Fw.d	For real input/output
Ew.d	For exponent form of real input/output
Aw	For character input/output
'h . . .'	Apostrophe form of character output
nHhhh. . .	H form of character output
/	Terminate record
Tc	Tabulate to character position c for next output
nx	Skip over n (+ or −) positions

Additional FORMAT edit descriptors are:

Iw.n	For output, n defines minimum number of digits. Leading zeros may be necessary. For example, a 3-digit output may be desired even if result is less than 100. The specification I5.3, if data is 7456, will print as 7456, but if data is 2, it will print as 002.
Gw.d	Same as F editing for input; compiler chooses E or F editing on output.
Dw.d	To define I/O for double-precision

Note that complex data (in two parts) is read by two F, E, D, or G edit descriptors.

:	Terminates format control if there are no more items in the input/output list.
±s	Specifies use of + sign for positive data + = print + − = do not print +

BN
BZ — During input BN specifies blank characters (no punches in card) are ignored: BZ specifies blanks are zeros (the normal case in FORTRAN).

nP — Used with F, E, D, and G fields. The scale factor is an integer constant or an integer constant signed with a minus. The scale factor of n on an F field for either input (if no exponent) or output increases the size of the number by 10^n. Once the scale factor is written, it applies to all succeeding real field descriptions. If normal scaling is to be reinstated, a zero scale factor is written.

The scale factor is most commonly used with an E field to shift the decimal point in the output. The P specification causes the decimal point to be shifted n places to the right (or left, if minus) and the exponent to be reduced by n. For example, if E15.8 causes an answer to be printed out as $0.34769334E + 05$, then 2PE15.6 will cause an output of $34.769334E + 03$.

Ew.dEe
Ew.dDe — Used for an exponent form in which the exponent is the power of e.

Lw — Logical field containing a T or F for true or false.

Additional Intrinsic Functions

A number of additional functions are available in FORTRAN. The entire set of functions is listed in the summary of the language. Note that there are separate functions for complex or double-precision arithmetic (function name preceded by C or D). The generic name or the specific name may be used. The specific names are generally most consistent with older FORTRAN versions.

Assigned GO TO

Since it is part of the language, the assigned GO TO will be explained, but good programming practice suggests that it should not be used. The reason for advising against its use is that it makes the logic of a program difficult to follow. The assigned GO TO feature is essentially a variable GO TO. There are two statements—the ASSIGN and the assigned GO TO. The ASSIGN statement assigns a statement number to an integer variable.

ASSIGN n to i

where n = a statement number
i = an integer variable

EXAMPLE   ASSIGN 13 TO KIX

The assigned GO TO lists the possible statement numbers to which the program may go and specifies the variable which contains the value to be used to specify the current transfer of control.

GO TO i(n₁,n₂, . . . ,nₙ)

where n_i = statement numbers to which control can transfer
i = integer variable containing value of one of statement numbers to which control is to be transferred.

As an example, suppose that the program might transfer to statements 13, 21, or 45 and that a variable KIX would specify which of these statements would be used, then the pair of statements to transfer control to 21 would be

ASSIGN 21 to KIX
GO TO KIX (13, 21, 45)

Run Time Specifications

In full FORTRAN, it is possible to read in FORMAT statements into an array. The FORMAT number in the input/output statements is replaced by a variable which references the array. The FORMAT statement is on a card and read into the array using an A FORMAT (without a statement number or the word FORMAT). The DATA initialization statement can also be used for this purpose. This allows the FORMAT to be decided at run time rather than specified when the program is written and compiled.

DIMENSION has been specified as an integer constant defining the maximum requirements. In a subprogram, the DIMENSION can be written with an integer variable. This variable must be an argument in the definition and be passed as a value when the subprogram is called.

The EXTERNAL statement is used to identify a subprogram that will be available to the program at run time. When a function name is used as an argument in a subprogram calling statement, the main program must have a statement which specifies that these functions exist outside the main program or subprograms.

List of FORTRAN Statements

Symbols used in list of statements:

d	Places to right of decimal in FORMAT
e	Expression
f	Function name; f(x) = function with dummy arguments
i	Integer variable
i*	Integer variable or integer value of an expression (full FORTRAN)
k	Constant of any type

m	Integer constant or integer variable (or in full FORTRAN, integer value of expression)
s	Statement label or FORMAT statement label
n	Stop or pause number
st	Statement
u	Unit designation (integer constant or variable) for I/O statement
c	Any type of constant
v	Variable name
w	Field width in FORMAT
[ ]	Optional

Executable Statements

Description of statement	Form
Assignment	v = e
Assignment of statement label	ASSIGN s TO i
Transfer of control	
Unconditional GO TO	GO TO s
Computed GO TO	GO TO $(s_1,s_2...,s_n)[,]i*$
Assigned GO TO	GO TO $i(s_1,s_2,...,s_n)$
Arithmetic IF	IF (e) s_1, s_2, s_3
Logical IF	IF (e) st
Block IF	IF (e) THEN st block
End of IF or ELSE IF	ELSE st block
	END IF
Nested block IF	ELSE IF (e) THEN st block
Stop with no restart	STOP [n]
Pause with restart	PAUSE [n]
End of program unit	END
Loop	
Establishing parameters	DO s[,]i = m_1, m_2[, m_3]
Define end of loop	CONTINUE
Input and output	
Read	READ (u, s) [list] or READ s, [list] or unformatted READ, [list] or READ (control list) [list]
Write	WRITE (u, f) [list] or unformatted WRITE, [list] or WRITE (control list) [list]
Print	PRINT s, [list]
Auxiliary files (see text for details)	REWIND, BACKSPACE, ENDFILE, OPEN, CLOSE, and INQUIRE
Subprograms	
Transfer to subroutine	CALL subroutine [list]
Return to calling program	RETURN

Nonexecutable Specifications or Declarations

Description of specifications or declaration	Form
Main program (optional)	PROGRAM name
Functions and subprogram declarations	
Statement	$f(x_1,x_2,...,x_n) = e$
Function subprogram	FUNCTION $f(x_1,x_2,...,x_n)$
Subroutine	SUBROUTINE f, or SUBROUTINE $(fx_1,x_2,...,x_n)$
Initialize named common	BLOCK DATA name
Optional entry into subprogram	ENTRY
Save data from subprogram	SAVE list
FORMAT of data	s FORMAT (specifications)
Initialization	DATA $/v_1,v_2,.../c_1,c_2,.../$
Dimension of maximum size of arrays	DIMENSION $v_1(k_1),v_2(k_1,k_2),v_3(k_1,k_2,k_3),...$
Define data-names in common storage	COMMON $v_1,v_2,...$
Define data-names as same	EQUIVALENCE $(v_1,v_2,...)$
Define type of data	INTEGER REAL COMPLEX $\Big\}$ $v_1,v_2,...,v_n$ LOGICAL DOUBLE PRECISION
Define type and length	CHARACTER [*length,] name
Define first letter as type	IMPLICIT type $(a_1,a_2,...a_n)$
Equate constant and name	PARAMETER name = constant
Define routine to be available	EXTERNAL list of routine names

FORMAT Specifications

Specification symbol	Form	Specifies
F	Fw.d	Floating point data
E	Ew.d	Data in exponent form
E	Fw.dEe	Exponent of e
I	Iw	Integer data
I	Iw.m	Integer data with at least m field length
A	Aw	Alphabetic data
H	wH	Hollerith field
X	wX	Skipping of field (can be negative in full FORTRAN)
T	Tc	Tabulating to character location c before printing
/	n/	Skip to next unit record, or skip over $n-1$ unit records
P		Scaling (nP precedes F, E, or D specification)
D	Dw.d	Double precision
D	Ew.dDe	Exponent of e for double precision
G	Gw.d	Either E or F depending on data

H	nH	Hollerith
' '	'characters'	Apostrophe
L	Lw	Logical
B	BN	Blanks on input ignored
B	BZ	Blanks on input are zero
S	[±]S	+ = print plus; − = do not print +
:	in FORMAT	Terminates FORMAT control if no more data items in list

List of Intrinsic Functions

FUNCTIONS TO CONVERT TYPE OR EXAMINE DATA

Definition	Generic	Specific	TYPE OF Argument	TYPE OF Function
Convert to integer	INT	INT	Real	Integer
		IFIX	Real	Integer
		IDINT	Double	Integer
Convert to real	REAL	FLOAT	Integer	Real
		SNGL	Double	Real
		REAL	Complex	Real
Convert to double precision	DBLE	DFLOAT	Integer	Double
		DBLE	Real	Double
Convert to complex	CMPLX	CMPLX	Real	Complex
Provide length of character data	LEN	LEN	Character	Integer
Imaginary part of complex argument	AIMAG	AIMAG	Complex	Real

ARITHMETIC FUNCTIONS

Definition	Generic name	TYPE OF ARGUMENT AND FUNCTION Real	Integer	Double precision	Complex
Square root	SQRT	SQRT		DSQRT	CSQRT
Exponential	EXP	EXP		DEXP	CEXP
Natural logarithms (to base e)	LOG	ALOG		DLOG	CLOG
Common logarithms (to base 10)	LOG10	ALOG10		DLOG10	

Truncation	AINT	AINT		DINT	
Nearest whole number	ANINT	ANINT		DNINT	
Nearest integer (function is integer value)	NINT	NINT		IDNINT	
Absolute value	ABS	ABS	IABS	DABS	CABS
Remaindering—Example: give remainder from division of x by 7 MOD (X,7)	MOD	AMOD	MOD	DMOD	
Transfer of sign—Example: transfer of sign to X from Y SIGN(X,Y)	SIGN	SIGN	ISIGN	DSIGN	
Positive difference—Example: positive difference between X and Y DIM(X,Y)	DIM	DIM	IDIM	DDIM	
Double-precision product (real to double)	DPROD				
Choose largest value—Example: choose largest of A, B, and C MAX (A, B, C)	MAX	AMAX1	MAX0	DMAX1	
		MAX1 (integer result)	AMAX0 (real result)		
Choose smallest value—	MIN	AMIN1	MIN0	DMIN1	
Example: MIN(A,B,C)		MIN1 (integer result)	AMIN0 (real result)		

TRIGONOMETRIC FUNCTIONS

		TYPE OF ARGUMENT AND FUNCTION			
Definition	Generic name	Real	Integer	Double precision	Complex
All angles in radians					
Sine	SIN	SIN		DSIN	CSIN
Cosine	COS	COS		DCOS	CCOS
Tangent	TAN	TAN		DTAN	
Arcsine	ASIN	ASIN		DASIN	
Arccosine	ACOS	ACOS		DACOS	
Arctangent, one argument	ATAN	ATAN		DTAN	
Arctangent, two arguments	ATANZ		ATANZ	DTANZ	
Hyperbolic sine	SINH	SINH		DSINH	
Hyperbolic cosine	COSH	COSH		DCOSH	
Hyperbolic tangent	TANH	TANH		DTANH	

Sample FORTRAN Programs

Three sample programs will illustrate the use of FORTRAN. The first program calculates two common statistics—the mean (average) and standard deviation for a set of numbers. The second program is numerical integration, a mathematical problem. The third is finding a rate of return, a calculation useful in business decisions.

Mean and Standard Deviation

The *mean* is the average of a set of numbers. Finding the mean is quite simple—sum the quantities and divide by the number of quantities. The *standard deviation* is a measure of the distribution of the data around the mean.

The following formulas define the statistics. In the definitions, n is the number of quantities in the array of data, X_i is an individual quantity in the array, and $\sum_{i=1}^{n}$ is the summation sign (called "sigma"), which means in these instances that the quantities in an array are to be summed, starting with the first ($i = 1$) and ending with the nth.

$$\text{Mean} = \frac{\sum_{i=1}^{n} X_i}{n}$$

$$\text{Standard deviation} = \sqrt{\frac{\sum_{i=1}^{n} x_i^2}{n}}$$

where small x_i is the difference of the individual X's from the mean; that is, $x_i = X_i - X$. In other words, it is the square root of the average of the squared deviations. For computational purposes, it will be simpler to use an alternative formulation.

$$\text{Standard deviation} = \sqrt{\frac{\sum_{i=1}^{n} X_i^2}{n} - \text{mean}^2}$$

This formula applies to a population. The formula for a sample is slightly different.

The program in Figure 18-10 calculates the mean and standard deviation. However, it should be noted that these computations can generally be obtained more easily from prewritten statistical programs than from user-coded programs.

In reading Figure 18-10, note the following features: (1) The program is divided into three logical parts. This division is also emphasized in the flowchart. (2) The input data on array size are validated as being greater than 0 and not greater than 100. (3) An error in array size terminates the program, and an error message is printed. (4) The input data is printed for visual verification. This is always a good practice.

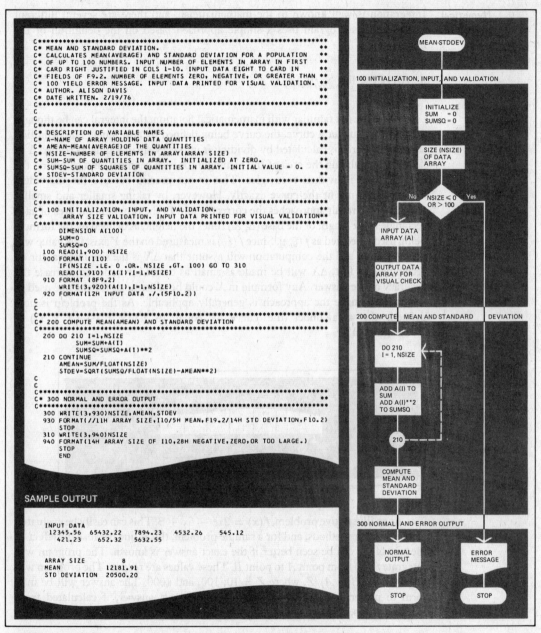

```
C****************************************************************
C* MEAN AND STANDARD DEVIATION.                                **
C* CALCULATES MEAN(AVERAGE) AND STANDARD DEVIATION FOR A POPULATION **
C* OF UP TO 100 NUMBERS. INPUT NUMBER OF ELEMENTS IN ARRAY IN FIRST **
C* CARD RIGHT JUSTIFIED IN COLS 1-10. INPUT DATA EIGHT TO CARD IN **
C* FIELDS OF F9.2. NUMBER OF ELEMENTS ZERO, NEGATIVE, OR GREATER THAN **
C* 100 YIELD ERROR MESSAGE. INPUT DATA PRINTED FOR VISUAL VALIDATION. **
C* AUTHOR. ALISON DAVIS                                        **
C* DATE WRITTEN. 2/19/76                                       **
C****************************************************************
C
C
C****************************************************************
C* DESCRIPTION OF VARIABLE NAMES                               **
C* A-NAME OF ARRAY HOLDING DATA QUANTITIES                     **
C* AMEAN-MEAN(AVERAGE)OF THE QUANTITIES                        **
C* NSIZE-NUMBER OF ELEMENTS IN ARRAY(ARRAY SIZE)              **
C* SUM-SUM OF QUANTITIES IN ARRAY.  INITIALIZED AT ZERO.      **
C* SUMSQ-SUM OF SQUARES OF QUANTITIES IN ARRAY. INITIAL VALUE = 0. **
C* STDEV-STANDARD DEVIATION                                    **
C****************************************************************
C
C
C****************************************************************
C* 100 INITIALIZATION, INPUT, AND VALIDATION.                  **
C*      ARRAY SIZE VALIDATION. INPUT DATA PRINTED FOR VISUAL VALIDATION **
C****************************************************************
      DIMENSION A(100)
      SUM=0
      SUMSQ=0
100   READ(1,900) NSIZE
900   FORMAT (I10)
      IF(NSIZE .LE. 0 .OR. NSIZE .GT. 100) GO TO 310
      READ(1,910) (A(I),I=1,NSIZE)
910   FORMAT (8F9.2)
      WRITE(3,920)(A(I),I=1,NSIZE)
920   FORMAT(12H INPUT DATA ,/,(5F10.2))
C
C
C****************************************************************
C* 200 COMPUTE MEAN(AMEAN) AND STANDARD DEVIATION              **
C****************************************************************
200   DO 210 I=1,NSIZE
         SUM=SUM+A(I)
         SUMSQ=SUMSQ+A(I)**2
210   CONTINUE
      AMEAN=SUM/FLOAT(NSIZE)
      STDEV=SQRT(SUMSQ/FLOAT(NSIZE)-AMEAN**2)
C
C
C****************************************************************
C* 300 NORMAL AND ERROR OUTPUT                                 **
C****************************************************************
300   WRITE(3,930)NSIZE,AMEAN,STDEV
930   FORMAT(//,11H ARRAY SIZE,I10/5H MEAN,F19.2/14H STD DEVIATION,F10.2)
      STOP
310   WRITE(3,940)NSIZE
940   FORMAT(14H ARRAY SIZE OF I10,28H NEGATIVE,ZERO,OR TOO LARGE.)
      STOP
      END
```

SAMPLE OUTPUT

```
 INPUT DATA
  12345.56    65432.22     7894.23     4532.26      545.12
    421.23      652.32     5632.55


 ARRAY SIZE          8
 MEAN            12181.91
 STD DEVIATION   20500.20
```

MEAN-STDDEV

100 INITIALIZATION, INPUT, AND VALIDATION

INITIALIZE
SUM   = 0
SUMSQ = 0

SIZE (NSIZE)
OF DATA
ARRAY

NSIZE ≤ 0
OR > 100

No   Yes

INPUT DATA
ARRAY (A)

OUTPUT DATA
ARRAY FOR
VISUAL CHECK

200 COMPUTE   MEAN AND STANDARD   DEVIATION

DO 210
I = 1, NSIZE

ADD A(I) TO
SUM
ADD A(I)**2
TO SUMSQ

210

COMPUTE
MEAN AND
STANDARD
DEVIATION

300 NORMAL   AND ERROR OUTPUT

NORMAL
OUTPUT

ERROR
MESSAGE

STOP   STOP

FIGURE 18-10 Program and flowchart for calculating mean and standard deviation.

Numerical Integration Integration is well known to the mathematician, and there are several different methods. This program uses a simple approach based on the definition of the integral.

$$\int_a^b f(X)\, dX = \lim_{\Delta \to 0} \sum_{k=1}^n f(\xi_k)\, \Delta_k X$$

For those not familiar with mathematical notation, the integral can be thought of as the area under a curve, the curve being defined by a formula. The definition says that the area is calculated by dividing it into very small segments (called Δ or "delta"), calculating the area of the rectangle for each segment, and summing the areas for the individual rectangles. This is not precise because the individual rectangles do not fit the curve exactly. However, by taking smaller and smaller segments, the result approaches the correct result. In the program, the area of each rectangle is the length of the base ($\Delta_k X$) times the height, as defined by the formula being used [specified as $f(\xi_k)$]. Since $f(\xi_k)$ is measured on the Y axis, this value will be termed Y_i, and the computation will assume that ΔX is the size interval for all rectangles. In fact, ΔX will be made as small as desired in order to increase the accuracy of the answer. Any formula in X could be substituted for the one used in the problem since the approach is generally applicable. As the problem is now defined, the area under the curve is equal to $(X \times Y_1) + (X \times Y_2) + \cdots + (X \times Y_n)$.

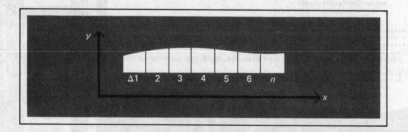

As an illustrative problem, $f(x) = 2x^2 - 5x + 3$. This can easily be evaluated by use of other methods, and for a sample problem, this is fine because the effect of the size of Δx can be seen better if the exact answer is known. The program will integrate $f(X)$ from point A to point B. These values are read in. The program will use an X of $(B - A)/Z$, where $Z = 10$, 100, and 1000. The answer will be in E form to preserve all digits of accuracy. The exact answer, if calculated from antiderivatives, is

$$\frac{2x^3}{3} - \frac{5x^2}{2} + 3x \Big]_3^9 = 306.0$$

The program for the numerical integration problem is given by Figure 18-11.

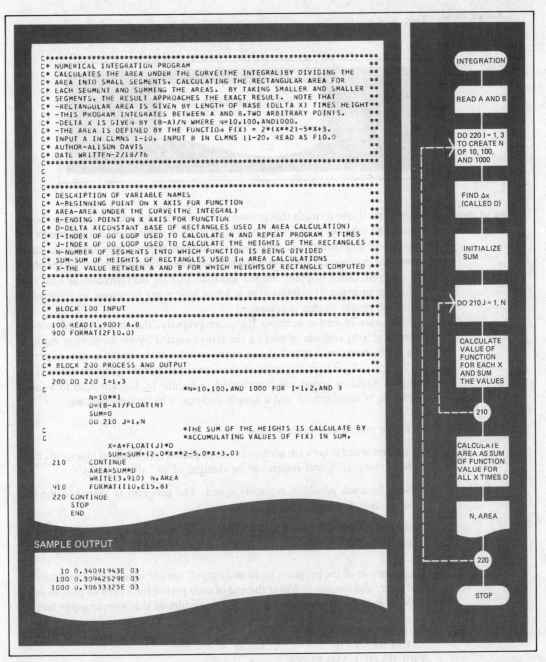

```
C*********************************************************************
C* NUMERICAL INTEGRATION PROGRAM                                   **
C* CALCULATES THE AREA UNDER THE CURVE(THE INTEGRAL)BY DIVIDING THE **
C* AREA INTO SMALL SEGMENTS, CALCULATING THE RECTANGULAR AREA FOR   **
C* EACH SEGMENT AND SUMMING THE AREAS.  BY TAKING SMALLER AND SMALLER**
C* SEGMENTS, THE RESULT APPROACHES THE EXACT RESULT.  NOTE THAT     **
C* -RECTANGULAR AREA IS GIVEN BY LENGTH OF BASE (DELTA X) TIMES HEIGHT**
C* -THIS PROGRAM INTEGRATES BETWEEN A AND B,TWO ARBITRARY POINTS.   **
C* -DELTA X IS GIVEN BY (B-A)/N WHERE N=10,100,AND1000.            **
C* -THE AREA IS DEFINED BY THE FUNCTION F(X) = 2*(X**2)-5*X+3.      **
C* INPUT A IN CLMNS 1-10, INPUT B IN CLMNS 11-20, READ AS F10.0     **
C* AUTHOR-ALISON DAVIS                                             **
C* DATE WRITTEN-2/18/76                                            **
C*********************************************************************
C
C
C*********************************************************************
C* DESCRIPTION OF VARIABLE NAMES                                   **
C* A-BEGINNING POINT ON X AXIS FOR FUNCTION                        **
C* AREA-AREA UNDER THE CURVE(THE INTEGRAL)                         **
C* B-ENDING POINT ON X AXIS FOR FUNCTION                           **
C* D-DELTA X(CONSTANT BASE OF RECTANGLES USED IN AREA CALCULATION) **
C* I-INDEX OF DO LOOP USED TO CALCULATE N AND REPEAT PROGRAM 3 TIMES**
C* J-INDEX OF DO LOOP USED TO CALCULATE THE HEIGHTS OF THE RECTANGLES**
C* N-NUMBER OF SEGMENTS INTO WHICH FUNCTION IS BEING DIVIDED       **
C* SUM-SUM OF HEIGHTS OF RECTANGLES USED IN AREA CALCULATIONS      **
C* X-THE VALUE BETWEEN A AND B FOR WHICH HEIGHTS OF RECTANGLE COMPUTED **
C*********************************************************************
C
C
C*********************************************************************
C* BLOCK 100 INPUT                                                 **
C*********************************************************************
100 READ(1,900) A,B
900 FORMAT(2F10.0)
C
C
C*********************************************************************
C* BLOCK 200 PROCESS AND OUTPUT                                    **
C*********************************************************************
200 DO 220 I=1,3
C                          *N=10,100,AND 1000 FOR I=1,2,AND 3
    N=10**I
    D=(B-A)/FLOAT(N)
    SUM=0
    DO 210 J=1,N
C                          *THE SUM OF THE HEIGHTS IS CALCULATE BY
C                          *ACCUMULATING VALUES OF F(X) IN SUM,
    X=A+FLOAT(J)*D
    SUM=SUM+(2.0*X**2-5.0*X+3.0)
210     CONTINUE
    AREA=SUM*D
    WRITE(3,910) N,AREA
910     FORMAT(I10,E15.8)
220 CONTINUE
    STOP
    END
```

SAMPLE OUTPUT

```
  10 0.34091943E 03
 100 0.30942529E 03
1000 0.30633325E 03
```

Flowchart:

```
INTEGRATION

READ A AND B

DO 220 I = 1, 3
TO CREATE N
OF 10, 100,
AND 1000

FIND Δx
(CALLED D)

INITIALIZE
SUM

DO 210 J = 1, N

CALCULATE
VALUE OF
FUNCTION
FOR EACH X
AND SUM
THE VALUES

210

CALCULATE
AREA AS SUM
OF FUNCTION
VALUE FOR
ALL X TIMES D

N, AREA

220

STOP
```

FIGURE 18-11 Program for numerical integration example.

Sample Input

> 3.0   9.0

Sample Output

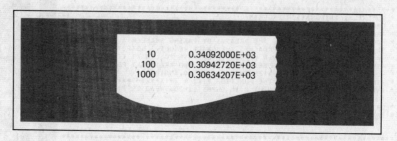

10	0.34092000E+03
100	0.30942720E+03
1000	0.30634207E+03

Rate of Return   There is no single formula that provides the solution of a rate-of-return problem. Rather, the solution is arrived at by a trial method in which each trial brings the result closer and closer. Since this iterative solution method may not find an exact answer, the precision of the answer at which iterations should stop must be specified. The program uses a stopping limit of less than .001 for the difference as a fraction of the sum invested. It is interesting to know how many iterations are required to obtain the result, so this is computed.

The rate-of-return problem (or more properly, the time-adjusted rate-of-return problem) consists of finding the return earned by an investment made at time T which returns a specified sum to the investor at the end of each time period $T_1, T_2, \ldots, T_n$. There are many sophisticated variations of this problem. This program, which is coded and flowcharted in Figure 18-12, will hold to a fairly simple set of assumptions and a simple analysis. The assumptions are

1   Entire investment made at time T_0.

2   Sum returned is net cash savings at end of period (problems of taxes, etc., have been eliminated, and return can be thought of as "after taxes").

3   Sum for each period is explicitly stated. The program is geared to the unequal-cash-flow problem.

4   Rate of return will not exceed 80 percent (an arbitrary figure which could be different).

As an example of the program input and output, sample input is an investment of $840 today and returns of $50 at the end of each period for 8 periods plus an extra $1000 at the end of the eighth period. The results of this sample input are:

PROBLEM NUMBER	1
INVESTMENT OF	840.00
PERIODS OF CASH FLOW	8
NUMBER TRIALS	11
RATE OF RETURN	7.77 PERCENT

```
C************************************************************************
C* RATE OF RETURN PROGRAM                                             **
C* CALCULATES THE RATE OF RETURN WHEN INITIAL INVESTMENT AND CASH     **
C* FLOWS ARE KNOWN. ASSUMPTIONS ARE:                                  **
C* -THE ENTIRE INVESTMENT IS MADE AT ONE TIME AT BEGINNING            **
C* -CASH FLOW IS NET CASH SAVINGS FOR A PERIOD(DAY,WEEK,MONTH,OR YEAR)**
C* -CASH FLOW FOR EACH PERIOD IS INPUT WITH LIMIT OF 100 CASH FLOWS   **
C* -ERROR IF RATE OF RETURN NEGATIVE OR GREATER THAN 80 PERCENT       **
C* CARD INPUT-                                                        **
C* -FIRST CARD--PROBLEM NO IN COLS 1-10 RIGHT JUSTIFIED               **
C*             --NUMBER OF CASH FLOWS IN COLS 18-20 RIGHT JUSTIFIED   **
C*               --SUM INVESTED IN COLS 21-30 INPUT AS F10.2          **
C* -SUCEEDING CARDS--CASH FLOWS EIGHT PER CARD IN FIELDS OF F9.2      **
C* AUTHOR-ALISON DAVIS                                                **
C* DATE WRITTEN-2/17/76                                               **
C************************************************************************
C
C
C************************************************************************
C* DESCRIPTION OF VARIABLE NAMES                                      **
C* BRATE-LOWER VALUE IN TRIAL AND ERROR CALCULATIONS, INITIAL VALUE 0 **
C* CASH-CASH FLOWS AS AN ARRAY                                        **
C* NFLOWS-NUMBER OF PERIODS OF CASH FLOWS.                            **
C* NTRIAL NUMBER OF TRIALS BEFORE CLOSE-ENOUGH RESULT OBTAINED        **
C* NUMPRO-PROBLEM NUMBER                                              **
C* PVC-PRESENT VALUE OF CASH FLOWS USING TRIAL RATE                   **
C* RATE-RATE OF RETURN                                               **
C* URATE-UPPER RATE FOR TRIAL AND ERROR CALCULATIONS,INITIAL VALUE 80 **
C* VESTMT-INVESTMENT                                                  **
C* VSUM-CASH FLOW ACCUMULATOR FOR DATA VALIDATION                     **
C************************************************************************
C
C
C************************************************************************
C*DIMENSION-AND-INITIALIZE FOR INTIAL TRIAL                           **
C************************************************************************
      DIMENSION CASH (100)
      URATE = .80
      BRATE = .0
      RATE = .40
C
C
C************************************************************************
C* 100 INPUT AND INPUT VALIDATION. ERROR OUTPUT FOR NEGATIVE RETURN   **
C* OR RETURN GREATER THAN 80 PERCENT.                                 **
C************************************************************************
  100 READ(1, 900) NUMPRO,NFLOWS,VESTMT
  900 FORMAT (2I10,F10.2)
      READ (1,910)(CASH(I),I=1,NFLOWS)
  910 FORMAT(8F9.2)
C                           *TEST FOR CASH FLOWS GR THAN INVESTMENT
      VSUM = 0
      DO 110 I=1,NFLOWS
         VSUM = VSUM + CASH(I)
  110 CONTINUE
      IF (VSUM .LE. VESTMT) WRITE (3,915) VSUM,VESTMT
  915 FORMAT (14H CASH FLOWS OF ,F10.2,18H AND INVESTMENT OF ,F10.2,
     -        21H MAKE NEGATIVE RETURN )
      IF (VSUM .LE. VESTMT) STOP
C                           *TEST FOR RETURN GREATER THAN 80 PERCENT
      PVC = 0
      DO 120 I=1,NFLOWS
         PVC = PVC + CASH(I)/(1.80**I)
```

continued

FIGURE 18-12 Program and flowchart for rate-of-return analysis.

```
    120 CONTINUE
        IF(PVC .GT. VESTMT) WRITE (3,920)
    920 FORMAT (39H RATE OF RETURN GREATER THAN 80 PERCENT)
        IF (PVC .GT. VESTMT) STOP
C                                    *ELSE CONTINUE BECAUSE DATA IN VALID
C
C
C*************************************************************************
C* 200 PERFORM COMPUTATION TO OBTAIN RATE OF RETURN USING TRIAL RATE. **
C* RATE ADJUSTED AND COMPUTATION REPEATED UNTIL RATE CLOSE ENOUGH.    **
C* CLOSE ENOUGH IS ABSOLUTE DIFFERENCE BETWEEN INVESTMENT AND PRESENT **
C* VALUE OF CASH FLOWS NOT MORE THAN .001 AS FRACTION OF INVESTMENT.  **
C* IF CLOSE ENOUGH NOT OBTAINED BY 100 TRIALS, STOP PROCESSING AND    **
C* GIVE MESSAGE                                                       **
C*************************************************************************
    200 DO 220 ITRIAL=1,100
        NTRIAL = ITRIAL
        PVC = 0
        DO 210 I=1,NFLOWS
            PVC=PVC+CASH(I)/((1.0+RATE)**I)
    210     CONTINUE
        DIFFR = VESTMT - PVC
        IF((ABS(DIFFR/VESTMT).LE..001).OR.(DIFFR.EQ. 0)) GO TO 300
        IF (DIFFR.LT.0)BRATE = RATE
        IF (DIFFR.GT.0)URATE = RATE
        RATE = (URATE + BRATE)/ 2.0
    220 CONTINUE
C                            *NORMAL LOOP EXIT MEANS RATE NOT CLOSE
C                            *ENOUGH BY 100 TRIALS. WRITE MESSAGE
        WRITE (3,925) DIFFR
    925 FORMAT (41H TERMINATION AT 100 TRIALS. DIFFERENCE OF F10.3)
C
C
C*************************************************************************
C* 300 PRINT RESULTS AND STOP RUN                                     **
C*************************************************************************
    300 RATE = RATE * 100.0
        WRITE (3,930) NUMPRO,VESTMT,NFLOWS,NTRIAL,RATE
    930 FORMAT(15H PROBLEM NUMBER I16,/ 14H INVESTMENT OF F20.2,/
       -21H PERIODS OF CASH FLOW I10 / 14H NUMBER TRIALS I17 /
       -15H RATE OF RETURN F19.2, 8H PERCENT //)
        WRITE(3,935)(CASH(I),I=1,NFLOWS)
    935 FORMAT (11H CASH FLOWS  /, (6F10.2))
        STOP
        END
```

SAMPLE OUTPUT

```
PROBLEM NUMBER              1
INVESTMENT OF            840.00
PERIODS OF CASH FLOW         8
NUMBER TRIALS               11
RATE OF RETURN            7.77 PERCENT

CASH FLOWS
    50.00      50.00     50.00     50.00     50.00     50.00
    50.00    1050.00
```

FIGURE 18-12 (Continued)

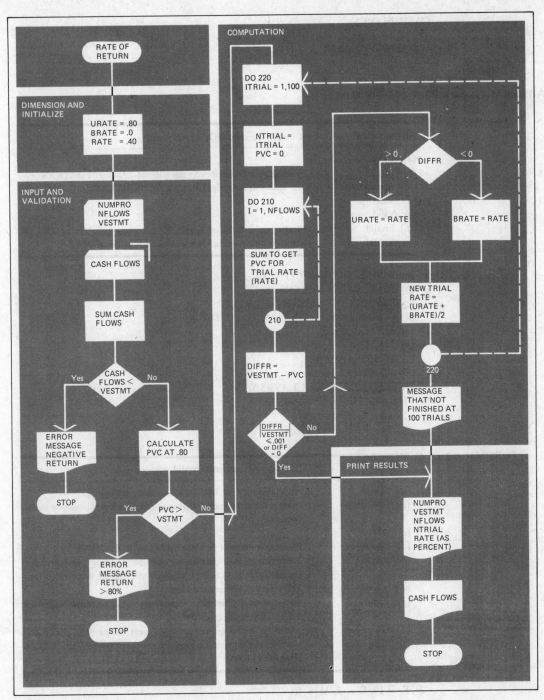

FIGURE 18-12 *(Continued)*

CASH FLOWS

50.00	50.00	50.00	50.00	50.00	50.00
50.00	1050.00				

Answers to Self-testing Quizzes

FORTRAN #7

1

Always valid	If invalid for some FORTRANs, why
(a) Valid	
(b) Invalid	Floating point subscript (X) not allowed in Subset FORTRAN
(c) Invalid	Not allowable subscript form in older FORTRANs
(d) Valid	
(e) Valid	
(f) Invalid	Floating point name not allowed as subscript in Subset FORTRAN
(g) Invalid	Not allowable form in older FORTRANs; should be I − 5

2   (a) DIMENSION ARRAY (100)
     (b) DIMENSION PERSNS (2, 10)
     (c) DIMENSION BUSNES (8, 15, 5)
     (d) DIMENSION A(15), B(15), C(15), D(15)

3   (a) A(2,2)
     (b) A(3,5)
     (c) CLASS (2,5,2)
     (d) CLASS (2,2,1)

4   DIMENSION A(5,5); CLASS(5,5,3)

5   Figure 18-13.

FORTRAN #8

1

Valid	If invalid or sometimes invalid, why
(a) Never	A variable may not be used as a statement number.
(b) Sometimes	Comma after statement number optional (or not allowed by older versions).
(c) Always	
(d) Sometimes	Parameters may not be signed for older FORTRANs.
(e) Always	Terminating value less than initial value. The new standard says execute zero times. Some processors will execute loop once.
(f) Always	The loop will be executed once.
(g) Always	The loop stops when the terminating value is exceeded. Therefore, this will be executed three times.
(h) Sometimes	Arithmetic expression not allowed except in new full FORTRAN.
(i) Sometimes	Control variable must be integer in Subset FORTRAN and in older FORTRANs.

2   K = 10, L = 5, M = 50

```
C************************************************************************
C* PROGRAM TO MULTIPLY ARRAYS A AND B                                 **
C* TO GIVE C. THEN PRINT ARRAY ELEMENTS.                              **
C* AUTHOR. G. DAVIS                                                   **
C* DATE  2-27-76.                                                     **
C************************************************************************
C
C
C************************************************************************
C* DIMENSION AND INITIALIZE                                           **
C************************************************************************
      DIMENSION A(5),B(5),C(5)
      I=1
      J=1
      K=1
C
C
C************************************************************************
C* READ DATA INTO ARRAYS                                              **
C************************************************************************
  100 IF(I .GT. 5) GO TO 200
      READ(1,900)A(I),B(I)
  900 FORMAT(F10.2,F10.2)
      I=I+1
      GO TO 100
C
C
C************************************************************************
C* PERFORM MULTIPLICATION OF A AND B TO GIVE C                        **
C************************************************************************
  200 IF(J .GT. 5) GO TO 300
      C(J) = A(J)* B(J)
      J=J+1
      GO TO 200
C
C
C************************************************************************
C* PRINT ARRAY ELEMENTS                                               **
C************************************************************************
  300 IF(K.GT. 5) GO TO 310
      WRITE (3,910)A(K),B(K),C(K)
  910 FORMAT(F10.2,F12.2,F12.2)
      K=K+1
      GO TO 300
  310 STOP
      END
```

SAMPLE OUTPUT

```
      10.50        12.80        134.40
      54.70        45.60       2494.32
      32.40        14.80        479.52
      36.30        85.00       3085.50
      14.30        85.10       1216.93
```

FIGURE 18-13 Simple program to use loops to read, multiply, and print array values.

3 (a) 1   (d) 2
   (b) 0*   (e) 3†
   (c) 5   (f) 6†
   * Pre-1977 versions often performed 1 time.
   † Not allowed by Subset FORTRAN and older FORTRANs.

4 ARRAY (1,1,1), (1,1,2), (1,2,1), (1,2,2), (2,1,1), (2,1,2), (2,2,1), (2,2,2)

5 The program will end with SUM = A(30)*B(30). The initializing of the accumulating variable name must be done outside the loop in which it is used.

6 Valid: *a*, *b*, *c*, *f*.

Invalid: *d* and *e*. Inner DO must be entirely within range of outer.

7
```
      ISUM = 0
      DO 150 I = 1,N
         ISUM = ISUM + LIX(I)*MIX(I)
150   CONTINUE
```

8
```
      BIG = 0               or   BIG = X(1)
      DO 100 I = 1,N             DO 100 I = 2,N
         IF (X(I).GT.BIG) BIG = X(I)   etc.
100   CONTINUE
```

9
```
      DO 160 I = 2,K,2
         WRITE (3,900) DAD(I)
160   CONTINUE
```

10
```
      TEMP = A(1)
      DO 100 I = 2,N
         A(I-1) = A(I)
100   CONTINUE
      A(N) = TEMP
```

11
```
      TEMP = A(25)          | Possible alternative in full FORTRAN
      DO 100 I = 1,24       | DO 100 I = 24,1,-1
         K = 25-I           |
         A(K+1) = A(K)      | A(I+1) = A(I)
100   CONTINUE             |
      A(1) = TEMP          |
```

FORTRAN #9 **1** (*a*) Repeat F6.0 with a new record for each use until list is exhausted.

(*b*) Uses 3 of I2, 4 of F10.0, and 3 of E15.8. Since this is greater than the capacity of a card, the list will, if used with units which read a card or punch a card, continue to read or punch on the following card, which will be part of a two-card set used by this FORMAT statement.

(*c*) The set I3, F10.0 is used 4 times.

(*d*) The first record has two variables using the I2 and I3 specifications. Remaining variables are one per record using I3 specifications.

(*e*) I7 and 10.0 are used once for the first record; F10.0 is repeated, with a new unit record for each repeat.

(*f*) I5 is used for value on first card or line, F10.0 for value on second. If list is not exhausted, the next card or line will use I5, etc.

(*g*) First card or line has one value F10.0, the next card or line is skipped, and then F10.0 is repeated for each unit record until list is exhausted.

(*h*) Skips three cards or lines and then uses F10.0. If repeated, it will skip three cards or lines again.

(*i*) Uses F10.0 and then skips five lines or cards.

(*j*) Printer control—spaces to top of page.

(*k*) Starts printing value of field described by F10.2 in column 40.

(*l*) Same as IH1—spaces to top of page.

2 (*a*) One hundred values for A will be read from cards. One value will be read from each card, arranged in natural (column) order—A(1,1), A(2,1), ...

(*b*) Twenty-five values for B will be read, eight to a card, in row order—B(1,1), B(1,2), ...

(*c*) Six values will be read from a card. These will form the first row of a 6 × 6 matrix.

(*d*) This will read an N × N × 3 array, punched one to a card and arranged in natural order. The row varies most rapidly, column next, and level last.

(*e*) The value read goes into the array as Y(2,J), where J is read previously.

(*f*) The 16-value array KIX will be printed out with four column values per line, double-spaced between lines.

3 DATA A,B,C,D/40.1,3.7,2*1.0/BETA/100*0/

4 DATA (ARRAY(I), I=15,49,2)/18*2.0/

5 Either a blank or a comma separates the data items.

6 READ (1) A,B,I,J,(C(I),I=1,5)

Five variable names could be listed instead of the loop.

7 WRITE (3) SQRT (A)

FORTRAN #10

1 CHARACTER ANAME*10, LNAME*10,

2 CHARACTER BARRAY(5)*6

3 IF (LNAME.EQ.'CLARK') GO TO 600

or for older compilers IF (LNAME.EQ.5HCLARK) GO TO 600

4 ABREV(LNAME(1:3))

5 CBREV = ABREV//'ABC'

6   CHARACTER NAMES(10)*8

    READ (1,900)(NAMES(I), I=1,10)

900   FORMAT (10A8)

7 DATA FNAME/'AARON'/

8 MISSIS

9   CHARACTER EMPNM*15

    READ (1,900) EMPNM

900   FORMAT (A15)

    WRITE (3,910) EMPNM

910   FORMAT (T45,A15)

FORTRAN #11

1

Access method	Order records read	File medium	Use of list-directed I/O	Use of end-of-file record
Sequential	Same order as written	Tape or disk	Not allowed	Yes
Stream	Same order as written	Tape or disk	Required	Yes
Direct	Any order	Disk	Not allowed	No

2 OPEN (8,ERR=600,NAME=PAY,STATUS=NEW,ACCESS=DIRECT, RECL=250)

READ (8,900,REC=IRNO,ERR=600)PAYNO,PAYRTE

CLOSE 8

3 OPEN (9,ERR=600,NAME=STUDNT,FORM=FORMATTED,STATUS=
NEW,ACCESS=SEQUENTIAL)
Note that status and access not required because new and sequential are default options.
WRITE (9,900,ERR=600) COURSE,GRADES
900 FORMAT (2F10.2)
BACKSPACE 9
READ (9,900,ERR=600) COURSE,GRADES
WRITE (3,900) COURSE,GRADES
CLOSE 9

FORTRAN #12

1 (a) A statement function definition.
 (b) The use of the statement function in line a.
 (c) The use of a function subprogram. If there is no definition for a statement function, it must reference a function subprogram.
 (d) A subroutine call with one value being transmitted (ALPHA) and one variable (BETA) assigned to receive the answer (this is known because of use of that variable in line e).
 (e) Shows that Z is receiving variable for value computed by subroutine CALC.

2 The function subprogram SUM sums the elements of a 100-entry array. The main program reads the array, takes the square root of the function, and prints the result.

3 A statement function can be only one statement, and it applies only to the program unit of which it is part. The FUNCTION subprogram does not have these restrictions.

4
```
      SUBROUTINE MOVE (N,B)
      DIMENSION B(20,20)
      DO 110 I = 1,N
         L = I + 1
         DO 100 J = L,N
            TEMP = B(I,J)
            B(I,J) = B(J,I)
            B(J,I) = TEMP
100      CONTINUE
110   CONTINUE
      RETURN (optional)
      END
```

5 CALL MOVE (KIX,ALPHA)

6
```
      FUNCTION ROOT (B,A,C)
      DESCR = B**2 − 4.0*A*C
      IF (DESCR.LE.0) ROOT = 0
      IF (ROOT.EQ.0) RETURN
      ROOT = −B + SQRT(DESCR)/(2.0*A)
      IF (ROOT.LT.0) ROOT = 0
      END
```

7 X = A**2 + ROOT(X,Y,Z)

8

Main program	COMMON	X,IOTA,CHI,DILLY
Subprogram	COMMON	X,IOTA,CHI,SILLY
Subprogram	COMMON	X,IOTA,CHI,SILLY

9 See Figure 18-14.

```
C*********************************************************************
C* PROGRAM TO READ DATA, PRINT THE DATA,                           **
C* ORDER THE DATA WITH A SUBROUTINE (FROM                          **
C* SMALLEST TO LARGEST, AND PRINT ORDERED                          **
C* LIST OF DATA ITEM. FOR FORTRAN QUIZ 12                          **
C* AUTHOR. GORDON DAVIS.                                           **
C* DATE. 3-15-76                                                   **
C*********************************************************************
C
C
C*********************************************************************
C* LIST OF VARIABLES                                               **
C* X-DATA ITEMS IN AN ARRAY                                        **
C* N-NUMBER OF ARRAY ELEMENTS                                      **
C*********************************************************************
C
C
C*********************************************************************
C* READ,PRINT,ORDER,AND PRINT                                      **
C*********************************************************************
      DIMENSION X(100)
      READ (1,900) N,(X(I),I=1,N)
  900 FORMAT (7X,I3,7F10.2,/ (8F10.2))
      WRITE(3,910)(X(I),I=1,N)
  910 FORMAT(5F10.2)
      CALL SMORDR(N,X)
      WRITE(3,920)(X(I),I=1,N)
  920 FORMAT(//,(5F10.2))
      STOP
      END
C
      SUBROUTINE SMORDR(N,B)
C*********************************************************************
C* SUBROUTINE TO ORDER AN N-ELEMENT ARRAY                          **
C* FROM SMALLEST TO LARGEST BY INTERCHANGE.                        **
C* B-ARRAY TO BE ORDERED                                           **
C* N-NUMBER OF ELEMENTS IN ARRAY                                   **
C* SAVIT-TEMPORARY LOCATION USED IN EXCHANGE SORTING               **
C*********************************************************************
      DIMENSION B(100)
      K=N-1
      DO 210 I=1,K
      L=I+1
      DO 200 J=L,N
          IF(B(I).LE.B(J))GO TO 200
          SAVIT=B(I)
          B(I)=B(J)
          B(J)=SAVIT
  200     CONTINUE
  210 CONTINUE
      RETURN
      END
```

SAMPLE OUTPUT

```
137.00      19.00     210.00      18.41      13.60
 47.10      18.90     165.00      11.40      84.60


 11.40      13.60      18.41      18.90      19.00
 47.10      84.60     137.00     165.00     210.00
```

FIGURE 18-14 Program to read data and, using a subroutine, order data from smallest to largest.

EXERCISES

1 What is the purpose of the DIMENSION statement?

2 Write the DIMENSION statements for the following:

(a) An array X with 59 entries

(b) An array YES with 39 rows and 10 columns

(c) An array to accept a threefold classification—by state, by 1 of 20 sizes of cities, and by one of two classes relating to the growth in past 10 years

3 Explain the difference between subscripts for full FORTRAN adopted in 1977 and subscripting in 1966 FORTRAN.

4 A company wishes to classify SALES by salesmen (10 of them), by size of company (4 size categories), and by product sold (8 of these). Set up the classification for SALES, and write a program segment to calculate totals by a salesman.

5 Explain the difference between the new FORTRAN and new Subset FORTRAN with respect to DO statements.

6

DO statement	Valid, invalid, or sometimes invalid	If invalid, or sometimes invalid, why
(*a*) DO 19 NIX = JIX,KIX,LIX		
(*b*) DO 100 FIX = 1,TRIX		
(*c*) DO 50 I = 1,N,L + 1		
(*d*) DO 30 I = 1,N,K		
(*e*) DO 17 I = 1,4,2		
(*f*) DO X J = I,K		

7 What is the purpose of the CONTINUE statement?

8 In what order will the first six subscripted variables be processed when N is 2 and M is 3?

```
        DO 102   I = 1,N
            DO 101   J = 1,N
                DO 100   K = 1,M
                    A (K,J,I) = · · ·
100                 CONTINUE
101             CONTINUE
102     CONTINUE
```

9 A matrix contains the number of A's, B's, etc., earned by each student in a class of 25. Each course is three credits.

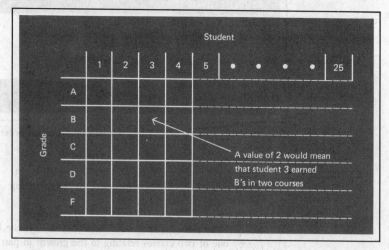

Write a program segment to calculate the grade point for each student and the grade-point average for the class.

10 What are the different ways that answers may be transferred from a subroutine to the main program?

11 Initialize the following variables using a DATA statement:

(a) Set array ALPHA to 0 (array has 15 entries)

(b) Set BETA to 4.5

(c) Set GAMMA to 3.1417

12 What is the effect of the following FORMAT statements?

(a) (1H0)   (f) (3F10.0,5E15.8)

(b) (3F10.0,3/)   (g) (I6,F10.0)

(c) (1F10.0)   (h) (I6/F10.0)

(d) (I6, (I7))   (i) 5(F10.0,I7)

(e) (3F10.0, (I3))   (j) (F10.4,F10.3,3/I6)

13 What is the effect of the following statements?

(a)   READ (1,900) (((A(I,J,K),K=1,3),J=1,5),I=1,3)

  900 FORMAT (F10.0)

(b)   DIMENSION BETA (5,5,5)

         READ (1,900) BETA

  900 FORMAT (F10.0/)

(c)   DIMENSION IOTA (8,8)

         WRITE (3,900) IOTA

  900 FORMAT (I10)

(d)   DO 4 J = 1,N

           WRITE (3,900) J,A(J)

    4 CONTINUE

  900 FORMAT (I10,F10.2)

(e)   READ (1,900) B(1,1),B(3,2),B(4,1)

  900 FORMAT (F10.0)

14 Write statements to read a 10-character heading from columns 36–45 on a punched card and to print it using the printer at columns 76–85. Use (1) an H field and (2) an apostrophe for the title and a T edit and an X edit to position the heading.

15 Read 10 five-character headings which will vary in their use, depending on the program.

16 Write onto magnetic tape one formatted record containing column 1 of a 10-row array. Backspace, read the same record, and print it.

17 What is the difference between the COMMON and the EQUIVALENCE statement?

18 What is the effect of each of the following statements or declarations?

(a) CALL WILMA

(b) CALL MOM (DAD, KIDS, SIS)

(c) EQUIVALENCE (TEEN,SILLY,CRAZY)

(d) FUNCTION NICE (I,J,K)

(e) SUBROUTINE COME (X,Y,Z,B)

(f) X = TALLY(GAMMA1,GAMMA2)

(g) INTEGER A,B,C

19 Write a program segment to define the day names, SUNDAY, etc., and to compare a character input data item (say, MONDAY) to find out which day it is.

20 Make X in a main program equal to $\sqrt[3]{A^2 + B^2}$. Do this step using three different methods—a statement function, a function subprogram, and a subroutine (using two methods for transferring the answer). Write complete subprograms, but show only the necessary segment of the main program.

21 Flowchart and write complete programs to solve each of the following problems. Specify input FORMAT. Make output neat and explanatory. Keep the solution general enough to handle all cases. The problems are grouped into three categories: general, statistical, and mathematical.

PROBLEMS

General Problems

1 For any given compound interest rate, prepare a table of the amounts to which $1 will accumulate if left for a specified number of periods. The input to the program is the specified interest rate and number of periods the table is to cover. The formula is:

$$S = P(1 + i)^n$$

where S is the compound amount, P is the amount invested ($1 in this case), i is interest rate, and n is number of periods.

2 Prepare a table showing the size of a loan that is possible from different monthly payments for a given number of months at different interest rates. Assume the monthly interest rate is one-twelfth of the yearly rate. The table might appear as shown below:

TERM IN MONTHS XX				
MONTHLY PAYMENT	RATE OF INTEREST 0.030	0.035	...	0.060
$100.00	XXXXX.	XXXXX.	...	XXXXX.
$105.00	XXXXX.	XXXXX.	...	XXXXX.
$150.00	XXXXX.	XXXXX.	...	XXXXX.

3 Prepare a present-value table for 25 years. Use the present value of a single payment n periods in the future.

$$PV = \frac{\text{Amount}}{(1 + i)^n}$$

Use interest rates starting at 15 percent and going by 5 percent jumps to 40 percent.

4 Prepare a table similar to the one called for in Problem 21(c) for the present value PV of an annuity.

$$PV = R\left(\frac{1 = (1 + i)^{-n}}{i}\right)$$

where R = the amount the annuity pays.

5 Compute the effect on time-adjusted rate of return of two rapid-depreciation methods—the sum-of-year digits method and the double-declining balance method. Use a tax rate of 50 percent. See Problem 21(*i*) for explanations.

6 Read a sentence and calculate the frequency of the characters T, H, and E.

7 Read a sentence and calculate the frequence of the word THE.

8 Data from a questionnaire filled out by customers has been punched into cards:

Columns	Data
1–2	Age (actual): 0 = no response
3	Sex: 1 = male, 2 = female
4	Homeowner: 1 = yes, 2 = no, 0 = no response
5–7	Income: in thousands, no income coded as 999, no response coded as 900
8	Political preference: 1 = Democrat, 2 = Republican, 3 = other, 0 = no response.

Tally responses and prepare the following tables:

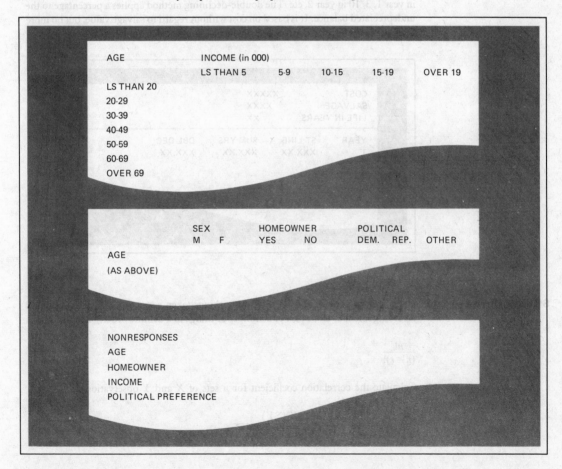

AGE	INCOME (in 000)				
	LS THAN 5	5-9	10-15	15-19	OVER 19
LS THAN 20					
20-29					
30-39					
40-49					
50-59					
60-69					
OVER 69					

	SEX		HOMEOWNER		POLITICAL		
	M	F	YES	NO	DEM.	REP.	OTHER
AGE							
(AS ABOVE)							

NONRESPONSES
AGE
HOMEOWNER
INCOME
POLITICAL PREFERENCE

9 Several methods of depreciation are allowed for tax purposes. The depreciation per year is given by the following formulas where C = cost, S = salvage value at end of life, and N = life in years.

Straight line $= \dfrac{C - S}{N}$

Sum-of-years digit $= (C - S)\left[i \Big/ \dfrac{N(N + 1)}{2} \right]$

where i goes from N to 1.

Double-declining method $= \dfrac{2}{N}(C - D)$ but no more than $C - S$ in total

where D is depreciation to date.

The sum-of-years digits method can be understood by example. If an asset has a life of 4 years, the sum-of-digits is 10 (4 + 3 + 2 + 1). The depreciation is 4/10 of $(C - S)$ in year 1, 3/10 in year 2, etc. The double-declining method applies a percentage to the undepreciated balance. It is based on cost without regard to salvage value, but no more than $(C - S)$ may be depreciated. Print out a table such as the following:

```
COST              XXXXX
SALVAGE           XXXX
LIFE IN YEARS     XX

YEAR    ST LINE    SUM YRS    DBL DEC
1       XXX.XX     XXX.XX     XXX.XX
2                  --         --
3                  --         --
```

Statistical Problems

10 Calculate the permutations of n different things taken r at a time. (A permutation is an arrangement of all or part of a number of things in a definite order.) The formula is

$$\frac{n!}{(n-r)!}$$

11 Calculate the correlation coefficient for n sets of X and Y observations.

$$r = \frac{n\Sigma XY - (\Sigma X)(\Sigma Y)}{\sqrt{[n\Sigma X^2 - (\Sigma X)^2][n\Sigma Y^2 - (\Sigma Y)^2]}}$$

12 Calculate the least-squares equation for a set of n data points. The formula is $a + bx$, where a is the y intercept, and b is the slope (change in x with change in y). The formula for finding b is:

$$B = \frac{\Sigma xy}{\Sigma x^2} \qquad A = \bar{Y} - B\bar{X}$$

where $x = (X - \bar{X})$
$\qquad y = (Y - \bar{Y})$
$\qquad \bar{x}$ and $\bar{y}$ refer to the means of X's and Y's.

An alternative formulation is

$$B = \frac{n\Sigma XY - (\Sigma X)(\Sigma Y)}{n\Sigma X^2 - (\Sigma X)^2}$$

13 Calculate a 12-month moving average covering n months.

14 Calculate the mode from an array of n numbers. If the distribution is bimodal, determine both. If more than bimodal, print out MORE THAN TWO and stop.

Mathematical Problems

15 Solve a quadratic equation. Use the formula

$$X = \frac{-b \pm \sqrt{b^2 - 4ac}}{2a}$$

If the roots are complex (have imaginary part from taking the square root of a negative number), print out a note to this effect but do not compute.

16 Repeat Exercise 20(a), but calculate the real and imaginary portions of the complex roots and show all roots properly labeled.

17 Program integration using, first, the trapezoidal rule and, second, Simpson's rule. The formulas are

$$\int_a^b f(x)\,dx, \text{ using trapezoidal rule} = \frac{D}{2}(y_1 + 2y_2 + \cdots + 2y_{n-1} + y_n)$$

$$\int_a^b f(x)\,dx, \text{ using Simpson's rule}$$

$$= \frac{D}{3}(y_1 + 4y_2 + 2y_3 + 4y_4 + 2y_5 + \cdots + 2y_{n-2} + 4y_{n-1} + y_n)$$

where $D =$ the division on the x axis chosen for the problem. This is assumed to be equal.

$$y_1 = f(a), y_2 = f(a + \Delta x), y_3 = f(a + 2\Delta x), \ldots, y_n = f(b)$$

18 Calculate the solution to a set of two simultaneous linear algebraic equations in two unknowns. Use Cramer's rule. The a's in the definition represent the coefficients of the variable. If the set of equations is described as

$$a_{1,1}x_1 + a_{1,2}x_2 = c_1$$

$$a_{2,1}x_1 + a_{2,2}x_2 = c_2$$

the solution is

$$x_1 = \frac{c_1 a_{2,2} - c_2 a_{1,2}}{a_{1,1} a_{2,2} - a_{2,1} a_{1,2}} \qquad x_2 = \frac{c_2 a_{11} - c_1 a_{2,1}}{a_{1,1} a_{2,2} - a_{2,1} a_{1,2}}$$

19 Use the Newton-Rapson method of finding the square root of a number. Print the result, the number of iterations required, and for comparison the same square root using the SQRT function.

$$S_c = \frac{S_{c-1} + (x/S_{c-1})}{2}$$

where S_c = current estimate of square root

S_{c-1} = prior estimate of square root; for starting out, use a value for S_{c-1} of 1

x = number

Continue to calculate using the formula until $(S_c - S_{c-1})$ is less than or equal to a stated limit. Use a limit of .001 for the program.

CHAPTER

19

ELEMENTARY COBOL

COBOL (an acronym for COmmon Business Oriented Language) is a high-level procedure-oriented language designed for coding business data processing problems. These types of problems are characterized by the use of large files, a high volume of input and output, and production of reports requiring editing and formatting of output data.

The method of presentation in this chapter is to explain the elementary features of the COBOL language and to guide the student in coding a simple COBOL program while progressing through the chapter. After completing this chapter, a student should grasp the basic format and flow of a COBOL program and be able to code a simple COBOL program. Chapter 20 explains the additional features which make COBOL a more versatile language. There are self-testing quizzes in the chapter. These include specifications for a program the student should write while studying the chapter. The answers to the self-testing quizzes are found at the end of the chapter.

Students of computers should be familiar with COBOL because it is the major language for business data processing. The language has been standardized, but there are provisions for change as programming needs evolve. COBOL compilers are available for almost all computers except those too small to support COBOL.

History of COBOL

Work on a common source language suitable to commercial (as opposed to scientific) data processing began in 1959. A committee composed of several large users, the federal government, computer manufacturers, and other interested parties was formed to develop the language. The CODASYL (Conference On DAta SYstems Languages) Committee developed the specifications for a language named COBOL.[1] Their report, issued in April 1960, contained the first version of COBOL, called COBOL-60. A maintenance committee was formed to initiate and review recommended changes to keep COBOL up to date. Subsequent revisions were published in 1961 (COBOL-61), 1963 (COBOL-61 Extended), and 1965 (COBOL, Edition 1965). Changes subsequent to the 1965 version have been published in the *COBOL Journal of Development*. Changes were issued in 1968, 1969, 1970, and 1973. Further revisions are expected.

COBOL has been established as a standard language by ANSI.[2] An initial standard, issued in 1968, was revised in 1974. The ANS COBOL is based on the COBOL specifications of the CODASYL committee. However, the American National Standard recognizes different levels of COBOL implementation and provides standards for each. The basic language elements are divided into Nucleus, level 1 (low level) and Nucleus, level 2 (high level), with level 2 having all basic COBOL elements, and level 1 being a restricted version. The same procedure is followed for functional processing modules which cover specific processing techniques. These functional modules are explained in Chapter 20.

The COBOL chapters are based on the 1974 COBOL standard, the version in

[1] See acknowledgement at end of Chapter 20.

[2] USA Standard COBOL, X3.23-1974, American National Standards Institute, New York, 1974.

use at the writing of this text. Almost all COBOL compilers adhere to the ANS standard, although some implementors provide nonstandard extensions to the language. If the compiler used by a student adheres to the 1965 ANS standard but is not updated for the 1974 standard, some language features will not be accepted.

Overview of the COBOL Language

COBOL provides a language for expressing business data processing procedures. A basic characteristic of business data processing is the existence of large files which are updated continuously or periodically. Business-type problems also tend to involve large volumes of transaction input and output of transaction documents and reports. In contrast, scientific problems usually require extensive processing but very limited input/output.

Like all procedure-oriented programming languages, COBOL requires a source language for coding instructions and a compiler to convert the source program into a machine-language object program. Thus, although the source language is common, the compiler is unique for each computer. It is usually supplied to users by the manufacturer as part of the software support. There may be an extra charge depending on the pricing policy of the manufacturer.

A COBOL program consists of four parts or divisions. These four divisions form a complete description of the program, including descriptions of the equipment required to run it, the form of the data files, and the processing steps to be performed.

Division	Purpose
IDENTIFICATION	Identification of the program
ENVIRONMENT	Description of the equipment to be used
DATA	Form and format of the data files
PROCEDURE	Processing steps to be performed

Each division has a specific form. The general hierarchy of structure is for a division to be divided into sections. Each section contains paragraphs, and each paragraph consists of entries (in the IDENTIFICATION, ENVIRONMENT, and DATA DIVISIONs) or sentences (in the PROCEDURE DIVISION). Entries are composed of clauses terminated by a period. Sentences are formed from a sequence of statements and end with a period.

Structure of COBOL division

Division
Section
Paragraph
Entry clauses
or
Sentence statements

The PROCEDURE DIVISION contains the processing instructions (Figure 19-1). These instructions are interpreted in the context of the equipment described by the ENVIRONMENT DIVISION and the files and records described by the DATA DIVISION. The PROCEDURE DIVISION is machine-independent, which means that it can be compiled and executed on different computers without any coding changes. The DATA DIVISION describes the format of the data and is also machine-independent. The ENVIRONMENT DIVISION specifies the equipment to be used and assigns files to file storage equipment. It is a link between the machine-independent PROCEDURE DIVISION and the specific physical characteristics of the computer system being used. It must be rewritten if the problem is to be run on another computer. The IDENTIFICATION DIVISION is for documentation purposes and does not affect the object program produced by the compiler. Each computer on which COBOL is implemented has a manual which describes the compiling procedures and details the way all computer-dependent features have been implemented for that computer. This manual is essential when using a computer to write, compile, and run a problem written in COBOL.

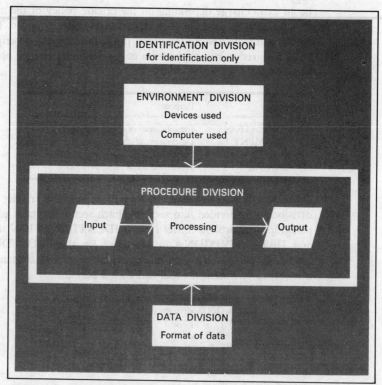

FIGURE 19-1 Purposes of COBOL divisions.

As an illustration, the program in Figure 19-2 is a simple but complete COBOL program to read 10 cards and print the contents of each card as a line of printed output. Note the placement of the four divisions on line 1, line 4, line 13, and line 22. The English-like character of COBOL is illustrated by statements in the PROCEDURE DIVISION such as READ CARD-FILE . . . and WRITE PRINT-LINE. The program is in the structured format described in Chapter 5. The advantages of COBOL can be summarized as follows:

1 *Wide use*   COBOL is the major data processing language.

2 *Documentation*   COBOL contains excellent features for self-documentation of programs.

3 *English-like*   The procedures in COBOL are expressed in English-like sentences.

4 *Machine-independent*   COBOL is sufficiently machine-independent to cross

```
00001            IDENTIFICATION DIVISION.
00002            PROGRAM-ID. CARD-LISTER.
00003         *
00004            ENVIRONMENT DIVISION.
00005            CONFIGURATION SECTION.
00006            SOURCE-COMPUTER. IBM-370-158.
00007            OBJECT-COMPUTER. IBM-370-158.
00008            INPUT-OUTPUT SECTION.
00009            FILE-CONTROL.
00010               SELECT CARD-FILE ASSIGN TO UT-S-INPUT.
00011               SELECT PRINT-FILE ASSIGN TO UT-S-OUTPUT.
00012         *
00013            DATA DIVISION.
00014            FILE SECTION.
00015            FD  CARD-FILE
00016               LABEL RECORD IS OMITTED.
00017            01  CARD-RECORD                 PICTURE X(80).
00018            FD  PRINT-FILE
00019               LABEL RECORD IS OMITTED.
00020            01  PRINT-LINE                   PICTURE X(132).
00021         *
00022            PROCEDURE DIVISION.
00023            MAINLINE-CONTROL-ROUTINE.
00024               PERFORM INITIALIZATION.
00025               PERFORM READ-AND-PRINT 10 TIMES.
00026               PERFORM CLOSING.
00027               STOP RUN.
00028            INITIALIZATION.
00029               OPEN INPUT CARD-FILE.
00030               OPEN OUTPUT PRINT-FILE.
00031            READ-AND-PRINT.
00032               READ CARD-FILE AT END STOP RUN.
00033               MOVE CARD-RECORD TO PRINT-LINE.
00034               WRITE PRINT-LINE.
00035            CLOSING.
00036               CLOSE CARD-FILE, PRINT-FILE.
```

FIGURE 19-2   COBOL program to read 10 punched cards and print the contents, one card per line.

computer-system lines. Programs compiled and run on the machine of one manufacturer may, with relatively minor modification, be compiled and run on the computer of another manufacturer.

5 *Standard* There is an accepted standard COBOL which is supported by ANSI.

6 *Growth* There are regular provisions for adding features to COBOL through the CODASYL committee.

7 *Support* COBOL was developed through the voluntary efforts of users and is supported by all manufacturers. The United States government requires COBOL compilers for all computers it uses for data processing. It is the most widely used language for data processing programs.

8 *Programming management* COBOL supports the adoption and enforcement of programming standards for effective programming management.

9 *Data control* COBOL offers strong capabilities in the areas of data handling and file management.

10 *Processing methods* COBOL modules support a variety of processing approaches.

11 *Communications* COBOL has a data communications module.

COBOL also has some disadvantages which limit its usefulness:

1 *Verbosity* COBOL is wordy because of its self-documenting features.

2 *Limited scope* COBOL lacks good facilities for scientific or mathematical processing. It lacks a few features useful in structured programming.

3 *For programmers* COBOL was designed for professional programmers, not the casual or occasional user. It is difficult to use COBOL without knowing a considerable part of the language.

On balance, then, COBOL is not for the casual user. But because of its predominant role in data processing, the characteristics of COBOL should be understood by those who are involved in data processing, and COBOL should be a part of the programming language skills of every professional programmer.

Programming in COBOL

The structure of the COBOL language is precise. Rules must be learned and applied exactly, or the intended result will not be obtained.

Conventions Used in Explanations The COBOL standards, COBOL implementation manuals, and this text use a set of standard conventions for explaining the form of COBOL statements.

1 All required (key) words in a format are underlined. If words are not underlined, they are used for readability and are not necessary.

2 All lowercase words represent items (COBOL names, literals, or entries) to be supplied by the programmer.

3 Alternatives enclosed in braces indicate that a choice must be made.

4 Features enclosed in square brackets are optional.

5 Commas and semicolons are always optional and are used only to improve readability.

For example, one COBOL format for a statement to add is described as follows:

$$\underline{ADD} \begin{Bmatrix} \text{data-name-1} \\ \text{literal-1} \end{Bmatrix} \underline{TO} \text{ data-name-2 } [\underline{ROUNDED}]$$
$$[;ON \underline{SIZE} \ \underline{ERROR} \text{ imperative sentence}]$$

This is interpreted as meaning that the words ADD and TO are required. The augend *must* be either a literal or a data-name. The addend must be a data-name. The sum is stored in the storage identified by data-name-2 in place of the addend. The rounding of the result is optional (enclosed in square brackets), but once the rounding option is chosen, the word ROUNDED is required. The ON SIZE ERROR to describe the action to take the case of arithmetic overflows is optional. If used, the word ON is optional, but the words SIZE and ERROR are required. The semicolon before ON is optional.

Coding Rules A line of coding is usually written so that it can be punched on an 80-column punched card, although source programs may be entered via terminals as well. The 80 positions are used as follows:

Column	Use
1-6	Coding line sequence number (optional).
7	An asterisk (*) identifies the line as a comment line. A stroke (/) in column 7 indicates comment plus page ejection to print the comment line at the top of the next page. A hyphen (-) in column 7 identifies the continuation of a literal or a coding word which was split because of lack of space on the preceding line. Continuation of a literal will be explained later in the chapter. In general, coding words should not be split. Leave unused spaces at the end of the line and begin the word on the following line. Continuation of a sentence does not require a hyphen unless a word was split.

8–72	Program coding. Generally stop at column 72 for statements on 80-column cards.
73–80	When source statements are punched on cards, this area is generally reserved for program identification and other purposes.

It is customary to use special COBOL coding paper when writing COBOL programs. Although not necessary, its use simplifies writing to the format required by COBOL. A typical coding sheet is shown in Figure 19-3.

The coding of statements starts on column 8 which is called the A margin. Column 12 is called the B margin. Some coding must begin in column 8; other coding must begin in column 12. The remaining items can begin in the B margin or beyond. Division names, section names, and paragraph names must be coded

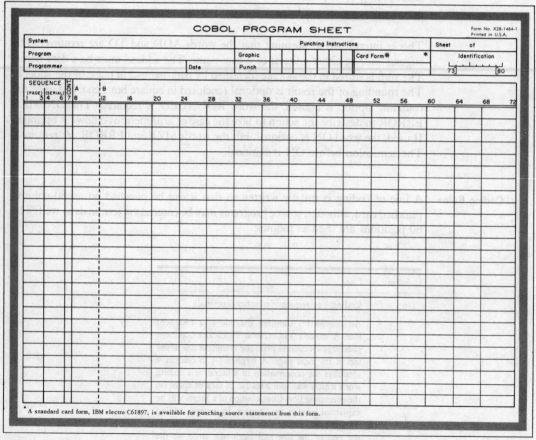

FIGURE 19-3 COBOL coding form.

beginning in the A margin at column 8. Other placements will be noted as the coding of specific items is explained. Coding can extend to include column 72 (or beyond, depending on the input medium and compiler).

Programs are coded in longhand by a programmer before being keypunched into cards. This means that certain alphabetic and numeric characters have a chance to be confused. There are standard coding conventions for clearly differentiating between these troublesome characters.

CODING TO DIFFERENTIATE BETWEEN LOOK-ALIKE CHARACTERS

Alphabetic	Numeric
I	1
O	0
Z	2
U	
V	

Note that the greatest possibility for mix-up is between I and 1, zero and O (oh), and Z and 2. However, it is also possible to mix up U and V. The zero and O are especially troublesome because some programmers slash the zero and other slash the O. This text uses the American National Standard of O for alphabetic O. Programmers should prepare a legible coding sheet and follow standard or generally accepted coding conventions. A period and a hyphen are particularly important punctuation marks in COBOL programming, so note their use in the explanations which follow.

A COBOL program always consists of the four divisions. Each division begins with the name of the division followed by the word DIVISION followed by a period. The division name starts at the A margin.

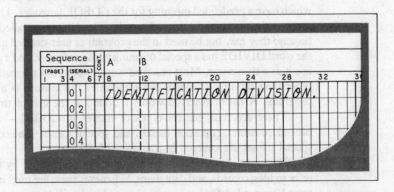

The divisions may be divided into sections, and sections may be divided into paragraphs. Both section and paragraph names begin at the A margin. No other statements appear on the line with a paragraph or section name. Sections contain a name followed by the word SECTION followed by a period.

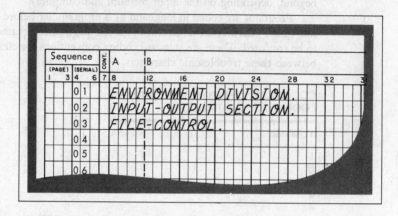

Characters, Words, and Names

Full COBOL uses the following 51 characters:

Alphabetic characters A through Z	; Semicolon
Digits 0 through 9	$ Currency sign (or £)
- Hyphen or minus sign	* Asterisk
Blank	+ Plus sign
' Quote mark (apostrophe)	= Equals sign
() Parentheses (left and right)	/ Stroke (slash or virgule)
. Period or decimal point	> Greater than symbol
, Comma	< Less than symbol

COBOL words consist of names established by the programmer and words which have a predefined meaning for the COBOL language. The predefined words are system names and reserved words. The latter are called "reserved words" because they may not be used in the program as user-defined names. For example, the word DIVIDE has a special meaning to the compiler, and a programmer cannot use it as a data-name. Most reserved words would not normally be used in a way other than the one intended, but sometimes this misuse is a source of error in programs. A list of reserved words is found at the end of this chapter.

There are four general types of names in COBOL—data-related names, procedure names, condition names, and special names. The condition names and special names are covered in the next chapter.

Data-related names are names which are formulated by the programmer to refer to files, records, and data items. Whenever these are used in the program, they must be named. A file has a name, a record in the file has a name (different than the file), and individual data items within records have data-names. A data-name refers to the current contents of a storage location. For example, PAY-AMOUNT refers to the quantity (say 094761) *currently* stored in the location called PAY-AMOUNT. The data-name PAGE-HEADING might refer to the alphabetic characters (say, THE ABC COMPANY) currently stored in the location called PAGE-HEADING. As will be explained later in more detail, all the data-related names are defined in the DATA DIVISION which describes the characteristics and format of the data.

Procedure names are used to refer to subdivisions of the PROCEDURE DIVISION. They are used so that computations which logically belong together can be referenced as a separate group. There are two types: paragraph names which refer to one or more instruction sentences which are grouped together, and section names which refer to a group of paragraphs.

A programmer can make up any name, but a descriptive name will make the coding more meaningful for others to read and to understand what the programmer is trying to accomplish. For example, if the data is gross pay, naming it GROSS-PAY is better than referring to it as X1. Each name must be unique. The same name cannot be used to refer to two different data items.

The rules for forming names are that a name may be a combination of no more than 30 alphabetic characters, numeric digits, and hyphens, and it may not begin or end with a hyphen. Although procedure names may be all numeric, all other names must contain at least one alphabetic character.

RULES FOR NAMES

A name may use

1 Any alphabetic character
2 Any numeric digit
3 Hyphens (-)

A name must

1 *Not* have any imbedded blanks; i.e., TOM JONES is not allowed
2 *Not* contain more than 30 characters
3 *Not* begin or end with a hyphen

Procedure-names may be all numeric, but data-names and other names must contain at least one alphabetic character (and must start with alphabetic in the lowest level of the standard COBOL).

Self-testing Quiz— COBOL #1

The following questions are provided to test your comprehension of the material you have just read. The answers are given at the end of the chapter.

1 COBOL was developed and updated by the _____ Committee; it is standardized as an American National Standard by the _____ _____ _____ _____.

2 List the four divisions of a COBOL program in the order in which they occur.
3 What is the major purpose of each of the divisions?
4 A COBOL program is composed of divisions which are made up of _____ which contain _____ that are formed from one or more sentences.

5 The A margin starts at column _____, and the B margin starts at column _____.

6 The section name appears as the only entry on a line and starts at column _____ or the _____ margin.

7 A word is a combination of not more than _____ alphabetic and numeric characters. A _____ may be used to connect two words used as a single name.

8 Which division in COBOL is least machine-independent?

9 Division names are always coded starting in what column?

10 At which margin does a paragraph name start?

11 What is wrong with the following data-names?
  (a) 12756 _____
  (b) DUE- _____
  (c) OLD NEW-BAL _____
  (d) -WORK-AREA _____

12 NET-PAY-TO-DATE is probably a _____-name.

13 5632 is a _____-name.

14 In the standard notation for describing COBOL, what does it mean for a word to be
  (a) Underlined?
  (b) Enclosed in braces?
  (c) Enclosed in square brackets?
  (d) Lowercase?

15 What do * and / mean when coded in column 7?

The IDENTIFICATION DIVISION

The chapter now examines the format and coding rules for each division in the same order they appear in the program. The first is the IDENTIFICATION DIVISION. This division is for identification purposes only. It does not affect the machine-language object program produced by the compiler. A minimum IDENTIFICATION DIVISION consists of the division-name and the PROGRAM-ID paragraph. The program-name in the PROGRAM-ID paragraph identifies the program. The name is formed according to the name rules specified earlier. Optional paragraphs which may be used to expand the IDENTIFICATION DIVISION are described in Chapter 20. Note that a period is used at the end of each sentence or entry. As in ordinary English punctuation, there is no space before the period, but a space always follows it. In the example (Figure 19-4) note the following:

1 The program is identified as CARD-LISTER

2 The use of the hyphen between PROGRAM and ID and in CARD-LISTER

3 The period after PROGRAM-ID and CARD-LISTER

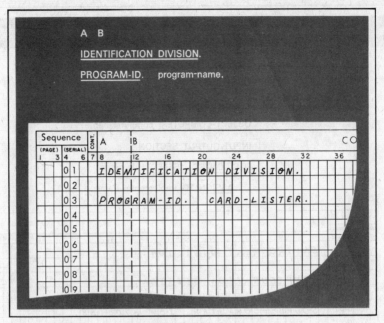

FIGURE 19-4 Basic IDENTIFICATION DIVISION and example.

The ENVIRONMENT DIVISION

The ENVIRONMENT DIVISION is the connection between the machine-independent DATA and PROCEDURE DIVISIONS and the specific equipment to be used for the program. The coding of clauses will vary depending on the computer system being used. Each manufacturer specifies certain clauses of this division. The examples will assume an IBM System/370 model 158. The ENVIRONMENT DIVISION has two sections—the CONFIGURATION SECTION and the INPUT-OUTPUT SECTION (Figure 19-5).

The CONFIGURATION SECTION   The CONFIGURATION SECTION specifies the computer on which the program is to be compiled, called the SOURCE-COMPUTER, and the computer on which it is to be run, called the OBJECT-COMPUTER. It is possible for these two to be different, but in most cases they will be the same. The example in Figure 19-5 specifies that both source and object computers are IBM System/370. Each manufacturer supplies the name to be used to refer to the computer in the CONFIGURATION SECTION.

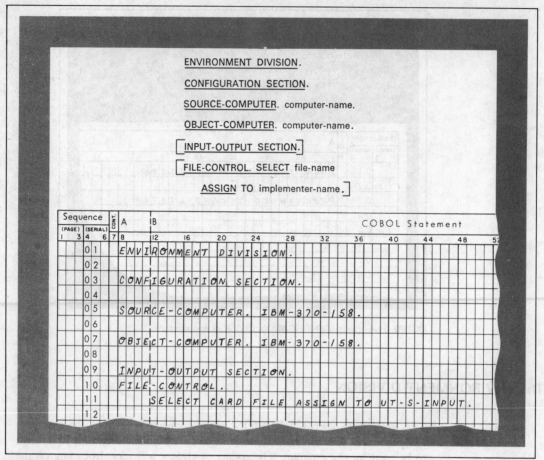

ENVIRONMENT DIVISION.

CONFIGURATION SECTION.

SOURCE-COMPUTER. computer-name.

OBJECT-COMPUTER. computer-name.

INPUT-OUTPUT SECTION.

FILE-CONTROL. SELECT file-name

ASSIGN TO implementer-name.

FIGURE 19-5 Basic ENVIRONMENT DIVISION and example.

The INPUT-OUTPUT SECTION

The INPUT-OUTPUT SECTION relates to transmission and handling of data between the computer and data files. The FILE-CONTROL paragraph associates files with the devices on which they are to be read or written and specifies the processing mode. The INPUT-OUTPUT SECTION in the example contains only one paragraph, the FILE-CONTROL paragraph. The entry in this paragraph names each of the data files that will be used in the program and assigns the data file to a particular hardware device. The format of the entry is the word SELECT followed by the file-name assigned by the programmer, then the term ASSIGN TO followed by the device-name specified by the manufacturer supplying the compiler. In the example, the programmer decided to call the first file to be assigned by the name CARD FILE. This is to be assigned to the card reader. IBM calls the card reader by a descriptive name. The complete IBM COBOL name for the card reader is UT-S-INPUT. The printer has an IBM COBOL name of UT-S-OUTPUT.

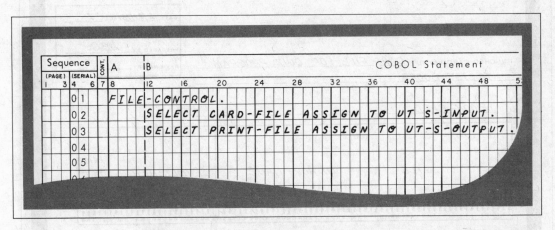

This short explanation will allow the writing of an ENVIRONMENT DIVISION for a simple program. Additional features of the ENVIRONMENT DIVISION are explained in Chapter 20.

Self-testing Quiz— COBOL #2

1 What is the minimum IDENTIFICATION DIVISION for a program? Make up all information needed and write one.

2 Before a period there are _____ spaces; after a period there is (are) at least _____ space (spaces).

3 What is the purpose of each of the two sections of the ENVIRONMENT DIVISION?

4 In the SELECT ASSIGN statement, which names are decided by the programmer and which names must be those supplied by the COBOL implementer?

5 Change the ENVIRONMENT DIVISION in the sample program in Figure 19-2 to run on the computer available to you. Punch the program, add necessary job control cards, add 10 data cards, and compile and execute the program. The data cards may contain any data. Start the data in column 2. The reason for this will be explained in Chapter 20. The program prints the card contents, one card per line.

6 Starting with this self-testing quiz, each quiz will include the writing of a portion of a simple program. The result will be a complete COBOL program ready to compile and execute. The program is to (1) read a deck of punched cards with data about books (author, title, publisher, and selling price), (2) print the data about each book in good form, and (3) sum the selling prices and print a total for the books. The card layout, printer layout, and sample output are shown in Figures 19-6 and 19-7. The answers to the self-testing quizzes can be used to check your coding, but do your own coding with your own names for data.

(a) Write the IDENTIFICATION DIVISION for the quiz problem explained above. Do the coding on a sheet of COBOL coding paper. Save it for later use.

(b) Write the ENVIRONMENT DIVISION for the quiz problem on a separate sheet of coding paper. Save it. Make up your own unique names for your files. There are

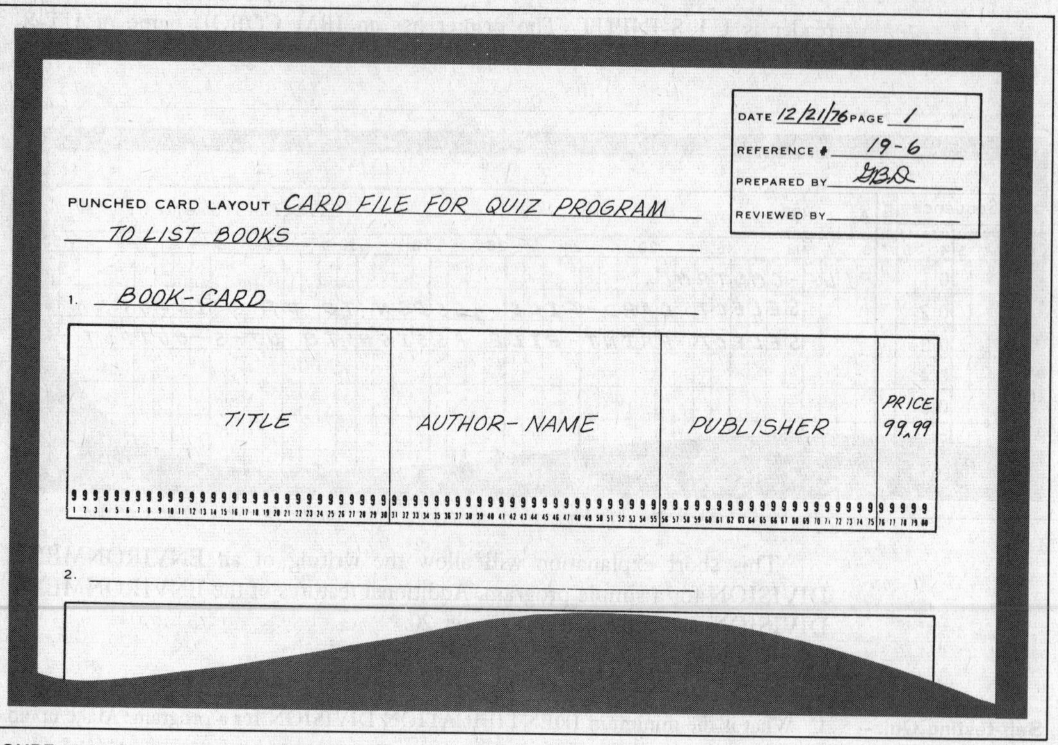

FIGURE 19-6 Card layout for chapter problem.

two files—the file of input cards for the reader and the file of output lines for the printer. (Although you may make up any names for the files, it may help in checking answers if everyone uses the same names, such as CARD-FILE and PRINT-FILE.) Obtain the implementer-names from either the manufacturer's manual or the instructor. Check your coding for correct use of hyphens and periods.

7 In addition to the chapter self-testing problem, a student may wish to begin writing a complete program for which answers are not given. Problem 1 at the end of the chapter has been structured to be written as the student proceeds through the chapter. Part (*a*) may be written at this time.

The DATA DIVISION

The DATA DIVISION describes the data to be processed by the instructions in the PROCEDURE DIVISION. There are five types of sections, but all of them need not be used in a particular program. The FILE-SECTION and WORK-ING-STORAGE SECTION are the most important for a simple program, and only these two are explained in detail in this chapter. Additional DATA DIVISION features in common use are explained in the next COBOL chapter.

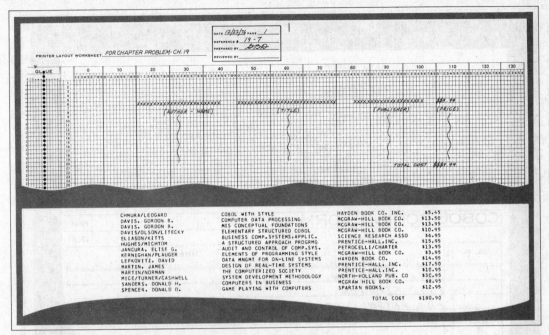

FIGURE 19-7 Printer layout for chapter problem plus sample output.

The
FILE SECTION

The first section of a DATA DIVISION is the FILE SECTION. In the FILE SECTION, there are file descriptions which completely describe each of the files used in the program (Figure 19-8). Each file description begins with a line which has the characters FD at the A margin followed by the file name starting at the B margin. After the file name is a file description which contains such information as labeling, blocking, record sizes, and names of all data records in file. The next entry after the FD (file description) clauses is the description of the first record.

In the example in Figure 19-8, the FD identifies this as a general input or output file (rather than as a file to be sorted). The name that the programmer has given to the file is PAYROLL-FILE. The payroll file has no file label record.

As explained previously in the text, a file is a collection of all records of a given type; a record contains all items related to an object of data processing; an item is a set of characters used together for some purpose. For example, a payroll record for an employee contains all items such as name, social security number relating to him or her for payroll processing. The collection of all such records for all employees is the payroll file.

The first record in a file may be a label record. Label records are important because they identify the file. When a file is originally written by a COBOL program, the first record will be a label record if LABEL RECORD IS STANDARD was specified. The format of the label is defined by the COBOL compiler implementer. For example, the label will contain the file name and other data about

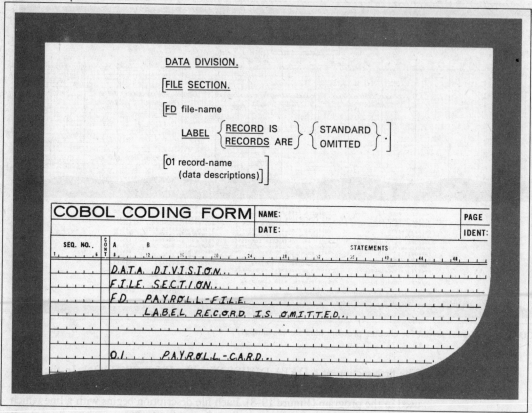

FIGURE 19-8 Basic structure of FILE SECTION and sample file description clauses.

the file. When a labeled file is read by a COBOL program, the program will check the label to see that the correct file is being used.

A COBOL file can consist of records stored on a variety of file media. (Figure 19-9). Examples of the most common are punched cards, lines on a printed output, magnetic tape, and magnetic disk.

File medium	Record	Label record
Punched cards	Data on one punched card or a set of punched cards.	First card in deck may be a label record describing the card file. The label record is frequently omitted for card files.
Lines on printed output	Generally one line but it is possible to have more than one in a record.	No label record.

| Magnetic tape | A block consists of data stored on section of tape between two interblock gaps. A block contains one or more records. | First record on tape may be a label record which identifies the file. |
| Magnetic disk | Data stored in blocks on section of a disk storage track. A block may contain one or more records. | A record may be identified as label record for the block. |

The way in which input from punched cards would be described in a COBOL program illustrates the overall flow of information in the computer program (Figure 19-10). The same principle applies to all files. The ENVIRONMENT DIVISION states that the file is on the card reader. The DATA DIVISION file description gives the characteristics of the file and states the name or names of records on the file. The next step is to provide the record entries to describe the record.

Record Description Entries

Records are made up of data items. Some items (we shall call them "group items") are composed of subitems (Figure 19-11). For example, an inventory code may contain subcodes within it. An item which is not subdivided is called an elementary item. In order to describe these relationships, COBOL uses level numbers (Figure 19-12). The 01 level refers to a full record; the next set of level numbers used (say, 02) refers to items in records; the next level (say, 03) specifies subitems within the group item. There can be many levels. Low-level COBOL allows use of 01 through 10; high-level COBOL uses 01 through 49. Each item at each level must have a data-name. The most elementary item, be it a full record, item, or subitem, must be defined with a data-description entry. The level numbers need not be continuous. Many programmers make it a practice to allow a space between level numbers because of the possibility of a need to insert some group name. For example, a programmer may assign level number 03 to group items and level 05 to items within the group. If an intermediate subgroup needs to be defined, it can be assigned 04 without renumbering all levels. Using that convention in Figure 19-12 would have resulted in level numbers 01, 03, and 05 instead of 01, 02, and 03.

When the data-name BIRTHDATE in the example in Figure 19-12 is used, it refers to the group item; DAY-OF-BIRTH refers only to the DAY-OF-BIRTH portion of BIRTHDATE. (The word DAY was not used because it is a reserved word. See the list of reserved words at the end of the chapter.) The data description entries are required only for the elementary items because, by describing the length and other characteristics of the most elementary items for each level, the group items are automatically defined.

In the explanation of COBOL names, it was emphasized that all COBOL names must be unique—a different name for each data item. In the case of subitems within a group item, the subitem name may be the same as a subitem in another group. The name is made unique by using the name followed by the word OF or

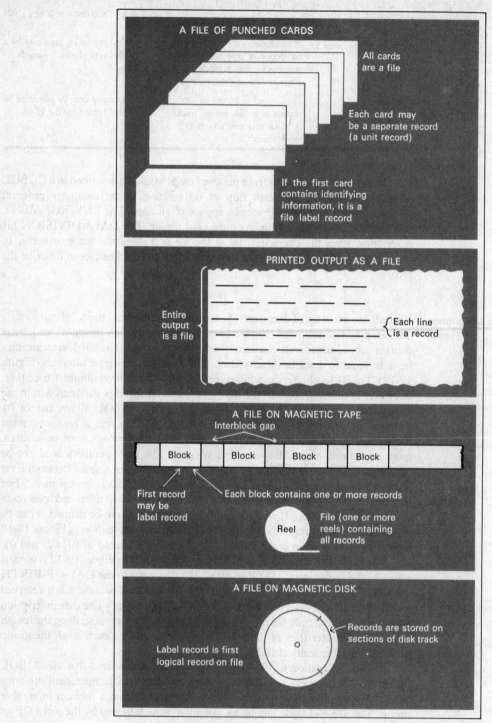

A FILE OF PUNCHED CARDS

All cards are a file

Each card may be a separate record (a unit record)

If the first card contains identifying information, it is a file label record

PRINTED OUTPUT AS A FILE

Entire output is a file

Each line is a record

A FILE ON MAGNETIC TAPE

Interblock gap

Block | Block | Block | Block

First record may be label record

Each block contains one or more records

Reel

File (one or more reels) containing all records

A FILE ON MAGNETIC DISK

Records are stored on sections of disk track

Label record is first logical record on file

FIGURE 19-9 Examples of a file in COBOL.

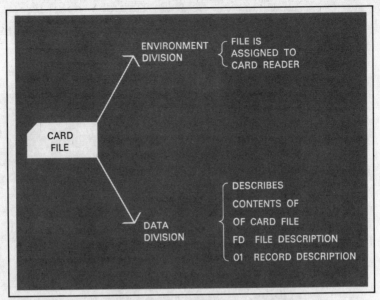

FIGURE 19-10 Describing input on punched cards to a COBOL program.

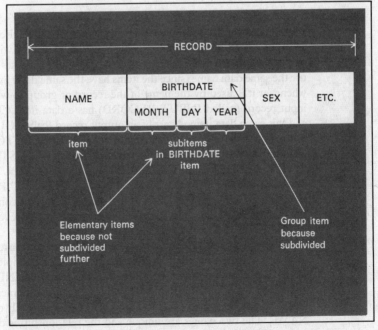

FIGURE 19-11 Illustration of record, group item, and elementary item.

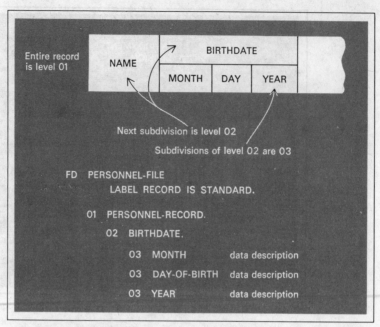

FIGURE 19-12 Use of level numbers in describing data.

IN followed by the group item name to which it belongs. For example, data from an input record is frequently moved to an output record without change, except perhaps editing to make the output item readable. It clarifies the program logic to use the same data name (since the items have the same data) but to qualify the name whenever it is used by the name of the record or group to which it belongs. If an input record (called INPUT-RECORD) has a data item CUSTOMER-NAME and this same data item is part of an output record (called OUTPUT-RECORD), it can be given the same name. Any use of the name CUSTOMER-NAME must include the group-item name to which it belongs—CUSTOMER-NAME OF INPUT-RECORD and CUSTOMER-NAME OF OUTPUT-RECORD. IN can be used in place of OF. CUSTOMER-NAME IN INPUT-RECORD is the same as CUSTOMER-NAME OF INPUT-RECORD. The concept of qualification can include more than one qualifier. An example of two levels of qualification is: MONTH IN DATE IN CUSTOMER-RECORD.

Some programmers prefer to use prefixes or suffixes instead of qualification to identify the same data items in different records. For example, the customer name in the input record might be given the data-name of INPUT-CUSTOMER-NAME or I-CUSTOMER-NAME while the same customer name in the output record might be named OUTPUT-CUSTOMER-NAME or O-CUSTOMER-NAME. The two names are unique and the relationship is defined by the prefix.

Data Description Pictures

For input, the data description entries define the size of the data item and, if the data item is numeric, describe the decimal location. The data description entries for output describe the format of the output and show where editing characters ($, . etc.) are to be inserted in the field. The basic form consists of the words PICTURE or PICTURE IS followed by the picture. The abbreviation PIC may be used instead of PICTURE. The picture consists of 9s, X's, or A's equal to the number of characters in the field. To avoid a long string of characters, a repeat number inside parentheses may be used. The 9 picture character is used for numeric input to be employed in computation. A V indicates the location of the assumed decimal point for numeric, computational input data. The decimal point is not usually punched in numeric input data (and COBOL assumes that it is not). An A picture character refers to data made up of alphabetic or space characters only. An X picture refers to data composed of any characters—numeric, alphabetic, or special. Numeric data not used in computation can be referred to by an X picture character. Since an X can always be used in place of an A, the A character is not as frequently used in practice as X. Note that a blank in an input item is not the same as a zero. Therefore, 0357 is not the same as b357.

BASIC DATA DESCRIPTION PICTURE CLAUSE FOR INPUT

level-no $\left\{ \begin{matrix} \text{data-name} \\ \underline{\text{FILLER}} \end{matrix} \right\}$ $\left\{ \begin{matrix} \underline{\text{PICTURE}} \\ \underline{\text{PIC}} \end{matrix} \right\}$ IS character-string

The picture consists of a string of characters which define the data.

9s for numeric data

X's for alphanumeric data

A's for alphabetic data (A to Z and space)

V for assumed decimal location

$\left\{ \begin{matrix} (\wedge) \text{ number indicates repeat} \\ \text{X(4) is same as XXXX} \end{matrix} \right.$

EXAMPLES

Data	PICTURE clause
123ᴧ45	PICTURE 999V99.
DAVIS	PICTURE AAAAA. or PICTURE XXXXX.
76546	PICTURE 99999. or PICTURE 9(5).

The programmer makes up names with which to refer to the data items, but sometimes no name is necessary because that portion of the record will never be referred to by name. In those cases, the term FILLER is used. It is defined by a picture as is any data item but cannot be referenced by a program. Suppose, for example, that the first 10 columns of an input card are not used, the next 5 are used, and the last 65 are not used. Only the five data columns need have a name. The unused columns must be accounted for because the entire record must be defined by the data description entries, so FILLER is used for these definitions. Note that the sum of all the pictures is equal to the size of the record. In the case of an 80-column Hollerith card, this will be 80 characters.

←	RECORD	→

Unused 1–10	Data 11–15	Unused 16–80

```
01  CARD RECORD.
    05  FILLER         PICTURE X(10).
    05  DATA-ITEM      PICTURE X(5).
    05  FILLER         PICTURE X(65).
```

The next step in data description is to define output data. Internally, there is no decimal point, no dollar sign, etc. For output, the data needs to be rearranged and edited (Figure 19-13). This is done by setting up output pictures and moving the computed data into these fields. The line containing the output pictures is then written.

The output picture uses the characters X, A, and 9, plus some additional report characters. The most used characters are explained here; the remainder are discussed in Chapter 20. A zero, comma, period, stroke, or dollar sign is inserted in the output merely by including the character in the desired position in the PIC-

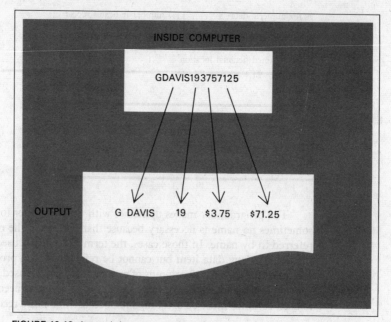

FIGURE 19-13 Internal data versus edited output.

TURE. The Z is used in place of a 9 to indicate that if a leading zero is found in that position, it will be replaced by a blank; a nonzero digit will output the same with a Z as for a 9 picture character.

It may not be desirable to have blanks between the dollar sign and the first nonzero character. In order to make the dollar sign float so that it is next to the first nonzero digit, the picture is written with dollar signs replacing the 9s or Z's for all positions over which the $ is to be allowed to float. Leading zeros in these positions will then be replaced by blanks, and the dollar sign will move over next to the first nonzero digit. Any inserted comma that is not needed because it separates leading zeros being suppressed will be eliminated during zero suppression.

BASIC PICTURE CHARACTERS FOR OUTPUT

X, A, and 9 same as for input

0
,
. } Insert this character in the position shown
/
$

Z in place of leading 9s in picture will replace leading zeros with blanks. Additional $ in place of 9s or Z's will cause leading zeros to be suppressed and the dollar sign to be situated in front of the first nonzero digit.

EXAMPLES

Internal data	To be output as	Picture
37ᐱ596	$37.596	$99.999
ᐱ0375	0.0375	0.9999
476532	476,532	999,999
00065	65	ZZZ99
0006ᐱ50	$6.50	$$$$9.99

The WORKING-STORAGE SECTION

The WORKING-STORAGE SECTION (notice the hyphen which makes a single name out of WORKING-STORAGE) consists of two parts—the first contains data descriptions of individual noncontiguous data items, the second consists of record description for items having subdivisions. The entries use 01, 02, etc., level numbers as do the file record entries (Figure 19-14). There are different level numbers for different purposes; the one used for general items stored individually is level 77. The level 77 entries may be before or after the 01 entries (but in older COBOL specifications they had to precede 01 entries).

The pictures in the WORKING-STORAGE SECTION follow the standard rules for pictures. An initial value of a WORKING-STORAGE data item can be defined by the use of the VALUE clause. The form consists of the words VALUE or VALUE IS followed by the value. The value can be stated as a numeric literal for a numeric data item, as a nonnumeric literal (enclosed in quote marks), or as a

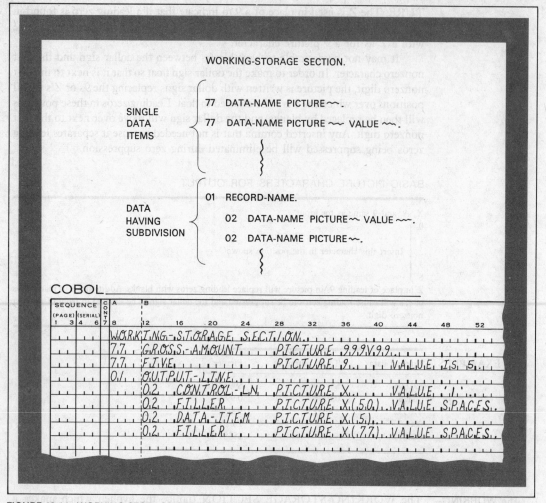

FIGURE 19-14 WORKING-STORAGE SECTION with example.

figurative constant. The following examples illustrate the use of the VALUE clause:

77	ALPHA	PICTURE 99V9	VALUE 39.7.
77	BETA	PICTURE 999V99	VALUE ZEROS.
77	PAGE-HEADING	PICTURE X(6)	VALUE 'REPORT'.
77	HEAD-1	PICTURE X(20)	VALUE SPACES.
01	REPORT-LINE.		
	02 DATA-ITEM	PICTURE $999.99.	
	02 FILLER	PICTURE X(125)	VALUE SPACES.

The first example illustrates a numeric value. The second is a numeric item that is set to zero. The third example is a nonnumeric literal which is enclosed in quote marks. PAGE-HEADING will contain the characters making up the word RE-PORT. The fourth example is a nonnumeric figurative constant. HEAD-1 is filled with the space character. In the last example, the 01 record level contains a data item, the remainder of the record is FILLER which is given a value of spaces, i.e., blanks.

A nonnumeric literal consists of alphabetic, numeric (not computational data), or alphanumeric characters enclosed in quote marks. If the literal will not fit on the coding line, it is broken at column 72 and continued on the next line by placing a hyphen in column 7 and a quote mark on or after column 12 (B margin) followed by the continuation of the literal and ended by a quote mark and period.

The use of figurative constants assists in the readability of COBOL. The figurative constants are words which are used to refer to constants. The most commonly used figurative constants are

ZERO, ZEROS, or ZEROES
SPACE or SPACES

Either the singular or plural can be used. The compiler automatically provides the correct size field. In all cases, the figurative constant is an alternative to writing out the constant. The two following definitions are identical in their effect:

77   SAMPLE PICTURE 999 VALUE IS ZEROES.
77   SAMPLE PICTURE 999 VALUE IS 000.

The use of the word ALL is another method of reducing coding. It specifies that the literal character or characters following ALL are to be repeated enough times to fill the field specified. The following pairs of definitions are identical in effect.

77   ONES-FIELD PICTURE X(6) VALUE ALL '1'.
77   ONES-FIELD PICTURE X(6) VALUE '111111'.

77   ALPHA-FIELD PICTURE X(8) VALUE ALL 'NO'.
77   ALPHA-FIELD PICTURE X(8) VALUE 'NONONONO'.

It has been explained that a file may be a set of lines on the printer, each line being a record. But there may be many different lines on a page—heading lines, detail lines, total lines, etc. If record definitions are used, this would require several different record definitions. This is allowed since a file may contain more than one record type. However, it simplifies programming to define a single output line (in the record definition for the print file). The entry defines a record equal to the printer line size. The different types of printed lines are defined in the WORK-ING-STORAGE SECTION, and when a line is to be printed, it is moved in total from WORKING-STORAGE to the output line record. The record in WORK-

ING-STORAGE is not changed by the move (copying) and is available for subsequent use without being restored (Figure 19-15). A sample definition for a line of output is shown in Figure 19-16. Note the use of quote marks around the nonnumeric literals and the use of figurative constants. The entire printer record (in this example, it has 132 positions) must be accounted for, and all positions which are to be blank (have spaces) must have that value specified.

Note that a VALUE clause can be used to insert data in the output line defined by FILLER. Since FILLER is not unique, the program cannot move data to FILLER or otherwise reference it. The headings in Figure 19-16 do not have names. In this line, it will not ever be necessary to reference the individual headings, so they do not need names, and FILLER is used.

Self-testing Quiz—
COBOL #3

1 What are the two sections in the DATA DIVISION described in this chapter?
2 What do the letters FD stand for in COBOL?
3 A label record for a file is the _____ record in the file.
4 Will *every* file-name in a SELECT/ASSIGN clause in the ENVIRONMENT DIVISION be described by a file description entry in the DATA DIVISION?

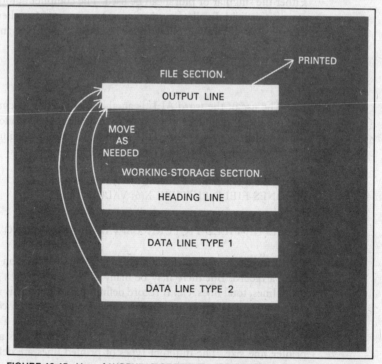

FIGURE 19-15 Use of WORKING-STORAGE records to format output records.

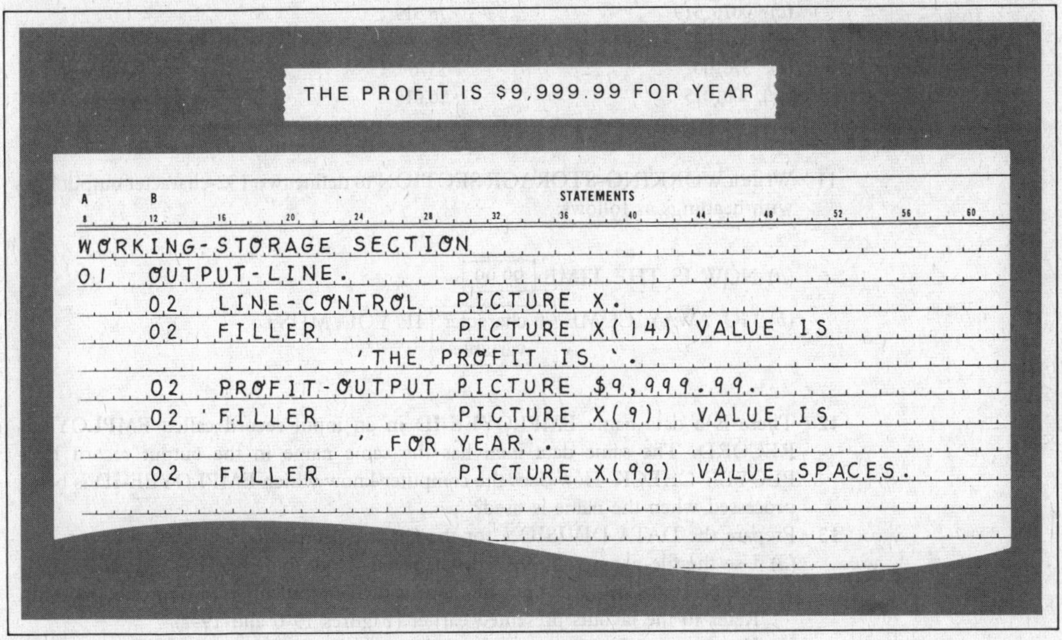

THE PROFIT IS $9,999.99 FOR YEAR

```
A      B                                    STATEMENTS
8      12      16      20      24      28      32      36      40      44      48      52      56      60
WORKING-STORAGE SECTION
01  OUTPUT-LINE.
    02  LINE-CONTROL  PICTURE X.
    02  FILLER        PICTURE X(14) VALUE IS
              'THE PROFIT IS '.
    02  PROFIT-OUTPUT PICTURE $9,999.99.
    02  FILLER        PICTURE X(9)  VALUE IS
              ' FOR YEAR'.
    02  FILLER        PICTURE X(99) VALUE SPACES.
```

FIGURE 19-16 The use of FILLER and VALUE to define a heading.

5 Assign level numbers to the data items in the record layout shown below.

A-RECORD					
B1	B2			B3	
C1	C2	C3	C4	C5	C6

6 Which of the data items in Question 5 are group items?

7 Which of the data items in Question 5 are elementary items?

8 A label record specification will normally state that it is either _____ or _____.

9 An output file consists of lines (records) on a printed page.
   (a) Where in the COBOL program would the fact that the records are to be written on the printer be specified?
   (b) Where would the records in the output file be named?

10 Fill in the following table:

Data	Input picture	Output	Output picture
(a) 364∧15		$364.15	
(b) ∧00001		.00001	

(*c*)	0076ᴧ519	76.519
(*d*)	001ᴧ00	$1.00
(*e*)	376ᴧ00	$376
(*f*)	000ᴧ015	$0.015

11 Write a WORKING-STORAGE SECTION to define two 132-character output lines with headings as follows:

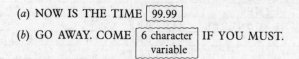

(*a*) NOW IS THE TIME 99.99

(*b*) GO AWAY. COME 6 character variable IF YOU MUST.

12 There is a data name EMPLOYEE-ID in an input record called EMPLOYEE-RECORD. The same data item has the same name in the output record EMPLOYEE-CHECK. How does the computer know which EMPLOYEE-ID is being processed when the name is used?

13 Prepare the DATA DIVISION for the chapter program.

(*a*) Use the file-name you selected when you wrote the ENVIRONMENT DIVISION. Both the card input file and printed output file will omit label records. Refer to the layouts presented earlier (Figures 19-6 and 19-7).

(*b*) Use the same data-name to refer to the same data item in the input record and the output record. (This is good practice but not necessary—completely unique names or names with prefixes or suffixes can be assigned which would avoid qualification when names are used.)

(*c*) There are only two types of output lines—define these in WORKING-STORAGE and define a single output line for the record in the print file.

(*d*) Use 132 spaces for the line if you have an IBM 1403 printer; use appropriate lengths for other printers.

(*e*) Define a level 77 data-name to use for summing the book prices.

(*f*) A special data item (to be explained later) should be defined by a 77-level entry. Call the data item MORE-CARDS with a picture of XXX.

14 Write part (*b*) of Problem 1 (p. 666).

The PROCEDURE DIVISION

The PROCEDURE DIVISION begins with the words PROCEDURE DIVISION at the A margin followed by a period. The division is divided into paragraphs, each of which has a paragraph name. Several paragraphs may be grouped together in a section with a section name. However, sections are not necessary in the PROCEDURE DIVISION. A paragraph name follows the same rules as other COBOL names, that is, up to 30 alphabetic or numeric characters with the hyphen used as a separator. The paragraph name may begin with, or consist entirely of, numerals, whereas data names must have an alphabetic character in them. A paragraph name is followed by a period. The body of the paragraph consists of one or more sentences, each ending with a period.

Basic verbs for writing the PROCEDURE DIVISION are explained in this chapter. Additional features are explained in Chapter 20. The verbs to be covered in this chapter are:

Procedure sequence control	PERFORM
	STOP
Input/Output	READ
	WRITE
	OPEN
	CLOSE
Data movement	MOVE
Arithmetic	ADD
	SUBTRACT
	MULTIPLY
	DIVIDE
Conditional	IF
	ELSE
	AT END

These verbs are sufficient for writing the PROCEDURE DIVISIONS of simple COBOL programs.

Structured Programming in COBOL

In Chapter 5, a disciplined approach to programming was presented; this included the concepts of top-down design, modular or block structure for programs, and straightforward coding using three basic patterns. With some exceptions (which will probably be remedied by CODASYL) the COBOL language has appropriate facilities for the structured, disciplined approach to program design. This chapter applies the structured approach to all examples and explanations. This means that

1 A COBOL program will be divided into modules or blocks. Each module will consist of a paragraph (or section of paragraphs) which performs a single function in the program.

2 There will be a hierarchy of modules. The first level is the mainline-control-routine which directs the execution of second-level modules. Second-level modules invoke third-level modules, etc.

3 Each module (paragraph or section) will have one entry point and one exit point.

4 There will be no use of the GO TO instruction. This instruction will, however, be explained.

5 Rules for indentation and comments will be followed to aid in clarity of documentation:

   (*a*) Each new sentence begins on a new line. Unless other indentation applies, it will be at the B margin (column 12).

   (*b*) The continuation of a sentence not fitting on one line is indented beyond the indentation of the beginning of the sentence. If the sentence starts at the B margin, the indentation for continuation might be column 16.

   (*c*) Statements within the range of an IF statement are indented beyond the indentation of the word IF. This will receive further explanation.

   (*d*) Comments (an asterisk or stroke in column 7) are used to document the purpose and relationship of program paragraphs and sections. For example, a blank comment card can be used before each paragraph to highlight the new function. Another comment line might explain the purpose of the paragraph (if it is not evident from the code).

Insofar as possible, the text explains and illustrates good programming style in COBOL. In the case of simple programs, disciplined, structured style will make the examples more complex. However, the approach very quickly provides less complex programs as the number of instructions increases.

The PERFORM and STOP Verbs

The PERFORM verb is an important COBOL instruction. In its several formats, it is used in coding:

1 The execution sequence of a modular program

2 The repetition (looping) code pattern (one of the three basic coding patterns)

Three forms of the PERFORM instruction are presented in this chapter; additional looping formats are explained in Chapter 20.

THREE FORMS OF PERFORM

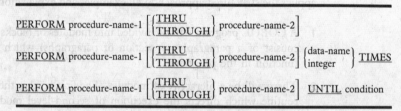

An instruction using the PERFORM verb calls for a procedure-name to be PERFORMed (executed). The procedure-name is a paragraph or section name. The PERFORM instruction in a sequence of instructions causes the computer to transfer control to the named (invoked) procedure, execute it, and then return to the instruction following the PERFORM (Figure 19-17). A set of contiguous procedures is executed by naming the first and last—procedure-1 THRU proce-

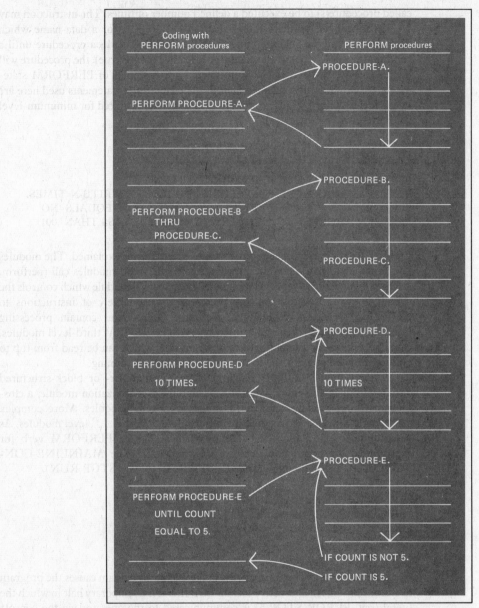

FIGURE 19-17 Different forms of the PERFORM verb.

dure-n. In structured programming, this form will generally not be used. For the first form of PERFORM, the procedure(s) named [paragraph(s) or section(s)] is (are) executed once, and then control is returned to the next executable instruction following the instruction with the PERFORM verb. The second form causes the called procedure(s) to be executed a defined number of times. The instruction may specify an integer (numeric literal such as 1, 2, 3, . . .) or a data-name which references an integer quantity. The third form PERFORMS a procedure until a condition exists (is true). If the condition already exists (is true), the procedure will not be PERFORMed at all. The following are examples of PERFORM statements. (Conditions are explained later in the chapter; the statements used here are self-evident.) The "UNTIL condition" format is not required for minimum-level COBOL (low-level nucleus).

PERFORM READ-AND-PROCESS.
PERFORM READ-PROCESS THRU PRINTOUT.
PERFORM PROCEDURE-READ-CARD 10 TIMES.
PERFORM PROCEDURE-READ THRU PROCEDURE-WRITE N TIMES.
PERFORM READ-PROCEDURE UNTIL MORE-CARDS EQUALS 'NO'.
PERFORM PROCESS-10 UNTIL TEST-AMOUNT IS LESS THAN .001.

In Chapter 5, the concept of a modular program was explained. The modules in a program form a hierarchy in which the higher-level modules call (perform, execute, invoke) the lower-level modules. The first-level module which controls the overall flow of the program may therefore consist largely of instructions to PERFORM second-level modules. Second-level modules contain processing instructions of various types plus instructions to PERFORM third-level modules, etc. This provides a straightforward program flow which can be read from top to bottom, in keeping with the ideas of structured programming.

Even a simple COBOL program using the modular- or block-structured design will have a mainline-control-routine plus an initialization module, a closing-procedures module, and one or more processing modules. More complex programs will have more modules with third, fourth, fifth, . . . , level modules. As an example of a simple structured program using the PERFORM verb for executing program modules, refer to Figure 19-2. The MAINLINE-CONTROL-ROUTINE contains three PERFORMS (plus a STOP RUN).

PERFORM INITIALIZATION
PERFORM READ-AND-PRINT 10 TIMES.
PERFORM CLOSING.
STOP RUN.

The STOP RUN command used in the example program causes the program to end execution. An alternative form STOP literal is a temporary halt in which the literal (say, ERROR-STOP-5) is communicated to the operator via the console display device (say, console typewriter). Execution will begin at the next statement following the STOP literal if the operator initiates a continuation of execution.

STOP $\begin{Bmatrix} \underline{RUN} \\ literal \end{Bmatrix}$ RUN is used for permanent termination; literal (nonnumeric or unsigned numeric) is used to display a temporary halt message to the operator

Self-testing Quiz— COBOL #4

1 The PROCEDURE DIVISION begins with the words _____ _____ starting at the _____ margin.

2 Each paragraph in the PROCEDURE DIVISION starts with a _____ _____.

3 The paragraph name begins at the _____ margin. The sentences on the following lines are coded at the _____ margin.

4 Each sentence must end with a _____.

5 Which of the following are not valid paragraph-names?

(*a*) PAYROLL-OUT   (*d*) 3.15
(*b*) NEXT1   (*e*) PAYROLL-$
(*c*) 45   (*f*) RECORD

6 In the sequence below, explain what happens.

MAINLINE	EDIT-IT
_____	_____
_____	_____
PERFORM EDIT-IT.	_____
STOP RUN.	_____

7 If the program contains the statement STOP 'ERROR-HALT-15' what will happen?

8 Write COBOL statements to:

(*a*) Execute a procedure called ERROR-MESSAGE.
(*b*) Execute 12 times a procedure READ-AND-PROCESS.
(*c*) Execute KOUNT times a procedure PRINT-LINES.

9 Which form of the PERFORM presented in the chapter is not required for the low-level nucleus?

10 Write the MAINLINE-CONTROL-ROUTINE for the chapter program. Assume there will be exactly 15 input cards. The program hierarchy to be used consists of the MAINLINE-CONTROL-ROUTINE plus three second-level routines.

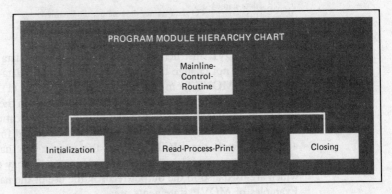

11 Write part (*c*) of Problem 1. No answer is provided.

The MOVE Instruction   As explained previously, a data-name refers to the current contents of storage locations to which the name has been assigned. The contents can be numeric data (such as 09376) or alphanumeric (such as $93.76 or YEAR ENDED). Data is placed in storage locations by:

1   A READ statement (to be explained later)
2   A VALUE clause for data items defined in WORKING-STORAGE
3   A MOVE statement

The MOVE statement puts data into a named storage location, the name being the data-name associated with the storage location. The MOVE statement can describe the data to be moved as a literal (a numeric literal, an alphanumeric literal, or a figurative constant), or the data to be moved can come from another storage location described by a data-name. Examples of internal moves are:

MOVE statement	Contents before MOVE	Contents after MOVE				
MOVE 3175 TO RATE.	Not known	RATE	3	1	7	5
MOVE 'NICE' TO HEADER.	Not known	HEADER	N	I	C	E
MOVE ZEROS TO TOTAL.	Not known	TOTAL	0	0	0	0
MOVE ZEROS TO TOTAL-1, TOTAL-2.	Not known	TOTAL-1	0	0	0	0
		TOTAL-2	0	0	0	0

MOVE INSTRUCTION

$$\text{MOVE} \begin{Bmatrix} \text{data-name} \\ \text{literal} \end{Bmatrix} \text{TO data-name, data-name, data-name, } \ldots$$

The MOVE instruction which moves (copies) data from one location to another does not change the contents of the sending data-name. Two important uses for the MOVE from one location to another are (1) data from a READ is moved before the next READ instruction places data in the same location, and (2) data to be output is moved into the output record location. The MOVE to an output record location also causes the data to be edited for the output report (in accordance with the PICTURE for the output data-name). Note that when subitems in two records are given the same name (as may occur with input items which are used also in the output record), the use of the names must be qualified. Examples of MOVE statements are:

MOVE INPUT-NAME TO OUTPUT-NAME.
MOVE NAME OF INPUT-RECORD TO NAME OF OUTPUT-RECORD.
MOVE ID-CODE TO MASTER-ID, OUTPUT-ID, STUB-ID. (Causes contents of ID-CODE to be copied into three data-name locations.)

The internal representation for a numeric data item for computation and the same numeric data item for displayed output may be quite different. A numeric data item can be moved to a field defined as numeric edited because this is the way data is edited for output. The reverse is not true; a numeric edited item should not be moved to a numeric field of any kind. Alphabetic data is not moved to numeric fields.

A special consideration when moving data is that the sending and receiving fields are not always the same size (in storage). The rules governing this situation differ for numeric (computational) items and nonnumeric items. If the data item is all numeric, the decimal point in the item being moved will be aligned with the decimal point position in the location into which it is being moved (described in the DATA DIVISION). If the item does not fit, excess digits will be truncated or extra positions zero-filled. If the item is nonnumeric, it will go in the receiving area from left to right, and the excess positions, if any, will be filled with spaces. If the receiving area is too small, a warning is usually given by the compiler when the instruction is being compiled.

Some examples will illustrate this statement. In the receiving-area description, 9s stand for numeric digits, and a caret ($_\wedge$) stands for the decimal point (the decimal point in numeric data is assumed and does not take up a memory position). X's stand for nonnumerics, and b's for blank spaces.

SENDING FIELD	RECEIVING FIELD	
	Description	Result
109$_\wedge$4375	9999V9999	0109$_\wedge$4375
109$_\wedge$100	999999V99	000109$_\wedge$10
986435$_\wedge$	99V9999	35$_\wedge$0000 and warning signal
ALPHA1	XXXXXXX	ALPHA1b

Descriptive Headings

At this point, it may be helpful to summarize the methods for providing descriptive headings for COBOL output. The two methods are the use of a record in WORKING-STORAGE and the use of a MOVE in the PROCEDURE DIVISION.

In the first approach, the descriptive line is formatted in the WORKING-STORAGE SECTION. The headings are defined by the VALUE IS clause. For example, the centered heading for a 132-character line reading PAYROLL REPORT will be defined as follows:

```
WORKING-STORAGE.
01  HEADING-LINE.
```

```
02   FILLER PICTURE X(59) VALUE SPACES.
02   FILLER PICTURE X(14) VALUE 'PAYROLL REPORT'.
02   FILLER PICTURE X(59) VALUE SPACES.
```

When the heading is to be printed, the record HEADING-LINE is moved to the output record and written.

The second method of providing descriptive headings is to move a literal into the heading area of the output line. For example, assume an output line which can be either of the two forms:

```
CUSTOMER OWES US $9,999.99
WE OWE CUSTOMER $9,999.99
```

The output line might be defined in WORKING-STORAGE as:

```
01   OUTPUT-LINE.
     02   FILLER          PICTURE X VALUE SPACE.
     02   MESSAGE-FIELD   PICTURE X(17).
     02   DATA-AMOUNT     PICTURE $9,999.99.
     02   FILLER          PICTURE X(105) VALUE SPACES.
```

When the correct message has been determined by the PROCEDURE DIVISION (say, the CUSTOMER OWES US message), a statement MOVE 'CUSTOMER OWES US' TO MESSAGE-FIELD will insert the correct heading. The above example assumes the record is defined in WORKING-STORAGE. If OUT-PUT-LINE was defined as a file record, VALUE clauses could not be used, and another method would be required to set the unused fields to blanks. It is incorrect to MOVE SPACES TO FILLER, so a name can be substituted for FILLER to allow spaces to be moved to these fields, or spaces could be moved to the entire record prior to moving the two data items.

Self-testing Quiz—
COBOL #5

1   Indicate whether correct or incorrect, and if incorrect, why.

Statement	Correct or incorrect	If incorrect, why
(a) MOVE A TO B.		
(b) MOVE A TO B, C, D.		
(c) MOVE 4.2 TO FICA.		
(d) MOVE 'TOTAL' TO TOTAL-LINE.		
(e) MOVE PAY-RATE TO 475.		
(f) MOVE SPACES TO LINE-PRINT		
(g) MOVE ZERO TO PAY-RATE.		
(h) MOVE LINE-UP TO SPACES.		

2 Each of the following data fields named QUAN-1 is to be moved to a data field named QUAN-2. The data description for both fields is given. Indicate the form of QUAN-2 after the transfer. X's stand for alphanumeric characters, and 9s for numeric characters.

Quantity in QUAN-1	Form of QUAN-2	Form of QUAN-2 after move
(a) AICPA01000	XXXXXXXXXXXX	
(b) 108ᴧ437	9999V9999	
(c) 4732	999V9	

3 An input record (called INPUT-RECORD) has a name in the form:

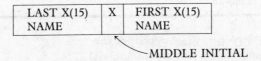

MIDDLE INITIAL

Write an input record description and a record description (call it OUTPUT-RECORD) for an output record defined in WORKING-STORAGE. Move the input name data to the output record name fields. Use different names in the input and output records. The output record should be in the form:

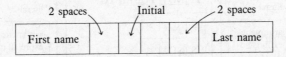

4 Repeat question 3 using the same data-names to refer to the same items in the input and output records.

5 An output line called MESSAGE-LINE has been set up in WORKING-STORAGE:

OUTPUT-MESSAGE X(20)	data etc.

On the basis of computations in the PROCEDURE DIVISION, the message is to be changed to OUTPUT QUANTITY IS. Write statements to make this change.

6 Write MOVES to accomplish the following:
(a) Move all 9s into CODE-FIELD. (CODE-FIELD is alphanumeric.)
(b) Move 3.1417 into PI.
(c) Move NAME into HEAD-1.
(d) Move blanks into ALPHA (PICTURE X(5)).
  (1) Using SPACES
  (2) Not using SPACES

The IF Statement   There are several forms of branching (transfer of control) instructions in COBOL. Only two are explained in this chapter—IF with simple conditional and AT END (to be explained in connection with input and output instructions).

The simple IF conditional statement executes one of two different program paths on the basis of the results of a test. The most common to be explained in this section are a relation comparison between quantities, a sign test of a quantity, and a class test.

IF STATEMENT

IF condition $\left\{ \begin{matrix} \text{Statement-1} \\ \underline{\text{NEXT}}\ \underline{\text{SENTENCE}} \end{matrix} \right\}$ $\left\{ \begin{matrix} \underline{\text{ELSE}}\ \text{Statement-2} \\ \underline{\text{ELSE}}\ \underline{\text{NEXT}}\ \underline{\text{SENTENCE}} \end{matrix} \right\}$

If the condition is true, execute statement-1 or <u>NEXT SENTENCE</u> (if specified); if condition is false, execute statement-2 or NEXT-SENTENCE as specified. ELSE NEXT SENTENCE may be omitted and will be implied.

COBOL CONDITIONAL EXPRESSIONS
(Items in boxes are part of Nucleus, level 2)

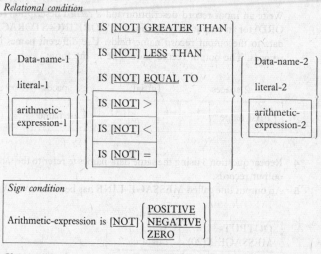

Relational condition

Sign condition

Class condition

The IF statement is used to code the basic IF . . . THEN . . . ELSE sequence control coding structure described in Chapter 5. IF the condition is true, one set of actions is to be taken; if false, another set is to be performed (ELSE . . .). In some cases there is no alternate set of actions for the ELSE. This is coded by leaving off the ELSE or by writing ELSE NEXT SENTENCE. There is no period for the IF sentence until the end of both sets of actions. The two examples which follow illustrate these two possibilities:

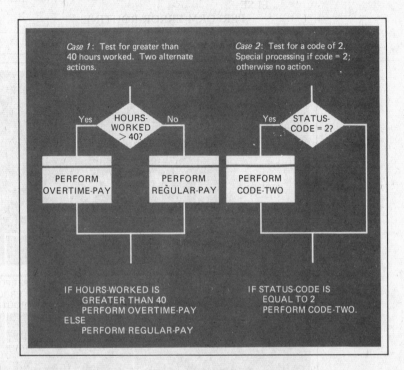

Case 1: Test for greater than 40 hours worked. Two alternate actions.

Case 2: Test for a code of 2. Special processing if code = 2; otherwise no action.

```
IF HOURS-WORKED IS
    GREATER THAN 40
    PERFORM OVERTIME-PAY
ELSE
    PERFORM REGULAR-PAY
```

```
IF STATUS-CODE IS
    EQUAL TO 2
    PERFORM CODE-TWO.
```

In the examples note that ELSE was indented to the same margin as the IF to which the ELSE applies. All statements following the IF are indented to show the range of the IF. The same applies to statements following the ELSE. ELSE is put on a separate sentence to set off the ELSE condition and statements following which belong to the ELSE condition. These are useful coding conventions for clear, understandable programs; they are not required by the COBOL language. The entire set of IF . . . ELSE . . . is one sentence terminated by a period. More than one condition can be handled by nested IFs (included in Nucleus, level 2). The use of indentation helps make the logic clear. For example, coding to select among four alternative processes might be written as shown:

COBOL coding

```
IF STATUS-CODE IS EQUAL TO '1'
    PERFORM CODE-ONE
ELSE
    IF STATUS-CODE IS EQUAL TO '2'
        PERFORM CODE-TWO
    ELSE
```

IF STATUS-CODE IS EQUAL TO '3'
    PERFORM CODE-THREE
ELSE
    PERFORM ERROR-ROUTINE.

Flowchart of logic

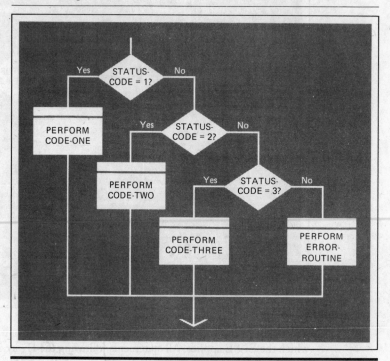

The examples have used the PERFORM verb as the action following the IF or ELSE. This is common in structured programming, but other imperative statements are used. Several statements may be used, each on a separate line for clarity, but the period is at the end of all statements. For example:

IF PAY-AMOUNT GREATER THAN MAXIMUM-PAY
    MOVE 'CHECK AMOUNT' TO ERROR-MESSAGE.

IF AMOUNT-DUE IS POSITIVE
    MOVE AMOUNT-DUE TO OUTPUT-AMOUNT
    MOVE MINIMUM-AMOUNT TO OUTPUT-MINIMUM
    MOVE DUE-DATE TO OUTPUT-DUE-DATE
ELSE
    MOVE CREDIT-MESSAGE TO OUTPUT-MESSAGE
    MOVE AMOUNT-DUE TO CREDIT-AMOUNT.

Program Flags and Programmed Switches in COBOL

There are many occasions in programming when the program needs to remember the result of a prior operation because it will affect a future processing path. The programming technique is a program flag or programmed switch. The concept is the same, so a flag will be used to refer to both terms. The flag is set by a MOVE statement which places a specified value in a storage location. The flag is tested by an IF statement which defines the two paths to follow depending on the value of the flag. A flag may be given a numeric value of 1, 2, 3, etc., or may be given an alphabetic or alphanumeric value such as 'YES', 'NO', or 'MORE'.

EXAMPLE

In a program some special processing is involved with the first record which should not be performed on subsequent records in the file. A flag is set initially to allow the first-record processing. The flag is then set to an off condition to suppress further use of the first-record procedures. The data-name for the flag is defined by a WORKING-STORAGE entry in the DATA DIVISION.

Set flag to initial value

```
INITIALIZATION.
      MOVE 'YES' TO FIRST-RECORD-FLAG.
PROCESSING.
      ————————
      ————————
```

Test flag]

```
IF FIRST-RECORD-FLAG IS EQUAL TO 'YES'
      PERFORM FIRST-RECORD-PROCESS
ELSE
      PERFORM SUBSEQUENT-RECORD-PROCESS.
```

Turn off flag after first record processed

```
FIRST-RECORD-PROCESS.
      ————————
      ————————
      MOVE 'NO' TO FIRST-RECORD-FLAG.
```

Self-testing Quiz— COBOL #6

1 How many statements can follow the IF or ELSE words?
2 Why is it recommended that the ELSE associated with an IF be coded on a separate line and indented to the same level as the IF?
3 What is the difference between a flag and a switch in programming in COBOL?
4 Write a statement to set a TEST-FLAG "on" where "on" equals 1 and "off" equals 2. TEST-FLAG is defined as PICTURE 9.
5 Write a statement to perform PROCEDURE-1 if TEST-FLAG (see question 4) is "on" and PROCEDURE-2 if it is "off."
6 Write IF statements for the following:
 (a) Perform ABC if TEST is greater than zero; perform DEF if it is not.
 (b) If TEST-ONE is less than or equal to TEST-TWO, perform PROCEDURE-M; otherwise do PROCEDURE-K.
 (c) If the quantity ORDER is greater than or equal to 1000.00, move 10 to DISCOUNT; then perform a procedure named BILLING. If ORDER is less than 1000.00, perform BILLING without any adjustment.

(*d*) If the quantity with the data-name BANK-BALANCE is positive or zero, continue with program; otherwise, perform a procedure named OVERDRAFT.

(*e*) If a candidate is less than 20 in AGE, has HAIR that is BROWN and less than 5.3 in HEIGHT, perform OUTPUT-ROUTINE; otherwise perform REJECT.

Arithmetic Statements

Arithmetic statements may be coded using words or using the $+, -, *, /$ symbols. This chapter explains the use of the arithmetic verbs; the COMPUTE verb (part of Nucleus, level 2) which allows symbols is presented in Chapter 20.

The basic formats for COBOL arithmetic are the GIVING format which specifies the data-name where the result is to be stored and the implied results format in which the result is stored in the location previously occupied by one of the operands in the arithmetic operation. As a reminder, a data name, if not unique, must be qualified. Commas and semicolons are optional and are used for clarity only.

ARITHMETIC STATEMENTS—BASIC GIVING FORMAT

$$\text{\underline{ADD}} \left\{ \begin{array}{l} \text{data-name-1} \\ \text{literal-1} \end{array} \right\}, \left\{ \begin{array}{l} \text{,data-name-2} \\ \text{,literal-2} \end{array} \right\} \left[\begin{array}{l} \text{,data-name-2} \\ \text{,literal-3} \end{array} \right] \ldots \text{\underline{GIVING}} \ \text{data-name-n}$$

$$\text{\underline{SUBTRACT}} \left\{ \begin{array}{l} \text{data-name-1} \\ \text{literal-1} \end{array} \right\} \left[\begin{array}{l} \text{,data-name-2} \\ \text{,literal-2} \end{array} \right] \ldots \text{\underline{FROM}} \ \text{data-name-n}$$

$$\text{\underline{GIVING}} \ \text{data-name-n}$$

$$\text{\underline{MULTIPLY}} \left\{ \begin{array}{l} \text{data-name-1} \\ \text{literal-1} \end{array} \right\} \text{\underline{BY}} \left\{ \begin{array}{l} \text{data-name-2} \\ \text{literal-2} \end{array} \right\} \text{\underline{GIVING}} \ \text{data-name-3}$$

$$\text{\underline{DIVIDE}} \left\{ \begin{array}{l} \text{data-name-1} \\ \text{literal-1} \end{array} \right\} \text{\underline{BY}} \left\{ \begin{array}{l} \text{data-name-2} \\ \text{literal-2} \end{array} \right\} \text{\underline{GIVING}} \ \text{data-name-3}$$

$$\text{\underline{DIVIDE}} \left\{ \begin{array}{l} \text{data-name-1} \\ \text{literal-1} \end{array} \right\} \text{\underline{INTO}} \left\{ \begin{array}{l} \text{data-name-2} \\ \text{literal-2} \end{array} \right\} \text{\underline{GIVING}} \ \text{data-name-3}$$

ARITHMETIC STATEMENTS—IMPLIED RESULTS

$$\text{\underline{ADD}} \left\{ \begin{array}{l} \text{data-name-1} \\ \text{literal-1} \end{array} \right\} \left[\begin{array}{l} \text{, data-name-2} \\ \text{, literal-2} \end{array} \right] \ldots \text{\underline{TO}} \ \text{data-name-n}$$

$$\text{\underline{SUBTRACT}} \left\{ \begin{array}{l} \text{data-name-1} \\ \text{literal-1} \end{array} \right\} \left[\begin{array}{l} \text{, data-name-2} \\ \text{, literal-2} \end{array} \right] \ldots \text{\underline{FROM}} \ \text{data-name-n}$$

$$\text{\underline{MULTIPLY}} \left\{ \begin{array}{l} \text{data-name-1} \\ \text{literal-1} \end{array} \right\} \text{\underline{BY}} \ \text{data-name-2}$$

$$\text{\underline{DIVIDE}} \left\{ \begin{array}{l} \text{data-name-1} \\ \text{literal-1} \end{array} \right\} \text{\underline{INTO}} \ \text{data-name-2}$$

The result of the computation is stored as the data-name location following TO, FROM, BY, and INTO.

ROUNDING AND OVERFLOW

[ROUNDED]	Placed immediately after the data-name where the result will be stored to cause rounding before dropping of the part of fractional results not able to be stored in the data-name location.
[ON SIZE ERROR imperative-statement]	Last phrase in arithmetic statement. Optional. Used to specify action to be taken if integer portion of result is greater than size of result data-name. Division by zero results in size error.

The formats provide the answers to various problems that arise with respect to arithmetic computations.

Problem	How handled in COBOL
Keeping track of the correct placement of the decimal point (scaling)	Scaling is handled automatically by the compiler using the data specifications contained in the DATA DIVISION.
Determining where the result of a computation will be stored	The location of the result of an arithmetic operation can be expressed or implied. The result either will be stored as the value for a separate data-name or will replace the value associated with one of the data-names being added, subtracted, etc. The word GIVING specifies the result as a separate data-name. If GIVING is not used, the order of the sentence will imply that the result will replace the last data-name specified (which therefore cannot be a literal).
An answer in which the number of places to the right of the decimal point exceeds the number of decimal places allowed for the answer	The decimal places in the answer are truncated to fit in the field specified for the answer. The word ROUNDED following the data-name used to store the result will cause the answer to be rounded before being truncated.
Overflow in which the integer places in the answer (places to the left of decimal point) exceed the number of integer places allowed for the answer	If overflow can occur, the clause ON SIZE ERROR is used in the arithmetic statement to indicate what the program should do if overflow does occur: for example, ON SIZE ERROR PERFORM SIZE-ERROR-MESSAGE.

There will be a short discussion of each of the arithmetic operations. Use of the instructions given allows the addition operation to be programmed in two ways, plus the option of ROUNDED and ON SIZE ERROR.

ADD A, B, GIVING C ⎤ ROUNDED
⎥ and/or
ADD A, B, TO C ⎦ ON SIZE ERROR . . .

The difference between the two examples is the way the location where the results are stored is specified (or implied). A statement should not specify or imply a literal as the location of the result.

Form	Location of result	What has happened
ADD A, B, C, GIVING D.	D	D replaced with sum of A, B, and C. The GIVING option specifies where the result is to be stored.
ADD A, B, TO C.	C	Contents of C replaced with sum of A, B, and C. The variable following TO is the location of the result. Note that the original value of C is no longer available since it has been replaced by A + B + C.

The ROUNDED and ON SIZE ERROR options are used if there is the possibility of the answer field not being large enough to contain the answer. Because overflow results in the loss of a significant digit, it is desirable to use the ON SIZE ERROR option on arithmetic statements if overflow is possible (and for good error control in some cases when it is thought not possible).

Examples of addition	Comments
ADD DATA-1, DATA-2 GIVING DATA-3 ROUNDED; ON SIZE ERROR PERFORM OVERFLOW-ROUTINE.	The sum of DATA-1 and DATA-2 is stored at DATA-3. The fractional result is rounded if it exceeds available storage places. If overflow occurs, OVERFLOW-ROUTINE is performed.
ADD 2.714 TO DATA-1.	The literal 2.714 will be added to the value of DATA-1 and the sum stored as the new value of DATA-1. No provision is made for rounding or overflow.

There are also two forms for subtraction. The ROUNDED and ON SIZE ERROR options can be used with either form.

Form of subtraction	Location of result
SUBTRACT A FROM B.	B
SUBTRACT A FROM B GIVING C.	C

Examples of subtraction	Comments
SUBTRACT DATA-1 FROM DATA-2 GIVING DATA-3 ROUNDED; ON SIZE ERROR PERFORM OVERFLOW-ROUTINE.	DATA-3 = DATA-2 − DATA-1 Provision is made for rounding decimal places and for overflow errors.
SUBTRACT A, B, C FROM D.	Subtract A, B, and C from D. The result is stored in D.
SUBTRACT A FROM 100.0 GIVING ANSWER.	ANSWER = 100.0 − A.

As with addition and subtraction, there are two basic forms for multiplication—one implies the location of the result, the other is the GIVING option which specifies the location of the result. ROUNDED and ON SIZE ERROR options may be used with either form.

Form of multiplication	Location of result
MULTIPLY A BY B.	B
MULTIPLY A BY B GIVING C.	C

Examples of multiplication	Comments
MULTIPLY A BY B GIVING C ROUNDED; ON SIZE ERROR PERFORM OVERFLOW-ROUTINE.	C = A × B with provision for rounding and overflow if the result field is too small for answer.
MULTIPLY A BY B.	The product of the multiplication is stored as the new value of B.
MULTIPLY A BY 99.4 GIVING PRODUCT	PRODUCT = 99.4 X A

Division can use the INTO format in either the GIVING form or the implied result form. The BY format is allowed only for the GIVING form.

Form of division	Location of result
DIVIDE A INTO B GIVING C.	C
DIVIDE A INTO B.	B
DIVIDE A BY B GIVING C.	C

Examples of division	Comment
DIVIDE A INTO B GIVING C ROUNDED; ON SIZE ERROR PERFORM OVERFLOW-ROUTINE.	C = B/A with provision for rounding and overflow.
DIVIDE A INTO B.	The quotient from B/A is stored as the new value of B.
DIVIDE 33.3 INTO B.	The quotient from B/33.3 is stored as the new value of B.
DIVIDE A BY B GIVING C.	C = A/B

Self-testing Quiz—
COBOL #7

1 Using the verbs ADD, SUBTRACT, MULTIPLY, DIVIDE, write statements to perform the following operations and to store the results where indicated:

Operation	Results stored at	Round	Provide for size error
(a) A + B + C	D	Yes	Yes
(b) A = B − C	A	Yes	No
(c) A/B	C	No	Yes
(d) A × B	X	No	No
(e) A + 2.7	A	No	No

2 Complete the following table:

COBOL statement	Result stored at	Result of A = 5, B = 10, and X = 9
(a) ADD B TO A.		
(b) ADD A TO B.		
(c) SUBTRACT A FROM B.		
(d) MULTIPLY A BY B GIVING X.		
(e) DIVIDE B BY A GIVING X.		
(f) DIVIDE B INTO A.		

3 What will be the results of the following COBOL statements, assuming ALPHA has a PICTURE of 999V99 and a value of 100.00, BETA has a PICTURE of 99V99 and a value of 75.55, and GAMMA has an initial value of 10.54 and a PICTURE of 99V99.

	Result	If size error
(*a*) ADD ALPHA, BETA GIVING GAMMA.		
(*b*) ADD ALPHA TO BETA; ON SIZE ERROR PERFORM OVERFLOW-ROUTINE.		
(*c*) DIVIDE BETA BY ALPHA GIVING GAMMA.		
(*d*) DIVIDE BETA BY ALPHA GIVING GAMMA ROUNDED.		

Input and Output   The input and output of a record requires three steps:

1   OPEN the files (before any READs or WRITEs).
2   The READ or WRITE statement.
3   CLOSE the files (after all READs and WRITEs).

The OPEN statements can properly be put in the initialization procedure; the CLOSE statements can usually be in a closing or ending procedure.

BASIC STATEMENTS FOR FILE INPUT AND OUTPUT

OPEN $\left\{\begin{array}{l}\underline{\text{INPUT}} \\ \underline{\text{OUTPUT}} \\ \underline{\text{I-O}}\end{array}\right\}$ file-name

<u>CLOSE</u> file-name

<u>READ</u> file-name RECORD [AT <u>END</u> imperative statement]

<u>WRITE</u> record-name

Each file must be opened before a record is read and closed after last record is read.

Files, especially those on magnetic tape and on disk storage, may have file labels. The label is a record at the beginning of the file. It is written when the file is created, and it is read and checked when the file is read. When the program is through with a file, there are housekeeping tasks to be performed such as rewinding, etc. COBOL specifies by the use of the OPEN and CLOSE verbs that these standard housekeeping tasks are to be performed. All files (whether or not they have labels) must be opened before the first use and closed after the last use (but before the program is terminated). The format of these statements is:

OPEN INPUT file-name, file-name, ...
OPEN OUTPUT file-name, file-name, ...

or

OPEN INPUT file-name, . . . OUTPUT file-name. . .

and

CLOSE file-name, file-name, ...

For example, if the file is an input file called PAY from which records are being read, the appropriate statement is OPEN INPUT PAY. If a disk file is to be used for both input and output, the statement reads OPEN I-O file-name. More than one file can be opened or closed with the same statement. For example, the statement to open two input files, ALPHA and BETA, plus an output file called CHECKS could read:

OPEN INPUT ALPHA, BETA OUTPUT CHECKS.

The close statement for the three files would be:

CLOSE ALPHA, BETA, CHECKS.

Input of a record (say, a punched card or a record from magnetic tape or magnetic disk) requires only the statement to READ file-name. Output requires WRITE record-name. Prior to the WRITE operation, the proper data will have been moved into the record to be output. Note that the statements are read a *file*, but write a *record*. The reason for this difference is that a file may contain more than one type of record. The command to READ file-name gets the record from the file, but the programmer must then determine which type of record it is (if there can be more than one type in the file). In such cases, there will need to be one field that is in the same position in both records to identify the type of record. In writing records onto a file, there may again be several types of records associated with the file. The file definition in the DATA DIVISION defined the records which belong with a file. The statement to WRITE a record will therefore write a record on the correct file.

What happens if the READ (next record from) file-name instruction is to be executed and there are no more records? The computer usually detects this by reading an end-of-file indicator. By adding an AT END clause to the READ sentence, the programmer can specify what is to happen. In the first example below, the computer is instructed to stop processing the program; in the second, the computer is instructed to PERFORM a paragraph named CLOSING. The CLOSING paragraph in this case specifies procedures to follow when the end-of-file (no more records) has been encountered.

READ PAYROLL-FILE AT END STOP RUN.
READ PAYROLL-FILE AT END PERFORM CLOSING.

The use of structured programming concepts is slightly complicated by the COBOL AT END statement. (Proposals have been made for modifications in this statement, but this text uses the current standard.) In order to achieve the hierarchical structure with the mainline control module controlling the performance of all second-level modules, one of which probably contains the READ, the AT END condition is programmed to set a flag which is tested by the mainline control module. In the example program in Figure 19-2, this problem was avoided by having the mainline control module PERFORM the READ-AND-PRINT paragraph 10 TIMES. But in most programs, the number of records is unspecified, and the end of the records is identified by the AT END condition. The PERFORM must therefore be able to repeat UNTIL the end of file. The program in Figure 19-2 can be altered to read and print any number of cards by making the following changes:

Original program	Revisions
(not needed)	(in WORKING-STORAGE) 77 MORE-CARDS-FLAG PICTURE X(3).
(not needed)	(in INITIALIZATION paragraph) MOVE 'YES' TO MORE-CARDS-FLAG.
PERFORM READ-AND-PRINT 10 TIMES.	(in MAINLINE-CONTROL paragraph) PERFORM READ-AND-PRINT UNTIL MORE-CARDS-FLAG EQUAL TO 'NO'.
READ CARD-FILE AT END STOP RUN. MOVE CARD-RECORD TO	(in READ-AND-PRINT paragraph) READ CARD-FILE AT END MOVE 'NO' TO MORE-CARDS-FLAG. IF MORE-CARDS-FLAG IS EQUAL TO 'YES' MOVE CARD-RECORD TO . . . .

The complete PROCEDURE DIVISION for the changed CARD-LISTER program now appears as shown on page 654. Only one change was made in the DATA DIVISION. If the revised CARD-LISTER program is used as an example, the steps in writing a READ when following a structured format can be summarized as:

1 Establish a flag in WORKING-STORAGE to use to indicate that there are no more records. Set to an initial value either by moving the correct value to the flag as part of initialization (preferred) or by a VALUE clause in WORKING-STORAGE.

2 Write the PERFORM in the mainline control routine as PERFORM read-routine UNTIL end-file-flag IS EQUAL TO code-for-end.

3 Write the READ as READ file-name AT END MOVE code-for-end-of-file TO end-file-flag.

There is more than one approach to coding the procedure. If the one illustrated

```
SEQ. NO.        A    B                              STATEMENTS
        PROCEDURE DIVISION.
        MAINLINE-CONTROL-ROUTINE.
            PERFORM INITIALIZATION.
            PERFORM READ-AND-PRINT UNTIL MORE-CARDS-FLAG EQUAL 'NO'.
            PERFORM CLOSING.
            STOP RUN.
        INITIALIZATION.
            OPEN INPUT CARD-FILE.
                 OUTPUT PRINT-FILE.
            MOVE 'YES' TO MORE-CARDS-FLAG.
        READ-AND-PRINT.
            READ CARD-FILE AT END MOVE 'NO' TO MORE-CARDS-FLAG.
            IF MORE-CARDS-FLAG EQUAL TO 'YES'
                MOVE CARD-RECORD TO PRINT-LINE
                WRITE PRINT-LINE.
        CLOSING.
            CLOSE CARD-FILE, PRINT-FILE.
```

above is used, there must be an IF end-file-flag IS EQUAL TO code-for-more-records . . . following the READ because the READ which detects the AT END condition should not be followed by the same action as the reading of a regular record. Another approach is to read the first card as part of the INITIAL-IZATION. This alters the logic to eliminate the test following the READ. It might be termed "initial read plus process before read." This second method will be illustrated in the self-testing exercises in this section.

Two additional features associated with READ and WRITE to be explained in this chapter are INTO and FROM and spacing of printer output.

ADDITIONAL READ AND WRITE PHRASES

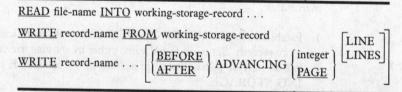

READ file-name INTO working-storage-record . . .

WRITE record-name FROM working-storage-record

WRITE record-name . . . $\left[\left\{\begin{matrix}\text{BEFORE} \\ \text{AFTER}\end{matrix}\right\} \text{ADVANCING} \left\{\begin{matrix}\text{integer} \\ \text{PAGE}\end{matrix}\right\} \left[\begin{matrix}\text{LINE} \\ \text{LINES}\end{matrix}\right]\right]$

The READ INTO is essentially a combination of a READ and MOVE, and the WRITE FROM a combination of MOVE and WRITE. The READ INTO instruction puts the record being read into a record defined in WORKING-STORAGE; the WRITE FROM takes a record set up in WORKING-STOR-AGE and moves it into the output record from which it is written. This is efficient because different output formats can be defined in WORKING-STORAGE, and all use the same output record area without programming a separate MOVE.

When writing a record into a printer, it is useful to be able to space to the top of a page before (or after) writing a line and to be able to skip lines. The ADVANCING PAGE allows this to be programmed as part of the WRITE instruction. (Caution: PAGE is not a part of older COBOLs.)

Self-testing Quiz—
COBOL #8

1 The OPEN verb must be used only for (select most appropriate and complete answer):
    (*a*) Input files   (*c*) Tape and disk files
    (*b*) Output files   (*d*) All files

2 Write a statement to close an input file NUTS and an output file BOLTS.

3 A file is called SALES-INVOICES; the records are called INVOICE.
    (*a*) Write a statement to open such a file to be used as input and a statement to read from the file (AT END STOP RUN).
    (*b*) Write a statement to open such a file for output. Write a statement to write a record on the file.

4 A file PERSONNEL has two types of records—OFFICE-TYPE and SHOP-TYPE. Write two statements to read both types of records (assuming the next two records include one of each). Assume AT END STOP RUN.

5 A file of punched cards called SALES is to be read one at a time. The only processing is to add a data-item SALE-AMOUNT to SUM-SALES. Write statements to initialize the end-file-flag, read the records, etc. Ignore all other coding, but show paragraph names. Show the entry in the WORKING-STORAGE which defines the flag.

6 Code the PROCEDURE DIVISION of the program in question 5 but change the logic to read the first record in the INITIALIZATION paragraph and to initialize the flag value in WORKING-STORAGE.

7 It is now possible to complete the coding of the chapter problem. Figure 19-18 details the logic of the four small modules making up the program. You should already have defined a data-name MORE-CARDS in WORKING-STORAGE. The return to the mainline routine is automatic; no instruction need be used.

8 Complete the coding of Problem 1 (answer not given).

Compiling and Executing a COBOL Program

After coding a COBOL program, the individual lines on the coding paper are punched into Hollerith cards—one line to a card. The resulting deck of punched cards is the source program deck. It must be in order by divisions—IDENTIFICATION, ENVIRONMENT, DATA, and PROCEDURE. Job control cards and data cards must be added to the source program deck to make a job deck.

·If you have a computer available, punch up the coding for your answers to the chapter problem, add control cards and data cards, and compile and execute. Rarely does a program compile and execute without correction. Make necessary corrections until this simple chapter program runs. Figure 19-19 is a sample output from the compilation and execution of the chapter problem. Some of the output from compilation used primarily in debugging has been omitted from the exhibit.

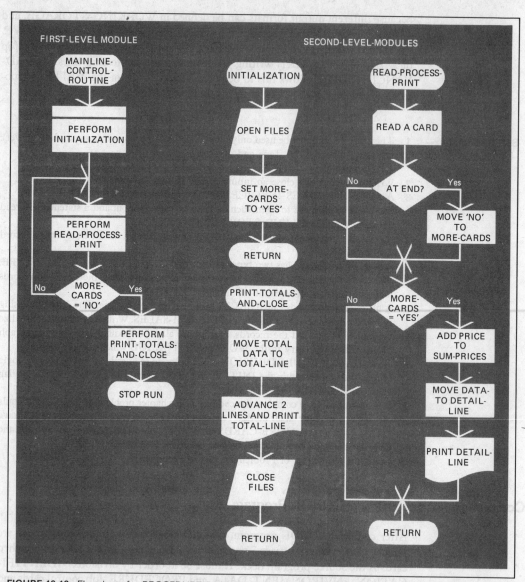

FIGURE 19-18 Flowcharts for PROCEDURE DIVISION of COBOL chapter problem.

With the information presented in this chapter, coding simple COBOL programs should be possible. Chapter 20 covers additional COBOL elements which are either useful or necessary in more complicated problems.

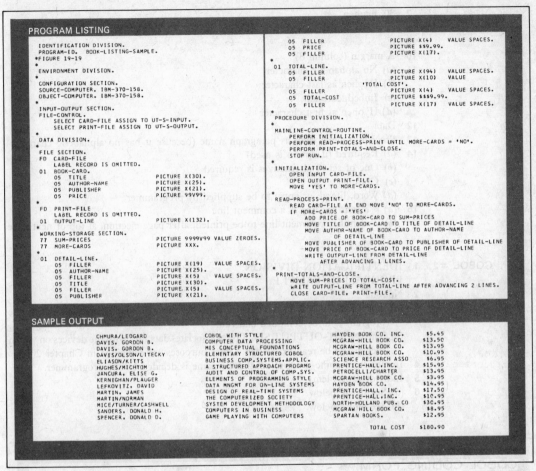

FIGURE 19-19 Program listing and sample output for chapter problem.

Answers to Self-testing Quizzes

COBOL #1

1. CODASYL; American National Standards Institute
2. IDENTIFICATION, ENVIRONMENT, DATA, and PROCEDURE
3. IDENTIFICATION: Identifies the program.
   ENVIRONMENT: Describes the equipment to be used and associates equipment with data files.
   DATA: Describes the form and format of the data.
   PROCEDURE: Defines the processing procedures.
4. Sections, paragraphs
5. 8, 12
6. 8, A

7 30, hyphen

8 ENVIRONMENT

9 8

10 A margin (column 8)

11 (*a*) No alphabetic character

(*b*) Hyphen as last character

(*c*) Imbedded blank

(*d*) Hyphen as first character

12 Data

13 Procedure-name such as paragraph name (because it has no alphabetic character)

14 (*a*) Required (if option is used)

(*b*) One of set of alternatives is required

(*c*) Optional

(*d*) Word, literal, or entry to be supplied by programmer

15 (*a*) * means the line is a comment line

(*b*) / identifies comment line to be printed, after page ejection, at top of next page

COBOL #2 **1** IDENTIFICATION DIVISION.

PROGRAM-ID. SAMPLE.

2 No, one

3 (*a*) The CONFIGURATION SECTION describes the equipment on which the program is to be compiled and run.

(*b*) The INPUT-OUTPUT SECTION associates data files with the devices on which they are to be read or written. Other purposes are explained in Chapter 20.

4 Implementer name is supplied; the file-name is decided by the programmer.

5 Individual problem

6 (*a*) See figure below.

(*b*) See figure below.

```
COBOL CODING FORM    NAME:                          PAGE        OF
                     DATE:                          IDENT:

SEQ. NO. | C | A   B                    STATEMENTS
         | O |
         | N |
         | T |

         IDENTIFICATION DIVISION.
         PROGRAM-ID. CHAPTER-19-PROBLEM.

         ENVIRONMENT DIVISION.
         CONFIGURATION SECTION.
         SOURCE-COMPUTER. IBM-370-158.
         OBJECT-COMPUTER. IBM-370-158.
         INPUT-OUTPUT SECTION.
         FILE-CONTROL.
             SELECT CARD-FILE ASSIGN TO UT-S-INPUT.
             SELECT PRINT-FILE ASSIGN TO US-S-OUTPUT.
```

COBOL #3 **1** (*a*) FILE SECTION
(*b*) WORKING-STORAGE SECTION
2 File description
3 First
4 Yes
5 01 A-RECORD.
    02 B1   PICTURE _____.
    02 B2.
        03 C1   PICTURE _____.
        03 C2   PICTURE _____.
        03 C3   PICTURE _____.
    02 B3.
        03 C4   PICTURE _____.
        03 C5   PICTURE _____.
        03 C6   PICTURE _____.
6 A, B2, and B3
7 B1, C1, C2, C3, C4, C5, and C6
8 STANDARD. OMITTED
9 (*a*) In the FILE-CONTROL paragraph in the INPUT-OUTPUT SECTION of the ENVIRONMENT DIVISION
(*b*) In the FD descriptions of the DATA DIVISION

10

Input	Output
(*a*) 999V99	$999.99
(*b*) V9(5)	.99999
(*c*) 9999V999	ZZ99.999
(*d*) 999V99	$$$9.99
(*e*) 999V99	$999
(*f*) 999V999	$$$9.999

11 WORKING-STORAGE SECTION.
01 HEADING-1.
    02   FILLER PICTURE X(17)   VALUE IS ' NOW IS THE TIME '.
    02   DATA-1 PICTURE 99.99.
    03   FILLER PICTURE X   VALUE '.'.
    02   FILLER PICTURE X(110)   VALUE SPACES.
01 HEADING-2.
    02   FILLER PICTURE X(15)   VALUE ' GO AWAY. COME '.
    02   DATA-2 PICTURE X(6).
    02   FILLER PICTURE X(13)   VALUE ' IF YOU MUST.'.
    02   FILLER PICTURE X(98)   VALUE SPACES.
12 The name EMPLOYEE-ID is qualified whenever used in the PROCEDURE DIVISION. It will read (OF can be used in place of IN)
EMPLOYEE-ID IN EMPLOYEE-CHECK
or
EMPLOYEE-ID IN EMPLOYEE-RECORD.
13 DATA DIVISION.

```
FILE SECTION.
FD   CARD-FILE
          LABEL RECORD IS OMITTED.
01   BOOK-CARD.
     02   TITLE              PICTURE X(30).
     02   AUTHOR-NAME        PICTURE X(25).
     02   PUBLISHER          PICTURE X(21).
     02   PRICE              PICTURE 99V99.
FD   PRINT-FILE
          LABEL RECORD IS OMITTED.
01   OUTPUT-LINE    PICTURE X(132).
WORKING-STORAGE SECTION.
77   SUM-PRICES     PICTURE 999V99 VALUE ZEROS.
77   MORE-CARDS     PICTURE XXX.
01   DETAIL-LINE.
     02   FILLER             PICTURE X(19)   VALUE SPACES.
     02   AUTHOR-NAME        PICTURE X(25).
     02   FILLER             PICTURE X(5)    VALUE SPACES.
     02   TITLE              PICTURE X(30).
     02   FILLER             PICTURE X(5)    VALUE SPACES.
     02   PUBLISHER          PICTURE X(21).
     02   FILLER             PICTURE X(4)    VALUE SPACES.
     02   PRICE              PICTURE $$9.99.
     02   FILLER             PICTURE X(17)   VALUE SPACES.
01   TOTAL-LINE.
     02   FILLER             PICTURE X(94)   VALUE SPACES.
     02   FILLER             PICTURE X(10)   VALUE 'TOTAL
                                             COST'.
     02   FILLER             PICTURE X(4)    VALUE SPACES.
     02   TOTAL-COST         PICTURE $$$9.99.
     02   FILLER             PICTURE X(17)   VALUE SPACES.
```

COBOL #4

1 PROCEDURE DIVISION. A

2 Paragraph-name

3 A, B

4 Period

5 (d) period special character not allowed

(e) special character $ not allowed

(f) RECORD is reserved word and cannot be used as paragraph-name

6 The execution of PERFORM EDIT-IT transfers control to the paragraph EDIT-IT which is executed. Control then returns to the MAINLINE to the next executable statement following the PERFORM EDIT-IT which is STOP RUN which causes the program to terminate.

7 The program execution will halt temporarily, a message ERROR-HALT-15 will be displayed at the console display device (typewriter or CRT). When the operator institutes a continuation, the program will continue with the statement following the STOP.

8 (*a*) PERFORM ERROR-MESSAGE.
(*b*) PERFORM READ-AND-PROCESS 12 TIMES.
(*c*) PERFORM PRINT-LINES KOUNT TIMES.
9 The PERFORM . . . . UNTIL condition.
10 PROCEDURE DIVISION.
MAINLINE-CONTROL-ROUTINE.
    PERFORM INITIALIZATION.
    PERFORM READ-PROCESS-PRINT 15 TIMES.
    PERFORM CLOSING.
    STOP RUN.

COBOL #5 **1** (*a*) Correct
(*b*) Correct
(*c*) Correct
(*d*) Correct
(*e*) Incorrect—cannot move a variable to a literal
(*f*) Incorrect—no period at end of sentence
(*g*) Correct
(*h*) Incorrect—cannot move a variable to figurative constant
2 (*a*) AICPA01000bb   b = space
(*b*) 01084370
(*c*) 7320 plus warning. Note loss of significant digit.
3 01 INPUT-RECORD.
    02 INPUT-FIRST-NAME   PICTURE X(15)
    02 INPUT-MIDDLE-INITIAL PICTURE X.
    02 INPUT-LAST-NAME   PICTURE X(15)
  01 OUTPUT-RECORD
    02 OUTPUT-FIRST-NAME   PICTURE X(15).
    02 FILLER   PICTURE X(2)   VALUE SPACES.
    02 OUTPUT-MIDDLE-INITIAL PICTURE X.
    02 PERIOD   PICTURE X   VALUE '.'.
    02 FILLER   PICTURE X(2)   VALUE SPACES.
    02 OUTPUT-LAST-NAME   PICTURE X(15).
    02 FILLER   PICTURE X(96) VALUE SPACES.
MOVE INPUT-FIRST-NAME TO OUTPUT-FIRST-NAME.
MOVE INPUT-MIDDLE-INITIAL TO OUTPUT-MIDDLE-INITIAL.
MOVE INPUT-LAST-NAME TO OUTPUT-LAST-NAME.
4 01 INPUT-RECORD.
    02 FIRST-NAME   PICTURE X(15).
    02 MIDDLE-INITIAL PICTURE X.
    02 LAST-NAME   PICTURE X(15).
  01 OUTPUT-RECORD.
    (Same as Question 3 without prefix OUTPUT)
MOVE FIRST-NAME OF INPUT-RECORD TO
    FIRST-NAME OF OUTPUT-RECORD.

```
        MOVE MIDDLE-INITIAL OF INPUT-RECORD
            TO MIDDLE-INITIAL OF OUTPUT-RECORD.
        MOVE LAST-NAME OF INPUT-RECORD
            TO LAST-NAME OF OUTPUT-RECORD.
```

5 MOVE 'OUTPUT QUANTITY IS' TO OUTPUT-MESSAGE.

6 (a) MOVE ALL '9' TO CODE-FIELD.

  (b) MOVE 3.1417 TO PI.

  (c) MOVE 'NAME' TO HEAD-1.

  (d) (1) MOVE SPACES TO ALPHA

      (2) MOVE '   ' TO ALPHA, or MOVE ALL ' ' TO ALPHA. (Five spaces in first literal, one in the second)

COBOL #6

1 No limit, but there must be only one period at the end of all statements.

2 To clearly show the range of the IF and the ELSE and all statements which belong to each.

3 No difference

4 MOVE 1 TO TEST-FLAG.

5 IF TEST-FLAG IS EQUAL TO 1

```
        PERFORM PROCEDURE-1
    ELSE
        IF TEST FLAG IS EQUAL TO 2
            PERFORM PROCEDURE-2.
        ELSE
            PERFORM TEST-FLAG-ERROR.
```

6 (a) IF TEST IS POSITIVE

```
        PERFORM ABC
    ELSE
        PERFORM DEF.
```

  (b) IF TEST-ONE IS NOT GREATER THAN TEST-TWO

```
        PERFORM PROCEDURE-M
    ELSE
        PERFORM PROCEDURE-K.
```

  (c) IF ORDER IS NOT LESS THAN 1000   or   IF ORDER IS NOT LESS

```
        MOVE 10 TO DISCOUNT              THAN 1000 MOVE
        PERFORM BILLING                 10 TO DISCOUNT.
                                            PERFORM BILLING.
    ELSE
        PERFORM BILLING.
```

  (d) IF BANK-BALANCE IS NEGATIVE

```
        PERFORM OVERDRAFT.
```

  (e) IF AGE IS LESS THAN 20

```
        IF HAIR IS EQUAL TO 'BROWN'
            IF HEIGHT LESS THAN 5.3
                PERFORM OUTPUT-ROUTINE
            ELSE
                PERFORM REJECT
        ELSE
            PERFORM REJECT
```

    ELSE
      PERFORM REJECT.

   or

    IF AGE NOT LESS THAN 20
      PERFORM REJECT
    ELSE
      IF HAIR IS NOT EQUAL TO 'BROWN'
        PERFORM REJECT
      ELSE
        IF HEIGHT IS NOT LESS THAN 5.3
          PERFORM REJECT
        ELSE
          PERFORM OUTPUT-ROUTINE.

COBOL #7 **1** (a) ADD A, B, C GIVING D ROUNDED; ON SIZE ERROR PERFORM SIZE-
       ERROR-ROUTINE.
     (b) SUBTRACT C FROM B GIVING A ROUNDED.
     (c) DIVIDE B INTO A GIVING C; ON SIZE ERROR PERFORM SIZE-
       ERROR-ROUTINE.
     (d) MULTIPLY A BY B GIVING X.
     (e) ADD 2.7 TO A.

2

Stored at		Result
(a)	A	15
(b)	B	15
(c)	B	5
(d)	X	50
(e)	X	2
(f)	A	.5 (or 0 if PICTURE for A allows only integers)

    3 (a) 75$_\wedge$55 and overflow. Control goes to next statement.
      (b) 75$_\wedge$55 and overflow. OVERFLOW-ROUTINE is performed.
      (c) 00$_\wedge$75 The remaining two digits were truncated as GAMMA is not large enough
         to hold them.
      (d) 00$_\wedge$76. The 00$_\wedge$7555 was rounded to 0076 before being stored in GAMMA.

COBOL #8 **1** d (all files)
     2 CLOSE NUTS, BOLTS.
     3 (a) OPEN INPUT SALES-INVOICES.
      READ SALES-INVOICES
        AT END STOP RUN.
      (b) OPEN OUTPUT SALES-INVOICES.
        WRITE INVOICE.

4   READ PERSONNEL AT END STOP RUN. { The statement reads the next re-
                                           cord. The program must deter-
     READ PERSONNEL AT END STOP RUN. mine the type.

5 WORKING-STORAGE SECTION.
    77   MORE-CARDS-FLAG   PICTURE X(3).

    PROCEDURE DIVISION.
    MAINLINE-CONTROL-ROUTINE.
        PERFORM INITIALIZATION.
        PERFORM READ-AND-ADD UNTIL MORE-CARDS-FLAG EQUAL
           TO 'NO'.

    INITIALIZATION.
        MOVE 'YES' TO MORE-CARDS-FLAG.
    READ-AND-ADD.
        READ SALES AT END MOVE 'NO' TO MORE-CARDS-FLAG.
        IF MORE-CARDS-FLAG EQUAL TO 'YES' ADD SALES-AMOUNT
           TO SALES-SUM.
6 WORKING-STORAGE SECTION.
    77   MORE-CARDS-FLAG   PICTURE X(3) VALUE 'YES'.

    PROCEDURE DIVISION.
    MAINLINE-CONTROL-ROUTINE.
        PERFORM INITIALIZATION.
        PERFORM ADD-AND-READ UNTIL MORE-CARDS-FLAG EQUAL
           TO 'NO'.

    INITIALIZATION.
        READ SALES AT END STOP RUN.

    ADD-AND-READ.
        ADD SALES-AMOUNT TO SALES-SUM
        READ SALES AT END MOVE 'NO' TO MORE-CARDS-FLAG.
7 See Figure 19-19.

EXERCISES

1 What are the advantages of using a common source language such as COBOL?
2 What is the mechanism for updating and revising the COBOL language?
3 What is the purpose of each of the four divisions in a COBOL program?
4 What is the purpose of a procedure-name?
5 What is a literal? How are literals defined in COBOL?
6 What is the general form of the IDENTIFICATION DIVISION? Illustrate a minimum division.
7 What is the general form of the ENVIRONMENT DIVISION? Illustrate a simple, but complete, division.
8 What is the general form of the DATA DIVISION?
9 What is the purpose of the FILE SECTION and WORKING-STORAGE SECTION?
10 Illustrate a simple, but complete, FILE SECTION for a card file.

11 What is the purpose of the level designation in a record description?

12 What is the purpose of the PICTURE?

13 In the PICTURE, what is meant by the following?
(a) a floating dollar sign
(b) zero suppression

14 Fill in the following table:

Data as read by computer	Actual value of data	Input picture	Data as it should appear in output	Output picture
(a) 9060	9.060		$9.06	
(b) 4375		99V99		$99.99
(c) 8190	.8190		$0.81	
(d) 6101	610100.		610,100	
(e) 9999	9999		9999	
(f) 6012		9(4)		$99,9(3).00
(g) 5329	.005329		.005329	
(h) 0101	0101		101.0	

15 What is the purpose of the VALUE IS clause? Illustrate its use for (a) a numeric value, (b) an alphanumeric value, and (c) a value using a figurative constant.

16 Write statements to do the following arithmetic operations. Have the answer in the location specified.

Operation to be performed	Location of result
(a) $(A+B)/D$	X
(b) $A+B$	B
(c) A/B	C
(d) $A \times B$	B
(e) A^2	X

17 How does COBOL provide for handling overflow in arithmetic?

18 Write statements to solve the following, providing for overflow and rounding.

$$X = \frac{(A + B)^2}{D}$$

19 Field X is 9999. What is the result of moving Y to X, where Y is
(a) 9999   (b) 1321   (c) 13   (d) 1441

20 Move the following data:
(a) Spaces into A, B, and C.
(b) Zeros into D, E, and F.
(c) The name CLARK into FIRST-NAME. If FIRST-NAME is defined as X(15), how will CLARK be located in the storage space? What will be done with the rest of the storage space?

21 The INPUT-RECORD has NAME, ADDRESS, and TELEPHONE. The OUT-

PUT-RECORD has the same data items with the same names, but in a different order. Move the data from the input record to the output record.

22 Write conditional statements to make the following tests:
  (a) If A is greater than B, perform an error routine; if not, perform a processing routine.
  (b) If A is less than or equal to B, do the edit procedure; if not, do the update procedure.
  (c) If A is greater than zero, perform a printing procedure.

23 What is the purpose of OPEN and CLOSE?

24 What is the purpose of the file label?

25 Write a complete PROCEDURE DIVISION to read the records from a payroll file and find if GROSS-PAY is greater than $4800. If it is, write the record on an analysis file; if not, read the next record. Stop when all records have been examined.

26 Rewrite the sample program in Figure 19-2 to read an unspecified number of records. Use the "initial read plus process before read" logic.

PROBLEMS

1 The pay rate report problem is designed to be written as the student progresses through the chapter. It is therefore divided into assignments which can be completed along with similar assignments for the self-testing chapter problem. This problem represents a slight increase in difficulty over the chapter problems, and the answer is not provided.

The Small Company wishes a periodic report showing the hourly rate and gross pay for 40 hours of work for each employee. There are about 15 employees, so the report fits easily on one sheet of printer paper. At the end of the list, the report should show the average rate and average gross pay for 40 hours' work for all employees. The input is available on punched cards. The report layout and input card layout are shown in Figure 19-20. To simplify the problem, the report is dated by hand when produced. Note that only the average figure has a dollar sign (a slight simplification from common report conventions). The assignments are:
  (a) Write the IDENTIFICATION and ENVIRONMENT DIVISIONS. There will be an input data file on punched cards (call it PAY-RATE-FILE) and an output file (call it PRINT-FILE).
  (b) Write the DATA DIVISION. There will need to be a file description for the two files. Neither has labels. The PAY-RATE-FILE has a card record. See Figure 19-20 for the card layout. The print line record is dependent on the printer (say, 132 positions). The three heading lines need to be defined in WORKING-STORAGE. See Figure 19-20 for the general layout of the report. Prepare a printer layout sheet as the basis for coding. Other WORKING-STORAGE items (77 level items) need to be defined to accumulate the count of employees, the calculation of 40-hour pay, the total rate, the total pay, and for the calculation of average pay rate and average 40-hour pay. Define a data-name as a read-switch (to be explained in the next chapter). Call it MORE-CARDS with a picture of XXX.
  (c) Write the MAINLINE-CONTROL module. See hierarchy chart (Figure 19-21) and flowcharts (Figure 19-22).
  (d) Write the three second-level modules. Use the flowcharts in Figure 19-22.

2 Make one or more of the following changes in the book list program presented in the chapter.
  (a) Add a title and column headings to the report. Skip two lines between report title and column headings and first detail lines.

(b) Count the number of lines per page and advance to a new page when the page is full (within five lines of the bottom of the page). The available lines per page may vary with installations—66 lines is typical. A smaller number of lines, say, 60, is actually printed.

(c) Combine (a) and (b) so that each new page begins with report heading and column headings. Add the page number for each page. Be sure to count heading lines and skipped lines.

(d) Add an input validation module to detect possible errors in the input. The module should check for the following errors:

(1) Title field is blank

(2) Author field is blank

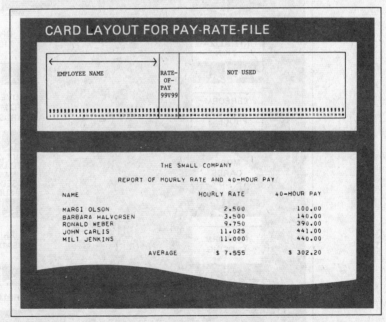

FIGURE 19-20 Layout of input card and report output for pay-rate report (Exercise problem 1).

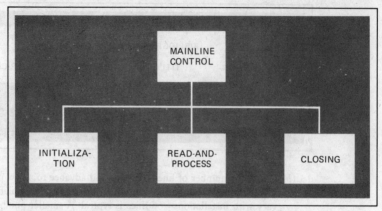

FIGURE 19-21 Hierarchy chart for Exercise problem 1.

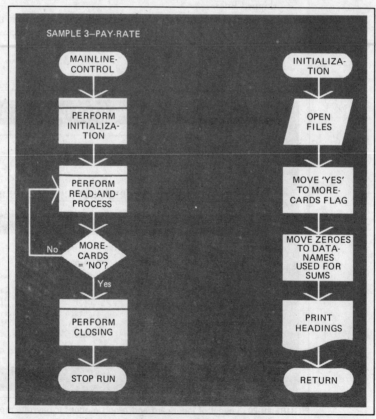

FIGURE 19-22 Flowcharts for Exercise problem 1.

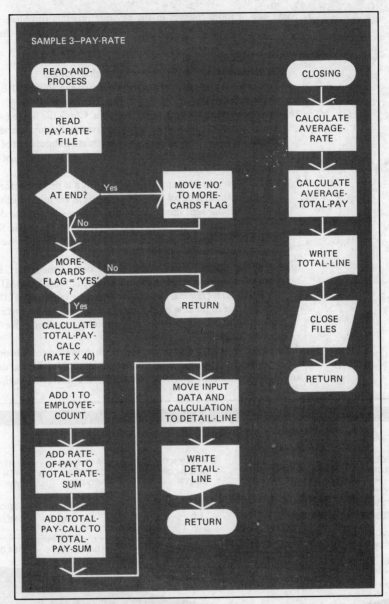

FIGURE 19-22 *(Continued)*

(3) Publisher field is blank
(4) Price is less than $3.00 or over $50.00
For each line in which an error condition occurs, print the message POSSIBLE ERROR in the space at the right of the detail line.

3 Make one or more changes in the pay rate program (problem 1):

(*a*) Include an input validation module to do simple error checking on input data. Check for:

(1) Blank name field

(2) Payrate less than $2.00 or greater than $10.00

Each time an error is detected, print the message 'POSSIBLE ERROR' to the right of the detail line.

(*b*) Include a crossfoot check in the program. Check the figure for the average 40-hour pay by summing the payrate column, dividing by the number of employees listed, and multiplying by 40 to provide an alternate computation of average 40-hour pay. (*Hint:* The crossfoot check should not be equality because of rounding errors. The check should be for ± a few cents.)

(*c*) Revise the report format so that a dollar sign is printed before the number in each column on the first detail line. No dollar signs are used on other lines until the total line. The dollar sign should be in the same position as the dollar sign in the total line. This is customary report form for typed reports. (*Hint:* Set up separate named fields in the detail line with an initial value of '$,' then move spaces to these fields after the print instructions.)

(*d*) Revise the report format to include the date of the report. Input the date of the report. Input the date on the first card in the form YYMMDD. Print the date as YY/MM/DD. (*Hint:* Define an 80-character record in WORKING-STORAGE with the date in the first six positions and the remainder spaces. READ the first file record INTO this working storage record and then move the date field to the appropriate fields in the output line.)

4 An insurance advisor prepares a report which shows the death benefits for a client under three conditions: nonaccident death (such as illness), accidental death by any accident, and death by accident in a common carrier (airplane, bus, taxi, etc.).

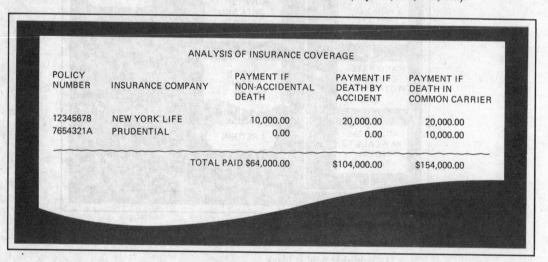

POLICY NUMBER	INSURANCE COMPANY	PAYMENT IF NON-ACCIDENTAL DEATH	PAYMENT IF DEATH BY ACCIDENT	PAYMENT IF DEATH IN COMMON CARRIER
12345678	NEW YORK LIFE	10,000.00	20,000.00	20,000.00
7654321A	PRUDENTIAL	0.00	0.00	10,000.00
	TOTAL PAID	$64,000.00	$104,000.00	$154,000.00

ANALYSIS OF INSURANCE COVERAGE

There is one input card per policy containing the policy number, the name of the insurance company, the base policy amount, and three factors (multipliers) by which the base policy amount is to be multiplied to yield the amount paid for each of the three conditions. For example, a policy of 10,000 and factors of $1_\wedge 00$, $2_\wedge 00$, and $2_\wedge 00$ will pay $10,000 for nonaccidental death, $20,000 for accidental death, and $20,000 for accidental death in a common carrier. The first factor (nonaccidental death) for an accident policy is therefore 0. Assume input data of 10 characters for policy number, 30 characters for company name, 9(7) for base amount, and 9V99 for each of the three factors. Write a program to prepare the report.

5 Prepare a simple payroll report for THE SMALL COMPANY showing the wages paid.

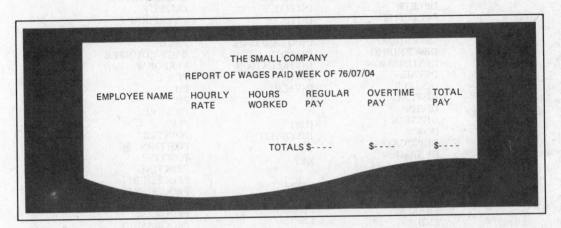

THE SMALL COMPANY

REPORT OF WAGES PAID WEEK OF 76/07/04

EMPLOYEE NAME	HOURLY RATE	HOURS WORKED	REGULAR PAY	OVERTIME PAY	TOTAL PAY
		TOTALS $- - - -		$- - - -	$- - - -

The first input card is a date card. See Problem 3(*d*) for hints on how to handle the date. The program should be written with a separate module to calculate overtime. Assume input record of 30 characters for name, 9(3) for hours worked, and 99V999 for rate of pay. Overtime is paid at rate of 1.5 times the regular rate for hours over 40.

List of COBOL Reserved Words

These words have a defined meaning in COBOL and must not be used as data or procedure names.

ACCEPT	ASSIGN	CHARACTER	CONTAINS
ACCESS	AT	CHARACTERS	CONTROL
ADD	AUTHOR	CLOCK-UNITS	CONTROLS
ADVANCING		CLOSE	COPY
AFTER	BEFORE	COBOL	CORR
ALL	BLANK	CODE	CORRESPONDING
ALPHABETIC	BLOCK	CODE-SET	COUNT
ALSO	BOTTOM	COLLATING	CURRENCY
ALTER	BY	COLUMN	
ALTERNATE		COMMA	DATA
AND	CALL	COMMUNICATION	DATE
ARE	CANCEL	COMP	DATE-COMPILED
AREA	CD	COMPUTATIONAL	DATE-WRITTEN
AREAS	CF	COMPUTE	DAY
ASCENDING	CH	CONFIGURATION	DE

DEBUG-CONTENTS
DEBUG-ITEM
DEBUG-LINE
DEBUG-NAME
DEBUG-SUB-1
DEBUG-SUB-2
DEBUG-SUB-3
DEBUGGING
DECIMAL-POINT
DECLARATIVES
DELETE
DELIMITED
DELIMITER
DEPENDING
DESCENDING
DESTINATION
DETAIL
DISABLE
DISPLAY
DIVIDE
DIVISION
DOWN
DUPLICATES
DYNAMIC

EGI
ELSE
EMI
ENABLE
END-OF-PAGE
ENTER
ENVIRONMENT
EOP
EQUAL
ERROR
ESI
EVERY
EXCEPTION
EXIT
EXTEND

FILE
FILE-CONTROL
FILLER
FIRST
FOOTING
FOR
FROM

GENERATE
GIVING
GREATER
GROUP

HEADING
HIGH-VALUE

HIGH-VALUES

I-O
I-O-CONTROL
IDENTIFICATION
INDEX
INDEXED
INDICATE
INITIAL
INITIATE
INPUT
INPUT-OUTPUT
INSPECT
INSTALLATION
INTO
INVALID

JUST
JUSTIFIED

KEY

LABEL
LAST
LEADING
LEFT
LENGTH
LESS
LIMIT
LIMITS
LINAGE
LINAGE-COUNTER
LINE
LINE-COUNTER
LINES
LINKAGE
LOCK
LOW-VALUE
LOW-VALUES

MEMORY
MERGE
MESSAGE
MODE
MODULES
MOVE
MULTIPLE
MULTIPLY

NATIVE
NEGATIVE
NEXT
NOT
NUMBER
NUMERIC

OBJECT-COMPUTER
OCCURS
OMITTED
OPEN
OPTIONAL
ORGANIZATION
OVERFLOW

PAGE
PAGE-COUNTER
PERFORM
PF
PH
PIC
PICTURE
PLUS
POINTER
POSITION
POSITIVE
PRINTING
PROCEDURE
PROCEDURES
PROCEED
PROGRAM
PROGRAM-ID

QUEUE
QUOTE
QUOTES

RANDOM
RD
READ
RECEIVE
RECORD
RECORDS
REDEFINES
REEL
REFERENCES
RELATIVE
RELEASE
REMAINDER
REMOVAL
RENAMES
REPLACING
REPORT
REPORTING
REPORTS
RERUN
RESERVE
RESET
RETURN
REVERSED
REWIND
REWRITE

RF
RH
RIGHT
ROUNDED
RUN

SAME
SD
SEARCH
SECTION
SECURITY
SEGMENT
SEGMENT-LIMIT
SELECT
SEND
SENTENCE
SEPARATE
SEQUENCE
SEQUENTIAL
SET
SIGN
SIZE
SORT
SORT-MERGE
SOURCE
SOURCE-COMPUTER
SPACE
SPACES
SPECIAL-NAMES
STANDARD

STANDARD-1
START
STATUS
STOP
STRING
SUB-QUEUE-1
SUB-QUEUE-2
SUB-QUEUE-3
SUBTRACT
SUM
SUPPRESS
SYMBOLIC
SYNC
SYNCHRONIZED

TABLE
TALLYING
TAPE
TERMINAL
TERMINATE
TEXT
THAN
THROUGH
THRU
TIME
TIMES
TO
TOP
TRAILING
TYPE

UNIT
UNSTRING
UNTIL
UP
UPON
USAGE
USE
USING

VALUE
VALUES
VARYING

WHEN
WITH
WORDS
WORKING-STORAGE
WRITE

ZERO
ZEROES
ZEROS

+
-
*
/
**
>
<
=

CHAPTER

ADDITIONAL FEATURES OF COBOL

This chapter describes additional features of COBOL. Some features are explained in detail; others are mentioned briefly. The purpose of the chapter is to explain additional features frequently used and to survey other features, so that the student has an awareness of the full range of COBOL capabilities.

American National Standard Functional Processing Modules

The American National Standard COBOL specifications are organized into a nucleus and eleven functional processing modules. Each module has one, two, or three levels of implementation. The highest level has all features; the lowest level eliminates some features. The following is a brief explanation of the nucleus and the 11 functional processing modules:

Functional processing module	Level	Explanation
Nucleus	Low	Elementary elements for internal processing.
	High	Full capabilities for internal processing.
Table handling	Low	Definition of fixed-length tables (up to three dimensions) and procedures to locate items using a subscript or index.
	High	Adds capability for variable-length tables and for searching of tables.
Sequential I-O	Low	Basic facilities for programming the use of sequential files.
	High	More complete facilities.
Relative I-O	Low	Capability to define and to randomly access records in mass storage files (say, disk storage) by means of relative record numbers.
	High	Random and sequential access processing in same COBOL program
Indexed I-O	Low	Basic facilities for random access to data records in mass storage via a key value and an index which relates the key value to storage locations.
	High	Alternate keys and both sequential and random access in same program.
Sort-Merge	Low	Basic sorting.
	High	Extended sorting and merging.
Report writer	One level	Semiautomatic production of reports based on specifications.
Segmentation	Low	Overlaying of COBOL program sections in memory during execution of the program to reduce main memory requirements—fixed segment limits.

	High	Variable segment limits.
Library	Low	Use COPY verb to include predefined COBOL text in a program.
	High	Alter COBOL statements to be copied by REPLACING phrases.
Debug	Low	Provides basic debug capabilities—selective output of data indicating progress of a program during execution.
	High	Full debug capabilities.
Interprogram communication	Low	Capability to transfer control to another program known at compile time and for both programs to have access to the same data.
	High	Communication with another program not known at compile time.
Communication	Low	Basic facilities to communicate (through a message control system) with local and remote communication devices—full messages only.
	High	More sophisticated capability such as segments of messages.

The minimum standard COBOL consists of level 1 for the nucleus, table handling, and sequential access processing modules. The elements of the minimum standard COBOL are described fully in the text; other modules receive less detailed explanation.

Remainder of Nucleus for IDENTIFICATION, ENVIRONMENT, and DATA DIVISIONS

The preceding chapter explained most features associated with the low-level nucleus. This section completes the description of the nucleus (including high-level features) for the IDENTIFICATION, ENVIRONMENT, and DATA DIVISIONS.

IDENTIFICATION DIVISION

The minimum IDENTIFICATION DIVISION consists of the division name and the PROGRAM-ID. Several other entries are allowed. These are for documentation and do not affect processing. The only one which is affected by compilation is DATE-COMPILED (high-level nucleus) in which the compilation process inserts the current date in place of the comment entry. The complete set of possible entries are shown in the table. The comment entry may use more than one line.

COMPLETE FORMAT FOR IDENTIFICATION DIVISION

IDENTIFICATION DIVISION.

PROGRAM-ID. Program-name.

[AUTHOR. [comment-entry] . . .]

[INSTALLATION. [comment-entry] . . .]

[DATE-WRITTEN. [comment-entry] . . .]

[DATE-COMPILED. [comment-entry] . . .]

[SECURITY. [comment-entry] . . .]

ENVIRONMENT DIVISION

The ENVIRONMENT DIVISION can have the following sections and paragraphs.

ENVIRONMENT DIVISION.
CONFIGURATION SECTION.
SOURCE-COMPUTER.
OBJECT-COMPUTER.   } Additional features in nucleus
SPECIAL-NAMES.   explained in this section.
INPUT-OUTPUT SECTION.   } Additional features explained
FILE-CONTROL.   in sections on processing
I-O-CONTROL.   modes.

The nucleus for OBJECT-COMPUTER contains two optional phrases—MEMORY SIZE and PROGRAM COLLATING SEQUENCE. The memory size phrase documents the memory requirements for the computer on which the program is run. The collating sequence phrase is used to define a different collating sequence that is native to the computer.

OBJECT-COMPUTER. computer-name

$$\left[, \underline{MEMORY} \text{ SIZE integer} \left\{ \begin{array}{l} \underline{WORDS} \\ \underline{CHARACTERS} \\ \underline{MODULES} \end{array} \right\} \right]$$

[, PROGRAM COLLATING SEQUENCE IS alphabet-name]

The SPECIAL-NAMES optional paragraph (not shown) has clauses which define names through which the program can refer to devices, assigns names to equipment switch settings, and defines the nonnative collating sequences. Two other SPECIAL-NAMES clauses are of interest internationally:

CURRENCY SIGN IS literal
DECIMAL-POINT IS COMMA

By the use of the first clause, a programmer may specify a currency symbol (e.g., £) to be used in place of $. Many countries exchange the use of the commas and period, so that 10,375.43 is expressed as 10.375,43. The DECIMAL-POINT IS COMMA clause causes the comma to be used as decimal point and the period to separate thousands, etc.

DATA DIVISION

The basic data description entry explained in Chapter 19 contains:

$$\text{level-number} \begin{Bmatrix} \text{data-name-1} \\ \underline{\text{FILLER}} \end{Bmatrix} \left[\begin{Bmatrix} \underline{\text{PICTURE}} \\ \underline{\text{PIC}} \end{Bmatrix} \text{ is picture} \right] \left[\underline{\text{VALUE}} \text{ IS literal} \right]$$

There are additional clauses available for data description. The clauses may be written in any order except that the data-name or FILLER must be first and REDEFINES (if used) must precede other clauses.

Optional clause	Explanation
REDEFINES data-name	Allows the same computer storage to be described by different data description entries; i.e., the same storage location will be used for different data items during the execution of a program. It is also useful in defining tables (to be explained later in this chapter).
[USAGE IS] $\begin{Bmatrix} \underline{\text{COMPUTATIONAL}} \\ \underline{\text{COMP}} \\ \underline{\text{DISPLAY}} \end{Bmatrix}$	Defines most common usage of a data-item to aid efficiency of internal representation. In most computers, a computational item may have a different representation than an item to be displayed (say, in output).
[SIGN IS] $\begin{Bmatrix} \underline{\text{LEADING}} \\ \underline{\text{TRAILING}} \end{Bmatrix}$ [SEPARATE CHARACTER]	Defines explicitly the operational sign (+ or −) in terms of position and whether it occupies a separate storage position. Not normally required.
$\begin{Bmatrix} \underline{\text{SYNCHRONIZED}} \\ \underline{\text{SYNC}} \end{Bmatrix} \begin{bmatrix} \underline{\text{LEFT}} \\ \underline{\text{RIGHT}} \end{bmatrix}$	Specifies the alignment of an elementary data item on the natural addressing boundaries of the computer memory. Used to improve object-code efficiency.
$\begin{Bmatrix} \underline{\text{JUSTIFIED}} \\ \underline{\text{JUST}} \end{Bmatrix}$ RIGHT	Standard usage is for alphabetic and alphanumeric data to be stored starting at left of the storage space; any excess positions are

filled with spaces and any extra characters are truncated. This clause moves the data in from the right with space fill or truncation at left. As an example, 'FUND' moved into a field defined as X(6): Without JUST

| F | U | N | D | | |

With JUST

| | | F | U | N | D |

'FUND' moved into a field defined as X(3): Without JUST

| F | U | N |

With JUST

| U | N | D |

BLANK WHEN ZERO

When a numeric or a numeric edited data item is zero, the storage area for the item will be filled with spaces. Normally used in connection with output where a zero result is to be displayed or printed as spaces.

Note that USAGE and SYNC are to promote efficiency in execution time; REDEFINES is to conserve storage.

Two new level numbers (66 and 88) are used for special cases. These cases are advanced nucleus features.

66 data-name-1 <u>RENAMES</u> data-name-2 $\left[\left\{ \begin{array}{l} \underline{\text{THROUGH}} \\ \underline{\text{THRU}} \end{array} \right\} \text{data-name-3} \right]$

This format is used to assign a new name to data already named. Different groupings of contiguous data items may be assigned new names. For example, assume the names of married women are defined as:

FULL-NAME		
FIRST-NAME	MAIDEN	LAST-NAME

‿ to be RENAMED MAIDEN-NAME

66 MAIDEN-NAME RENAMES FIRST-NAME THRU MAIDEN.

The use of MAIDEN-NAME will obtain the two fields, whereas FULL-NAME will continue to reference all three fields.

88 condition-name $\left\{ \begin{array}{l} \underline{\text{VALUE}} \text{ IS} \\ \underline{\text{VALUES}} \text{ ARE} \end{array} \right\}$ literal-1 $\left[\left\{ \begin{array}{l} \underline{\text{THROUGH}} \\ \underline{\text{THRU}} \end{array} \right\} \text{literal-2} \right] \ldots$

The 88-level entry allows a name to be assigned to a condition value. For example, assume that a program flag to indicate more input cards or no more input cards is defined as explained in Chapter 19 but that names are to be assigned to the two conditions. This is done by 88-level entries:

```
77   CARDS-FLAG PICTURE IS X(3).
     88     MORE-CARDS VALUE 'YES'.
     88     END-CARDS VALUE 'NO'.
```

The statement to initialize the flag would be MOVE 'YES' to CARDS-FLAG. The statement to perform the read routine would be PERFORM READ-ROUTINE UNTIL END-CARDS. The read statement would include the clause AT END MOVE 'NO' TO CARDS-FLAG. The test following the read statement would be IF MORE-CARDS . . . . Another instance when 88 level may be used is in assigning names to codes; for example, assume a code of 1, 2, 3, and 4 for freshmen, sophomores, etc.

```
03   STUDENT-CODE PICTURE X.
     88     FROSH   VALUE '1'.
     88     SOPH    VALUE '2'.
     88     JUNIOR VALUE '3'.
     88     SENIOR VALUE '4'.
```

A statement to see if the student record refers to a senior would be coded IF SENIOR . . . . Note that the 88 entry VALUE clause can state either specific values or a range of values. This is illustrated by a data-name SCHOOLING which has the number of years of school completed. Codes might be assigned names as follows (note use of ERROR-1):

```
02   SCHOOLING PICTURE 99.
     88     GRADE-SCHOOL VALUES ARE 1 THRU 6.
     88     JUN-HIGH        VALUES ARE 7 THRU 9.
     88     HIGH-SCHOOL   VALUES ARE 10 THRU 12.
     88     ERROR-1          VALUES ARE 0 AND 25 THRU 99.
```

Additional Picture Characters

As explained in Chapter 19, the PICTURE clause provides a simplified way of specifying the form of data items. The PICTURE itself is a set of characters which define the data item. A few picture characters are presented in Chapter 19. The entire set is summarized in Table 20-1.

The size of a PICTURE is the number of characters used in the PICTURE (limited to 30 picture characters). The size of the data item defined by the PICTURE is the number of characters actually stored in memory. Thus, assumed decimal points and signs are not part of the size of the data string in storage, but inserted characters such as the inserted decimal point do take up storage positions.

It is recommended that the operational sign S be included in the PICTURE for items which might assume a negative value. In input from punched cards, a negative input item normally has an 11 overpunch on the rightmost digit of the

TABLE 20-1 CHARACTERS AND SYMBOLS USED IN PICTURE CLAUSE

Character	Explanation of use	Example	Comments on example
Characters representing size and class			
A	To represent alphabetic character	PICTURE IS AAA	Data item is three alphabetic characters
X	To represent alphanumeric character	PICTURE IS XXX	Three alphanumeric characters
9	To represent numeric character	PICTURE IS 9999	Four numeric characters
c(i)	Indicates a repeat of preceding character i times	PICTURE IS X(4)	Same as XXXX
Operational symbols (not counted in size of item)			
S	Causes operational sign to be part of word	PICTURE IS S9999	Sign will be included in storage
V	Assumed decimal point	PICTURE IS 99V99	Locates decimal point for compiler
P	Number of leading or trailing zeros depending on which end of picture P appears	PICTURE IS P(3)999	Quantity is ∧000375
	Decimal point assumed to right or left of zeros specified by P	PICTURE IS 999P(6)	Quantity is 375000000∧

For stored quantity of 375

Character	Explanation of use	Example	Comments on example
Zero suppression symbols			
Z	Causes leading zero to be suppressed	PICTURE IS ZZ99	Indicates first two characters may be zero and, if so, should be replaced by blanks in outputs
*	Causes leading zero to be suppressed and replaced by check protection symbol (*)	PICTURE IS **99	Same as Z except leading zeros replaced by*
Characters to be inserted for output editing (if used, class of item is alphanumeric)			
$	To insert dollar sign. If more than one is used, it will be floating (see explanation in text)	PICTURE IS $999	Dollar sign inserted as part of item
,	To insert comma	PICTURE IS 999,999	Comma inserted in item in location shown
.	To insert actual decimal point	PICTURE IS 99.99	Actual decimal inserted
B	To insert a blank space	PICTURE IS 99B99	Will print as 41 67
O	To insert a zero	PICTURE IS 99099	Will print as 41067
/	To insert stroke symbol	PICTURE IS XX/XX	ABCD will print as AB/CD

For stored quantity of 4167

Character	Explanation of use	Example	Comments on example
Report signs			
−	To insert a minus if item is negative	PICTURE IS −9999	Will be blank if positive
+	To insert the sign of the quantity	PICTURE IS +9999	+ if positive, − if negative
CR	CR printed only if quantity is negative	PICTURE IS 9999CR	Will be blank if positive
DB	DB printed only if quantity is negative	PICTURE IS 9999DB	Will be blank if positive

data field; for example, −43 is 4̄3̄. Defining the input item with the S picture character ensures a correct interpretation of the negative number. Likewise, there should be provisions for a negative sign on output if it is possible for the data to be negative. The use of the PICTURE clause is illustrated by the following examples. Table 20-1 explains the use of P, B, CR, etc.

Data as read by computer	Actual value of data	Input picture	Data as it should appear in output	Output picture
5000	5000	9(4)V	$5000.00	$9(4).99
5000	50.00	S99V99	+50.00	+9(2).9(2)
485̄9̄	−485,900	S9(4)P(2)	−485,900	−9(3).9(2)
4859	4.859	9V9(3)	$ 4.859	$B9.9(3)
4859	0.4859	V9(4)	0.4859	0.9(4)
485̄9̄	−0.004859	SP(2)9(4)	$00.004859 CR	$00.9(6)BCR
0010	00.10	9(2)V9(2)	$0.10	$$9.99
0100	100	9(4)V	*100	*9(3)
X545	X545	X(4)	X/545	X/XXX

**Self-testing Quiz—
COBOL #9**

1   What is included in minimum COBOL?
2   In France, 17,377.82 is written as 17.377,82. How does COBOL provide for programming a report in French?
3   What is the difference between RENAMES and REDEFINES?
4   A 4-character alphanumeric item (NUTS) is moved into a field that has only two characters. What will be stored? How would JUSTIFY in the data description for this receiving field change this storage?
5   Code clauses to do each of the following:
   (a) Assume the following record:
```
        01  REC-A.
            02    ITEM-1
            02    ITEM-2
            02    ITEM-3
            02    ITEM-4
```
   Give the last three the name SUB-A.
   (b) In a listing of SALES-BY-CUSTOMER, customers for which there are no sales are to have the sales blank on the output.
   (c) Position an alphabetic name in a storage field called NAME-FIELD as follows:

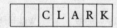

   (d) Item A and item B, each with two subitems (X,Y and W,V), are to occupy the same storage locations at different times in the execution of the program. Item-A subitems are numeric 9(6) and 9(10) while item-B subitems are X(10) and X(6).
6   (a) Write a data description for a numeric data item of nine characters called PAY-AMOUNT and then assign the storage locations to another item called PAY-GROSS.

(b) Define PAY-AMOUNT as computational and stored beginning on a storage boundary.

7 Specify that input data ALPHA 9(5) has minus sign for negative quantities.

8 Complete the following table:

Actual value of data	Data as read by computer	Input area picture	Data as displayed	Output area picture
(a) 450.5	4505		$450.50	
(b) 986,000	9860			9(3),9(3)
(c)	5743	VP(3)9(4)	$0.0005743	
(d) 8	0008		$8.00	
(e)	9040	9V9(3)		+9.9(3)
(f) 88	0088		$99.99	
(g)	453̄0	S9(3)V9	453 CR	
(h) 96.54	9654		$***96.54	
(i) 1.981	1981		1.90801	
(j) 1.476	1476			$9.99
(k) HOLD-OUT	HOLD-OUT			X(6)
(l) K1767		X(5)	K1767	
(m) K1765	K1765		K/1765	

9 A set of program statements read:
IF MARRIED
    IF OVER-40
        IF UNDER-25
            PERFORM TALLEY-IT.
The data being tested has a code of 2 for a MARITAL-STATUS of currently married (1 for single, 3 for divorced, 4 for widowed). AGE is the actual age. Write data descriptions to support the use of the procedure statements.

10 The statement to perform a read module states PERFORM READ-MODULE UNTIL END-RECORDS. What must the statement do to initialize the end-of-record flag (called RECORD-END-FLAG) if the code for the condition END-RECORD is 1 and the code for condition MORE-RECORDS is 0? Also show the data description for the RECORD-END-FLAG.

Remainder of Nucleus for PROCEDURE DIVISION

The basic features of the PROCEDURE DIVISION, corresponding roughly with level 1 of the nucleus, are described in Chapter 19. The remaining nucleus features are covered in this section, some in detail, others in summary.

The COMPUTE Statement and Other Arithmetic

The high-level nucleus provides for a compact computational instruction consisting of the COMPUTE verb plus arithmetic expressions composed of data-names, numeric literals, arithmetic operators, the equals sign, and parentheses. An example is: COMPUTE X = − A − B + C / D ** 2.

Arithmetic operators	Meaning
+	Addition
−	Subtraction
*	Multiplication
/	Division
**	Exponentiation

Plus or minus signs may be used in front of data-names or literals to indicate a positive or negative value. The arithmetic operators and plus or minus signs must be preceded by a space and followed by a space. A minus in front of a data-name means multiplication of the value by −1 (which results in a positive value if the data is already negative). Parentheses are used to eliminate ambiguities because operations inside parentheses are performed first. In the absence of parentheses, the operations are from left to right with all exponentiations first, then multiplication and division, and finally addition and subtraction.

The COMPUTE statement is used not only to write complex computations (such as formulas) but can also set a data-name to a value (a literal or value of another data-name). The latter is an alternative to a MOVE statement.

THE COMPUTE VERB

$$\underline{\text{COMPUTE}} \text{ data-name } [\underline{\text{ROUNDED}}] = \begin{cases} \text{arithmetic expression} \\ \text{literal} \\ \text{data-name} \end{cases}$$

[; ON $\underline{\text{SIZE}}$ ERROR imperative statement]

ROUNDED refers only to the final results.

Example	Comment
COMPUTE X ROUNDED = (A / B) ** 2 ON SIZE ERROR PERFORM OVERFLOW-ROUTINE.	$X = \left(\dfrac{A}{B}\right)^2$ with provision for rounding and overflow.
COMPUTE X = (A / B) ** 2.	$X = \left(\dfrac{A}{B}\right)^2$ with no rounding or overflow.
COMPUTE X = 3.1417.	Define value of X as 3.1417.
COMPUTE X = A + B / C + D ** 2.	$X = A + \left(\dfrac{B}{C}\right) + D^2$
COMPUTE X = A + (B / C) + (D ** 2).	Same as above.

The high-level nucleus allows arithmetic expressions using either COM-PUTE or the GIVING format to define multiple data-names where the result is to be stored.

Example	Explanation
ADD A, B GIVING C, D, E.	The sum of A + B will be stored in each of three locations C, D, and E.
COMPUTE C, D, E = A + B.	Same as above.

The high-level nucleus provides for the remainder from a division to be available. A clause is inserted following the GIVING data-name-3 [ROUNDED] which says <u>REMAINDER</u> data-name-4. The remainder is placed in data-name-4.

EXAMPLE   The sum of employee pay equal to $3012 is divided by the number of employees (say, 14) yielding average pay of $215 (rounded). The remainder is $2. The remainder is defined as the dividend (3012) − [quotient (215) × divisor (14)]. The COBOL statement would read:

DIVIDE SUM-PAY BY NO-EMPLOYEES GIVING AVERAGE-PAY ROUNDED
    REMAINDER PAY-REMAINING
    ON SIZE ERROR PERFORM ERROR-16.

**The
CORRESPONDING
Phrase**

As noted in Chapter 19, it is possible to use the same name for the data items in different records, but each use of the data-name would have to be qualified by the name of the group item to which it belonged. Two records with EMPLOYEE-NAME would be differentiated as EMPLOYEE-NAME OF INPUT-RECORD and EMPLOYEE-NAME IN OUTPUT-RECORD. Not only does this provide clear documentation, it also simplifies certain statements if the CORRESPOND-ING feature can be used (high-level nucleus). CORRESPONDING can be used with ADD TO, SUBTRACT FROM, and MOVE TO.

$$\left\{ \begin{array}{l} \underline{MOVE} \\ \underline{ADD} \\ \underline{SUBTRACT} \end{array} \right\} \underline{CORRESPONDING}\ identifier\text{-}1 \left\{ \begin{array}{l} \underline{TO} \\ \underline{TO} \\ \underline{FROM} \end{array} \right\} identifier\text{-}2$$

Identifier-1 and identifier-2 are group items with data-names some or all of which are the same. The CORRESPONDING phrase causes all pairs of same data-names in the group items to be operated upon—MOVED, ADDED TO, or SUB-TRACTed FROM. As examples, assume input and output records:

```
01  INPUT-RECORD       01  OUTPUT-RECORD
    03    NAME-ID          03    CLASSIF
    03    RATE             03    FILLER
    03    CLASSIF          03    NAME-ID
```

03	JOB-CODE	03	FILLER
		03	RATE
		03	FILLER
		03	etc.

MOVE CORRESPONDING INPUT-RECORD TO OUTPUT-RECORD will move NAME-ID, RATE, and CLASSIF to the corresponding fields in OUTPUT-RECORD. JOB-CODE is not moved because there is no corresponding named output field; other fields in the output record are not affected. The data-items need not be in the same order in the group-items.

As another example, assume an employee current pay record and a cumulative pay record. Fields in the current pay are to be added to the cumulative pay.

01	CURRENT-PAY	01	CUMULATIVE-PAY
03	GROSS-PAY	03	GROSS-PAY
03	DEDUCTIONS	03	DEDUCTIONS
03	NET-PAY	03	NET-PAY

ADD CORRESPONDING CURRENT-PAY TO CUMULATIVE-PAY will add the three current pay items to the corresponding cumulative pay items.

More on Conditional Statements

In the low-level nucleus, relation conditions must use words such as GREATER, LESS, EQUAL. The high-level nucleus allows the use of relational characters:

Use of relational characters	Same as
IS [NOT] >	IS [NOT] GREATER THAN
IS [NOT] <	IS [NOT] LESS THAN
IS [NOT] =	IS [NOT] EQUAL TO

Complex conditions are formed from simple conditions connected by logical operators:

Logical operator	Meaning
AND	Condition is true if both conditions connected by AND are true.
OR	Condition is true if either of conditions connected by OR are true.
NOT	Reverses the truth of the condition.

Some examples will illustrate the complex conditions:

Complex condition	Meaning
IF AGE > 40 AND MARITAL-STATUS = 'SINGLE' PERFORM LISTING.	List all records when age is greater than 40 and marital status is single.

IF AGE > 40
    OR MARITAL-STATUS = 'SINGLE'
    PERFORM LISTING.

List all records where either age is greater than 40 or marital status is single.

IF NOT (AGE > 40
    OR MARITAL-STATUS = 'SINGLE')
    PERFORM LISTING.

List all records except those listed in example above.

Note the use of parentheses to group conditions in the last example. In evaluation of a compound statement, the conditions inside parentheses are evaluated first. Then the conditions are grouped and evaluated first according to AND and second by OR, proceeding from left to right. Notice the difference in the following examples:

Compound conditional statement	Effect
(A AND B) OR C	True when C is true or A and B are true or when all three are true.
A AND (B OR C)	True when A and one or both of B and C are true.

C AND D AND E
    OR F
    OR G AND H AND I
    OR J.
(C AND D AND E)
    OR F
    OR (G AND H AND I)
    OR J.
	Equivalent. True when one or more of the following are true: C, D, and E; G, H, and I; F; J.

Complex condition statements can be abbreviated by allowing certain portions to be understood. In such cases, the compiler will take the missing terms from the nearest preceding relation which explicitly states the subject, relation, and object. Examples are:

1   Subject omitted   IF A = B OR = C OR = D . . . .
2   Subject and relational operator omitted   IF A = B OR C OR D . . . .

In both of the examples, the meaning is:

IF A = B OR A = C OR A = D . . . .

Self-testing Quiz—
COBOL #10

1   Write COMPUTE statements to solve the following:

(a) $x = \left(\dfrac{a + b}{c}\right)^3$

(b) $x = \left(\dfrac{a}{b}\right) c^2$

(c) $x = \dfrac{(a + b)^2}{c}$

(d) Place the sum of A + B + C in X, Y and Z.

(e) Put the value of X in Y.

2 Use arithmetic words to do the following:

(a) Place sum of X and Y in A, B, and C.

(b) Place product of X and Y in A, B, and C.

3 A data group called FARM has data items HORSES, COWS, and PIGS. Write a statement to MOVE these items to RANCH which uses the same names but has the data items in reverse order.

4 The contents of TABLE-A are to be added to TABLE-B. The entries in each table are labeled A, B, C, and D. TABLE-B also has E and F. Write a statement to do the addition.

5 In an examination of input data, HOURS must be greater than zero but less than 60; SHIFT must be 1, 2, or 3; and SENIORITY must be positive but less than or equal to 11 or a code of 99. Write a statement to do the test. If it passes, perform PERSON-NEL-PROCESSING.

6 Write WORKING-STORAGE entries to define the condition-names for each code and then write complex conditional statements to perform the following processing: From among a large list of coeds, a male student wishes to select those meeting certain criteria as possible dates. When one is found, perform GIRL-NAME-PRINT.

Condition or data-name		Code	Student's criteria
EYES	BROWN	N	
	BLACK	K	brown or blue
	BLUE	E	
	GRAY	Y	
HEIGHT (in inches)			Between 60.0 and 66.0 inches
WEIGHT (in pounds)			Between 100.0 and 130.0 pounds
GRADE-POINT			Between 2.5 and 3.5
AGE			Between 17 and 22
HAIR	BLOND	D	
	BROWN	N	blond, brown, or red
	RED	R	
	BLACK	K	

Low-Volume Input and Output   The low-volume input/output verbs ACCEPT and DISPLAY are used in connection with accepting input data from the console typewriter, console display device, card reader, etc., and with displaying output information on the console typewriter, console display device, card punch, or printer. The manufacturer's manual for a particular COBOL compiler will specify the devices which may be used with the ACCEPT and DISPLAY verbs. Usually, standard devices are assigned to these verbs, and if no equipment name is used, the standard device is assumed. The form of the ACCEPT and DISPLAY verbs is:

ACCEPT AND DISPLAY STATEMENTS

ACCEPT data-name [<u>FROM</u> mnemonic-name for input device]

ACCEPT data-name <u>FROM</u> $\begin{Bmatrix} \underline{DATE} \\ \underline{DAY} \\ \underline{TIME} \end{Bmatrix}$

DISPLAY $\begin{Bmatrix} literal \\ data\text{-}name \end{Bmatrix}$ $\begin{bmatrix} , \begin{Bmatrix} literal \\ or \\ data\text{-}name \end{Bmatrix} \end{bmatrix}$ ... [<u>UPON</u> mnemonic-name for output device]

The device-name (high-level nucleus) is optional because frequently there will be only a standard device, and in such cases the specification of the device is not needed. If a mnemonic-name is used, it is defined in the SPECIAL-NAMES paragraph in the ENVIRONMENT DIVISION. The form of the data referred to by the data-names is described in the DATA DIVISION of the program. Two examples illustrate the ACCEPT and DISPLAY verbs:

DISPLAY INVOICE-NUMBER.

ACCEPT CORRECTED-NUMBER. } Assumes a standard device

In a program which uses an ACCEPT statement for the typewriter or other input device, it may be necessary to insert a DISPLAY instruction before the ACCEPT is to be executed in order to let the users (such as computer operators) know that they are expected to type some data on the typewriter. For example, if a control total is to be inserted using the typewriter, a pair of instructions would be necessary.

DISPLAY 'TYPE CONTROL TOTAL'.
ACCEPT CONTROL-TOTAL.

In some cases, the compiler will automatically provide a message indicating a response is required.

The ACCEPT . . . DATE, DAY, or TIME is a high-level nucleus feature which provides a standard form for input of day, date, or time figures. The data called for is placed in the storage assigned to the data-name by the DATA DIVISION.

Specification	Input format
DATE	Year of century, month, day of month; for example, July 4, 1976, is 760704.
DAY	Year of century, day of year counting from January 1; for example, July 4, 1976, is 76186. (July 4 is the 186th day of the year in a leap year.)
TIME	Hours, minutes, seconds on 24-hour clock. 3:31:08 P.M. would be 153108.

The PERFORM VARYING Statement

The high-level nucleus has two forms of the PERFORM statement—the UNTIL form explained in Chapter 19 and the VARYING form to be described in this section. The VARYING format repeats the execution of one or more procedures augmenting a data-name or an index-name by a stated value each time the procedure(s) are executed until a condition is met. A maximum of three sets of data-names/index-names to be varied, initial values, augmenting values (called BY values), and terminating conditions may be used to control the execution of the PERFORM VARYING. The full power of the statement is most apparent in table handling to be explained later in the chapter.

PERFORM VARYING STATEMENT

PERFORM procedure-name-1 $\left[\left\{ \begin{array}{l} \text{THROUGH} \\ \text{THRU} \end{array} \right\} \text{procedure-name-2} \right]$

VARYING $\left\{ \begin{array}{l} \text{data-name-1} \\ \text{index-name-1} \end{array} \right\}$ FROM $\left\{ \begin{array}{l} \text{data-name-2} \\ \text{index-name-2} \\ \text{literal-1} \end{array} \right\}$

BY $\left\{ \begin{array}{l} \text{data-name-3} \\ \text{literal-2} \end{array} \right\}$ UNTIL condition-1

An additional controlling variable may be added by the AFTER clause indicating that after the first condition is satisfied, the next variable is to be used.

$\left[\text{AFTER} \left\{ \begin{array}{l} \text{literal-4} \\ \text{index-name-3} \end{array} \right\} \text{FROM} \ldots \text{BY} \ldots \text{UNTIL} \ldots \right]$

There can be a third AFTER specification for execution AFTER the second variable is satisfied.

As an example of PERFORM VARYING, a program which is to perform accounts receivable aging analysis (determine how long the invoices have remained unpaid) on every tenth customer account, where the accounts are numbered sequentially from 01000 to 55000, might read:

PERFORM AGING VARYING CUSTOMER-ACCOUNT-NO
    FROM 01000 BY 10
    UNTIL CUSTOMER-ACCOUNT-NO IS GREATER THAN 55000.

As shown by the flowchart, the varying option tests for the condition, executes the procedure if the condition is not satisfied, augments the data-name with its BY value, and begins the loop again. The condition should, therefore, be stated so that when it is satisfied, the loop has already been executed the requisite number of times.

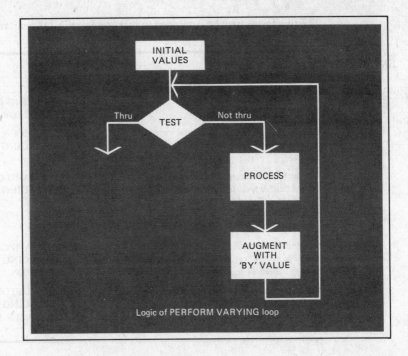

Logic of PERFORM VARYING loop

INSPECT, STRING, and UNSTRING Statements

The INSPECT, STRING, and UNSTRING statements provide COBOL facilities to do some text editing and manipulation of character strings.

The INSPECT statement instructs the computer to tally, replace, or tally and replace single characters (or groups of characters in high-level nucleus) in a data item.

INSPECT STATEMENT

INSPECT data-name-1 <u>TALLYING</u> $\left\{\begin{array}{l}\text{data-name-2 (which} \\ \text{stores results of} \qquad \underline{\text{FOR}} \\ \text{tallying)}\end{array}\right.$

$\left\{\text{,}\left\{\begin{array}{l}\left\{\begin{array}{l}\underline{\text{ALL}} \\ \underline{\text{LEADING}} \\ \underline{\text{CHARACTERS}}\end{array}\right\} \left\{\begin{array}{l}\text{data-name-3} \\ \text{literal-1}\end{array}\right\}\end{array}\right\}\left[\left\{\begin{array}{l}\underline{\text{BEFORE}} \\ \underline{\text{AFTER}}\end{array}\right\}\text{INITIAL}\right.\right.$

$\left.\left.\left.\left\{\begin{array}{l}\text{data-name-4} \\ \text{literal-2}\end{array}\right\}\right]\right]\cdots\right\}\cdots$

INSPECT data-name-1 <u>REPLACING</u>

$\left\{\begin{array}{l}\underline{\text{CHARACTERS}} \ \underline{\text{BY}} \left\{\begin{array}{l}\text{data-name-2} \\ \text{literal-3}\end{array}\right\}\left[\left\{\begin{array}{l}\underline{\text{BEFORE}} \\ \underline{\text{AFTER}}\end{array}\right\}\text{INITIAL}\left\{\begin{array}{l}\text{data-name-3} \\ \text{literal-4}\end{array}\right\}\right]\end{array}\right.$

$\left.\text{,}\left\{\begin{array}{l}\underline{\text{ALL}} \\ \underline{\text{LEADING}} \\ \underline{\text{FIRST}}\end{array}\right\}\text{,}\left\{\begin{array}{l}\text{data-name-4} \\ \text{literal-5}\end{array}\right\}\underline{\text{BY}}\left\{\begin{array}{l}\text{data-name-6} \\ \text{literal-6}\end{array}\right\}\left[\left\{\begin{array}{l}\underline{\text{BEFORE}} \\ \underline{\text{AFTER}}\end{array}\right\}\text{etc.}\right]\right\}$

The two forms may be combined to make an inspect, tallying, replacing statement.

EXAMPLES	Operation to be performed	
	How many characters in the mailing street address? Put answer in CHARACTER-TALLY.	INSPECT STREET-ADDRESS TALLYING CHARACTER-TALLY FOR CHARACTERS.
	Keypunch operator punched zeros instead of alphabetic Os for a program. Make the change.	INSPECT PROGRAM-LINE REPLACING ALL 'ZEROS' BY 'O'.
	A deck of punched cards was punched on an old machine which uses the code for # instead of =, % in place of (, and ⊐ instead of). Recode to produce correct output.	INSPECT CARD-CONTENTS REPLACING ALL "#" BY "=" "%" BY "(" "⊐" BY ")".
	An input data item SAMPLE-DATA was punched in the card field with blanks (spaces) instead of leading zeros.	INSPECT SAMPLE-DATA REPLACING LEADING SPACES BY ZEROS.
	The customer name is stored with a blank as a delimiter between the first and last name. Isolate the first name and blank out the rest of the characters.	INSPECT CUSTOMER-NAME REPLACING CHARACTERS BY SPACES AFTER INITIAL SPACE.

The STRING statement allows the placing of two or more data items into a single data item. This is a form of text editing. For example, assume that the computer is being used to print contracts in which some of the lines are variable and must be composed by assembling the correct words. The words can be moved in the right order into data-names which are to hold them. The STRING statement puts them all together as a single character string.

STRING STATEMENT

STRING $\begin{Bmatrix} \text{data-name-1} \\ \text{literal-1} \end{Bmatrix}$ $\begin{bmatrix} \text{data-name-2} \\ \text{literal-2} \end{bmatrix}$ . . . DELIMITED BY $\begin{Bmatrix} \text{data-name-3} \\ \text{literal-3} \\ \underline{\text{SIZE}} \end{Bmatrix}$

(can repeat data-names, etc., with new delimiter)

INTO data-name-4 [WITH POINTER data-name-5]

[ON OVERFLOW imperative-statement]

DELIMITED BY data-name or literal means that the movement of data from the list into the receiving field will stop at the character specified. BY SIZE will cause transfer to stop when the receiving or sending field is exhausted. POINTER is a counter in a data-name which indicates the character storage location in the receiving field where the next character is to be stored. The programmer can change the value of the pointer, thereby changing the storage of the data.

In the example of a contract, five variable fields, called WORD-1, WORD-2, etc., are defined and correct characters moved into them. The CONTRACT-LINE-1 would be assembled by:

STRING WORD-1, WORD-2, WORD-3, WORD-4,
    WORD-5 DELIMITED BY SIZE INTO
       CONTRACT-LINE-1.

UNSTRING is essentially the opposite of STRING. The format will not be explained in detail. The simplest form (without a number of optional clauses) is:

UNSTRING STATEMENT

UNSTRING data-name-1 $\left[\underline{\text{DELIMITED}}\text{ BY }[\underline{\text{ALL}}]\left\{\begin{array}{l}\text{data-name-2}\\\text{literal-1}\end{array}\right\}\left[\underline{\text{,OR}}\text{ }[\underline{\text{ALL}}]\right.\right.$

$\left.\left.\left\{\begin{array}{l}\text{data-name-3}\\\text{literal-2}\end{array}\right\}\right]\right]\ldots\right]$ INTO data-name-4 . . .

For example, an English-language text to be stored word by word might be programmed as:

UNSTRING TEXT-LINE DELIMITED BY SPACES
    INTO WORD-1, WORD-2, ...

Other Nucleus Statements

In order to complete the discussion of the nucleus, four statements are described: ENTER, EXIT, GO TO, and GO TO DEPENDING ON. In many COBOL explanations, the GO TO statements would have been introduced early and used extensively. The concept of structured programming followed in this text does not normally require the use of a GO TO. The GO TO may still be useful in certain situations, but its misuse can complicate programs and make them difficult to maintain.

ENTER language-name allows a programmer (subject to implementer restrictions) to include other language coding. For example, some coding in assembly language might be used. The first instruction would be to ENTER ASSEMBLY-LANGUAGE followed by the assembly language code followed by ENTER COBOL. This feature is very dependent upon the individual compiler.

EXIT is used to provide a common end point for a series of procedures. It does not cause any processing. It appears in a separate paragraph as the only sentence in the paragraph.

The GO or GO TO procedure-name statement transfers control (branching) from one part of the PROCEDURE DIVISION to another (to a paragraph-name or section-name). When used, the GO TO can transfer control backward or forward in the coding. Unlike a PERFORM which returns control to the statement following the PERFORM, the GO TO transfers control with no return.

Perform	Go to
ADD A TO B ON SIZE ERROR PERFORM SIZE-ERROR-ROUTINE.	ADD A TO B ON SIZE ERROR GO TO SIZE-ERROR-ROUTINE.
NEXT	
SIZE-ERROR-ROUTINE.	SIZE-ERROR-ROUTINE.

In the simple GO TO, only one procedure-name is specified to which control can transfer. It is possible to have a GO TO which branches to a procedure-name based on the results of processing.

GO TO procedure-name-1 [, procedure-name-2 . . . procedure-name-n]
DEPENDING ON data-name.

The data-name is defined in the DATA DIVISION as a numeric elementary item without positions to the right of the decimal. If the data-name has a value of 1, control transfers to procedure-name-1; if 2, to procedure-name-2, etc.

Self-testing Quiz—
COBOL #11

1 Write a statement to print a message GO HOME on the console typewriter (the standard device).

2 The date is July 24, 1976. What input should be provided when the instruction for receipt of date is ACCEPT DATE?

3 A procedure called INTEREST-TABLE prepares an interest table. The computations for each set of years are five different interest rates, .01, 02, . . . , 05. Write a PERFORM VARYING loop to compute the five interest rates.

4 Perform a reorder routine to place inventory replenishment orders until the amount on hand, plus the amount on order, equals the maximum. Because of minimum-size orders, the last order placed may cause the on-hand plus on-order amounts to exceed the maximum. This is considered satisfactory.

5 Perform a computation procedure which sums quantities, keeping track of the number of loops by a data-name COUNT-1. Cause it to sum 100 quantities.

6 What is the content of the COUNTIT (5-character field) after each of the following commands is executed if DATA-1 is 0094399 (seven characters in size in display format)?

(a) INSPECT DATA-1 TALLYING COUNTIT FOR CHARACTERS BEFORE INITIAL '9'.

(b) INSPECT DATA-1 TALLYING COUNTIT FOR ALL '9'.

(c) INSPECT DATA-1 TALLYING COUNTIT FOR LEADING '0'.

7 What is the result of the following commands on data-word TODAYS-DATE, which is in the form JUNE 16?

(a) INSPECT TODAYS-DATE REPLACING FIRST '1' BY '2'.
INSPECT TODAYS-DATE REPLACING FIRST '6' BY '2'.

(b) INSPECT TODAYS-DATE REPLACING CHARACTERS BY SPACES BEFORE INITIAL '1'.

8 Input for a program is in free form, i.e., the data need not be in fixed fields on the input card. The data items are punched in the order in which they are to appear but are separated by a space or a comma. Write a statement to obtain the data-items and put them in DATA-1, DATA-2, ...

9 Write a statement to leave a computational routine and execute error routine 15. Do not return to the computational routine.

10 A code with 4 values from 1 to 4 is analyzed by the program. If the code is 1, control goes to P-1; if 2, to P-2; if 3 or 4, to P-3-4. Write a GO TO DEPENDING ON to direct this transfer.

Table Handling

The table-handling module of COBOL provides facilities for defining tables and for accessing items within tables. A table is a set of data items, homogenous with respect to some characteristic, and arranged in a logical order. Placing data items in tables serves two purposes:

1 It clarifies, from a documentation standpoint, the similarity of a set of data items.

2 It simplifies programming to arrange data in a table. The data items can then be addressed by their position in the table rather than by unique data-names. For example, a data item can be identified as the tenth item in a table.

The table-handling module provides language elements for defining tables in the DATA DIVISION, for referencing table items by the use of subscripting or indexing, and for searching a table. Table handling can become quite complex; this section will serve as an introduction to the COBOL table-handling facilities rather than a comprehensive exposition.

Subscripting   Subscripting and indexing are methods for identifying the position of a data item within a table. A reference to a table item must always have subscripts or an index-item associated with it.

Subscripts are numeric positive integer literals, data-names having positive integer values, or index-names. In each case, the integer value is 1 or greater because it refers to one of the items in the table. Subscripts are written following the data-name, enclosed in parentheses. There may be a maximum of three subscripts to reference a maximum of three levels of the table. The subscripts are separated by a space or a comma. Examples are:

SALES-BY-CUSTOMER (3)
SALES-CUSTOMER-AREA (5, READ)
SALES-CUSTOMER-AREA-SALESMAN (CUSTOMER, AREA, SALESMAN)

The table can have one, two, or three levels or dimensions. These can frequently be thought of as single, double, or triple classification. As an example, assume a table of sales. A first-level classification might include customer identification and amount of sales to the customer:

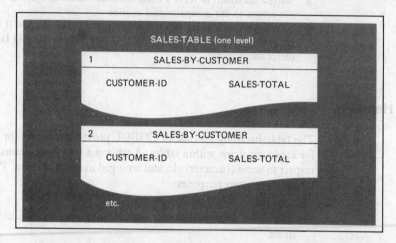

A reference to the group item SALES-BY-CUSTOMER (2) obtains the CUS-TOMER-ID and SALES-TOTAL for the second customer in the table. A reference to an elementary item uses IN or OF. CUSTOMER-ID OF SALES-

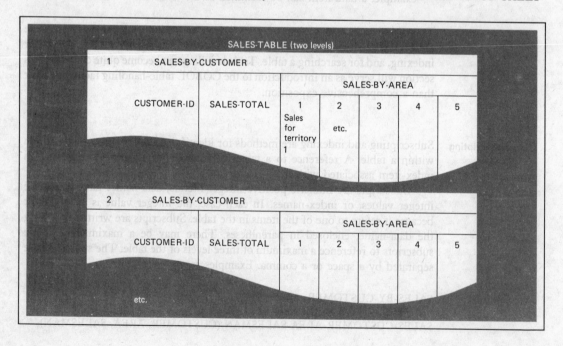

BY-CUSTOMER (2) obtains the ID for the second customer. If the SALES-AMOUNT is further subdivided into SALES-BY-AREA and there are five territories, the table becomes as visualized at the bottom of page 696. A reference to the group item SALES-BY-CUSTOMER(2) now obtains CUSTOMER-ID, SALES-TOTAL, and all five of the entries for SALES-BY-AREA for the second customer in the table. SALES-BY-AREA(2,3) obtains the elementary data item SALES-BY-AREA for area 3 by customer 2.

If a second-level item is divided into subitems, a reference to a single third-level elementary item must have three subscripts. For example, if sales by territory are subdivided into sales by product, the SALES-BY-CUSTOMER entry in the SALES-TABLE would be as follows:

A reference to SALES-BY-AREA(2,1) will now obtain the three product sales for area 1 for customer 2. If the sales for product 3 in area 1 for customer 2 are desired, the reference is PRODUCT-SALES(2,1,3). Note that the total sales of product 1 to customer 2 (for each of five areas) consists of PRODUCT-SALES(2,1,1) + PRODUCT-SALES(2,2,1) + PRODUCT-SALES(2,3,1) + PRODUCT-SALES(2,4,1) + PRODUCT-SALES(2,5,1). The use of the PERFORM VARYING is an effective way to code such computations:

```
PERFORM PRODUCT-SUM VARYING AREA-NO FROM 1 BY 1
    UNTIL AREA-NO > 5.
PRODUCT-SUM.
    ADD PRODUCT-SALES(2,AREA-NO,1) TO SUM-PRODUCT-SALES.
```

If the intention is to prepare a two-level table of sales by the five areas for each of 50 customers, the three product sales must be summed for each area for each customer.

```
PERFORM AREA-SUM VARYING
    CUSTOMER-NO FROM 1 BY 1 UNTIL CUSTOMER-NO > 50
    AFTER AREA-NO FROM 1 BY 1 UNTIL AREA-NO > 5
```

> AFTER PRODUCT-NO FROM 1 BY 1 UNTIL PRODUCT-NO > 3.
> AREA-SUM.
> ADD PRODUCT-SALES(CUSTOMER-NO,AREA-NO,PRODUCT-
> NO) TO SUM-PRODUCT-SALES(CUSTOMER-NO,AREA-NO).

Note that the innermost VARYING cycle, the one repeated most often (PRODUCT-NO in this case) is written last; the outermost cycle which varies least is written first.

The OCCURS Clause for Defining a Table

A table is defined in the DATA DIVISION by an OCCURS clause. The OCCURS is placed following the data name but before the PICTURE clause (if that is used). It is used for any repeating set of items which are to be referenced by subscripting (or indexing). It may *not* be used at the 01 level.

OCCURS CLAUSE

Option 1
OCCURS integer-1 TIMES

Option 2
OCCURS integer-2 TO integer-3 TIMES [DEPENDING ON data-name-1]

The first option defines a fixed table; the second option indicates that the size of the table may vary with the actual limit, unless otherwise stated, being found in data-name-1.

In the example of the SALES-TABLE used previously, the DATA DIVISION might read:

Case 1   Single-level table:

```
01   SALES-TABLE.
     05   SALES-BY-CUSTOMER OCCURS 50 TIMES.
          10   CUSTOMER-ID PICTURE X(10).
          10   SALES-AMOUNT PICTURE 999V99.
```

Case 2   Two-level table:

```
01   SALES-TABLE.
     05   SALES-BY-CUSTOMER OCCURS 50 TIMES.
          10   CUSTOMER-ID PICTURE X(10).
          10   SALES-TOTAL PICTURE 999V99.
          10   SALES-BY-AREA OCCURS 5 TIMES PICTURE 999V99.
```

Case 3   Three-level table:

```
01  SALES-TABLE
    05   SALES-BY-CUSTOMER OCCURS 50 TIMES.
         10   CUSTOMER-ID PICTURE X(10).
         10   SALES-TOTAL PICTURE 999V99.
         10   SALES-BY-AREA OCCURS 5 TIMES.
              15   PRODUCT-SALES OCCURS 3 TIMES PICTURE 999V99.
```

Redefining for Table Definition

It is not legal to use a VALUE clause in the data definition of a data name which has an OCCURS clause. The definition and filling of a table with entries can therefore be cumbersome. For example, a table of codes to be used in identifying forty 2-digit product codes and described as follows needs to have the codes inserted, but VALUE IS cannot be used.

```
01  PRODUCT-CODE-TABLE.
    02   PRODUCT-CODE OCCURS 40 TIMES PICTURE XX.
```

A method to overcome this restriction is to define the content of the table and to then redefine the same storage area as a table. For example:

```
01  PRODUCT-CODE-TABLE.
    02   TABLE-VALUES.
         03   FILLER PICTURE XX VALUE 'YA'.
         03   FILLER PICTURE XX VALUE 'YB'.
              etc. for all 40 entries.
    02   FILLER REDEFINES TABLE-VALUES.
         03   PRODUCT-CODE OCCURS 40 TIMES PICTURE XX.
```

These entries allow the table values to be inserted in a storage area that is then redefined as a table with each entry being referenced as PRODUCT-CODE (subscript). This approach can be even more efficient if it is noted that RE-DEFINES need not have the same picture. For example, the TABLE-VALUES could have been inserted (or could be read in from an input card) as a string of 80 characters.

```
01  PRODUCT-CODE-TABLE.
    02   TABLE-VALUES PICTURE X(80)
         VALUES 'YAYB . . . .'.
    02   FILLER REDEFINES TABLE-VALUES.
         03   PRODUCT-CODE OCCURS 40 TIMES PICTURE XX.
```

Indexing

Individual items in a table may be referenced by indexing (in addition to subscripting but not at the same time). Indexing is the use of a specially designated index-name to refer to a level (dimension) of a table. A single-dimension table uses a single index-name, a two-level table uses two index-names (one for each level).

The handling of tables by indexing is similar to subscripting, but the indexes are initialized and controlled by a PERFORM VARYING statement or by two special statements SET and SEARCH. The major advantage of indexing is in searching a table.

Indexing is defined by appending an INDEXED BY index-name to each data-item having multiple occurrences in a table (which therefore has an OCCURS clause). The INDEXED BY phrase is placed after OCCURS and before PICTURE (when used). The index-name is not defined elsewhere. For example, in Case 3 for the SALES-TABLE, the addition of index-names would be coded as follows:

Case 4   Three-level table with indexing:

```
01   SALES-TABLE.
     05   SALES-BY-CUSTOMER OCCURS 50 TIMES INDEXED BY
          CUSTOMER-INDEX.
          10   CUSTOMER-ID PICTURE X(10).
          10   SALES-TOTAL PICTURE 999V99.
          10   SALES-BY-AREA OCCURS 5 TIMES INDEXED BY AREA-INDEX.
               15   PRODUCT-SALES OCCURS 3 TIMES INDEXED BY
                    PRODUCT-INDEX PICTURE 999V99.
```

The indexes can be used in a PERFORM VARYING in the same way as subscripts. For example, the prior coding to prepare a two-level table of sales by the five areas for each of 50 customers would be coded with indexes as follows (assuming Case 4 data description):

```
PERFORM AREA-SUM VARYING
     CUSTOMER-INDEX FROM 1 BY 1 UNTIL CUSTOMER-INDEX > 50,
     AFTER AREA-INDEX FROM 1 BY 1 UNTIL AREA-INDEX > 5
     AFTER PRODUCT-INDEX FROM 1 BY 1 UNTIL
          PRODUCT-INDEX > 3.
AREA-SUM.
     ADD PRODUCT-SALES(CUSTOMER-INDEX,AREA-INDEX,
          PRODUCT-INDEX) TO SUM-PRODUCT-SALES
          (CUSTOMER-INDEX,AREA-INDEX).
```

Searching for an Item in a Table   There are many data processing situations in which a table needs to be searched to locate data items meeting one or more conditional criteria. This search can be programmed with the SEARCH statement. When a data-item meeting the criteria is found, the index-name for the table item is set to identify the one that has been located. The use of the SEARCH statement, therefore, requires that the table being searched is indexed. Format 2 also requires the table be defined with a KEY phrase (to be explained). The difference is that format 1 searches on the basis of the index name while format 2 searches sequentially on the basis of the record key.

SEARCH STATEMENT

Format 1
<u>SEARCH</u> table-dimension-name [<u>VARYING</u> index-name] [; AT <u>END</u> imperative-statement-1]

$$\underline{\text{WHEN}} \text{ condition-1} \begin{Bmatrix} \text{imperative-statement-2} \\ \underline{\text{NEXT SENTENCE}} \end{Bmatrix} [\underline{\text{WHEN}} \text{ condition-2 etc.}]$$

Format 2
<u>SEARCH</u> <u>ALL</u> table-dimension-name [; AT <u>END</u> imperative-statement-1]

$$\underline{\text{WHEN}} \begin{Bmatrix} \text{data-name-1} \\ \text{condition-name-1} \end{Bmatrix} \begin{Bmatrix} \text{IS } \underline{\text{EQUAL}} \text{ TO} \\ \text{IS} = \end{Bmatrix} \begin{Bmatrix} \text{data-name-2} \\ \text{literal-1} \\ \text{arithmetic expression} \end{Bmatrix}$$

$$\left[\underline{\text{AND}} \begin{Bmatrix} \text{data-name-3, etc.} \\ \text{condition-name-2} \end{Bmatrix} \right] \begin{Bmatrix} \text{imperative-statement-2} \\ \underline{\text{NEXT}} \text{ } \underline{\text{SENTENCE}} \end{Bmatrix}$$

As an example, the SALES-TABLE (defined as being indexed by CUS-TOMER-INDEX) might be searched for a customer having a TOTAL-SALES greater than 1000 by the following statement:

SEARCH SALES-BY-CUSTOMER; WHEN SALES-TOTAL > 1000 PERFORM SALES-ANALYSIS.

When a SALES-TOTAL greater than 1000 is found, the search stops. The index for the table (CUSTOMER-INDEX) contains the table entry number, and so a reference in processing to SALES-BY-CUSTOMER (CUSTOMER-INDEX) will provide all data about the customer meeting the specifications.

The SEARCH ALL format requires a table-dimension name with a KEY phrase in its description. The KEY phrase is an optional phrase in the OCCURS clause.

$$\left[\begin{Bmatrix} \underline{\text{ASCENDING}} \\ \underline{\text{DESCENDING}} \end{Bmatrix} \text{KEY is data-name} \right]$$

This phrase is used to indicate a set of data items in a sequence based on a key contained in a subitem within each. For example, the key item for sequencing an inventory file might be part number. A table is searched using the key. Multiple search criteria may be specified for the search.

The index for a search or other table operation can be manipulated by the SET statement.

SET STATEMENT

$$\underline{\text{SET}} \text{ index-name } \underline{\text{TO}} \begin{Bmatrix} \text{data-name} \\ \text{index-name} \\ \text{integer} \end{Bmatrix}$$

$$\underline{\text{SET}} \text{ index-name } \begin{Bmatrix} \underline{\text{UP}} \text{ } \underline{\text{BY}} \\ \underline{\text{DOWN}} \text{ } \underline{\text{BY}} \end{Bmatrix} \begin{Bmatrix} \text{data-name} \\ \text{integer} \end{Bmatrix}$$

Self-testing Quiz— COBOL #12

1 Define a table to hold population data. There will be 50 states with income and population, within each state a maximum of 100 cities with income and population, and within each city the population of four income groups.

STATE						
State income	State population	CITY 1				
		City income	City population	Income Group		
				1	2	3	4

2 Write statements to obtain a total income and total population for all 50 states.

3 Given the following data definition, what is referenced by the variable names?

```
01    TABLE-OF-STUDENTS.
    05    STATE-CLASS OCCURS 50 TIMES.
        10    S-CLASS PICTURE 9(2) OCCURS 5 TIMES.
```

(*a*) S-CLASS (48,2)

(*b*) S-CLASS (IX,NIX)

(*c*) STATE-CLASS (42)

4 Referring to the definition in Question 3, what is performed by the following?

```
P-1. PERFORM ROUTINE-X VARYING STATE FROM 1 BY 1 UNTIL
        STATE IS GREATER THAN 50 AFTER C-LASS FROM 1 BY 1 UNTIL
        C-LASS IS GREATER THAN 5.
ROUTINE-X. ADD S-CLASS (STATE, C-LASS) TO TOTAL-STUDENTS.
```

5 Change whatever statements in the table definition for Question 1 that need to be changed to use indexing.

6 Define a DISCOUNT-TABLE of 40 DISCOUNT-ENTRIES. Use indexes.

DISCOUNT-ENTRIES

CUSTOMER TYPE	PRODUCT-TYPE		
	DISCOUNT-TYPE	DISCOUNT-TYPE	DISCOUNT-TYPE

7 Using the table from question 6, write statements to search customer type to match with an input customer type code, then to search product type to match an input product type code. When the two matches are completed, perform a discount calculation.

Sequential Input and Output

The sequential I-O module of COBOL provides language facilities for writing files in sequential order and for reading records from such a file in the same order they were written. All problems to this point have been using the sequential file module because, unless otherwise specified, COBOL assumes a file arranged sequentially. There are a low-level and a high-level sequential model; the low-level is required for basic COBOL. The features explained in Chapter 19 were all from the low-level module.

The sequential I-O module is not based on any specific storage medium. For example, it clearly applies to punched card input or output, printed output, and magnetic tape input or output, but it is also applicable to direct access storage such as disk storage, if this storage medium is used for a sequential writing and a corresponding sequential reading of records. Some instructions are, however, applicable only to magnetic tape files.

Additional ENVIRONMENT DIVISION Entries for Sequential Input and Output

The ENVIRONMENT DIVISION has the CONFIGURATION SECTION (already fully explained) and the INPUT-OUTPUT SECTION. The latter section has a generally used FILE-CONTROL and an optional I-O-CONTROL paragraph, each of which can have additional clauses related to sequential file processing.

Clause in FILE-CONTROL paragraph	Explanation
SELECT [OPTIONAL] file-name ASSIGN TO implementer-name . . .	Used to indicate files which may not always be present.
$\left[\text{RESERVE integer-1} \left[\begin{matrix} \text{AREA} \\ \text{AREAS} \end{matrix} \right] \right]$	Used to reserve more input-output areas than standard. May allow more efficient processing.
[ORGANIZATION IS SEQUENTIAL]	If not specified, sequential organization is implied.
[ACCESS MODE IS SEQUENTIAL]	If not specified, sequential access is implied.
[FILE STATUS IS data-name]	Defines a data-name for a file status indicator.

The SELECT clause must appear first; the others may appear in any order. The OPTIONAL in the SELECT clause and all the other clauses are optional. The two SEQUENTIAL clauses are used for completeness of documentation because they are implied. The OPTIONAL and RESERVE clauses are the high-level module; the others are the low-level module.

The optional I-O CONTROL paragraph, when used, follows the FILE-CONTROL paragraph. It specifies reruns, same areas for files, and multiple files on the same magnetic tape reel. These are surveyed briefly.

I-O-CONTROL PARAGRAPH

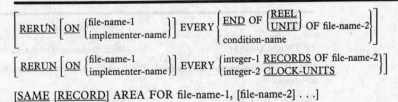

$$\left[\text{RERUN} \left[\text{ON} \left\{ \begin{matrix} \text{file-name-1} \\ \text{implementer-name} \end{matrix} \right\} \right] \text{EVERY} \left\{ \begin{matrix} \text{END OF} \left\{ \begin{matrix} \text{REEL} \\ \text{UNIT} \end{matrix} \right\} \text{OF file-name-2} \\ \text{condition-name} \end{matrix} \right\} \right]$$

$$\left[\text{RERUN} \left[\text{ON} \left\{ \begin{matrix} \text{file-name-1} \\ \text{implementer-name} \end{matrix} \right\} \right] \text{EVERY} \left\{ \begin{matrix} \text{integer-1 RECORDS OF file-name-2} \\ \text{integer-2 CLOCK-UNITS} \end{matrix} \right\} \right]$$

[SAME [RECORD] AREA FOR file-name-1, [file-name-2] . . .]

[<u>MULTIPLE</u> <u>FILE</u> TAPE CONTAINS file-name-1 [<u>POSITION</u> integer-1] file-name-2 [<u>POSITION</u> integer-2] . . .]

The RERUN statement is significant to processing efficiency. In a long processing run, an error toward the end of the run will require the entire run to be repeated unless provision has been made to back up and start at a rerun point. A rerun capability is obtained by recording status data on a rerun file. The RERUN statement defines the file to be used (file-name-1 or a standard file defined by the COBOL implementer) and the basis for writing status data: end of reel, end of unit, every so many records, every so many clock units, or condition of the file status indicator (defined in FILE-CONTROL).

A SAME AREA clause may be used in the I-O-CONTROL paragraph to define a single input or output area as being used for more than one file. The object is to conserve storage. If two or more files are not active (i.e., not OPEN) at the same time, there is no reason to have different input or output areas. The concept is the same as REDEFINES (in the DATA DIVISION). Not only may input and output areas be shared, but the area where the current logical record is processed may be shared by two or more files. Sharing of record space can include files that are open at the same time. The SAME AREA sharing is a low-level feature; the SAME RECORD AREA sharing is a high-level sequential I-O feature.

If there is more than one file on a single reel of tape, special processing procedures are required. The condition is specified by the MULTIPLE FILE clause (a high-level feature). The POSITION phrase need be used only if all files on the tape are not listed in sequential order.

Additional DATA DIVISION Entries for Sequential Input and Output

The file description presented so far contained only the required FD file-name and LABEL clause:

FD file-name

LABEL $\begin{Bmatrix} \underline{RECORD} \text{ IS} \\ \underline{RECORDS} \text{ ARE} \end{Bmatrix}$ $\begin{Bmatrix} \underline{STANDARD} \\ \underline{OMITTED} \end{Bmatrix}$.

The file description may include a number of optional clauses. These optional clauses, if used, can appear in any order. The first four clauses will be explained in this section, LINAGE will be explained later in the chapter, while CODE-SET is quite specialized and will receive no further explanation.

Clause	Explanation or comment
DATA RECORD(S)	Documentation of different records in a file.
VALUE OF implementor-data-item-in-label IS	Specifies a value for a data item in file label.
BLOCK CONTAINS	Specifies blocking of records.

RECORD CONTAINS	Specifies variable length for records.
LINAGE IS	For page format—explained in later section of chapter.
CODE-SET IS	Specifies code set that is not native to computer being used.

The DATA RECORDS clause is useful for documentation purposes; it is not required. It specifies the names of all record types contained in the file.

$$\left[\underline{\text{DATA}} \; \begin{Bmatrix} \underline{\text{RECORD}} \text{ IS} \\ \underline{\text{RECORDS}} \text{ ARE} \end{Bmatrix} \text{ record-name-1, record-name-2, } \ldots \right]$$

The required LABEL RECORD clause specifies that the standard label is either present or omitted. If the label is present, the standard label is created or read during processing. The COBOL implementater may include one or more data items in the standard label, assign implementer names to them, and allow the programmer to place a value in them (as a literal or value associated with a data-name). The appropriate clause to associate the label data item with the program data item is the VALUE OF clause.

$$\left[\underline{\text{VALUE}} \; \underline{\text{OF}} \text{ implementer-name-1 IS } \begin{Bmatrix} \text{data-name-1} \\ \text{literal-1} \end{Bmatrix} \left[\text{ ,implementer-name-2 IS} \right. \right.$$
$$\left. \left. \begin{Bmatrix} \text{data-name-2} \\ \text{literal-2} \end{Bmatrix} \right] \ldots \right]$$

Blocking of records is combining of several records (logical records) into a single physical record (block). A physical record or block is the unit for reading or writing a storage medium. Blocking of records is an important operating consideration because it reduces the total time required to obtain from or write records to a storage medium such as magnetic tape or magnetic disk. The discussion uses magnetic tape because the operating characteristics of tape make blocking especially important to efficient performance.

A magnetic tape file consists of blocks of data written on magnetic tape. Each block (physical record) on the tape contains one or more logical records. A logical record is the record defined in the DATA DIVISION. Blocks are separated by interblock gaps which define the amount of tape to be read by a read-from-tape instruction. The READ instruction in the PROCEDURE DIVISION causes a logical record to be provided to the program from the block but it does not necessarily read from the tape. For example, if a block contains five records, the first READ instruction will cause the physical record block to be read into internal storage and provide the first logical record in the block to the program. The next execution of a READ instruction gets the next record from the block (the block need not be read because it is already in memory). The opposite procedure is followed for output using the WRITE instruction. COBOL performs the blocking and unblocking of records on the basis of a specification of a BLOCK CONTAINS file description clause. The clause is not required if there is only one record per block.

$$\left[\underline{\text{BLOCK}} \text{ CONTAINS [integer 01 } \underline{\text{TO}} \text{] integer-2 } \begin{Bmatrix} \text{CHARACTERS} \\ \underline{\text{RECORDS}} \end{Bmatrix} \right]$$

A block need not contain a fixed number of records, in which case the integer TO option is used and the range is specified. Examples of the BLOCK clause are:

BLOCK CONTAINS 5 RECORDS
BLOCK CONTAINS 3 TO 5 RECORDS
BLOCK CONTAINS 156 CHARACTERS

Records within blocks need not be of fixed length. If variable in length, this may be documented by a RECORD CONTAINS clause. The clause is never required because the definition is in the data description entry.

[<u>RECORD</u> CONTAINS [integer-1 <u>TO</u>] integer-2 CHARACTERS]

Additional PROCEDURE DIVISION for Sequential Input and Output

In the PROCEDURE DIVISION in Chapter 19, the basic CLOSE and OPEN statements were presented. The high-level CLOSE statement has additional elements for tape files or other units.

$$\underline{\text{CLOSE}} \text{ file-name } \left[\begin{Bmatrix} \underline{\text{REEL}} \\ \underline{\text{UNIT}} \end{Bmatrix} \begin{bmatrix} \text{WITH } \underline{\text{NO}} \ \underline{\text{REWIND}} \\ \text{FOR } \underline{\text{REMOVAL}} \end{bmatrix} \right] \left[\text{WITH } \begin{Bmatrix} \underline{\text{NO}} \ \underline{\text{REWIND}} \\ \underline{\text{LOCK}} \end{Bmatrix} \right]$$

The REEL or UNIT option specifies that the CLOSE refers only to the current reel or unit. The NO REWIND option causes the current reel or unit to be left in its current position; otherwise, CLOSE causes a rewind or return to its physical beginning. FOR REMOVAL specifies the unit is to be removed. LOCK repositions the unit and prevents it from being used again during the program as part of the file.

The high-level OPEN statement can also specify that an input tape file should be read in reverse order from back to front or that the tape should not be rewound before processing begins.

$$\underline{\text{OPEN}} \begin{Bmatrix} \underline{\text{INPUT}} \text{ file-name } \begin{bmatrix} \underline{\text{REVERSED}} \\ \text{WITH } \underline{\text{NO}} \ \underline{\text{REWIND}} \end{bmatrix} \\ \underline{\text{OUTPUT}} \text{ file-name [WITH } \underline{\text{NO}} \ \underline{\text{REWIND}}] \\ \underline{\text{I-O}} \text{ file-name} \\ \underline{\text{EXTEND}} \text{ file-name} \end{Bmatrix}$$

The I–O means a sequential file is used for both input and output, such as a disk file. EXTEND means to position the file immediately following the last record of that file. This allows records to be added to a file already written.

A REWRITE statement is available to write a record (say, in a disk file) back in the same position occupied by the record just read. It is used instead of WRITE.

REWRITE record-name.

Providing Multiple-Page Output

When an output spans more than one page of output, there must be programming to put report headings at the beginning of the report, to put page headings on each page, to write detail lines until a page is filled, to write any page footings at the end of each page, and to write the report footings at the end of the report. Footings are used to refer to text used at the bottom of a page or end of a report in much the same way a heading is used at the beginning of the report and the beginning of each page. There are special page instructions in the sequential I–O module for this purpose. The report writer module is especially designed for report formatting, but that module is beyond the scope of this text.

A simple low-level instruction for page control is the PAGE phrase.

$$\text{WRITE} \ldots \left[\left\{ \begin{array}{l} \underline{\text{BEFORE}} \\ \underline{\text{AFTER}} \end{array} \right\} \text{ADVANCING} \left\{ \begin{array}{l} \text{mnemonic-name} \\ \underline{\text{PAGE}} \end{array} \right\} \right]$$

In order to make use of this feature, the programmer must write instructions to count the number of lines printed. When the end of the page is reached, the instruction to WRITE includes the PAGE phrase. For example, if the beginning of each page is a heading line, the program (when it had determined that the current page was filled) would execute a statement such as the following:

WRITE OUTPUT-LINE FROM HEADER-LINE AFTER ADVANCING PAGE.

In older COBOL versions, a mnemonic-name was used in place of PAGE.

The high-level sequential I–O module has the LINAGE feature which simplifies the handling of multiple-page output. In order to use this feature, there must be a DATA DIVISION entry plus a clause with the WRITE statement. In the DATA DIVISION, an optional clause in the file description for an output file specifies the use of the LINAGE feature.

$$\left[\underline{\text{LINAGE}} \text{ IS} \left\{ \begin{array}{l} \text{data-name-1} \\ \text{integer-1} \end{array} \right\} \text{LINES} \left[\text{WITH} \underline{\text{FOOTING}} \text{ AT} \left\{ \begin{array}{l} \text{data-name-2} \\ \text{integer-2} \end{array} \right\} \right] \right.$$

$$\left. \left[\text{LINES AT} \underline{\text{TOP}} \left\{ \begin{array}{l} \text{data-name-3} \\ \text{integer-3} \end{array} \right\} \right] \left[\text{LINES AT} \underline{\text{BOTTOM}} \left\{ \begin{array}{l} \text{data-name-4} \\ \text{integer-4} \end{array} \right\} \right] \right]$$

The terms in the linage clause apply to a logical page (which may be different than the physical medium being used, but generally will be the same, such as a printed page or CRT screen). On a printed page, the terms apply as follows:

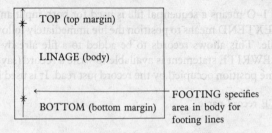

When this linage clause is included in the DATA DIVISION output file description, the WRITE statement can contain the END-OF-PAGE phrase.

$$\left[AT \begin{Bmatrix} \underline{\text{END-OF-PAGE}} \\ \underline{\text{EOP}} \end{Bmatrix} \text{imperative statement} \right]$$

This phrase causes the imperative statement to be executed instead of the writing of the current record when the write statement would cause printing or spacing within the footing area of the page body. If the writing of the current record would enter the bottom margin (such as when footing data is not defined), there is an automatic advance to the next page where the line is printed as the first line in the body (following the top margin). For example, assume 66 possible lines on the page with a top margin of 10 lines followed by a heading and then two spaces before the detail lines. There are a maximum of 43 lines in the body below the heading of which three are reserved for footing lines and spaces. The bottom margin is 10 spaces.

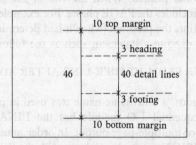

The detail line, footing line, and heading line are defined in
WORKING-STORAGE.

```
DATA DIVISION.
FILE SECTION.
FD OUTPUT-REPORT-FILE
    LABEL RECORD IS OMITTED
    DATA RECORD IS OUTPUT-LINE
    LINAGE IS 46 LINES
        WITH FOOTING AT 43,
        LINES AT TOP 10,
        LINES AT BOTTOM 10.
```

PROCEDURE DIVISION.

WRITE OUTPUT-LINE FROM DETAIL-LINE
AT END-OF-PAGE PERFORM PAGE-FOOTING-AND-HEADING.

PAGE-FOOTING-AND-HEADING.
WRITE OUTPUT-LINE FROM FOOTING-LINE BEFORE
ADVANCING PAGE.
WRITE OUTPUT-LINE FROM HEADING-LINE BEFORE
ADVANCING 2 LINES.

Note that it was unnecessary for the programmer to write coding to keep track of the number of detail lines that had been printed.

Self-testing Quiz— COBOL #13

1 What is the purpose of RERUN? Write a statement to write rerun data on RERUN-FILE at the end of every reel.

2 File-A is used at the beginning of the program; file-B is used at the end. Write a statement to cause both files to use the same input-output storage areas.

3 Write statements to:
(*a*) Define a file for output with a block size of five records.
(*b*) Write a logical record into the physical block.
(*c*) Write the physical block itself.

4 Write all necessary statements to read a PAY-RECORD record from an I-O file (on disk) called PAYROLL-FILE and then write a revised record into the same location.

5 Define a report page with five lines of top heading, five lines of bottom margin, and 56 lines of body. There are no heading or footing lines.

Direct Access Input and Output

The sequential I-O module assumes a file that can be accessed only serially. The technical constraints on magnetic tape and punched cards mean that only sequential access is feasible. Direct access storage devices such as magnetic disk allow for direct access (also called "random access"). However, the direct access devices are flexible so that files stored on them can be arranged to allow sequential access, random access, or a combination (termed "dynamic access" in COBOL).

The two direct access modules provide two somewhat different approaches to access—relative and indexed. The relative approach uses a file organization in which a file is assumed to consist of logical records in storage positions numbered from 1 to the limit of the file. A record is accessed by means of the logical storage position number. For an indexed file, on the other hand, there is an index which is separate from the file. The index relates record keys to storage locations. Access to the location for a record is through the record key which allows the storage location to be found in the index.

Relative Input and Output

The relative I-O module provides facilities for accessing records on a direct access storage file medium (say, a disk file) in either a sequential, random, or dynamic (mixed sequential and random) manner. A relative file consists of a serial string of logical storage areas, each capable of holding one record. Each of the record storage areas is identified by a record number. Records are stored or retrieved by the use of the logical storage area number. The first record in a relative file has a relative record number of 1; the tenth, a relative record number of 10. Not all storage positions need be filled.

When a file has a relative organization, it may be accessed sequentially (in ascending order of the relative record numbers) or randomly. Random access is controlled by the program; the record to be accessed is identified by its relative record number. This is a fairly simple organization compared with the indexed I-O to be explained later.

The instructions to read or write the relative organization are the same as those for sequential files with a few exceptions and additions. The FILE-CONTROL paragraph in the INPUT-OUTPUT SECTION of the ENVIRONMENT DIVISION defines the file as RELATIVE and specifies the access mode.

FILE-CONTROL PARAGRAPH FOR RELATIVE I/O

FILE-CONTROL.

SELECT ... ASSIGN ...

ORGANIZATION IS RELATIVE

$$\left[\text{ACCESS MODE IS} \left\{ \begin{array}{l} \text{SEQUENTIAL} \\ \text{RANDOM} \\ \text{DYNAMIC} \end{array} \right\} \text{[RELATIVE KEY IS data-name-1]} \right]$$

[FILE STATUS IS data-name-2]

ACCESS MODE is the way the file records will be accessed—sequentially (in which case the RELATIVE KEY is optional), randomly using the relative key, or dynamic (mixed sequential and random). Sequential access and relative access are part of the low-level relative I-O module, dynamic access is in the high-level module. The RELATIVE KEY (associated with the ACCESS MODE clause) is used in processing to contain the relative record number of a record to be read or written. It can be accessed by its data-name.

The following I-O statements and clauses in the relative I-O module are essentially identical to the sequential I-O module:

The I-O-CONTROL paragraph with the RERUN clauses. MULTIPLE FILE TAPES does, of course, not apply.

File description clauses in the DATA DIVISION:
BLOCK CONTAINS
RECORD CONTAINS
LABEL RECORD

VALUE OF
DATA RECORDS

PROCEDURE DIVISION statements:
CLOSE . . . [WITH LOCK] (but not REWIND AND REMOVAL)
OPEN (but not EXTEND or REVERSED or REWIND)
USE AFTER STANDARD ERROR or EXCEPTION (Not explained in the chapter—this statement is used to specify programmed error handling when an I-O error is detected.)

Several statements are somewhat different for the relative I-O reading and writing. START is a high-level feature.

INPUT/OUTPUT STATEMENTS FOR RELATIVE I/O

READ file-name RECORD [INTO data-name] [INVALID KEY imperative-statement]

WRITE record-name [FROM data-name] [INVALID KEY imperative-statement]

REWRITE record-name [FROM data-name] [INVALID KEY imperative-statement]

DELETE file-name RECORD [INVALID KEY imperative-statement]

$$
\text{START file-name} \left[\underline{\text{KEY}} \left\{ \begin{array}{l} \text{IS } \underline{\text{GREATER}} \text{ THAN} \\ \text{IS } > \\ \text{IS } \underline{\text{EQUAL}} \text{ TO} \\ \text{IS } = \\ \text{IS } \underline{\text{NOT}} \underline{\text{LESS}} \text{ THAN} \\ \text{IS } \underline{\text{NOT}} < \end{array} \right\} \text{data-name} \right]
$$

[INVALID KEY imperative-statement]

Note the INVALID KEY phrase. This must be used for RANDOM and DYNAMIC access files to specify what is to be done if the key that is being used for reading or writing is invalid. The phrase is not written when the file is accessed sequentially. The DELETE clause is used to logically remove a record from the file.

When a relative file is opened, the relative key is set to the value of the beginning record pointer for the file. This allows sequential access through the relative file. The program may alter the relative key to another value to randomly obtain records. This is accomplished by moving a value into the data-name associated with the relative key. Or, the START statement sets the relative KEY to a value which is equal to, greater than, or greater than or equal (same as not less than) to a value stored in a data-name. START thus positions the relative key and provides a basis for subsequent sequential retrieval of records.

EXAMPLE A file of inventory code parts with 10,000 records is stored in a COBOL relative file containing 15,000 storage positions. A record for a part is stored in a relative file position based on a computation performed on the part number which produces a random number in the range from 1 to 15,000. As explained in Chapter 9, the randomizing (or hashing) procedure for obtaining a relative storage address sometimes results in synonyms in which two part numbers yield the same address, thus requiring an algorithm for handling the collision. The following program statements are required to locate an inventory record, given the part number, when the records have been stored in a relative file by randomizing.

```
ENVIRONMENT DIVISION.
INPUT-OUTPUT SECTION.
FILE-CONTROL.
    SELECT INVENTORY-FILE ASSIGN TO DISK-FILE-1
    ORGANIZATION IS RELATIVE
    ACCESS MODE IS DYNAMIC
    RELATIVE KEY IS INV-KEY.
PROCEDURE DIVISION.

    OPEN I-O INVENTORY-FILE.

    COMPUTE INV-KEY =        Hashing formula using part number

    READ INVENTORY-FILE INTO INVENTORY-RECORD-TEST,
        INVALID KEY PERFORM READ-ERROR-ROUTINE.
```
Comparison of part number in record located with part number being sought. If record found, perform processing; if not found, assume a synonym and locate by overflow procedure.

| Indexed Input and Output | The indexed I-O module provides a COBOL capability for randomly (or sequentially) storing and retrieving records from a direct access file device using one or more unique keys in the record as a basis for retrieval. Examples of keys are employee number, part number, customer account number, and student identification number. The key may be alphabetic, numeric, or alphanumeric, but must be unique. |

When an indexed file is created, an index is established which provides a facility for locating a record based on the record key. The method for establishing the index may vary with the implementer. If more than one key might be used as the basis for access, a separate index is established for each.

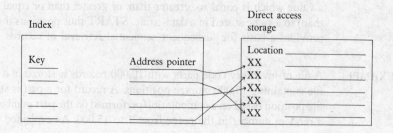

The instructions in the ENVIRONMENT DIVISION FILE-CONTROL paragraph to establish an indexed file are the same as for a relative file with only a few exceptions.

UNIQUE FILE-CONTROL PARAGRAPH ENTRIES FOR INDEXED I/O

ORGANIZATION IS INDEXED

RECORD KEY IS data-name-1

[ALTERNATE RECORD KEY IS data-name-2 [WITH DUPLICATES]]

Instead of RELATIVE KEY as in relative I-O, the access is by means of a RECORD KEY. This must be unique for a record. Alternate keys may also be used for retrieval.

The DATA DIVISION clauses for indexed I-O are identical to relative I-O. The following PROCEDURE DIVISION statements are the same. In all cases, the KEY in the statement (such as INVALID KEY phrase) is the record key.

INPUT-OUTPUT STATEMENTS FOR INDEXED I/O

Same as Relative I/O

CLOSE	START	WRITE
DELETE	USE	REWRITE
OPEN		

Unique Statements for Indexed I/O

READ file-name [NEXT] RECORD [INTO data-name] [AT END imperative-statement]

READ file-name RECORD [INTO data-name] [KEY IS data-name], [INVALID KEY imperative-statement].

The first read format is used for files in sequential access mode; NEXT is specified if records from a dynamic access file are being retrieved sequentially. The second read format is used for random access. The KEY phrase is used to establish the record key (where alternatives are specified) to be used as the reference for this retrieval. In dynamic access mode, a record key once specified continues until a different key is established. If KEY is not specified, the prime record key is assumed.

Self-testing Quiz—
COBOL #14

1 Explain the difference between the KEY in relative I-O and the KEY in indexed I-O.

2 In the example coding for a relative file, some of the unique coding for a relative file is given. Show replacement statements which would need to be used if the INVEN-TORY-FILE has an indexed organization.

3 Write statements to read a CUSTOMER-RECEIVABLE record from a RECEIVA-BLES-FILE into RECEIVABLE-WORK-RECORD (assume updating), then write the record back in the same storage location.

(a) Write statements if ACCESS is SEQUENTIAL.

(b) Write statements if ACCESS is RANDOM.

Hint: The difference is in the use of INVALID KEY for random access.

Additional COBOL Modules

It is beyond the scope of these chapters to cover all features of COBOL. This section briefly describes additional modules.

Sort-Merge The low-level portion of the sort-merge module provides for ordering one or more files of records according to a set of designated keys within each record. The higher-level portion of the sort-merge module provides a facility for combining two or more files which are ordered on the same keys. Depending on the verbs used, some processing can be performed on the records before or after sorting or merging. The sort-merge is implemented by defining a sort file in the DATA DIVISION and by fairly simple statements in the PROCEDURE DIVISION. For example, a sort might be specified in the PROCEDURE DIVISION by:

```
SORT PAYROLL-SORT-FILE ON ASCENDING KEY EMPLOYEE-ID
     USING PAYROLL-FILE
     GIVING SORTED-PAYROLL-FILE.
```

Report Writer The 1974 COBOL standard has a substantially revised report writer module. This module provides facilities for producing reports by specifying the physical format of the report. This is in contrast to the approach of writing procedures to produce the report. In general, a report will consist of some of or all the following: report heading at beginning of report, page heading for each page, control heading for each group of output, the detail lines, control footing for each group of output, footing lines at the end of each page, and report footing lines at the end of the report. For example, a report listing sales by salesmen but with subtotals for the salesmen in each state would use sales by state as the basis for a control heading (state) and a control footing (total for state), as shown in figure on page 715. Report writer defines each of these elements of a report by clauses in a report description in the REPORT SECTION of the DATA DIVISION. The PROCEDURE DIVISION requires only a few statements to produce the report.

```
OPEN report-files
INITIATE report-names (to initialize)
GENERATE report-name (to produce report)
TERMINATE report-name (to produce report footings)
CLOSE report-file
```

A few other statements are also available.

Segmentation A program may be too large for the storage allocated to it. One solution is to segment the program in some logical fashion. Segment 1 occupies storage until it is completed, then segment 2 is brought into the same area, overlaying segment 1,

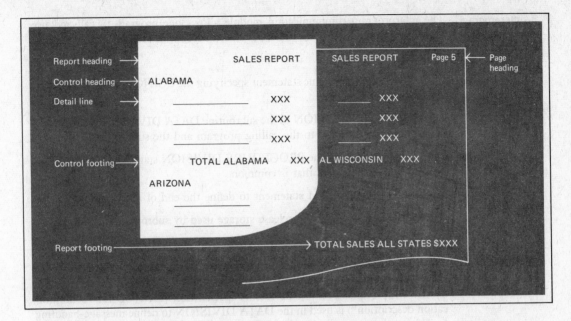

etc. In order to do segmentation, the mainline control routine and other procedures needed throughout the program are defined as fixed permanent segments; other procedures are defined as independent segments (which can be overlaid). Section numbers following the section name and word SECTION are used to code the type of segment into which the section is classified.

Library The library module allows a program to include prewritten program statements by copying the statements from a library into the program. Copying can be done without changing the statements being copied, or the text can be changed by replacing the library text (names, literals, words) by new text for these items. This feature is very useful. Any programs which access a file already defined can COPY the existing file description. Prewritten modules to perform tasks common to many programs can be copied, etc.

Debug The debug module allows the program to trace the execution of a program. Temporary output is provided whenever a specified procedure (or all procedures) is executed or when reference is made to a specified communication-name, a file-name, or a data-name. Special debugging lines can be added to the program by putting a D in the indicator area (column 7). The debugging line is deactivated and becomes like a comment when the debugging mode is not specified. This mode is specified in the SOURCE-COMPUTER paragraph by appending WITH DE-BUGGING MODE.

Interprogram Communication The interprogram communication module allows one program to call and use another program. This is the COBOL closed subroutine facility. These facilities include:

1 A CALL program-name statement specifying the USING of data items by the subroutine.

2 A LINKAGE-SECTION in the subroutine DATA DIVISION for specification of data common to the calling program and the subroutine.

3 A USING clause in the PROCEDURE DIVISION statement of the subroutine to name the data that is common.

4 An EXIT PROGRAM statement to define the end of a subroutine.

5 A CANCEL statement to release storage used by subroutine (for efficiency).

Communications The data communication module provides COBOL program statements to access, process, and create messages and to communicate through a Message Control System with local and remote devices. A special description (CD for "communication description") is used in the DATA DIVISION to define message-handling facilities such as message queues, destination, and text length. The PROCEDURE DIVISION has statements to ENABLE transmission, RECEIVE a message, SEND a message, etc.

Self-testing Quiz— COBOL #15

1 A sort requires what coding (all places in program)?
2 What is required (all places) in a program to implement report writer?
3 Several programmers are working on programs which will access the same file. How can COPY assist in this?
4 The SOURCE-COMPUTER has a clause WITH DEBUGGING and a list of section-names. What will happen when the program is executed?
5 A program calls another. How does the called program know what data to use?

Sample Program

The buyer for the PETIT IMPORT CO. arranges most of the purchases in the local currency of the country in which the purchase is made. Because of currency fluctuations, a report is prepared each evening summarizing the dollar value of the foreign currency purchases. The report is also used by the company treasurer to decide on the timing of purchases of foreign exchange to pay for the goods. The body of the report is triple-spaced and has a bottom margin of 15 lines in order to allow notations by the buyer and treasurer. Because of this spacing, the report frequently runs several pages. There is also a heading on each page after the first. The first and second pages are formatted as follows:

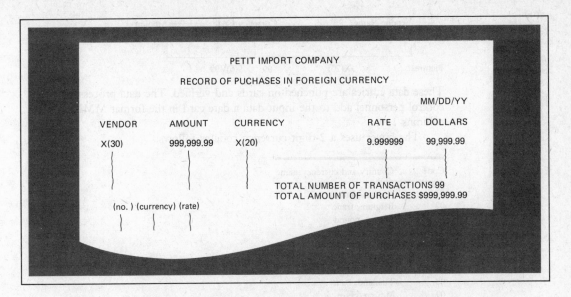

PETIT IMPORT COMPANY

RECORD OF PUCHASES IN FOREIGN CURRENCY

MM/DD/YY

VENDOR	AMOUNT	CURRENCY	RATE	DOLLARS
X(30)	999,999.99	X(20)	9.999999	99,999.99

(no.) (currency) (rate)

TOTAL NUMBER OF TRANSACTIONS 99
TOTAL AMOUNT OF PURCHASES $999,999.99

FOREIGN PURCHASES MM/DD/YY PAGE 2

(column headings are repeated)

At the end of the report, a list of all currencies and rates is printed. There is no validation of input, so this table is used for both reference and input error control. A member of the treasurer's staff reviews the rate table to check accuracy of input before the report is released.

The input for the program come from two sources:

1   The treasurer's office which prepares on a form a list of exchange rates for the 10 currencies of countries the company deals with (format 9V9):

AUSTRIA SHILLING	BELGIUM FRANC	BRITAIN POUND	DENMARK KRONE

2   The buyer who writes each purchase on a line on a preprinted form as shown:

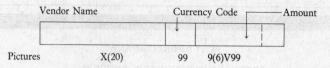

| Pictures | X(20) | 99 | 9(6)V99 |

These data entries are punched on cards and verified. The data processing input control personnel add to the input data a date card in the format MMDDYY in columns 1–6.

The buyer uses a 2-digit currency code as follows:

Code	Country and currency name
01	Austria, shilling
02	Belgium, franc
03	Britain, pound
04	Denmark, krone
05	Finland, markka
06	Italy, lira
07	Japan, yen
08	Thailand, baht
09	Mexico, peso
10	West Germany, mark

There are no plans to add any new countries.

For illustrative purposes, the program is somewhat restricted. For example, in practice it would be better to read in the codes and currency name descriptions in order to allow currencies to be added or dropped without changing the program.

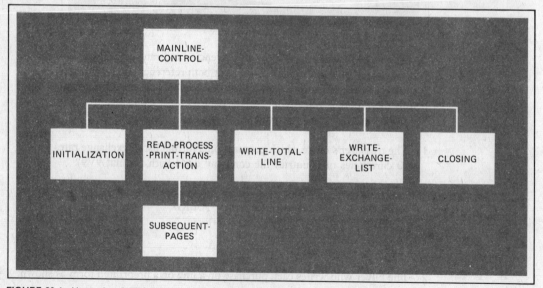

FIGURE 20-1 Hierarchy chart for sample program to prepare foreign purchases report.

NARRATIVE
FOREIGN-PURCHASES-REPORT Program

Completed: 11/21/75
Author: G. B. Davis
Requested by: G. Dickson, Treasurer

The program prepares a report of foreign purchases with the amount of the purchases in dollars. It is used by the treasurer in planning foreign exchange purchases and by the foreign goods buyer in reviewing purchase commitments.

Input is from:
1. List of rates from treasurer's office
2. Transactions from purchasing
3. Date card by input control

Output is distributed to the treasurer and purchasing. Corrections and reruns are authorized by the treasurer.

Error control: Input control compares record count of report with record count provided by purchasing. Control over input data and correctness of processing is by a printout of all input data with each detail line plus a list of rates that were input. The treasurer's office has responsibility for review of the rates.

FIGURE 20-2 Program narrative as part of documentation for program to prepare foreign purchases report.

The documentation of the program includes a hierarchy chart (Figure 20-1), a program narrative (Figure 20-2), the program in structured format (Figure 20-3), and sample output (Figure 20-4). Layout charts are omitted. Program flowcharts are not needed because the logic can be clearly seen from the coding.

Note the following features of the coding for this application:

1 A table is defined for the currency rates using an OCCURS (line 41). By having a fixed-form input, the input data is easily moved into this table.

2 A table is defined for the currency names. The table is filled with a single string of values and then divided into strings referenced by subscripts through the use of REDEFINES (line 70).

3 To position the printer three lines from the column headings for the first detail line (in INITIALIZATION), a blank line is written by moving spaces to the PRINT-LINE and writing after advancing three lines (lines 169–171).

4 The currency code input with the PURCHASES-DATA is used as a subscript to get all necessary data to process and print the line (lines 185 and 190).

5 The printout of the exchange rate data in a list at the end of the report is used for after-processing input validation (lines 221–226).

6 TOP-OF-PAGE is used instead of PAGE to advance to top of new page (lines 160 and 206). TOP-OF-PAGE is defined as synonymous with page control (called C01 by IBM) in SPECIAL-NAMES (lines 9–10).

```
00001          IDENTIFICATION DIVISION.
00002          PROGRAM-ID. FOREIGN-PURCHASES-REPORT.
00003          AUTHOR. G. B. DAVIS.
00004     ****
00005     ENVIRONMENT DIVISION.
00006     CONFIGURATION SECTION.
00007     SOURCE-COMPUTER. IBM-370-158.
00008     OBJECT-COMPUTER. IBM-370-158.
00009     SPECIAL-NAMES.
00010          C01 IS TOP-OF-PAGE.
00011     INPUT-OUTPUT SECTION.
00012     FILE-CONTROL.
00013          SELECT DATE-RATE-PURCHASE-INPUT-FILE ASSIGN TO UT-S-INPUT.
00014          SELECT PRINT-FILE ASSIGN TO UT-S-OUTPUT.
00015     ****
00016     DATA DIVISION.
00017     FILE SECTION.
00018     FD  DATE-RATE-PURCHASE-INPUT-FILE
00019          LABEL RECORD IS OMITTED.
00020     01  INPUT-RECORD               PICTURE X(80).
00021     ****
00022     FD  PRINT-FILE
00023          LABEL RECORD IS OMITTED.
00024     01  PRINT-LINE                 PICTURE X(132).
00025     ****
00026     WORKING-STORAGE SECTION.
00027     01  FLAGS-COUNTERS-INDEX.
00028          02  MORE-CARDS            PICTURE XXX.
00029          02  PAGE-NO               PICTURE 99    VALUE 01.
00030          02  LINE-COUNT            PICTURE 99    VALUE ZEROES.
00031          02  TRANSACTION-COUNT     PICTURE 999   VALUE ZEROES.
00032          02  RATE-NO               PICTURE 99.
00033     01  CALCULATION-RESULTS.
00034          02  DOLLARS-CALCULATED    PICTURE 9(7)V99.
00035          02  TOTAL-CALCULATED      PICTURE 9(8)V99
00036                                                  VALUE ZEROES.
00037     01  DATE-CARD.
00038          02  DATE-OF-TRANSACTIONS  PICTURE X(8).
00039          02  FILLER                PICTURE X(74).
00040     01  RATE-VALUE-CARD.
00041          02  EXCHANGE-RATE         PICTURE 9V9(6) OCCURS 10 TIMES.
00042          02  FILLER                PICTURE X(10).
00043     01  PURCHASE-DATA.
00044          02  VENDOR-NAME           PICTURE X(20).
00045          02  CURRENCY-CODE         PICTURE 99.
00046          02  PURCHASE-AMOUNT-FOREIGN PICTURE 9(6)V99.
00047          02  FILLER                PICTURE X(50).
00048     01  NAMES-STRING-TABLE.
00049          02  NAMES-STRING.
00050               05  STRING-1         PICTURE X(20)
00051                    VALUE 'AUSTRIA SHILLING    '.
00052               05  STRING-2         PICTURE X(20)
00053                    VALUE 'BELGIUM FRANCS      '.
00054               05  STRING-3         PICTURE X(20)
00055                    VALUE 'BRITAIN POUND       '.
00056               05  STRING-4         PICTURE X(20)
00057                    VALUE 'DENMARK KRONE       '.
00058               05  STRING-5         PICTURE X(20)
```

FIGURE 20-3 Listing of program to prepare foreign purchases report.

```
00059                         VALUE 'FINLAND MARKKA       '.
00060            05  STRING-6            PICTURE X(20)
00061                         VALUE 'ITALY LIRA          '.
00062            05  STRING-7            PICTURE X(20)
00063                         VALUE 'JAPAN YEN           '.
00064            05  STRING-8            PICTURE X(20)
00065                         VALUE 'THAILAND BAHT       '.
00066            05  STRING-9            PICTURE X(20)
00067                         VALUE 'MEXICO PESO         '.
00068            05  STRING-10           PICTURE X(20)
00069                         VALUE 'WEST GERMANY MARK   '.
00070         02  CURRENCY-NAME REDEFINES NAMES-STRING
00071                         PICTURE X(20) OCCURS 10 TIMES.
00072     01  HEADING-COMPANY-NAME.
00073         02  FILLER               PICTURE X(58) VALUE SPACES.
00074         02  FILLER               PICTURE X(16) VALUE
00075                         'PETIT IMPORT CO.'.
00076         02  FILLER               PICTURE X(58) VALUE SPACES.
00077     01  HEADING-REPORT-TITLE.
00078         02  FILLER.              PICTURE X(46) VALUE SPACES.
00079         02  FILLER               PICTURE X(39) VALUE
00080                         'RECORD OF PURCHASES IN FOREIGN CURRENCY'.
00081         02  FILLER               PICTURE X(47) VALUE SPACES.
00082     01  HEADING-REPORT-DATE.
00083         02  FILLER               PICTURE X(111)
00084                                  VALUE SPACES.
00085         02  DATE-OF-TRANSACTIONS PICTURE X(8).
00086         02  FILLER               PICTURE X(13) VALUE SPACES.
00087     01  HEADING-COLUMNS.
00088         02  FILLER               PICTURE X(20) VALUE SPACES.
00089         02  FILLER               PICTURE X(6)  VALUE 'VENDOR'.
00090         02  FILLER               PICTURE X(21) VALUE SPACES.
00091         02  FILLER               PICTURE X(6)  VALUE 'AMOUNT'.
00092         02  FILLER               PICTURE X(16) VALUE SPACES.
00093         02  FILLER               PICTURE X(8)  VALUE 'CURRENCY'.
00094         02  FILLER               PICTURE X(18) VALUE SPACES.
00095         02  FILLER               PICTURE X(4)  VALUE 'RATE'.
00096         02  FILLER               PICTURE X(13) VALUE SPACES.
00097         02  FILLER               PICTURE X(7)  VALUE 'DOLLARS'.
00098         02  FILLER               PICTURE X(13) VALUE SPACES.
00099     01  TOTAL-LINE.
00100         02  FILLER               PICTURE X(30) VALUE SPACES.
00101         02  FILLER               PICTURE X(30) VALUE
00102                         'TOTAL NUMBER OF TRANSACTIONS   '.
00103         02  OUT-TRANSACTION-COUNT PICTURE ZZ9.
00104         02  FILLER               PICTURE X(17) VALUE SPACES.
00105         02  FILLER               PICTURE X(27) VALUE
00106                         'TOTAL AMOUNT OF PURCHASES   '.
00107         02  TOTAL-OUTPUT         PICTURE $$$,$$$,$$9.99.
00108         02  FILLER               PICTURE X(11) VALUE SPACES.
00109     01  HEADING-FOLLOWING-PAGES.
00110         02  FILLER               PICTURE X(82) VALUE SPACES.
00111         02  FILLER               PICTURE X(19) VALUE
00112                         'FOREIGN PURCHASES   '.
00113         02  DATE-OF-TRANSACTIONS PICTURE X(8).
00114         02  FILLER               PICTURE X(8)  VALUE '  PAGE  '.
00115         02  PAGE-NO-HEADING      PICTURE Z9.
00116         02  FILLER               PICTURE X(13) VALUE SPACES.
```

FIGURE 20-3   (*Continued*)

```
00117          01   DETAIL-LINE.
00118               02   FILLER                      PICTURE X(13) VALUE SPACES.
00119               02   VENDOR-NAME                 PICTURE X(20).
00120               02   FILLER                      PICTURE X(10) VALUE SPACES.
00121               02   PURCHASE-AMOUNT-FOREIGN     PICTURE ZZZ,ZZZ.ZZ.
00122               02   FILLER                      PICTURE X(10) VALUE SPACES.
00123               02   CURRENCY-NAME-OUTPUT        PICTURE X(20).
00124               02   FILLER                      PICTURE X(10) VALUE SPACES.
00125               02   EXCHANGE-RATE-OUTPUT        PICTURE 9.999999.
00126               02   FILLER                      PICTURE X(7)  VALUE SPACES.
00127               02   DOLLARS-OUTPUT              PICTURE ZZZZ,ZZZ.99.
00128               02   FILLER                      PICTURE X(13) VALUE SPACES.
00129          01   EXCHANGE-LIST-OUTPUT.
00130               02   FILLER                      PICTURE X(13) VALUE SPACES.
00131               02   RATE-NO-LIST                PICTURE 99.
00132               02   FILLER                      PICTURE X(5)  VALUE SPACES.
00133               02   CURRENCY-NAME-LIST          PICTURE X(20).
00134               02   FILLER                      PICTURE X(5)  VALUE SPACES.
00135               02   EXCHANGE-RATE-LIST          PICTURE 9.9(6).
00136               02   FILLER                      PICTURE X(79) VALUE SPACES.
00137     ****
00138          PROCEDURE DIVISION.
00139     ****
00140          MAINLINE-CONTROL.
00141               PERFORM INITIALIZATION.
00142               PERFORM READ-PROCESS-PRINT-TRANSACTION UNTIL MORE-CARDS
00143                    IS EQUAL TO 'NO'.
00144               PERFORM WRITE-TOTAL-LINE.
00145               PERFORM WRITE-EXCHANGE-LIST VARYING RATE-NO FROM 1 BY 1
00146                    UNTIL RATE-NO GREATER THAN 10.
00147               PERFORM CLOSING.
00148               STOP RUN.
00149     ****
00150          INITIALIZATION.
00151               OPEN INPUT DATE-RATE-PURCHASE-INPUT-FILE.
00152               OPEN OUTPUT PRINT-FILE.
00153               READ DATE-RATE-PURCHASE-INPUT-FILE
00154                    INTO DATE-CARD
00155                    AT END DISPLAY 'INPUT ERROR'.
00156               MOVE DATE-OF-TRANSACTIONS OF DATE-CARD TO
00157                    DATE-OF-TRANSACTIONS OF HEADING-REPORT-DATE,
00158                    DATE-OF-TRANSACTIONS OF HEADING-FOLLOWING-PAGES.
00159               MOVE SPACES TO PRINT-LINE.
00160               WRITE PRINT-LINE AFTER ADVANCING TOP-OF-PAGE.
00161               WRITE PRINT-LINE FROM HEADING-COMPANY-NAME
00162                    AFTER ADVANCING 3 LINES.
00163               WRITE PRINT-LINE FROM HEADING-REPORT-TITLE
00164                    AFTER ADVANCING 2 LINES.
00165               WRITE PRINT-LINE FROM HEADING-REPORT-DATE
00166                    AFTER ADVANCING 2 LINES.
00167               WRITE PRINT-LINE FROM HEADING-COLUMNS
00168                    AFTER ADVANCING 2 LINES.
00169               MOVE SPACES TO PRINT-LINE.
00170               WRITE PRINT-LINE
00171                    AFTER ADVANCING 3 LINES.
00172               MOVE 13 TO LINE-COUNT.
00173               READ DATE-RATE-PURCHASE-INPUT-FILE
00174                    INTO RATE-VALUE-CARD
```

FIGURE 20-3 (Continued)

```
00175                    AT END DISPLAY 'INPUT ERROR'.
00176              MOVE 'YES' TO MORE-CARDS.
00177              READ DATE-RATE-PURCHASE-INPUT-FILE
00178                  INTO PURCHASE-DATA
00179                  AT END MOVE 'NO' TO MORE-CARDS.
00180          ****
00181          READ-PROCESS-PRINT-TRANSACTION.
00182              IF LINE-COUNT IS GREATER THAN 60
00183                  PERFORM SUBSEQUENT-PAGES.
00184              MOVE CORRESPONDING PURCHASE-DATA TO DETAIL-LINE.
00185              MOVE CURRENCY-NAME (CURRENCY-CODE) TO
00186                  CURRENCY-NAME-OUTPUT.
00187              COMPUTE DOLLARS-CALCULATED ROUNDED =
00188                  PURCHASE-AMOUNT-FOREIGN OF PURCHASE-DATA *
00189                      EXCHANGE-RATE (CURRENCY-CODE).
00190              MOVE EXCHANGE-RATE (CURRENCY-CODE) TO
00191                  EXCHANGE-RATE-OUTPUT.
00192              MOVE DOLLARS-CALCULATED TO DOLLARS-OUTPUT.
00193              ADD DOLLARS-CALCULATED TO TOTAL-CALCULATED.
00194              ADD 1 TO TRANSACTION-COUNT.
00195              WRITE PRINT-LINE FROM DETAIL-LINE
00196                  BEFORE ADVANCING 3 LINES.
00197              ADD 3 TO LINE-COUNT.
00198              READ DATE-RATE-PURCHASE-INPUT-FILE
00199                  INTO PURCHASE-DATA
00200                  AT END MOVE 'NO' TO MORE-CARDS.
00201          ****
00202          SUBSEQUENT-PAGES.
00203              ADD 1 TO PAGE-NO.
00204              MOVE PAGE-NO TO PAGE-NO-HEADING.
00205              MOVE SPACES TO PRINT-LINE.
00206              WRITE PRINT-LINE AFTER ADVANCING TOP-OF-PAGE.
00207              WRITE PRINT-LINE
00208                  AFTER ADVANCING 2 LINES.
00209              WRITE PRINT-LINE FROM HEADING-FOLLOWING-PAGES
00210                  BEFORE ADVANCING 2 LINES.
00211              WRITE PRINT-LINE FROM HEADING-COLUMNS
00212                  BEFORE ADVANCING 3 LINES.
00213              MOVE 7 TO LINE-COUNT.
00214          ****
00215          WRITE-TOTAL-LINE.
00216              MOVE TRANSACTION-COUNT TO OUT-TRANSACTION-COUNT.
00217              MOVE TOTAL-CALCULATED TO TOTAL-OUTPUT.
00218              WRITE PRINT-LINE FROM TOTAL-LINE
00219                  BEFORE ADVANCING TOP-OF-PAGE.
00220          ****
00221          WRITE-EXCHANGE-LIST.
00222              MOVE RATE-NO TO RATE-NO-LIST.
00223              MOVE CURRENCY-NAME (RATE-NO) TO CURRENCY-NAME-LIST.
00224              MOVE EXCHANGE-RATE (RATE-NO) TO EXCHANGE-RATE-LIST.
00225              WRITE PRINT-LINE FROM EXCHANGE-LIST-OUTPUT
00226                  BEFORE ADVANCING 1 LINES.
00227          ****
00228          CLOSING.
00229              CLOSE DATE-RATE-PURCHASE-INPUT-FILE,   PRINT-FILE.
```

FIGURE 20-3   *(Continued)*

PETIT IMPORT CO.

RECORD OF PURCHASES IN FOREIGN CURRENCY

10/21/76

VENDOR	AMOUNT	CURRENCY	RATE	DOLLARS
BELGE EXPORT S. A.	95,000.00	BELGIUM FRANCS	0.025550	2,427.25
DANMARK AKTIEBOLAG	40,510.00	DENMARK KRONE	0.165500	6,704.41
CROWN JEWEL LTD	6,095.40	BRITAIN POUND	1.652500	10,072.65
ESSO ITALIA	800,000.00	ITALY LIRA	0.001469	1,175.20
SUNDMUSIKEN	400,050.00	AUSTRIA SHILLING	0.054500	21,802.73
ITALIA INTL	405,900.00	ITALY LIRA	0.001469	596.27
LAPLANDER	200,500.00	FINLAND MARKKA	0.260000	52,130.00
FINLANDIA	5,000.00	FINLAND MARKKA	0.260000	1,300.00
AHSO EXPORTERS	95,600.00	JAPAN YEN	0.003303	315.77
NOTSONY	10,000.00	JAPAN YEN	0.003303	33.03
BANGKOKALORA	15,000.00	THAILAND BAHT	0.051000	765.00
DAISTEIN	10,000.00	WEST GERMANY MARK	0.385600	3,856.00
CHICHEN-ITZA	200,000.00	MEXICO PESO	0.080060	16,012.00
BRITISH SHIPPING	467.00	BRITAIN POUND	1.652500	771.72
V W EXPORTERS	100,640.00	WEST GERMANY MARK	0.385600	38,806.78
MARSUPIAL EXPORTERS	6,600.00	AUSTRIA SHILLING	0.054500	359.70

FOREIGN PURCHASES 10/21/76 PAGE 2

VENDOR	AMOUNT	CURRENCY	RATE	DOLLARS
KRUMKAKES INTER	123.00	FINLAND MARKKA	0.260000	31.98
SAKI BOTTLING CORP	4,360.00	JAPAN YEN	0.003303	14.40
SUMBRARO LIMITED	456.00	MEXICO PESO	0.080060	36.51

TOTAL NUMBER OF TRANSACTIONS 19   TOTAL AMOUNT OF PURCHASES $157,211.40

01	AUSTRIA SHILLING	0.054500
02	BELGIUM FRANCS	0.025550
03	BRITAIN POUND	1.652500
04	DENMARK KRONE	0.165500
05	FINLAND MARKKA	0.260000
06	ITALY LIRA	0.001469
07	JAPAN YEN	0.003303
08	THAILAND BAHT	0.051000
09	MEXICO PESO	0.080060
10	WEST GERMANY MARK	0.385600

FIGURE 20-4 Sample output from program to prepare foreign purchases report.

Answers to Self-testing Quizzes

COBOL #9

1 The first level of:
(*a*) Nucleus   (*b*) Table handling   (*c*) Sequential I-O

2 By a DECIMAL-POINT IS COMMA clause in the SPECIAL-NAMES paragraph of the CONFIGURATION SECTION of the ENVIRONMENT DIVISION

3 RENAMES assigns a new name to data already named (or to different groupings of data already named). REDEFINES assigns a second set of data to storage locations which have already been assigned to a set of data. REDEFINES is appropriate only if the two data sets can occupy the storage at different times.

4 Normally, NU will be stored. With JUSTIFY, TS will be stored.

5 (*a*) 66 SUB-A RENAMES ITEM-2 THRU ITEM-4.
(*b*) 02 SALES-BY-CUSTOMER PICTURE 999.99 BLANK WHEN ZERO.
(*c*) 02 NAME-FIELD PICTURE X(7) JUSTIFIED RIGHT.
(*d*) 02 ITEM-A.
      03   X PICTURE 9(6).
      03   Y PICTURE 9(10).
   02 ITEM-B REDEFINES ITEM-A.
      03   W PICTURE X(10).
      03   V PICTURE X(6).

6 (*a*) 02 PAY-AMOUNT PICTURE 9(7)V99.
   02 PAY-GROSS REDEFINES PAY-AMOUNT.
(*b*) 02 PAY-AMOUNT PICTURE 9(7)V99 USAGE IS
          COMPUTATIONAL SYNCHRONIZED.

7 02 ALPHA PICTURE 9(5) SIGN IS LEADING SEPARATE CHARACTER.

8

Actual value of data	Data as read by computer	Input area picture	Data as displayed	Output area picture
(*a*)		9(3)V9		$9(3).99
(*b*)		9(4)P(2)	986,000	
(*c*)	.0005743			$0.9(7) or $9.9(7)
(*d*)		9(4)V		$$$9.99 or $$$9.00
(*e*)	9.040		+9.040	
(*f*)		9(4)	$88.00	
(*g*)	−453.0			9(3)BCR
(*h*)		99V99		$***99.99
(*i*)		9V9(3)		9.90909
(*j*)		9V9(3)	$1.47	
(*k*)		X(8)	HOLD-O	
(*l*)	K1767			X(5)
(*m*)		X(5)		X/X(4)

9 77 MARITAL-STATUS PICTURE X.
   88   SINGLE   VALUE '1'.
   88   MARRIED   VALUE '2'.
   88   DIVORCED VALUE '3'.
   88   WIDOWED VALUE '4'.

```
77  AGE PICTURE 99.
    88    UNDER-25          VALUES ARE 00 THRU 24.
    88    AGE-25-THRU-40 VALUES ARE 25 THRU 40.
    88    OVER-40           VALUES ARE 40 THRU 99.
10 INITIALIZE
    MOVE ZERO TO RECORD-END-FLAG.
77  RECORD-END-FLAG PICTURE 9.
    88    END-RECORDS   VALUE 1.
    88    MORE-RECORDS VALUE 0.
```

COBOL #10

1 (a) COMPUTE X = ((A + B) / C) ** 3.
(b) COMPUTE X = (A / B) * C ** 2.
(c) COMPUTE X = (A + B) ** 2 / C.
(d) COMPUTE X, Y, Z = A + B + C.
(e) COMPUTE Y = X.

2 (a) ADD X, Y GIVING A, B, C.
(b) MULTIPLY X BY Y GIVING A, B, C.

3 MOVE CORRESPONDING FARM TO RANCH.

4 ADD CORRESPONDING TABLE-A TO TABLE-B.

5 IF HOURS > 0 AND < 60
        AND SHIFT = 1 OR 2 OR 3
        AND SENIORITY > 0 AND < 12 OR = 99
        PERFORM PERSONNEL PROCESSING
    ELSE . . . .

6 WORKING-STORAGE.

```
01    GIRL-RECORD.
    02    GIRL-NAME              PICTURE X(30).
    02    EYES                  PICTURE X.
        88  BROWN-EYES VALUE 'N'.
        88  BLACK-EYES VALUE 'K'.
        88  BLUE-EYES   VALUE 'E'.
        88  GRAY-EYES   VALUE 'Y'.
    02    HEIGHT                PICTURE 99V9.
    02    WEIGHT                PICTURE 999V9.
    02    GRADE-POINT-AVERAGE PICTURE 9V9.
    02    AGE                   PICTURE 99.
    02    HAIR                  PICTURE X.
        88  BLOND       VALUE 'D'.
        88  BROWN       VALUE 'N'.
        88  RED         VALUE 'R'.
        88  BLACK       VALUE 'K'.
PROCEDURE-DIVISION.
———
GIRL-SELECTION.
IF (BROWN-EYES OR BLUE-EYES)
        AND (HEIGHT NOT LESS THAN 60.00 AND NOT
            GREATER THAN 66.0)
```

AND (WEIGHT NOT LESS THAN 100.0 AND NOT GREATER
            THAN 130.0)
AND (GRADE-POINT NOT LESS THAN 2.5 AND NOT
            GREATER THAN 3.5)
AND (AGE NOT LESS THAN 17 AND NOT GREATER THAN 22)
AND (BLOND OR BROWN OR RED)
PERFORM GIRL-NAME-PRINT
    ELSE . . . .

COBOL #11   **1** DISPLAY 'GO HOME'.
            2 760724
            3 PERFORM INTEREST-TABLE VARYING INTEREST-RATE FROM .01 BY
                   .01 UNTIL INTEREST-RATE GREATER THAN .05. Note that COBOL tests for
                   termination before execution. If the above were written UNTIL INTEREST-RATE
                   EQUAL TO .05, the .05 condition would cause an exit and not be processed.
            4 PERFORM REORDER UNTIL AMOUNT-ON-HAND + ON-ORDER IS
                   GREATER THAN OR EQUAL TO MAXIMUM.
            5 PERFORM COMPUTATION VARYING COUNT-1 FROM 1 BY 1 UNTIL
                   COUNT-1 IS GREATER THAN 100.
            6 (a) 00002
                   (b) 00003
                   (c) 00002
            7 (a) JUNE 22
                   (b)   16
            8 UNSTRING INPUT-CARD DELIMITED BY SPACES OR ';' INTO
                   DATA-1, DATA-2, ...
            9 GO TO ERROR-ROUTINE-15.
           10 GO TO P-1, P-2, P-3-4, P-3-4 DEPENDING ON CODE-NUMBER.

COBOL #12   **1** 01 POPULATION.
                       05   STATES OCCURS 50 TIMES.
                           10   STATE-INCOME PICTURE 9(9)V99.
                           10   STATE-POPULATION PICTURE 9(8).
                           10   CITY OCCURS 100 TIMES.
                               15   CITY-INCOME PICTURE 9(9)V99.
                               15   CITY-POPULATION PICTURE 9(8).
                               15   INCOME-GROUP OCCURS 4 TIMES PICTURE 9(6).
            2 PERFORM TOTALING VARYING STATE-NO FROM 1 BY 1 UNTIL
                   STATE-NO > 50.
                   TOTALING.
                       ADD STATE-INCOME (STATE-NO) TO TOTAL-INCOME.
                       ADD STATE-POPULATION (STATE-NO) TO TOTAL POPULATION.
            3 (a) The value for the second S-CLASS of the forty-eighth STATE-CLASS
                   (b) The value of the NIX S-CLASS for the IX STATE-CLASS
                   (c) The five values composing all S-CLASSes for the forty-second STATE-CLASS
            4 All entries in the TABLE-OF-STUDENTS are added to obtain the sum called
                   TOTAL-STUDENTS.

5 05 STATES OCCURS 50 TIMES INDEXED BY STATE-INDEX.
    10 CITY OCCURS 100 TIMES INDEXED BY CITY-INDEX.
    15 INCOME-GROUP OCCURS 4 TIMES INDEXED BY INCOME-
        GROUP-INDEX.
6 01 DISCOUNT-TABLE.
    05 DISCOUNT-ENTRIES OCCURS 40 TIMES INDEXED BY
        DISCOUNT-INDEX.
        10 CUSTOMER-TYPE PICTURE X(4).
        10 PRODUCT-TYPE.
            15 DISCOUNT-TYPE OCCURS 3 TIMES INDEXED
               BY DISCOUNT-INDEX PICTURE XX.
7 SEARCH DISCOUNT-ENTRIES
    AT END PERFORM TABLE-CLOSING
  WHEN CUSTOMER-TYPE = INPUT-CUSTOMER-TYPE
    SEARCH PRODUCT-TYPE
      AT END PERFORM TABLE-CLOSING
    WHEN PRODUCT-TYPE = INPUT-TYPE
      PERFORM DISCOUNT-CALCULATION.

COBOL #13 **1** Rerun preserves status data so that a job need not be restarted from the beginning.
I-O CONTROL.
RERUN ON RERUN-FILE EVERY END OF REEL.
2 I-O-CONTROL.
SAME AREA FOR FILE-A, FILE-B.
3 (a) DATA DIVISION.
    FILE SECTION.
    FD OUTPUT-FILE
        LABEL RECORD IS STANDARD
        BLOCK CONTAINS 5 RECORDS
        DATA RECORD IS DETAIL-RECORD. (optional)
  (b) WRITE DETAIL-RECORD.
  (c) The physical record block is written automatically when it is filled with logical
     records by the statement WRITE DETAIL-RECORD.
4 PROCEDURE DIVISION.
    OPEN I-O PAYROLL-FILE.
    READ PAYROLL-FILE AT END . . .
    REWRITE PAY-RECORD.
5 DATA DIVISION.
FILE SECTION.
FD OUTPUT-FILE
    LABEL RECORD IS STANDARD
    DATA RECORD IS OUTPUT-LINE (optional)
    LINAGE IS 56 LINES,
    LINES AT TOP 5,
    LINES AT BOTTOM 5.

COBOL #14 **1** The KEY in relative I-O is the relative key which identifies the logical record position
(1, 2, 3, . . . , n) in the file. A key of 50 references the fiftieth record. The KEY in

indexed I-O refers to a field in the record which uniquely identifies the record, e.g., customer number, social security number.

2 ORGANIZATION IS INDEXED (changed)
ACCESS MODE IS DYNAMIC (same)
RECORD KEY IS INVENTORY-NUMBER (changed)
PROCEDURE DIVISION.
OPEN I-O INVENTORY-FILE. (same)
(no search key computation required)
READ INVENTORY-FILE INTO CURRENT-INVENTORY RECORD
INVALID KEY PERFORM READ-ERROR-ROUTINE.
(Note that KEY IS INVENTORY-NUMBER is optional since prime key is implied. The search procedure need not be programmed because the search of the index is provided by the read routine.)

3 (a) Access is sequential.
READ RECEIVABLES-FILE INTO RECEIVABLE-WORK-RECORD
AT END PERFORM CLOSING.
REWRITE CUSTOMER-RECEIVABLE FROM RECEIVABLE-WORK-
RECORD.
(b) Access is random.
READ RECEIVABLES-FILE INTO RECEIVABLE-WORK-RECORD
INVALID KEY PERFORM KEY-ERROR-ROUTINE.
REWRITE CUSTOMER-RECEIVABLE FROM RECEIVABLE-WORK-
RECORD
INVALID KEY PERFORM KEY-ERROR-ROUTINE.

COBOL #15

1 A definition of a sort file and a SORT statement in the PROCEDURE DIVISION.
2 A REPORT SECTION in the DATA DIVISION with report description; a set of statements in the PROCEDURE DIVISION: INITIATE,GENERATE,TERMI-NATE.
3 A common DATA DIVISION can be written once and then accessed in all programs via the COPY verb.
4 During execution, the results of each of the sections will be output for debugging tracing.
5 The CALL statement specifies the data-names in the USING clause of the CALL statement.

EXERCISES

1 Explain the purpose of each of the functional modules in COBOL.
2 How is the date that the program was compiled included in the program documentation?
3 How does COBOL handle international differences in currency and comma-period conventions?
4 Explain each of the following storage consideration features of COBOL:
(a) REDEFINES   (c) SAME RECORD AREA
(b) SAME AREA   (d) Segmentation
5 What is the difference between JUSTIFIED and SYNCHRONIZED?
6 Write statements to define condition names for three answers to a questionnaire—YES,

NO, DONT KNOW coded as 1, 2, and 3. Then write at least one statement to use the condition names to tally responses.

7 Using the COMPUTE verb, write statements to:

(*a*) Put value of ITEM-A into RESULT.

(*b*) Calculate $X = A + B / C^3$

8 Place the result of $A + B + C$ into the storage for L, M, N.

9 In what order is a compound conditional using AND, OR, and NOT executed?

10 In coding of survey data, the following codes are used:

Homeowner 1 = yes, 2 = no

Years at location = actual

Construction 1 = brick, 2 = wood, 3 = other

Number of bedrooms = actual

Air conditioning 1 = yes, 2 = no

Heating 1 = gas, 2 = oil, 3 = coal, 4 = wood

Write DATA DIVISION entries to define descriptive names for each condition. Write a PROCEDURE DIVISION statement to select and tally the number who are homeowner, 3 or more years at location, not brick construction, three or more bedrooms, with air conditioning, and use gas or oil heat.

11 The entries in TABLE-1 and TABLE-2 have the same names:

A-1, A-2, A-3, and A-4.

(*a*) Add the entries in TABLE-1 to the same-named entries in TABLE-2 without using CORRESPONDING.

(*b*) Add the table entries of TABLE-1 to TABLE-2 using CORRESPONDING.

12 How can the program obtain the current date, day, or time?

13 A tally based on an analysis of personnel data by the HEW Co. has been placed in a table with the following criteria:

Sex (men, women), race (five categories), and job class (six categories).

(*a*) Prepare the DATA DIVISION entries to define the table.

(*b*) Write a PERFORM to sum the number of persons represented by the table.

14 What is the purpose of INSPECT, STRING, and UNSTRING? Write a statement to count the number of blanks in a line (called OUTPUT-LINE).

15 What is the difference between indexing and subscripting?

16 Input data for invoicing includes a product code on each item ordered. The printed invoice contains the code plus a description of the product. The descriptions for the invoice output are obtained from a table of codes and descriptions.

(*a*) Define such a table with 30 codes (9(3)) and descriptions (X(20)).

(*b*) Write statements to search the table to obtain a code description.

17 Discuss the value of the LINAGE feature in reducing coding requirements.

18 Explain the difference between relative I-O and indexed I-O organization.

19 Under what conditions would the following be used or useful?

(*a*) Segmentation

(*b*) Library

(*c*) Interprogram communication

(*d*) Report writer

(*e*) Debug

20 Write single-line statements for a PROCEDURE DIVISION for each of the following:

(*a*) Write a line (OUTPUT-LINE) and space the paper to the top of the next page.

(*b*) Write a message GO HOME on the console typewriter.

(c) Write LINE-OUT if SEX is MALE and AGE is OVER-30 (assume condition names have been defined). If neither condition applies, perform TRY-AGAIN.

(d) Rewind a magnetic tape used for FILE-7.

(e) Insert a library procedure called FIND-OUT into the program.

(f) Execute an ANALYSIS procedure until the record with key 998 has been processed. (Make sure you process 998.)

(g) Execute a procedure ANALYSIS on every other one of 1000 items (ANALYSIS-ITEMS) in a table (ANALYSIS-TABLE).

(h) Read a record (TRANSACTION) from a file (TRANSACTION-FILE) assuming relative organization and dynamic access.

(i) Read same record as (h) but assume sequential access.

PROGRAMMING PROBLEMS

1 Prepare a table of present values.

(a) The table of present values is to be for a given number of periods (not greater than 40) at a specified interest rate between 01 and 99. Input the number of periods and the interest rate from a punched card using the ACCEPT statement. Use a PERFORM VARYING statement for the loop to generate the values. The form of the output should be:

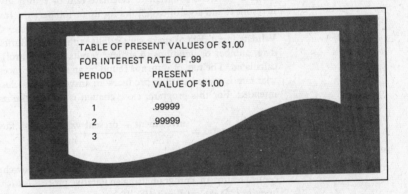

TABLE OF PRESENT VALUES OF $1.00

FOR INTEREST RATE OF .99

PERIOD	PRESENT VALUE OF $1.00
1	.99999
2	.99999
3	

Be sure to validate the input data. The limits for the number of periods is 40, so if N is greater than 40, print only 40 periods plus an error message. The interest rate can range from 01 to 99 but may not be zero.

Hint: Since any interest rate except 00 is valid, check only for a rate of zero. A zero rate will abort the job. The formula for present value is $1/(1 + i)^n$ where i is interest rate and n is period for which calculation is being made. If a table is being computed, each value can be calculated as the prior present value divided by $(1 + i)$.

(b) The table of present values is to be for 20 periods using rates of .05, .10, .15, .20, and .25. The output should be as shown on page 732 (single-spaced).

Utilize the following COBOL features in preparing the table:

(1) Define a table of rates and insert interest rate values using REDEFINES

(2) Define the table of present values using OCCURS (subscripted)

(3) Compute the entire table using PERFORM VARYING and then print it

TABLE OF PRESENT VALUES OF $1.00
FOR FIVE INTEREST RATES

PERIOD	WITH INTEREST RATE OF				
	05	10	15	20	25
1	.99999	.99999	.99999	.99999	.99999
2	.99999	.99999	.99999	.99999	.99999
3					.99999

(c) Put the table in 1(b) on two pages of output, double-spacing each line. Use the LINAGE feature to define a page and to cause the program to advance to the second page.

2 Write a COBOL program to calculate rate of return given an input of an initial investment and a set of cash flows for up to 100 periods. Investment and cash flow are less than $10 million. Program limits should allow a rate of return between 0 and 80. Validate input data to make sure it falls within these limits. Output should list input data, number of iterations to achieve results (as a control), and the rate of return as calculated. The rate of return is found by an iterative process using trial rates, and the trial rate is varied until it produces an answer that is close enough for the purpose intended. For this program, close enough is .001 as the difference ratio.

$$\text{Difference ratio} = \frac{\text{investment} - \text{present value of cash flows using trial rate}}{\text{investment}}$$

The logic of this iterative process is described in a flowchart on page 589. An error control feature of a program using an iterative process is to put a limit on the number of iterations. Make this limit 100. If iterations reach 100, stop the process and print the trial rate. Print the number of iterations as a control in all cases.

3 Write a program to create a file on tape or disk and then write records from the file.

(a) Read an unspecified number (between 25 and 29) of records from cards, 20 alphanumeric characters per record. The input data can be any alphanumerics, but names are suggested. Display each record. Write the records onto a labeled tape file in blocks of 10. After the records have been written, close the tape file, rewind, reopen the file, and read and display each record. Display an appropriate message before and after both the file creation and the file read. *Note:* Since the last block of tape records is not full, the block will not write until the CLOSE instruction, at which time the operating system will mark the end of the records in the block and write it on the tape.

(b) Read and display records from cards [as in 3(a)]. Count the records as they are read and display a record number alongside each record. Write the records onto a relative file on a disk. This will require a field in the output record for a record number. The first record is 1, the next is 2, etc. After all records have been written, each with a record number, read and display the record number and contents of record for record numbers 17, 5, and 10 (in that order). If an invalid key occurs, display an error message.

(c) Update the relative file created in 3(b). The input cards will have the relative record number plus the new value of the data-field for the record. Access each record to be changed replacing its contents with the new data. Print the record number, the contents of the record before the change, and the contents of the record after the change. If there is an invalid key for any record, print the record number and an error message. *Hint:* A program switch may be useful in programming the selection of the error output.

4 Write a COBOL program to prepare a grade report for a professor. The report contains the student names, student ID numbers, scores of quizzes (assume 4), the total score of all quizzes, and the grade assigned on the basis of the total score. At the end of the report, print the number of students and average for all students.

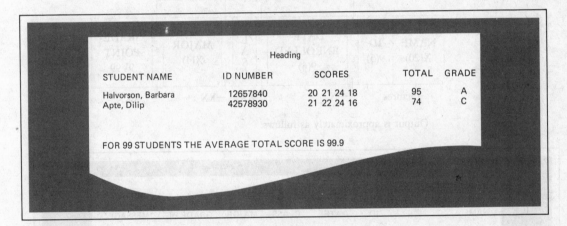

```
                              Heading

STUDENT NAME          ID NUMBER        SCORES        TOTAL  GRADE

Halvorson, Barbara    12657840      20 21 24 18        95    A
Apte, Dilip           42578930      21 22 24 16        74    C


FOR 99 STUDENTS THE AVERAGE TOTAL SCORE IS 99.9
```

The input record is a punched card:

Student name X(20)	ID Number X(10)	Filler X(5)	Scores 1	2	3	4	Filler X(37)

Picture 99 for each

Grades should be assigned as follows:

90–100	A
80–89	B
70–79	C
60–69	D
Below 60	F

Hint: 88-levels can be used to define a name for the ranges. The four scores on each card can be defined as a list using OCCURS. The scores can then be added using a PERFORM VARYING.

5 Write a COBOL program to examine student records and on the basis of certain criteria

accept or reject each student for a special educational program. The criteria for acceptance are:

(*a*) Date of enrollment is not before January 1, 1974

(*b*) The student is classified as a junior (JR) or senior (SR)

(*c*) The student is majoring in Business (BUS)

(*d*) Grade point is at least 3.00

Print a report listing each student record processed plus the comment *ACCEPTED*, *REJECTED*, or *ERROR* at the right of the detail line. *ERROR* is printed if the input validation module finds a possible error. All input fields should be checked. *Hint:* Check for blank field, grade-point average greater than 4.0, etc. Keep a count of the number of students processed, the number accepted and rejected, and the number of records in error. Print this data at the end of the report.

Input is on punched cards:

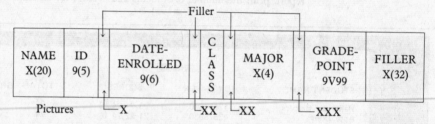

Output is approximately as follows:

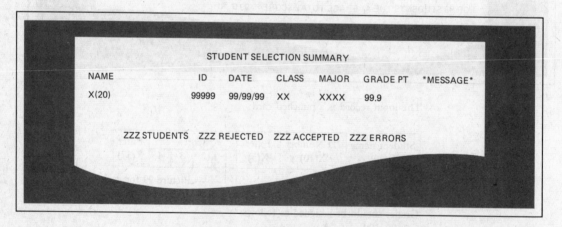

6 Write a COBOL program which selects students as described in Problem 5, but read the criteria as input to the program (a more flexible program design). Input a parameter card containing each of the values against which a student is to be compared. Allow up to four different classes (FROSH, etc.) to be acceptable and up to three different majors. *Hint:* Make parameters for class and majors subscripted variables (using OCCURS). Use a PERFORM varying to compare the appropriate field on the student record with each acceptable value for that field. Be sure to print out input values for visual validation.

7 Write a program to build a table and print it out. A retail store is organized into 12 departments. Each item stocked by the store is identified by a department number and an item number. The store wishes to create (for later access) a table of descriptions of the items using the department and item numbers. Assume a maximum of 10 items per department. Write a COBOL program to create a table of items by department. The data record to build the table is on punched cards. Each card contains a department number 9(6), item number 9(4), and description of the item X(10). Assume that the cards are in order by department number and item number within department. A card with department number of all 9s is used to signify the end of the data. After building the table, print it out. *Hint:* The table has two levels—the first is the department; the second is the item number. Use PERFORM . . . VARYING . . . UNTIL . . . AFTER . . . UNTIL . . . to read the items and to print the table.

8 Modify the program from Problem 7 to accept requests giving a department and an item number in order to access the description of the item requested. *Hint:* Index the table, search first for department, and then search for item within the department.

COBOL Acknowledgment

COBOL is an industry language and not the property of any company or group of companies, or of any organization or group of organizations.

No warranty, expressed or implied, is made by any contributor or by the CODASYL Programming Language Committee as to the accuracy and functioning of the programming system and language. Moreover, no responsibility is assumed by any contributor, or by the committee, in connection therewith.

The authors and copyright holders of the copyrighted material used herein

FLOW-MATIC (trademark of Sperry Rand Corporation), Programming for the UNIVAC® I and II, Data Automation Systems copyrighted 1958, 1959, by Sperry Rand Corporation; IBM Commercial Translator Form No. F 28-8013, copyrighted 1959 by IBM; FACT, DSI 27A5260-2760 copyrighted 1960 by Minneapolis-Honeywell.

have specifically authorized the use of this material in whole or in part, in the COBOL specifications. Such authorization extends to the reproduction and use of COBOL specifications in programming manuals or similar publications.

APPENDIX

Punching without Use of Automatic Features

Punching with AUTO FEED

Punching with a Program Card

Other Keys and Controls

HOW TO USE
THE CARD PUNCH

Students of computer data processing frequently need to be able to operate the keydriven card punch, either to keypunch their programs or to make corrections in previously punched card decks. The purpose of this appendix is to aid the student in these activities. It, therefore, covers only the basic elements of using the card punch.

The three most common card punches are the IBM Model 129, the IBM Model 29, and the IBM Model 26 printing card punches (Figure A1-1). The Model 26 was the standard card punch until 1960; the Model 29 was introduced in 1960 in conjunction with IBM's System/360 computers; the Model 129 is similar to the Model 29 in keyboard but uses an internal buffer (memory) to hold the card contents as they are being keyed. In the Model 129 (and other buffered card punches), when the keying of data is complete for a card (and corrections have been made, if necessary), the card is punched from the data in the buffer. The punching occurs while the next card is being keyed, thus reducing the waiting time found on the nonbuffered 26 and 29 models. The features of the Model 129 buffered card punch are most significant for commercial keypunching. Occasional users are more likely to use a Model 29 (or a Model 26 because many of these older units are still in service). Other vendors supply keypunches with the same (and additional) features. The explanation in this appendix concentrates on the IBM Model 29 but with some details of the IBM Model 26.

The alphabetic characters on the keypunch keyboard are identical to those on a typewriter. This means that a person who can type can keypunch alphabetics

Model 26 keydriven card punch   Model 29 keydriven card punch

FIGURE A1-1   IBM card punches. (*Courtesy of International Business Machines Corporation.*)

without learning any new keying. The numbers 1 to 9 are arranged so they can be punched with three fingers of the right hand. The special characters are different for the Model 29 (and 129) and the older Model 26.

On Models 29 and 129 there are different punches for each of 28 special characters, and each has a unique position on the keyboard. The Model 26 has only 11 special characters with the same punch codes being used for five pairs of different characters—one set of characters termed "commercial" and the other set identified as "scientific." The differences in the keyboards for Model 26 are as follows:

Commercial	Scientific (FORTRAN)
#	=
&	+
%	(
⌑	)
@	' (apostrophe)

The punches are the same in the Model 26 for either of each pair of characters; the difference is only in the keytop character and in the printing character which is printed on top of the card when it is punched. This means that a user needing to punch the FORTRAN statement X = Y + (A/B) on a Model 26 with a commercial keyboard can get the correct punches by keying X # Y & % A/B ⌑. The Model 29 uses the same keys as the Model 26 for the commercial characters; the scientific characters are on new keys. Figure A1-2 shows the keyboards of a Model 26 and a Model 29.

The use of the card punch is facilitated by features which perform functions that otherwise must be done manually. The beginner may wish to start by punching without using these features and then, as more proficiency is developed, begin to use these aids to punching speed. The use of the card punch will therefore be described at three levels.

1 Punching without making use of automatic features
2 Punching using the automatic feed but not a program card
3 Punching with a program card

Punching without Use of Automatic Features

The on-off switch for the card punch is on the inside of the right leg for the Model 29 and at the upper left in the card stacker for a Model 26. The Model 26 requires a warm-up period before it will operate.

On the panel directly above the keytops, there are six switches on a Model 29 and three toggle switches on a Model 26 (Figure A1-3). Turn the AUTO SKIP DUP and AUTO FEED switches off (down). Turn the PRINT switch on. On a Model 29, the LZ print should be on; the PROG SEL and CLEAR are not needed

IBM Model 29

IBM Model 26

FIGURE A1-2 Keyboards of IBM model 29 and 26 card punches.

by the occasional user. In the upper part of the card punch, directly below the window showing a cylinder (program drum), there is a small program control lever. Depress this lever to the right to deactivate the program card mechanism.

Blank cards to be punched are placed in the card hopper at the upper right; cards which have been punched are moved by the card punch into a card stacker at the upper left from which they can be removed. The path of a card through the card punch is shown in Figure A1-4.

Note in Figure A1-2 the three keys at the right-hand side of the keyboard labeled REL, FEED, and REG. These are the release, feed, and register keys. Using these keys, punching a card is performed as follows:

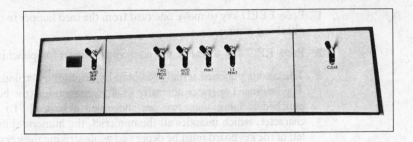

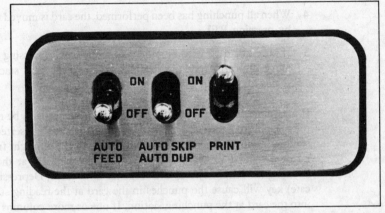

FIGURE A1-3 Functional control switches for card-punch model 29 (top) and model 26 (bottom).

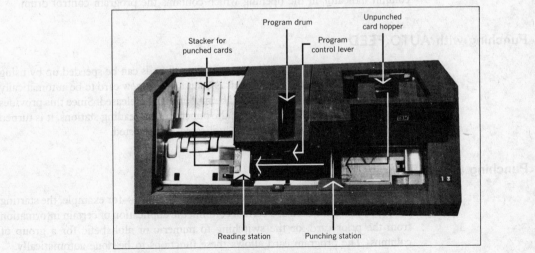

FIGURE A1-4 Path of the card through the card punch.

1   Press FEED key to move one card from the card hopper to the entrance to the punching station.

2   Press REG key to move the card into position for punching.

3   The card is punched serially (column by column) by striking the proper keys. The keyboard operates normally in alphabetic mode (the bottom character is punched if more than two are shown on a keytop). To obtain the upper character, which includes all the numerics, the numeric shift key at the lower left of the keyboard must be depressed while striking the keys. Columns may be skipped by depressing the space bar.

4   When all punching has been performed, the card is moved to the reading station by pressing REL.

5   If only one card is to be punched, immediately pressing REL and REG will move the card from the reading station to the card stacker where it can be removed.

If a card needs to be corrected, a damaged card needs to be replaced, or a card is to be duplicated, the card to be reproduced is manually inserted against the reading station, leaving only a slight space. A blank card is brought from the card hopper by depressing FEED (or a card is inserted manually at the punching station). Pressing the REG key will then register both cards. Depressing the DUP (duplicate) key will cause the punches in the card at the reading station to be punched into the card at the punching station. If one or more columns are to be omitted or altered from what is found in the card being reproduced, the operator depresses the space bar or keyboard characters instead of the duplicate key for the columns to be omitted or altered. The next column to be punched or duplicated is read from the column indicator in the opening which contains the program control drum.

Punching with AUTO FEED

If many cards are to be punched, the feeding of cards can be speeded up by using the AUTO FEED option. When this is on, it causes a new card to be automatically fed and registered each time the card being punched is released. Since this provides a continuous supply of cards at both the punching and reading stations, it is turned off in order to insert a card to be duplicated or corrected.

Punching with a Program Card

In punching applications, there are repetitive operations—for example, the starting of the punching of a field at a certain column, the duplication of certain information from the prior card, or the switching to numeric or alphabetic for a group of columns. The program card allows these functions to be done automatically.

The program card is a regular punched card which is wrapped around the program drum. Control punches in the top five rows are read by program star wheels (Figure A1-5), and cause certain functions to be automatically performed. On a Model 29, a second program may be punched lower in the same card. The second program is selected by the PROG SEL switch. This should be on ONE to use the control cards explained here. A small lever on the keypunch is depressed to the left to activate the program card and to the right to deactivate it. Some common control punches are

Punch	Function
None	Beginning of field to be manually punched.
1	Shifts keyboard to alphabetic mode with program control; the keyboard is in numeric unless this control punch is used.
0	Starts automatic duplication.
11	Starts automatic skipping.
12	Defines the columns for which the preceding punches apply.

AUTO SKIP DUP toggle switch must be "on" for duplication or skipping.

FIGURE A1-5 (a) Program drum and (b) program drum engaged. (*Courtesy of International Business Machines Corporation.*)

An example will illustrate the use of a control card. In punching a FORTRAN program, the first five columns are for a statement number (numeric). Column 6, indicating a continuation of a statement, is rarely used. Columns 7–72 are for alphanumeric punching, with alphabetics the most common. Columns 73–80 are for identification. The identification in this example is assumed to be a four-character alphabetic program identifier to be duplicated in every card and a four-digit numeric sequence number. The program card should therefore put the card punch in numeric mode for columns 1–5, in numeric mode for column 6, and in alphabetic mode for columns 7–72, should duplicate columns 73–76, and should put the punch in numeric mode for columns 77–80. The control card is illustrated in Figure A1-6. Remember that the use of the control card shifts the punch to numeric mode. When punching FORTRAN under program card control (and AUTO SKIP DUP switch on), there will be no need to manually space the card to column 7 (if there is no statement number to be punched); merely pressing SKIP twice will position the card at the third field (7–72). If the FORTRAN statement is completed at column 61, pressing SKIP will move the card to column 73 and will duplicate columns 73–76. The keypuncher can then punch the card numbers in columns 77–80. If there were to be no identification in columns 73–80, the program card would use an 11 punch in column 73 and 12 punches in 74–80, and the punch would then automatically skip over columns 73 to 80 when column 73 is reached.

Other Keys and Controls

The MULT PCH (multiple punch) key is for use when a punch combination not found for the machine is to be punched. If, for example, an 11, 5, 8 punch combination is to be punched on a Model 26, the MULT PCH key is depressed, and 11, 5, and 8 are punched. The multiple punch key keeps the card from advancing to allow the three keys to punch in one column.

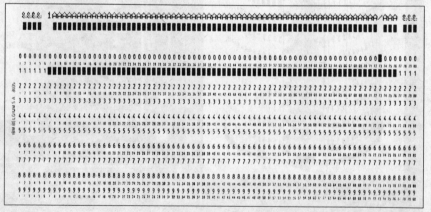

FIGURE A1-6 Example of a program card for punching FORTRAN statements on a card punch.

The backspace control is a small rectangular button between the reading station and the punching station. Depressing the control backspaces one column.

On the Model 29, but not on the Model 26, there are two additional switches not normally used by the student. If the LZ PRINT is off, it suppresses the printing of leading zeros in a field. The switch should usually be on for the student user. The CLEAR switch is a spring switch which causes all cards then in process to be moved through to the stacker without any new cards being fed.

APPENDIX

Computer Organizations

Selected Periodicals

Getting Started

GUIDE TO
UNITED STATES
COMPUTER
ORGANIZATIONS
AND PERIODICALS

There are a number of active computer organizations and journals in countries other than the United States, but this appendix surveys only those in the United States. The major world organization is the International Federation for Information Processing (IFIP), 3, Rue du Marche, 6H-1204 Geneva, Switzerland. It has constituent societies from 34 countries. IFIP includes an Administrative Data Processing Group (IAG) which is devoted to organizational data processing uses of computers.

Computer Organizations

American Federation of Information Processing Societies (AFIPS) 210 Summit Avenue, Montvale, N.J. 07645. This is a federation of societies representing the information processing community. AFIPS represents the United States in a similar international group (IFIP). A major activity of AFIPS is to sponsor the National Computer Conference (NCC). This consists of sessions at which papers are presented and a large equipment show at which manufacturers display their latest equipment. Proceedings of the conference are published. AFIPS has also sponsored research such as studies of the computing industry. A person receives AFIPS notices by being associated with one of its member societies—ACM, IEEE, AICPA, etc.

Association for Computing Machinery (ACM) 1133 Avenue of the Americas, New York, N.Y. 10036. This organization, founded to advance the science and arts of information processing, holds an annual meeting (usually in August), sponsors special-interest groups on various topics, organizes seminars, and publishes six journals—*Journal of the Association for Computing Machinery* (quarterly), *ACM Transactions on Database Systems* (quarterly), *ACM Transactions on Mathematical Software* (quarterly), *Communications of the ACM* (monthly), *Computing Reviews* (monthly), and *Computing Surveys* (quarterly). ACM tends to be oriented toward scientific problems, algorithms for solutions, etc. ACM chapters are active in many cities and on a number of college campuses. Annual dues include subscriptions to *Communications of the ACM* plus one other journal. There is a special student membership rate.

Association for Educational Data Systems (AEDS) 1201 16th Street N.W., Washington, D.C. Founded by professional educators, this association has a membership consisting of individuals interested in exchanging information about the impact of modern technology upon the educational process. The association provides a monthly publication, a quarterly journal, a national convention, regional chapters, etc., and operates the AEDS National Center for Educational Data Processing.

Association for Systems Management 7890 Brookside Drive, Cleveland, Ohio 44138. A national organization of persons interested in systems work. It has local chapters, publishes a journal (*Journal of Systems Management*), promotes educational programs, and holds an annual meeting with an accompanying equipment exposition.

Data Processing Management Association (DPMA) 505 Busse Highway, Park Ridge, Ill. 60068. The membership of this organization is concerned mainly with business methods and their mechanization. The association has local chapters, publishes a monthly journal, holds an annual conference and exposition, publishes the proceedings of this conference, and sponsors educational programs.

EDP Auditors Association P.O. Box 15562, Los Angeles, Calif. 90015. This organization is concerned with control and audit of EDP systems. The association has local chapters, an annual meeting, and a quarterly journal (*The EDP Auditor*).

Society for Management Information Systems (SMIS) One First National Plaza, Chicago, Ill. 60670. This society holds annual meeting, sponsors research, distributes papers, etc. It has student memberships. SMIS is cosponsor of a journal, *The MIS Quarterly.*

Interested organizations A number of organizations have an active computer-interested constituency. As examples:

> IEEE (Institute of Electrical and Electronics Engineers)
> AIDS (Association for Decision Sciences)
> TIMS (The Institute of Management Science)

Selected Periodicals

Collected Algorithms from ACM Quarterly Loose-leaf collection of algorithms for solving problems using the computer.

Communications of the ACM A monthly journal of ACM. Reports ACM activities plus technical articles on a wide range of subjects.

Computer Decisions New York, N.Y. Articles on administration and use of computers. Free to qualified individuals.

Computer Digest Detroit, Mich. 48226. A monthly digest of articles from over 400 journals and other publications in computers.

Computers and the Humanities Queens College Press, Flushing, N.Y. 11367. Monthly publication emphasizing applications in the humanities.

Computerworld Chicago, Ill. A comprehensive weekly newspaper covering developments in the computer community.

Computing Newsletter for Schools of Business University of Colorado, Colorado Springs, Col. 80907. Monthly newsletter of special interest to educators and students.

Computing Surveys A quarterly publication of ACM for tutorial and survey articles.

Computing Reviews A monthly publication of ACM devoted to reviews of books and papers in the computing field.

Data Base A quarterly publication of ACM Special Interest Group on Business Data Processing (SIGBDP).

Data Comm User Monthly. Deals with problems of users of data communications.

Datamation New York, N.Y. Circulated without charge to individuals (by name and title) who qualify. Also available on a subscription basis. It is a basic source of information on current and prospective developments in the computer field. Mixed technical and user material.

Data Processing Digest Los Angeles, Calif. A monthly service which reviews publications relevant to business data processing.

EDP Analyzer Vista, Calif. Monthly reports on specific topics. Highly regarded in the industry.

EDP Auditor Quarterly publication of EDP Auditors Association.

EDPACS Reston, Va. Monthly updating publication in the field of EDP audit, control, and security.

Electronic News Fairchild Publications, Inc., New York, N.Y. Weekly newspaper oriented toward hardware and technical developments.

IBM Systems Journal Armonk, N.Y. Quarterly journal of technical articles by IBM authors. Generally of high quality with a bias toward technical topics in hardware and software.

ICP Quarterly International Computer Programs, Inc., Indianapolis, Ind. Listing of available software programs. Very complete and valuable reference.

Infosystems Wheaton, Ill. Monthly publication oriented to data processing management and other management personnel. Free to subscribers who qualify.

Journal of the Association for Computing Machinery Baltimore, Md. A quarterly publication devoted to research papers.

Journal of Data Management Park Ridge, Ill. Published monthly by DPMA. Articles are oriented to business data processing.

Journal of Systems Management Cleveland, Ohio. Monthly publication of the Association for Systems Management. Contains articles on a variety of topics related to analysis and design of information and management systems.

MIS Quarterly Blegen 93 University of Minnesota, Minneapolis, Minn. 55455. Quarterly journal cosponsored by the Society for Management Information

Systems (SMIS) and the Management Information Systems Research Center at the University of Minnesota (MISRC). Contains both practitioner and academic articles of a scholarly nature.

Mini-Micro Systems Hudson, Mass. Formerly *Modern Data*. Monthly user-oriented nontechnical publication emphasizing minicomputers and applications of microprocessors.

SIG Publications Many of the special interest groups (SIGs) of the ACM have publications. Members of ACM may also join the SIGs.

Small Systems World Canoga Park, Calif. Monthly publication covering problems of small business system computer users.

Transactions on Database Systems (*TODS*) Published quarterly by ACM. Papers on database development and research.

Transactions on Mathematical Software (*TOMS*) Published quarterly by ACM; significant research and development in fundamental algorithms and associated hardware.

Other publications Other interested organizations have journals which contain articles of interest. Examples are *Decision Sciences* and *Management Sciences*.

Getting Started

The person who is starting a career in computers and information processing should maintain an awareness of the field by reading computer periodicals and by associating with computer organizations. It is difficult for the novice to know where to start. Each journal and each organization has a purpose, but there are logical places to begin. The beginner should start with a subscription to *Computerworld* and a general-coverage journal such as *Infosystems, Computer Decisions,* or *Datamation*. A student with a scholarly interest should consider the *MIS Quarterly* and *Computing Surveys*. In terms of computer organizations, the largest is ACM, but a student who has a business orientation will also want to consider DPMA and the Association for Systems Management.

APPENDIX

Requirements

How to Apply

THE CERTIFICATE IN DATA PROCESSING

3. Pass the CDP examination. The examination may be taken prior to completing the experience requirement.

3. Principles of management
4. Quantitative methods
5. Systems analysis and design

One of the problems in data processing has been the lack of professional standards and of academic training to qualify persons to do programming and other data processing work. The formal academic programs directed toward employment in data processing are few, and most persons in the field have gained their training through computer manufacturer seminars and on-the-job experience. The heterogeneity of background and training makes it difficult to assess even minimum capabilities in the data processing area.

One method for achieving minimum standards of competence and professional orientation, a certification program, was initiated by the Data Processing Management Association (DPMA). A Certificate in Data Processing (CDP) was begun in 1962; a Registered Business Programmer (RBP) examination was first offered in 1970 (and suspended in 1974). In 1973, DPMA turned the CDP examination over to an independent organization sponsored by eight computer societies. The organization, the Institute for the Certification of Computer Professionals (ICCP), prepares and administers the business-oriented CDP examination. The ICCP has developed a code of ethics for data processing professionals and may develop other tests as well as the CDP. It plans to reinstate the programmer examination. In 1976 there were approximately 15,000 holders of the CDP. Another organization, The Society of Certified Data Processors (SCDP), a voluntary organization for CDP recipients, provides a program of assistance for those planning to take the CDP examination.

Requirements

The CDP certificate is awarded to individuals who meet the following qualifications:

1 Acquire 5 years of direct experience in data processing. Possible reduction for academic courses, based on an evaluation of the transcripts by ICCP.

2 Possess high character (as evidenced by references).

3 Pass the CDP examination. The examination may be taken prior to completing the experience requirement.

Persons who hold the certificate are entitled to use the designation "CDP" after their names.

The examination (as of 1976) consists of 300 multiple-choice questions divided into five 50-minute sections.

1 Data processing equipment
2 Computer programming and software
3 Principles of management
4 Quantitative methods
5 Systems analysis and design

The candidate need not take all sections. If a section is passed, it need not be taken again, except that all sections must be passed within 4 years, or the sections passed prior to 4 years must be retaken and repassed.

How to Apply

The CDP examination is offered annually (about the third Saturday in February). The application deadline has been about November 15. Cost in 1976 was $45 and $85, depending on the number of sections taken. Application blanks and study guides are available from:

Institute for Certification of Computer Professionals (ICCP)
304 East 45th Street
New York, N.Y. 10017

Information on a program for preparing for the examination is available from:

The Society of Certified Data Processors
500 12th Street
Washington, D.C. 20024

SELECTED REFERENCES

Since the field of computing is changing rapidly, many items in any list of references will be shortly out-of-date. The student of computers or computer data processing needs an approach to the discovery of recent articles and books. The usual library reference services are, of course, useful. Another valuable source is *Computing Reviews,* published monthly by the Association for Computing Machinery (ACM). The journal reviews books, articles, proceedings, etc., from a wide range of sources. The major topics for reviews are:

General topics and education
Computing milieu
Applications
Software
Mathematics of computation
Hardware
Analog computers
Functions

Various updating services are available which seek to keep subscribers abreast of developments in the field of computers and computer data processing. If available, they form a ready source of information about significant, current developments. Examples are Datapro and Auerbach reports.

The selected references have been restricted to a sample of recent articles and books (generally since 1975) plus a few older references that are not outdated, such as historical surveys or methods not affected by changes in technology. The references are grouped by the five parts of the text.

Part 1 Introduction

There are a considerable number of articles reporting on applications of computers. A rich source of such descriptions is the IBM publication, *Data Processor.* IBM also produces application briefs describing specific, interesting applications in organizations using IBM equipment. Other manufacturers also produce similar descriptions.

Alpert, D. A., and D. L. Bitzer: "Advances in Computer-based Education," *Science,* vol. 167, March 20, 1970, pp. 1582-1590.

Bassler, Richard A., and Edward O. Joslin (compilers): *Applications of Computer Systems,* Arlington, Va.: College Readings, 1974.

Bigelow, Robert P., and Susan H. Nycum: *Your Computer and the Law,* Englewood Cliffs, N.J.: Prentice-Hall, 1975.

Cashman, Michael: "The IBM System/32," *Datamation,* vol. 21, no. 2, February 1975, pp. 67-68.

"Computers in Manufacturing," *Infosystems,* vol. 23, no. 4, April 1976, pp. 39-43.

Davis, Gordon B.: *Management Information Systems: Conceptual Foundations, Structure and Development,* New York: McGraw-Hill, 1974.

———— and Gordon C. Everest: *Readings in Management Information Systems,* New York: McGraw-Hill, 1976.

Dilorio, Anthony M.: "EFT Today," *Computer Decisions,* vol. 8, no. 3, March 1976, pp. 20-24.

Goetz, Martin A.: "What's Inside the Software Industry?" *Computer Decisions,* vol. 7, no. 6, June 1975, pp. 18-21.

Goldstine, Herman: *The Computer from Pascal to von Neumann,* Princeton, N.J.: Princeton University Press, 1968.

Head, Robert V.: "The Elusive MIS," *Datamation,* September 1, 1970, pp. 22-27.

Nievergelt, J., and J. C. Farrar: "What Machines Can and Cannot Do," *Computing Surveys,* vol. 4, no. 2, June 1972, pp. 81-96.

Ouellette, R. P., R. S. Greeley, and J. W. Overbey II: *Computer Techniques in Environmental Science,* New York: Petrocelli, 1975.

Randell, Brian (ed.): *Origins of Digital Computers,* 2d ed., New York: Springer-Verlag, 1975.

Rosen, Saul: "Electronic Computers: A Historical Survey," *Computing Surveys,* March 1969, pp. 6-36.

Science, vol. 167, March 20, 1970. Several articles on computer-assisted instruction.

Seidel, Robert J., et al.: *Learning Alternatives in U.S. Education: Where Student and Computer Meet,* Englewood Cliffs, N.J.: Educational Technology Publications, 1975.

Weiss, Eric A. (ed.): *Computer Usage/Applications,* New York: Computer Usage Company, 1970.

Withington, Frederic G.: *The Real Computer: Its Influence, Uses, and Effects,* Reading, Mass.: Addison-Wesley, 1969.

Yasaki, Edward K.: "Microcomputers in System Design," *Datamation,* vol. 22, no. 2, February 1976, pp. 71-76.

————: "The Mini: A Growing Alternative," *Datamation,* vol. 22, No. 5, May 1976, pp. 139-142.

Part 2   The Development of Computer Applications and Computer Programs

Baker, F. T.: "Chief Programmer Team Management of Production Programming," *IBM Systems Journal,* vol. 11, no. 1, 1972, pp. 56-73.

Benjamin, Robert I.: *Control of the Information System Development Life Cycle,* New York: Wiley, 1971.

Bohm, C., and C. Jocopini: "Flow Diagrams, Turing Machines, and Languages with only Two Formation Rules," *Communications of the ACM*, vol. 9, no. 3, May 1966, pp. 366–371.

Brooks, Frederick P., Jr.: *The Mythical Man-Month: Essays on Software Engineering*, Reading, Mass.: Addison-Wesley, 1975.

Brown, P. J.: "Programming and Documenting Software Projects," *Computing Surveys*, vol. 6, no. 4, December 1974, pp. 213–220.

Chapin, Ned: "Flowcharting with the ANSI Standard: A Tutorial," *Computing Surveys*, June 1970, pp. 119–146.

Couger, J. D.: "Evolution of Business System Analysis Techniques," *Computing Surveys*, vol. 5, no. 3, September 1973, pp. 167–198.

Dijkstra, Edger W.: *A Discipline of Programming*, Englewood Cliffs, N.J.: Prentice-Hall, 1976.

"Education Related to the Use of Computers in Organizations," *Communications of the ACM*, September 1971, p. 577. Table 1 is a presentation of various life cycles.

Flowchart Symbols and Their USAGE in Information Processing (ANSI X3.5-1970), New York: American National Standards Institute, 1970.

Goetz, Martin A.: "Soup-up Your Programmers with COBOL Aids," *Computer Decisions*, vol. 5, no. 3, March 1973, pp. 8–12.

"Improved Programming Technologies—An Overview," GC20-1850, White Plains, N.Y.: International Business Machines Corporation, October 1974.

Kernighan, B. W., and P. J. Plauger: "Programming Style: Examples and Counterexamples," *Computing Surveys*, vol. 6, no. 4, December 1974, pp. 303–319.

—— and ——: *The Elements of Programming Style*, New York: McGraw-Hill, 1974.

—— and ——: *Software Tools*, Reading, Mass.: Addison-Wesley, 1976.

Knuth, Donald E.: *Fundamental Alogrithms*, 2d ed. (vol. I of *The Art of Computer Programming*), Reading, Mass.: Addison-Wesley, 1973.

——: *Seminumerical Algorithms* (vol. II of *The Art of Computer Programming*), Reading, Mass.: Addison-Wesley, 1973.

——: "Structured Programming with GO TO Statements," *Computing Surveys*, vol. 6, no. 4, December 1974, pp. 261–301.

Lee, John A. N.: *The Anatomy of a Compiler*, New York: Van Nostrand Reinhold, 1974.

Lucas, Henry C., Jr.: *The Analysis, Design and Implementation of Information Systems*, New York: McGraw-Hill, 1976.

Pollack, S., H. Hicks, Jr., and W. Harrison: *Decision Tables: Theory and Practice*, New York: Wiley, 1971.

Rubin, M.: *Introduction to the System Life Cycle*, Princeton, N.J.: Auerbach, 1970.

Stevens, W. P., G. J. Myers, and L. L. Constantine: "Structured Design," *IBM Systems Journal*, vol. 13, no. 2, 1975, pp. 115–139.

Yohe, J. M.: "An Overview of Programming Practices," *Computing Surveys*, vol. 6, no. 4, December 1974, pp. 221–245.

Yourdon, Edward: "Making the Move to Structured Programming," *Datamation*, vol. 21, no. 6, June 1975, pp. 52–56.

——: *Techniques of Program Structure and Design*, Englewood Cliffs, N.J.: Prentice-Hall, 1976.

Weinberg, Gerald M.: *The Psychology of Computer Programming*, New York: Van Nostrand Reinhold, 1971.

Part 3 Computer Technology

Abdel-Fattah, M., and Arnold C. Meltzer: *Principles of Digital Computer Design,* vol. I, Englewood Cliffs, N.J.: Prentice-Hall, 1976.

"Data Communications Report," *Infosystems,* vol. 23, no. 2, February 1976, p. 27, and vol. 23, no. 3, March 1976, pp. 29–35.

Date, C. J.: *An Introduction to Database Systems,* Reading, Mass.: Addison-Wesley, 1975.

Denning, Peter: "Virtual Memory," *Computing Surveys,* vol. 2, no. 3, September 1970.

Fry, J. P., and E. H. Sibley: "Evolution of Database Management Systems," *Computing Surveys,* vol. 8, no. 1, March 1976, pp. 7–42.

Granholm, Jackson W.: "Interactive Hardcopy Terminals," *Datamation,* vol. 21, no. 11, November 1975, pp. 51–56.

Gray, James P., and Charles R. Blair: "IBM's Systems Network Architecture," *Datamation,* vol. 21, no. 4, April 1975, pp. 51–56.

Guidelines for General System Specifications for a Computer System, New York: American Institute of Certified Public Accountants, 1976.

Hunter, John J.: "Pointers in Data Base Management," *Computer Decisions,* vol. 7, no. 1, January 1975, pp. 41–46.

Katzan, Harry, Jr.: *Computer Data Management and Data Base Technology,* New York: Van Nostrand Reinhold, 1975.

Knuth, Donald E.: *Sorting and Searching* (vol. III of *The Art of Computer Programming*), Reading, Mass.: Addison-Wesley, 1973.

London, Keith: *Techniques for Direct Access,* New York: Petrocelli/Charter, 1976.

Lorin, Harold: *Sorting and Sort Systems,* Reading, Mass.: Addison-Wesley, 1976.

McEnroe, P. V., et al.: "Overview of the Supermarket System and the Retail Store System," *IBM Systems Journal,* vol. 14, no. 1, 1975, pp. 3–15.

Martin, James: *Principles of Data Base Management,* Englewood Cliffs, N.J.: Prentice-Hall, 1976.

————: *Telecommunications and the Computer,* 2d ed., Englewood Cliffs, N.J.: Prentice-Hall, 1976.

Mattson, Donald: "Understanding Media," *Computer Decisions,* vol. 8, no. 3, March 1976, pp. 44–46.

"Micrographics Report," *Infosystems,* vol. 22, No. 4, April 1975, pp. 33–35.

Musgrave, Bill: "Minding the Storage," *Computer Decisions,* vol. 7, no. 3, March 1975, pp. 26–30.

Nievergelt, J.: "Binary Search Trees and File Organization," *Computing Surveys,* vol. 6, no. 3, September 1974, pp. 195–207.

Presser, Leon: "Multiprogramming Coordination," *Computing Surveys,* vol. 7, no. 1, March 1975, pp. 21–44.

Ritchie, Robert O.: "Intelligent Terminals and Distributed Processing," *Computer Decisions,* vol. 7, no. 2, February 1975, pp. 36–40.

Selection and Acquisition of Data Base Management Systems, New York: Association for Computing Machinery, 1976.

Snyders, Jan: "Data Entry, Intelligent Terminals and OCR," *Computer Decisions,* vol. 8, no. 2, February 1976, pp. 38–40.

Teicholz, Eric: "Interactive Graphics Comes of Age," *Datamation*, vol. 21, no. 12, December 1975, pp. 50–53.

Tenkhoff, P. A., and J. C. Collard: "The Common Carriers' Uncommon Offerings," *Datamation*, vol. 21, no. 4, April 1975, pp. 44–47.

Testa, Charles J., and Sheldon J. Laube: "How Do You Choose a Data Base Management System? Carefully!" *Infosystems*, vol. 22, no. 1, January 1975, pp. 41–46.

Totaro, J. Burt: "Communications Processor Survey," *Datamation*, vol. 22, no. 5, May 1976, pp. 151–170.

Tremblay, Jean Paul, and Paul Gordon Sorenson: *Introduction to Data Structures with Applications*, New York: McGraw-Hill, 1976.

Yasaki, Edward K.: "Bar Codes for Data Entry," *Datamation*, vol. 21, no. 5, May 1975, pp. 63–68.

Part 4 Effective Operation and Use of the Computer

Buying Software, Carmel, Ind.: International Computer Programs, Inc., 1976.

Chadwick, H. A.: "Burning Down the Data Center," *Datamation*, vol. 21, no. 10, October 1975, pp. 60–64.

Computer Audit Guidelines, Canadian Institute of Chartered Accountants, 1975.

Computer Control Guidelines, Canadian Institute of Chartered Accountants, 1970.

Donovan, J. J., and S. E. Madnick: "Hierarchical Approach to Computer System Integrity," *IBM Systems Journal*, vol. 14, no. 2, 1975, pp. 188–202.

"Facilities Management Report," *Infosystems*, vol. 22, no. 11, November 1975, pp. 27–30.

Ghanem, S. B.: "Computing Center Optimization by a Pricing-Priority Policy," *IBM Systems Journal*, vol. 14, no. 3, 1975, pp. 272–291.

Goldstein, Robert C.: "The Costs of Privacy," *Datamation*, vol. 21, no. 10, October 1975, pp. 65–69.

Hammer, Glen B.: "Cutting Time-sharing Costs," *Datamation*, vol. 21, no. 7, July 1975, pp. 36–39.

Hillegass, John R.: "As Timesharing Goes By," *Computer Decisions*, vol. 7, no. 4, April 1975, pp. 56–60.

Jacobson, R. V., W. F. Brown, and P. E. Browne: *Guidelines for Automatic Data Processing, Physical Security and Risk Management*, Federal Information Processing Standards Publication 31, 1974.

Jancura, Elise G., and Arnold Berger: *Computers: Auditing and Control*, New York: Petrocelli/Charter, 1976.

Laven, Kenyon: "Timesharing Grows Up," *Infosystems*, vol. 22, no. 2, February 1975, pp. 32–34 and 53.

Lucas, Henry C., Jr.: "Performance Evaluation and Monitoring," *Computing Surveys*, vol. 3, no. 3, September 1971.

McFarlan, F. Warren, and Richard Nolan (eds.): *Information Systems Handbook*, Homewood, Ill.: Dow Jones-Irwin, 1975.

Martin, James: *Security, Accuracy and Privacy in Computer Systems*, Englewood Cliffs, N.J.: Prentice-Hall, 1973.

Mooney, John W.: "Organized Program Maintenance," *Datamation,* vol. 21, no. 2, February 1975, pp. 63–64.

Parker, Donn B.: *Crime by Computer,* New York: Scribner, 1976.

Patrick, R. L.: *Security Systems Review Manual,* Montvale, N.J.: AFIPS Press, 1974.

Siegel, Paul: *Strategic Planning of Management Information Systems,* New York: Petrocelli, 1975.

Szatrowski, Ted: "Rent, Lease, or Buy?", *Datamation,* vol. 22, no. 2, February 1976, pp. 59–68.

Timmreck, E. M.: "Computer Selection Methodology," *Computing Surveys,* vol. 5, no. 4, December 1973, pp. 199–222.

Wheeler, T. F., Jr.: "OS/VS1 Concepts and Philosophies," *IBM Systems Journal,* vol. 13, no. 3, 1974, pp. 213–229.

Part 5 Computer Programming Languages

There are a large number of programming language texts, and no attempt has been made to list texts for the major languages of BASIC, COBOL, and FORTRAN. The extent of available texts for these languages is indicated by the numbers in the end-of-1975 Couger list of programming texts dated 1971–1975 (J. Daniel Couger, ed., *Computing Newsletter for Schools of Business,* vol. 9, no. 5, January 1976).

BASIC	31
COBOL	38
FORTRAN	76

The listing below concentrates on standards, selected references for languages other than the three major ones, useful references, and very helpful articles and texts. In studying a programming language, it is often helpful to select and read a second text as a supplement. The second explanation, from any well-written text, seems to clear up difficult-to-understand points. A question to consider in selecting a text is whether it adheres to the new standard (for COBOL or FORTRAN). The COBOL standard is dated 1974 (issued in 1975), and the new FORTRAN standard dates from 1977. Also, the use of a structured or disciplined approach to programming is relatively new (say, 1974 to 1976). Therefore, any programming text in COBOL dated before 1976 is probably not up-to-date with the new COBOL standard and structured programming practices. Any FORTRAN dated before 1977 may not meet the new FORTRAN standard.

Ahl, David H.: *BASIC Computer Games,* Maynard, Mass.: Digital Equipment Corp., 1973. Listing of BASIC instruction code for 100 computer games.

American National Standard FORTRAN (X3.9-1977), New York: American National Standards Institute, 1977.

American National Standard Programming Language COBOL (X3.23-1974), New York: American National Standards Institute, 1974.

American National Standard Programming Language Minimal BASIC (Draft of Proposal), Washington, D.C.: Computer and Business Equipment Manufacturers Association, 1976.

Bates, Frank, and Mary L. Douglas: *Programming Language/One: With Structured Programming,* 3d ed., Englewood Cliffs, N.J.: Prentice-Hall, 1975.

Davis, Gordon B., Margrethe H. Olson, and Charles R. Litecky: *Elementary Structured COBOL*, New York: McGraw-Hill, 1977. An unusual instructional approach.

Griswold, Ralph E., Ivan P. Polonsky, and James F. Poage: *The SNOBOL4 Programming Language*, 2d ed., Englewood Cliffs, N.J.: Prentice-Hall, 1976.

Hellerman, Herbert, and I. A. Smith: *APL/360 Programming and Applications*, New York: McGraw-Hill, 1976.

Kernighan, Brian W., and P. L. Plauger: *The Elements of Programming Style*, New York: McGraw-Hill, 1974. Excellent reference on programming style.

Klecka, William, Norman H. Nie, and C. Hadlai Hull: *SPSS Primer*, New York: McGraw-Hill, 1975.

Ledgard, Henry F. and William C. Cave: "COBOL under Control," *Communications of the ACM*, vol. 19, no. 11, November 1976, pp. 601-608.

Lientz, Bennet P.: "A Comparative Evaluation of Versions of BASIC," *Communications of the ACM*, vol. 19, no. 4, April 1976, pp. 175-181.

Nie, Norman H., et al.: *Statistical Package for the Social Sciences*, 2d ed. New York: McGraw-Hill, 1975.

Polivka, Raymond P., and Sandra Pakin: *APL: The Language and Its Usage*, Englewood Cliffs, N.J.: Prentice-Hall, 1975.

Sammet, Jean E.: "Roster of Programming Languages for 1974-75," *Communications of the ACM*, vol. 19, no. 12, December 1976, pp. 655-669.

Schucany, W. R., B. S. Shannon, Jr., and P. D. Minton: "A Survey of Statistical Packages," *Computing Surveys*, vol. 4, no. 2, June 1972, pp. 65-79.

Slysz, W. D.: "An Evaluation of Statistical Software in the Social Sciences," *Communications of the ACM*, vol. 17, no. 6, June 1974, pp. 326-332.

Struble, George W.: *Assembler Language Programming: The IBM/360 and 370*, 2d ed., Reading, Mass.: Addison-Wesley, 1975.

Symposium on Structured Programming in COBOL—Future and Present, New York: Association for Computing Machinery, 1975.

Tenny, Ted: "Structured Programming in FORTRAN," *Datamation*, vol. 20, no. 7, July 1974, pp. 110-115.

Yohe, J. M.: "An Overview of Programming Practices," *Computing Surveys*, vol. 6, no. 4, December 1974, pp. 221-243.

Other: Current and Projected Developments and Societal Implications

"Distributed Computing—A Growing Concern," *Infosystems*, vol. 22, no. 8, August 1975, pp. 32-34.

Dolotta, T. A., et al.: *Data Processing in 1980-1985*, New York: Wiley, 1976.

Frank, Werner L.: "The Second Half of the Computer Age," *Datamation*, vol. 22, no. 5, May 1976, pp. 91-100.

Gilchrist, Bruce, and Milton R. Wessel: *Government Regulation of the Computer Industry*, Montvale, N.J.: American Federation of Information Processing Societies, Inc., 1973.

Hoffman, L.: "Computers and Privacy: A Survey," *Computing Surveys*, vol. 1, no. 2, 1969.

Kriebel, Charles H.: "MIS Technology: A View of the Future," *Proceedings of the Spring Joint Computer Conference*, 1972, pp. 1173-1180.

Martin, James, and Adrian Norman: *The Computerized Society,* Englewood Cliffs, N.J.: Prentice-Hall, 1970.

Mumford, Enid, and Harold Sackman: *Human Choice and Computers,* New York: American Elsevier, 1975.

Patrick, Robert L.: "Decentralizing Hardware and Dispersing Responsibility," *Datamation,* vol. 22, no. 5, May 1976, pp. 79–84.

Rosenberg, N. (ed.): *Perspectives on the Computer Revolution,* Baltimore: Penguin, 1971.

Sackman, Harold, and J. Borko (eds.): *Computers and the Problems of Society,* Montvale, N.J.: American Federation of Information Processing Societies, Inc., 1973.

―――― and Norman Nie: *The Information Utility and Social Choice,* Montvale, N.J.: American Federation of Information Processing Societies, Inc., 1973.

Salzman, Roy M.: "The Computer Terminal Industry: A Forecast," *Datamation,* vol. 21, no. 11, November 1975, pp. 46–50.

Silverstein, Jamie Ellen: "Outlook for the Industry," *Computer Decisions,* vol. 8, no. 1, January 1976, pp. 34–39.

Wagner, Frank V.: "Is Decentralization Inevitable?" *Datamation,* vol. 22, no. 11, pp. 86–97.

――――: "The Next (and Last?) Generation," *Datamation,* May 1972, pp. 71–74.

Withington, Frederick G.: "Future Computer Technology," *Database,* vol. 7, no. 4, Spring 1976, pp. 7–14.

"Word Processing Report," *Infosystems,* vol. 22, no. 10, October 1975, pp. 29–32.

GLOSSARY

The glossary contains definitions for a selected list of terms used in the field of computers and data processing. The definitions are consistent with the two glossaries having official status.

International Federation for Information Processing, *IFIP Guide to Concepts and Terms in Data Processing,* Ian Gould, ed., North-Holland Publishing Company, Amsterdam, 1971. Distributed in the United States and Canada by AFIPS, Montvale, N.J.

American National Standards Institute, *American Standard Vocabulary for Information Processing,* USA Standard X3.12-1970, New York, 1970.

In preparing the selected glossary for the first edition of the text, the *Glossary of Automatic Data Processing,* published by the U.S. Bureau of the Budget, 1962, was used in choosing the terms to include and in preparing many of the definitions. Many terms have since been revised, and additional terms have been added to the second and third editions. Terms in the glossary appear in alphabetical order by the key word. Thus the term "double precision" appears under "precision, double."

A

absolute address See *address, absolute*.

access, direct Pertaining to the process of obtaining information from or placing data in storage where the access to the storage location is independent of the location most recently accessed. An example of direct access storage medium is disk storage. Direct access is in contrast to serial access, in which access is dependent on the position of the storage location in a set of storage locations that must be processed serially. An example of a serial access storage medium is magnetic tape.

access, random Same as *access, direct*.

access, serial See *access, direct*.

accumulator A register and associated equipment in the arithmetic unit of the computer where arithmetic and logical operations are performed.

acronym A word formed from the initial letter or letters in a name or phrase. An example is FORTRAN for FORmula TRANslator.

address A number, symbol, name, or label which identifies a register or location in storage.

address, absolute A machine-language address of a specific storage location.

address, base See *address, relative*.

address, immediate An instruction in which the address portion of the instruction is the operand itself rather than the address of the operand.

address, indirect An address which references a storage location containing the address of the operand needed. This is in contrast to direct addressing in which the address references the location of the operand.

address, relative An address which is translated into an absolute address by adding a base address to it. If, for example, a relative address were 390 and the base address were 4000, the absolute address would be 4390.

ADP Automatic Data Processing.

ALGOL An acronym for ALGOrithmic Language, an international algebraic, procedure-oriented language. Similar in concept and content to FORTRAN. Widely used in Europe.

alphanumeric (or alphameric) A contraction for alphabetic and numeric. A set of alphanumeric characters will usually include special characters such as the dollar sign and comma.

analog computer See *computer, analog*.

AND gate or AND circuit See *gate*.

application A specific task on which the computer is used. Examples are payroll, order entry, and inventory management.

arithmetic, fixed point Arithmetic in which the computer does not consider the location of the radix. For example, all numbers are considered to be integers. See *arithmetic, floating point*, for contrasting system.

arithmetic, floating point Arithmetic which automatically keeps track of the scaling for the results. In floating point operations, the numbers consist of two parts—a signed mantissa and an integral exponent. Arithmetic is performed on both the mantissas and the exponents in order to form a mantissa and exponent for the result. It is contrasted with fixed point arithmetic in which the programmer must keep track of the decimal point.

ASCII An acronym for American Standard Code for Information Interchange, a 7-bit (or 8-bit compatible) used when transmitting data between computers.

assembler Also called an "assembly program" or "assembly routine." A computer routine which translates computer instructions written in machine-oriented symbolic coding into machine-language instructions.

associative memory See *storage, associative*.

asynchronous Not synchronized. Operating independently.

auxiliary storage See *storage, secondary*.

B

background program See *multiprogramming*.

baud A unit of signaling speed equal to 1 bit per second. The Baudot code is a 5-bit code sometimes used in data communications. It has generally been replaced by the ASCII code.

binary-coded decimal code A system in which individual decimal digits are represented by a group of binary digits. A minimum of four binary digits is necessary to represent a decimal digit.

binary number system A number system having a radix of 2. Absolute values are 1 and 0; the positional values are powers of 2.

bit An abbreviation for binary digit.

bit, parity A bit added to a group of binary digits in order to detect the loss of a bit from the group during processing. Also called a *check bit*. In an odd-parity check, for example, a 1- or 0-bit is added to the group of digits to make the number of 1-bits odd.

bits, zone Two to four bits added to the four bits in a binary-coded decimal group in order for the group to represent alphabetic and special characters.

block A group of records, characters, or digits handled as a unit by input and output.

blocking Combining two or more records into a single physical block to reduce read or write time.

Boolean algebra An algebra for dealing with the truth of logical propositions. Operators are AND, OR, NOT, EXCEPT, IF . . . THEN. Named after George Boole, English mathematician (1815–1864).

branch Another name for a transfer-of-control instruction which causes the selection of one, two, or more possible program paths.

breakpoint A point in a program at which the program can be halted and the results to that point analyzed or preserved for a later continuation of the program. Used primarily in debugging.

buffer Storage used to compensate for differences in the rate of flow of data or to allow devices to operate asynchronously. For example, intermediate storage between an input or output device and the computer.

bug A mistake in a program or an equipment malfunction.

byte A group of adjacent binary digits operated upon as a unit. In many computers, it is an 8-bit set encoding one alphanumeric character or two decimal digits.

C

call A transfer to a subroutine.

central processing unit (CPU) The device containing the arithmetic unit, control unit, and main memory. Also referred to as the "main frame."

channel (1) A path along which information can flow, e.g., an input/output channel which connects input/output units to the central processor; (2) one of the parallel tracks on magnetic tape or bands on a magnetic drum.

charts, HIPO Hierarchy plus input-process-output charts. They are a method of planning and documenting a program. Associated with structured programming.

check, echo An error-control procedure in which information transmitted to an output device such as a printer is transmitted back to the computer for comparison with the original information.

clock In a synchronous computer, a circuit which emits pulses at equal intervals. The pulses are used to schedule the operation of the computer.

clock, realtime A clock which records the passage of time. It can be set and read by program instructions.

COBOL An acronym for COmmon Business Oriented Language, a high-level language oriented toward organizational data processing procedures.

collate To merge two or more sequenced files into a single sequenced file.

COM Computer-output microfilm.

compile To produce a machine-language program by translating a set of instructions written in a high-level language, such as FORTRAN or COBOL.

compiler A computer program to compile a high-level source language program into an object language.

computer, analog A computer which operates by using an electrical representation of the variables in the problem.

computer, asynchronous A computer in which an operation begins as a result of the signal that the previous operation is completed or that the part of the computer needed is available.

computer, synchronous A computer in which operations are performed in set intervals of time fixed by pulses from a clock.

console The control panel used by the computer operator. It typically contains a typewriter or visual display for operator communications and may contain register displays, switches, etc.

control card A punched card which is part of a set of job control cards which direct the execution of a job on the computer.

coupler, acoustic A modem which converts data into a sequence of tones that are sent over the telephone voice line.

CRT Cathode-ray tube display device.

D

DASD Direct access storage device.

data administrator Person responsible for defining, updating, and controlling access to a database.

database An integrated file of data used by many processing applications.

database management system Comprehensive

software system to build, maintain, and access a database.

data management system Software system to access files and prepare reports.

data set A set of data records (a file). Also used to refer to a modem.

DBMS Database management system.

debug To locate and correct errors in a program or malfunctions in equipment.

decimal, binary-coded See *binary-coded decimal code.*

decision table A description of decision rules in which sets of conditions are related to actions to be taken.

demodulator See *modem.*

density The number of characters which can be stored per unit of length, such as an inch of magnetic tape.

detail file See *file, detail.*

development, top-down An approach to program development in which high-level modules are coded first.

digit, check A redundant digit added to a group of digits to detect errors. When used in connection with an identification number, the check digit provides a means for detecting invalid numbers. Also used to refer to a check bit.

disk, magnetic A rotating metal disk having a magnetized surface on which data may be stored. Direct access storage. Also spelled disc.

double precision See *precision, double.*

drum, magnetic A rapidly revolving cylinder which stores information as small polarized spots on its surface. The data is stored or obtained by means of a read-write head. Provides direct access storage.

dump, storage A transfer of the contents of a storage device to another media, such as punching cards, printout, etc. Frequently used in debugging when the contents of memory need to be listed.

duplex (1) Pertaining to a pair or a two-in-one situation; (2) a channel which allows simultaneous transmission in both directions; (3) a stand-by unit to be used in the event of equipment failure.

E

EBCDIC Abbreviation for extended binary-coded decimal interchange code. An 8-bit code identified with IBM System/360 and 370.

echo check See *check, echo.*

edit To modify the form or format of data for output by inserting dollar signs, blanks, etc. To validate and rearrange input data.

emulator Stored logic that enables a computer to execute machine-language instructions for another computer of dissimilar design.

equipment, peripheral Auxiliary machines which may be placed under the control of the computer.

F

facilities management The use of an independent service organization to operate and manage a data processing installation.

factor, scale The coefficient in the scale factor method of scaling. A number is put into a given range of magnitude (such as between $+1$ and -1), and the scale factor is the coefficient necessary to convert the normalized number back to the original number.

field An assigned area in the storage defined for a record.

file An organized collection of records having a common feature or purpose.

file, detail A file containing transaction data. Frequently used to update a master file.

file, inverted A file organized so it can be accessed by characteristic rather than by record key.

file maintenance See *maintenance, file.*

file, master A file containing relatively permanent data.

fixed point arithmetic See *arithmetic, fixed point.*

fixed word length See *word.*

flag A program indicator which informs a part of the program about a condition that occurred earlier.

flip-flop A bistable device capable of storing a bit of information.

floating point arithmetic See *arithmetic, floating point.*

foreground See *multiprogramming.*

FORTRAN An acronym for FORmula TRANslator, a programming language designed for writing programs to solve problems which can be stated in terms of arithmetic procedures. This is the most popular of the algebraic procedure-oriented languages.

frame, main See *central processing unit.*

frontend See *processor, communications.*

full duplex See *duplex.*

G

gap (1) An interval of space or time which separates words, records, or files on a magnetic tape. For example, an interblock gap is a space between blocks of records which permits start-stop operations and keeps blocks separate; (2) a space between a read-write head and the recording medium.

gate A circuit which provides an output signal dependent on past or present input signals. An AND gate provides an output pulse only if there is an input pulse on all inputs. An OR circuit has the property that an input pulse on any input line will cause an output pulse.

generator, program A routine which writes a program based on a set of specifications. The specifications may be a set of parameters (such as the characteristics of a report to be prepared) or problem-oriented instructions. The generator program essentially puts together instructions from a library, making changes as necessary.

generator, report A routine to write a program to produce a specified report from a specified set of data.

H

half-adder A circuit which adds two binary digits but does not provide for a carry. Two circuits, plus a delay, form an adder, so that a half-adder is half of an adder.

half duplex See *duplex.*

hash total See *total, hash.*

header See *label.*

heuristic Serving to discover or invent. The term pertains to a guided trial-and-error method for problem solving.

hexadecimal number system A number system with the base 16. The 16 absolute values of the system are usually represented by the numbers 0 to 9 and the letters A to F.

Hollerith Refers to the 80-column punched card and related equipment originally designed by Herman Hollerith. Also character output in FORTRAN.

housekeeping In computer programming, the setup and initialization procedures (setting up constants, variables, and switches, and clearing locations, etc.) performed prior to the processing steps of the program.

I

immediate address See *address, immediate.*

index register See *register, index.*

index sequential Data organization in which records are organized in sequential order and also referenced directly via an index based on some characteristic.

indirect address See *address, indirect.*

informatics Theory and practice associated with analysis, design, and application of computer-based information systems in organizations. The term is popular in Europe.

input Reading of data from storage medium or entry of data from terminal.

input validation See *validation.*

instruction A set of characters which define an operation to be performed and the data or unit of equipment to be used.

instruction, macro An instruction which is translated into a set of object language instructions for performing the operation specified by the macro.

instruction, one-address An instruction with an operation code and the address for one operand.

instruction, symbolic An instruction using a symbolic operation code and symbolic addresses. It is usually translated into a single machine-language instruction.

instruction, two- or three-address A machine-oriented instruction with an operation code and two or three addresses which specify operands and/or the address where results are to be stored.

interblock gap See *gap.*

interface A common boundary or connection between computer systems or parts of a single system.

interpretative routine See *routine, interpretative.*

interrupt To stop the current operation to perform some other operation, after which control may be resumed at the point where it was stopped.

IOCS (Input/Output Control System) A standard set of routines which initiate and control input and output processes.

item A contiguous set of data treated as a unit. A part of a record.

K

key An item which identifies a record.

L

label (1) A name attached to or written alongside an entity to identify it; (2) a header label record at the beginning of a file to identify the file and selected characteristics and a trailer label at the end of the file to identify the number of records, hash totals, etc.

language, algorithmic A procedure-oriented language suited for stating numerical procedures.

language, business-oriented A procedure-oriented language especially suited for business file processing. Refers specifically to COBOL.

language, object The language which results from the translation of procedure-oriented language statements. These are typically machine-language instructions.

language, procedure-oriented A machine-independent language designed for ease in stating the procedures by which a problem is to be solved. Examples are FORTRAN, COBOL, and PL/1.

length, block The number of records, characters, or words contained in one block.

length, word The number of bits in a computer word.

library Organizational function which maintains custody of programs, disks, tapes, and documentation.

library routine See *routine, library.*

list Organization of data using indexes and pointers to allow for nonsequential retrieval.

loader A routine which loads programs into internal storage for execution.

loop A series of instructions which repeat a set of computations a number of times, modifying some variable each time. The looping is terminated when a test indicates that a termination condition is satisfied. Repetition program structure.

M

maintenance, file The updating of a file with corrections and nonperiodic changes.

maintenance, program The correction, modifying, and updating of a computer program.

Management Information System See *MIS.*

map A list of storage areas used by elements of a program.

mark sensing See *sensing, mark.*

masking Extracting a group of characters from a computer word or words.

merge To combine two separate sequenced files into a single sequenced file.

MICR Magnetic Ink Character Recognition. Coding using magnetically readable ink. Primarily for check processing.

micrologic The use of a permanent stored program to interpret instructions in a micro-

program. Besides lower hardware cost, the advantage of micrologic is that it can be used when a computer needs to execute the instructions of another, possibly larger, computer. The same as stored logic.

microprocessor The basic logic and storage elements required to do processing. Generally on one or two chips containing integrated circuits.

microprogram A sequence of instructions which will be translated by micrologic hardware in the computer.

microsecond One millionth of a second.

millisecond One thousandth of a second.

minicomputer A small and inexpensive but typically fast computer with limited input and output capabilities.

MIS (Management Information System) An information processing system oriented toward providing information for management. The concept requires a data-base and substantial analysis and retrieval capabilities.

mnemonic As an aid to human memory. Use of codes which sound like the function, e.g., SUB for subtraction and DIV for division.

modem (modulator-demodulator) Device to interface between processing equipment and communications system.

monitor To supervise the operation of a program by a diagnostic routine.

monitor, communications A software system to supervise and manage data communications.

multiplex To make simultaneous use of a single communications channel to transmit a number of messages.

multiprocessor A computer system with more than one arithmetic and logic unit for simultaneous use.

multiprogramming A technique for running several programs simultaneously by interleaving their operations. If one of the programs must provide realtime response and therefore must have priority, it is frequently termed a "foreground program." The nonpriority program is then termed a "background program."

N

nanosecond One billionth of a second (i.e., one thousandth of a millionth of a second, or 10^{-9} second).

normalize In programming, to adjust the exponent and fraction of a floating point quantity so that the fraction is within a prescribed range.

O

OCR Optical Character Recognition.

octal number system A number system to use the base 8. Binary-coded octal represents octal numbers by groups of three binary digits.

offline Not under the control of the central processing unit.

online Under the control of, and connected to, the central processing unit.

operand A unit of data in a storage location or an equipment unit which the instruction operation will use.

overflow The loss of a digit when the results of an arithmetic operation exceed the capacity of the register or memory location where the result is to be stored.

overhead The time and space for nonproductive operations in a computer system. Includes the time and space taken by the functions of the operating system.

overlay The technique for putting a routine into memory when it is needed by a program and for using as storage location the positions occupied by a routine which is no longer needed. Used where the entire program cannot fit in memory at once.

P

pack To put several data items into one fixed-length computer word.

packet-switching Transmission of data over a communications network. Each group (packet) of data has destination identification so data to be sent to a variety of locations can be intermixed in transmission.

page A segment of a program or data which can be moved in and out of storage in multiprogramming.

parallel Handled simultaneously using separate facilities.

parity bit See *bit, parity*.

pass A processing cycle in which data is read, processed, and written out.

patch To correct a program in a rough or expedient way.

PL/1 (Programming Language, Version 1) A combined algebraic and business language introduced by IBM in connection with its System/360.

pointer A data item associated with an index, a record, or other set of data which contains the address of a related data item or record. Allows data to be related and referenced.

precision, double The use of twice as many digits to represent a quantity as the computer normally operates on. If the computer normally uses 32-bit words, double precision would use a pair of 32-bit words to represent a quantity, thus increasing the number of significant digits obtainable in processing.

processing, batch Periodic processing of items after a number of like items have been gathered together.

processing, file The periodic updating of a file with current data, such as transaction data.

processing, online The processing of transactions when received—in contrast to batch processing where items must accumulate before processing. To accomplish online processing requires that all equipment be online and that data records be accessible directly.

processing, parallel Concurrent running of two or more programs stored in the memory.

processing, realtime The processing of information as received and in time for the result to be available for influencing the process being controlled.

processor (1) A hardware unit—the CPU; (2) an assembler or compiler translator routine.

processor, communications A small computer dedicated to handling data communications for a larger computer. Also called a "front-end."

processor, micro See *microprocessor*.

program (1) The set of instructions to solve a problem; (2) to plan the procedures for solving a problem.

program generator See *generator, program*.

program, object The coding which results from the translation by a compiler of a source program written in a source language, such as FORTRAN or COBOL.

programming, structured A structured approach to coding of a computer program. Generally assumes top-down design and modular hierarchy of program.

programming, symbolic Programming using symbolic addresses and mnemonic operation codes. The symbolic program is converted to a machine-language program by a symbolic assembly system.

protocol, communications The coding and decoding of messages to/from terminals to obtain and provide all routing and control information.

R

radix The base of a number system.

rate, clock The time rate at which pulses are emitted from the timing circuit. This rate governs all operations in a synchronous computer.

read-only storage See *micrologic.*

realtime system See *processing, realtime.*

record A collection of related items of data.

redundancy Added characters, bits, or operations not required for the message being sent or operation being performed but added for checking purposes.

reentrant Pertaining to a routine that can be used by two or more independent programs at the same time. Used in multiprogramming and timesharing.

register A hardware device for holding data (usually a computer word) to be operated upon.

register, index A register used to modify an instruction during the instruction cycle.

report generator See *generator, report.*

routine A set of instructions which direct the computer to perform a particular process.

routine, executive A routine to control the loading of programs, relocation of programs in memory, scheduling of runs, and other functions requiring manual intervention when an executive routine is not available. Also called a "monitor" or "supervisory" routine.

routine, interpretive A routine to decode and immediately execute instructions written in a high-level code.

routine, library A prewritten, standard routine for use in programs.

RPG Report Program Generator. See *generator, report.*

run A performance of a specific process on a file of data.

S

scale factor See *factor, scale.*

semiconductor As used in computer circuitry and storage, consists of circuits etched on a small silicon chip.

sensing, mark Using a pencil to mark a box on a punch card. The markings can be sensed by special equipment, translated, and punched as regular punches.

sequence, collating The sequence in which the computer will order the set of characters used by it.

serial Pertaining to the handling of arithmetic, data transmission, etc., a digit at a time.

simplex Transmission in only one direction at a time. Contrast with duplex.

software The programming aids available for a computer. These include library routines, assembly routines, utility routines, compilers, and applications programs. Contrasted to hardware.

storage, associative A content-addressable storage in which storage locations are identified by their contents rather than by name or position.

storage, auxiliary See *storage, secondary.*

storage, buffer See *buffer.*

storage protection Protection against one program writing in or reading from the storage assigned to another program.

storage, secondary A storage device providing storage in addition to the main storage of a computer. The secondary storage is typically less expensive and with slower access than the main memory. Examples are magnetic tape, disk files, cartridge files, and magnetic drums.

storage, virtual Use of storage segments in a hierarchy of storage devices which allow the programmer to ignore physical limits on main memory.

storage, working A portion of the internal storage set aside for data being operated upon.

subroutine A set of computer instructions to carry out a predefined computation. Subroutines are either open or closed. An open subroutine is put in as an integral part of the main program. A closed subroutine is arranged so that control may be transferred to it, and after computation control will return to the main program. A closed subroutine is used (1) to avoid repeating the coding for a set of computational steps applied more than once; (2) for modular programming.

switch (1) A hardware switch; (2) a program flag that causes a selection from among alternative sequences.

System, Management Information See *MIS.*

system, operating A set of routines for supervising the operations of a computer system. The routines provide for loading of programs, relocation of programs, sequencing of operations, assembly, compilation, accounting, diagnostics, etc. The operating system automatically brings in the proper routines and keeps the computer operating without the need for manual intervention.

T

table look-up The operation of obtaining a value from a table in computer storage, where the value obtained (value of the function) is dependent on the data (value of the argument).

telecommunications Data communications using communications facilities.

throughput The total amount of work during a given time period.

time, access The time required to locate data in storage and transfer it to the arithmetic unit for processing.

timesharing Carrying out two or more functions during the same time period by allocating small divisions of the total time to each function in turn. It allows many users to use the computer at the same time.

total, hash A sum of the numbers in one field of a batch of records. The numbers are not normally added, such as account numbers. The sum is used as a control total.

trace A diagnostic technique to provide an analysis of the results after each instruction (or a certain type of instruction) is executed.

track The recording paths on a recording medium.

trail, audit The means for identifying the processing performed. The audit trail may consist of transaction listings, batch references, input document references, terminal input transaction identification, etc. Provides processing trail so any input can be traced to output and any output traced back to constituent inputs.

U

unbundling Separate pricing of hardware and software.

unpack To separate parts of a tape record or computer word and store in separate locations.

update To incorporate changes in a program, master file, etc.

V

validation To test data for correctness, completeness, and readiness to be processed. Also termed input validation or input editing.

virtual memory See *storage, virtual.*

W

word An ordered set of characters handled as a unit by the computer. The word may be fixed or variable in length. In a fixed word-length computer, the number of characters in a word does not vary, and an address will typically refer to one set of characters. In a variable word-length computer, each character or byte has an address, and the word utilized by the computer can include a variable number of characters. The length of the variable word is generally specified by the instruction which calls for it.

Z

zone (1) On Hollerith punch cards, the top three positions, used for indicating alphabetic and special characters; (2) the part of a computer word or the bits in a byte used for alphabetic and special character representations.

INDEX